Human Trafficking Handbook: Recognising Trafficking and Modern-Day Slavery in the UK

For my son Kamran, with love,

- and -

For those who have been trafficked and lost:

We wrote this book for you

Human Trafficking Handbook: Recognising Trafficking and Modern-Day Slavery in the UK

General Editor

Parosha Chandran,
LLB (Hons.), LLM (Lond.), Diplôme in Human Rights (International Institute of Human Rights, Strasbourg), Barrister of Lincoln's Inn

With a team of specialist contributors

 LexisNexis®

Members of the LexisNexis Group worldwide

United Kingdom	LexisNexis UK, a Division of Reed Elsevier (UK) Ltd, Halsbury House, 35 Chancery Lane, LONDON, WC2A 1EL, and 4 Hill Street, EDINBURGH EH2 3JZ
Argentina	LexisNexis Argentina, BUENOS AIRES
Australia	LexisNexis Butterworths, CHATSWOOD, New South Wales
Austria	LexisNexis Verlag ARD Orac GmbH & Co KG, VIENNA
Canada	LexisNexis Butterworths, MARKHAM, Ontario
Chile	LexisNexis Chile Ltda, SANTIAGO DE CHILE
Czech Republic	Nakladatelství Orac sro, PRAGUE
France	Editions du Juris-Classeur SA, PARIS
Germany	LexisNexis Deutschland GmbH, FRANKFURT, MUNSTER
Hong Kong	LexisNexis Butterworths, HONG KONG
Hungary	HVG-Orac, BUDAPEST
India	LexisNexis Butterworths, NEW DELHI
Ireland	LexisNexis, DUBLIN
Italy	Giuffrè Editore, MILAN
Malaysia	Malayan Law Journal Sdn Bhd, KUALA LUMPUR
New Zealand	LexisNexis Butterworths, WELLINGTON
Poland	Wydawnictwo Prawnicze LexisNexis, WARSAW
Singapore	LexisNexis Butterworths, SINGAPORE
South Africa	LexisNexis Butterworths, DURBAN
Switzerland	Stämpfli Verlag AG, BERNE
USA	LexisNexis, DAYTON, Ohio

ISBN 978-1-4057-6559-6

9 781405 765596

Printed and bound in Great Britain by Hobbs the Printers, Brunel Road, Totton, Hampshire, SO40 3WX

Visit LexisNexis UK at http://www.lexisnexis.co.uk

Acknowledgments

There are many inspirational figures behind the scenes. People that I know or knew or read about during my studies and internships or met through my work; my husband, our son, and our families, my close friends and colleagues. All these interactions have contributed towards the vision or completion of this book and I thank you all. My respect and gratitude goes to all the distinguished contributors who have co-written the Human Trafficking Handbook. It has been a privilege to work with you and I have learned so much. I am also profoundly grateful to the inspirational Sir Nicolas Bratza, Vice-President and President-elect of the European Court of Human Rights, for writing the Foreword to this book and indeed for encouraging me to pursue my dream of becoming a human rights barrister nearly 20 years ago. I also thank all at LexisNexis, particularly our publisher James Kearns and our editor Vickie Tomlinson, for their support, insight and dedication to producing and publishing this Handbook. A special mention also goes to Nigel Roberts, Director of Global Associations for LexisNexis and to Jennifer Rosen.

I would like to acknowledge the support of my close colleagues Nadine Finch and Klara Skrivankova with whom I founded the Trafficking Law and Policy Forum in 2007 and I also thank all the members of the Forum who have created a great community by attending our meetings and sharing their knowledge on human trafficking issues.

Last but not least, I acknowledge on behalf of all the contributors to this Handbook all the victims and survivors of human trafficking, some of whose paths have crossed with ours. Your courage and bravery has no doubt inspired us all.

Appendices

The Council of Europe Convention on Action against Trafficking in Human Beings 2005 is reproduced by kind permission of the Council of Europe.

The Explanatory Report to the Council of Europe Convention on Action against Trafficking in Human Beings 2005 is reproduced by kind permission of the Council of Europe.

London Safeguarding Trafficked Children Guidance, March 2011 is reproduced with the permission of the London Safeguarding Children Board (http://www.londonscb.gov.uk/trafficking/).

Position from ACPO Lead's on Child Protection and Cannabis Cultivation on Children and Young People Recovered in Cannabis Farms, August 2010 reproduced by kind permission of Association of Chief Police Officers of England, Wales and Northern Ireland: ACPO Child Protection and Abuse Investigation Working Group C/o The Child Exploitation and Online Protection (CEOP) Centre.

Anti-Trafficking Monitoring Group 'Wrong Kind of Victim?' Summary report, June 2010 reproduced by kind permission of the Anti-Trafficking Monitoring Group.

UNODC Human Trafficking Indicators are reproduced by kind permission of the United Nations, Copyright UNODC, 2011. For further information see: http://www.unodc.org/ and http://www.ungift.org.

The Protocol to Prevent, Suppress and Punish Trafficking in Persons, especially Women and Children, supplementing the United Nations Convention against Transnational Organized Crime (Palermo Protocol 2000) is reproduced by kind permission of the United Nations, Copyright United Nations, 2011.

Foreword

Human trafficking constitutes, in the words of the Preamble to the Council of Europe Convention on Action against Trafficking in Human Beings of 2005, 'a violation of human rights and an offence to the dignity and the integrity of the human being'. There can indeed be few graver violations of human rights and fundamental freedoms than the trafficking of human beings, whether for sexual exploitation, forced labour, domestic servitude or other contemporary forms of exploitation. Article 4 of the European Convention on Human Rights, which prohibits all forms of slavery and servitude and forced or compulsory labour has been held to enshrine one of the basic values of the democratic societies making up the Council of Europe, a special status which is reflected in the fact that, in common with the prohibition of torture or inhuman and degrading treatment in Article 3 of the Convention, the obligation imposed by Article 4 makes no provision for exceptions and is non-derogable. It is, therefore, perhaps surprising that, despite the cardinal place occupied by the Article within the Convention, cases before the European Court of Human Rights relating to human trafficking have been both few in number and recent in date. Two judgments alone have addressed the issue in any detail. The landmark cases of *Siliadin v France* in 2005 and *Rantsev v Cyprus and Russia* in 2010, both served to underline the positive obligation imposed on Member States under Article 4 to ensure the practical and effective protection of victims and potential victims of trafficking by putting in place a legislative and administrative framework and by adopting effective measures for the investigation and prosecution of those responsible.

As this Handbook vividly demonstrates, the comparative paucity of Strasbourg case-law should not be seen as any indication of the prevalence or scale of the problem of human trafficking or of a lack of need for more effective measures to combat this modern form of slavery, whether in the United Kingdom or elsewhere.

The modest title 'Handbook' might suggest that this work is no more than a practical manual for those directly concerned with the subject-matter of human trafficking. Certainly the book has all the virtues of a manual, containing as it does a mine of information and clear and practical guidance. But it is much more than that. It is a book which examines all aspects of human trafficking in separate chapters, contributed by acknowledged experts in the field – doctors, children's services, domestic and international trafficking specialists, legal practitioners, police and prosecutors and members of organisations dedicated to the support of victims of trafficking. The diversity of the contributors is matched by the diversity of the topics covered in the chapters, each with its own valuable summary – the identification of victims and potential victims of trafficking and their treatment and support, including the special problems relating to child victims; the international rights and duties affecting the protection of victims; the problematic issue of remedial measures for victims, including the right to compensation; and the legislative and operational measures in the United Kingdom relating to the non-criminalisation of victims and the investigation and prosecution of human traffickers. A common theme and a continuing concern of all the experts is to ensure that respect for the human rights of all victims of trafficking must underpin all anti-trafficking measures.

Parosha Chandran, the General Editor as well as one of the contributors, and herself an advocate of distinction in the field, is to be warmly congratulated on having assembled authors of the highest quality and having combined, in a single volume, such a wealth of learning and experience.

The picture painted by the book illustrates the stark reality that, despite the important advances which have been made in the United Kingdom in recent years, much remains to be done to respond more effectively to the threat and consequences of human trafficking, both of which are still disturbingly real. This excellent Handbook will not only contribute to a better understanding of the challenges presented by human trafficking but it will become an indispensable resource for all concerned with combating this pernicious trade.

Nicolas Bratza, Vice-President

European Court of Human Rights

Strasbourg

August 2011

Preface

In October 2006 the Joint Committee on Human Rights, a Parliamentary body appointed by the House of Lords and the House of Commons to consider matters relating to human rights in the United Kingdom, published its report on Human Trafficking [HL Paper 245, HC 1127] following an inquiry into the scale and nature of human trafficking in the UK. The evidence it received indicated that there were at least 4,000 victims of trafficking for sexual exploitation in the UK during 2003 but no reliable figures existed to show the numbers of adults and children trafficked for labour exploitation. In its report the Committee gave detailed consideration to the provisions of the Council of Europe Convention on Action against Trafficking in Human Beings 2005 ('the Trafficking Convention'). It concluded that the Government should sign and ratify the Treaty. The Committee, having heard and considered evidence on the consequences of human trafficking, specifically its impact on trafficked victims in the UK, the domestic criminal provisions then in force and also the residency arrangements made for trafficked victims in Italy, found no realistic likelihood that the protections under the Convention for victims of trafficking would operate as a pull factor to inspire false claims of trafficked status, which formed the central plank of the Government's objection to signing the Convention. The Committee determined that, in accordance with human rights standards, 'the effective protection of victims must be the starting point from which all other policies relating to trafficking should flow' and advised that, although the Government had started taking some significant steps to improve the protection of victims, 'the current level of protection as a whole is still far from adequate'. Amongst its many conclusions it found that 'either through legislation or other means, effective protection of trafficking victims must be put on a far more reliable basis in order to meet the UK's human rights obligations'. Some five months later, in March 2007, the Government bowed to pressure and signed the Trafficking Convention. Over a year later, in December 2008, it ratified the Treaty and the Trafficking Convention entered into force in the UK on 1 April 2009.

Two years after the Trafficking Convention opened for signature in Warsaw in 2005 and shortly before the UK had agreed to sign it in 2007, inspired by the Committee report and the protections that the Trafficking Convention sought to provide to victims of trafficking, myself and two other trafficking specialists in the UK, Klara Skrivankova, the head of the anti-trafficking programme at Anti-Slavery International and Nadine Finch, a leading barrister at Garden Court Chambers, decided to set up an informal group which we named the Trafficking Law and Policy Forum (the Trafficking Forum). We wanted to create an educational think-tank comprising a network of support and understanding amongst professionals whose work involved trafficking issues, no matter how broad or brief the overlap with their other work, with a view to discussing such issues amongst ourselves and also raising awareness of related matters, including trafficking law and policy, as it developed in the UK and abroad. Our first meeting of the Trafficking Forum was held on a rainy Thursday afternoon in London, in a room above a pub in the Spring of 2007. Over 50 invited guests from non-governmental and inter-governmental organisations, from the legal and medical professions, the judiciary, social services, academia, the police and the Crown Prosecution Service, attended. The level of the discussions that took place between us then were as intense, informative and thought-provoking as they still are at our quarterly meetings today and many successful partnerships have been forged over the past four years between Trafficking Forum members from diverse backgrounds which have directly impacted on the protection of individual victims of trafficking in the UK whom we have, in our individual professions, cared for, or given advice in respect of, or represented in court proceedings.

In the Spring of 2009 and then again in 2010 I was approached by LexisNexis to submit a book proposal on human trafficking in the UK, given my experience as a barrister in the field. On those occasions the time was not right for me but in March of this year I accepted a publication commission from LexisNexis under its corporate social responsibility banner. Hence it came to be, on another rainy afternoon in London, that I met with certain members of the Trafficking Forum, selected for their individual or group expertise covering a breadth of learning, to invite them to share in the book-writing with me. All agreed without exception or hesitation. These colleagues, who have been joined by one or two key individuals along the way, are the specialist contributors to this Handbook.

What is this Handbook? It is not, as I have been asked, a textbook. Nor is it a definitive guide which covers all aspects of trafficking and exploitation in the United Kingdom. What it provides instead, for the first time, is a compilation of the perspectives of various leading trafficking experts from diverse fields all of whom have a richness of experience in understanding the plight of victims of trafficking in the UK. In their chapters each specialist shares with us for example, sometimes in an acute way, their findings on the protection gaps which exist under current domestic law and practice in terms of securing respect for the human rights of trafficked victims, their techniques for achieving protection and/or their recommendations on ways to improve the protection position of victims of trafficking in the UK.

Part I of this Handbook places the identification of victims of trafficking in the UK firmly under the spotlight. Klara Skrivankova from Anti-Slavery International (on the complexities of forced labour identification), Dr Michael Korzinski of the Helen Bamber Foundation (on recognising and understanding trauma-based harm), Philip Ishola from the London Borough of Harrow Children's Services (on the statutory duties on local authorities to protect trafficked children) and Kalvir Kaur from ECPAT UK (on obtaining evidence from traumatised trafficked persons) have joined me (on interpreting human trafficking and on the identification of victims of trafficking) in writing chapters which highlight the crucial need for accurate identification of trafficked victims from a human rights perspective and the many obstacles which exist to achieving such identification. We each provide our recommendations in our respective roles and from our diverse backgrounds ranging from law, policy, medicine, local government and children's rights, on what needs to be better understood or done to aid better victim identification with a view to achieving tangible help and protection for trafficked victims in the UK.

Part II covers human trafficking in Scotland and Northern Ireland. Written by lawyers Piya D. Muqit (on Scotland) and Lois Hamilton and Catherine Robinson (on Northern Ireland) these chapters provide what may be unprecedented: consolidated, detailed assessments by specialist lawyers in their fields on all relevant matters pertaining to human trafficking in these parts of the UK. The depth and breadth of their knowledge is quite staggering.

Part III of the Handbook relates to the support of victims of trafficking. Christine Beddoe, Kayte Fairfax and Andrew Howard have, as child rights specialists who work or have worked with ECPAT UK, written vital, practical guidance on the need for safe accommodation for trafficked children in the UK. Sally Montier and Silva Hove's comprehensive chapter on the support and safety needs for victims of trafficking for sexual exploitation draws upon their immense experience as support providers at the Poppy Project since the time it was set up. Jenny Moss and Kate Roberts' detailed commentary on protecting the needs of victims of domestic servitude is equally specialist, arising from their work at the leading migrant workers' support organisation in the UK, Kalayaan.

Part IV covers the legal recognition of rights and duties in relation to victims of trafficking. Nadine Finch's chapter raises much-needed attention to the international legal protection of child victims of trafficking whilst Adam Weiss and Saadiya Chaudary, writing in their specialist roles at the AIRE Centre, expertly unravel and clearly explain the UK's obligations to trafficked victims under ECHR and EU law. In the final chapter of Part IV, Nadine Finch and I cover the rights to residence for victims of trafficking, including to asylum and human rights protection.

Part V of the Handbook examines in an extremely crucial way the right to compensation for victims of trafficking. Klara Skrivankova's chapter provides an overview of the right to compensation as a form of restitution under international law, what that right ought to precisely comprise and the major pitfalls which prevent most compensation claims from being brought by trafficked victims in the UK. The situation on the ground is then expertly examined in detail by lawyers Jawaid Luqmani (civil claims against traffickers), Jamila Duncan-Bosu (employment claims against traffickers) and Giles Hogan and Harriet Dykes (compensation for trafficked victims under the statutory Civil Injuries Compensation Scheme).

Finally, in Part VI, the UK's criminal law and practice relating to trafficking is comprehensively examined from a number of different perspectives. Pam Bowen, in her specialist role as head of policy at the Crown Prosecution Service (CPS), provides a detailed overview of trafficking related criminal legislation in the UK. The three chapters which then follow, written by police experts from the Metropolitan Police Service, complement this overview by describing the writers' experiences of investigating human traffickers in the UK from various angles, namely from the helm of the Human Exploitation and Organised Crime Command, Serious Crime Directorate 9 (Detective Chief Superintendent Richard Martin and Detective Chief Inspector Nick Sumner), from leading Operation Golf in terms of the successful investigation of the Roma traffickers of children into the UK (Retd. Superintendent Bernie Gravett and Chief Inspector Colin Carswell) and from the perspective of investigating the traffickers of children who were exploited for their labour by way of domestic servitude (Detective Constable Sarah Wood). The final two chapters of the Handbook, which are intended to be read together, examine the issue of the criminalisation of victims of trafficking for trafficking-dependent crimes and have been written by Pam Bowen (who summarises the relevant CPS Legal Guidance on adults and children) and by Peter Carter QC and myself (where we examine in detail the non-punishment and non-prosecution legal obligations on the UK, including under Article 26 of the Trafficking Convention).

One clear conclusion can be drawn from the experiences and learnings of the expert authors that are showcased in this Handbook and that is, in the words of Sir Nicolas Bratza in his Foreword:

> 'The picture painted by the book illustrates the stark reality that, despite the important advances which have been made in the United Kingdom in recent years, much remains to be done to respond more effectively to the threat and consequences of human trafficking, both of which are still disturbingly real.'

When I was a law student I read a book called The Alchemy of Race and Rights (Harvard University Press, 1991), written by the now highly-acknowledged law professor of Columbia University, Patricia J Williams. In documenting the experiences of slaves in the USA and their absence of any opportunity for hundreds of years to change their enslaved predicament she determined that 'rights are islands of empowerment'. Those words have resonated in my mind throughout my studies and throughout my practice as a human rights lawyer in the UK. In the context of the protection of victims of trafficking in the UK, and taking into account the findings, advice and conclusions of the Joint Committee on Human Rights in its report on Human Trafficking in 2006 as briefly addressed above, the UK is, as a State Party to both the Palermo Protocol and the Trafficking Convention, still a frighteningly long way from recognising or accepting the dire need for express legislation to translate the rights of victims of trafficking as set out in those legal instruments into islands of empowerment. Without the legal recognition of their rights, victims are still highly unsafe, if no longer directly at the hands of traffickers, then as applicants for recognition under the uneven, piecemeal and often unreliable formal identification and assistance procedures that exist under UK policy, not law. Such processes, as many of the expert authors of this book confirm, are very often likely to hinder and not help trafficked victims by maintaining and exacerbating their fears and subjecting them to the real risk of misidentification. The UK's adoption of detailed domestic criminal legislation since 2003, to prosecute and punish traffickers is both necessary and commendable as the police chapters in this Handbook show; however its reliance on mere policy to protect the rights of the victims of human trafficking is not, and this urgently needs to be addressed. It is hoped that this Handbook may serve to demonstrate that victims have, under international, Council of Europe and European law, the right to receive via lawful, fair procedures a legal recognition of their trafficked status that will enable them to receive a safer route to recovery, justice and restitution than the UK currently provides. Trafficked adults and children, as victims of significant human rights abuses and in many cases as victims of modern-day slavery, need their rights to be recognised, protected and respected under domestic law: their rights must be brought home.

Parosha Chandran

1 Pump Court Chambers

Elm Court

Temple

London

August 2011

Contributors

General Editor

Parosha Chandran, General Editor

LLB (Hons.), LLM (Lond.), Diplôme in Human Rights (International Institute of Human Rights, Strasbourg), Barrister of Lincoln's Inn

Parosha Chandran is an award-winning human rights barrister at 1 Pump Court Chambers in London whose work has led to several advances in the law governing victims of human trafficking. A member of Lincoln's Inn, with 14 years' experience at the Bar, she acts for both adult and child victims of trafficking in the UK and is a recognised, leading specialist in the fields of forced labour and human trafficking for sexual and labour exploitation. Her ground-breaking and precedent-setting trafficking cases include the non-punishment related criminal appeal in *R v O* [2008] EWCA Crim 2835, the refugee-recognition trafficking appeal in *SB (PSG, Protection Regulations, Reg 6) Moldova CG* [2008] UKAIT 00002 and *M v UK*, 16081/08 [2009] ECHR 1229, the first successful human trafficking-related claim against the UK to be taken to the European Court of Human Rights. She recently acted in the significant gang-related trafficking protection appeal in *PO (Nigeria) v Secretary of State for the Home Department* [2011] EWCA Civ 132.

Her human rights and human trafficking expertise stems from her practice at the Bar and from having undertaken study and work placements at several leading human rights organisations including the British Institute of Human Rights (London, 1993-5), the AIRE Centre (London, 1996), the former European Commission for Human Rights, Strasbourg (1996), the UNHCR in London (1997) and the UN International Criminal Tribunal for the Former Yugoslavia in The Hague where she worked for the Office of the Prosecutor (1999). She won, in 1994, the coveted Diplôme in Human Rights at the International Institute of Human Rights in Strasbourg: she was the youngest recipient of the award at the time. Her first book, '*A Guide to the Human Rights Act*' was published by Butterworths in 1999. She has been consulted on numerous trafficking-related publications and was a specialist contributor to the *Anti-trafficking Toolkit* (IAS, 2007).

Working from her base in London, Parosha's legal practice often involves the bringing of 'test cases' on human trafficking issues which she has identified, so as to encourage law and policy to be developed and refined. She also provides expert legal training to numerous organisations and works closely with many key NGOs to promote and protect the rights of victims of human trafficking and victims of forced labour in the UK. These include Anti-Slavery International, the Poppy Project, the AIRE Centre, ECPAT (UK), Kalayaan and the Helen Bamber Foundation.

In 2008 Parosha was named 'Barrister of the Year' by the Law Society's Excellence Awards and in 2009 she won the Society of Asian Lawyers' 'Pro Bono/Human Rights Lawyer of the Year' Award. That same year she was selected as a Woman of Achievement by the Woman of the Year Awards 2009. She, together with Klara Skrivankova of Anti-Slavery International and Nadine Finch of Garden Court Chambers founded the Trafficking Law and Policy Forum in early 2007, an educational think-tank which meets quarterly in the UK with specialists to discuss emerging developments in domestic and international human trafficking law and policy. Parosha is a member of 'The Times' Law Panel, a list of the 100 most influential lawyers in the UK. She is ranked by the Chambers and Partners Law Directory and by the Legal 500 as a leader in her fields.

Contributors

Christine Beddoe

Christine Beddoe, the Director of ECPAT UK, has been working with the international ECPAT network for over 15 years in UK, Australia and Asia. She has campaigned extensively on the prevention of child sexual exploitation, participating in landmark campaigns to change laws for the protection of children. Between 1999 and 2004 Christine designed and led an innovative programme across South East Asia developing partnerships with governments and private sector partners to protect vulnerable children from sexual abuse and trafficking. Since joining ECPAT UK in 2004 Christine has driven forward the campaign to combat the trafficking of children into the UK, working with government and other stakeholders to expose the extent of the exploitation of children in prostitution, domestic servitude, forced labour and organised criminal activity across Britain. Christine was awarded a Winston Churchill Research Fellowship in 2003 and her MA research dissertation focussed on the sexual exploitation of boys in Sri Lanka.

Pam Bowen

Pam Bowen has worked for the Crown Prosecution Service since 1986. Having worked in CPS Merseyside for many years she moved to East Midlands in 1993 and then the CPS Headquarters in 1999 to work on a national re-organisation. After a 12 month secondment to HM CPS Inspectorate she joined the Policy Directorate as a senior policy advisor in 2001. Her work has involved a wide range of topics, mostly supporting victim initiatives. She has worked on developing policy regarding human trafficking, organised immigration crime and prostitution since 2006.

Colin Carswell

Colin Carswell is a Chief Inspector in the Metropolitan Police Service (MPS) in London having served for over 22 years in a variety of roles. He joined the MPS in 1989 and served for a number of years in uniform throughout South and West London. In 2000 he was accepted into the MPS Anti-Corruption Command working on high profile Police corruption investigations. In 2004 he was promoted to Inspector and he led the Policing team for Oxford Street, the busiest retail street in Europe with 200 million visitors a year. In January 2007, as Detective Chief Inspector in the MPS Specialist Crime Directorate, he delivered international capacity building projects in Romania, Bulgaria, Vietnam, Tanzania and UAE, much of this funded by external partners. In late 2007 Colin was recruited to operationally lead the MPS response to Romanian organised criminals trafficking and exploiting Roma children, an investigation known as 'Operation Golf'. He regularly runs training days and workshops on trafficking for Local Authorities and Police 'Public Protection Units'. He recently carried out training on Joint Investigation Teams for the United Nations Office of Drugs & Crime (UNODC) and the European Police College (CEPOL). He is currently the MPS' Team Leader for a Joint Investigation with Bulgarian Law enforcement into organised crime involving thefts on London's transport network.

Peter Carter QC

Peter Carter was called to the Bar by Gray's Inn in 1974 and was appointed Queen's Counsel in 1995. He is a Master of the Bench of Gray's Inn. He undertakes all types of criminal law work either for defence or prosecution, but with the principal emphasis upon fraud, terrorism, homicide and trafficking.

He is on the panel of Special Advocates and acted as special advocate in the case of *Bourgass and others* at the Old Bailey (the ricin case).

His interest in, and knowledge of, international human rights law adds another area to his practice. He has appeared before the Inter-American Court of Human Rights, the UN Human Rights Council and the Social Rights group of the EU Parliament as well as the Privy Council.

He frequently lectures on domestic and international criminal law and human rights law.

He is a trustee of the British Institute of Human Rights and of Fair Trials International, a patron of Amicus, and a member of the British Institute of International & Comparative Law, of the Society for Advanced Legal Studies and of the Poetry Society.

He acted for the victim of trafficking in the landmark non-punishment related criminal appeal of *R v O* [2008] EWCA Crim 2835.

Saadiya Chaudary

Saadiya Chaudary is the Legal Project Manager at the AIRE Centre and co-ordinates the Centre's Human Trafficking and Domestic Violence Law Project. Saadiya undertakes third-party interventions and litigation before UK courts and tribunals, the European Court of Human Rights and the Court of Justice of the European Union. She also provides advice on these issues through the Centre's advice service. Saadiya has delivered a number of training sessions on aspects of international and European human rights law and on trafficking, and has authored publications on human rights and EU law.

Saadiya is a qualified Solicitor in the UK and holds an LLM in International Law.

Jamila Duncan-Bosu

Jamila Duncan-Bosu is a Solicitor, based at the North Kensington Law Centre (NKLC) since 2006. Her practice includes all areas of Employment and Discrimination Law. During her time at NKLC she has developed unique expertise in representing Migrant Domestic Workers in relation to their complaints of domestic servitude, She is currently instructed in an appeal to the Employment Appeals Tribunal regarding the application of the family worker exemption that is contained in national minimum wage legislation. She has appeared on national media to speak on domestic servitude and employment law to a lay audience. She was broadcast speaking on this subject on Radio 4's File on Four programme.

Kayte Fairfax

Kayte Fairfax is a consultant who has worked in Europe, Asia, Africa and Australia to develop strategies and frontline tools to better protect child victims of trafficking. She successfully advocated for the inclusion of child rights in Australia's federal law on human trafficking. Recent UK work has focused on the identification and safeguarding of suspected child Victims. Over two years, Kayte was involved in the development, implementation and monitoring of the London Safeguarding Children Board Child Trafficking Toolkit that was piloted across 12 UK local authorities. She implemented the Toolkit in Southwark council, designed a child trafficking indicators screening tool for social workers and authored the national monitoring report of the Toolkit pilot project.

Nadine Finch

Nadine Finch was called as a barrister in 1991 and practises in children's rights, immigration and community care law at Garden Court Chambers, 57–60 Lincoln's Inn Fields, London WC2A 3LS. She has also been a fee paid Immigration Judge since December 2006.

As a barrister she regularly represents migrant and trafficked children at all levels of the Tribunal and court. She has also delivered lectures and training courses on human trafficking for a wide range of organisations, including the Immigration Law Practitioners Association, the NSPCC, CFAB, IAS, RMJ, the Bar Conference, the International Bar Association and Garden Court Chambers.

She was a contributor to the Fifth, Sixth and Seventh Editions of *Macdonald's Immigration Law & Practice* (Lexis Nexis), a co-author of *Putting Children First: A guide for immigration practitioners* (LAG) and *Seeking Asylum Alone: Unaccompanied and Separated Children and Refugee Protection in the U.K.* (Harvard University Committee on Human Rights Studies), *Seeking Asylum Alone: Unaccompanied and Separated Children and Refugee Protection in Australia, the U.K. and the U.S.* (Themis Press) and *Levelling the Playing Field: A UNICEF report into provision of services to unaccompanied or separated migrant children in three local authority areas in England* (UNICEF UK March 2010).

She is also a member of the advisory group to the NSPCC's Child Trafficking Advice and Information Line and founded the Trafficking Law and Policy Forum with Parosha Chandran and Klara Skrivankova. In addition she is a Trustee of *Statewatch*.

She is presently undertaking contracts on behalf of UNHCR and UNICEF relating to the best interests of children, including trafficked children, in Europe.

Bernie Gravett (Superintendent Retired)

Bernie Gravett is a retired Police Superintendent from the Metropolitan Police. He created and led 'Operation Golf', an investigation into Romanian Roma Organised Crime Networks which traffick and exploit children who are forced to beg and steal across the UK and Europe. Golf was a formal Joint Investigation Team with Romania under EU law and is the first such operation in Europe. The operation concluded in December 2010 with over 130 members of the criminal network prosecuted in the UK and Romania. This was unique in policing history, thoroughly dismantling the network and reducing trafficking of children across the whole of Europe. Operation Golf achieved the first conviction in the UK for the trafficking of a child for criminal exploitation and also for 'internal' trafficking within the UK for criminal exploitation. Four people were sentenced for a total of 24 years in prison.

Retired Superintendent Gravett advises the Home Office on trafficking of human beings and Romanian Organised Crime. He has developed THB training for law enforcement officers that has been delivered to the Serious Organised Crime Agency, UK Police forces, Europol, Interpol, Eurojust and the UNODC.

He is an accredited Eurojust expert on Joint Investigation Teams.

Bernie Gravett is now the Director of Specialist Policing Consultancy Ltd. The company specialises in training on human trafficking and organised crime issues to the 3rd sector and police across Europe. It is also able to advise on applications for European Commission funding and a wide range of security, risk management and policing issues.

Lois Hamilton

Lois Hamilton attended Queens University Belfast and qualified as a solicitor in 1998. After spending time in private practice she began work in Northern Ireland (NI) in 2000 in the voluntary legal sector with Law Centre (NI) where she continues to work. She was initially employed as an employment lawyer before moving to the immigration team where she continues to specialise in immigration law cases involving human rights, asylum, unaccompanied minors, applications under EU law and victims of human trafficking. In October 2008 Lois was invited to Washington D.C. by the Office for Democratic Institutions and Human Rights Department as a UK representative to participate in a seminar held by the American Bar Association on Civil Remedies for Human Trafficking Victims. Since then she has become one of the leading lawyers in NI representing in this particular area of law. Lois contributed a NI legal perspective to the Anti-Trafficking Monitoring Project report into the UKs compliance with the Trafficking Convention and continues to lobby the Justice Minster in NI to implement the recommendations. She was one of the guest speakers at a recent conference held in Belfast alongside statutory and non-statutory agencies including members of the Police forces both North and South of Ireland.

Hogan Lovells

Hogan Lovells is an international law firm with a 40 year commitment to pro bono work, delivering over 100,000 hours of pro bono advice a year. The firm's anti-human trafficking practice has succeeded in establishing the first ever compensation awards for victims of human trafficking and continues to work to support the victims of this largely underestimated crime. The firm partners with the UK's leading NGOs in the area: Kalayaan, the Poppy Project and Anti-Slavery International. **Giles Hutt** is a Professional Support Lawyer in Hogan Lovells' London office, specialising in commercial litigation. He has handled numerous statutory compensation cases, including claims brought by victims of the July 2005 London bombings.

Silva Hove

Silva Hove has worked in the Social Care sector for over 10 years. Through her work with vulnerable women, including women who have been trafficked and exploited in prostitution, she has acquired a wealth of knowledge on gender issues and developed expertise of working with women trafficked and exploited in prostitution, their backgrounds, their experiences of prostitution and the impact of prostitution on their (mental) well-being.

Silva Hove is one of the original staff members of the Poppy Project, and worked for Poppy from 2004 to 2011. She has over seven years' experience of providing support to female victims of trafficking and has contributed to shaping the support model developed within Poppy. Silva's roles have included managing the Accommodation and Support (Acute) services of the Poppy Project and Team Leader for the Poppy Outreach Service which co-ordinated the outreach support for female victims of trafficking throughout the UK.

Silva Hove has contributed to a number of significant research studies on trafficking by Eaves Housing including: 'When women are trafficked – quantifying the gendered experience of trafficking in the UK' (2004) and she participated in a European Research project on the Health Impacts of Trafficking (2005) led by Catherine Zimmerman.

Andrew Howard

Andrew Howard joined ECPAT UK in January 2010 as Campaigns Officer, bringing with him a range of campaigning and political lobbying experience on a variety of issues, including animal welfare at the International Fund for Animal Welfare, climate change at Operation Noah and international development at ActionAid UK. Prior to this he spent two years working as a parliamentary researcher for two Labour MPs. Andrew has also worked in the Foreign Office and at the Foreign Policy Centre, a centre-left think-tank. Andrew's interest in children's issues started when he was an English teacher at a junior high school in Japan in the late 1990s. As a researcher in Parliament he worked on issues such as access to early years' education and child poverty. Since starting his role as Campaigns Officer, Andrew has undertaken a wide range of tasks. He has greatly improved ECPAT UK's use of social networking and has built a strong supporter base for ECPAT UK issues in Parliament.

Philip Ishola

Philip Ishola has worked within the local and central government field of child protection and child and adult safeguarding for 18 years, extensively focused around safeguarding unaccompanied children and families seeking asylum in the UK. As part of these roles Philip has led the development of a range of care, integration transition and safe returns policies, procedures and strategies incorporating a strong safeguarding focus. Philip is currently Harrow Council's Separated Children and Leaving Care Children's Service Manager and Member of the Local Harrow Safeguarding Children Board. Philip chairs the London Safeguarding Children Board (London SCB) Trafficked Children Group and the London SCB 2012 Olympics (safe games for children) Group and he is an advisor on safeguarding children matters (including child trafficking) to the Greater London Authority 2012 Olympic Network. As part of this role Philip holds the counter child trafficking portfolio for the Association of Directors of Children Services National Asylum Task Force. He is the former Deputy chair of the Victim Care Group of the UK Human Trafficking Centre (Serious Organised Crime Agency SOCA-UKHTC) and is a member of the UK Government National Referral Mechanism Strategic Monitoring Group advising on safeguarding children matters.

Kalvir Kaur

Kalvir Kaur, a solicitor by qualification, is Project Officer (Child Trafficking) at ECPAT UK. Her reputation as a solicitor known for her extensive experience in representing refugee children and victims of trafficking was recognised when in 2008 she was the recipient of the Immigration Legal Aid Lawyer of the Year Award. In her current role, Kalvir takes forward this expertise in ECPAT's legal work, liaising with legal representatives across the immigration, welfare and criminal fields and preparing expert legal reports. She is particularly renowned for her ability to effectively interview child victims of trafficking.

Dr Michael Korzinski PhD

Michael is a co-founding Director of the Helen Bamber Foundation. He has worked with survivors of torture, trafficking and other forms of human cruelty since 1990. He was a lead clinician in the first organisation in the United Kingdom, founded by Helen Bamber, specialising in the care and treatment of victims of torture. He has been directly involved in the rehabilitation of hundreds of survivors of gross human rights' violations and thousands more through his training and consultation work. As a therapist he advanced new methods to treat survivors of torture and is a recognised expert in the field of trauma and recovery. He has authored several works on the subject. He is a consultant to trauma services, Governmental and Non-Governmental Organisations in the UK and worldwide. His international work included the development of a project in Afghanistan utilising story telling and drama as a means of providing therapeutic support for women traumatised by war and torture. His recent work includes providing direct therapeutic support as well as developing projects to assist former Guantanamo Bay detainees to reintegrate into society. He is currently acting as specialist consultant to the OSCE on human trafficking and is a member of Mayor's Office for the City of New York working party on human trafficking. He has extensive experience in treating survivors of human trafficking in the UK as well as acting as an expert witness and preparing reports for the court.

Jawaid Luqmani

Jawaid Luqmani is a senior partner at Luqmani Thompson & Partners and has been involved in migration related work for over 20 years. His firm is very well regarded and his client and peer feedback is exemplary. He was Treasurer for the Immigration Law Practitioners' Association (ILPA) between 2002–2007. He was appointed by the Law Society as Chief Assessor to the Immigration and Asylum Accreditation Scheme in 2011 and previously served as a member of the Advisory Panel to the Immigration Services Commissioner from 2001–2005. He has lectured extensively for ILPA and provided in house training for a number of non-governmental organisations, charities and individual law firms in the UK and abroad. He has been involved in lobbying work in the UK and the European Parliament. Published work includes chapters in 'Defending Suspects at Police Stations' and 'Support for Asylum seekers and other Migrants'. He has provided written updates in immigration law for Legal Action Group for over 15 years. Cases include a wide range involving the interplay between migration related issues and education, crime, terrorism and discrimination. He has been listed in Chambers and Partners since 1997 and continues to be regarded as a significant leader in his field.

Detective Chief Superintendent Richard Martin

Detective Chief Superintendent Richard Martin is the Operational Command Unit (OCU) Commander for SCD 6, the Economic and Specialist Crime Command, and SCD 9, the Human Exploitation and Organised Crime Command within London. These specialist commands comprise over 700 specialist detectives and staff tackling local, national and international criminal networks. Richard began his career in the British Army in 1983 before embarking on a policing career in the West Midlands Police in 1994. In June 2002 Richard was seconded to the National Criminal Intelligence Service (NCIS) as a Detective Chief Inspector responsible for conducting covert operations aimed at tackling serious and organised crime. During this period he transferred to London to create and lead a new operational team to support London and South East Police Forces in tackling criminal networks working with the US Drug Enforcement Agency and other key enforcement partners. Richard transferred to the Metropolitan Police in December 2004, initially carrying out the Head of Uniform Operations role before becoming, as Detective Superintendent, Head of the Crime Command responsible for all criminal investigations within the London borough of Lewisham. In 2006 he took on the role of Borough Commander leading a team of 850 police officers and police staff. Following this role and prior to becoming the OCU Commander for SCD 6 and 9, Richard led a joint operation together with the United Kingdom Border Agency, tackling the most harmful gang members in London using both police and immigration powers to reduce harm within London communities. This operation led to the arrests and detention of 80 of the most harmful offenders in London.

Sally Montier

Sally Montier joined the Poppy Project as a Senior Support Worker in 2003 and through direct work, gained extensive experience of supporting women who have been trafficked, promoting client-centred, safe, sustainable support. In 2009 she moved to the role of Team Leader, managing the accommodation service. In July 2011 she took up the post of Training and Capacity Building Worker within the Poppy Team. Sally has worked with both statutory and non-statutory agencies to raise awareness of trafficking and improve best practice in victim care. She has also been involved in training external agencies and services to respond to trafficking on a national and international level and contributed to research and consultations influencing trafficking-related policies.

Jenny Moss

Jenny Moss is a Community Advocate at Kalayaan where she has worked for three years giving advice to migrant domestic workers, and campaigning with them, helping them to raise their voices to policy makers. Jenny worked previously for Toynbee Hall delivering financial inclusion workshops at domestic violence refuges, prisons and drug treatment centres, as well as contributing to financial inclusion policy for banks and Government departments. Jenny has also worked in public health research in Bangladesh and the UK.

Piya D. Muqit

Piya D. Muqit was called to the English Bar in October 2001 and completed pupillage with Doughty Street Chambers and Garden Court Chambers. Since then she has worked for ECRI in the Directorate of Human Rights, Council of Europe, the Capital Post Conviction Project of Louisiana in New Orleans and Ain o Salish Kendra in Dhaka. In the UK she was a legal officer for Refugee and Migrant Justice and is currently the children's law and policy officer at Freedom from Torture, the Medical Foundation for the Care of Victims of Torture, where she works on policy and legal issues affecting children, young people and families who have suffered torture.

She qualified at the Scottish Bar in 2005 and practices as a barrister with the Murray Stable, Faculty of Advocates, specialising in asylum and immigration law, child law, public law and human rights. She has extensively trained UK lawyers and practitioners from other disciplines in human rights law, in particular on the rights of children, and organises legal training for practitioners working in the immigration and asylum field in Scotland on behalf of the Murray Stable and the Scottish Refugee Council.

Kate Roberts

Kate Roberts has worked at Kalayaan since 2005. Her role as a Community Advocate involves direct client advice as well as policy and campaign work. Prior to working at Kalayaan, Kate was employed as a Community Development Worker in a Sure Start Local Programme in Haringey. Kate has also worked in International Development and has volunteered with refugees in the UK. Kate has an LLM in Human Rights from Birkbeck University, for which she was awarded a Distinction.

Catherine Robinson

Catherine Robinson qualified as a solicitor in 2006 having completed her training contract at an international law firm. Subsequently she joined the

Immigration Department of Fisher Meredith LLP. She has undertaken a wide-range of immigration cases from judicial reviews, appeals at all levels including the Court of Appeal, initial applications for leave to remain (asylum and non-asylum), fresh asylum and human rights claims and applications to the European Court of Human Rights. She was ranked as an 'Associate to Watch' by Chambers & Partners 2011 in the category Immigration: Personal: London. She acted as solicitor, jointly with the AIRE Centre and Counsel Parosha Chandran in the case of *M v UK* (Application No: 16081/08), the first human trafficking-related claim from the UK to be brought to the European Court of Human Rights. Catherine is cross-qualifying as a barrister and from October 2011 she will be undertaking her pupillage at 1 Pump Court Chambers.

Klara Skrivankova

Klara Skrivankova has been working in anti-trafficking since 2000 and has since been involved in assistance to numerous victims. In 2005, she joined Anti-Slavery International, the world's oldest international human rights organisation and the only UK charity solely dealing with modern day slavery. She leads Anti-Slavery's anti-trafficking programme, managing research, advocacy and projects to eliminate all forms of trafficking. Her most recent work has focused on trafficking for forced labour and access to justice for trafficked persons. Klara frequently provides expert witness statements in British courts. She acted as an expert (2005–2008) with the Council of Europe, assisting the campaign to promote the Convention on Action against Trafficking in Human Beings. In 2007 she co-founded with Parosha Chandran and Nadine Finch the Trafficking Law and Policy Forum. She was a member (2008–2011) of the EU Experts Group on Trafficking, advising the European Commission. Since 2009, she has served on the Advisory Board of the Forced Labour and Modern Day Slavery Programme of the Joseph Rowntree Foundation. In 2009, she was appointed to the Board of Trustees of the UN Voluntary Trust Fund on Contemporary Forms of Slavery and in 2010 to the Board of the UN Voluntary Trust Fund for Victims of Trafficking in Persons.

Detective Chief Inspector Nick Sumner MA

Nick Sumner began his police career in the Metropolitan Police Service in 1989 when he joined as a police cadet. His first posting was to South Norwood in South London where he soon began his career as a Detective. In 1999 he was posted to the Homicide Command before being promoted to Detective Sergeant in 2001 and transferring to the Royal Borough of Kensington and Chelsea. Nick returned to the world of homicide in 2005, was promoted to the rank of Detective Inspector and became qualified as a Senior Investigating Officer. Whilst on the Homicide Command he led the investigation into a number of murders across London and achieved promotion to the rank of Detective Chief Inspector in 2010. In his current post Nick is the operations manager for the MPS Human Exploitation and Organised Crime Command (SCD9) that investigate human trafficking cases within London.

Adam Weiss

Adam Weiss is the Assistant Director of The AIRE Centre and is involved in all of the Centre's work on migration issues, including numerous cases before the European Court of Human Rights as well as the vast majority of the AIRE

Centre's advice work. He conducts training on human trafficking, domestic violence, asylum and immigration and EU free movement law in the UK and widely throughout Europe. Adam studied law in the USA and the UK and is a Member of the New York State bar. He is a part-time lecturer at Webster Graduate School, Regent's College where he teaches public international law and grant-writing to masters students. Adam has published various articles on the free movement of persons as well as human rights and equality law.

Detective Constable Sarah Wood – Metropolitan Police

Sarah Wood is a Detective Constable with the Metropolitan Police Service (MPS) and currently works on the Child Abuse Investigation Command as a trainer. Her current work involves training police officers and social workers in child abuse investigation and interviewing children.

Having lived and worked in Greece and Portugal, Sarah began her police career with Nottinghamshire Police in 1993. Sarah moved to work for a national police unit in London in 2001 and in 2004 transferred to the Metropolitan Police and worked in a team investigating child abuse. Her interest in child trafficking became a focus when she became one of the founder members of the award winning Paladin Team (a joint MPS and United Kingdom Border Agency team dedicated to safeguarding children at London ports) whilst working at London Heathrow airport.

During her time working with the Paladin Team, Sarah became particularly interested in interviewing children for whom English is not their first language and developed enhanced awareness of how cultural factors influence victims of child abuse and trafficking.

After four years safeguarding children at Heathrow airport Sarah left the Paladin Team in early 2010 and moved to become a trainer. Sarah is currently a full time trainer in the Child Abuse Investigation Command of the Metropolitan Police in London teaching child protection and safeguarding subjects to a variety of professionals including police officers and social workers and regularly speaks at conferences and seminars on the subject of child trafficking.

Organisations

The AIRE Centre

The AIRE Centre (Advice in Individual Rights in Europe) is a London-based NGO whose mission is to promote awareness of European law rights and assist marginalised individuals and those in vulnerable circumstances to assert those rights. The Centre runs an advice service providing free legal advice to individuals and representatives on European Law (particularly EU migrant law) and also takes cases to the European Court of Human Rights. The Centre also frequently intervenes as a third party before national and European courts including the Court of Justice of the European Union. The AIRE Centre has been involved in the litigation of nine cases before the European Court of Human Rights involving the rights of trafficking victims. For further information see: www.airecentre.org/.

Anti-Slavery International

Anti-Slavery International, founded in 1839, is the world's oldest international human rights organisation and the only charity in the UK to work exclusively against modern day slavery and related human rights abuses. Anti-Slavery International is committed to eliminating slavery throughout the World. Slavery, servitude and forced labour are violations of individual freedoms, which deny millions of people their basic dignity and fundamental human rights. Anti-Slavery International works to end these abuses by exposing current cases of slavery, campaigning for its eradication, supporting the initiatives of local organisations to release people, and pressing for more effective implementation of international and national laws against slavery. Anti-Slavery International has been working on the issue of trafficking in human beings since the early 1990s, documenting the problem and campaigning to ensure that trafficking is brought on the international agenda and that laws put in place to deal with this modern form of slavery. The organisation continues to work on trafficking, most recently focussing especially on forced labour, access to justice and compensation and monitoring of implementation of laws. In 2009, Anti-Slavery International with its partners was instrumental in lobbying the British Government to introduce a stand-alone criminal offence of forced labour. For further information see: www.antislavery.org.

ECPAT UK

ECPAT UK (End Child Prostitution, Child Pornography and the Trafficking of Children for Sexual Purposes) is a leading child rights organisation campaigning against the exploitation of children, including child trafficking and the sexual abuse of children by British sex offenders who travel abroad. ECPAT UK was established in 1993 and has led ground breaking campaigns to change legislation and influence public opinion. ECPAT UK achieves its aims by undertaking research, training professionals and working with young people to ensure that all campaigns are evidence based. ECPAT UK is constantly in demand for speaking to media, providing policy advice and working with Local Authorities to provide a safe environment for children. ECPAT UK is also the advisor to the All Party Parliamentary Group on Human Trafficking and is the UK representative of the global ECPAT movement. The ECPAT UK Youth Group is a weekly support group for child victims of trafficking and has created an opportunity for children and young people affected by trafficking to contribute their voice to public policy. The Youth Group projects include a training video for Foster Carers about what makes good foster care for trafficked children. For further information see: www.ecpat.org.uk/.

The Helen Bamber Foundation

The Helen Bamber Foundation, founded by Helen Bamber OBE and Dr Michael Korzinski in 2005, is a UK-based human rights charity providing medical consultation, therapeutic care, human rights advocacy and practical support to survivors of gross human rights violations, torture, political oppression, trafficking for sexual exploitation and other forms of extreme cruelty. Amongst the organisations addressing the issue for human trafficking, the Helen Bamber Foundation holds a unique role in offering long-term clinical treatment to thousands of male, female and child survivors of human trafficking. For further information see www.helenbamber.org.

Kalayaan

Kalayaan is a registered charity that gives advice and support to migrant domestic workers and campaigns with them to improve their rights and their ability to enforce those rights in the UK. Kalayaan, domestic workers and the Unions have, since 1987, campaigned for migrant domestic workers to be given an immigration status independent of their employer, with recognition as a worker and the right to change employer as a measure of protection against exploitation and abuse. These rights were won in 1998 and preserved when under threat in 2008. Kalayaan is currently campaigning against proposals to remove these rights, which would make hundreds of workers more vulnerable to trafficking for domestic servitude. For further information see: www.kalayaan.org.uk/.

The Poppy Project

The Poppy Project is part of the charity Eaves which has more than 30 years' experience supporting women affected by homelessness, violence and exclusion. The Poppy Project has accommodated and supported female trafficked victims since 2001 and was funded by the Government to provide these services to women trafficked into England and Wales since 2003. Poppy's services have contributed to the development of the UK's position in terms of a victim-led, human rights-based response to human trafficking. Since July 2011 the Poppy Project has been independently funded. For further information see: www.eaves4women.co.uk/POPPY_Project/POPPY_Project.php.

SCD9

SCD 9 is a specialist Metropolitan Police Service (MPS) Operational Command Unit (OCU) which provides guidance and operational support to the MPS around a number of key areas of criminality. The key areas of responsibility for the OCU are: tackling organised immigration crime; human trafficking for sexual exploitation, domestic servitude and forced labour; the policing of the night time economy of nightclubs, licensed premises and casinos; on-street and off-street prostitution and obscene publications including the investigation of the electronic sharing of indecent images of children. SCD 9 has pan-London responsibility but also operates both nationally and, at times, internationally within these key areas.

Contents

APPENDICES

Contents

Table of Cases

Table of Cases

S

Decisions of the European Court of Justice are listed below numerically. These decisions are also included in the preceding alphabetical list.

Table of Statutes

References printed in **bold** type indicate where the section of an Act is set out in part or in full.

Other Jurisdictions

Australia

Table of Statutory Instruments

References printed in **bold** type indicate where the Statutory Instrument is set out in part or in full.

Table of European Legislation

Paragraph references printed in **bold** type indicate where the Legislation is set out in part or in full.

Table of European Legislation

Table of International Legislation

References printed in **bold** type indicate where the Legislation is set out in part or in full.

Part I

PERSPECTIVES ON IDENTIFICATION

Contents

1

A COMMENTARY ON INTERPRETING HUMAN TRAFFICKING

Parosha Chandran

THE NEED TO IDENTIFY WHAT HUMAN TRAFFICKING MEANS

1.1 Through the experience of representing the rights of trafficked and other vulnerable victims and survivors for many years I have learned never to assume the meanings of legal words or phrases but to seek out authoritative, or rational, interpretations of them. My objective, like that of many other lawyers, has been always to seek equal and fair treatment and protection for some of the most vulnerable children and adults in our society.

To commence any stage of the victim identification process it is vital that the definition of human trafficking is applied to what is known about an individual's case. Disclosure by trafficking victims is never straightforward, if ever complete. For this reason it is absolutely crucial that those who conduct the identification process on behalf of the State are trained professionals in human trafficking, as is fully expected by the Council of Europe in its Convention on Action against Trafficking in Human Beings 2005 ('Trafficking Convention')[1] and that such persons act in partnership with support organisations, including local authorities and NGOs, in identifying victims. All professionals therefore need to have a clear understanding of what obstacles may prevent or hinder a victim's disclosure[2], they need to be aware of the need to build a relationship of trust with the individual and above all they must be aware that the individual might not be able to fully, or even partly if the victim is a child, understand or explain what actions led to them being trafficked and, where applicable, exploited. Experience in correctly identifying victims of trafficking is a vital tool, although for newcomers, dedicated identification training and the use of human trafficking indicators, such as are included in the Appendices to this book[3], will assist in the identification process. Notwithstanding these safeguards however, if the definition of human trafficking is not applied or is not applied correctly to what is objectively or factually known about an individual's case a real risk of misidentification will ensue.

Central to the identification process is therefore how to determine whether the act of human trafficking took place. Something that needs to be openly discussed in the UK is how to define and thereby interpret the meaning of the words that form the three core elements of the trafficking definition itself. What do words such as 'recruitment', 'deception', 'coercion', 'abuse of a position of vulnerability', 'slavery', 'forced labour' actually mean? Has the meaning of any of these words changed over time, and if so what do they mean now? What is, for example, contemporary slavery? Has 'exploitation' been defined and if so does the exploitation of a child differ from that of an adult? Are there common definitions of these terms in any one document which apply to States that are bound by the Protocol to Prevent, Suppress and Punish Trafficking in Persons, Especially Women and Children, supplementing the United Nations Convention against Transnational Organized Crime 2000 ('the Palermo Protocol') and/or the Trafficking Convention? If the answer to this question is 'no', and it is no, are there any forms of authoritative international or European guidance which States can consult and potentially adopt in order to better streamline and co-ordinate their actions to protect victims via their accurate identification, to achieve intelligence and witness testimony to successfully prosecute and punish traffickers, including by way of cross-border collaborative police operations, and use to enforce the prevention of trafficking, all in collaboration with specialist organisations and experienced NGOs in the UK?

[1]   See Appendix to this book. Article 10(1) of the Trafficking Convention provides, so far as is relevant: 'Each Party shall provide its competent authorities with persons who are trained and qualified in preventing and combating trafficking in human beings, in identifying and helping victims, including children, and shall ensure that the different authorities collaborate with each other as well as with relevant support organisations, so that victims can be identified in a procedure duly taking into account the special situation of women and child victims . . . '.

[2]   See **CHAPTER 2** of this book and also **CHAPTER 4** as a whole.

[3]   For example, the United Nations Office on Drugs and Crime (UNODC) human trafficking indicators, the UK's National Referral Mechanism (NRM) trafficking indicators as contained within the NRM referral forms and the guidance on the criminal offences of slavery and forced labour which is to be found in the Court Circular on s 71 of the Coroners and Justice Act 2009.

THE UNODC MODEL LAW AGAINST TRAFFICKING IN PERSONS

1.2 In 2009 the United Nations Office on Drugs and Crime (UNODC)[1] developed its Model Law against Trafficking in Persons[2]. The Model Law was developed in particular to assist States in implementing the provisions contained in the Palermo Protocol 2000. The Model Law was therefore designed in such a way as to adapt to the needs of each State, whatever its legal tradition and social, economic, cultural and geographical conditions.

This Model Law helpfully provides an extensive set of definitions[3] which explain the meanings of many of the words that are used in the three core elements which comprise the act of human trafficking under the Palermo Protocol and they therefore may apply equally to understanding the act of human trafficking as defined in identical terms under the Trafficking Convention[4]. This is particularly relevant when one considers that neither of these two instruments, including the Explanatory Report to the Trafficking Convention, provide many key definitions themselves. Indeed the new EU Directive 2011/36/EU[5] ('the EU Trafficking Directive') is also silent in terms of many such definitions. The value of the definitions proposed under Article 5 of the

UNODC Model Law is, to my mind, that they are perfectly suited as an aid to interpretation for all three trafficking instruments[6]. The extensive list of highly-researched Model Law definitions also includes, in some places, detailed commentary which explains the terms used in an essentially trafficking-specific context. As one will soon see, ordinary words have a special meaning when looked at through the human trafficking lens. Hence, many vital terms, including deception, coercion, sexual exploitation, abuse of a position of vulnerability, forced labour and slavery are defined under the Model Law in such a way as to enable us to achieve a greater understanding of what the words used to define the act of human trafficking encompass and mean and consequently they will assist us in learning how these words ought to apply to all trafficking cases in a uniform but case-specific manner. This understanding should enable both accurate victim identification and meaningful victim protection to be achieved in the UK and, in consequence, an increase in the successful investigation, prosecution and punishment of human traffickers leading to the prevention of this abhorrent crime.

[1] As explained by the UNODC the creation of the Model Law arose following the General Assembly's request to the Secretary-General of the UN to promote and assist the efforts of Member States to become party to and implement the United Nations Convention against Transnational Organized Crime and the Protocols thereto. See Model Law, p 1.

[2] The mandate and work of the United Nations Office on Drugs and Crime (UNODC) is to assist UN Member States to fight organised crime, illicit drugs, corruption and international terrorism within the respective UN conventions and universal instruments. The UNODC is the guardian of the United Nations Convention against Transnational Organized Crime and its supplementary protocols on human trafficking and migrant smuggling, including the Palermo Protocol. The primary goal of the UNODC is to promote global adherence to these universal instruments and assist States to effectively implement them. See further http://www.unodc.org.

[3] The definitions under Article 5 of the UNODC Model Law are listed in alphabetical order and are not confined to the words used in the common definition of trafficking: numerous other words and phrases are also defined which are relevant to other aspects of the Model Law. For the purposes of introducing into the UK a detailed exposition of what the actual act of human trafficking engages and prohibits, my Commentary is restricted to providing an explanation of the definitions and trafficking-related meanings of only the key words that are used in the Palermo Protocol and Trafficking Convention common definition of trafficking. It does not extend to other aspects of the UNODC's Model Law: these are certainly also relevant for consideration by States and civil society organisations but are outside the scope of this chapter.

[4] The act of human trafficking has a shared definition under the Palermo Protocol and the Trafficking Convention, which is termed in my Commentary as 'the common definition of trafficking'. Hence Article 4(a) of the Palermo Protocol and Article 3(a) of the Trafficking Convention provide: '"Trafficking in human beings" shall mean the recruitment, transportation, transfer, harbouring or receipt of persons, by means of the threat or use of force or other forms of coercion, of abduction, of fraud, of deception, of the abuse of power or of a position of vulnerability or of the giving or receiving of payments or benefits to achieve the consent of a person having control over another person, for the purpose of exploitation. Exploitation shall include, at a minimum, the exploitation of the prostitution of others or other forms of sexual exploitation, forced labour or services, slavery or practices similar to slavery, servitude or the removal of organs.' See further para **1.5** below. The EU Trafficking Directive does not share the exact wording of the common defitnion of trafficking as it has an amended, extended definition of human trafficking: See further para **1.5** fn 1, below.

[5] Directive 2011/36/EU of the European Parliament and of the Council of 5 April 2011 on preventing and combating trafficking in human beings and protecting its victims, and replacing Council Framework Decision 2002/629/JHA. See Appendix to this book.

[6] Namely, the Palermo Protocol, the Trafficking Convention and the EU Trafficking Directive.

RECENT GUIDANCE FROM THE OSCE ON THE IDENTIFICATION OF VICTIMS

1.3 The OSCE[1] published in June 2011 a guidebook for police entitled 'Trafficking in Human Beings: Identification of Potential and Presumed Victims A Community Policing Approach' ('the Policing Guidebook'). In the Guidebook's 'Clarification of Terms' list the OSCE adopts many of the key trafficking-related definitions that are proposed in the UNODC's Model Law of 2009, confirming the authoritative status of many of the definitions that are set out in my Commentary below. For certain words however the OSCE promotes revised definitions which are also highly relevant in the context of recognising modern-day trafficking and slavery. The OSCE Policing Guidebook, as a whole, provides excellent, practical yet detailed advice on all aspects of victim identification for all who are engaged in the proocess, including how to assess and understand the issues of recruitment and transfer in the exploitation phases[2] and I highly recommend the Guidebook as essential further reading.

[1] Organization for Security and Co-operation in Europe. The OSCE is a pan-European security body which has 56 participating states, including the UK, the USA and spans from Vancouver to Vladivostok. It is recognised as a regional arrangement under Chapter VIII of the United Nations Charter and is a primary instrument for early warning, conflict prevention, crisis management and post-conflict rehabilitation in its areas. It addresses a wide range of security-related concerns including human rights, arms control, confidence and security building measures, national minorities, democratisation, policing strategies, counter-terrorism and economic and environmental activities. The OSCE hosts the Office of the Special Representative and Co-Ordinator for Combating Trafficking in Human Beings. See further http://www.osce.org.

[2] See OSCE Policing Guidebook, at pp 51–64 and 87 in particular.

THE METHODOLOGY USED IN THIS COMMENTARY

1.4 By using a personal methodology to provide a Commentary on the meaning of the words and terms used in the common definition of human trafficking it is sought not only to introduce definitions where there are none in the Palermo Protocol and the Trafficking Convention, via direct references to the definitions and guidance provided in the Model Law and terms that are clarified in the OSCE Policing Guidebook, but also to raise attention to other explanations for words, phrases and terms that are provided in the detailed Explanatory Report to the Trafficking Convention and in the Recital to the EU Trafficking Directive. I have also provided my own explanatory notes and in some relevant places my analysis of comparative European and international jurisprudence.

It is hoped that this Commentary will assist all those who work with victims of trafficking. Ideally the adoption and use of common terms may promote a common understanding of the meaning of essential trafficking terms amongst professionals in all sectors whose work directly or indirectly involves victim identification and in so doing this may enable victims of trafficking in the UK to be accurately identified, without re-traumatisation or criminalisation[1], by the operation of fair, efficient processes leading to their protection and assistance as recognised victims of serious crimes and of human rights violations in this country, and maybe beyond.

¹ See **CHAPTERS 24** and **25** of this book.

The Common Definition of Trafficking in Human Beings

1.5 The act of human trafficking is defined in identical terms in the Palermo Protocol and in the Trafficking Convention: to that extent they share a common definition of trafficking.

> '"Trafficking in human beings" shall mean the recruitment, transportation, transfer, harbouring or receipt of persons, by means of the threat or use of force or other forms of coercion, of abduction, of fraud, of deception, of the abuse of power or of a position of vulnerability or of the giving or receiving of payments or benefits to achieve the consent of a person having control over another person, for the purpose of exploitation. Exploitation shall include, at a minimum, the exploitation of the prostitution of others or other forms of sexual exploitation, forced labour or services, slavery or practices similar to slavery, servitude or the removal of organs.'¹

¹ Palermo Protocol 2000, Article 3(a); Council of Europe Convention on Action against Trafficking in Human Beings 2005 ('the Trafficking Convention'), Article 4(a). An extended definition of trafficking is provided in the new EU Directive 2011/36/EU which enters into force in the opting-in States of the EU on 13 April 2013. The UK has announced its intention to opt in. Article 2(1) of the Directive thus provides that human trafficking is: 'The recruitment, transportation, transfer, harbouring or reception of persons, <u>including the exchange or transfer of control over those persons</u>, by means of the threat or use of force or other forms of coercion, of abduction, of fraud, of deception, of the abuse of power or of a position of vulnerability or of the giving or receiving of payments or benefits to achieve the consent of a person having control over another person, for the purpose of exploitation.' [new words underlined]

COMMENTARY ON INTERPRETING THE DEFINITION OF HUMAN TRAFFICKING

1.6 The human trafficking definition can be broken down into three core elements, namely (1) the act; (2) the means and (3) the purpose. The common definition of trafficking therefore entails the following:

'1   The act of the:
  –   Recruitment
  –   Transportation
  –   Transfer
  –   Harbouring or
  –   Receipt of persons:
2   By means of:
  –   the threat or use of force, or
  –   other forms of coercion,
  –   of abduction,
  –   of fraud,
  –   of deception,
  –   of the abuse of power or of a position of vulnerability, or
  –   of the giving or receiving of payments or benefits to achieve the consent of a person having control over another person
3   For the purpose of exploitation. Exploitation includes at a minimum:
  –   the exploitation of the prostitution of others

> – or other forms of sexual exploitation,
> – forced labour or services,
> – slavery or practices similar to slavery,
> – servitude
> – or the removal or organs.'

As succinctly explained by the United Nations Office on Drugs and Crime (UNODC)[1], the 'act' explains what is done; 'the means' describe how it is done and 'the purpose' explains why it is done. Under the human trafficking definition the trafficking of an adult takes place when all three core elements above are present. The trafficking of a child occurs when core elements 1 and 3 are present: there is no requirement to establish that any of the specified 'means' were used. For some details on the issue of consent in adult cases see below at paras 1.13 and 1.14 and for further detail on the special definition of child trafficking and on the irrelevance of consent in both adult and child cases, which are not covered here, see further **CHAPTER 2**, for example, at paras **2.7, 2.8, 2.11**.

[1] See further http://www.unodc.org/unodc/en/human-trafficking/.

The act of the: Recruitment

1.7 Explanatory Report to the Trafficking Convention, at para 78:

> 'The actions the Convention is concerned with are "recruitment, transportation, transfer, harbouring or receipt of persons". The definition endeavours to encompass the whole sequence of actions that leads to exploitation of the victim.'

And further at para 79:

> 'The drafters looked at use of new information technologies in trafficking in human beings. They decided that the Convention's definition of trafficking in human beings covered trafficking involving use of new information technologies. For instance, the definition's reference to recruitment covers recruitment by whatever means (oral, through the press or via the Internet).'

Transportation

1.8 Explanatory Report to the Trafficking Convention at para 80:

> 'As regards "transportation", it should be noted that, under the Convention, transport need not be across a border to be a constituent of trafficking in human beings. Similarly Article 2, on the Convention's scope, states that the Convention applies equally to transnational and national trafficking. Nor does the Convention require, in cases of transnational trafficking, that the victim have entered illegally or be illegally present on national territory. Trafficking in human beings can be involved even where a border was crossed legally and presence on national territory is lawful.'

Transfer, Harbouring or Receipt of persons

1.9 These words are not separately defined in the Palermo Protocol, the Trafficking Convention or the EU Trafficking Directive. They are also, similarly to the words 'recruitment' and 'transportation' above, not defined in a trafficking-specific context in the UNODC Model Law against Trafficking in Persons or in the OSCE Policing Guidebook, although the latter provides excellent guidance on how to assess recruitment and transfer in the pre-exploitation and exploitation phases of trafficking[1].

Of note is that in the EU Trafficking Directive under the human trafficking definition Article 2(1) provides that core element 1, namely the 'act of', includes the addition of the words 'including the exchange or transfer of control over [such] persons', ie the Directive covers: 'The recruitment, transportation, transfer, harbouring or reception of persons, including the exchange or transfer of control over those persons . . . '. This widens the scope of the criminal offence of trafficking in persons under EU law and thereby also broadens the identification of who is a victim of the criminal act(s) in question.

[1]   OSCE Policing Guidebook, pp 51–64, 87.

By means of: The threat or use of force, or other forms of coercion

1.10 UNODC Model Law against Trafficking in Persons, Article 5(1)(e):

'"Coercion" shall mean use of force or threat thereof, and some forms of non-violent or psychological use of force or threat thereof, including but not limited to: (i) Threats of harm or physical restraint of any person; (ii) Any scheme, plan or pattern intended to cause a person to believe that failure to perform an act would result in serious harm to or physical restraint against any person; (iii) Abuse or any threat linked to the legal status of a person; (iv) Psychological pressure.'[1]

The Model Law Commentary on the trafficking-specific coercion definition provides:

'This is one example of how to define "coercion". Many variations are possible, focusing on the objective situation or on the situation as perceived by the coerced person.'[2]

The OSCE Policing Guidebook adopts an almost identical definition of 'coercion' at p 7. None of the texts seek to define the term 'threat or other use of force' in a trafficking-specific way.

[1]   UNODC cited source: US State Department Model Law to Combat Trafficking in Persons, 2003.
[2]   UNODC Model Law, p 11.

Abduction

1.11 Under the heading 'coercion' the OSCE Policing Guidebook advises that '[p]eople may be coerced into prostitution, forced labour, etc., through abduction or kidnapping' (p 7). None of the texts however seek to define abduction in a trafficking-specific way.

Fraud

1.12 Explanatory Report to the Trafficking Convention, at para 82:

'Fraud and deception are frequently used by traffickers, as when victims are led to believe that an attractive job awaits them rather than the intended exploitation.'

An explanation of the use of fraud as a means by which control is achieved over a trafficking victim is contained within the UNODC Model Law commentary on the 'deception' definition, below.

Deception

1.13 UNODC Model Law against Trafficking in Persons, Article 5(1)(f) offers a choice of trafficking-specific definitions of 'deception', which includes:

'"Deception" shall mean any conduct that is intended to deceive a person;
or
"Deception" shall mean any deception by words or by conduct [as to fact or as to law], [as to]: (i) The nature of work or services to be provided; (ii) The conditions of work; (iii) The extent to which the person will be free to leave his or her place of residence; or [(iv) Other circumstances involving exploitation of the person.'

The Model Law commentary on the trafficking-related deception definitions explains that:

'Deception or fraud can refer to the nature of the work or services that the trafficked person will engage in (for example the person is promised a job as a domestic worker but forced to work as a prostitute), as well as to the conditions under which the person will be forced to perform this work or services (for instance the person is promised the possibility of a legal work and residence permit, proper payment and regular working conditions, but ends up not being paid, is forced to work extremely long hours, is deprived of his or her travel or identity documents, has no freedom of movement and/or is threatened with reprisals if he or she tries to escape), or both. Under the United Kingdom Theft Act 1968, s 15(4), the statutory definition provides that "deception" means "any deception (whether deliberate or reckless) by words or by conduct as to fact or as to law, including a deception as to the present intentions of the person using the deception or any other person"'[1].

The OSCE Policing Guidebook, at page 8 draws upon the second of the UNODC's Model Law's definitions as set out above, but prefers a definition of deception in everyday language as follows:

'Deception is understood as misleading a person by words of conduct about the nature of work or services to be provided (ie, promises of legitimate work), the conditions of work, the extent to which the person will be free to leave his or her place of residence, or other circumstances involving exploitation of the person.'

---

[1] UNODC Model Law, commentary, p 12.

Of the abuse of power or of a position of vulnerability

1.14 Explanatory Report to the Trafficking Convention at para 83:

'By abuse of a position of vulnerability is meant abuse of any situation in which the person involved has no real and acceptable alternative to submitting to the abuse. The vulnerability may be of any kind, whether physical, psychological, emotional, family-related, social or economic. The situation might, for example, involve insecurity or illegality of the victim's administrative status, economic dependence or fragile health. In short, the situation can be any state of hardship in which a human being is impelled to accept being exploited. Persons abusing such a situation flagrantly infringe human rights and violate human dignity and integrity, which no one can validly renounce.'

The EU Trafficking Directive expressly defines this term in the following way under Article 2(2):

'A position of vulnerability means a situation in which the person concerned has no real or acceptable alternative but to submit to the abuse involved.'

See also however one of the definitions proposed by the UNODC Model Law against Trafficking in Persons, Article 5(1)(a):

'"Abuse of a position of vulnerability" shall refer to any situation in which the person involved <u>believes</u> he or she has no real and acceptable alternative but to submit.'[1] [Author's emphasis].

The Model Law's commentary on the definition of abuse of a position of vulnerability provides:

'Many other definitions of abuse of a position of vulnerability are possible, including elements such as abuse of the economic situation of the victim or of dependency on any substance, as well as definitions focusing on the objective situation or on the situation as perceived by the victim. It is recommended to include a definition of this crime element in the law, as in practice it appears to pose many problems. In order to better protect the victims, Governments may consider adopting a definition focusing on the offender and his intention to take advantage of the situation of the victim. These may also be easier to prove, as it will not require an inquiry into the state of mind of the victim but only that the offender was aware of the vulnerability of the victim and had the intention to take advantage of it.[2]'

The OSCE, at page 7 of its Policing Guidebook, and drawing upon the same interpretative notes as those relied upon by the UNODC in its Model Law, advises:

'Abuse of a position of vulnerability is understood as taking advantage of the vulnerable position a person is placed in as a result of: having entered the country illegally or without proper documentation; pregnancy or any physical disease or disability, including addiction to the use of any substance; reduced capacity to form [judgments] by virtue of being a child or due to illness, infirmity or physical or mental disability; promises made or sums of money or other advantages given to those having authority over the person; or being in a precarious situation from the standpoint of social survival or other relevant factors.'

---

[1] UNODC cited source: Interpretative notes for the official records (travaux préparatoires) of the negotiation of the United Nations Convention against Transnational Organised Crime and the Protocols thereto (A/55/383/Add.1), para 63.

[2] UNODC Model Law, pp 9–10.

Of the giving or receiving of payments or benefits to achieve the consent of a person having control over another person

1.15 None of the texts provide any trafficking-specific definitions of these words.

3 For the purpose of exploitation

1.16 The term 'exploitation' is defined in an inclusive, not exclusive, manner in both the Palermo Protocol and the Trafficking Convention: each contain an identical list of the types of exploitation that, 'as a minimum', must be prohibited under a State's criminal laws. It is well recognised that the prohibited forms of trafficking-related exploitation are not limited to only those in the list. Article 4(a) of the Trafficking Convention and Article 3(a) of the Palermo Protocol therefore provide:

> 'Exploitation shall include, at a minimum, the exploitation of the prostitution of others or other forms of sexual exploitation, forced labour or services, slavery or practices similar to slavery, servitude or the removal of organs.'

The Explanatory Report to the Trafficking Convention provides some guidance as to what this means, at para 85:

> 'The purpose must be exploitation of the individual. The Convention provides: "Exploitation shall include, at a minimum, the exploitation of the prostitution of others or other forms of sexual exploitation, forced labour or services, slavery or practices similar to slavery, servitude or the removal of organs". National legislation may therefore target other forms of exploitation but must at least cover the types of exploitation mentioned as constituents of trafficking in human beings.'

The UNODC Model Law does not define the word 'exploitation' itself, but does define sexual forms of exploitation as to which see below at paras **1.17** and **1.18**. However, the OSCE Policing Guidebook, at page 8, provides the following, inclusive, definition:

> 'Exploitation includes: the prostitution of others or other forms of sexual exploitation; forced or coerced labour or services (including bonded labour and debt bondage); slavery or practices similar to slavery; servitude; the removal of organs; and other forms of exploitation defined in national law.'

It is highly relevant to recall at this point however that the prohibited act of human trafficking takes place in advance of any actual exploitation occuring: it is the trafficker's purpose of exploitation that forms the third constituent element of the act of human trafficking, not the exploitation itself. Of course if there is exploitation this should be encompassed within the criminalisation of the prohibited act of human trafficking, but it may also, depending on how the individual was controlled by the trafficker give rise to independent consideration of whether the individual was in law and fact subjected to modern-day slavery if not forced labour. However, for the purposes of the human trafficking definition, where there is no identifiable exploitation the act of human trafficking will have been made out where, in adult cases, the three core elements (namely being the act of, by means of, for the purposes of exploitation) are present. As the Explanatory Report to the Trafficking Convention puts it:

> '87. Under the definition, it is not necessary that someone have been exploited for there to be trafficking in human beings. It is enough that they have been subjected to one of the actions referred to in the definition and by one of the means specified "for the purpose of" exploitation. Trafficking in human beings is consequently present before the victim's actual exploitation.'

Of course in children's cases this also applies albeit there is no legal requirement to establish that any of the specified 'means', ie core element two, were used by a trafficker for the act of human trafficking to have taken place.

As to the forms of expressly prohibited exploitation, at para 86 the Explanatory Report explains:

'The forms of exploitation specified in the definition cover sexual exploitation, labour exploitation and removal of organs, for criminal activity is increasingly diversifying in order to supply people for exploitation in any sector where demand emerges.'

Child exploitation as a specific form of exploitation is not expressly defined in the Palermo Protocol, the Trafficking Convention, the EU Trafficking Directive or in the UNODC Model Law. However, the OSCE Policing Guidebook, at p 7, provides a free-standing, inclusive, child-specific definition of exploitation:

'Child exploitation includes: procuring or offering a child for illicit or criminal activities (including the trafficking or production of drugs and begging); using children in armed conflict; work that by its nature or the circumstances in which it is carried out is likely to harm the health or safety of children, as determined by the national legislation or authority; the employment or use for work of a child who has not yet reached the applicable minimum working age for the said employment or work; other forms of exploitation, and illegal adoption.'

As to illegal adoption as a form of child exploitation, the Trafficking Convention's Explanatory Report both accepts and advises us, at para 94 that:

'The definition of trafficking in human beings does not refer to illegal adoption as such. Nevertheless, where an illegal adoption amounts to a practice similar to slavery as defined in Article 1(d) of the Supplementary Convention on the Abolition of Slavery, the Slave Trade, and Institutions and Practices similar to Slavery, it will also fall within the Convention's scope.'

The types of prohibited exploitation which fall under the human trafficking definition have been expressly extended by the EU Trafficking Directive which, at Article 2(1) adds 'begging [and] the exploitation of criminal activities' to the list shared by the Palermo Protocol and the Trafficking Convention. The Recital to the EU Trafficking Directive provides, at para 11, that this 'broader concept' of what should be considered as trafficking in human beings includes forced begging as a form of forced labour and services, as defined in the ILO Forced Labour Convention No 29 of 1930, that will involve the use of 'a trafficking-dependent person for begging'. The Recital, at para 11, continues:

'The expression "exploitation of criminal activities" should be understood as the exploitation of a person to commit, inter alia, pick-pocketing, shop-lifting, drug trafficking and other similar activities which are subject to penalties and imply financial gain.'

As to other forms of trafficking-dependent exploitation the Recital advises, again at para 11, that:

'The definition also covers trafficking in human beings for the purpose of the removal of organs, which constitutes a serious violation of human dignity and physical integrity, as well as, for instance, other behaviour such as illegal adoption or forced marriage in so far as they fulfil the constitutive elements of trafficking in human beings.'

Exploitation includes at a minimum: the exploitation of the prostitution of others

1.17 UNODC Model Law against Trafficking in Persons, Article 5(1)(h):

'"Exploitation of prostitution of others" shall mean the unlawful obtaining of financial or other material benefit from the prostitution of another person'[1].

The Model Law commentary on the sexual exploitation definition provides:

'This is one example of a definition, but many other definitions are possible.'[2]

The reason as to why there is no definition of 'the exploitation of prostitution of others' and of 'sexual exploitation' in the Palermo Protocol, and why such a definition is now necessary has been clearly explained by the UNODC in its Model Law commentary in the following way:

' . . . The terms "exploitation of prostitution of others" and "sexual exploitation" have been intentionally left undefined in the Protocol in order to allow all States, independent of their domestic policies on prostitution, to ratify the Protocol. The Protocol addresses the exploitation of prostitution only in the context of trafficking (interpretative notes . . . (A/55/383/Add.1), para. 64). There is no obligation under the Protocol to criminalize prostitution. Different legal systems—whether or not they legalize, regulate, tolerate or criminalize (the exploitation of the prostitution of others) non-coerced adult prostitution—comply with the Protocol. The term "unlawful" was added to indicate that this has to be unlawful in accordance with the national laws on prostitution. If using these terms in the law, it is advisable to define them.[3]'

The Trafficking Convention is also absent a definition of these terms for a similar reason, as the Explanatory Report to the Trafficking Convention, at para 88, explains:

'As regards "the exploitation of the prostitution of others or other forms of sexual exploitation", it should be noted that the Convention deals with these only in the context of trafficking in human beings. The terms "exploitation of the prostitution of others" and "other forms of sexual exploitation" are not defined in the Convention, which is therefore without prejudice to how States Parties deal with prostitution in domestic law.'

[1] UNODC cited source: Trafficking in Human Beings and Peace Support Operations: Trainers Guide, United Nations Interregional Crime and Justice Research Institute, 2006, p 153.
[2] UNODC Model Law, commentary, p 13. In fact the OSCE Policing Guidebook adopts the same definition, at p 8, to that proposed by the UNODC Model Law.
[3] UNODC Model Law, commentary, pp 13 and 14.

Or other forms of sexual exploitation

1.18 UNODC Model Law against Trafficking in Persons, Article 5(1)(s):

'"Sexual exploitation" shall mean the obtaining of financial or other benefits through the involvement of another person in prostitution, sexual servitude or other kinds of sexual services, including pornographic acts or the production of pornographic materials.'[1]

[1] UNODC cited source: Trafficking in Human Beings and Peace Support Operations: Trainers Guide, United Nations Interregional Crime and Justice Research Institute, 2006, p 153. The

OSCE Policing Guidebook, at p 10, adopts the same definition as that proposed by the UNODC Model Law.

Forced labour or services

1.19 Neither the Palermo Protocol nor the Trafficking Convention define 'forced labour' but the Explanatory Report to the Trafficking Convention, at para 88, refers to several international relevant instruments on forced labour, including the Universal Declaration on Human Rights, the International Covenant on Civil and Political Rights, the ILO Forced Labour Convention No 29 and the ILO Convention concerning the Abolition of Forced Labour No 105. The Explanatory Report at paras 89–93 also considers the forms of prohibited acts under Article 4 ECHR and relevant ECtHR case law which existed at the time such as *Van der Mussele v Belgium (Application 8919/80)*[1] (concerning the issue of the validity of consent in forced labour cases and the ECtHR's finding that forced labour is to be given a broad meaning so as to encompass forced services – see Explanatory Report, paras 90 and 92) and the Commission's decision in *Van Droogenbroeck v Belgium (Application 8919/80)*[2] on the definition of servitude: see Explanatory Report, para 95.

It is highly relevant to note that the Trafficking Convention opened for signature on 16 May 2005, that is two months prior to the ECtHR's judgment on 26 July 2005 in the landmark Article 4 ECHR case of *Siliadin v France (Application 73316/013)*[3]. This I find accounts for the absence of any mention of *Siliadin* in the Explanatory Report to the Trafficking Convention and the limited mention of the Trafficking Convention in *Siliadin*. The facts and findings of the ECtHR in *Siliadin* are summarised in **CHAPTER 12** on ECHR and EU Protections for Victims of Trafficking but in brief summary the applicant was a Togolese minor who was forced, against her will and with no respite, to work in France as a domestic servant in the private household of her 'employers' for no pay and her case in the ECtHR highlighted her lack of protection against her exploiters under the existing French criminal law.

In *Siliadin* the Court of Human Rights found of 'slavery' that the 'classic' meaning of was that in the 1927 Slavery Convention, namely '[s]lavery is the status or condition of a person over whom all or any rights of the powers attaching to the right of ownership are exercised'[4]; that 'servitude' prohibits a particularly serious denial of freedom and 'includes the obligation to provide one's services that is imposed by the use of coercion, and is to be linked with the concept of slavery described earlier'[5]; and of 'forced or compulsory labour', as it had earlier found in *Van Droogenbroek* in which the Court followed and applied the definition in the ILO Forced Labour Convention No 29, 'forced or compulsory labour' is 'all work or service which is exacted from any person under menace of any penalty and for which the said person has not offered himself voluntarily'[6]. The Court also found that for forced or compulsory labour to arise there must therefore be some physical or mental constraint, as well as some overriding of the person's will[7].

On the facts of the case in *Siliadin* the Court found that the applicant had been subjected to servitude[8] and forced and compulsory labour[9] but that her treatment had fallen short of slavery because, in the Court's judgment, the people that she had been forced to work for had not exercised 'a genuine right of ownership' over her which reduced her to the status of an 'object'[10].

More recently, the Court albeit briefly considered its findings in *Siliadin* in the context of the first substantive human trafficking case to be heard by it, *Rantsev v Cyprus and Russia, (Application 26965/04)*[11], judgment of 7 January 2010. The facts and findings of the ECtHR in *Rantsev*, including its important significance for all victims of trafficking in the UK are detailed in **CHAPTER 13**.

In *Rantsev*, which principally concerned the positive and procedural duties on States to protect trafficked victims and also investigate trafficking allegations the Court took into account the international criminal law judgment of the UN's International Criminal Tribunal for the Former Yugoslavia in *Prosecutor v Kunarac, Vukovic and Kovac*[12] of 12 June 2002, which was the first case to deal substantively with the definition of enslavement for sexual exploitation as a crime against humanity. Having considered the Tribunal's findings in *Kunarac* the ECtHR in Rantsev observed that:

'280. [T]he International Criminal Tribunal for the Former Yugoslavia concluded that the traditional concept of "slavery" has evolved to encompass various contemporary forms of slavery based on the exercise of any or all of the powers attaching to the right of ownership . . . . In assessing whether a situation amounts to a contemporary form of slavery, the Tribunal held that relevant factors included whether there was control of a person's movement or physical environment, whether there was an element of psychological control, whether measures were taken to prevent or deter escape and whether there was control of sexuality and forced labour . . . '

The ECtHR in *Rantsev* held:

'281. The Court considers that trafficking in human beings, by its very nature and aim of exploitation, is based on the exercise of powers attaching to the right of ownership. It treats human beings as commodities to be bought and sold and put to forced labour, often for little or no payment, usually in the sex industry but also elsewhere . . . It implies close surveillance of the activities of victims, whose movements are often circumscribed . . . It involves the use of violence and threats against victims, who live and work under poor conditions . . . It is described by Interights and in the explanatory report accompanying the . . . Trafficking Convention as the modern form of the old worldwide slave trade . . . ' [Author's emphasis].

And further:

'282. There can be no doubt that trafficking threatens the human dignity and fundamental freedoms of its victims and cannot be considered compatible with a democratic society and the values expounded in the Convention. In view of its obligation to interpret the Convention in light of present-day conditions, the Court considers it unnecessary to identify whether the treatment about which the applicant complains constitutes "slavery", "servitude" or "forced and compulsory labour". Instead, the Court concludes that trafficking itself, within the meaning of Article 3(a) of the Palermo Protocol and Article 4(a) of the Anti-Trafficking Convention, falls within the scope of Article 4 of the [European] Convention [on Human Rights]' [Author's emphasis].

Returning to *Kunarac*, I note that there the ICTY had observed that the traditional (or 'classic') concept of slavery has evolved to encompass contemporary forms of slavery, observing that:

'117. . . . the traditional concept of slavery, as defined in the 1926 Slavery Convention and often referred to as 'chattel slavery' has evolved to encompass various contemporary forms of slavery which are also based on the exercise of any or all of the powers attaching to the right of ownership. In the case of these various contemporary forms of slavery, the victim is not subject to the exercise of the more extreme rights of ownership associated with "chattel slavery", but in all cases, as a result of the exercise of any or all of the powers attaching to the right of ownership, there is some destruction of the juridical personality; the destruction is greater in the case of "chattel slavery" but the difference is one of degree . . . ' (Cited in *Rantsev*, para 142).

The ICTY had concluded:

'119. . . . the question whether a particular phenomenon is a form of enslavement will depend on the operation of the factors or indicia of enslavement [including] the "control of someone's movement, control of physical environment, psychological control, measures taken to prevent or deter escape, force, threat of force or coercion, duration, assertion of exclusivity, subjection to cruel treatment and abuse, control of sexuality and forced labour". Consequently, it is not possible exhaustively to enumerate all of the contemporary forms of slavery which are comprehended in the expansion of the original idea . . . ' (Cited in Rantsev at para 143).

In reaching its conclusions on the facts before it the ICTY in *Kunarac* had found that enslavement was not limited to chattel slavery[13] and that conditions of de facto control and ownership were relevant in a modern day assessment of slavery, as opposed solely to de jure ownership[14]. In reaching these findings the ICTY held that enslavement is a crime against humanity under customary international law[15].

In the High Court of Australia's landmark judgment in 2008 on contemporary slavery in *R v Tang*[16], on appeal from the Court of Appeal[17], the High Court conclusively determined the criminal liability of the defendant, Ms Tang, who had earlier been convicted of five counts of possessing slaves and five counts of using slaves in relation to five Thai female sex workers who had travelled from Thailand to Australia voluntarily for sex work. The Court of Appeal had quashed those convictions and this decision was appealed by the Prosecutor to the High Court. As to the applicable slavery law, the Australian criminal law against slavery that was introduced via an amendment to the Criminal Code in 1999, under s 270, is extensive and includes a prohibition on the possession of a slave or the exercise over a slave any powers attaching to the right of ownership. Under the Code the definition of slavery is very similar to the definition of slavery under the Slavery Convention 1926 but it also includes situations where the right or exercise of ownership over a slave arises 'from a debt or contract'. In *Tang*, the High Court provided a detailed summary of the important facts in this trafficking case, including that the women had each been 'purchased' for AU$ 20,000, that they were treated as being 'owned' by those who had procured their passage from Thailand to Australia and they each had to pay back AU$ 45,000 to work off their debt[18]. The Court described how:

'14 . . . [E]ach complainant was to work in the respondent's brothel . . . serving up to 900 customers over a period of four to six months. The complainants earned nothing in cash while under the contract except by working on the seventh, 'free', day each week, they could keep the $50 per customer that would, during the rest of the week, go to offset their contract debts.'

The Court also noted that the women were not aware of terms of their debt, upon their arrival in Australia their passports and return tickets were removed from them by Tang and found that although they were well-fed and provided for and were 'not kept under lock and key' they were effectively restricted to the premises. The Court also noted that when two of the five women had eventually paid off their debts their passports and tickets were returned to them and they were given free choice of working hours and accommodation: they chose to stay on and work in Tang's brothel[19].

The High Court of Australia compared the ECtHR's somewhat brief findings in *Siliadin* that the offence of slavery was not made out on the facts of Miss Siliadin's case as 'no rights of ownership' were found by the ECtHR to have been operated over her, with the ICTY's findings regarding the conditions of de facto enslavement in *Prosecutor v Kunarac*[20]. Observing that in Australia the legal status of slavery no longer existed[21], as the High Court assumed would also to have been the case in France at the time of the *Siliadin* judgment, the High Court noted that in *Siliadin* the ECtHR had not determined in detail the slavery question on the basis of the applicant's employers' apparent comprehensive de facto (ie factual) control over the applicant's condition, but had rested its judgment rather on their lack of de jure (ie lawful) ownership over her. Preferring *Kunarac* the High Court in a detailed judgment in *Tang* held that conditions of slavery had existed in respect of the Thai victims who having gone to Australia voluntarily, had subsequently had restraints placed on their movement and freedoms and were in fact possessed and used by the defendant as if she 'owned' them[22]. The defendant's convictions of five counts of possessing a slave and utilising a slave contrary to s 270.3(1)(a) of the Criminal Code were thereby restored[23].

It is important to note that on facts such as these the offence of slavery was made out on the basis of the de facto control that *Tang* had exercised over her clients. The fact that the victims were not confined to the premises and were well fed and accommodated were all taken into account by the High Court but these findings did not undermine its conclusion and recognition that in this case slavery, the most egregious form of exploitation, had been committed. The facts in *Tang* indicate that in law such control as was exercised by *Tang* amounted to conditions of slavery for the victims and this justified the successful prosecutions for that offence. This judgment, like that in *Kunarac*, moves the boundaries of the classic definitions of slavery, forced and compulsory labour and of servitude and highlights that slavery in its contemporary form, control without chains, must also be given high legal prominence in the UK. Those who make modern-day slaves of human beings should be judged and punished and the introduction of the free-standing slavery and forced labour offences (under s 71 of the Coroners and Justice Act 2009) will hopefully enable this to be achieved. One hopes therefore that *Kunarac* and *Tang*, taken together with the vital *Rantsev* judgment will greatly aid our judiciary when determining slavery and human trafficking cases, particularly in the context of criminal prosecutions against traffickers and exploiters in the UK.

For an excellent and highly insightful summary of the facts and the legal issues engaged in the *Tang* case see Jean Allain, 'R v Tang: Clarifying the Definition of 'Slavery' in International Law [2009] 10(1) Melbourne Journal of International Law 246.

The terms, 'forced labour and services' are also defined in the UNODC Model Law against Trafficking in Persons by Article 5(1)(i):

'"Forced labour or services" shall mean all work or service that is exacted from any person under the threat of any penalty and for which the person concerned has not offered him- or herself voluntarily'[24].

In explaining in general terms 'forced labour, slavery, practices similar to slavery and servitude' the Model Law Commentary provides:

'Article 14 of the [Palermo] Protocol takes note of the existence of other international instruments in interpreting the Protocol . . . [and these] concepts . . . are elaborated upon in a number of international conventions and should, where applicable to States concerned, guide the interpretation and application of the Protocol'[25].

In explaining 'forced labour and services' more specifically the Model Law Commentary provides:

'The notion of exploitation of labour in the definition allows for a link to be established between the Protocol and ILO Convention concerning Forced Labour and makes clear that trafficking in persons for the purpose of exploitation is encompassed by the definition of forced or compulsory labour of the Convention. Article 2, paragraph 1, of the Convention defines "forced labour or services" as: "All work or service which is exacted from any person under the menace of any penalty and for which the said person has not offered himself voluntarily." While the Protocol draws a distinction between exploitation for forced labour or services and sexual exploitation . . . [it should also be recalled that] [c]oercive sexual exploitation and forced prostitution fall within the scope of the definition of forced labour or compulsory labour (ILO, Eradication of Forced Labour, International Labour Conference, 2007, p. 42). Since the coming into force of Convention No. 29, the ILO Committee of Experts has treated trafficking for the purpose of commercial sexual exploitation as one of the forms of forced labour'[26].

In describing 'work or service' the Model Law Commentary provides:

'A forced labour situation is determined by the nature of the relationship between a person and an "employer", and not by the type of activity performed, the legality or illegality of the activity under national law, or its recognition as an "economic activity" (ILO, Global Report 2005, p. 6). Forced labour thus includes forced factory work as well as forced prostitution or other forced sexual services (also when prostitution is illegal under national law) or forced begging'[27].

In explaining 'voluntarily' the Model Law commentary provides:

'Legislatures and law enforcement have to take into account that the seemingly "voluntary offer" of a worker/victim may have been manipulated or was not based on an informed decision. Also, the initial recruitment can be voluntary and the coercive mechanisms to keep a person in an exploitative situation may come into play later. Where (migrant) workers were induced by deceit, false promises, the retention of travel or identity documents or use of force to remain at the disposal of the employer, the ILO supervisory bodies noted a violation of the Convention. This means that also in cases where an employment relationship was originally the result of a freely concluded agreement, the worker's right to free choice of employment remains inalienable, that is, a restriction on leaving a job, even when the worker freely agreed to enter into it, can be considered forced labour (ILO Guidelines on Human Trafficking and Forced Labour Exploitation, 2005; ILO, Eradication of Forced Labour, International Labour Conference, 2007, pp. 20-21). One way to deal with the difficulty the use of the term may cause is to include in the definition the use of means such as force or threat. This has been the approach taken by several national legislators . . . The Model Law includes an optional definition that refers back to the "means" element.[28]'

As to the meaning and consequences of 'any penalty' The Model Law commentary states:

'The threat of a penalty can take multiple forms ranging from (the threat of) physical violence or restraint, (threats of) violence to the victim or his or her relatives, threats to denounce the victim to the police or immigration authorities when his or her employment or residence status is illegal, threats of denunciation to village elders or family members in the case of girls or women forced into prostitution, (threat of) confiscation of travel or identity papers, economic penalties linked to debts, the non-payment of wages, or the loss of wages accompanied by threats of dismissal if workers refuse to work overtime beyond the scope of their contract or national law. (ILO, Global Report 2005, pp. 5-6; ILO, Eradication of Forced Labour, International Labour Conference, 2007, p. 20). In its report "Human trafficking and forced labour exploitation – guidance for legislation and law enforcement", ILO identifies five major elements that[29] can point to a forced labour situation:

–   (Threat of) physical or sexual violence; this may also include emotional torture like blackmail, condemnation, using abusive language and so on;
–   Restriction of movement and/or confinement to the workplace or to a limited area;
–   Debt bondage/bonded labour; withholding of wages or refusal of payment;
–   Retention of passport and identity papers so that the worker cannot leave or prove his or her identity and status;
–   Threat of denunciation to the authorities.[30]'

[1]   (1983) 6 EHRR 163, [1983] ECHR 8919/80, ECtHR.
[2]   (1983) 13 EHRR 546, ECtHR, (1982) 4 EHRR 443, ECtHR.
[3]   (2005) 43 EHRR 287, 20 BHRC 654, ECtHR.
[4]   (2005) 43 EHRR 287 at para 122, 20 BHRC 654, ECtHR.
[5]   (2005) 43 EHRR 287 at para 123–124, 20 BHRC 654, ECtHR.
[6]   (2005) 43 EHRR 287 at para 116, 20 BHRC 654, ECtHR.
[7]   (2005) 43 EHRR 287 at para 117, 20 BHRC 654, ECtHR.
[8]   *Siliadin v France (Application 73316/01)* (2005) 43 EHRR 287 at para 129, 20 BHRC 654, ECtHR.
[9]   *Siliadin v France (Application 73316/01)* (2005) 43 EHRR 287 at para 120, 20 BHRC 654, ECtHR.
[10]   (2005) 43 EHRR 287at para 122, 20 BHRC 654, ECtHR.
[11]   *Rantsev v Cyprus and Russia (Application 25965/04)* (2010) 28 BHRC 313, [2010] ECHR 25965/04, ECtHR.
[12]   *Prosecutor v Kunarac, Vukovic and Kovac (Kunarac appeal judgment)* – *IT-96-23 & IT-96-23/1-A*, International Criminal Tribunal for the former Yugoslavia (ICTY), 12 June 2002.
[13]   (12 June 2002, unreported).
[14]   (12 June 2002, unreported).
[15]   (12 June 2002, unreported).
[16]   [2008] HCA 39, 28 August 2008.
[17]   A judgment which appears not to have been considered by the ECtHR in *Rantsev*.
[18]   *R v Tang* [2008] HCA 39 at paras 7, 8, 10, 25 BHRC 35.
[19]   *R v Tang* [2008] HCA 39 at paras 16, 17, 25 BHRC 35.
[20]   *Kunarac appeal judgment* – *IT-96-23 & IT-96-23/1-A*, International Criminal Tribunal for the former Yugoslavia (ICTY), 12 June 2002.
[21]   *R v Tang* [2008] HCA 39 at para 25, 25 BHRC 35.
[22]   See for example, *R v Tang* [2008] HCA 39 at paras 50, 25 BHRC 35.
[23]   *R v Tang* [2008] HCA 39, 25 BHRC 35.
[24]   UNODC cited source: ILO Convention No 29 concerning Forced or Compulsory Labour of 1930, articles 2, paragraph 1, and 25. The OSCE Policing Guidebook also adopts this

definition, at p 8, but with one amendment, namely that the forced labour or work may be 'any' rather than 'all' work or service that is exacted from the person under the conditions described.

25 UNODC Model Law, p 14.
26 UNODC Model Law, p 14.
27 UNODC Model Law, p 14.
28 UNODC Model Law, pp 14–15.
29 Author's note: Individually or cumulatively.
30 UNODC Model Law, p 15.

Slavery or practices similar to slavery

1.20 See para **1.19** above for a detailed Commentary on recent international and European jurisprudence relating to developments in understanding the concept of modern-day slavery in the human trafficking context.

UNODC Model Law against Trafficking in Persons, Article 5(1)(t):

> '"Slavery" shall mean the status or condition of a person over whom any or all the powers attaching to the right of ownership are exercised'[1].

Or

> '"Slavery" [as a contemporary definition] shall mean the status or condition of a person over whom control is exercised to the extent that the person is treated like property.'

The Model Law commentary on the slavery definition provides:

> 'The definition in the Slavery Convention may cause some difficulties today, as there could be no rights of ownership for one person over another. In order to solve this difficulty, an alternative definition is included here, which instead requires that the person is "treated like property" . . . '[2].

This resonates perfectly with the findings of the High Court of Australia in *Tang*[3], at para **1.19**, above. The OSCE Policing Guidebook, at p 10, also defines 'slavery' in a highly contemporary way:

'Slavery means the status or condition of a person over whom control is exercised to the extent that the person is treated like property'. Placement or maintenance in a position of slavery occurs when use is made of violence, threat, deceit or abuse of power, or when anyone takes advantage of a situation of physical or mental inferiority and poverty; or when money is promised, payments are made or any kinds of benefits are promised to those who are responsible for the person in question[4]. As to defining the term 'practices similar to slavery', the UNODC Model Law against Trafficking in Persons, Article 5(1)(l), provides that:

> '"Practices similar to slavery" shall include debt bondage, serfdom, servile forms of marriage and the exploitation of children and adolescents.'

The Model Law commentary advises that:

> 'The Supplementary Convention on the Abolition of Slavery does not contain a definition, but specifically prohibits debt bondage, serfdom, servile forms of marriage and the exploitation of children and adolescents.'[5]

The OSCE Policing Guidebook, at page 9, also provides a definition of 'practices similar to slavery' which takes into account the UNODC Model Law proposed definition and refines it:

"Practices similar to slavery means the economic exploitation of another person on the basis of an actual relationship of dependency or coercion, in combination with a serious and far-reaching deprivation of fundamental civil rights, and includes debt bondage, servile marriage, the exploitation of children and adults."

As to the definitions of 'debt bondage, serfdom and servile forms of marriage' these terms are defined in the Model Law as follows.

UNODC Model Law against Trafficking in Persons, Article 5(1)(g):

"'Debt bondage' shall mean the status or condition arising from a pledge by a debtor of his or her personal services or those of a person under his or her control as security for a debt, if the value of those services as reasonably assessed is not applied towards the liquidation of the debt or if the length of those services is not limited and defined⁶'.

The OSCE Policing Guidebook, at page 8, refers to the same source as that which supports the UNODC Model Law definition but the Guidebook provides:

"Debt bondage refers to a system by which a person is kept in bondage by making it impossible for him or her to pay off actual or imagined debts."

In my view both of these definitions may justify revision in light of what we now know about the facts in *Tang*, a case which starkly illustrates modern forms of persuasive psychological control by traffickers over their victims and shows that debt bondage may occur in fact even where unreasonable debts are imposed to bond a person to labour in such a way that the proceeds of their labour go towards liquidating a debt and even entirely extinguishing it.

Regarding 'serfdom' the UNODC Model Law against Trafficking in Persons, Article 5(1)(q) provides:

"'Serfdom' shall mean the condition or status of a tenant who is by law, custom or agreement bound to live and labour on land belonging to another person and to render some determinate service to such other person, whether for reward or not, and is not free to change his or her status'⁷.

On 'servile marriage', the UNODC Model Law against Trafficking in Persons, Article 5(1) (j) provides:

"'Forced or servile marriages' shall mean any institution or practice in which: (i) A woman [person] or child without the right to refuse is promised or given in marriage on payment of a consideration in money or in kind to her [his] parents, guardian, family or any other person or group; or (ii) The husband of a woman, his family or his clan has the right to transfer her to another person for value received or otherwise; or (iii) A woman on the death of her husband is liable to be inherited by another person'⁸.

The Model Law commentary advises that:

'The definition derived from the above-mentioned Convention refers solely to the practice of forced or servile marriages in relation to women. Legislators may consider updating this definition to include practices in which both women/girls and men/boys can be the subject of forced or servile marriages. This may cover trafficking for marriage and certain forms of "mail order bride" practices.'[9]

[1] UNODC cited source: Slavery Convention of 1926 as amended by the 1953 Protocol, article 1, paragraph 1.
[2] UNODC Model Law, Commentary, p 19.
[3] [2008] HCA 39.
[4] OSCE cited source: Penal Code of Italy, Article 600.
[5] UNODC Model Law, commentary, p 17.
[6] UNODC cited source: Supplementary Convention on the Abolition of Slavery, the Slave Trade, and Institutions and Practices Similar to Slavery, article 1.
[7] UNODC cited source :Supplementary Convention on the Abolition of Slavery, article 1. Serfdom is not separately defined in the OSCE Policing Guidebook. It is difficult to see how conditions of serfdom would not amount to conditions of classic and/or contemporary slavery under the UNODC and the OSCE's definitions of those legal concepts.
[8] UNODC cited source: Supplementary Convention on the Abolition of Slavery, article 1.
[9] UNODC Model Law, commentary, p 17. A substantially similar definition is adopted by the OSCE in its Policing Guidebook at pp 8–9.

Servitude

1.21 UNODC Model Law against Trafficking in Persons, Article 5(r):

'"Servitude" shall mean the labour conditions and/or the obligation to work or to render services from which the person in question cannot escape and which he or she cannot change.'

In the UNODC Commentary on the servitude definition the following is stated:

'Servitude is prohibited by, among other instruments, the Universal Declaration of Human Rights (1948) and the International Covenant on Civil and Political Rights (1966). Neither of these international instruments contains an explicit definition of servitude. The definition given is based on an interpretation of the Universal Declaration and the Covenant listed. In its 2005 judgement in the case of *Siliadin v France* the European Court of Human Rights defined servitude as: "An obligation to provide one's services that is imposed by the use of coercion, and is to be linked to the concept of slavery." (ECHR, 26 July 2005, No. 73316/01).'[1]

[1] UNODC Model Law, Commentary, p 18. The OSCE Policing Guidebook, at p 10, adopts the *Siliadin* definition of servitude.

Or the removal of organs

1.22 The Explanatory Report to the Trafficking Convention provides, at para 96:

'Exploitation also includes "removal of organs". The principle that it is not permissible for the human body or its parts as such to give rise to financial gain is established Council of Europe legal acquis. It was laid down in Committee of Ministers Resolution (78) 29 and was confirmed, in particular, by the final declaration of the 3rd Conference of European Health Ministers (Paris, 1987) before being definitively established in Article 21 of the Convention on Human Rights and Biomedicine (ETS No.164). The principle was then reaffirmed in the protocol to that convention concerning transplantation of organs and tissues of human origin (ETS No.186), which was opened for signature in January 2002.

Article 22 of the protocol explicitly prohibits traffic in organs and tissues. It should also be recalled that the Parliamentary Assembly of the Council of Europe adopted a Report on "Trafficking in organs in Europe" (Doc. 9822, 3 June 2003, Social, Health and Family Affairs Committee, Rapporteur: Mrs Ruth-Gaby Vermot-Mangold, Switzerland, SOC) and Recommendation 1611 (2003) on trafficking in organs in Europe.'

CONCLUDING REMARKS

1.23 As someone once said, times change and we change with them. Sadly, the types of criminal exploitation that are intended for victims of human trafficking in this country and abroad have massively proliferated over recent years and as the above Commentary indicates it is now recognised that forced begging, illegal adoption, forced marriage, drug trafficking and production, shoplifting and pick-pocketing are in need of being recognised as constituting the prohibited purposes of exploitation, in addition to those which are expressly included in the Palermo Protocol's original exploitation list. In the trafficking context both the UNODC and the OSCE, as world leaders in the field of international policing, are expressly aware of the need to shed light on how to understand human trafficking and how to assist all concerned in recognising and thereby protecting trafficked victims, including by way of securing justice against their traffickers, and the Model Law and the Policing Guidebook are excellent resources for us all. In terms of trafficking, slavery and forced labour, which includes domestic servitude in *Siliadin* style cases, what is shown by recent comparative jurisprudence is that a recognition of contemporary slavery arises in all trafficking cases (cf. ECtHR in *Rantsev* at para 281) and also that in assessing the conditions of modern-day slavery this ought not to be limited to an enquiry as to whether an individual was genuinely owned by the trafficker or exploiter under the 'classic' definition of slavery, which in many States will be impossible to establish anyway, but must extend to whether the person who exercised control over the individual did so 'as if' he or she owned them (*Kunarac, Tang*). The fact that an individual was not in chains, may have had some liberty, and presumably therefore may have been able to escape, did not in the High Court of Australia's judgment in *Tang*, undermine its conclusive finding, on five counts, that slavery took place. These landmark legal judgments which emanate, respectively, from Strasbourg, The Hague and from Australia will, I hope, form vital guidance for the UK courts in determining trafficking, slavery and forced labour cases in the future. Finally, what I hope this Commentary has been able to highlight is the importance of applying the definition of human trafficking to what is known about an individual's case. As I wrote at the beginning of this chapter, ordinary words have a special meaning when looked at through the trafficking lens. The descriptions in this Commentary of the key words that are used in the trafficking definition, placing reliance on the authoritative guidance from the UNODC, the OSCE, the Explanatory Report to the Trafficking Convention and the EU Trafficking Directive and its Recital will hopefully not only assist us in understanding how to interpret human trafficking and what roles, for example, deception or coercion may play, but will equip us all with powerful tools, via the meaning of words, to recognise human trafficking and modern-day slavery in the UK.

2

THE IDENTIFICATION OF VICTIMS OF TRAFFICKING

Parosha Chandran

'Precise and careful identification of presumed victims of trafficking in human beings is above all necessary to protect their physical safety and their rights and to ensure that they receive access to vital services. It should also ensure access to justice for those who are victims of crime. Proper identification of trafficked persons can also lead to more criminal investigations and may help disclose other crimes . . . [t]imely identification of potential victims of human trafficking is also an effective preventative measure against this crime.'

1   OSCE, *'Trafficking in Human Beings: Identification of Potential and Presumed Victims A Community Policing Approach'*, June 2011.

INTRODUCTION

2.1 This book is concerned with recognising human trafficking and modern-day slavery in the UK. Hence all the chapters in this book relate in one way or another to victim identification as highlighted by the grouping of chapters into different parts. The special cases of child trafficking and identification are addressed in **CHAPTERS 5, 9** and **12**.

This chapter forms the backdrop against which many of the other chapters can be read. It is however specifically intended to be read in conjunction with **CHAPTER 1** on Interpreting Human Trafficking. As the UN Special Rapporteur on trafficking in persons, especially women and children, advised in her report to the United Nations General Assembly in 2009[1]:

'Understanding the definition of human trafficking and the important elements contained therein may prove fundamental for the proper identification of trafficked victims and for responding effectively to their situation. The definition of trafficking as encompassed in the Palermo Protocol underscores the fact that trafficking is a process that involves a number of interrelated actions rather than a single act at any given time.'

Indeed, in the context of the UK, the authoritative report by the Anti-Trafficking Monitoring Group (ATMG) in June 2010 *'Wrong Kind of Victim? One year on: an analysis of UK measures to protect trafficked persons'*[2] which provided a detailed critique of the UK in terms of its obligations under the Trafficking Convention a year after the Convention entered into force in the UK in April 2009 and the impact on victims, found that:

'The analysis reveals that one of the key problems is the incorrect application of the trafficking definition when assessing a victim. Too often the authorities fail to apply the Convention and do not define as victims all those who were subject to the crime of trafficking. Instead, the system creates a narrow, legally dubious, interpretation of a victim, and attaches conditions that have been proven to impede identification, and have also been found to undermine prosecution in some cases.'[3]

Hence, the vital need for the human trafficking definition to be applied correctly by the UK Government to the cases of trafficked victims in the UK cannot be overemphasised.

In this chapter some of the UK's legal obligations under the Palermo Protocol[4] and the Council of Europe Convention on Action against Trafficking in Human Beings 2005 ('the Trafficking Convention') are put under the spotlight, including the formal arrangements under the National Referral Mechanism (NRM) for identification decision-making, the conditions for the grant of residence permits under Article 14 of the Trafficking Convention and the standards of proof by which reasonable and conclusive identification decisions are made under the NRM scheme. The chapter also provides a summary of who is a victim of trafficking and includes guidance on the barriers to victim identification. The chapters which follow in Parts I, II and III of this book each contain detailed examinations of the identification and support needs of victims of trafficking in the UK and document the experiences, often negative, of victims of trafficking under the National Referral Mechanism (NRM).

The findings and the recommendations made by the ATMG in its June 2010 report[5] are endorsed by the author of this chapter. To avoid unnecessary overlap or repetition this chapter therefore provides a snapshot of the NRM scheme in the UK, but with the inclusion of updated trafficking-related identification statistics, and it addresses some selected practices under existing UK policy which not only continue to risk undermining respect for individuals' rights under the Trafficking Convention but which indicate the UK's continuing failure in certain areas to adhere to its international obligations as a State Party to that Treaty.

It is recalled that the stated purposes of the Palermo Protocol[6] and the Trafficking Convention are to prevent and combat trafficking in human beings[7], to protect and assist the victims of such trafficking and respect their human rights[8] as well as to ensure effective investigation and prosecution of traffickers[9] whilst promoting international co-operation to meet these objectives and to secure action against trafficking in human beings[10]. These three 'P's, as they have been commonly known (ie the prevention of human trafficking, the protection of victims and the prosecution of perpetrators) have been joined by a fourth P, under recognition by the international community, namely 'partnerships' towards ending human trafficking. Indeed the Trafficking Convention gives high prominence to the role of non-governmental and other support organisations in achieving the purposes addressed above[11].

A recognised key to achieving all the purposes of the Trafficking Convention is therefore a vital partnership between the State's agencies and civil society, particularly through the often-expert support of Non-Governmental Organisations (NGOs). Many of the experiences described by the expert authors of the chapters in this book, including **CHAPTERS 21** to **23** which are written by the police, are testament to the need for such partnerships to exist.

It is crucial that victims of trafficking are correctly identified by lawful procedures in the UK so as to enable their human rights to be protected and respected and for victims to benefit from the multitude of protection and assistance measures that the Palermo Protocol and the Trafficking Convention intends they should receive as presumed/potential, and then as fully identified, victims of the serious crime of human trafficking. Of course when victims are, and feel, protected and safe they are also more likely to be willing to provide intelligence or evidence to the police to enable the successful prosecution and punishment of their trafficker(s) to take place. Successful prosecutions and deterrent sentences are relevant also to the aim of preventing human trafficking in any given country. Identifying the victim before the exploitation occurs will of course fulfil the dual purposes of protection and prevention.

In terms of the express recognition in both legal instruments that the human rights of victims must be respected and protected, and in light of the recognised need for a comprehensive framework for the protection and assistance of victims and witnesses as introduced under the Trafficking Convention, it follows, in theory at least, that the accurate identification of victims of trafficking in the UK as victims of crime is the gateway to the protection of their human rights[12].

[1] Report of the Special Rapporteur on trafficking in persons, especially women and children, 12 August 2009, A/64/290, at para 93.

[2] The ATMG comprises nine UK-based organisations, namely Amnesty International UK, Anti-Slavery International, ECPAT UK (End Child Prostitution, Child Pornography and the Trafficking of Children for Sexual Purposes), Helen Bamber Foundation, Immigration Law Practitioners' Association (ILPA), Kalayaan, POPPY Project (of Eaves Housing), TARA (The Trafficking Awareness Raising Alliance, of Glasgow Community and Safety Services), UNICEF UK. The Summary Report of the ATMG is included in the Appendices to this book. Its full report was expressly taken into account by the United States Department of State in its most recent Trafficking in Persons Report on the UK, published in June 2011.

[3] ATMG '*Wrong Kind of Victim One year on: an analysis of UK measures to protect trafficked persons*' report, June 2010, at page 12, see also page 5 of the Summary Report.

[4] Protocol to Prevent, Suppress and Punish Trafficking in Persons, especially Women and Children, supplementing the United Nations Convention against Transnational Organized Crime 2000.

[5] See ATMG Summary Report, at page 6, in the Appendices to this book. Most of the recommendations have not been implemented by the Government although the new CPS Legal Guidance on Smuggling and Trafficking, published in May 2011 and addressed in **CHAPTERS 24** and **25** of this book, ought to impact on improving the non-prosecution of victims of trafficking in the UK as per ATMG recommendation no 4 and the UK will, as an opting-in Member State to the EU's Trafficking Directive 2011/36/EU have to introduce a protection/guardianship scheme for trafficked children by 2013 under the Directive: this will address the ATMG's recommendation no 5.

[6] The Protocol to Prevent, Suppress and Punish Trafficking in Persons, especially Women and Children, supplementing the United Nations Convention against Transnational Organized Crime 2000.

[7] Palermo Protocol, Article 2(a); Trafficking Convention, Article 1(1)(a).

[8] Palermo Protocol, Article 2(b); Trafficking Convention, Article 1(1)(b), which is to be obtained by 'a comprehensive framework for the protection and assistance of victims and witnesses'.

[9] Trafficking Convention, Article 1(1)(b).

[10] Palermo Protocol, Article 2(c); Trafficking Convention, Article 1(1)(c).

[11] For example, Article 35 of the Trafficking Convention provides, under the heading 'co-operation with civil society' as follows: 'Each Party shall encourage State authorities and public officials, to co-operate with non-governmental organisations, other relevant organisations and members of civil society, in establishing strategic partnerships with the aim of achieving the purpose of this Convention'.

12   Identification is also the gateway to the protection of the civil rights of victims of trafficking, including the right to compensation which is addressed in detail in Part V of this book. Access to this right in the UK will often depend on a NRM conclusive decision.

THE IDENTIFICATION PROCEDURE UNDER THE TRAFFICKING CONVENTION

2.2   The two-stage identification scheme under the Trafficking Convention by which decisions on the identification of a trafficking victim are made which can trigger measures to assist and support the victim, including immediate assistance, recovery and reflection and the eligibility for a renewable residence permit, is well-summarised in the Explanatory Memoranda that was presented to the UK Parliament in 2008 prior to the Government's ratification of the Trafficking Convention:

'8. The assessment that there are reasonable grounds to believe that a person is a victim is the gateway to a range of provisions intended to help a trafficked person escape from the influence of traffickers and begin a process of recovery. Under Article 13, such a victim must be given a recovery and reflection period of at least 30 days[1] to allow the person to recover and escape from the influence of the traffickers and to take an informed decision about co-operating with the competent authorities. During this time a person is authorised to stay in the UK[2], where such permission is needed. Under Article 10(2), the person shall not be removed from the UK until the conclusive identification process has been completed. The person is also entitled to support and assistance provided for in Article 12(1) and (2) – including: appropriate and secure accommodation; psychological and material assistance; access to emergency medical treatment; counselling and information on their legal rights and services available to them; translation and interpretation services; assistance to enable their rights and interests to be presented and considered at appropriate stages of criminal proceedings; and access to education for children. Members States are obligated to take due account of the victim's safety and protection needs. (Article 10(2)).

9. The Convention requires that following the identification process and where a competent authority has established conclusively that an individual is a victim of trafficking, renewable residence permits should be granted in one or both of the following circumstances: where it is deemed necessary owing to "their personal situation"; or because a victim is co-operating with an investigation or criminal proceedings (Article 14). But being recognised as a victim of trafficking does not automatically lead to a residence permit. It is entirely possible to be identified as a victim and have no right to remain in the UK simply on that basis beyond the period required for recovery and reflection. Where an identified victim is granted a residence permit, they are entitled to all of the support and assistance listed in Article 12(1) and (2) (as specified in paragraph 7). Additionally it will provide access to the provisions of Articles 12 (3) and (4) which place obligations on Member States to provide necessary medical care and access to the labour market, vocational training and education.'[3]

---

1   The UK provides a 45-day period of recovery and reflection for victims of trafficking. See para **2.3**, below.
2   The authorisation is in the form of 'temporary admission' to the UK by which a person is lawfully present in the country but is not lawfully resident.
3   Explanatory Memoranda to Command Paper Number: CM 7465, entitled *EM on Council of Europe Convention on Action against Trafficking in Human Beings*, presented to Parliament in 2008 and updated on 30 September 2009. Accessed 18 July 2011 at http://www.fco.gov.u

k/en/publications-and-documents/treaty-command-papers-ems/explanatory-memoranda/expl
anatory-memoranda-2008/humantrafficking.

THE IDENTIFICATION PROCESS IN THE UK UNDER THE NATIONAL REFERRAL MECHANISM

2.3 The Government's National Referral Mechanism (NRM) has operated since 1 April 2009, the date on which the Trafficking Convention entered into force in the UK[1]. The NRM in the UK is a creature of policy, not statute: it was not created by law. Its objective is to formally identify victims of trafficking in the UK and it provides statistics[2] on the number of individuals, adults and children, who have been referred to it and the identification decisions it has made in respect of those persons. Despite its name it is not a referral body: whilst, under its arrangements, it receives requests to identify victims of trafficking from specified organisations it refers no victims to services or assistance for trafficked victims.

The method by which victims of trafficking in the UK are identified under the UK's National Referral Mechanism was quite recently summarised by the Government's own representatives who attended the Second Expert Meeting on Human Rights Protection in the return of trafficked persons to countries of origin on 14 April 2010, Warsaw, convened by the OSCE Office for Democratic Institutions and Human Rights (ODIHR) Anti-Trafficking Program. In its report of that meeting the ODIHR has reported[3]:

'The UK Government representatives, from the UK Border Agency (UKBA), focused on the identification of victims of trafficking and voluntary return programmes. They summarised how the newly introduced identification and referral mechanism (NRM) functioned. It included a wide number of organizations (UKBA, UKHTC (UK Human Trafficking Centre), police, local authorities, NGOs and other agencies) acting as 'first responders'[4]. First responders identified indicators of human trafficking and made referrals of possible victims to a 'competent authority'[5] who determined whether there were 'reasonable grounds'[6] to consider someone a victim and provide them with a reflection delay. Following this appraisal, a 'conclusive grounds'[7] decision could be made which could trigger different residence options. The NRM procedure applied irrespective of the immigration status of the person and was not an immigration procedure[8]. If there was an immigration issue with a victim then the UK Border Agency would take the decision, otherwise the UKHTC acted. Adults needed to consent to be included in the NRM, but for children the NRM was regarded as a safeguard. The UK provided 45 days of reflection period that could be extended for a number of reasons, such as information gathering, issues of disclosure, and the needs of an individual victim to access services before a conclusive grounds decision. The return of a victim was not considered until a conclusive grounds decision had been made. If the conclusive grounds decision was positive, the personal circumstances of the victim would be taken into account (meaning Art. 8 of ECHR (private and family life) and questions of non-refoulement and discretionary leave could be given. Police could make an application for a residence permit for a year which could then be extended for another year. If discretionary leave was granted, it was possible to apply for further leave to remain, in consideration of the personal circumstances.'

---

[1]   The Trafficking Convention was signed by the UK in March 2007, was ratified by the UK on 17 December 2008 and its implementation date was 1 April 2009. Regarding the legal status of the Trafficking Convention in the UK, in *R v LM* [2010] EWCA Crim 2327 a case involving

criminal appeals by five asserted victims of trafficking, Lord Justice Hughes, the Vice President of the Court of Appeal Criminal Division said of the Trafficking Convention, at para 2: 'The United Kingdom is bound by this treaty. At the time of *R v O* [2008] EWCA Crim 2835 [in September 2008, the UK] had signed but not ratified the [Trafficking Convention] and was thus subject to the attenuated obligation under Article 18 of the Vienna Convention on the Law of Treaties to refrain from acts which would defeat its object and purpose. Now however, this country has ratified the Convention . . . and is fully bound by it'. [Author's emphasis].

2   Statistics can be found on the website of the Serious Organised Crime Agency (SOCA): http://www.soca.gov.uk.

3   *ODIHR, Anti-Trafficking Programme, Report, Second Expert Meeting on Human Rights Protection in the return of trafficked persons to countries of origin, 14 April 2010, Warsaw,* at pages 2–3. A detailed analysis of the operation and effectiveness of the UK's NRM in terms of victim identification is outside the scope of this chapter. However, it is hoped that this and other chapters in this book, will highlight the need for accurate victim identification in the UK: many of the specialist authors' have described their own and their organisations' experiences of the NRM in terms of victim identification. For a detailed critique of victim identification under the NRM in the UK please see the full report of the Anti-Trafficking Monitoring Group (ATMG), *Wrong Kind of Victim?* of June 2010. The summary report of the ATMG, which contains its key findings and recommendations in respect of the NRM, is included as an Appendix to this book.

4   First Responders cannot formally identify victims of trafficking under the UK's NRM, despite many of the named First Responders being specialist agencies in terms of victim identification, often through years of experience. Their role under the NRM is limited to referring possible victims to the two named 'Competent Authorities' in the UK for the reasonable grounds assessment and the conclusive decisions to be made: see note 6 below. The named First Responders in the UK are: the Police, UK Border Agency (UKBA), Serious Organised Crime Agency (SOCA), Local Authorities/Social Services, Gangmasters Licensing Authority (GLA), Poppy Project, Trafficking Awareness Raising Alliance (TARA), Migrant Helpline, Kalayaan, Medaille Trust, Salvation Army and (following the announcement in the Government's *Human Trafficking: the Government's Strategy*, July 2011), the NSPCC Child Trafficking Advice and Information Line (CTAIL) and another children's charity, Barnardo's.

5   The UK has designated only two bodies as being 'the Competent Authorities' for the purpose of formal victim identification under the NRM. These are the UKBA for non-EEA citizens, and for EEA nationals, the United Kingdom Human Trafficking Centre (UKHTC), a police body which forms part of the Serious Organised Crime Agency (SOCA). One of the UK's two Competent Authorities, the United Kingdom Border Agency (UKBA), had little if indeed any exposure to the requirements of human trafficking identification under the Palermo Protocol or the Trafficking Convention prior to 1 April 2009. The police, some forces more than others, may have had experience in interviewing victims of trafficking from 2003 when trafficking-related criminal laws first were introduced in the UK: See **CHAPTERS 19** to **23** of this book. The UK's restriction on which 'competent authorities' can fulfil its victim identification obligations under Article 10 of the Trafficking Convention does not reflect the Convention's intention that the role of identification should be multi-agency, as addressed below.

6   The 'reasonable grounds' test is intended by the Trafficking Convention to be set very low in order to enable rapid identification and thereby swift assistance to be given to the presumed victim. As explained in its Explanatory Report at para 135: '135. Even though the identification process may be speedier than criminal proceedings (if any), victims will still need assistance even before they have been identified as such. For that reason the Convention provides that if the authorities "have reasonable grounds to believe" that someone has been a victim of trafficking, then they should have the benefit, during the identification process, of the assistance measures provided for in Article 10(1) and (2).' The European Court of Human Rights has found, in the landmark judgment of *Rantsev v Cyprus and Russia* [2010] ECHR 22 that human trafficking is a violation of Article 4 ECHR (prohibition on slavery, servitude, forced and compulsory labour) and that States have positive obligations both to identify and to remove victims of trafficking from locations or the immediate risk of harm. See **CHAPTERS 1, 13** and **25**. The Court found: '286 . . . Article 4 may . . . require a State to take operational measures to protect victims, or potential victims, of trafficking . . . In order for a positive obligation to take operational measures to arise in the circumstances of a particular case, it must be demonstrated that the State authorities were aware, or ought to have been aware, of circumstances giving rise to a credible suspicion that an identified individual had been, or was at real and immediate risk of being, trafficked or exploited within the meaning of Article 3(a) of the Palermo Protocol and Article 4(a) of the Anti-Trafficking Convention. In

the case of an answer in the affirmative, there will be a violation of Article 4 of the Convention where the authorities fail to take appropriate measures within the scope of their powers to remove the individual from that situation or risk . . . ' [Author's emphasis]. The author notes that all public authorities in the UK have a positive obligation to protect victims of trafficking from harm. This necessitates rapid accurate identification. See too the OSCE's guidance at para **2.13** of this chapter. It follows that the NRM scheme ought to be reviewed so as to allow, in line with the UK's pre-existing legal obligations, specialist trafficking NGOs and other organisations (such as the First Responders) to directly collaborate with the two designated Competent Authorities in determining the victim status of all children and adults who are referred into the NRM scheme. This will enable swift, accurate assessments at the 'reasonable grounds' stage and it will form a tighter safety-net against misidentifications at the full identification stage. See also, for example, ATMG report 2010, *Wrong Kind of Victim*, at chapter 6 of that report. It is to be noted that breaches by the Government of its positive obligations under *Rantsev*, may give rise to serious damages-based litigation, as illustrated by the recent High Court's judgment in *OOO and others v Commissioner of Police for the Metropolis* [2011] EWHC 1246 (QB) in which the Court, applying and approving *Rantsev*, in a severe condemnation of the way in which four victims of trafficking had been ignored as potential victims by the police, granted each victim an award of damages for breaches of their Article 3 and 4 ECHR rights. It is now also essential in terms of victim protection for the 'reasonable grounds for believing' identification test under the NRM to be interpreted in such a way as to comply with the *Rantsev* identification test of 'circumstances giving rise to a credible suspicion': this will also accord with the Trafficking Convention's intention that the test should be set very low as it is just the starting point for the full identification process to begin: see also para **2.13** below.

[7] The UK, again via policy not law, insists on a civil standard of proof for 'conclusive' ie full identification decisions on trafficking, thereby requiring the Competent Authorities to decide this on a balance of probabilities. Is this standard of proof too high for trafficking identification? The Trafficking Convention is itself silent on the appropriate standard of proof that ought to applied by States in reaching the full identification decision. However the Explanatory Report to the Convention, at para 27, recognises the complexities in achieving full identification and advises that: '127. . . . Failure to identify a trafficking victim correctly will probably mean that victim's continuing to be denied his or her fundamental rights and the prosecution to be denied the necessary witness in criminal proceedings to gain a conviction of the perpetrator for trafficking in human beings. Through the identification process, competent authorities seek and evaluate different circumstances, according to which they can consider a person to be a victim of trafficking'. It is well-recognised that when victims of trafficking escape or are freed from their traffickers they may remain terrified and silent about what has happened to them. Disclosure, when it occurs, may be piecemeal, may be slow and may be at times inconsistent (See further para **2.13** below, the OSCE Policing Guidebook, June 2011, Part II, pages 21–30 and **CHAPTER 4** of this book). The UK recognises that the civil standard of proof is too high for the lawful assessment of another vulnerable category of individuals in the UK, namely those who seek recognition of their rights under the Refugee Convention 1951. In asylum cases the decision maker, be it the SSHD or the UK's courts and tribunals, will reach all relevant assessments including the credibility of facts past and present claims, on the basis of 'a reasonable degree of likelihood': this is known as the *Sivakumaran* standard of proof and is much lower than the civil standard. See **CHAPTER 14** The UK's judiciary reaches decisions, in the context of asylum claims by victims of trafficking, on whether a person has been trafficked by applying this standard. In light of this fact and to achieve consistency in decision-making by the State, taken together with a recognition of the tremendous number of obstacles to full disclosure by victims of trafficking as highlighted for example in para **2.13** and in **CHAPTER 4**, the decision as to whether a person is fully/conclusively identified as a victim of trafficking ought to also be reached on the lower, *Sivakumaran* standard. A review by the Government of the standard of proof for the conclusive identification decision is necessary. Furthermore, as highlighted in the ATMG report of June 2010, negative NRM decisions, which are disclosable in criminal proceedings, may impact on the successful prosecutions of traffickers. The Trafficking Convention, under Article 3, prohibits discrimination in the implementation of all its provisions. The Article 10 identification process must not enable a State to discriminate against victims of trafficking on account of their status and yet by requiring victims of trafficking in the UK to prove their identification on a balance of probabilities this exposes those who cannot meet this standard to discrimination as being recognised victims and witnesses of crime.

8   To the extent that negative NRM identification decisions, which are routinely served by the SSHD in asylum appeals in the UK and are indeed often written by the same UKBA case owner who wrote the asylum refusal letter for the victim (albeit such decisions reached, ostensibly, on different standards of proof) are relied upon at all by the SSHD in asylum appeals is a serious cause for concern. Whereas the use by the SSHD of a negative NRM decision is specifically used for prejudicial purposes namely to discredit an asylum seeker's account, this is a potentially unlawful practice in view of the the 'savings clauses' in both the Palermo Protocol, Article 14, and the Trafficking Convention, Article 40, which provide *inter alia* that nothing in the in the Protocol or the Convention shall affect the right of individuals under international law including the Refugee Convention 1951.

Residence Permits

2.4 As one might immediately notice, the Government's description to the ODIHR of the eligibility for a residence permit for a confirmed victim of trafficking, as being dependent on either an Article 8 ECHR assessment or a police request, does not marry with the Trafficking Convention's requirements. Article 14 of the Trafficking Convention provides for the grant of a residence permit in two circumstances, first, where it is necessary owing to the victim's personal situation and, secondly, where it's necessary for the victim to co-operate with the police. There is also the proviso in children's cases that the residence permit, when legally necessary, (ie presumably where the conditions for a grant under either limb of Article 14(1) are met), shall be issued where the best interests of the child require it.

The text of Article 14(1) and (2) is as follows:

'1.   Each Party shall issue a renewable residence permit to victims, in one or other of the two following situations or in both:
    a   the competent authority considers that their stay is necessary owing to their personal situation;
    b   the competent authority considers that their stay is necessary for the purpose of their co-operation with the competent authorities in investigation or criminal proceedings.
2   The residence permit for child victims, when legally necessary, shall be issued in accordance with the best interests of the child and, where appropriate, renewed under the same conditions.'

It is also necessary to consider what the Explanatory Report provides in terms of the aim of a residence permit under Article 14(1):

'182 . . . The aim of these requirements is to allow Parties to choose between granting a residence permit in exchange for cooperation with the law-enforcement authorities and granting a residence permit on account of the victim's needs, or indeed to adopt both simultaneously.'

And further, in respect of the test for eligibility under the personal situation category the Explanatory Report confirms the appropriate test:

'183 . . . the victim's personal circumstances must be such that it would be unreasonable to compel them to leave the national territory . . .
184. The personal situation requirement takes in a range of situations, depending on whether it is the victim's safety, state of health, family situation or some other factor which has to be taken into account.'

Hence, the test for a residence permit under Article 14(1)(a) is whether, owing to a person's circumstances it would be 'unreasonable to compel the individual to leave the UK'. The personal matters that are expressly to be taken into account include health, safety and family issues or 'some other factor', which ought presumably to include a statutory claim for compensation under Article 15 of the Trafficking Convention (in respect of which the Government was notably silent at the ODIHR meeting above), or for example a claim for breach of contract, unpaid wages or for personal injury, loss and damages against a trafficker in the Employment Tribunal or in the civil courts respectively. This 'personal circumstances' test, under Article 14(1)(a) does not engage a proportionality-based balancing exercise, as is required under an Article 8 ECHR assessment, despite the Government's reference to Article 8 ECHR to the ODIHR: the Trafficking Convention and the European Convention on Human Rights are both Council of Europe Treaties but the tests under Article 14(1)(a) of the Trafficking Convention and under Article 8 ECHR are entirely different. To the author's mind there may therefore be a need to remind the Government of its duties under Article 14(1) of the Trafficking Convention. Certainly those who represent victims of trafficking who have been conclusively identified under the NRM may wish, where suitable, to encourage them to seek residence permits under Article 14(1)(a) on the basis of the express terms identified above. See also **CHAPTER 14**.

Statistics

NRM referrals and decisions 1st April 2009 – 31st March 2011

2.5 The following is a brief analysis[1] of the most recent NRM figures that were released in July 2011[2]. The analysis below broadly follows the methodology adopted by the ATMG in its June 2010 report.

The UKHTC reported in its published statistics that between 1st April 2009 and 31st March 2011 the cases of 1481 potential victims of trafficking had been referred to the NRM. Those referred into the NRM came from a total of 90 countries. However, by far the largest contributors were Nigeria (262 people), China (167 people) and Vietnam (145 people), a significant proportion of whom are believed to have been children. The next three countries (in terms of the numbers of people who were referred) were all EU countries (totalling 179 people), whilst the country with the next largest number of people referred was the UK itself, with 52.

Out of the 1481 people who were referred, 1066 (72%) were women or girls and 415 (28%) were men or boys. 390 were said to be children (ie under 18) at the time they were referred (26 % of the total), of whom 55% were below the age of 16, and 45% were aged 16 or 17.

The statistics were disaggregated according to the forms of exploitation that were reported: sexual exploitation, labour exploitation, domestic servitude and unknown exploitation. A total of 506 adults and 115 children were reported to have been trafficked for sexual exploitation, accounting for 42% of all the referrals. A total of 331 adults and 134 children were referred as presumed trafficked for labour exploitation, (31%), and 52 adults and 201 children for domestic servitude, (17%). 89 adults and 53 children were referred as presumed trafficked for unknown exploitation.

Of the 1481 referrals, 896 (60%) received a positive reasonable grounds decision, and 30% a negative decision, the balance accounted for by 5% of referrals where a decision had yet to be made and 5% withdrawn or suspended.

Of the 896 referrals which received a positive reasonable grounds decision, 497 (55%) received a positive conclusive grounds decision, 17% a negative decision and 9% remained undecided. The balance of 3% were suspended. Hence the conclusive identification rate is just over 30% of the total.

[1]   The analysis of the NRM figures has kindly been provided by Clive Daykin.

[2]   The tables of statistics are available here: http://www.soca.gov.uk/about-soca/about-the-ukht c/statistical-data. Owing to time restrictions in terms of this book going to print no commentary can be provided in this chapter by way of comparing and contrasting the new NRM figures with those that were documented in the ATMG June 2010 report.

The need for partnership in identification

2.6 Many of the other chapters in the Identification section of this book refer to the NRM and its outcomes in terms of victim identification and a common theme which arises, namely the risk of mis-identification as a victim of trafficking, including for those referred under the NRM scheme by specialist support organisations, is clearly linked to the absence of any UK law or policy which requires collaboration on determining victim identification, rather than the mere referral by specialist organisations for identification by the Government. Of concern therefore is that the UK is failing to meet its legal obligations under Article 10 of the Trafficking Convention which requires State's Parties to involve a range of different authorities and specialist organisations, including NGOs, in the identification determination process. As Article 10(1) provides:

> 'Each Party shall provide its competent authorities with persons who are trained and qualified in preventing and combating trafficking in human beings, in identifying and helping victims, including children, and shall ensure that the different authori-ties collaborate with each other as well as with relevant support organisations, so that victims can be identified in a procedure duly taking into account the special situation of women and child victims and, in appropriate cases, issued with residence permits under the conditions provided for in Article 14 of the pres-ent Convention'. [Author's emphasis].

The UK's legal duty to involve non-state parties in victim identification is also reiterated under Article 10(2) of the Trafficking Convention, clearly to underline the point. Article 10(2) hence provides so far relevant:

> 'Each Party shall adopt such legislative or other measures as may be necessary to identify victims as appropriate in collaboration with other Parties and relevant support organisations . . . '[Author's emphasis]

Indeed, as recently advised by the OSCE in its June 2011 publication *Trafficking in Human Beings: Identifcation of Potential and Presumed Vic-tims, A Community Policing Approach* ('Policing Guidebook'), at page 46, there are numerous professionals who can identify victims of trafficking in any given country:

> 'The range of people and institutions that can identify trafficked persons is rather broad, particularly if they are trained and if a system of referral is in place. They include: law enforcement [including the police] and government actors, NGOs, local

social welfare organizations, hospital staff and psycho-social medical specialists, [trade] unions, labour inspections and other labour-related agencies [ie in the context of the UK the Gangmasters Licensing Authority], as well as embassy officials.'

Moreover, as highlighted in the ATMG *Wrong Kind of Victim* report of June 2010, the UK's arrangements for the establishment and operation of its NRM scheme do not correspond with what the OSCE expects of a national referral mechanism for victims of trafficking as set out in the OSCE Handbook on National Referral Mechanisms of 2004[1]. Indeed it is notable that the OSCE has very recently in June 2011 reiterated its clear definition of what a national referral system must encompass:

'National Referral Mechanism (NRM) is defined as a co-operative framework through which State actors fulfil their obligations to protect and promote the human rights of trafficked persons, co-ordinating their efforts in a strategic partnership with civil society. The basic aim of an NRM is to ensure that the human rights of trafficked persons are respected and to provide an effective way to refer victims of trafficked to needed services. At the core of every NRM is the process of locating and identifying likely victims of trafficking who are generally known as 'presumed trafficked persons'. This process includes all the different organizations involved in a NRM, which should co-operate to ensure that victims are offered assistance through referral to specialized services'[2].

Certainly, in terms of victim identification at the very least, the OSCE definition of a NRM corresponds with the UK's, thus far unimplemented, legal obligations under Article 10 of the Trafficking Convention to allow collaboration in determining victim identification, as highlighted above. Indeed, following the establishment of the NRM in the UK, Eva Biaudet, the OSCE's Special Representative for Combating Trafficking in Human Beings had advised:

'I welcome recent efforts to revise the UK National Referral Mechanism aimed at improving identification and treatment of trafficked persons. However, I recommend looking into whether law enforcement and immigration authorities who currently are assigned as 'competent authorities' to identify victims, such as the UK Human Trafficking Centre and the UK Border Authority, are alone best equipped for this task,"
"Based on experience from other OSCE participating States, I recommend a multi-agency approach to determining victim status and referral to services, involving child protection professionals and representatives from specialized NGOs providing support to victims.'[3]

That recommended multi-agency approach to determining victim identification, as opposed to the current arrangement whereby specialist or support bodies in the UK, merely refer victims to the NRM for Government-dependent identification outcomes, still remains aspirational in the UK.

[1] See ATMG Wrong Kind of Victim full report, pages 25–26.
[2] See OSCE, 'Trafficking in Human Beings: Identification of Potential and Presumed Victims A Community Policing Approach', June 2011, at p 36.
[3] LONDON, 18 June 2009 http://www.osce.org/cthb/51058.

UNDERSTANDING HUMAN TRAFFICKING IDENTIFICATION

2.7 The critical issues that are of crucial importance to an understanding of the issues relating to trafficking victim identification are:

(1)   what constitutes the act of human trafficking; and
(2)   who therefore are the victims of such acts.

(1) The act of human trafficking

2.8 The act of human trafficking is defined under the Palermo Protocol 2000, Article 3, and the Council of Europe Convention on Action against Trafficking in Human Beings 2005 ('the Trafficking Convention'), Article 4:

> '"Trafficking in human beings" shall mean the recruitment, transportation, transfer, harbouring or receipt of persons, by means of the threat or use of force or other forms of coercion, of abduction, of fraud, of deception, of the abuse of power or of a position of vulnerability or of the giving or receiving of payments or benefits to achieve the consent of a person having control over another person, for the purpose of exploitation. Exploitation shall include, at a minimum, the exploitation of the prostitution of others or other forms of sexual exploitation, forced labour or services, slavery or practices similar to slavery, servitude or the removal of organs.'

This definition can be broken down into three core elements, namely the act, the means and the purpose. As succinctly explained by the United Nations Office on Drugs and Crime (UNODC), the 'act' explains what is done; 'the means' describe how it is done and 'the purpose' explains why it is done[1].

Hence the definition of human trafficking can be subdivided as consisting of the following:

'1   The act of the:
    –   Recruitment
    –   Transportation
    –   Transfer
    –   Harbouring or
    –   Receipt of persons
2   By means of:
    –   the threat or use of force, or
    –   other forms of coercion,
    –   of abduction,
    –   of fraud,
    –   of deception,
    –   of the abuse of power or of a position of vulnerability, or
    –   of the giving or receiving of payments or benefits *to achieve the consent of a person having control over another person*
3   For the purpose of exploitation. Exploitation includes at a minimum:
    –   the exploitation of the prostitution of others
    –   or other forms of sexual exploitation,
    –   forced labour or services,
    –   slavery or practices similar to slavery,
    –   servitude
    –   or the removal or organs.'

With this human trafficking definition in mind there are two additional legal issues that must be recognised:

- Consent: where all the three core elements are present there has been trafficking in persons (adults) and if any of the above means in core element (2) have been used[2] by the trafficker to obtain the adult victims' consent to their trafficking, that consent by the victim is thereby rendered irrelevant ie the victim is still a victim if they consented in any of those circumstances. The process which leads to the irrelevance of the consent of a victim to their trafficking[3] has been well described by the UNODC[4] in the following way:

> 'When looking at the definition included in the [Palermo Protocol], the fact that the victim may have consented in any way to the process of human trafficking is irrelevant if any of the means listed above are used. A trafficked person cannot "consent" to being trafficked if the consent occurs as a result of threats, force, abduction, fraud, etc. As such, a human trafficker's contention the trafficked person agreed to the conditions is irrelevant. If any of the means are present the victim's consent is no defen[c]e for the accused. For instance, if a person agreed to migrate and engage in sex work but is held by force and coerced to perform sex work for long hours and not paid as promised, that person has been trafficked. The fact the person agreed to go but is then held by force and coerced nullifies the presence of consent. The person has been, in fact, trafficked.'[5]

- Children's cases: where core elements (1) and (3) are present, there has been trafficking in persons (children). There is no legal requirement to establish that any of the means described in core element (2) were used in order for the act of human trafficking of a child to have taken place[6]. Hence, a child cannot consent to their trafficking or their exploitation.

The definition engages a number of processes, as explained by the United Nations High Commissioner for Refugees (UNHCR):

> 'An important aspect of this definition is an understanding of trafficking as a process comprising a number of interrelated actions rather than a single act at a given point in time. Once initial control is secured, victims are generally moved to a place where there is a market for their services, often where they lack language skills and other basic knowledge that would enable them to seek help. While these actions can all take place within one country's borders, they can also take place across borders with the recruitment taking place in one country and the act of receiving the victim and the exploitation taking place in another. Whether or not an international border is crossed, the intention to exploit the individual concerned underpins the entire process.'[7]

The act of human trafficking can therefore be broken down into separate assessments or phases: the recruitment phase and transfer phase (which take place pre-exploitation), an assessment of the means of control over victims in the exploitation phase and the phase of exploitation itself. An identification methodology which applies these phases and assessments to what is known about the facts involving the experiences of any a victim of trafficking is therefore advised. See too OSCE Policing Guidebook at pp 51–78.

The recent EU Directive 2011/36/EU of the European Parliament and of the Council of 5 April 2011 on preventing and combating trafficking in human beings and protecting its victims, and replacing Council Framework Decision 2002/629/JHA ('the EU Trafficking Directive') incorporates the same three core elements as those contained in the human trafficking definition adopted in the Palermo Protocol and the Trafficking Convention. However the definition of human trafficking is developed under the Directive in a number of ways[8].

First, the Directive definition of the 'act of' includes the addition of 'the exchange or transfer of control over [such] persons'. This widens the scope of the criminal offence of trafficking in persons and thereby also broadens the identification of who is a victim of the criminal act(s) in question.

Secondly, the Directive defines what is meant by a position of vulnerability[9]:

> 'A position of vulnerability means a situation in which the person concerned has no real or acceptable alternative but to submit to the abuse involved.'[10]

It appears that the addition of this explanatory definition may well be linked to the realisation that this form of 'means', ie the abuse of a person's vulnerability, is very often used by traffickers but is frequently overlooked or misunderstood by States and their identification mechanisms.

Misidentification of a victim will impact not only on the rights of a trafficked person to receive assistance and respect for their human rights but on a State's ability to adequately investigate and prosecute human trafficking offences. It is a straightforward matter of cause and consequence that if individual or group traffickers are not prosecuted and trafficking rings are not dismantled, leading to the prosecution and punishment of the main criminal players, the human trafficking industry will continue to be a low risk, highly profitable black market trade in the UK. The modern day trade of trafficking human beings for exploitation is proliferating around the World. Indeed, as the EU Parliament and Council recently recognised in presenting its new Directive 2011/36/EU to the Member States of the European Union:

> '[T]he objective of this Directive, namely to fight against trafficking in human beings, cannot be sufficiently achieved by the Member States and can therefore, by reason of the scale and effects of the action [can] be better achieved at Union level . . . '[11]

There is also a growing realisation of the need for deterrent sentences to be imposed on human traffickers. Hence, the EU Trafficking Directive requires that where an offence is committed against a particularly vulnerable victim, which should at least include all children, the criminal penalty should be more severe[12].

Further, the Directive extends the definition of 'exploitation' to expressly include 'begging . . . or the exploitation of criminal activities'[13].

According to the Recital[14] to the EU Trafficking Directive 'this broader concept of exploitation' is to tackle recent developments in the phenomenon of human trafficking. The Recital advises that 'forced begging' should be understood as a form of forced labour or services as defined in the ILO Convention no 29 of 1930 and that 'the exploitation of criminal activities' should be understood as being the exploitation of a person to commit *inter alia* pick-pocketing, shop-lifting, drug trafficking and other similar activities which are subject to penalties and imply financial gain for the trafficker[15].

Finally, the Directive, in what appears to be an express recognition of the tensions that arise when States have duties and obligations under legal instruments to provide residency or residence permits[16] to non-EEA nationals, including those who are victims of trafficking, expressly provides that:

'This Directive establishes specific protection measures for any victim of trafficking in human beings.'[17]

And, that:

'Consequently, this Directive does not deal with the conditions of the residence of the victims of trafficking in human beings in the territory of the Member States.'[18]

Hence, under the EU Trafficking Directive a trafficked victim is a victim who is entitled to all the protection measures that are established under it: eligibility is therefore absolute and is not affected, or potentially undermined, by any national identification mechanism which is designed to select or root out those who should be granted a residence permit from those who should not[19].

Under all three instruments the intentional act of human trafficking is a crime[20].

Under UK and Scottish law there are various crimes of trafficking in respect of which a human trafficker can be prosecuted and convicted[21]: readers are referred to **CHAPTER 19** in this book on Trafficking-Related Criminal Legislation.

It is important to note that the list of the types of exploitation (core element (3), above) for which a person might be trafficked under the Palermo Protocol and the Trafficking Convention is an inclusive one. Hence even before the implementation date of the EU Trafficking Directive in April 2013 the trafficking of persons into and within the UK for the purposes of exploitation through enforced criminality including forced begging, cannabis farming/cultivation, volume theft and benefit fraud and the trafficking of persons, usually children, for the purposes of forced marriage or illegal adoption are as much prohibited forms of trafficking-related crimes as those which are expressly listed under 'exploitation' in Article 3 of the Palermo Protocol and Article 4 of the Trafficking Convention: therefore the victims of all these acts are the victims of human trafficking.

[1] See further http:/www.unodc.org/unodc/en/human-trafficking/.
[2] Palermo Protocol, Art 3(b); Trafficking Convention, Article 4(b); EU Trafficking Directive, Article 2(4).
[3] And its relevance to the prosecution of a trafficker.
[4] The mandate and work of the United Nations Office on Drugs and Crime (UNODC) is to assist UN Member States to fight organised crime, illicit drugs, corruption and international terrorism within the respective UN conventions and universal instruments. The UNOCD is the guardian of the United Nations Convention against Transnational Organized Crime and its supplementary protocols on human trafficking and migrant smuggling, including the Palermo Protocol. The primary goal of the UNODC is to promote global adherence to these universal instruments and assist States to effectively implement them.
[5] UNODC *A Comparative Analysis of Human Trafficking Legislation and Case Law: Suggestions for Best Practices in Creating Laws against Human Trafficking* 2009, at p 5.
[6] Palermo Protocol, Article 3(c); Trafficking Convention, Article 4(c); EU Trafficking Directive, Article 2(5). The punishable acts of adult and child trafficking are subsumed within the common trafficking definition. A common theme in the Palermo Protocol, the Trafficking Convention and the EU Trafficking Directive is that where a child is concerned no possible consent should ever be considered valid.
[7] *UNHCR Guidelines on International Protection: The application of Article 1A(2) of the 1951 Convention and/or 1967 Protocol relating to the Status of Refugees to victims of trafficking and persons at risk of being trafficked*, at para 10. The interpretative guidance in this paragraph has been accepted as being relevant to the identification of victims of trafficking by the UKBA in numerous trafficking-related policy documents including in its APPU Guidance to Competent Authorities, 2011, at page 8.

8   Article 2(1) of the EU Directive provides that the following intentional acts are punishable: 'The recruitment, transportation, transfer, harbouring or reception of persons, including the exchange or transfer of control over those persons, by means of the threat or use of force or other forms of coercion, of abduction, of fraud, of deception, of the abuse of power or of a position of vulnerability or of the giving or receiving of payments or benefits to achieve the consent of a person having control over another person, for the purpose of exploitation.'

9   An explanatory definition of this term is contained within the Explanatory Memorandum of the Trafficking Convention, at para 83, but is not defined within Article 3 of the Trafficking Convention itself. The term is not defined in the Palermo Protocol.

10   Directive 2011/36/EU, Article 2(2).

11   Directive 2011/36/EU, Recital (32).

12   Directive 2011/36/EU, Article 4(2), explained in Recital (12).

13   Directive 2011/36/EU, Article 2(3). Article 2(1) provides that the following intentional offences of trafficking in human beings shall be punishable: 'The recruitment, transportation, transfer, harbouring or reception of persons, including the exchange or transfer of control over those persons, by means of the threat or use of force or other forms of coercion, of abduction, of fraud, of deception, of the abuse of power or of a position of vulnerability or of the giving or receiving of payments or benefits to achieve the consent of a person having control over another person, for the purpose of exploitation.'

14   Directive 2011/36/EU, Recital (11).

15   Directive 2011/36/EU, Recital (11).

16   See comments made earlier at para **2.4**.

17   Directive 2011/36/EU, Recital (17).

18   Directive 2011/36/EU, Recital (17).

19   And a victim status is therefor also not dependent on an NRM mechanism which attempts to decide, by a process of identification, those who should be granted the Chapter III-style assistance measures under the Trafficking Convention from those should not.

20   Palermo Protocol, Article 5; Trafficking Convention, Article 18; EU Trafficking Directive Article 2.

21   And as summarised by the United States' Trafficking in Persons report on the UK, June 2011: 'The UK prohibits all forms of trafficking through its 2009 Coroners and Justice Act, 2003 Sexual Offences Act, and its 2004 Asylum and Immigration Act, which prescribe penalties of a maximum of 14, 14, and [14 – amendment added] years' imprisonment, respectively.'

(2) Who is a victim of trafficking?

2.9 Under the Trafficking Convention, a victim of human trafficking is a person who has been subjected to the act of human trafficking. The Trafficking Convention, Article 4(e) defines a victim in the following way:

'"Victim" shall mean any natural person who is subject to trafficking in human beings as defined in this article.'

The Explanatory Report to the Trafficking Convention provides further guidance:

'Definition of "victim"
99. There are many references in the Convention to the victim, and the drafters felt it was essential to define the concept. In particular the measures provided for in Chapter III are intended to apply to persons who are victims within the meaning of the Convention.
100. The Convention defines "victim" as "any natural person who is subjected to trafficking in human beings as defined in this Article". As explained above, a victim is anyone subjected to a combination of elements (action – means – purpose) specified in Article 4(a) of the Convention. Under Article 4(c), however, when that person is a child, he or she is to be regarded as a victim even if none of the means specified in Article 4(a) has been used.'

Chapter III of the Trafficking Convention, as referred to in paragraph 99 of the Explanatory Report, above, contains the measures that have been introduced by the Trafficking Convention to protect and promote the rights of victims. Chapter III of the Trafficking Convention therefore establishes the following protection measures[1]: Identification (Article 10); Protection of Private life (Article 11); Assistance to victims (Article 12); Recovery and reflection period (Article 13); Residence Permit (Article 14); Compensation and legal redress (Article 15); Repatriation and return of victims (Article 16); Gender equality (Article 18).

The OSCE definition of a victim of trafficking is as follows:

'A victim of human trafficking is any natural person who has been subject to trafficking in persons, or who the competent authorities including the designated non-governmental organizations where applicable reasonably believe is a victim of trafficking in persons, regardless of whether the perpetrator is identified, apprehended, prosecuted or convicted.'[2]

Hence a person is a victim in advance of whether or not their trafficker has been identified, charged or punished by the criminal justice system.

As to who is, generally, a victim of crime, which would therefore include trafficked victims, the OSCE has advised:

'Victims of crime are persons who, individually or collectively, have suffered harm, including physical or mental injury, emotional suffering, economic loss or substantial impairment of their fundamental rights through acts or omissions that are in violation of criminal laws including those laws proscribing criminal abuse of power.'[3]

---

[1] See the Trafficking Convention which is an Appendix in this book.
[2] OSCE, *Trafficking in Human Beings: Identification of Potential and Presumed Victims A Community Policing Approach* June 2011, at p 11, which draws on and develops the definition that is adopted by the United Nations Office on Drugs and Crime in its *Model Law against Trafficking in Persons*, Vienna 2009, Article 5(1)(v).
[3] OSCE, *Trafficking in Human Beings: Identification of Potential and Presumed Victims A Community Policing Approach* June 2011, at p 10, drawing upon and developing the definition adopted by the UN General Assembly, Res 40/34, annex, Declaration of Basic Principles of Justice for Victims of Crime and Abuse of Power, 29 November 1985, at p 1.

PRACTICAL LEGAL TOOLS TO IDENTIFY A VICTIM

(1) Who is an adult victim of trafficking?

2.10 Where all three of the core elements in the trafficking definition exist, the person who was subjected to such treatment is entitled to be recognised as a victim of trafficking. Although there is a requirement to show that one of 'the means' of trafficking occurred in the cases of trafficked adults in order to establish that 'the crime' of human trafficking took place and thereby to successfully prosecute a trafficker, in terms of deciding who is an adult victim of the crime of trafficking it matters not whether the adult victim consented to their trafficking if any of the means listed in the definition were used to obtain that consent[1].

---

[1] See for example, Trafficking Convention, Article 4(b) which provides: 'The consent of a victim of "trafficking in human beings" to the intended exploitation set forth in subparagraph (a) of

this article shall be irrelevant where any of the means set forth in subparagraph (a) have been used'. A similar provision is included in the EU Trafficking Directive, under Article 2(4) albeit the reference 'to the intended exploitation . . . ' in the Trafficking Convention is more precisely defined under the Directive, which instead provides 'to the exploitation, whether intended or actual . . . '.

(2) Who is a child victim of trafficking?

2.11 Where, on the objective and/or subjective facts of a case, core elements (1) and (3) in the trafficking definition exist, and the person who was subjected to such treatment was under 18 years old at the time, that person is a child victim of trafficking. In the case of child victims there is no requirement at all to establish that any of the means identified in the trafficking definitions were used by the trafficker individual or group to enable a successful prosecution for 'the crime' of child trafficking to take place[1]. Hence there is no requirement to prove that a child was deceived, coerced or forced into the human trafficking scenario. The Recital to the EU Trafficking Directive confirms that:

> '[W]hen a child is concerned, no possible consent should ever be considered valid.'[2]

A child cannot consent to their trafficking and cannot consent to their exploitation: any child moved or recruited into a place for the purposes of exploitation is a victim of trafficking.

[1] Trafficking Convention, Article 4(c), which provides: 'The recruitment, transportation, transfer, harbouring or receipt of a child for the purpose of exploitation shall be considered "trafficking in human beings" even if this does not involve any of the means set forth in subparagraph (a) of this article'. The Explanatory Report to the Trafficking Convention helpfully explains: '76. For there to be trafficking in human beings ingredients from each of the three categories (action, means, purpose) must be present together. There is, however, an exception regarding (trafficked) children: under Article 4(c) recruitment, transportation, transfer, harbouring or receipt of a child for the purpose of exploitation is to be regarded as trafficking in human beings even if it does not involve any of the means listed in Article 4(a). Under Article 4(d) the word "child" means any person under 18 years of age.'

[2] Directive 2011/36/EU, Recital (11).

(3) When are the elements of 'the crime' of human trafficking met?

2.12 In all cases of human trafficking, the crime of human trafficking will take place before the exploitation begins, albeit the crime of human trafficking will also encompass the act(s) of the actual exploitation if the intended exploitation of the victim has already occurred.

As the Explanatory Report to the Trafficking Convention provides:

> '87. Under the definition, it is not necessary that someone have been exploited for there to be trafficking in human beings. It is enough that they have been subjected to one of the actions referred to in the definition and by one of the means specified "for the purpose of" exploitation. Trafficking in human beings is consequently present before the victim's actual exploitation.'

Of course there is no requirement to prove that any of the specified means were used in the case of a child.

GENERAL INDICATORS OF TRAFFICKING AND BARRIERS TO VICTIM IDENTIFICATION

2.13 There are numerous publications in the UK and in the international domain which provide indicators that assist in the identification of victims of trafficking.

The National Referral Mechanism forms[1] which are to be completed by the named First Responders[2] in the UK list many general indicators of human trafficking and these should be referred to. These Indicators are reproduced in the Appendices.

Practitioners are also referred to the 'Human Trafficking Indicators' of the United Nations Office on Drugs and Crime which are reproduced in full as an Appendix. This is an extensive list which provides both a detailed list of general indicators that a victim of trafficking may exhibit and/or disclose and also lists of trafficking or exploitation-specific indicators with regard to identifying child victims and victims of trafficking for the purposes of the following forms of exploitation: domestic servitude; sexual exploitation; labour exploitation; begging and petty crime.

As advised by the OSCE in its Policing Guidebook, at page 45:

'Misperceptions of who is likely to be a victim, how victims should behave and where they come from can all hinder victim identification. Common myths about victims [include:] they do not take opportunities to escape and therefore there was no coercion; if they say they have a better life than previously, then they have not been trafficked; they are not victims when they reject help. These myths and false perceptions do not consider that victims may have legitimate reasons for choosing not to escape or to reject assistance (e.g. fear of reprisals, vulnerability, lack of knowledge of the environment.) Even if their life in their country of origin might have been worse than their trafficking experience, that still does not mean that they have not been trafficked.'

And at page 47:

'Preliminary identification [Author's note: which appears to correspond with the test for the reasonable grounds decision under Article 10 of the Trafficking Convention] should support the conclusion that there is a reasonable assumption that a person might have been trafficked. This assumption should be based on the presence of relevant indicators. Indicators are signs that suggest the possibility of human trafficking. They can be discovered through incidents associated with criminal activity, statements from the victim or signs of harm associated with trafficking. Some indicators are obvious, others are not'.

In terms of the barriers and difficulties in victim identification these have been documented in detail in by numerous international and domestic organisations and NGOs but for the purposes of this chapter the following, paraphrased, observations of the OSCE in its Policing Guidebook at pages 48-50 are highlighted:

- Victims are usually unaware of their rights as victims, do not understand the laws of the country and often do not speak the local language – all of which help traffickers to control the victims and keep the crime.
- The interaction between the trafficker and victim is multifaceted because in many cases the perpetrator is also 'protecting' the victim from the authorities if the victim has irregular residence or work-related

status. The victim may feel dependent on, and bound to, the trafficker (eg debts). In many cases a trafficker uses the negotiation of the terms of the victim's exploitative conditions (eg sharing the victim's earnings) as a strategy to strengthen the victims' sense of indebtedness to the trafficker and/or to make the victim feel complicit in his or her own exploitation.

- Methods of controlling victims do not necessarily involve physical violence. Sophisticated forms of psychological pressure, pressure and manipulation are increasingly common in trafficking cases. In many situations they have completely replaced physical violence.

- In cases of both sexual and labour exploitation, shame is another powerful mechanism of control. The trafficker may threaten to reveal to the victim's family that she has been working as a prostitute. [In terms of both women and men], victims feel ashamed for 'being so naive or weak', or they may have hoped their entrapment in a human trafficking situation is some kind of misunderstanding and that they will get paid if they comply with the trafficker's requirements.

- Victims of trafficking may manifest symptoms of post-traumatic stress disorder that may make their identification even more difficult. Traumatised victims may deny that they have been trafficked; they may experience difficulty in remembering what actually happened; they may fill in blanks in their memory by making up plausible elements of the traumatic situation; and they may refuse to co-operate upon their detection.

- Another reason why individuals choose not to identify themselves as victims of human trafficking is that they may be told that co-operating with the police will provide them with a short term of residence before they are returned home, which means a return to the misery they tried to escape.

The OSCE therefore advises, at page 50 of the Policing Guidebook:

'Given the complexity of both victim identification and the crime of human trafficking, authorities should give the benefit of the doubt to a person claiming to have been subjected to exploitation possibly related to trafficking. A person presumed to have been trafficked should be considered and treated as a victim as soon as the competent authorities have the slightest indication that he or she has been subject to the crime of trafficking.'

[1]   There are separate NRM referral forms for adult and child victims – see the Appendices in this book
[2]   Which are the Police, UK Border Agency (UKBA), Serious Organised Crime Agency (SOCA), Local Authorities/Social Services, Gangmasters Licensing Authority (GLA), Poppy, Trafficking Awareness Raising Alliance (TARA), Migrant Helpline, Kalayaan, Medaille Trust, and Salvation Army. New First Responders include the NSPCC's specialist trafficking identification group, the Child Trafficking Advice and Information Line (CTAIL) and Barnardo's (as announced by the Government in its *Human Trafficking: the Government's Strategy*, July 2011, at p 27).

CONCLUDING REMARKS

2.14 Misidentification can have grave consequences for victims of trafficking and therefore the human rights of all victims of trafficking in the UK deserve careful recognition. The UK's ratification of the Palermo Protocol in 2006 and of the Trafficking Convention in 2008 means that it is subject to a raft of legal obligations as contained within those instruments. However, two years after the entry into force of the Trafficking Convention in the UK the real risk of misidentification for many victims of trafficking still exists as the chapters which follow will in some cases starkly demonstrate. There are no corners that can be cut when implementing safeguards for trafficked victims. The UK's National Referral Mechanism must be reviewed in terms of how it operates and consideration must be given by the Government on how to reform the NRM arrangements for victim identification so as to bring to its heart the collaborative human rights approach to identification and assistance that its namesake, the OSCE, intended all NRMs to have. In respect of reasonable grounds decisions these must be reached rapidly on the basis of human trafficking indicators alone, taking also into account a victim's rights under *Rantsev* and Articles 3 and 4 ECHR to have their trafficking circumstances or allegations promptly investigated by the police. The need for a firm understanding of the human trafficking definition by all identification decision-makers is a prerequisite to victim safety. As for the final identification decisions, not only must these be determined, as with the reasonable grounds decisions, in partnership with relevant agencies and NGOs but an appropriate legally relevant standard of proof must be applied to the assessment of the UK's, notably non-judicial, conclusive NRM decisions, particularly, in view of all the well-known obstacles to victim disclosure, and therefore to victim identification. As the EU Parliament and the Council have implicitly recognised in the EU Trafficking Directive 2011/36/EU, if there is no required relationship between trafficking victim identification and residence permits the legal recognition of a 'victim' is, in political terms, a lighter, less encumbered task, enabling all victims of trafficking in the territories of the opting-in States of the EU to achieve entitlement to all measures under the Directive regardless of their immigration status. One cannot help wonder if the absence of an expressed right to a residence permit under the Trafficking Convention for confirmed victims would have impacted on the current NRM arrangements in the UK, particularly conclusive decision-making, and if so, how. Notwithstanding, the legal obligations under the Trafficking Convention are firm and the UK, as a State Party to this treaty is, in the words of the Lord Justice Hughes in *R v LM*[1], 'fully bound by it.' With this in mind it is hoped that reform of the NRM scheme takes place imminently so that, in particular, the astonishingly low rate of confirmed trafficking victims in the UK, at just over 30% of the total number of persons referred into the NRM on present figures rises to more accurately reflect the numbers of trafficked victims in the UK. A different standard of proof for the conclusive identification decisions, which victims could more fairly and realistically meet, would enable this. For with legal recognition comes rights, including enhanced care, safety and support, a path to justice and the right to compensation for recognised victims of serious crime.

[1] [2010] EWCA Civ 2327.

3

FORCED LABOUR: UNDERSTANDING AND IDENTIFYING LABOUR EXPLOITATION

Klara Skrivankova

This chapter focuses on the forms of exploitation outside of the sex industry that occur in the context of trafficking. It highlights some of the challenges which relate to defining and understanding the situations in which victims find themselves and the remedies that are available within the law.

THE REALITY OF TRAFFICKING AND FORCED LABOUR – DO WE NEED A NEW DEFINITION OF EXPLOITATION?

3.1 Unlike cases of trafficking for sexual exploitation, most trafficking for labour occurs in regular sectors (such as agriculture, hospitality, cleaning, fishing, care or domestic work) where exploited workers can in some instances be found alongside workers who are not exploited. Trafficking for forced begging or illegal activities are of course exceptions. Given the limited scope of this chapter, these specific forms of labour trafficking will not be addressed here. This should not however be taken as meaning that they are less important – rather the contrary – as newer or newly recognised forms of exploitations, forced begging and trafficking for criminal activities require particular attention and further examination.

In seeking to describe what constitutes exploitation, the array of situations that exist in and around a workplace need to be examined. If the working conditions of different persons are to be compared, one will find a wide range of situations, from non-exploited workers (who enjoy good working conditions), to workers who are subject to some exploitation (which may relate to the violation of employment laws and regulations) to workers who suffer extreme exploitation (forced labour). While all these three situations exist, they are not clearly defined categories and the lines between them are rather blurred by a variety of other situations that might be found in between. Extreme forms of labour exploitation (eg forced labour) constitute a crime both within the international legal framework and within the UK domestic legislation.

In terms of trafficking, the UK is bound by the definition of the Palermo Protocol and Council of Europe Convention on Action against Trafficking in Human Beings. The definitions in both treaties are identical, and define trafficking as a three-stage process, the purpose of which is exploitation that at minimum includes '. . . . . forced labour or services, slavery, practices similar to slavery, servitude . . . ''[1]. Section 71 of the Coroners and Justice Act 2009, as to which see further below, is also relevant as this criminalises forced labour in the UK as a free-standing offence and as one which takes place irrespective of whether the person was trafficked. Consequently, situations of forced labour are legislated against, either as linked with trafficking (if forced labour is an outcome of a process of interrelated actions intended purpose of which is forced labour) or as a stand-alone offence.

Most recently, the European Union in its new trafficking Directive[2] decided to adopt similar wording of the recognised international definition of trafficking and to further extend the definition to include **forced begging and forced criminal activities** among the purposes of exploitation. The Directive will enter into force on 6 April 2013 and the UK shall be bound by it, as the Government announced in March 2011 its decision to opt-in to the treaty[3].

Compared to trafficking, forced labour is an older concept within the international legal framework. It dates back to the first half of the 20th century. The principal definition of forced labour was set by the International Labour Organisation (ILO) in its Convention No 29 of 1930 and defines forced labour as:

(a)   all work or service;
(b)   which is not voluntary;
(c)   and is exacted under the menace of a penalty[4].

At the time of the conception of the Convention, the situation in the world was different from today and the ILO has since provided further clarification, see below, as to how to understand the forced labour definition in the 21st century – these clarifications are particularly key to identifying situations of trafficking for forced labour. Generally, however there are two common features that situations of forced labour share: the exercise of coercion and the denial of freedom[5].

According to the ILO, menace of penalty does not always mean that some form of direct punishment is applied by the trafficker or exploiter to obtain the victim's work; subtle forms of menace exist, sometimes of a psychological nature; or it may take the form of a loss of rights or privileges[6]. The ILO's guidance is very significant, as many cases of trafficking for forced labour today do not include elements of harsh physical violence, but rather psychological abuse, control and manipulation – as will further be demonstrated.

The domestic legislation in the UK also criminalises trafficking for forced labour. However, unlike the crime of human trafficking for sexual exploitation which is contained within criminal legislation[7], the offence of 'human trafficking for labour exploitation' is contained within immigration legislation[8], namely in the Asylum and Immigration (Treatment of Claimants, etc.) Act 2004, s 4, as amended[9].

In recognition of the fact that the s 4 trafficking offence did not cover all instances of forced labour, such as where no trafficking was involved or where the exploitation occurred before December 2004 when s 4 entered into force in the UK, a new criminal offence of holding another person in slavery or servitude or requiring them to perform forced or compulsory labour was introduced in the Coroners and Justice Act 2009, s 71. The offence came into force on 6 April 2010.

Section 71 provides that a person (D) commits an offence if:

> 'D holds another person in slavery or servitude and the circumstances are such that D knows or ought to know that the person is so held, or; D requires another person to perform forced or compulsory labour and the circumstances are such that D knows or ought to know that the person is being required to perform such labour.'

In Scotland, this offence was introduced in the Criminal Justice and Licensing (Scotland) Act 2010, s 47, which came into force in March 2011.

The legislation that is now in place as well as the level of penalties provided for by the legislation suggest that the crimes of labour trafficking and forced labour are to be treated as being very serious. However, is the dedicated legislation sufficient to deal effectively with the reality of labour exploitation in the UK? How are the definitions applicable in practice? Is there a common understanding of what constitutes exploitation or what are the constitutive elements of forced labour?

The absence of a clear definition of exploitation and the problems derived from this absence have been the subject of international debate ever since the introduction of the common definition of trafficking in the Palermo Protocol in December 2000.

States (including the UK), as well as international organisations, including the ILO (which is the UN agency responsible for labour standards) have routinely been using the expression 'trafficking for labour exploitation', without defining what constitutes exploitation beyond the list of examples given in the Palermo Protocol trafficking definition.

The body of ILO Conventions and their legal interpretations are an example of a continuous effort to define and re-define labour exploitation – and an attempt to revise the interpretation of it to the changing reality[10].

The problem we are now faced with is the complexity of the reality, the ever changing nature of trafficking, new forms of trafficking and the more subtle methods of coercion applied by the traffickers.

For those addressing a particular case of a potentially trafficked person, this process is complicated not only by the dynamic nature of the problem, but also by complex external and individual circumstances. The complexities of the situation in which a particular presumed trafficked person is found include: understanding the legal framework, identifying labour market functions and failures, whether the worker is a victim, the impact of his or her immigration status, individual agency and personal status. While there might be some commonalities in people's experiences of exploitation, the personal experiences of workers tend to differ and it is difficult to simply compare individual realities and consider them as binary values: either forced labour or not forced labour, with nothing in between. The plethora of the realities of exploitation that exist means that the issue we are dealing with is a complex social phenomenon[11].

Countries within the EU have adopted various approaches in dealing with the lack of clarity as to what constitutes exploitation. Some countries, such as the Netherlands, have left it to the discretion of their courts to interpret what such an act entails (with the risk that the concept of trafficking maybe interpreted too broadly and the severity of the crime eroded), while others, like Belgium, have focused on the concept of a violation of human dignity as the fundamental aspect of exploitation[12].

One possible way to determine exploitation in a particular given case is to compare the situation of the worker who we consider is exploited, to the situation of the non-exploited standard. A similar comparative approach has been adopted in Germany[13]. Interesting to consider is also the definition of 'particularly exploitative working conditions' contained in Article 2 of the EU Sanctions Directive[14]. According to the Directive, such conditions mean: ' . . . . working conditions, including those resulting from gender based or other discrimination, where there is a striking disproportion compared with the terms of employment of legally employed workers which, for example, affect workers' health and safety, and which offends against human dignity.' While the Directive is aimed at combating irregular migration within the EU, it contains some provisions that could be beneficial for exploited workers. However, the UK has not opted into this Directive and in May 2011, the Minister of State for Immigration, Damian Green, confirmed that the UK will maintain its opt-out position[15].

Within the UK domestic legislation, there is an attempt to define exploitation in the Asylum and Immigration (Treatment of Claimants, etc.) Act 2004, s 4 labour exploitation trafficking offence where it is defined as: slavery or forced labour; use of threats, force or deception to obtain a service; or the use of or attempt to use someone to undertake an activity that someone who was not young, disabled or a family member would be likely to refuse[16].

This definition is useful, although it is obvious that it misses the majority of labour trafficking cases where the abuse of the worker's position of vulnerability is present but is more often related to other circumstances than those included in the above definition, such as the status of the person (eg irregular immigration status) or the existence of a debt. It appears that in defining more precisely what acts constitute exploitation in cases of trafficking, there will be a need for further interpretation by the courts and it will be for those lawyers dealing with the cases to raise awareness about the circumstances and situations that those in forced labour endure.

The judgment of the Court of Appeal in November 2010 of *R v Khan, Khan and Khan*[17] provides some important clarification as to what factors should be taken into account when considering the severity of exploitative conduct:

> 'The nature and the degree of deception or coercion exercised upon the incoming worker. Coercion will be an unusual aggravating feature in a case of economic exploitation. The gravamen of the offence committed against economic migrants is the deceitful promise of work on favourable term;
> The nature and degree of exploitation exercised upon the worker on arrival in the work place. This will involve a consideration both of the degree to which what is

promised is in fact denied on arrival and the extent to which the treatment in the workplace offends the common standards within the United Kingdom;
The level and methods of control exercised over the worker with a view to ensuring that he remains economically trapped;
The level of vulnerability of the incoming worker, usually physical, psychological and financial;'[18].

Judgments like these are vital in informing the practitioner, when it is still debated and difficult to find an answer to the question: how severe does the exploitation need to be for it to qualify as forced labour?

The next two sections will offer some ideas as to how to overcome the definitional vacuum.

[1]   Council of Europe Convention on Action against Trafficking in Human Beings (Warsaw, 2005), Article 4; Protocol to Prevent, Suppress and Punish Trafficking in Persons, especially Women and Children to the UN Convention against Transnational Organized Crime (Palermo, 2000), Article 3.

[2]   Directive 2011/36/EU on preventing and combating trafficking in human beings and protecting its victims.

[3]   The UK is currently engaged in parliamentary processes which will determine how it is to implement the EU Directive.

[4]   ILO Convention No 29 of 1930, Article 2.

[5]   Skrivankova, K.: *Between decent work and forced labour: examining the continuum of exploitation* (2010) Joseph Rowntree Foundation.

[6]   A global alliance against forced labour. ILO, Geneva, 2005.

[7]   Namely the Sexual Offences Act 2003, ss 57–59.

[8]   The location of this particular offence in immigration, as opposed to criminal, legislation has often been cited in trafficking forums as the reason why it has so rarely been enforced by the police and the CPS.

[9]   Section 4 states:

'(1)   A person commits an offence if he arranges or facilitates the arrival in the United Kingdom of an individual (the "passenger") and—
   (a)   he intends to exploit the passenger in the United Kingdom or elsewhere, or
   (b)   he believes that another person is likely to exploit the passenger in the United Kingdom or elsewhere.

(2)   A person commits an offence if he arranges or facilitates travel within the United Kingdom by an individual (the "passenger") in respect of whom he believes that an offence under subsection (1) may have been committed and—
   (a)   he intends to exploit the passenger in the United Kingdom or elsewhere, or
   (b)   he believes that another person is likely to exploit the passenger in the United Kingdom or elsewhere.

(3)   A person commits an offence if he arranges or facilitates the departure from the United Kingdom of an individual (the "passenger") and—
   (a)   he intends to exploit the passenger outside the United Kingdom, or
   (b)   he believes that another person is likely to exploit the passenger outside the United Kingdom.

(4)   For the purposes of this section a person is exploited if (and only if)—
   (a)   he is the victim of behaviour that contravenes Article 4 of the Human Rights Convention (slavery and forced labour),
   (b)   he is encouraged, required or expected to do anything as a result of which he or another person would commit an offence under the Human Organ Transplants Act 1989 (c. 31) or the Human Organ Transplants (Northern Ireland) Order 1989 (S.I. 1989/2408 (N.I. 21)),
   (c)   he is subjected to force, threats or deception designed to induce him—
      (i)   to provide services of any kind,
      (ii)   to provide another person with benefits of any kind, or
      (iii) to enable another person to acquire benefits of any kind, or
   "(d)   a person uses or attempts to use him for any purpose within subparagraph (i), (ii) or (iii) of paragraph (c), having chosen him for that purpose on the grounds that—

(i)   he is mentally or physically ill or disabled, he is young or he has a family relationship with a person, and

(ii)   a person without the illness, disability, youth or family relationship would be likely to refuse to be used for that purpose."

(5)   A person guilty of an offence under this section shall be liable—

     (a)   on conviction on indictment, to imprisonment for a term not exceeding 14 years, to a fine or to both, or

     (b)   on summary conviction, to imprisonment for a term not exceeding twelve months, to a fine not exceeding the statutory maximum or to both.'

[10] Rijken, C.(ed).: *Combating Trafficking in Human Beings for Labour Exploitation* (2011) Wolf Legal Publishers, Netherlands, p 471.

[11] Skrivankova, K.: *Between decent work and forced labour: examining the continuum of exploitation* (2010) Joseph Rowntree Foundation, p 16.

[12] Rjken, C.(ed).: *Combating Trafficking in Human Beings for Labour Exploitation* (2011) Wolf Legal Publishers, Netherlands.

[13] Skrivankova, K.: *Between decent work and forced labour: examining the continuum of exploitation* (2010) Joseph Rowntree Foundation.

[14] Directive 2009/52/EC of the European Parliament and of the Council of 18 June 2009 providing for minimum standards on sanctions and measures against employers of illegally staying third-country nationals.

[15] http://www.theyworkforyou.com/wms/?id=2011-05-24a.50WS.1&s=border+agency#g50W S.2.

[16] Skrivankova, K.: *Trafficking for forced labour – UK country report* (2006) Anti-Slavery International, London.

[17] *A-G's Reference (Nos 37, 38 and 65 of 2010), R v Khan, Khan and Khan* [2010] EWCA Crim 2880.

[18] *A-G's Reference (Nos 37, 38 and 65 of 2010), R v Khan, Khan and Khan* [2010] EWCA 2880, para 17.

NON-COMPLIANCE VERSUS FORCED LABOUR

3.2 Non payment of wages, long working hours, lack of protective clothing, workers with little or no command of English – all or some of these factors may accumulate and point to employment laws being violated: but they could also be indicators of forced labour. How though do we tell what situation the worker is in, what are his or her entitlements and where in the law they ought to look for a remedy?

This section will provide a brief insight into how situations of exploitation in the workplace can be classified using either employment laws or indicators of forced labour.

For the sake of simplicity, the chapter with operate only with the term 'forced labour', understanding that forced labour could be both an outcome of trafficking or a stand-alone offence. Whichever way the worker arrived in the situation of exploitation, it is the very situation of exploitation that is the determining factor. **Not** the process that led to it.

Forced labour as experienced in the UK is a dynamic phenomenon. Forms of coercion employed by traffickers are constantly changing – exploiters apply more often subtle forms of violence, psychological threats and control. Some manage to create such a level of dependency of their victims and exercise such a level of control over them, that the victims feel incomprehensible loyalty to the 'employer' and may even return back to the situation of exploitation. This scenario was exemplified in *R v Khan, Khan and Khan*[1]. Paragraph 18 of the judgment states that victims had returned back to the UK from their country of origin, as the trafficker promised improvement in their treatment and working conditions if they returned. The judge concluded that the victims were: 'lead to believe they were valued employees . . . .' and that the fact that they returned, attested to the control they were under and was 'evidence of further exploitation by the offenders of personal circumstances of which they knew they could take advantage of'.

These very specific and subtle forms of coercion that relate to the personal circumstances of the victims and the way they are manipulated and controlled by the exploiters seem to be at the heart of most cases of forced labour in Europe, according to service providers and legal representatives. The UK is not an exception in this sense. And it is in dealing with these cases that the obstacles arising from a missing definition of exploitation become apparent.

It is however important to highlight that there are cases where physical violence is present – both in cases concerning men and women. Victims of forced labour can also be subject to sexual violence. In cases of domestic servitude, where the victims are predominantly (but not exclusively) women, many are raped by the male members of the family. In these cases, sexual abuse is used as a means of control and assertion of power[2].

Another known reality is that an individual experience can begin as an acceptable work situation but conditions subsequently deteriorate into forced labour (often as a consequence of the worker's vulnerable immigration status). Furthermore, other factors, such as the subjective assessment of the situation, or the agency of an individual worker, play an important role and must not be overlooked – many of those in forced labour do not see themselves as victims[3].

In order to assist in the identification of a situation of forced labour, in 2004 the ILO provided six indicators. Usually, there is a combination of indicators inflicted on a worker. The ILO argues that if two or more are present, there is a strong indication of forced labour:

- Threats of or actual physical or sexual violence.
- Restriction of movement and confinement, to the workplace or to a limited area;
- Debt bondage: where a worker works to pay off debt or loan, and is not paid for his or her services;
- Withholding of wages, refusing to pay the worker at all or excessive wage reductions;
- Retention of passports and identity documents;
- Threat of denunciation to the authorities[4].

Across Europe, indicators are the most commonly used method of identification of forced labour in practice. In addition to this initial set of indicators, the ILO further developed a Delphi[5] model to be applied to identify a situation of forced labour as an outcome of trafficking – this model is now used in some European countries as well (eg Ireland)[6].

Sets of indicators are also used for identification of trafficking for forced labour in the UK and are included in the referral forms of the National Referral Mechanism. There are also lists of indicators of forced labour that UK judges are advised to consider and apply when dealing with criminal trials involving the s 71 stand-alone forced labour offence[7].

The use of indicators is common and provides guidance for various actors and enforcers, however their use is not without difficulties. The application of indicators is often problematic in practice when it comes to determining the extremity of a situation. This is because the majority of cases occupy the middle ground between the two extremes and are hard to fit into a straight-forward 'exploitation – yes/no' category[8].

The question remains, how severe does the exploitation need to be for it to qualify as forced labour? And if no forced labour is found, what should be done?

It is important to remember that not all unacceptable working conditions constitute forced labour and there is a thin line between a sub-standard employer and a human trafficker who exploits others[9]. Still even in a case with facts that do not appear to be severe enough to constitute labour exploitation under the trafficking crime or forced labour under s 71, it may be likely that the case involves an employer's non-compliance with various employment laws and that those laws have been violated. In such instances, the State has the obligation to enforce the laws and to protect those whose rights have been abused.

Moreover, a remedy can often be found under employment legislation for both non-compliance and forced labour for a number of acts, including: breaches of health and safety regulations, breaches of contract, working-time regulations, low-wages, sick and holiday pay, etc.

From the perspective of prevention as well as protection of rights, it is important to deal even with the 'lesser forms of exploitation'. Where impunity for employment law violations is permitted, labour standards erode and the labour rights of workers are not respected – such a situation could over time result in labour exploitation and has often been described by forced labour experts as an underlying factor of forced labour.

Added to that, it has been argued by the ILO, as well as by legal professionals and trade unions, that approaching situations of forced labour solely from the perspective of the criminal law is rather limiting and fails to address the critical underlying factors of such violations.

Furthermore, a sole criminal justice approach does not necessarily benefit those in forced labour; nor does it address the sum of complex and dynamic situations and their causes or achieve the aim of affronting the antithesis of decent work[10]. In fact, enforcement of employment law in cases of forced labour can later influence or instigate a criminal investigation – in several cases of forced labour for domestic servitude in the UK, the case was first dealt with by an Employment Tribunal and subsequently the employer was investigated within the criminal justice framework.

Combining criminal justice with labour justice in tackling forced labour and related exploitation provides us therefore, not only with an opportunity to prosecute, but with an added opportunity for regulation and monitoring. Rigorous enforcement against non-compliance with employment laws and rigorous criminal law enforcement are clear deterrents to exploitation.

[1]   *A-G's Reference (Nos 37, 38 and 65 of 2010), R v Khan, Khan and Khan* [2010] EWCA 2880.

2   *Unprotected Work, Invisible Exploitation: Trafficking for the Purpose of Domestic Servitude* Office of the Special Representative and Co-ordinator for Combating Trafficking in Human Beings. OSCE, Vienna, 2011.

3   Skrivankova, K.: *Between decent work and forced labour: examining the continuum of exploitation* (2010) Joseph Rowntree Foundation.

4   See ILO (2004) Human Trafficking and Forced Labour Exploitation: Guidelines for Legislators and Law Enforcement in Anderson and Rogaly (2005) p 16.

5   Operational indicators of trafficking in human beings: Results from a Delphi survey implemented by the ILO and the European Commission. Geneva: ILO, 2009. http://www.ilo.org/wcmsp5/groups/public/—ed_norm/—declaration/documents/publication/wcms_105023.pdf.

6   Skrivankova, K.: *Between decent work and forced labour: examining the continuum of exploitation* (2010) Joseph Rowntree Foundation.

7   See Ministry of Justice Court Circular 2010/07 of March 2009, 'Slavery, Servitude and forced or compulsory labour: Implementation of section 71 of the Coroners and Justice Act 2009'.

8   See Ministry of Justice Court Circular 2010/07 of March 2009, 'Slavery, Servitude and forced or compulsory labour: Implementation of section 71 of the Coroners and Justice Act 2009'.

9   Rjken, C.(ed).: *Combating Trafficking in Human Beings for Labour Exploitation* (2011) Wolf Legal Publishers, Netherlands, p 430.

10 Skrivankova, K.: *Between decent work and forced labour: examining the continuum of exploitation* (2010) Joseph Rowntree Foundation.

CONTINUUM – A MODEL TO DESCRIBE THE REALITY OF EXPLOITATION AND REMEDY THE ABUSE?

3.3 When presenting a case, it is important to focus on the situation of exploitation itself, rather than on the process of how a person arrived in it. Examining a work situation through that lens will give us an indication of whether it is a case of forced labour (trafficked or not), or whether the violations fall within the scope of other legislation – criminal or employment laws. One of the contributions of the stand-alone forced labour offence in the UK is that it focuses precisely at the core of the criminal act – the act of exploitation.

As mentioned above, there is a blurred line between the point at which a situation transgresses from labour exploitation to forced labour. The absence of a definition of exploitation makes it difficult to draw clear marking points. Moreover, due to the lack of clarity in defining an individual worker's situation, potential victims of trafficking might fail to be correctly identified if their circumstances do not fall neatly within the scope of the National Referral Mechanism. Another problem is the sole focus on identifying the extreme condition of either trafficking or forced labour. Consequently, those whose employment rights might have been violated are left without a remedy, despite the fact that those who violated their rights will be in breach of employment laws.

In general, labour exploitation is work under conditions that violate international and European labour standards, as related to labour and/or human rights. Furthermore, principles of universal human rights apply to all workers. And while some workers might be limited in their access to labour rights due to their immigration status, they should all have their basic human rights protected[1].

It has been previously suggested by the ILO and others that in order to understand and describe the reality of forced labour and exploitation the

57

concept should be looked at as a continuum. Using a continuum in practice means that all situations that are not decent work are redressed, contributing to the heightening of standards and eliminating the environment conducive to forced labour.

This idea of a continuum has further been developed in the work of the Joseph Rowntree Foundation's programme on forced labour[2]. The next section introduces an abridged version of the continuum concept from the paper *Between decent work and forced labour: examining the continuum of exploitation*[3] published by the Joseph Rowntree Foundation in November 2010. In the paper, the following scheme of a continuum of exploitation was suggested:

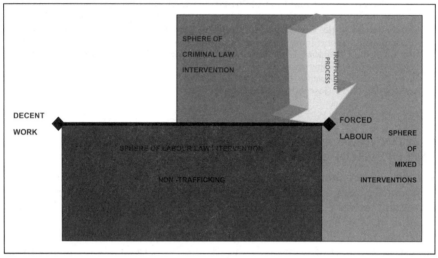

The scheme represents the continuum of exploitation, demonstrating situations in which workers might find themselves, ranging from the positive extremity (decent work), to the negative extremity (forced labour). For explanation of the concept, it should be assumed that 'all other things are equal'[4].

The concept of a continuum should not however be understood as a replacement of the missing definition of exploitation. The continuum helps us define what labour exploitation entails within a spectrum that ranges from a situation where no exploitation is found, ie a decent work situation to a situation where the most serious form of labour exploitation is found, ie forced labour. It further illustrates how the denial of rights to certain categories of workers (allowing for their exploitation) fills the space between the desirable (non-exploitative work) and the unacceptable (forced labour) and reinforces the argument that enforcement against non-compliance has a deterrent effect for those who engage in all levels of exploitation.

> 'It has been established that any acts that have the effect of lowering standards will inadvertently affect the general level of standards for all workers. By that token, the continuum represents a sum of situations that need to be addressed in order to:
> * uphold the obligations of the state to promote decent work and protect rights;
> * protect persons from forced labour;
> * provide a deterrent for those that derive their profit from violations.

. . . [T]he continuum of exploitation captures not only the complex combination of situations that exist between decent work and forced labour (an environment that permits the existence of sub-standard working conditions), but also an individual work situation, as it evolves over time. The continuum of exploitation aids understanding of the persistent problem of the changing reality of work, captures various forms of exploitation up to forced labour and assists in identifying ways of addressing it. It can be applied also to forced labour situations that are an outcome of trafficking.'[5]

According to the ILO, sub-standard working conditions are not forced labour *per se*; neither is the lack of viable economic alternatives that makes people stay in such situations (unless those are actively abused to induce and control the victim, as found in *R v Khan, Khan and Khan*[6] mentioned above). A situation in which a person finds themselves and and which leads or influences them into engagement by the trafficker needs to be examined from the perspective of vulnerability that can be abused to obtain consent, and *de facto* negate the principle of freedom of choice, the absence of which is one of the elements of forced labour. The continuum scheme above covers all such situations.

'The scheme functions between two extremes and the space between those on the scheme is filled with situations that do not comply with the principles of decent work and represent some form of violation of standards, starting from more benign forms (eg discrimination, payment under minimum wage, breach of contract), with increasing severity, leading to the most serious form of violation, forced labour. The scheme further indicates where trafficking is present and where not, operating with the concept of trafficking as a process, where forced labour can be one of the outcomes. The situation of decent work and trafficking cannot correlate. However, the purpose of trafficking is exploitation that is achieved through a series of exploitative and coercive actions, one of its forms being forced labour. Cases where forced labour is an outcome of trafficking are signified by the point on the scheme where trafficking and forced labour correlate.

The scheme also shows areas of interventions/remedy provided for by the law, in particular criminal and labour law. Individual situations and elements of violations can be indicated on the scheme, which will then point to a form of intervention that could be available. In practical terms, the continuum can be used in a number of ways.'[7]

These ways include:

(1)   To note individual elements of exploitation and identify which area of law covers those – the above scheme uses the examples criminal or labour law as single avenues of remedy or the combination of both legal routes. Some acts that are found in cases of trafficking and forced labour, such as the withholding of a passport or the false imprisonment of the worker are criminal offences in their own right in the UK and can be prosecuted separately. If these acts are combined with other acts, such as withholding wages and requiring the worker to undertake excessive working hours, they indicate a forced labour situation that entails elements of both criminal conduct and violations of employment legislation – the interaction of the two would consequently fall within the sphere of mixed intervention on the scheme.

(2)   'For comparative analysis of a real situation against the extremities of a desirable and undesirable situation. For instance:

- To evaluate a situation against the premise of decent work (a situation of freedom, eg freedom to leave, freedom of choice), security, dignity, protected rights, adequate remuneration and social protection and against the designation of forced labour (involuntary work under the menace of penalty).
- To evaluate compliance with basic labour rights eg national minimum wage, working hours, terms and conditions;
- To identify whether any of the forced labour indicators are present;
- To identify whether any of the indicators that are criminal offences in their own right are present;
- To discuss whether the remedies available are accessible for the individual in question, pointing out any systemic barriers and underlying problems[8] (such as any obstacles for trafficked persons with irregular status to successfully bring a claim in the Employment Tribunal[9])'.

To conclude, cases of trafficking and forced labour occur within the complex environment of causes and contributing factors; forced labour should be addressed both as an issue of labour rights (including human rights) as well as through the criminal justice system. The very situation of exploitation is the key determining factor that will point to the most appropriate intervention in the particular case. Using the concept of the continuum of exploitation, four key possibilities have been identified:

(1) Where labour standards are violated, remedies are provided for by employment law.

(2) Where a situation of trafficking occurs, remedies are provided for by the criminal law.

(3) Where a situation of forced labour occurs (as an outcome of trafficking or not), remedies available include both employment law and criminal law. Someone who subjects another person to forced labour can be prosecuted for committing the offence of forced labour, but can also be taken to the Employment Tribunal for failure to comply with employment laws.

(4) Where an indicator that constitutes a distinct criminal offence (such as withholding of passport) is present, but no forced labour can be established, the remedy can still be found in the criminal law[10].

This section has demonstrated how in the absence of a clear definition of exploitation, the concept of a continuum can be utilised to describe and tackle the complex reality stretching from labour exploitation (non-compliance with labour laws) to forced labour (the extreme form of exploitation). The concept can be applied both to analyse the subjective and objective situation of an individual as well as to identify the remedies that the law ought to and should apply. From the perspective of a practitioner, it could potentially serve as a guide to identify available remedies. Like every theoretical concept, it lends itself to further testing and improvements.

[1] Skrivankova, K.: *Between decent work and forced labour: examining the continuum of exploitation* (2010) Joseph Rowntree Foundation, p 19.
[2] http://www.jrf.org.uk/work/workarea/contemporary-slavery.
[3] Skrivankova, K.: *Between decent work and forced labour: examining the continuum of exploitation* (2010) Joseph Rowntree Foundation.

⁴ Skrivankova, K.: *Between decent work and forced labour: examining the continuum of exploitation* (2010) Joseph Rowntree Foundation, p 19.
⁵ Skrivankova, K.: *Between decent work and forced labour: examining the continuum of exploitation* (2010) Joseph Rowntree Foundation, p 19.
⁶ A-G's Reference (Nos 37, 38 and 65 of 2010), R v Khan, Khan and Khan [2010] EWCA 2880.
⁷ Skrivankova, K.: *Between decent work and forced labour: examining the continuum of exploitation* (2010) Joseph Rowntree Foundation, p 20.
⁸ Skrivankova, K.: *Between decent work and forced labour: examining the continuum of exploitation* (2010) Joseph Rowntree Foundation, p 20.
⁹ See **CHAPTER 17** on Employment Claims in this Handbook, however it should be noted that the chapter only deals with ET claims by victims of domestic servitude, not victims of other forms of forced labour in the UK or exploited persons who are self-employed. In those latter two cases there may indeed be insurmountable hurdles to bringing a claim to the ET on the basis of their illegal status or unprotected status.
¹⁰ Skrivankova, K.: *Between decent work and forced labour: examining the continuum of exploitation* (2010) Joseph Rowntree Foundation, p 21.

CONCLUSION

3.4 Trafficking in human beings and forced labour are significant problems in the UK today. Hundreds of people were identified as victims of these modern forms of slavery last year according to the data from the National Referral Mechanism. The Crown Prosecution Service has confirmed that more than a dozen defendants are currently awaiting prosecution under the stand-alone forced labour offence. Still, these cases represent just the tip of the iceberg. Specialist NGOs as well as Parliament's Home Affairs Select Committee[1] estimate that thousands of people are in forced labour in the UK, either as a result of trafficking or without having been trafficked. Those who have their labour rights violated represent an even larger group.

In order to significantly reduce the occurrence of modern day slavery in the UK, cases of forced labour and the underlying causes need to be effectively addressed and links should be established between the various forms of exploitation and the regulatory environment that surrounds those. Importantly, responses that combine criminal justice with employment law solutions need to be strengthened – as they go to the heart of the problem. Where cases of non-compliance with employment laws are left without punishment, even more severe forms of exploitation are free to develop over time. A combined response provides both the remedy for the exploited worker, as well as a deterrent to those who build their businesses on the premise of making profit though the violation of labour rights and standards.

The concept of a continuum as presented here offers a method that captures the broad spectrum of realities that are encountered in practice. It further promotes the approach of focusing on the core: examining the situation of exploitation as the key determinant – the essential point being that worker's human rights and employment rights have been violated (although the levels of violation might differ).

Whilst the concept is mainly meant to inform, and assists policy-making in addressing forced labour and trafficking, it could be useful also for service providers and legal representatives – both in dealing with concrete cases as well as in testing the law with the aim of overcoming practical barriers. This is relevant in particular in developing jurisprudence that would help overcome the obstacles faced by many migrant workers who, owing to their immigration status, may be less able than others to assert their rights in Employment Tribunals if their wages are being withheld.

It is important to acknowledge that in practice limited time and a lack of information available about a specific situation can complicate a thorough identification assessment; the use of continuum might also not be realistic or the most appropriate in certain situations[2].

Added to this, the agency of workers is a very important element in each case. Many of those in forced labour do not see themselves as victims, nor do they want to be labelled as such. They regard themselves as workers, an active party and want to participate in the resolution of their problem – which at times might mean returning back to the exploitative working situation, if an appropriate remedy is not accessible.

There is a diverse spectrum of exploitative labour situations that can be found in the UK today. While some are more extreme than others, none of them are compatible with the principles of a democratic society. Although the absence of a clear definition of exploitation makes it difficult to delineate the individual forms of exploitation, legal frameworks do exist to address them. It is imperative that these be utilised as a means of looking at the reality of a worker's situation in its totality. The concept of a continuum of exploitation and intervention is a tool that offers itself to testing for these purposes.

[1] Home Affairs Committee – Sixth Report, The Trade in Human Beings: Human Trafficking in the UK, 24 May 2009.
[2] Skrivankova, K.: *Between decent work and forced labour: examining the continuum of exploitation* (2010) Joseph Rowntree Foundation.

4

IDENTIFYING AND RESPONDING TO TRAUMA IN VICTIMS OF TRAFFICKING AND EXPLOITATION

Dr Michael Korzinski PhD

'I didn't know I was a slave until I found out I couldn't do the things I wanted.'
Frederick Douglass[1]

[1] *Narrative of the Life of Frederick Douglass, an American Slave, Written by Himself* in June 1845. Frederick Douglass (1818–1895) rebelled against his enslavement in the South of the United States of America and became a leader of the abolitionist movement. He was highly respected for his incisive writings and his skilled oratory. When many Northerners refused to believe that this eloquent orator could have been a slave, he responded by writing an autobiography, the *Narrative of the Life of Frederick Douglass, an American Slave, Written by Himself* in June 1845 which identified the men who once had owned him, by name. The *Narrative* was published in 1845: he was just 27 years old. Douglass was known in his lifetime as a being a great writer, orator and statesman. The *Narrative*, which was the first of his three autobiographies, has been recognised as being one of the most influential autobiographies of 19th century American literature. Douglass passionately believed in the equality of all people, whatever their colour, race or nationality. He said: 'I would unite with anybody to do right and with nobody to do wrong.'

FROM SLAVERY TO TRAFFICKING: VOICES PAST AND PRESENT

4.1 Human trafficking is the modern day criminal manifestation of a problem that has vexed humanity from the beginning of recorded history. Slavery was as fundamental to the way of life of the Egyptian Pharaoh, as it was to the Plantation owner of the American South. The suffering of their slaves is captured in works of literature as diverse as Homer's Iliad and Odyssey to Mark Twain's Huckleberry Finn. Slaves had no 'rights' other than those accorded to slaves. One such 'right' was the right to be tortured. Torture was defined in Roman Law as a 'certain kind of inquisition made for the purposes of tearing out the truth (erundae veritaitis) by torments and bodily pain.'[1] The pernicious cruelty of the act relegated its use solely to slaves until 2 AD. Confessions extracted under torture were considered the highest form of 'truth'. A confession of a slave was only valid if it was extracted under torture on the assumption that slaves could not be trusted to reveal the truth voluntarily[2]. In more modern times science also played a part in reinforcing and perpetuating the rationale for slavery. Samuel G Morton was an anthropologist who collected and measured hundreds of human skulls and documented his research in books such as *Crania Americana* (1839), *An Inquiry into the Distinctive Characteristics of the Aboriginal Race of America and*

Catalogue of Skulls of Man (1840), and *Crania Egyptica* (1844). He used his influence to make the case for black inferiority and in doing so 'scientifically' rationalise the enslavement of Africans[3]. The 20th century saw the emergence of new forms of 'slavery' in which millions of people were reduced to 'worthless prisoners' in the Nazis' concentration camps or in Stalin's Gulags. The brutality meted out against the poor souls who fell prey to these regimes was unprecedented in modern history.

It has taken thousands of years for the world to recognise that slavery, like torture, is wrong and in doing so create the moral and legal framework for it to be abolished. Today's victims unlike our ancestors have a sophisticated network of professionals supported by national and international laws designed to protect the victim and punish the perpetrators. The modern day survivor has rights. A concept unknown to our ancestors[4]. Modern day slavery generates huge profits for modern day slave owners. Each generation confronts new forms of these ancient practices that despite our best efforts remain extremely difficult to eradicate. What has not changed is our capacity to dehumanise and exploit vulnerable groups of people and in the process perpetrate extreme acts of cruelty that in many cases is tantamount to torture. Fredrick Douglass over 160 years ago recounted his experiences at the hands of Mr Covey, a 'slave breaker' whose job it was to 'tame' slaves:

> 'I was broken in body soul and spirit. My natural elasticity was crushed, my intellect languished, the disposition to read departed, the cheerful spark that lingered about my eye died; the dark night of slavery closed in upon me; and behold a man transformed into a brute.'[5]

Over a century later his voice is indistinguishable from the young men and women who visit my consulting room today.

[1] Peters, Edward *Torture* (1985) New York: Basil Blackwell Inc.
[2] Peters, Edward *Torture* (1985) New York: Basil Blackwell Inc.
[3] This was form of biological racism. In fact Frederick Douglass was the living embodiment of the intellectual capacity of a slave to become an American citizen.
[4] However it was only a short time after the bombing of the World Trade Centre and the tragic loss of 2,996 innocent lives on 11 September 2001 that the Bush administration began to rationalise the use of torture as key weapon in the new 'war on terror'.
[5] Fredrick Douglass, *Narrative of the Life of Fredrick Douglass, An American Slave* Ed Benjamin Quarles Cambridge Mass., (pp 94–95).

UNDERSTANDING AND IDENTIFYING THE IMPACT: 200 YEARS OF SUFFERING. TEARS OF UNDERSTANDING. TEARS OF DENIAL AND DISBELIEF. 'WHY SHOULD I TELL THE TRUTH?'

4.2 I read Fredrick Douglass' words to a young woman whose experiences at the hands of her trafficker left her feeling broken, alone and unable to 'trust anybody'. Tatiana straightened up listening intently to every word. She asked the meaning of a few words. 'What is a "brute"', she asked. I replied, 'it is like an animal.' She replied, 'He understands how I feel. I think they even treat animals better than I was treated. What happened to him? Where is he from?' I said it was written over a century ago by an American slave. She burst into tears. I asked if her tears had any words. She said, 'When I listened, I thought he expresses himself so well. I wish I could speak like that. It is how I feel. But when you said it was written over a 100 years ago it hit me this has been going on a long time. Long before I was born. It is so sad.' I said 'it is interesting, he is a 200 year African American man but he seems to understand you better than your Home Office case owner'. She burst out laughing. 'Yes that is exactly right. In between the tears and laughter she managed to blurt out, 'It is painful but I am not alone.' She slowly gathered herself. Her breathing became more regular, she paused, smiled and said, 'do you think he had someone who listened to him?' She burst out laughing again. I joined her. She said, 'I feel better. Thank you'. She responded to genuine concern for her pain. Trafficking victims feel degraded isolated and unreachable. This is of course exactly what the trafficker wants the victim to feel. As a therapist it is one's job to listen but also demonstrate in the here and now that she is not alone.

It is interesting to note that Frederick Douglass' accounts of his ill-treatment at the hands of Mr Covey were considered by many to be unbelievable because he was 'an unlearned and rather an ordinary Negro.' Here again he shares an experience that is not dissimilar to the modern day victim who often finds his or her account being questioned by the authorities and judged 'not credible'. Mr Douglass responded to his doubters in the following way:

'Well, I have to admit I was rather an ordinary Negro when you knew me, and I do not claim to be a very extraordinary one now . . . It was when I lived with Mr. Covey, the Negro-breaker, and member of the Methodist Church. I had just been living with master Thomas Auld, where I had been reduced by hunger. Master Thomas did not allow me enough to eat. Well, when I lived with Mr. Covey, I was driven so hard, and whipt so often, that my soul was crushed and my spirits broken. I was a mere wreck. The degradation to which he subjected me, as I now look back to it, seems more like a dream than a horrible reality. I can scarcely realize how I ever passed through it, without quite losing all my moral and intellectual energies. I can easily understand that you sincerely doubt if I wrote the narrative; for if any one had told me, seven years ago, I should ever be able to write such a one, I should.'[1]

Modern day trafficking victims fear they will not be believed. Many do not have the capacity to formulate their response in the composed and lucid manner of Mr Douglass. The fear of having their experience denied, the requirement to tell the story over and over again to different people simply confirms the victim's worst nightmare. The trafficker reinforces a fear of authority that often already exists within the victim. Whether it is the fear of a parent, husband, boyfriend, relative, police force, or a Government the victim will have had many experiences of the abuse of power by some authority. They meet 'new' people with the same scripts running in their heads that authorities are not to be trusted. One young woman after a year of treatment at the Helen Bamber Foundation put it in the following way:

'Why should I tell the truth? It is the biggest mistake in my life. If you want to get help you have to lie. I will do something bad.
"We believe you and why did you not tell the immigration person you were trafficked?" What is wrong with these . . . people? If they could know what it's like to be in my skin, they would not ask these stupid questions. Why do they write one thing in my refusal letter – and in my file something different? I want to kill somebody. I want to destroy everything. Why do I have to prove myself? Let's humiliate her again again and again.
When I see the court building I cannot go in I feel so claustrophobic. All of them are my destroyers. I will lose control. I am going to smash people. The judge must have a beautiful life. How [can a Judge] judge me if he has never tasted my life? Nothing is going to help. Speak with the barrister again. Speak with the solicitor again. I am

65

not a person with a good reputation. I am a piece of ****. Two years have destroyed me. I just need to feel safe. A place to recover and help myself.'

This was her truth. Her experience needed to be acknowledged. She needed someone to hear it unconditionally without 'judgment'. The abusive process produces in the mind of the abused a sense of themselves as rubbish. After two years of being sexually violated, held captive, physically and morally degraded she needed to take out what had been put it into her without being humiliated again. Her anger sounded big, but as a person she felt so small. She was fighting with what little she had to even remember. She had the right to say that what happened to her was wrong, First and foremost to herself. Then to me as her therapist. She was not ready to say it aloud.

[1]   Philip Sheldon Foner, Yuval Taylor *Frederick Douglass: Selected Speeches and Writings By Frederick Douglass* (1999) Lawrence Hill Books at p 21.

PROTECTION, SELF BLAME AND SHAME – 'AT LEAST I COULD KEEP THE MONEY'

4.3 A young woman is battered by her boyfriend in Moldova. She goes to the police. The officer responds, 'what did you do to deserve it?' As a woman in her country she felt as if she were a subclass of humanity not worthy of protection. When she was trafficked to the UK she was arrested and the Home Office removed her back to Moldova. It was the final betrayal. She described her experience in the following way:

'I had a very loving supportive family and a wonderful childhood. My father died when I was only 13, which made life very difficult financially and being the oldest of five children I felt that I had the responsibility to go and get a job and help to support my family, as there was no other help from the local authority.
At the age of 14 I got a job as market trader and continued to support my mother and my other siblings. At the time I had a boyfriend who was very violent and abusive, every day I was beaten up and went to work with black eyes, I have approached the police on several occasions but they did nothing to help me and only to be told that I must have done something to deserve it. This did nothing for my confidence and made me feel vulnerable.
One day one of my trusted regular customers who always bought products from my stall over the years offered me the opportunity to come to England. At that time it sounded a very good idea to escape the abuse and to start a new beginning.
I have taken the opportunity but when I got to England I have found my whole situation worse than the situation I have left behind me. I had to have sex with 40 men a day, these men were as old as my uncle and as young as my brother for as little as £20 pounds and when I refuse to have sex with them the traffickers told me that I had to pay back £20,000 and I was not allowed to leave the country until the debt was cleared or my family would be killed.
After three months of sex slavery I have been arrested and deported back to my home country with no money at all. I felt dirty, ashamed and helpless. I could not look in my mother eyes; I felt that she and everyone around me knew that I have been used as a prostitute. I could not approach anyone to tell my sorrow, which made it difficult, and I felt like I did not belong there any longer. What else could I do with my life? Next time I would sell myself. At least I could keep the money!'

She was later re-trafficked to the UK.

Many years later she questioned whether anyone could ever love her. 'Michael', she said, 'I have [been forced to have sex with] so many men. How could anybody love me.' She reckoned it had been in the thousands. She hated the prostituted part of herself. It became the split off, disowned part of her personality that needed to be welcomed home. The question was not how could anyone else love her but could she ever love herself again.

DUTY: THE POWER OF CULTURE FAMILY AND PERSONAL BELIEFS: 'WHY WEREN'T MY PARENTS LIKE YOU?'

4.4 I am currently working with a young woman from China who was sold to a snakehead gang by her stepmother and her father. At first she had no words to express how she felt. Her responses were monosyllabic. As a girl she had learned early in her life that what she felt was of no consequence. It was alien to her that someone should be interested in how she felt. She felt angry that her brother was treated differently. She longed to be treated in the same way he was. She listened to the conversations her stepmother had with others in her village about selling her. She eventually found the words, 'I felt that I owed my father a debt for bringing me into this world. I hated my stepmother but I loved my father. I thought that after I paid this debt I would be free. My life would be my own.' She looked at me her eyes filled with tears, 'you are a stranger but you have shown me more kindness than my own parents. Why? Why do you do this? It is not right. Why did all these terrible things have to happen to me? Why do I have to come all this way to find kindness? Why weren't my parents like you?' 'That it is a good question', I replied. We take compassion for granted but it is something is as precious as the air we breathe.

OPENING REMARKS – TRAFFICKING AND TRAUMA: UNDERSTANDING AND IDENTIFYING THE IMPACT

4.5 I have been asked to write a chapter on the 'trauma' of the trafficking victim. I have begun this chapter by bringing forward their voices rather than theories and putting their trauma in a historical context that spans millenniums and millions of victims. They are able to articulate their hurt just as Fredrick Douglass did over a century ago. They may not be able to use or understand the word 'trauma' but they know what it feels like to be hurt. The other word used in the title of this chapter is 'identify'. There are countless documents that have been written to help us identify victims. I will leave it to other experts to discuss 'trafficking indicators' such as does he or she have freedom of movement, are they allowed to keep their wages, are they forced to pay off an excessive, often irrational debt. This chapter focuses on identifying and understanding the psychological truth of a victim's experiences. The impact that the experience has upon their identity, the sense of their own body and their place in the world.

EXPLOITATION OF TRUST BY THE TRAFFICKER

4.6 The trauma the victim experiences has its origins in human relationships. Human trafficking is different from the trafficking of arms or drugs because human beings make choices. One does not need to build a relationship with narcotics to control it and transport it from place to place. But one needs to build a relationship with 'human cargo' to transport it. The trafficker must identify and understand the victim's needs in order to exploit those needs, drive the victim's decisions and ensure that the victim complies. Establishing trust and then betraying that trust is central to the relationship between the victim and perpetrator. Once the victim's mind is moved, ie they are prepared to take the decisions that will set their journey in motion, the transportation of the 'body' from one place to another becomes a simple matter of logistics.

Traffickers are adept at targeting the very basic things that people are conditioned to want and need such as trust, love, attention, positive feedback, affection, dreams, protection, safety and rewards. The wanton exploitation and violation of these needs assaults one's basic humanity. The victim feels less than human. The fact that so many victims describe themselves as feeling less than an animal is testimony to the brutal success of the process The perpetrator takes the decision in which his or her own self interests are more important than propriety, rules, regulations and common morality.

MODERN-DAY METHODS OF VICTIM CONTROL AND CHOICES: 'I HAD A HAND IN MY ENSLAVEMENT.'

4.7 The *control* of the victim is of paramount importance. Stripping the person of their humanity is the way that slaves have been broken and controlled for centuries. The fact that the modern day victim has choices that slaves in the past did not have only adds to the psychological complexity of the situation. However these 'choices' are as much conscious as they are unconscious often rooted in a person's attachment system and developmental dependencies and needs. It is the modern day victim's own choices that have played a part in the individual being enslaved. The notion internalised by the victim that 'I had a hand in my own enslavement' is as fundamental to 'breaking' the person, as is whatever additional brutality that is meted out against the victim once the true intention of the perpetrator reveals itself. The victim's own self-loathing and shame breaks him or her from the inside. Long before a person arrives at their destination the seeds of their undoing are already sown in the decision to trust in the intentions of their fellow human being at the beginning of the journey. The betrayal of all that is good and decent in human relationships strips the individual of their humanity and is fundamental to breaking the trafficking victim. The victim becomes convinced of their own 'sub-humanity'. That is not to say that trafficking victims do not demonstrate extraordinary resilience and capacity to survive in the most harrowing of circumstances. But survival always comes at a cost. It always involves 'choices'. Survivors experience many complex feelings. Survival may be a matter of luck or circumstance, or the consequence of resilience and ingenuity. Survival may come at a terrible cost, and experienced with profound feelings of guilt and shame. I have never met a victim where this issue did not dominate his or her inner world. It is *their part* in making the 'choices' that represents rock against which the person is shattered.

Such as in the case of the Chinese woman mentioned at para **4.4**. From the time that she was born it was clear that she had no choices. She was conditioned as a girl within her culture to obey, respect her elders and honour the 'traditions' of her village, even if one of those traditions is the selling of their sons and daughters abroad to earn money. It is difficult to not think of such parents as 'monsters'. Many believe or want to believe that they are sending their children to a better life. However this is an egregious error in judgment that transcends the normal ebb and flow of the mistakes that every parent makes. It is a tragic irony that the first time a young victim understands that there is a world which operates with a different value system is when they exit the trafficking situation and begin to form new relationships with people whose duty it is care for and protect them. The gradual awakening that one has rights is a fragile revelation. Fragile because it has been their experience that they inhabit and immoral universe where the rules of social reciprocity have broken down and one cannot expect decent treatment even from one's parents much less strangers.

The betrayal experienced by the victim can happen at the level of a State that fails to meet its international obligations to protect vulnerable groups such as women and children. Cultural attitudes towards woman within certain societies represents a betrayal within that culture of a woman's right to be treated equally. The betrayal is perpetrated by the hands of an individual who flourishes in such conditions and targets the vulnerable. The betrayal may come all at once or take a long time but when it hits, it is the psychological equivalent of a tsunami in which the emotional and relational foundations upon which we have built our lives is, in some cases irredeemably, destroyed.

One victim I worked with put in the following way:

> 'The traffickers and the pimps are very good at controlling. You don't even realise it at the beginning. He has a simple conversation with you, but he's learning all about you. Then it starts to become more heavy. He controls when you wake up, who you see, who you talk to, calling on your mobile 24/7.
> In the beginning he asked me if I wanted to use his mobile phone to call my family. I was really happy thinking he was generous and kind. I didn't have much money at the time so I was really grateful. Afterwards he would ask me questions about my family and other stuff. But once he had all my numbers everything changed. He said he'd talked to my sister and my mother. He said he'd told them that I was working as a prostitute[1]. I was horrified. Then he laughed. Did he call my sister and my mother? I didn't know. He had beaten me with his mind. I felt it physically even though he didn't touch me. My body collapsed. If my family knew I would kill myself. I did everything he wanted after that but the pressure never ended. Bad people always win. What is the point of goodness? Spend one week with these shit people who play with your mind and I guarantee you Dr. Michael you will go down.'

---

[1] She wasn't. This was before she was trafficked.

UNDERSTANDING AND MISUNDERSTANDING PERSONAL CHOICES: 'WHY DIDN'T SHE JUST RUN AWAY?'

4.8 The 'needs' that the trafficker exploits in the victim may be socio-economic, cultural or rooted in our earliest stages of development such as the need to feel safe, loved and secure. Here there are similarities between the trafficker and torturer. The torturer is also seeking to identify and exploit the victim's vulnerabilities. However, whereas the objective of the torturer, namely to inflict torture, is clear, the aim of the trafficker remains hidden until is too late for the victim to effectively respond. The fact that the victim *has* made choices albeit in hindsight poor ones, or, does not even believe that they even have a choice intensifies the feelings of self hatred. 'How could I have been so stupid? Looking back I can see now it was all a big setup.' The victim's own sense of incredulity is mirrored by officials who often find that he or she was a 'willing victim' because it is simply not believable that the victim did not reach out to ask for help.

The same culture of disbelief which victims of domestic violence suffered 30 years ago is not dissimilar to what is faced by modern day trafficking victims. People then and now struggle with the question as to why people remain trapped in violent and abusive relationships? Why don't they simply leave? Over the 20 years that I have been working with victims who have suffered egregious violations of their human rights and dignity these two questions consistently come up in relation to human trafficking. Unlike the case of a person who is imprisoned, shut off from the world and tortured, victims of human trafficking often come into contact with members of the public and the authorities. However they do not necessarily identify themselves as victims, may fear to seek assistance, or in some cases don't even see themselves as having the capacity to ask 'please help me' to a stranger.

'She was not "imprisoned". She was "walking around". Why didn't she just ask for help?' It is counter-intuitive, for those who commence an assessment with personal disbelief, to accept that a victim would remain in an exploitative relationship when there appears to have been many avenues through which the victim could have escaped if he or she had really wanted to. I was giving a talk once in which I was presenting a case study of a victim of human trafficking. A member of the audience raised his hand and asked the following question. 'How could she [the victim] be so stupid?' I replied, 'She was young, naive and fell victim to a predator. But not stupid. Their trauma is rooted in betrayal and a desperation that blinds them to the risks of their journey in the hope that whatever happens it cannot be worse than the life they are leading at moment.'

THE DESTRUCTION OF BY DESIGN. 'SOMEWHERE OVER THE RAINBOW'

4.9 Trafficking and torture share the same aim of breaking down the victim's defences. The victim of trafficking, however, is *made* to *feel safe* by design. As was pointed out earlier, human cargo, requires one to relate to it, encourage it, to get it to believe that the choices are good ones. The victim in essence must feel safe and trust the perpetrator to begin the journey. The idea is nurtured that 'somewhere over the rainbow' there is safe world where, 'dreams come true'. The myth is created and then destroyed. One is reminded of Dorothy in the Wizard of the Oz. She is an orphan raised by her Auntie Em on a bleak farm in Kansas. She dreams of a place somewhere over the rainbow where skies are blue and dreams come true. When Dorothy is transported by a tornado to Oz, a magical technicoloured land of new possibilities, she is confronted by the Wicked Witch of the West. Her new world comes crashing down just like her house did when it fell from the sky. In the real world when the betrayal is played out by the trafficker and the victim is faced with the 'Wicked Witch of the West', whether it is in the form of brutal physical torture and/or psychological coercion, the destruction of the belief in one's self and the loss of faith one holds in others is profound and in many cases complete. Self hatred, toxic self blame and shame are the outcomes.

Trafficking is designed to force the victim into a position of isolated helplessness, in which the victim's own decision-making process is used against her. The only person to whom the victim can turn for relief from his or her suffering is the perpetrator who is implacable, hostile or even gratified by the victim's experience. Trafficking is the total abuse of power. Trafficking is the abolition of love. The trafficker must strip the other's humanity. He or she must not see in the eyes of the victim the eyes of his daughter, son, sister, mother, or brother. How could they do what they do if they did? It is the annihilation of empathy. Why was it that the Nazis didn't find it that difficult to get people to run their death camps? What was it that allowed the camp guard to go home and tuck his own children into bed while committing genocide against the children of his neighbours? It seems that throughout history there have been and will be the Mr Covey's of this world. A god-fearing member of the Methodist Church capable of whipping a man until the poor soul's humanity is flayed away along with his skin. I remember the story that was recited to me by a young trafficking victim who had screamed at her trafficker as she was being raped by him, 'Think of your sister. How can you do this? Please stop.' It only intensified and fuelled the man's rage. The rape was a way of destroying the very thing that she was asking him to remember, that she, like his sister, was a human being. She never said it again.

The trafficker creates scenarios that are as unpredictable as they are dangerous, in which the victim eventually learns that ultimately there is no possibility of influencing the outcome. So-called compliance leads only to another level of manipulation. A victim might be strong and resolute yet the psychological pain can destroy the integrity of a person's mind and body, and their loyalty to friends and ideals. It is a dehumanising process designed to deconstruct the person's sense of identity. Core to the experience is the victim's terrifying sense of an all-consuming sense of helplessness, and the devastating recognition that the harm done to him/her is *intentional* rather than accidental. The most basic adult decision-making processes are systematically undermined. Deprived of her liberty she is deprived of all that is natural about her bodily functions, for example she may not even be able to decide when or where to go to the toilet. This may seem trivial, until the victim is forced to soil herself. She will be told by her trafficker to insert a sponge during her menstrual cycle so she can continue to service the customers. A young Vietnamese boy will be locked up in a house 24/7 to tend cannabis plants. He has no access to the outside world until the house is raided by the police. Trafficking represents the total loss of the control of one's world. It is designed to take the person back to his earliest stages of development in a process of enforced psychological regression. The objective is to break down the victim by making him or her childlike and dependent so that mature defences crumble. The only escape is into the most primitive defensive survival mechanisms. The victim becomes completely reliant on the trafficker for her survival, analogous to the extreme cases of child abuse and domestic violence. Trafficking robs the victim of the most basic modes of relating to reality. The sense of time is warped by sleep deprivation. The victims have nothing familiar to hold on to: family, home, personal belongings, loved ones, language, name. Gradually, they lose their mental resilience and sense of freedom. They feel alien – unable to communicate, relate, attach, or empathise with others[1].

The aim is not only to break the person in a conventional sense, but to reformulate the personality by an assault on connections between one's mind and body and on the victim's relationships to other human beings. The victim's sense of attachment (relationship) to other human beings, developed over years from infancy (Bowlby, 1969) is destroyed, damaging a person's capacity to form and maintain relationships. The damage to a person's capacity to form and maintain relationships, together with enduring personality change, helps to explain the profound problems faced by trafficking victims in rebuilding their lives after release[2]. The loss of safety, direction, and the ability to detect or respond to cues of danger can set off a chain of events leading to subsequent or repeated trauma exposure throughout adult life. There are powerful analogies to be made between the experiences of victims of trafficking, victims of domestic violence and in certain cases victims of State sponsored torture.

[1] Bowlby, J *Attachment and Loss. Volume 1, Attachment* (1969) New York: Basic Books.
[2] The release from the exploitative trafficking scenario may of course arise from accident or design.

CLINICAL CLASSIFICATIONS OF TRAUMA-BASED HARM; FROM SOLDIER'S HEART TO COMPLEX TRAUMA

4.10 Descriptions of the after effects of traumatic events are contained in the works of some of our greatest playwrights and writers, such as William Shakespeare's 'Coriolanus' and Charles Dickens' 'A Tale of Two Cities'. There have been a variety of attempts to formulate the ways in which human beings respond to images and experiences of catastrophic violence and loss. A classification of these responses has evolved over time and reflect the historical social and cultural contexts in which the observations were made. Palpitations suffered by soldiers under combat conditions during the American Civil war were known as 'Soldier's Heart'. 'Da Costa's syndrome', or 'Soldier's Heart' as it is colloquially known, is generally classified as a physical manifestation of an anxiety disorder, or a somatoform autonomic dysfunction. It was first observed in Union Soldiers in hospitals away from the field. Da Costa believed that the symptoms developed due to the level of stress that was maintained during a Civil War soldier's active duty. These symptoms were primarily cardiac in nature, including: chest pains, palpitations, breathlessness, and extreme fatigue with or without physical exertion[1]. The term 'shell shock' was used by psychiatrists to describe the presenting symptoms of soldiers who had been subjected to the relentless bombing and intense hand to hand combat in the trenches in WWI[2]. The British psychiatrist CS Meyers, who in 1915 coined the term 'shell shock', described soldiers' reactions to trauma during World War I as follows: 'The normal personality [is] replaced by an "emotional" personality. Gradually or suddenly an "apparently normal" personality returns-normal, save for the lack of all memory of the [traumatic] events, normal, save for the manifestation of somatic, hysteric disorders indicative of mental dissociation.'[3]. Doctors argued that a bursting shell creates a vacuum, and when the air rushes into this vacuum it disturbs the cerebro-spinal fluid and this can upset the working of the brain. However the reality was that the horrors of watching comrades being blown to bits, maimed and the killing of another human being at close quarters had more to do with complete psychological and physical breakdown than 'bursting shells'. When Abram Kardiner recorded his observations of World War I veterans, noting that on return to civilian life 'the subject continues to behave as if the original traumatic situation was still in existence,' the foundation was set for the inclusion of Post Traumatic Stress Disorder (PTSD) in the Diagnostic and Statistical Manual of Mental Disorders, Versions III (DSM-III) and IV(DSM-IV)[4]. Throughout history other terms have been used such as 'battle fatigue', 'concentration camp syndrome' and 'war neurosis'.

[1] http://ptsd.kpaulmedical.com/2011/04/a-history-of-ptsd-part-1-a-soldiers-heart/.
[2] Abram Kardiner *The Traumatic Neuroses of War* (1941) New York: Paul B Hoeber.
[3] Psychiatric Times Vol 14 No 3 (1 March, 1997).
[4] Abram Kardiner *The Traumatic Neuroses of War* (1941) New York: Paul B Hoeber.

POST TRAUMATIC STRESS DISORDER

4.11 Post Traumatic Stress Disorder (PTSD) emerged in relation to the symptoms that were exhibited by young men returning from the Vietnam war in the United States[1]. As much as it was a medical diagnosis it also allowed people to inhabit the sick role with dignity[2]. Now psychologists are applying their understanding to the experiences of the 'victims' of the modern day slave trade[3]. However, whereas the examples may appear to be profoundly different, I am reminded how betrayal featured in the experiences of the young men returning to the United States after the Vietnam war. What they believed they were fighting for and what they found on the ground were two different things. Their world view imploded along with napalm that maimed and killed thousands of innocent Vietnamese men, women and children. Is this what it meant to fight for freedom and democracy? Post Traumatic Stress Disorder was in my view as much a response to the helplessness these men felt and the horror that they witnessed, and were indeed part of, as it was in the betrayal of values that they had been taught about freedom, democracy and the 'American Way'. Their trauma was compounded by the same society that turned their back on them labelling them baby killers and losers[4].

According to the DSM-IV[5], a traumatic event has occurred if, 'the person experienced, witnessed, or was confronted with an event or events that involved actual or threatened death or serious injury, or a threat to the physical integrity of self or others' and 'the person's response involved intense fear, helplessness, or horror.' Originally published in 1994 by the American Psychiatric Association, it was released in 2000 as a text revision. Earlier versions of the DSM date back to 1952. The Handbook is used by mental health professionals for diagnosing mental illness. The current diagnostic formulation of PTSD derives primarily from observations of survivors of relatively circumscribed traumatic events: combat, disaster, and rape. In contrast to the circumscribed traumatic event, prolonged, repeated trauma can occur only where the victim is in a state of captivity, unable to flee, and under the control of the perpetrator. Examples of such conditions include prisons, concentration camps, and slave labour camps. According to Judith Herman:

'Such conditions also exist in some religious cults, in brothels and other institutions of organized sexual exploitation, and in some families. Captivity, which brings the victim into prolonged contact with the perpetrator, creates a special type of relationship, one of coercive control. This is equally true whether the victim is rendered captive primarily by physical force (as in the case of prisoners and hostages), or by a combination of physical, economic, social, and psychological means (as in the case of religious cult members, battered women, and abused children). The psychological impact of subordination to coercive control may have many common features, whether that subordination occurs within the public sphere of politics or within the supposedly private (but equally political) sphere of sexual and domestic relations.'[6]

Experienced clinicians have observed that, 'victims of car accidents and natural disasters often have quite different clinical presentations than those who experienced abuse, deprivation, and/or neglect at the hands of their caregivers. In addition, the age at which the trauma occurred also shapes subsequent adaptation patterns. While the symptomatology of victims of single-incident traumas are fairly well captured in the DSM-IV diagnosis of PTSD, victims of interpersonal trauma present with a more complex picture'[7].

[1] Edgar Jones, and Simon Wessely 'Psychological trauma: A Historical Perspective' Psychiatry Volume 5, Issue 7, July 2006, pp 217–220, Trauma and stress-related disorders.
[2] Edgar Jones, and Simon Wessely 'Psychological trauma: A Historical Perspective' Psychiatry Volume 5, Issue 7, July 2006, pp 217–220, Trauma and stress-related disorders.
[3] Cathy Zimmerman, Mazeda Hossain, Kate Yun, Brenda Roche, Linda Morison, and Charlotte Watts *Stolen smiles: The physical and psychological health consequences of women and adolescents trafficked in Europe.* (2006) The London School of Hygiene and Tropical Medicine.
[4] Barnett Hoffman *Baby Killers Vietnam Veterans of America* (2011) Lake County. Ch 951.
[5] Diagnostic and Statistical Manual of Mental Disorders (DSM) American Psychiatric Association 1994.
[6] 'Complex PTSD: A Syndrome in Survivors of Prolonged and Repeated Trauma' Journal of Traumatic Stress, Vol 5, No 3, 1992.
[7] Toni Luxenberg, PsyD, Joseph Spinazzola, PhD, and Bessel A. van der Kolk, MD 'Complex Trauma and Disorders of Extreme Stress (DESNOS) Diagnosis, Part One: Assessment' Vol 1, Lesson 25, Directions in Psychiatry, 2001.

COMPLEX POST TRAUMATIC STRESS DISORDER (DESNOS)

4.12 The concept of Complex Post Traumatic Stress Disorder – Disorders of Extreme Stress Not Otherwise Specified (DESNOS) was first introduced by Judith Lewis Herman and others such as BA Van der Kolk[1,2]. Both are leaders in the field of treating survivors of extreme forms of traumatic experience rooted in interpersonal violence and relational trauma. It has been argued that experiences of prolonged totalitarian control such as where the victim is in state of captivity, unable to flee and under the control of the perpetrator causes a disorder that is more severe, more complex and more enduring than what is defined in the current DSM defined classification. Symptoms associated with Complex Post Traumatic Stress Disorder include:

- Difficulties regulating emotions, including symptoms such as persistent sadness, suicidal thoughts, explosive anger, or inhibited anger;
- Variations in consciousness, such as forgetting traumatic events, reliving traumatic events, or having episodes of dissociation (during which one feels detached from one's mental processes or body);
- Changes in self-perception, such as a sense of helplessness, shame, guilt, stigma, and a sense of being completely different than other human beings;

- Varied changes in the perception of the perpetrator, such as attributing total power to the perpetrator or becoming preoccupied with the relationship to the perpetrator, including a preoccupation with revenge;
- Alterations in relations with others, including isolation, distrust, or a repeated search for a rescuer;
- Loss of, or changes in, one's system of meanings, which may include a loss of sustaining faith or a sense of hopelessness and despair.

The usefulness of the concept of Complex PTSD has been well demonstrated in clinical practice and therefore can contribute to a better understanding of clinical management and support needs of this population[3]. New diagnostic categories are needed to better account for the range of symptom constellations that can result from chronic traumatisation. This move beyond simple psychiatric diagnoses into the realms of complex trauma reactions is helpful because it moves the survivor away from a sense of being reduced simply to a naïve categorisation of symptoms and allows the individuality of the experience and, importantly, its social, political, economic and cultural context to be considered. However, in taking this step, it is also important that the advances which have been made in the understanding of some of the simple trauma reactions and their treatment are not ignored. It is important to find the right balance, acknowledging that these conditions (especially PTSD and depression) are common in victims of trafficking[4] and that they may be treatable, whilst at the same time recognising the complex and human nature of the experience and of the response and the limits of existing treatment paradigms.

DESNOS[5] is not a coded diagnosis in the DSM-IV, although its symptom constellation has been identified in numerous research studies and it's explanatory power is recognised by clinicians throughout the world[6]. One needs to look to ICD 10, see below, for a formerly coded diagnosis that covers similar clinical ground to what is being addressed by DESNOS. Enduring personality change after catastrophic experience (EPCACE) is a diagnostic category included in the International Statistical Classification of Diseases and Related Health Problems, 10th revision (ICD-10), as one of the adult personality disorders. Preliminary investigation suggests there is considerable endorsement in principle for this new category amongst experts. 'Enduring personality change is present for at least two years, following the exposure to catastrophic stress. The stress must be so extreme that it is not necessary to consider personal vulnerability in order to explain the profound effect on the personality. The disorder is characterised by a hostile or distrustful attitude toward the world, social withdrawal, feelings of emptiness or hopelessness, a chronic feeling of being on edge and estrangement. Post Traumatic Stress Disorder (F43.1) may precede this type of personality change.'[7] Examples of the types of events that can cause the personality change include: Concentration camp experiences, disasters, prolonged captivity with an imminent or possibility of being killed, exposure to life threatening situations such as being a victim of terrorism, and torture. Trafficking would also fall within this category.

[1] Herman JL. 'Complex PTSD: A syndrome in survivors of prolonged and repeated trauma' (1992) JTrauma Stress 5:377–391.
[2] Van der Kolk BA, Roth S, Pelcovitz D, Mandel F. 'Complex PTSD: Results of the PTSD Field Trial for DSM-IV' (1993) Washington, DC: American Psychiatric Association.
[3] Van der Kolk, B.A. Mcfarlane, A. D. & Weisaeth (Eds). 'Traumatic Stress: The effects of overwhelming experience on mind, body, and society' (1995) New York: Guilford Press.

4   Cathy Zimmerman, Mazeda Hossain, Kate Yun, Brenda Roche, Linda Morison, and Charlotte Watts *Stolen smiles: The physical and psychological health consequences of women and adolescents trafficked in Europe.* (2006) The London School of Hygiene and Tropical Medicine.

5   As stated earlier: Complex Post Traumatic Stress Disorder – Disorders of Extreme Stress Not Otherwise Specified (DESNOS).

6   Bessel A. van der Kolk, Susan Roth, David Pelcovitz, Susanne Sunday, and Joseph Spinazzola, Journal of Traumatic Stress, Vol 18, No 5, October 2005, pp 389–399 (C _ 2005).

7   The ICD-10 Classification of Mental and Behavioural Disorders. F 62.0 Enduring personality change after catastrophic experience.

MEMORY: TOO PAINFUL TO REMEMBER TOO HARD TO FORGET

4.13 Memory is the mental faculty that enables one to retain and recall previously experienced sensations, impressions, information, and ideas. Our ability to recall an event is influenced by a wide range of variables. How we feel on a given day; whether we are bored, afraid, who we were with, feeling distracted or unwell are just a few of the variables that impact how and what we remember. Our memory is affected by the nature of an event and the importance that we attach to it. Was it a special occasion or another dreary day at the office. We have all experienced a moment where we are able to remember something that happened years earlier in vivid detail. 'As if it happened yesterday', one will say. Transient observations such as what one was wearing, ate for breakfast, something funny the cat did, all come flooding back. Yet at the same time we forget to buy the milk, a person's name escapes us, or one cannot remember where he put keys just as he is rushing out the door. There are times when we remember things differently. I remember giving what I considered to be a full and accurate account of an incident only for the person who was with me to say, 'I remember it differently.' A police officer shared with me that when he takes a statement from two or more people who witness the same incident they invariably remember it in different ways. He went on to say that if the descriptions match exactly, it raises concerns about the witnesses having spoken to each other in order to get their accounts straight.

Memory is fallible at the best of times. There are times when we remember things accurately, other times when we do not and times we simply forget. This is part of the ordinary ebb and flow of memory in everyday life. If memory is fallible at the best of times what happens at the worst? There are patterns of forgetting and memory loss that are anything but ordinary. Highly charged traumatic events can leave one feeling distressed at the very thought of being asked to remember. The memory is fragmented; seemingly inaccessible to person who is being asked to recall it. Loss of memory can indicate an underlying neurological disease or a brain injury. One must be careful not to assume that a person's memory problems are purely psychological or rooted in trauma. Brain tumours are also known to affect memory and personality. To confuse the two can have catastrophic consequences for the the person. It is easy to do given that there may be significant overlaps in the symptoms that can only be delinated through specific medical tests. With this picture of memory in my mind it is not surprising that the accounts of many victims are filled with omissions, distortions, and outright contradictions. Many struggle to recall what happened or how and why they behaved in the way they did. I have found in clinical practice that the the capacity to recall is often inextricably bound with the victim's capacity to *comprehend* what happened to him or her. I have been recently working with a young trafficking victim who literally could not recall her name. The only name she used was the name her trafficker gave her. She is unable to comprehend the enormity of the abuse to which she has been subjected. She bangs her head against the wall and cuts herself as way of controlling herself and her memories. 'When I bang my head against the wall the pain stops. I feel better. I wash my body until my skin is raw but I cannot clean my mind'.

The integration and recall of painful traumatic experiences and events is extremely complex. It is as much related to the neurology of trauma as it to the simple fact one feels ashamed. One victim once said to me, 'Everyone wants to know my secrets. It feels bad to talk about it. I feel ashamed. I try to keep myself busy to block it. But I can't.' I remember saying to her that, 'no one is that strong. What happened to you must feel as if it has taken on a life of its own.' 'Yes' she said, 'I hate the night. I get tired and cannot control it. It hits me from every direction. I watch the television until 4 or 5 in the morning. I do not want to dream. My life is nightmare. "Why did I do this. Why did I do that". I don't know. What happened . . . "try to remember.". I can't. I just can't. When I start to remember it is like it happening again I just shut down. I feel so humiliated. His voice is always in my head. No one will believe you. We will take your sister. The men just look through you as if you are not there... It is too painful to remember.' I replied, 'but it's too hard to forget.' She took a deep breath and said, 'true.'

When a person is faced with a horrific experience they naturally try to disconnect through splitting and dissociation. Dissociation has long been associated with trauma exposure[1].

The victim will describe how she 'fled' from her 'body' or 'went somewhere' in her head 'to escape'. Dissociation serves to keep the experience at a distance from the self thus avoiding a form of psychological death. If the person is dissociating during the experience it has an impact on how the memory is laid down. The memory of the event is recalled in the way that it was experienced. It is split off from the self as if it happened to someone else. A victim once said, 'I looked in the mirror and it was not me.' A pioneering study explored the relationship between dissociation, memory and betrayal within the context of traumatic events in which the person is known to the victim. Their research suggests that the closer victim is the perpetrator the more intense the experience of betrayal. '.. . . . high dissociators reported significantly more trauma history and significantly more betrayal trauma (abuse by a caregiver) than low dissociators. These results are consistent with the proposal that dissociation may aid individuals with histories of betrayal traumas to keep threatening information out of awareness'. The study then goes on to suggest that recall of specific words related to the trauma is impaired[2].

The 'memories' may be experienced in a non-verbal form. The therapist must help the patient to decode these messages and reconnect the mind and body that is so often torn apart by the violations experienced by the victim. In 1990 the Medical Foundation for the Care of Victims of torture began to develop a method for torture survivors who had lost all conscious connection to their bodies[3].

The body had become something unknowable and dangerous. Bad things happened to it. One survivor succinctly put it, 'My body no longer belongs to me.' Memories do exist but in the form of bodily experiences that at the beginning may not be accessible to the individual or others. The experience can be so overwhelming that all one can be left with is chaotic, fragmented images, somatic affects, and bodily enactments[4,5,6, 7].

On a neurobiological level the effects of trauma on memory and body are well documented[8]. The flooding of stress hormones released in a state of shock knocks declarative memory (chronological recall of events) situated at the hippocampus, out of action, whereas the amygdala is intensely activated, which elicits a fear response, without a memory of the event. Dissociation is frequent, coupled with high levels of arousal, a fight–flight state, rendering the trauma unassimilated, it thus remains 'a speechless terror' (Van der Kolk 1989). The person has what can be described as part memories in which he or she may oscillate between an almost amnesic lack of recall on the one hand with a reasonable capacity to remember events on the other. One must understand that these memories may represent split off and disowned aspects of the self that have not been fully integrated. and may for the first time be relived in your presence.

Memory does not occur in a vacuum. One must search his or her own motives for asking someone to remember when she is desperate to forget. Memories come in many forms; some as described above are somatic, others are verbal, or, felt in other ways. As a therapist one operates under the assumption of the value of 're-membering', putting things together, finding meaning and integrating the experience. However I have also been a staunch believer in recovery in the context of ordinary living. Let people get on with the business of living. See what happens. People are capable of recovering from horrendous life experiences if given the opportunity to do so. Therapy has a place but a person must feel the need for it. A bit like mother's milk. However there are so many things that mitigate against such a process. The limit of a victim's leave to remain in the country creates an underlying uncertainty that cuts across the fundamental need to have a place that someone can call home. The need for a victim to give evidence to prosecute the trafficker runs headlong into all of what has been described above. The same holds true when the victim is asked to give an account to an immigration official.

1 Putnam, F.W. (1997). Dissociation in children and adolescents. New York: Guilford Press.
2 Anne P. DePrince and Jennifer J. Freyd (2003) Forgetting Trauma Stimuli PSYCHOLOGICAL SCIENCE Volume 15 — Number 7.
3 One can find a detailed description of what at the time I described as Somatic PsychoTherapy in my PhD thesis entitled Mind and body: the treatment of the sequelae of torture using a combined somatic and psychological approach (1998) Korzinski, MichaelAnn Arbor: UMI Dissertation Services, 1998.
4 'Dissociation, Affect Dysregulation & Somatization the complex nature of adaptation to trauma' American Journal of Psychiatry, 1996 153(7), Festschrift Supplement, 83-93.
5 Yovell, Y. 'From hysteria to post traumatic stress disorder: Psychoanalysis and the neurobiology of traumatic memories' (2000) Neuro-Psychoanalysis, 2: 171–181.
6 Schore, A.N. 'Affect regulation and the origin of the self: The neurobiology of emotional development' (1994) Mahwah, NJ: Erlbaum.
7 Schore, Alan 'Affect regulation and the repair of the self' (2003) New York: W.W. Norton and Co.
8 CF Van der Kolk 1996, Yovell 2000, Schore 1994, 2003a, 2003b.

THE RELATIONSHIP BETWEEN VICTIM AND PERPETRATOR: ATTACHMENT AND THE TRAUMA THAT BONDS

4.14 It is clear that the attachment the victim forms with the perpetrator is complex and powerful. It has been discussed throughout the medical literature on trauma. The question of why victims seem to choose to remain in abusive relationships – a response that appears illogical – has been posed by many researchers. One of the most difficult behaviours to comprehend is when the victim seems to have formed an emotional attachment to the perpetrator. At the Foundation we have cases of women who remain loyal and continue to 'commit' to the men who trafficked and sexually exploited them through prostitution. In domestic violence cases the victim continues to love the man who batters her. Such women may not even relate to the idea that they are a victim.

A young woman from central Africa who was trafficked to the UK for the purposes of labour exploitation called her mother on a regular basis to tell her mother of the abuse that she was being subjected to at the hands of her 'employer'. She was desperate to go home but her mother told her to remain. The victim made it clear that she was being subjected to physical and psychological abuse, that the working conditions were brutal, and that she was told to sleep in the closet under the stairs like a dog. The promise of attending school was broken. She wanted to come home. However she obediently complied with her mother's wishes and remained in a position of enforced servitude. She was in fact referred to the Helen Bamber Foundation because the police were puzzled as to why they young woman kept on saying that she was 'guilty' even though they had all the evidence required to prosecute her trafficker. It took this young woman several months of treatment before she began to see that there was anything strange or wrong with her moth-er's behaviour. We later discovered that her 'guilt' was born out of a sense that she must have done something to displease her mother. Otherwise why would her mother have sent her to this terrible place? In her mind, she must *deserve* to be punished.

As far back as 1936, Anna Freud in her book *The Ego and the Mechanisms of Defence* attempted to understand the identification of victim with the aggressor. When threatened with repeated violence, whether it is within a family or concentration camp. Freud postulated that the victim will emotionally identify with the aggressors rather than resist them. It is a form of psychological defence designed to preserve the victim's sanity.

Ferenczi (1933) felt that when we feel overwhelmed by an inescapable threat, we 'identify with the aggressor'[1]. Hoping to survive, we sense and 'become' precisely what the attacker expects of us – in our behaviour, perceptions, emotions, and thoughts. Other theories such as Traumatic Bonding, Stockholm Syndrome and Learned Helplessness, which are described below, have come forward in more recent times to try and explain the bond formed between the victim and perpetrator.

Donald Dutton and Susan Painter's paper 'Emotional Attachments in Abusive Relationships: A Test of Traumatic Bonding Theory' published in 1993 was seminal work on traumatic bonding theory. They postulated that, 'traumatic bonding, [is where] powerful emotional attachments are seen to develop from two specific features of abusive relationships: power imbalances and intermittent good-bad treatment'.[2] Dutton and Painter (1981) liken this attachment process to an elastic band which stretches away from the abuser with time and subsequently 'snaps' the woman back[3]. These behaviours have a neurological basis as sustained and overwhelming states of helplessness and fear produce actual changes in the brain that make it extremely difficult for the victim to free him or herself from the state psychological bondage that has been created with the perpetrator[4,5]. Attachment deepens with terror. Furthermore the idea that attachment is strengthened by intermittent good/bad treatment is counterintuitive and still 'beyond the ken' of the average jury member (Ewing and Aubrey, 1987)[6]. Hence, part of the role of expert witnesses who testify in battered women self-defence cases is to clarify the role of traumatic bonding in contributing (along with threats from the batterer, financial pressures, etc) to the overall difficulty battered women have in leaving abusive relationships. There is a compelling correlation to be made between the experiences of many victims of trafficking and those of domestic violence. One could argue that our understanding of domestic violence and what has developed over the past 25 years, as best practice models, are highly relevant to work with victims of trafficking.

The theory of learned helplessness was based on research initially conducted with dogs. Martin Seligman, a psychologist, placed dogs in cages and administered random shocks to them. Like most domestic violence and trafficking situations, the 'shocks' were not based on the dogs' behaviour in any way. The dog tried to escape from cages and tried to avoid the shocks, but nothing worked. Eventually they stopped trying since their attempts were repeatedly unsuccessful. Even when researchers tried to teach the dogs to escape the dogs were hesitant. It wasn't until repeated efforts were made by researchers (eg dragging the dogs to their escape) that the dogs finally learned to escape and avoid the shocks. One important aspect of the theory is that even when it was apparent that the dogs could escape they did not do so because of learned helplessness. They had reached a point where they had been conditioned that nothing they did would help them to prevent the shocks[7]. Similarly, outsiders often fail to understand why abused women do not simply leave. The battered or trafficked woman's perception of her own control over her own situation has a great deal to do with it. Even if she were able to escape, if she believes that she cannot leave or survive on her own, she will not leave. Walker (1979)[8] theorised that some women remained in physically and psychologically abusive relationships because of extreme fear and the belief that there is no escape. The victim also feels as though she has no choice but to remain in an abusive situation. This syndrome develops over time, as the cycle of violence occurs and the person loses hope and feels unable to deal with the situation. The victim may continue to try and attempt, within the abusive situation, to minimise the abuse but the actual thought of leaving recedes as a possibility. Core to the helplessness includes both the lack of control and failure. Learned helplessness response is a consequence of repeated exposure to (a) traumatic events and stimuli that were as unpredictable as they were dangerous; (b) in which there was zero possibility of the victim influencing the outcome of the events. It is essentially the experience of uncontrollable failure to solve a problem originally perceived as solvable. Crucial to understanding human learned helplessness, one should analyse the meaning a person attaches to the uncontrollable failure.

1   Prax Kinderpsychol Kinderpsychiatr. 1996, Jul–Aug; 45(6):198–205.
2   Donald Dutton and Susan Painter's 'Emotional Attachments in Abusive Relationships: A Test of Traumatic Bonding Theory. Violence and Victims' (1993) Springer Publishing Company Vol 8, No 2,1993.
3   Dutton, DG and Painter, S. L. 'Traumatic Bonding: The development of emotional attachments in battered women and other relationships of intermittent abuse' (1981) Victimology: An International Journal, 7(4), pp 139–155.
4   Robert Post., 'Tansduction of Psychosocial into the Neurobiology of Recurrent Affective Disorder' (1992)American Journal of Psychiatry 149, no 8 pp 999–1010.
5   Yehuda R. 'Linking the neuroendocrinology of post-traumatic stress disorder with recent neuroanatomic findings' (1999) Seminars in Clinical Neuropsychiatry 4:256–265.
6   Ewing, C P., and Aubrey, M. 'Battered women and public opinion: Some realities about the myths' (1987) Journal of Family Violence, 2, 257–264.
7   Peterson, C., Maier, S., Seligman, M 'Learned Helplessness: A Theory for the Age of Personal Control' (1993) Oxford University Press.
8   Walker, L. 'The Battered Woman' New York: Harper and Row.

REFLECTIONS AND REMARKS

4.15 In writing this chapter I realise that my audience will reflect the diversity of people who have contributed to this book. You may be an experienced professional or just starting to explore this work. It is important to remember that we bring our own values, born out of our upbringing, culture, and professionalism. We may find it incomprehensible that children should be bought and sold by their parents or turned into child soldiers. In our culture JuJu or witchcraft is a simple superstition but for the young victim from Nigeria the power it holds over her is real and trying to convince her otherwise can make things worse. Whether one is a police officer, immigration official, lawyer, judge, feminist, psychologist, NGO specialist or social worker we bring who we are to the problem including our own problems.

The psychologist is typically concerned about the victim's trauma. He or she will be asked to prepare a report and provide a diagnosis. There are models of good practice in preparing reports such as the Istanbul Protocol the Manual for Effective Investigation and Documentation of Torture and Other Cruel, Inhuman or Degrading Treatment or Punishment 1999 (Istanbul Protocol). An important tool in the prevention of torture and fight against impunity is the effective investigation of torture. The same should apply in trafficking cases. Are the physical and psychological findings consistent with the alleged report of trafficking? What physical conditions contribute to the clinical picture? Are the psychological findings expected or typical reactions to extreme stress within the cultural and social context of the individual? Why were they late in disclosing crucial details related to their claim? What clinical reasons could there be for inconsistencies? What kind of treatment will they require? These are just a few questions that a mental health professional might be expected to answer with respect to a victim's allegation that he or she might have been trafficked. However simply cutting and pasting the Istanbul Protocol and applying it to the case of victims of trafficking would be a grave mistake but it does serve as model for good practice and a solid starting point on which to build a more specific protocol related to human trafficking.

The police investigating will rightfully be concerned about the evidence trail, the testimony and prosecuting the trafficker. He or she will have been building a case that hopefully does not rely completely on the victim's testimony. However he or she recognises the victim may be coming from a country in which their experience of the police has not been positive. Officers recognise they have big hurdles to overcome if they are to demonstrate to the victim that they are different than the police in the victim's home country. The immigration department in all countries, such as the UK Border Agency in this country, is tasked with protecting the nation's borders. However, the skills necessary to identify victims are highly specialised and one must seriously question whether the identification of victims of trafficking is to be left to this department. The primary concern of the department is the authenticity of the claim. 'Is this person a genuine trafficking victim?', or, 'if they are a victim is it safe to send them back?'. It is not the aim of UK Border Agency caseworkers to build a relationship of trust with the 'applicant'. They will want to know whether or not the victim is co-operating with the police. Is the victim's story consistent? They will measure the case against existing case law and, hopefully, their obligations under the law. Why was the victim late in disclosing crucial details about their trafficking? The Home Office case worker may raise doubts about the victim's credibility that are often at odds with facts that have already been confirmed by the police or expertly commented upon by trafficking specialists from NGOs. The legal representative wants to ensure their client is properly represented but may find it difficult to get a coherent story. He or she will refer the client to the psychologist or other mental health professional for an opinion. The victim is having to tell her story multiple times to different people all of whom have different agendas. Universally the victim finds this profoundly difficult as more and more people get to know about their shameful and degrading secrets. Often the retelling reproduces harm and pain.

CONCLUDING COMMENTS

4.16 Trafficking is an abuse of power. It is a betrayal of all of that is good and decent in human relationships. As Fredrick Douglass put it over 160 years ago, 'behold a man transformed into a brute.' Trafficking strips the victim of his or her humanity. It is an experience that teaches people harsh lessons about the innate cruelty of their fellow human beings. Many of these lessons are first learned in the family. The family is where we learn to be a person. Many of the victims we see have had difficult beginnings in their own families. Time and time again we hear how the family of origin story is marred by neglect, poverty, abuse and cruelty. Others are not. These lessons are often repeated with different people and in different forms. The family analogy extends to us as well. As you can see from the preceding paragraph there are many different and at times, competing, interests when it comes to our responses to victims of human trafficking. We must not mirror the dysfunctions that have blighted the victim's life. If we do, we compound their trauma and confirm that they are living in a world that is as unpredictable as it is dangerous, and one where they should expect no decent and fair treatment from their fellow human beings. When we work well together we have the power to transform the victim's experience of authority into something that is positive and compassionate.

Dorothy survived her ordeal in Oz because she met in others the qualities of the heart, courage and mind as embodied in the tin-man, the lion and the scarecrow. The Good Witch of the North brought her own special skills to the situation, including wisdom, kindness and understanding. We would do well to remember these qualities as we go about our work with those who have been trafficked. As Martin Luther King once said, 'With this faith, we will be able to hew out of the mountain of despair a stone of hope.'[1] That is what we have to offer every survivor. Let's work together to make this dream a reality.

[1] Martin Luther King's speech 'I Have a Dream', delivered 28 August 1963, at the Lincoln Memorial, Washington D.C.

5

ASSESSMENT, IDENTIFICATION AND CARE FOR SUSPECTED VICTIMS OF CHILD TRAFFICKING: A CHILDREN SOCIAL CARE APPROACH

Philip Ishola

INTRODUCTION

5.1 Since 2008, a number of local authorities have embarked on a top to bottom review of their child trafficking responses in their areas. These local authorities formed part of a pilot group looking at identification procedures, enhanced victim care procedures, multi-agency training and multi-agency investigations and assessment mechanisms with a view to developing detailed policies and procedures to bring agencies closer together to protect child victims of trafficking. Has it succeeded? In my view it has. Although significant challenges for both practitioners and senior managers across all local authorities remain, there is a marked improvement in the capacity of local authority Children's Services[1] to respond to child trafficking and therefore the protection for suspected and confirmed victims is improving.

In this chapter I will explore how the legal framework supports and hinders the response, how we protect victims and, how current practice can be improved in order to better protect child victims of trafficking in the UK whilst never losing sight of the need to protect all vulnerable children (girls or boys).

As a Senior Manager in Harrow Council Children's Social Care (CSC)[2], I have been privileged to be part of a team with a passion to protect victims. This has led to a wealth of home grown expertise in Harrow, enabling us to respond to the needs of children and young people suspected of being trafficked. For many years, Harrow Council's Separated Children's Service (ie the Unaccompanied Asylum Seeking Child's department) in particular has been at the cutting edge of this work, establishing close links with local authorities across the UK and in Europe to share good practice and intelligence and to enhance and co-ordinate efforts to identify and safeguard suspected or confirmed victims in accordance with the Solace Report 2009[3]. The Council has helped to build a national abuser (trafficker) profile[4] and a data-based Operations Matrix in order to assist Harrow Children's Services in the identification of individual or trafficking networks that may be operating in the locality and elsewhere in the

UK, working with the police and other law enforcement agencies as part of the Victim Track Trace and Recover Model[5] (TTR).

The TTR is an extension of the London Safeguarding Children Board's 'Good Practice Guidance for Trafficked Children in Care'[6] and requires a case-specific agreement to be reached between relevant agencies and on its implementation, a close working arrangement with the local police that is specifically designed to locate a trafficked child who has gone missing from care. The Track response looks specifically at the routes that a child victim of trafficking may have been taken through, the type of transport which may have been used and if the child has a mobile phone it involves requesting assistance from the police to trace the location of that mobile phone in order to potentially identify the whereabouts of the missing child. The Trace response overlays the 'Track' mapping process with additional intelligence obtained during the Children's Services assessment of the child (and information that the child may disclose at a later point) with that of intelligence from other agencies. This information may relate to known addresses, individuals associated with a trafficking network or traffickers operating on their own. The 'Recover' response is initiated when the information about the whereabouts of the missing child is confirmed or it is suspected the child may be at a specific location. The TTR response must be agreed at the earliest stages of the multi-agency planning stage and must form part of the care and safety plan for a trafficked child in care (and must be a joint police and, Children's Services response, with the police leading on the wider context of missing children).

In Harrow, trafficked children are placed with foster carers, some of whom have been trained in safeguarding trafficked children and all of whom have been provided with support and guidance from the allocated social worker and the designated Child Trafficking Senior Practitioner in order to assist the designated foster carer to implement the additional safety and security response detailed in the Good Practice Guidance for Trafficked Children in Care. The designated Child Trafficking Senior Practitioner is responsible for co-ordinating the trafficking response across all agencies involved in the child's care and protection. At a strategic level, the Council is taking an active role in the Local Safeguarding Children Boards' Safeguarding Trafficked Child Co-ordination Group (comprising of other local, regional, Scottish and Welsh authorities, the Metropolitan Police, Serious Crime Directorate 9 (Human Exploitation and Organised Crime Command) Operation Paladin part of Serious Crime Directorate 5 (Child Abuse Investigation Command), the UK Border Agency, Serious Organised Crime Agency (SOCA), the Home Office, and the Greater London Authority (GLA).

[1]   The term 'Children's Services' will be used throughout this chapter to describe the 'Children's Social Care' departments of local authorities in the UK.
[2]   Philip is currently a Service Manager within Harrow Children's Service and is a member of the Harrow Safeguarding Children Board. On behalf of the London Safeguarding Children Board, he led the 2009/10 Safeguarding Trafficked Children Toolkit national pilot team and has worked within the field of asylum seeker support to families, single adults and separated children in both central and local government for 14 years. Through his management of Children's Services teams and the Harrow Child Protection Trafficking Operations team, membership of the Association of Directors of Children Service Asylum Task Force, former deputy chair of the UKHTC Victim Care Group (currently the UKHTC, SOCA Protection Group of which he remains a member), the NRM Strategic Monitoring Group, Chair of the London Safeguarding Children Board Child Trafficking Monitoring Group and chair of the

London Safeguarding Children Board Olympics Safe Games for Children Group, Philip has been able to contribute to the local and national response to safeguard victims of trafficking.

3   '*"Solace Report" The role of local authorities in addressing human trafficking'* 2009; The report explores how Local Authorities can improve their response to the crime of human trafficking, in particular in the area of identifying and assisting victims. This is a timely study, as the Council of Europe Convention on Action against Trafficking in Human Beings 2005 ('the Trafficking Convention') came into force in the UK on 1 April 2009, providing all victims of human trafficking (both adults and children) with minimum rights and protection.

4   National abuser (trafficker profile): The trafficker profile is based on information provided by individual child victims of trafficking and intelligence obtained from a range of local and national agencies in the UK. All information held is cross-referenced enabling the Operations Matrix to be populated with data identifying where activity maybe taking place (hot spots), trafficking routes used to move children and, in some cases addresses where exploitation may be occurring.

5   In summary, the TTR model involves building, with the police, a rapid response model for tracking a missing child's likely movements by, for example, identifying routes the child may take or may be picked up from by a trafficker. This Model requires close working relationships and agreements between victim support providers and law enforcement (police).

6   *Good Practice Guidance For Trafficked Children In Care*– updated February 2011; This guidance is designed to aid Social Care and Education professionals, foster carers and residential staff to meet to the needs of trafficked children in care provision. This document has been developed within the context of the London Safeguarding Children Board Trafficked Children 2011 Toolkit. It is intended as a practice guide only and not as compulsory procedures for services. Please refer to the London Safeguarding Trafficked Children Guidance 2011 [included in the Appendices] and London Safeguarding Children Board Trafficked Children Toolkit 2011 for more detailed guidance and details of support services/agencies.

LEGAL FRAMEWORKS

5.2 Domestic and international law classifies children as people who are aged under 18[1]. An age dispute case refers, in the UK, to an asylum applicant who claims to be a child with little or no evidence to support their claimed age and their physical appearance or demeanour very strongly suggests that they are significantly over 18 years of age. In most instances, this dispute first arises at the Initial Screening Interview with the UK Border Agency, triggering a local authority age assessment in order to establish eligibility for services and to assist the UK Border Agency in its determination of eligibility for leave to remain. In cases specific to human trafficking where the age of a victim is uncertain (irrespective of immigration status), special measures under international law exist where there are reasons to believe that the victim is a child (pending verification of their age)[2].

1   Such as under the UK's domestic law via the Children Act 1989 and internationally under the Convention on the Rights of the Child 1989, the Palermo Protocol 2000 and the Council of Europe Convention on Action against Trafficking in Human Beings 2005.

2   Trafficking Convention Article 10(3) on the identification of child victims. The Explanatory Report to the Traficking Convention provides: '136. The point of paragraph 3 is that, while children need special protection measures, it is sometimes difficult to determine whether someone is over or under 18. Paragraph 3 consequently requires Parties to presume that a victim is a child if there are reasons for believing that to be so and if there is uncertainty about their age. Until their age is verified, they must be given special protection measures, in accordance with their rights as defined, in particular, in the United Nations Convention on the Rights of the Child.'

CONSENT

5.3 The Palermo Protocol (ratified by the UK in 2006)[1] defines child trafficking as 'The recruitment, transportation, transfer, harbouring or receipt of a child for the purpose of exploitation'. The same definition of child trafficking applies under the Council of Europe Convention on Action against Trafficking in Human Beings 2005 ('the Trafficking Convention'). Under the common definition deception, coercion, threat or any other means is not required in order to establish that a child was trafficked and therefore rules out the possibility for children to give their informed consent to being trafficked.

It is also important to note that in all cases of child trafficking, a child cannot consent to their own exploitation. The Palermo Protocol definition of child trafficking has thus been highly influential in developing Children's Services response to victims since, if the definition is applied correctly and in a timely manner in the case of a child, it will directly affect whether a child is protected by Children's Services and/or the police eg non-intervention may mean a child remains in a place of exploitation. Unfortunately it has been known for agencies with responsibility to safeguard and protect children, to assume that if the child has not objected to their exploitative situation (exemplified by a child undertaking domestic servitude, sometimes on their birth parent's agreement, in order to have somewhere to live, food to eat and possibly a small amount of money provided to them) that for all intents and purposes, they are not at risk of harm and therefore do not meet the threshold which defines them as a Child In Need[2]. This approach completely misses identifying the child as being a victim of the criminal act of trafficking and that the trafficked child may be at continuing risk of exploitation, at current risk of being seriously or fatally harmed or resold into a similar or other type of exploitation. The provision of specialist trafficking training for social workers and importantly their managers has proved to be highly effective in enabling agencies to see trafficking for what it is: child abuse. As such, this type of training can focus the analytical skills of these professionals in understanding the indicators of trafficking and the needs of trafficked victims in order to quickly safeguard and protect the victims.

The London Child Protection Procedures (4th Edition, December 2010) and the supplementary procedures on Safeguarding Trafficked and Exploited Children set out the measures required by all London agencies, groups and individuals in promoting and safeguarding the welfare of children and are endorsed by the 33 London Local Authorities[3].

Whether or not the child is already in receipt of public services, all agencies, groups and individuals have a responsibility to refer a child to Children's Services when it is believed or suspected that the child has or is likely to suffer significant harm. The development of a trafficking Risk Assessment Matrix[4] and a tool for child trafficking assessments (as well as a range of additional tools and practice guidance) as part of the London Safeguarding Children Board Toolkit 2011[5] are there to assist agencies to capture their concerns and enable Children's Services to assess the risks towards the immediate and ongoing needs of a trafficked child. Put simply, if a person or agency is concerned that a child is at risk of harm then they should immediately call the police on 999 and/or contact the local Children's Services department who will work in partnership with the police to investigate[6]. The 2011 Toolkit, which provides tools for identifying child victims of trafficking and assessing their needs, assists with capturing the often hidden issues of trafficking and assists the referral process to protection agencies.

Every statutory agency and every agency or organisation which has contact with children has a crucial role to play in the identification of child victims of trafficking. Health and education departments and schools have a wealth of knowledge which may be crucial in identifying trafficked children and lead to referrals into Children's Services. The expertise of these professionals could be critical in triggering the trafficking and child protection investigations. For example, supporting information within a referral to Children's Services from a school might include information that a child that is continually late for school or is notable for non- attendance, that there is evidence of a lack of care, that unidentified children or adults pick the child up from school, that the child acts as a carer for other children or drops off and picks up children from school but does not attend themselves. Alternatively, health professionals such as health visitors might provide information which includes that suspected children acting as main carers for other children, children who should be at school but are not when a health visit is carried out or observing differing adult (alleged parents) interactions between adults and children in the households. All of which can be indicators of a range of potential issues other than trafficking but if the professional is both trafficking trained and child protection trained, then by adding these to other indicators and analysing all the information in the context of trafficking the trained professional's identification and assessment and partnership approach could save a child from potential or actual exploitation.

[1]   The United Nations Protocol to Prevent, Suppress and Punish Trafficking in Persons, especially Women and Children, supplementing the United Nations Convention against Transnational Organized Crime (the 'Palermo Protocol'), ratified by the UK in 2006. The Protocol defines child trafficking and provides the following guidance on the issue of consent:

'It is not considered possible for children to give informed consent to being trafficked. Any child transported for exploitative reasons is considered to be a trafficking victim – whether or not they have been subjected to threats, force coercion, abduction or fraud. Even when a child understands what has happened they may still appear to submit willingly to what they believe to be the will of their parents or caregiver in their home country'

[2]   Child In Need Definition: A child with high or complex needs **significantly** affecting their health, development or well being. Children in Need are defined in the Children Act 1989, s 17. They can be any age from 0–16 (older if disabled). The approach to working with Children In Need is multi-agency, normally with social care as the lead agency.

[3]   In 2010, a pledge was signed by the chair of the London Safeguarding Children Board, London Councils, all local authorities in the capital, NHS London, the Metropolitan Police Authority, the Government Office for London and voluntary sector partners which underlined progress made on safeguarding children in the capital. It represented a commitment from agencies to continue to work closely in order to share experience and best practice.

[4]   The Risk Assessment Matrix is a tool contained within the London Safeguarding Trafficked Children Toolkit 2011 which assists professionals and practitioners to use all available information in order to discuss the risk of harm (through trafficking) to a child. This may include deciding that the available information is not enough to form a sound judgment about the risk.

[5]   To test how well the draft London Safeguarding Children Board Trafficked Children Toolkit worked in practice, a pilot scheme was carried out in 2009 involving 12 local authorities, seven of which were in London. The aim was to identify ways in which the assessment framework in the toolkit facilitated or hindered the identification, assessment and support of trafficked children. One of the main findings was that multiple interviews with various agencies can be

traumatic for young victims so a single multi-agency assessment was preferred, with teams of agencies needing to work more closely together and be more proactive in sharing information quickly.

6 In 2010, The Department for Children Schools and Families (DfCSF) published the guidance *Working together to Safeguard Children*. It sets out how organisations and individuals should work together to safeguard and promote the welfare of children and young people in accordance with the Children Act 1989 and the Children Act 2004. It builds upon the *Framework for the Assessment of Children in Need and their Families* (Department of Health, 2000) which outlines the principles for analysing, understanding and recording what is happening to children and young people within their families and communities.

ASSESSMENT

5.4 Where a child (irrespective of nationality or immigration status) is at risk of significant harm as a suspected victim of trafficking, local authorities (with the explicit co-operation of their statutory partners) are required to undertake an initial and/or subsequent Core Assessment using the Risk Assessment Matrix[1] as a tool where possible to ascertain whether any action is necessary. Good practice dictates the child protection procedure described as a Section 47 investigation (s 47 of the Children Act 1989[2]) should be initiated at the earliest stage of the process to ensure a child can be protected while investigations proceed.

The additional specialist trafficking assessment tool under the London Safeguarding Trafficked Children Toolkit 2011 was developed for Children's Services social workers and the Police to use as part of a Section 47 investigation and can be used both prior to and/or as an outcome of a Section 47 investigation or even much later in the care provision process where a child may have been in Local Authority Children's Services care for some time but discloses trafficking much later. The assessment tool can be used in full or in part depending on the 'trafficking' knowledge of the assessing social worker and whether the key trafficking indicators and assessment approach have been incorporated into the Local Authority's Common Assessment Framework for Children and Young People (CAF) and whether there has been the designation of a children local contact.

1 Risk Assessment Matrix refer to para **5.3**, footnote 4.
2 This is a child protection enquiry. See http://www.legislation.gov.uk/ukpga/1989/41/section/4.

PROTECTION AND PREVENTION

5.5 There are a range of powers available to local authorities and their statutory partners to take emergency action via the courts where required. This includes the use of Emergency Protection Orders[1], Exclusion Requirements[2] and Police Protection[3] with accommodation and support being provided subject to eligibility for a Child in Need or leaving care service. It is the responsibility of each local authority to bring together the relevant stakeholders to improve the well being of all children in their area and to establish data collection and sharing mechanisms (limited to the information stipulated by the Secretary of State) in order to promote and safeguard a child's welfare. In so far as reasonably practical (and consistent with the welfare of the child), due consideration should be given to his or her wishes and feelings before determining what services to provide or what action to take. However where there is a suspicion that a child is a victim of trafficking or has been identified as a victim of human trafficking, statutory guidance[4] deems that local police and Children's Services are informed at the earliest opportunity. Unless there is a careful assessment by statutory agencies of the facts of a child's case, including whether there exist indications of exploitation, there is a real risk not only that the child will not be identified as having been trafficked but also that the child may in some cases be treated as a criminal offender rather than as the victim of human trafficking offences. For example a child recovered from a cannabis farm may be charged with a drug related offence or a child arrested for pick pocketing may be charged with theft.

Where exploitation is present, statutory child protection and safeguarding responses should be applied and a referral should be made to the National Referral Mechanism. Notably, under Article 10 of the Trafficking Convention and therefore via the NRM, the Government is obliged to *provide its competent authorities* (acting under the National Referral Mechanism) *with persons who are trained and qualified in preventing and combating trafficking in human beings, in identifying and helping victims, including children.* Article 12 of the Trafficking Convention also requires assistance for potential trafficked children and adults which takes many forms[5]. By Article 16(2) of the Trafficking Convention any return of a trafficked person to their home country, including child, must take place preferably voluntarily and in all cases with due regard for their rights, safety and dignity. Generally the Articles of the Trafficking Convention referred to provide a framework to ensure identified victims are afforded protection from harm and exploitation in the UK and that any removal from a host country should not take place without appropriate safeguarding measures in place to remove or at least significantly minimise the potential risk of re-trafficking.

As part of the NRM process if a child receives a positive reasonable grounds decision then a 45 day reflection period comes in to effect, together with the grant of temporary admission into the UK for that duration of time. This 'reflection period' is designed to allow First Responders under the NRM (which are, in the case of children, Children Services, the police and members of designated Local Safeguarding Children Boards) to investigate, safeguard and protect the suspected child victim. The 45 day reflection period can be extended on request of the First Responder or the Competent Authority. If a child later receives a positive conclusive decision under the NRM, by which they are formally recognised as being a victim of trafficking under the Trafficking Convention, the child may then be entitled to the grant of a one year renewable Residence Permit, in line with one of the two grounds under Article 14 of the Trafficking Convention[6]. A complicating feature is that if an unaccompanied child has also made an (unsuccessful) claim for asylum in the UK then, under Home Office policy, the child will be granted leave to remain in the UK only up to the age of 17½. In such cases, where for example the child was 17 at the time of being formally recognised via a positive conclusive decision under the NRM, the child may not be eligible for a Residence Permit and hence may not achieve any obvious and immediate benefit from the NRM, in terms of leave to remain in the UK. However as a young adult there may be some benefit in so far as their trafficked status will have been formally recognised by the UK and so, if they were to be considered for return to their home country following a negative outcome of their asylum or human rights application and any appeal, then, under the requirements of the Trafficking Convention, a range of safety and support measures will need to be in place before they can be returned.

It is very important to note that there is currently no statutory responsibility on First Responders (which are for children, as already explained, the police, Children Services and designated persons within local Safeguarding Children Boards) to refer any child to the NRM who is suspected of being a victim of trafficking. It is my view that this compounds the problem of statutory agencies failing to identify and protect child victims and it skews the figures on the total number of child victims of trafficking the UK. This reinforces the incorrect view that there is no substantial problem of child trafficking in the UK. However, as covered below, the current arrangements may in some cases lead to unwarranted negative NRM reasonable grounds decisions. These instances also skew the NRM figures on the actual numbers of identified trafficked children in the UK.

[1] Emergency Protection Orders (EPOs) were introduced in the Children Act 1989 to replace Place of Safety Orders following concerns expressed in the Review of Child Care Law (1985) and the Cleveland Inquiry. They are intended to provide for the immediate protection of children in a genuine emergency.

[2] Exclusion Requirements refer specifically to the Children Act 1989, ss 38 and 44; and can be made alongside an EPO to specify that certain people who should be excluded from living where the child is resident. The court may attach a power for the police to arrest anyone suspected to be in breach of an exclusion requirement which ceases when the EPO ends.

[3] Police Protection; Home Office Circular 017/2008 sets out the duties and powers of the Police under the Children Act 1989. Section 46 of the Children Act 1989 empowers a police officer who has reasonable cause to believe that a child would otherwise be likely to suffer significant harm, to:
(a)   remove the child to suitable accommodation and keep him/her there; or
(b)   take such steps as are reasonable to ensure that the child's removal from any hospital, or other place, in which he/she is being accommodated is prevented.

[4] Working Together to Safeguard Children: A guide to inter-agency working to safeguard and promote the welfare of children. 'Next steps – suspicion that a child is suffering, or is likely to suffer, significant harm'; Where it is suspected that a child is suffering, or is likely to suffer, significant harm the local authority is required by the Children Act 1989, s 47 to make enquiries to enable it to decide whether it should take any action to safeguard and promote the welfare of the child. A section 47 enquiry should be carried out through a core assessment (see paragraph 5.62). The *Framework for the Assessment of Children in Need and their Families* provides a structured framework for collecting, drawing together and analysing available information about a child and family within and between the following three domains: (i) the child's developmental needs; (ii) parenting capacity; and (iii)family and environmental factors.

[5] Such as appropriate and secure accommodation, psychological and material assistance.

[6] In practice however the Residence Permit is usually only granted in cases where the victim is assisting the police in investigating the trafficker.

CURRENT PRACTICE

5.6 All agencies working with children and families share the commitment to safeguard and promote the welfare of a child. Whilst child trafficking is becoming better recognised as a form of child abuse, applying the legal framework in practice is problematic. The London Safeguarding Children Board's supplementary procedures on Safeguarding Trafficked and Exploited Children[1] (launched on 3 February 2011) integrated the process of assessing child victims of trafficking within mainstream Child Protection Procedures however the process is underused, particularly where a suspected victim is not assessed as being at imminent risk of harm or where family abuse has not been identified. This is compounded by a lack of specialist resources, trained specialists and an overlapping of legal frameworks which inhibits the progress of crucial time-enhanced activities regarding identification, protection and prevention. As such in my experience the child protection framework as it is currently configured under UK legislation[2] does not meet the needs of trafficked child victims and should be amended to include a specific reference to the protection of child victims of trafficking, and the hidden aspects it entails, so as to ensure in all cases where trafficking is suspected, a robust and immediate child protection response is initiated following the child protection framework.

[1]   See http://www.londonscb.gov.uk/procedures/supplementary_procedures/safeguarding_traffic ked_and_exploited_children.htm.

[2]   Notably the NRM itself is a creature of policy, not law, as it was not introduced by legislation.

IDENTIFICATION

5.7 There are some children's service practitioners who inherently do not believe that child trafficking is a problem in their geographical area but rather that child trafficking is a problem only in large cities or less developed countries. However the vast majority of professionals are learning to respond to a wide variety of indicators of trafficking, including those which relate to trafficking for sexual exploitation, forced labour (including enforced criminality), domestic servitude and forced marriage. Children who have been trafficked rarely make themselves known to the police or local authorities voluntarily. In many cases, they may not understand the concept of trafficking let alone understand that they may have become a victim of it. More often than not, they are only brought to the attention of law enforcement agencies and Children's Services following local concerns or investigations into illegal or anti-social activities. Even after being rescued, child victims of trafficking may not be able to comprehend the exploitative nature of their experiences and it is often days, weeks or even months before they are able to understand that what happened to them was wrong and was unlawful. At the same time, with the appropriate support, guidance and advice, they may start to understand their rights, feel empowered to share their thoughts and relinquish any remaining trust they had once, if at all, inadvertently bestowed to their traffickers.

With this background in mind many trafficked children will often give disparate and varying (ie inconsistent) accounts of their experiences. There are a multitude of reasons for this: many such children will have been told by their trafficker that they are debt-bonded (which owing to the child's vulnerability is likely to make them comply with any instruction of the trafficker, often also thinking that their parents made this decision for them) and they therefore, psychologically, have no hope of release. Others suffer from exploitation or harm-based trauma, and/or mistrust of anyone, including the authorities, particularly where they have been told or assume they are 'illegal' with no immigration status in the UK. Some children suffer from continuing intimidation by adults and many will fear reprisals or repercussions by disclosing their history and/or fear being stigmatised by their societies. Some children may also lack sufficient language skills, owing to their age, maturity or cognitive abilities, to enable professionals to respond effectively or adequately to any signs of suspected exploitation or abuse. Although the gathering of all the necessary information by Children's Services is part of the trafficking evidential background that Children's Services will undertake in its capacity of First Responder for the NRM referral of a child, independently of this, and hence while the child's case is being considered under the NRM, Children's Services will conduct its own child risk assessment, will formalise the child's needs assessment and care plan and will determine for itself whether or not it recognises the child as a victim of trafficking. Hence, whilst the NRM reasonable grounds decision and/or conclusive decision may be of assistance; if either decision was negative and at variance with the view of Children's Services that the child had been trafficked then Children's Services would still proceed on the basis that the child was trafficked and provide support, including accommodation. This is because human trafficking falls within the child protection legal framework and as such the identification of a trafficked child, together with an assessment of that child's needs, are matters which fall squarely within the remit of child care agencies such as Children's Services.

However the current configuration of the NRM does not include Children's Services as a Competent Authority. Instead, the UK's designated Competent Authorities sit only within the UKHTC, for the identification of European Economic Area (EEA) nationals, and the UKBA (comprising of designated UK Border Agency officials) for the identification of non-EEA nationals. Social workers and other Children's Services professionals (who are best placed to carry out interviews and investigations with children) are to a great extent sidelined and confined to a paper-based exercise unless they are responding to child trafficking under the child protection framework where children who they suspect are victims can and must be protected using the statutory Child Protection Procedures.

However, where the Child Protection Procedures are not followed or are delayed, lengthy assessments by Children's Services can ensue and, in some cases, undue consideration is given to the age of suspected victims (child or adult) and their immigration status. This increases the risk of young people going missing from temporary accommodation (pending the need or availability of safe placements) and heightens the risk of the child being re-trafficked.

As at the moment only very few Local Authorities in the UK use the child protection approach when presented with a suspected trafficked victim. This is not due to a lack of will, more to the restrictive thresholds defining what triggers a child protection investigation and possibly also a lack of awareness amongst all statutory agencies that child trafficking is a child protection issue that can trigger such an investigation, particularly where there has been no specific training on trafficking which can lead to an understanding and partnership on such issues between Children's Services and the police. The tools within the London Safeguarding Children Board Toolkit 2011 were created in line with the safeguarding and child protection statutory framework. So everything is aligned but the connection between the two child abuse approaches requires a lock to ensure the needs of child victims of trafficking are identified and met.

PROTECTION AND PREVENTION

5.8 Failure to intervene immediately and protect children at risk of significant harm endangers preventative measures from being adopted in a timely manner. Such measures include the enhanced process within the London Safeguarding Children Board Trafficked Children Toolkit (March) 2011 and the Harrow Good Practice Guide for Trafficked Children in Care (February) 2011, which both include the provision of safe accommodation for a child which is located away from the trafficker(s). Such preventative measures are aimed at removing the child from the contact and control of the trafficker and mitigating the risks of children being re-trafficked. Children who have been trafficked require a high level of care and protection in the aftermath of being rescued. Despite the UK's ratification of the Council of Europe Convention on Action against Trafficking in Human Beings which under Article 12 includes the provision of *appropriate and secure accommodation, psychological and material assistance*, most vulnerable children in the UK suspected of being trafficked continue to be denied safe accommodation[1]. Furthermore, whilst both domestic legislation and international law have made it explicit that individual assessments of a child's circumstances should take their views, needs and concerns into account as part of the process of identifying suitable support arrangements, it remains the case that safe accommodation (from the perspective of the child) is difficult to provide to the child for a number of reasons, possibly due to the high cost of such accommodation, but certainly owing to the lack of child trafficking specialisms that will be required to protect the child whilst in the safe placement. In some circumstances, ascertaining the wishes of the child is also impeded by disputes pertaining to trafficked victims' age; which in itself can hamper a child's access to the necessary levels of care and support. Children who may have been trafficked will often not have identification documents, may have false documents or have been instructed by their traffickers to lie about their age. If a child's age is disputed, they can be in limbo for months or even years until it is settled. The assessment of age by a local authority plays a crucial role both in the asylum process and for school admissions and defines what type of service a child may receive from the local authority. Age assessments also have a bearing on the safety of the child and other children in placements and schools as it is important to place the child in an appropriate environment that meets their needs and protects them and other children.

[1] See further ECPAT UK's excellent set of Principles and Practice points on the provision of safe accommodation for trafficked children, 2011 which are set out in **CHAPTER 9** of this book.

WAYS FORWARD

5.9 In light of the Munro Review[1] to improve child protection and suggestions for procedural change collected as part of the London-wide consultation of Children's Social Care (CSC) in 2010, significant amendments to the Child Protection Procedures are imminent. Whilst the recommendation that is aimed at simplifying the current arrangements is welcomed in the context of a single, holistic framework, there are a number of ways in which the current practice could also be improved. Professionals must be able to respond to a wide variety of indicators of child exploitation, including children who may have been trafficked. The danger is that if child protection intervention is not immediate the child will continue to remain under the control of the exploiter (abuser, trafficker) and he or she will continue to be exploited and at risk.

Given the difficulties in identifying the nature and extent of child trafficking, establishing aggregate and disaggregated information-sharing mechanisms between agencies is crucial both in terms of contributing towards the strategic threat assessment and as an important information tool for practitioners to effectively assess the risks and needs of potential victims. It is recommended that as a first step, global indicators of child abuse should be incorporated into domestic definitions of abuse with a view to both educating professionals and establishing new triggers for a full Section 47 investigation in all cases as part of mainstream child protection procedures. As part of this, the Risk Assessment Matrix[2] Profile could be enhanced (in partnership with the police and other agencies) based on the effective use of intelligence gathered during the risk profiling. This will also lead to the development of a structured, multi-agency preventative model which takes into account any suspicion (or soft intelligence) suggesting that a child may be a victim of sexual or other form of exploitation and uses the Assessment Framework to intervene.

The role that the Police's Child Exploitation and Online Protection Centre (CEOP) has played in bringing agencies together, and will play after 1 July 2011 when 'missing children' becomes part of its responsibility, will potentially transform the way all agencies work together in this area. CEOP's new role will bring greater understanding as to why children go missing, will build the capacity of all agencies to intervene early and will put 'trace and recover' systems in place via a multi-agency approach. In accordance with best practice to enhance the skills of practitioners, it may also bring added benefit for the National Referral Mechanism if the NRM were to have a specialist child system within it comprising of social care professionals to deal with the cases of children who may have been trafficked. This would allow local authorities and others responsible for child protection to have the authority to make decisions as to whether a child has been trafficked. Multi-agency child safeguarding teams should also be encouraged to operate at main UK ports to identify and respond to concerns about children and young people arriving or leaving the UK. It would also be prudent (as has been achieved in Harrow) to designate a lead Children's Services manager for child trafficking in every local authority to ensure leadership, responsibility and direction to professionals coming into contact with children who may have been trafficked. A multi-disciplinary approach is encouraged, specifically to help remedy issues pertaining to the identification of a trafficked child, the age of a potential victim, their immigration status, health and psychological needs as well as to help assess whether the parents of some migrant children are indeed their parents, and whether, even if they are the parents, they may have been involved in the trafficking of their own children.

[1] The Munro Review of Child Protection: Final Report A child-centred system, May 2011 – 'Chapter three: A system that values professional expertise'; Recommendation 1: The Government should revise both the statutory guidance, Working Together to Safeguard Children and The Framework for the Assessment of Children in Need and their Families and their associated policies to: (i) distinguish the rules that are essential for effective working together, from guidance that informs professional judgment; (ii) set out the key principles underpinning the guidance; (iii) remove the distinction between initial and core assessments and the associated timescales in respect of these assessments, replacing them with the decisions

that are required to be made by qualified social workers when developing an understanding of children's needs and making and implementing a plan to safeguard and promote their welfare; (iv) require local attention is given to timeliness in the identification of children's needs and provision of help; the quality of the assessment to inform next steps to safeguard and promote children's welfare; and the effectiveness of the help provided; (vi) give local areas the responsibility to draw on research and theoretical models to inform local practice; (v) remove constraints to local innovation and professional judgment that are created by prescribing or endorsing particular approaches, for example, nationally designed assessment forms, national performance indicators associated with assessment or nationally prescribed approaches to IT systems.

2   Risk Assessment Matrix, refer to para **5.3**, footnote 4.

Protection and Prevention

5.10 Where a potential child victim has been identified, safe placements (including but not exclusively specialist foster care) and a system of guardianship for child victims of trafficking should be established in order to reduce the risk of a child going missing from care. Such a system would also mean that every child victim of trafficking would have someone other than a corporate parent to care and support them based on their personal best interests. Furthermore, it is recommended that a non-age specific emergency response service should be developed to keep potential victims safe and prevent children from going missing during investigative stages. This would be in keeping with the UK's obligations under the Trafficking Convention[1]. In my view, the Trafficking Convention's child protection requirements and a robust Children's Service child protection strategy and framework are brought together within the 2011 Guidance and Toolkit[2] and the recommendations within the final monitoring report[3].

In building a safe accommodation model a number of local authority Children's Services are using the Trafficked Child Good Practice Guide, updated February 2011[4] which was created by Harrow UASC Service (November 2009) to assist in the protection of trafficked children in care. That Guide also recommended that an integrated, multi-agency trafficking response be developed, including the effective use of the Track Trace and Recover model for all trafficked children who go missing. This should include implementing the Contact and Recover model in partnership with the police within a local authority boundary or outside of a local authority boundary if the child is known to the local authority but is in another part of the UK. The Contact and Recover response should be triggered whenever a missing child may have been identified. Expanding the current joint working between agencies (such as the police, health authorities, UKBA, schools and faith and community groups) and senior CSC managers and practitioners at all levels should be encouraged. In time a national body should also be created to oversee good practice and guide local authorities in implementing appropriate Child Protection Procedures. In the longer term, I would strongly recommend that an intelligence led trafficking activity matrix, by which dedicated trafficking intelligence data can be stored and analysed, be built in each local area in order to assist in the prosecution of traffickers and exploiters and to disrupt both small groups or larger organised criminal gangs. This would create better effective protection and intervention models in partnership with the police. This would also help facilitate the development of a national and international specialist child protection rapid response mechanism to all cases where a child or children are at risk of being trafficked or re-trafficked. The locally specific intelligence could also be analysed at a regional and national level and fed in to international trafficking assessments.

[1] Trafficking Convention, Article 10 relates to the victim's safety and protection needs. Article 13 states that victims must be given a recovery and reflection period of at least 30 days (45 days have been given by the UK) to allow the person to recover and escape from the influence of the traffickers; during which time, Article 10 (stating that the person shall not be removed from the UK until the conclusive identification process has been completed) and Article 12 (stating that the victim is also entitled to emergency support and assistance) applies.

[2] The London Safeguarding Children Board Trafficked Children Toolkit 2011.

[3] Final Monitoring Report; London Trafficked Children Pilot Toolkit 2011.

[4] The Trafficked Child Good Practice Guide (created in November 2009 and regularly updated, most recent update February 2011) is designed to aid Social Care and Education professionals, foster carers and residential staff to meet to the needs of trafficked children in care provision. This document has been developed within the context of the London Safeguarding Children Board Trafficked Children Toolkit 2011 and is intended as a non-statutory practice guide.

THE WAY FORWARD

5.11 Having chaired the London SCB child safeguarding group/pilot group and monitoring group for over three years I have been able to look in detail at the difficulties that all statutory agencies face when trying to identify a child victim of trafficking. In 2008 we created the London Trafficked Children Initiative to assist with this, following in the footsteps of the UK Government's signing of the Trafficking Convention[1] a year earlier in February 2007. This 18 month project had three aims, namely to: (1) Develop and share good practice in local safeguarding responses to trafficked children for London Local Safeguarding Children Boards and their partner agencies; (2) Assist the integration of national trafficked children mechanisms with existing safeguarding children procedure and practice (still in progress); (3) Contribute to the redrafting of the 2006 London Child Protection Committee – Safeguarding Trafficked Children Guidance incorporating learning from the 2009/10 pilot project (now complete). In pursuit of these aims, the London SCB developed the *London SCB Trafficked Children Toolkit 2009* to provide guidance and tools for local multi-agency responses to trafficked children. From January 2009 to May 2010 12 local authorities across the UK agreed to pilot the toolkit: Camden, Croydon, Glasgow, Harrow, Hillingdon, Hounslow, Islington, Kent, Manchester, Slough, Solihull and Southwark. In March 2010 the pilot phase was completed. The tools developed for the pilot have now been evaluated and have proved invaluable to statutory agencies which are endeavouring to identify, safeguard and protect child victims of trafficking.

[1] With Article 10 relating to the identification and protection of victims of trafficking.

KEY FINDINGS

5.12 Overall, the *London SCB Trafficked Children Toolkit 2009* has helped pilot authorities to develop, implement and strengthen good practice in the safeguarding of trafficked children. Certain tools and sections of the guidance were widely used in this identification. However, rather than just being a set of discrete tools, the Toolkit offered to the pilot authorities a comprehensive framework in which to approach the safeguarding of trafficked children. At the heart of this framework is multi-agency working, which recognises that trafficking is a complex form of child abuse and requires a pro-active response supported by specialist training and input from a variety of professionals, voluntary groups and community agencies alike. These factors include strong leadership, staff specialism, robust identification and assessment processes, multi-level inter-agency training and consistent, informed multi-agency engagement throughout the safeguarding process. These factors and others are captured in the following six key findings, which particularly address the persistent challenges faced by pilot authorities in developing and maintaining a multi-agency approach.

Firstly, the identification of trafficked children is a major challenge for pilot local authorities in a context of low public awareness, professional reluctance to accept child trafficking as a live issue in the UK, inconsistent levels of multi-agency engagement, and the rapid speed with which trafficked children can go missing. Second, some trafficked children face strong pressure to go missing, (to return to the trafficker or trafficking network) within 24 hours of being identified. All agencies need to recognise the challenges faced in safeguarding these children and the importance of the first 'golden hour' in rapidly implementing safeguarding measures for newly identified trafficked children. Third, many authorities compare trafficking to other child protection issues such as child sexual abuse, showing that extensive training and awareness building is needed across all agencies and the general public to build an acceptance of trafficking as being a particular form of child abuse and to develop skills to respond to it. Child trafficking needs to be recognised as a highly complex area of child protection that requires an intensive, concerted and *resourced* response. Fourth, pilot authorities rated the 'Risk Assessment Matrix[1] *for children who may have been trafficked*' as the most useful tool, considered a 'must-have' by two-thirds of the pilot local authorities, though it may be problematic for younger children: a concern exists where the Risk Assessment Matrix is being used instead of the more appropriate trafficking assessment. Fifth, the assessment of children suspected of being trafficked can be problematic. For example short assessment timescales employed in order to speed up a referral to the National Referral Mechanism [NRM] do not recognise the complexities of disclosure, and can reduce the quality of the trafficking assessment and traumatise children. Potentially, this could lead to the risk of a weak NRM assessment in some children's cases leading unnecessarily to a negative reasonable grounds decision. A significant problem then may occur when additional information, as is often the case, emerges after initial investigations, and Children's Services practitioners find there are difficulties in disseminating newly disclosed information on cases of child trafficking to the NRM following initial negative NRM decisions. However where a positive reasonable grounds decision is reached under the NRM this risk can be mitigated by the fact that the 45-day reflection period that follows can and is often extended at the request of Children's Services or the Competent Authority allowing time for their complex victim centred assessments to continue. In all cases, however, multiple interviews by various agencies can be traumatic for a child: more streamlined information-gathering through a single, holistic, multi-agency interview is preferred.

Finally, age assessments remain a controversial issue for child protection and asylum teams. Initial decisions about the age of trafficked children should always be made by specialist, trained social workers through an holistic assessment of age which includes social interaction and assessments which relate to subjective and objective factors. In this context it is very important to pay regard to the fact that in January 2006 an Age Assessment Joint Working Protocol was agreed by the Immigration and Nationality Directorate(IND) of the Home Office and the Association of Directors of Social Services. By the terms of that protocol, IND agreed that local authorities (ie via their Children's Social Care Services, formally known as Children's Social Services) was the best placed agency to assess the age of a child. It follows that the determination of age by Children's Services ought to be respected by the UKBA in reaching its trafficking identification decisions under the NRM in pursuance of Article 10 of the Trafficking Convention: the matter of the age of the child is one for Children's Services to undertake by using its specialist skills via a holistic assessment of age[2].

The future arrangements for trafficked children have improved over the last three years but in my view further considerable effort is still required in order to protect some of the most vulnerable children in this country. This can only be achieved through the closest partnership working arrangement between all agencies. Based on my experience in this field, co-operation between frontline agencies to safeguard and protect child victims of trafficking in the UK, together with the development of strong local, regional, national and international strategies and policies will provide victims with optimum protection.

It is sometimes difficult to quantify just how the creation of strategies and policies impact on actual child protection interventions. A good example of where they have, for children, is through the influence of the protection measures in the Council of Europe Convention on Action against Trafficking in Human Beings. The Trafficking Convention has lowered the threshold of the trigger by which Children's Services could respond to a trafficked victim from cases where it could be proven that a child was trafficked (which was almost impossible without the conviction of the trafficker), to the present situation where the trafficked status of a child is suspected but not proved.

This change enables a local authority's Children's Services in the first instance to respond under s 47 of the Children Act 1989 and provide the enhanced specialist trafficking protection measures developed during the piloting of the London-SCB Trafficked Children Toolkit 2009[3] and subsequent Guidance and Toolkit developed from the pilot which was launched on 3 February 2011. However these protection measures only work where trafficking is recognised as a child protection concern within statutory agencies, where staff are trained to identify victims and we are all able to competently work in partnership.

---

[1] The London Safeguarding Children Board Trafficked Children Toolkit 2011 assists professionals and practitioners to use all available information in order to discuss the risk of harm (through trafficking) to a child. This may include deciding that the available information is not enough to form a sound judgment about the risk.

[2] Age Assessment Joint Working Protocol between the Immigration and Nationality Directorate of the Home Office (IND) and the Association of Directors of Social Services (ADSS) January 2006. Available online.

[3] Following the UK Government's ratification of the Council of Europe Convention on Action against Trafficking in Human Beings in December 2008, a National Referral Mechanism

(NRM) was implemented for adults and children trafficked into and within the UK. To accompany this mechanism the London Safeguarding Children Board developed an assessment framework and guidance to support practitioners and policy makers working with suspected victims of child trafficking. This framework and guidance was piloted as the *London SCB Trafficked Children Toolkit 2009* (from January 2009 to July 2010) in 12 local authority areas across the UK and monitored by a national monitoring group comprising of representatives of various interested stakeholders. The pilot aims were to:(a) develop and share good practice local safeguarding responses to trafficked children for London LSCB's and their partner agencies; (b)pilot this work in a number of London and Regional LSCB areas and in Scotland, with Wales and a number of other LSCB's across the UK forming part a wider group using the toolkit but not formally part pf the Pilot; and (c) and to assist with the integration of national trafficked children mechanisms (particularly the newly developed national referral mechanism) with existing safeguarding children procedure and practice.

AUTHOR'S NOTE

5.13 The legislation referred to in this chapter is current and is used by agencies to meet their statutory duties as defined by the relevant legislation referred to. The specific pieces of guidance referred to are either statutory or non-statutory. Statutory guidance is delivered by UK Government departments and is included in statutory body responses as per the legislative framework referred to above. The non-statutory guidance is referred to as good practice and has influenced the development of the London SCB Toolkit and guidance and broader responses and raised awareness within local authorities. All guidance directly referenced within the Toolkit is current.

Legal Framework

- Council of Europe Convention on Action against Trafficking in Human Beings (2005)
- UK Government: Children Act 1989;
- UK Government: Children Act 2004;
- UN Convention on the Rights of the Child 1989;
- UN Convention against Transnational Organized Crime 2000;
- UN Protocol to Prevent, Suppress and Punish Trafficking in Persons, especially Women and Children 2000, otherwise referred to as the 'Palermo Protocol' which forms part of the Convention against Transnational Organized Crime 2000.

Statutory Guidance

- London Child Protection Committee London Child Protection Procedures (2006);
- London Safeguarding Children Board London Child Protection Procedures (4th edition April 2011);
- Department for Children Schools and Families (DCSF), Working Together to Safeguard Children 2006;
- Department for Education Working Together to Safeguard Children 2010;
- Department of Health (DOH), Framework for the Assessment of Children in Need and their Families 2000;

- Home Office Circular 017/2008 which forms part of the Children Act 1989.

Non-Statutory Guidance

- Solace, The role of local authorities in addressing human trafficking (2009);
- London Safeguarding Children Board (London SCB), Trafficked Children Toolkit (March 2011) which includes the risk assessment matrix and assessment framework;
- London SCB, Trafficked Children Guidance (March 2011) supplementary guidance to the *London Safeguarding Children Board London Child Protection Procedures (4th edition April 2011)*;
- London Borough of Harrow, The Trafficked Child Good Practice Guide (2011);
- London Borough of Harrow, Good Practice Guidance For Trafficked Children In Care (February 2011);
- IND/ADSS, Age Assessment Joint Working Protocol (2006).

6

OBTAINING EVIDENCE FROM TRAUMATISED TRAFFICKED PERSONS

Kalvir Kaur

INTRODUCTION

6.1 This chapter explores how the fundamental principle of the right to be heard in legal matters is maintained whilst working with traumatised trafficked persons[1]. The techniques discussed herein are not exhaustive but merely suggestive of that which encompasses best practice.

Whilst there are inevitably common factors to be borne in mind when obtaining evidence from adult and child trafficked persons, there are also distinct factors for trafficked children.

[1]   The term traumatised trafficked person is used here to describe a person who is overwhelmed by the trafficking experience and is as a result unable to coherently and/or accurately recount that persecution or related events with or without accompanying physiological, psychological or psychiatric symptoms.

BEST PRACTICE IN OBTAINING EVIDENCE FROM TRAUMATISED TRAFFICKED PERSONS

6.2 The legal process for a traumatised trafficked person involves a range of statutory and non-statutory bodies. It may involve a statutory decision making body, such as the United Kingdom Border Agency (UKBA), in matters concerning trafficking identification and irregular immigration status, and may involve the police in cases where the individual is helping with a trafficking-related investigation. Ideally in all cases the process should also involve a legal representative and it may also involve a care worker from a specialist NGO, a foster parent or another primary caregiver in the case of a child, an independent advisor or befriender and also the court service. Each and every one of these parties should be ensuring that all that can be done is done in order that the trafficked person's voice is heard and accorded due weight.

LEGAL REPRESENTATIVES

6.3 This chapter will focus on exploring how legal representatives should be seeking to obtain best evidence from traumatised trafficked persons and give effect to their right to be heard in asylum proceedings. It is not intended to be an exhaustive checklist of points but rather as a foundation to be built upon and altered according to need of the trafficked persons and individual style of the interviewer. As will be seen, however, many parts of the suggested processes which are discussed below can apply equally to interviews that are conducted by other professionals from different agencies: one of our ultimate goals will surely be the same, namely to achieve as full and as accurate a picture of the experiences of the traumatised trafficked person in order to reflect what really happened to them – to that end the procedures we all adopt to assist the trafficked person to provide their best evidence should, ideally, have considerable overlap.

The legal representative

6.4 The difficulties in eliciting good quality evidence from traumatised trafficked persons should not get in the way of allowing their voice to be heard in proceedings that affect them. However, a legal representative can only act on instructions of their client.

One of the crucial elements of ensuring a traumatised trafficked person's voice is heard in the whole asylum process is effective interviewing by the legal representative. What may or not be elicited by the legal representative will have consequences for the rest of the process. Poor interviewing can lead to the full substance and detail of the claim never being heard by the decision maker and any attempt thereafter to remedy this failure may lead to adverse credibility findings. Poor interviewing may also be indicative of the legal representative's failure to adapt their interviewing technique and conduct to one that is more suitable for this highly traumatised group of clientele. It will undoubtedly mean that the client's voice, even if partially heard, has been restricted.

It will be common for the trafficked person seeking legal assistance to be referred to a legal representative by a third party. This may be the police, the social worker, a NGO or in the instance of a child, perhaps the foster parent. With trafficked children it can easily be forgotten that it is not the adult who is your client, rather it is the child and remains the child at all times. Working with children requires a shift from our instinct of engaging with the adult to the exclusion of the child.

Of course that is not to say that the referrer must not be engaged with at all, to the contrary their role is crucial. Firstly it is from the referrer that you will gain initial details of your prospective clients such as name, date of birth, nationality, language, whether there has been any claim made already to UKBA (or one is to be made) and preferred gender of representative and any interpreter. Second, in the case of children, it is likely that the referrer will also act as the responsible adult (a person who is independent of the Secretary of State and who has responsibility for the child) for the child during the whole asylum process.

It must however be borne in mind throughout that there is a real possibility that the trafficked person remains under the control of the trafficker who may be presenting as a concerned individual. As such all avenues must be exhausted and the necessary checks[1] complied with in order to satisfy yourself that the accompanying person is who they claim to be. Any suspicion must be acted upon, with the safety of the trafficked person informing your actions.

In order to properly represent the client, the following factors require careful consideration.

[1] For example, at a minimum by way of checking personal identity documents or organisation identity card, noting any recurrent attendance as accompanying person by one individual for many clients, body language indicating control and fear whilst in presence of accompanying person, sounds made by accompanying person after questions asked possibly indicating how the question should be responded to or reinforcing potential repercussions if a script is not adhered to.

Are you the right legal representative for the client?

6.5 Specific criteria apply before one can assume conduct of a vulnerable person's case. From my experience, trafficked clients are inherently vulnerable. All solicitors who are registered with the Law Society of England and Wales and case workers who provide immigration and asylum advice and services must be a member of the Immigration and Asylum Accreditation Scheme[1] to be eligible to work and receive payments for work carried out under a Legal Aid contract in the immigration category[2].

Under this scheme one must achieve, at a minimum, the status of senior caseworker in order to conduct work on vulnerable client's cases; this means to be accredited to Level 2[3].

Likewise, to assume conduct of a child's case one must also be accredited to Level 2 status. In addition, under the 2010 Standard Civil Contracts[4], providers are subject to new contract provisions when providing advice to separated children seeking asylum. The key provisions require that all such work is carried out by a Level 2 senior caseworker or above, and for any new cases opened on or after 15 November 2010, the representative must have had an enhanced Criminal Records Bureau check in the two years before instruction and records of the check must be available to the Legal Services Commission on request.

For solicitors and non-solicitors alike, it is best practice to bear in mind Rule 2.01(1)(b) of the Solicitor's Code of Conduct throughout conduct of all matters which states that you must refuse to act or cease to act for a client where you have insufficient resources or lack the competence to deal with the matter. This means having both the appropriate legal knowledge and skills. Acting for both trafficked children and adults can become testing at times; if during any stage you feel that you are not best placed to do justice to the case and properly represent the client, serious consideration must be given to transferring the matter to another fee-earner[5] who possesses the necessary mix of knowledge and skills base.

[1] http://www.legalservices.gov.uk/civil/immigration/accreditation.asp.
[2] The specific rules will be different for legal representation in Scotland and Northern Ireland but the guidance in this chapter applies to all legal representatives in the UK.

³ This will require the sitting of three exams initially, consisting of a written paper, a drafting
   paper and a client interview.
⁴ http://www.legalservices.gov.uk/civil/8758.asp.
⁵ If necessary, in another firm.

The interpreter

6.6 Most trafficked persons do not speak English as their first language and in order to listen to and hear their voice fully an interpreter will need to be employed. The role of the interpreter is vital. The consequences of poor interpreting are obvious: distortion of instructions, confusion, inaccuracy, the full claim never being in front of the UKBA and seemingly internal contradictions.

Always use a reputable, professional interpreting agency. Never use friends or family members to interpret. Not only does this increase the scope for mistakes, as such people are not likely to be professional interpreters[1], but it can often place your client in a very difficult position as they may not want to disclose matters that form part of the claim owing to embarrassment or fear of loss of ties with their community.

As stated above, and reiterated, there remains the real risk that an individual who accompanies the trafficked person and seems, in the first instance, helpful and accommodating and presents as a concerned humanitarian or a friend, may actually be the trafficker. This danger is emphasised again owing to the known tactics employed by traffickers to keep a trafficked person under their control[2]. Even if your enquiries satisfy you that the person is who he or she claims to be[3]; indicators such as not allowing the client to speak for him or herself, in the presence of an interpreter, should be acted upon immediately.

Equally and related is the real concern that cultural norms may dictate it unacceptable or taboo to talk of certain matters to others outside of the community or indeed to be spoken of at all. Legal representatives must ensure that they provide the necessary tools for the trafficked person to speak freely without fear, embarrassment or hindrance.

A choice as to the gender of the interpreter is a must; it may be that a female trafficked for sexual exploitation does not feel comfortable with a male interpreter and thus not feel she is able to disclose her whole claim. A male child or adult trafficked from Vietnam for cannabis cultivation might also prefer a female interpreter, but for different reasons: the client may subjectively[4] fear that a Vietnamese male interpreter might disclose the client's whereabouts to the trafficker. In other cases, where a male client has for example been exploited for domestic servitude he might prefer a male interpreter in order to reassert his masculine status.

At the start of the interview, ensure the client is made fully aware of the role of the interpreter. Namely this is to provide an impartial, complete and confidential rendition of everything that is said and that the interpreter is not to offer opinion, comment or answer questions on behalf of the client.

If both you and the client are satisfied with the interpreter, it is good practice to retain the same interpreter for all future appointments with the client. This will allow the client to feel more at ease with the interpreter and consequently more at ease in disclosing his or her experiences.

It is of great importance that despite the involvement of the interpreter, you must conduct every appointment by asking questions directly to the client in the first person. For example, 'can you tell me what happened that day?' rather than asking questions of the interpreter such as 'can you ask him what happened that day?'. You have employed an interpreter to ensure that your non-English speaking client is placed on an equal footing with those who understand English, so speak to your non-English speaking client as you would to your English speaking client.

When acting for a trafficked person, and particularly so if acting for a trafficked child, you must remain vigilant to any modulation in the interpreter's voice; this can sometimes be a sign of a reproaching or a disbelieving attitude on the part of the interpreter, or irritation. People who have been exploited, abused, whose trust has been broken and who feel that they have no control over their own lives are less likely to indicate that they have any difficulties or unease with an interpreter than those who have not been the victims of such experiences. Remain aware of the non-verbal indicators such as body language and facial expressions and if required, terminate the appointment.

Following this, re-arrange a further appointment within a very short time period with a different interpreter. Inform the client, and in case when acting for a child, the appropriate adult, why there has been a change in interpreter and enquire whether there had been any consequential problems with the first interpreter, do not just assume there had been. Stress to the client the importance of ensuring that they are comfortable and are able to speak at their own pace with the interpreter. If the client seems hesitant in his or her response, emphasise that they have done nothing wrong and that it is not a problem for you as their legal representative to book different interpreters until they feel at ease with any particular one. It is only then that you can proceed knowing that you have ensured that this element has been duly executed to aid the flow of instructions.

[1] And as such will not have been trained in understanding the terminology that may be used by lawyers in providing advice.

[2] There have been instances where traffickers have been known to force their victims to make false asylum claims in the UK as a means of being able to continue to exert their control and exploitation of the victim once asylum status has been fraudulently obtained, through no fault of the victim.

[3] Traffickers are not always male.

[4] Ie this fear might be objectively lacking in foundation but it is the client's perception of the risk of disclosure, that should be a paramount consideration for the lawyer. However, despite the assurances of a lawyer, and even with an interpreter in the case (male or female) which the client has agreed on, there are well-documented risks of Vietnamese trafficked children going missing from local authority care: this is something which the legal advisor ought to be aware of. See '*Missing Out: A Study of Child Trafficking in the North-West, North-East and West Midlands*', ECPAT 2007. And the CEOP report of December 2010: '*Strategic Threat Assessment, Child Trafficking in the UK*'.

The interviewing room

6.7 Prior thought to the layout of the interview room can aid effective communication and avoid subtle non-verbal messages which may undermine the relationship of trust yet to be established.

UNHCR's training document on interviewing clients[1] explains the best placing of parties attending an interview in order to facilitate an optimal environment. Try to arrange the seating so that the interpreter is to the side of the interview and slightly withdrawn which will allow the interviewer and applicant to communicate face to face. The document recommends that in the case of a child, that the interpreter sits closer to the child than the interviewer to avoid any perception of authority.

To aid concentration, ensure the interviewing room is free, as far as possible, from distracting noises such as ringing telephones and other secondary noise. Try to arrange seating all on one level to avoid perceptions of authority and do not have your client seated in such a position that they are facing a source of light, such as a window, in order to avoid 'blinding' light. All this will achieve is for your client to suffer from a headache from the blind light resulting in loss in concentration and consequently greater risk of errors and inaccuracies[2].

Refreshments are important and ensure they are at hand or easily accessible; although initially you may find that the trafficked person is very hesitant to accept anything from you, ensure that you ask at every appointment and during the course of every appointment. It is this kind of repetitive action that allows familiarity to develop which can lead to breaking down barriers.

It is common for young children not to drink tea or coffee. However experience has shown that they are more willing to accept hot chocolate! Equally popular are diluted fruit drinks.

WHO's Ethical and Safety Recommendations for Interviewing Trafficked Women 2003[3] make a number of important recommendations when interviewing trafficked women; it is the author's view that these recommendations are equally applicable to *all* trafficked persons irrespective of gender or age. In summary, and in modified form to address all trafficked persons, the 10 recommendations are:

(1) Do no harm;
(2) Know your subject and assess the risks;
(3) Prepare referral information – do not make promises you cannot fulfil;
(4) Adequately select and prepare interpreter and co-workers;
(5) Ensure confidentiality;
(6) Ensure consent is informed and real;
(7) Listen to and respect each trafficked person's assessment of their situation and risks to their safety;
(8) Do not re-traumatise;
(9) Be prepared for emergency intervention;
(10) Put information collected to good use.

---

[1] http://www.unhcr.org/3ae6bd670.html.

[2] Later on, if the client's case requires the assistance of a barrister, for example if there is to be an asylum appeal which requires a case conference, consideration should be given to the venue of that conference with the client's needs in mind. The formal, unfamiliar surroundings of the

barrister's chambers might not be appropriate in all cases for the client. Ask the barrister to come to your offices if that is where you think the client will feel more comfortable and safe.
³ http://www.who.int/gender/documents/en/final%20recommendations%2023%20oct.pdf.

Your appearance

6.8 Many traumatised trafficked people have in some way or form, been exploited, deceived and abused by an adult or an adult in a position of authority and/or trust. You should consider how your dress impacts on the client. Is it stating you too are an adult in a position of authority or is it stating that you are an adult who the trafficked person can trust? Stuffy suits and sterile offices do not always provide the best environment for interviewing vulnerable, traumatised adults and children.

Starting the interview

6.9 Once you are in the position to start interviewing, the following points should be borne in mind in order to create a positive initial meeting; the first meeting is crucial and will set the tone for all subsequent appointments.

Put your client at ease

6.10 Employ steady, friendly visual expressions, maintain good eye contact, open body language and appropriate vocal tone. Explain who you are and who all other parties in the room are and their roles. Check that client is comfortable with all parties present.

Ownership

6.11 Emphasise to the client that you are their representative and you will be working for them, irrespective of the number of people in the interviewing room; that it is the client who is the most important person there and it is them that you want to hear from. Whilst this may seem like a trivial thing, do not forget that traumatised trafficked persons will rarely have felt in control of any given situation; you must do your utmost to ensure that your client is the one with the power in the relationship and is given every tool to exercise it.

In the situation of a child, give the child your contact details, as opposed to simply providing them to the appropriate adult, and make certain that the child is aware that he or she can talk to you at any time in confidence and call you whenever they need to. Utilise modern methods of communication to facilitate your relationship; encourage the child to text you or 'miss call' you; this simple process will make you more accessible by means which most young people are familiar with. Constantly encourage the child to ask questions of you.

Plan your time

6.12 Lengthy appointments are not appropriate for traumatised adults or children; two hours for any appointment is more than sufficient at any one time. Traumatised people are not able to retain focus for any prolonged period and frequent breaks are a must; on average a 10 minute break after 45 minutes should be enforced. Plan your time accordingly.

Managing expectations

6.13 Define your boundaries and explain everyone's role. Do not promise that which you cannot deliver. Be honest. Whilst one can show empathy, being emotional is unhelpful.

Assumptions

6.14 Do not assume that all traumatised trafficked persons of a particular country must have certain experiences; not all Nigerian children of a certain age will have been trafficked for the purposes of domestic servitude. Doing the best for each client means not pre-judging or making assumptions.

Taking instructions

6.15 Interviewing traumatised trafficked adults or children is one of the hardest skills to master. Each action of the interviewer must be informed by the common factor of this group of clientele – ie they have all been victims of trafficking. This means that they are inherently vulnerable by virtue of their profile, history and experience. As someone who has been under the control of another, has had no power in decision making and most likely will have been exploited, it is common that traumatised trafficked persons will very often defer to those in positions of authority, including the legal representative, and follow the line of least resistance. Some trafficked persons will be at a complete loss when having to make the simplest of decisions.

There may be feelings of having done wrong and of immense shame, the legal representative as interviewer may often reveal an agenda, sometimes inadvertently, and the trafficked person may simply seek to please the interviewer, therefore leading questions may well elicit the response sought by the questioner. All of this will mean that the true voice of the traumatised trafficked person is suppressed since the optimal environment has not been fostered to allow the client to give instructions freely without any fear[1].

[1] For more information on how to interview refugee children and the additional factors that need to be considered see: ILPA Working with Refugee Children Current Issues in Best Practice, specifically the chapter 'Voice of the Child', May 2011.

Techniques and tips

6.16 The following may assist in conducting an effective, productive interview that sets the client at ease and maximises their opportunity to have their voice heard.

(i) **Body language:** It is of the utmost importance that you remain self-aware of your body language, your own facial expressions, tone of voice and any other non-verbal indicator of displeasure, frustration, disbelief, judgment or lack of patience. Whilst of equal importance for all clients, this is particularly so when acting for a traumatised victim of trafficking who most likely may have, for a period of time, been verbally and physically abused, spoken to in an authoritarian manner and any resistance translated into displeasure on the part of the trafficker. Interviewers must remain acutely aware at all times that they do nothing to replicate the trafficking experience in any way.

(ii) **Appropriate language:** It is of course an obvious point that language must be appropriate for the audience. When interviewing a traumatised trafficked person however we must also ensure that language employed is at the same time sensitive and precise, as well as accepting that some words will be of a character which are not frequently used, such as highly emotive sexual terms.

If acting for a trafficked child, ensure language is child friendly and jargon-free: it is highly unlikely that the child will understand you if you employ the same vocabulary as you would for an adult. Find analogies if you struggle to make yourself clear. Constantly reiterate and emphasise that there is no 'right' or 'wrong' answer but simply the answer that is in the child's knowledge. Remind the child that it is perfectly acceptable to say 'I cannot remember/I do not know/I do not want to talk about it or can I tell you about this later'.

(iii) **Interviewing techniques:** There are many interviewing techniques, such as the Phased Interview, on which, for more information, see Ministry of Justice Achieving Best Evidence in Criminal Proceedings: Guidance on Interviewing Victims and Witnesses, and Guidance on Using Special Measures March 2011[1] and The Cognitive Interviewing of Children by the Institute of Forensic Expert Opinion, Krakow, 2005[2].

Common to most interviewing techniques are the following limbs:

- Personalise the interview and establish rapport;
- Explain the goals of the interview to the child;
- Re-instating the context;
- Asking questions;
- Closure.

Whichever interviewing method is opted for, it is crucial that every interview has a closure phase ensuring that the client is in a positive frame of mind and not distressed by the process. This may be achieved by ending the appointment by talking about neutral topics unrelated to the trafficking experience.

Traumatised trafficked people may struggle to find the correct words to describe their experiences. This can be perpetuated if interpretation is not accurate. The right to be heard does not mean simply mean that which is said is taken at face value. You must investigate, clarify, probe and expand instructions received.

Effective questioning includes the use of appropriate language whilst creating an environment in which the trafficked person does not feel scared, embarrassed, or inhibited by feelings of wrongdoing. Without probing, especially round difficult subjects such as vaginal and anal rape, forced abortions and torture of the genitalia, there remains the real possibility that an accurate account of the trafficking experience will not have been elicited.

1   http://www.justice.gov.uk/guidance/docs/achieving-best-evidence-criminal-proceedings.pdf.
2   http://www.canee.net/files/The%20Cognitive%20Interview%20of%20Children.pdf.

Obstacles to effective interviewing

6.17 There will be times when, despite your best endeavours, your carefully planned appointment simply does not fulfil the objective you had hoped due to the lack of any real instructions. Trafficked persons going through the asylum process may have distinct reasons which impact on their ability at any one given time to give instructions. Some of these may be:

(1)   **Repetition.** You may not be the first person to whom the client has had to reveal part or all of their experiences. By the time a legal representative is instructed it is probable that the client has had to disclose information to at least two people if not more; such as the police or a support group. Patience is required to avoid re-traumatisation.

(2)   **Disjointed testimony and late disclosure.**

'When I am investigating these cases I am more suspicious of the highly detailed account told from beginning to end that never changes than I am of the one that moves all over the place and has gaps and changes a number of times'[1]

Owing to the trafficking experience, fear, shame, lack of trust and trauma, amongst other factors, it is common for the trafficked person to convey extremely disjointed and/or late testimony. This may mean that appointments may necessarily need to be frequent as old instructions are revisited.

(3)   **Safe environment.** Interviews should take place where the client feels safe; this does not necessarily mean at an office. If appropriate, identify another safe space.

A victim of trafficking would have a near breakdown like reaction when attempting to attend the office of her legal representative for a pre-arranged appointment. It became apparent from the limited instructions received that the trafficked person history involved abuse and exploitation in or emanating from an office environment. As any office space invoked the same physical and mental reaction; all future legal appointments were conducted in a discreet coffee shop or in a quite corner of parkland[2].

(4)   **Other fears.** There may be specific barriers which are hampering effective communication and stifling the voice of the trafficked person. These may include a professional relationship devoid of trust, fear of

those in positions of authority, fear of interpreters and any related ties, anger and fear of having to divulge their experiences through fear of shame and reprisals.

Of particular concern is the use of juju, voodoo and hoodoo as a common means of silencing those who have been victims of trafficking.

- Juju (pronounced dzudzu)
  Supernatural power attributed to a charm of fetish, especially of a type used by some West African people.

- Voodoo (pronounced vudu)
  A black religious cult practiced in the Caribbean and the southern USA, combining elements of the Roman Catholic ritual with traditional African magical and religious rites, character-ised by sorcery and spirit possession.

- Hoodoo (pronounced hudu)
  A run of bad luck associated with a person or activity.

In one particular case where the young woman was under severe fear of juju, the legal representative recognised that it would take a long time before the individual was able to summon enough courage to overcome her own fears. Until such time, the legal representative did not force the issue and let the individual tell her in her own time[3].

(5) **Trauma.** In addition to the above potential factors, trauma is a common factor amongst most trafficked people. The UNHCR Guidelines on Evaluation and Care of Victims of Trauma and Violence[4] found that manifestation of trauma included but was not limited to 'shut down' consisting of uncontrollable weeping, self-blame, head down and disengagement.

In such a scenario you may wish to make a referral to a specialised counselling service with consent of your client[5].

[1] Comments of an experienced investigator:http://www.unodc.org/documents/human-traffickin g/TIP_module8_Ebook.pdf.
[2] Personal experience with client – 2011.
[3] Personal client – January 2010.
[4] UNHCR 'Guidelines on Evaluation and Care of Victims of Trauma and Violence', Geneva, December 1993.
[5] The following specialised counselling services, amongst others, accept referrals of those who have been victims of trafficking: The Helen Bamber Foundation; the Medical Foundation for the Care of Victims of Torture; the Traumatic Stress Clinic; Women and Girls Network; The Baobab Centre for Young Services in Exile.

Limited instructions

6.18 There may be occasions when the client will not be able to give instructions relating to his or her claim at all, or only partly. In such circumstances the following suggestions may be useful:

- Ask the client to write out their statement in their own language if they are able to do so to be translated for read back and clarification. This should then stand to serve as the foundation for a more comprehensive statement further to clarification and expansion by your interviewing.

- Rely on third party sources such as social workers' assessments, medical evidence, educational psychologist assessment, NGO reports, country expert reports and your own statement detailing the difficulties in taking instructions and objective evidence in order to draft detailed representations in support.

- Make clear in the client's statement that he or she was not able to speak about *xyz* at this point in time. This will serve to protect the client to a degree against allegation of bolstering by the UKBA if at a later date the client feels able to disclose to you.

- Some clients may feel more comfortable in conveying their experiences by drawing. If so this should be encouraged and the drawing to stand as part of the statement.

- In cases involving juju, it may be that when the client reaches the point that they are ready to divulge to you their experience, it may be stated at such a speed all at once in order to finish the action which they most feared – ie disclosing. In such a scenario it is unlikely that any typed or hand written notes could be made with any degree of accuracy owning to the speed of instructions, however, a taped interview would be ideal since it would allow the client to speak in a free account without any interruption. Ask your client if they agree to be taped.

There may be circumstances where your client is so traumatised that he or she cannot provide you with any instructions. In such circumstances one needs to make the relevant application to the Court of Protection[1].

[1] See further: http://www.direct.gov.uk/en/Governmentcitizensandrights/Mentalcapacityandthel aw/UsingtheCourtofProtection/DG_176235.

Vicarious trauma

6.19 This secondary trauma can result in unconscious messages being conveyed, acting as obstacles to effective interviewing, such as anger, rage and depression. To do the best for the traumatised trafficked person means being aware of our own limitations.

CONCLUSION

6.20 This chapter's aim was to share practical solutions on how we can ensure that the traumatised trafficked person's voice is heard throughout the asylum process, irrespective of age or gender. It is of course equally applicable to any interviewing scenario involving traumatised trafficked people. Working with and acting as advocates for traumatised trafficked people is not easy; however this should never stop us from seeking to hear their voices and listening to them – this chapter stands to merely serve as a foundation on how to achieve that, to be adapted, modified and discarded according to need.

ACKNOWLEDGMENT

6.21 This chapter relies heavily upon the ILPA[1] Working with Refugee Children Current Issues in Best Practice. ILPA is thanked for kindly agreeing to share it for the purposes of this Handbook.

[1]   The Immigration Practitioners' Network.

Part II

PERSPECTIVES ON HUMAN TRAFFICKING IN SCOTLAND AND NORTHERN IRELAND

Contents

7

THE PROTECTION OF TRAFFICKING VICTIMS IN SCOTLAND

Piya D. Muqit

INTRODUCTION

7.1 Scotland was an independent sovereign state that joined the rest of the United Kingdom in 1707. Scotland has a population of 5,168,500[1] and shares a border with England to the south and is bounded by the North Sea to the east, the Atlantic Ocean to the north and west and the North Channel and Irish Sea to the southwest, and includes over 790 islands[2]. Upon accession in 1707, the country retained a separate legal system and continues to constitute a separate jurisdiction in public and private, civil and criminal law.

The Court of Session, Outer and Inner House, is the supreme civil court based in Edinburgh. The High Court of Justiciary is the supreme criminal court and a court of first instance hearing murder, rape, drug trafficking, armed robbery and serious sexual violence cases particularly involving children. Sheriff Courts around the country hear criminal and civil matters with their decisions appealable to the Court of Session and the High Court of Justiciary. District Courts hear minor offences and small claims.

The police, Crown Office and the Procurator Fiscal's office[3] are responsible for the arrest and prosecution of traffickers. There is a Scotland and Northern Ireland regional division of the UK Border Agency (UKBA) based in Glasgow although there is no separate National Referral Mechanism or branch of the UK Human Trafficking Centre (UKHTC) in Scotland.

Following a referendum in Scotland in 1997, the Scottish Parliament was established in 1999 with responsibility over education, economic development, health, justice and home affairs, rural affairs and transport. The UK Parliament continues to legislate for Scotland in broadcasting, immigration and asylum, foreign policy and international relations, social security and tax. The Scotland Office represents the UK Government in Scotland on reserved matters. The First Minister is the leader of the Scottish Parliament who heads the Scottish cabinet who are responsible for developing and implementing Scottish government policy[4]. The Scottish Parliament must ensure that Scotland is compliant with the provisions of the Council of Europe Convention on Action against Trafficking in Human Beings (the Trafficking Convention)[5] and every Act of the Parliament must be compliant with the Human Rights Act

1998.

[1] http://www.scotland.org/facts/population/.
[2] Scottish Executive, *Scotland in Short.* 17 February 2007.
[3] http://www.crownoffice.gov.uk/news/releases/2005/12/historical-development-office-procurat or-fiscal.
[4] http://www.scotland.gov.uk/About/18060/11552.
[5] 'Tackling Human Trafficking, Update to the UK Action Plan on tackling human trafficking', October 2009.

GEOGRAPHICAL CONTEXT

7.2 Glasgow has the largest population of any other Scottish city[1] and is the only city in Scotland to which the UKBA disperses asylum seekers[2]. Glasgow City Council was the first city council in the UK to receive asylum seekers in 1999 through the dispersal scheme and the Scottish Refugee Council was required to grow significantly to meet the demand of their services. As a direct result of dispersal, specialist non- governmental organisations (NGOs), legal service providers and specialist statutory services developed in Glasgow, some of those with a remit to cover the whole of the country.

[1] Population is 577,980. Population of Scotland is 5,168,500 http://www.scotland.org/facts/po pulation/.
[2] UKBA policy since 1999 was to move asylum seekers out of London and the South East to relieve pressure on services in those areas. Local authorities were required to apply for funding to house and support asylum seekers.
http://www.ukba.homeoffice.gov.uk/sitecontent/documents/policyandlaw/asylumsupportbulle tins/dispersal/pb31?view=Binary.

TRAFFICKING IN THE SCOTTISH CONTEXT

7.3 The perception for a long time was that Scotland did not have a trafficking problem until research[1] undertaken in 2008, and published in 2009, involving a retrospective social work case file analysis suggested that approximately 25% (21 children) of unaccompanied asylum seeking children in Glasgow had probably been trafficked[2]. This was followed by interview-based research by the Scottish Government[3] which identified 79 individual adults across Scotland thought to have been the victims of trafficking[4]. This report suggested that the absence of convictions in Scotland for trafficking was probably a combination of:

'An unclear intelligence picture; low levels of awareness among the public; absence of witnesses; difficulties with translation during debrief of witnesses; further training needs among police and prosecution professionals; and some difficulties in obtaining warrants, including a perceived tendency for Sheriffs to favour the familiar language of brothel-keeping instead of newer legislation relating to human trafficking'.[5]

In 2010 Glasgow Child Protection Committee published a report[6] documenting the experiences of frontline practitioners working on trafficking issues that, 'indicated positive developments, but only the embryonic stages of an understanding and response to the complexities of trafficking.'[7] The Scottish Government's Equal Opportunities Committee (EOC) undertook an inquiry into migration and trafficking in 2010 wherein, amongst the NGOs which gave evidence, Amnesty International Edinburgh spoke of research they had carried out in 2008[8] where they had found that trafficking was not just a sexual exploitation issue but extended to domestic servitude and forced labour, with the Association of Chief Police Officers (ACPO) in Scotland estimating that Scotland had 13.5% of the UK's trade in trafficking. The Amnesty International report and the Scottish Government's own research in 2009[9] highlighted that anti-trafficking measures were focused on sexual exploitation of adult women and not forced labour or domestic servitude. The findings of the EOC inquiry were reported[10] on 7 June 2010. The Committee found that despite Government initiatives, exploratory research projects and the work of specialist agencies like TARA[11] there remained little indication of the full extent of trafficking in Scotland and, 'It is difficult to identify the true nature, scale and extent of human trafficking as it affects Scotland'[12].

[1]   Rigby, P, *'Child Trafficking in Glasgow: Report of a Case File Analysis of Unaccompanied Asylum Seeking Children – Glasgow Child Protection Committee 14'* (2009).
http://www.glasgowchildprotection.org.uk/NR/rdonlyres/F4470FF7-1586-4ADB-821703A0
E45EA07A/0/GCPC_child_traffic_2009.pdf.

[2]   A sample group of 75 unaccompanied asylum seeking children known to the social work asylum assessment team in 2007 was used in the retrospective case file analysis. The sample consisted of 38 females and 37 males, aged between 12 and 17 on their first contact with social work services in Glasgow.

[3]   Lebov, K, *'Human Trafficking in Scotland 2007/08, Scottish Government Social Research'* (2009).

[4]   The study took place between April 2007–March 2008.

[5]   Lebov, K, *'Human Trafficking in Scotland 2007/08'* (2009) Scottish Government Social Research, p 14.

[6]   Rigby, P *'Child Trafficking in Glasgow 2: The Views of Professionals Glasgow Child Protection Committee'* (2010).
http://www.glasgowchildprotection.org.uk/NR/rdonlyres/C3597A7A-8D4C-4F98-B846-76A
6F7CB1D1C/0/GCPC_child_traffic_research2010.pdf.

[7]   Rigby, P *'Human Trafficking- a role for youth and criminal justice workers? Towards Effective Practice Paper 11'* (June 2010). http://www.cjsw.ac.uk/cjsw/files/TEP%2011%20June%202010.pdf.

[8]   Amnesty International, *'Scotland's Slaves'* (2008) http://www.amnesty.org.uk/news_details.asp?NewsID=17865.

[9]   Lebov, K, *'Human Trafficking in Scotland 2007/08'*, Scottish Government Social Research (2009).

[10]   http://www.scottish.parliament.uk/s3/committees/equal/reports-10/eor10-05-00.htm.

[11]   TARA stands for the 'Trafficking Awareness Raising Alliance' Project.

[12]   Scottish Parliament 'Equal opportunities committee inquiry into migration and trafficking' (2010).
http://file:///D:/Trafficking%20research/The%20Scottish%20Parliament%20%20Equal%20
Opportunities%20Committee%20Report.htm.

PROSECUTION – TRAFFICKERS AND THEIR VICTIMS

7.4 Seventy nine individuals believed to be victims of trafficking had come into contact with agencies in Scotland between April 2007 and March 2008[1]. To date there has not been a single prosecution of human trafficking[2] in Scotland. In 2010 the Lord Advocate[3] reported to the Scottish Parliament Equal Opportunities Committee that[4]:

'We are simply not having cases reported to us under section 4 of the Asylum and Immigration (Treatment of Claimants, etc) Act 2004 or section 22 of the Criminal Justice (Scotland) Act 2003[5], which are the two main acts that relate to trafficking. There have been very few cases. Four cases have arisen, but because of the sufficiency of evidence we were able to initiate proceedings in only two of them. We took one case to trial at the High Court, but again because of the evidential difficulties, which are significant in such cases, it was not successful.'

However there have been prosecutions in relation to immoral earnings, keeping brothels and a variety of different offences, where the Procurator Fiscal and Crown Office have not had sufficient evidence of trafficking itself but which have been effective in disrupting trafficking activity. Crown Office has appointed a national lead in human trafficking who is an advocate depute[6] and more than 500 prosecutors have been trained in sexual crime, which includes human trafficking. In 2010 prosecutors specialised in human trafficking were appointed and trained by other specialist trafficking agencies who work with Crown Office. As soon as a sexual crime is reported to the police, the specialist prosecutors in Crown Office are involved together with the specialist Procurator Fiscal. In terms of the risk of prosecution, not protection, of victims of trafficking Crown Office has produced guidance for prosecutors[7] which identifies credible indicators that should be taken into account by a prosecutor before reaching the decision to prosecute a victim of trafficking. However, as in the case of the CPS guidance which applies to England and Wales, no blanket statement is made that a victim of trafficking would not be prosecuted per se. There has also been no training for criminal defence solicitors which is problematic as there have been cases where victims have, often on advice, pleaded guilty to offences relating to cannabis cultivation or possession of false documents where they should have been advised to plead not guilty[8]. The Anti-Trafficking Monitoring Group[9] found cases:

> 'which proved that trafficked persons in Scotland are still being arrested and convicted for offences that they have committed while in a trafficking situation, the most common offences being for possession of illegal documentation and for cannabis cultivation. In one particular case, a young female was convicted for cannabis cultivation despite disclosing details of her trafficking to her solicitor, who advised her to plead guilty to the charges against her, despite an expert report presented during court proceedings about her trafficking experience.'[10]

A key feature of Scottish criminal law, in contrast to that of England, Wales and Northern Ireland, and indeed a possible explanation as to the lack of prosecutions for human trafficking in Scotland, is the requirement for corroboration, namely two individual pieces of evidence, before a prosecution can go ahead[11]. This is challenging in the context of trafficking cases where a lapse of time, fear of removal or deportation, psychological trauma or the impact of the use of witchcraft[12] are all barriers to trafficking victims disclosing that they have been trafficked and providing corroboration. There are three verdicts open to a jury in Scotland – guilty, not guilty or not proven[13] which is unique to the jurisdiction.

[1]   Lebov, K, '*Human Trafficking in Scotland 2007/08*' (2009) Scottish Government Social Research.
[2]   This was the position as of 2 June 2011.
[3]   The Lord Advocate is the right hon Elish Anglioni QC, chief legal officer of the Scottish Government and the Crown in Scotland for both civil and criminal matters that fall within the devolved powers of the Scottish Parliament. She is the chief public prosecutor for Scotland and all prosecutions on indictment are conducted by the Crown Office, nominally in her name.
[4]   http://www.scottish.parliament.uk/s3/committees/equal/or-10/eo10-1702.htm#Col2086.
[5]   Both attract convictions of up to 14 years.
[6]   The Lord Advocate appoints practising advocates (barristers), called advocates depute, to assist in conducting cases in the High Court of Justiciary.
[7]   Guidance on Human Trafficking Offences, COPFS, 29/10/10.

8 Case study provided by Legal Services Agency on 20 April 2011.
9 Anti-Trafficking Monitoring Group, '*Wrong Kind of Victim? One year on: an analysis of UK measures to protect trafficked persons*' (2010) London, Anti-Trafficking Monitoring Group.
10 Anti-Trafficking Monitoring Group, '*Wrong Kind of Victim? One year on: an analysis of UK measures to protect trafficked persons*' (2010) London, Anti-Trafficking Monitoring Group, p 109.
11 http://www.scotland.gov.uk/About/CarlowayReview/CRconsSuffOfEvid#_edn2; Hume Commentaries II, 383; *O'Hara v Central SMT Co Ltd* 1941 SC 363, LP (Normand) at 379.
12 Such as Ju Ju which is very often used by Nigerian traffickers to instill absolute fear of disobedience in their trafficked victims.
13 The 'not proven' verdict is when the judge or jury does not have enough evidence to convict but is not sufficiently convinced of the defendant's innocence for a 'not guilty' verdict.

LEGAL SERVICES PROVISION FOR TRAFFICKING VICTIMS

7.5 The Legal Services Agency (LSA) in Glasgow is the only specialist law centre in Scotland which has a dedicated women and children's refugee project (the Project). The four lawyers working in the Project offer advice to women and children who have suffered gender and child based persecution in their country of origin and/or in the UK and have an unresolved immigration or asylum case. The LSA's Project also has a remit to deliver and contribute to training, research and policy on issues that directly affect its client group at a local and national level within Scotland. The Project is based on a holistic model of service provision founded on a human rights based approach. The Project has an Advisory Group made up of key representatives from the Scottish Refugee Council, the British Red Cross, the Medical Foundation for the Care of Victims of Torture, the NHS, Glasgow City Council Social Work Department, members of the Department's client group, Rape Crisis, Women's Aid, the Scottish Guardianship Service and the Trafficking Awareness Raising Alliance (TARA).This Advisory Group has contributed to the devleopment of the Project's model of service provision. The Project uses its work to inform other agencies and increase knowledge and awareness in an effort to improve protocols and practice for women and children.

From April 2010 to March 2011, the Project assisted a total of 93 clients. Of this total figure, 35 (38%) of the clients disclosed that they had been trafficked to the UK and 28 (80%) of that number have disclosed trafficking for the purposes of commercial sexual exploitation[1]. 144 case files on asylum, welfare, child protection and trafficking, have been opened for these clients demonstrating the range of complex legal and social issues. The casework is funded by the Scottish Legal Aid Board, and the Scottish Government and Comic Relief fund the rest of the work of the Project. There is no other comparable legal service in Scotland for adult men. In the last three years the Project has initiated three judicial reviews involving procedural flaws within the NRM with all three conceded by the Secretary of State.

In addition to casework, the Project has been involved in research[2] training, policy and advocacy work on the issue of human trafficking. The Project is a member of the Advisory Group to the Equalities and Human Rights Commission's (EHRC) Inquiry into Human Trafficking in Scotland, the Advisory Group to the Scottish Commissioner for Children and Young People's Scoping Study into Child Trafficking in Scotland, the Operational Committee of the Scottish Separated Children Guardianship Pilot

Project, Sub Group on Child Trafficking, Child Protection Committee of Glasgow City Council and the Inter-Agency group on Human Trafficking, West of Scotland led by Strathclyde Police.

The challenge facing the Project is the lack of capacity to expand to the rest of Scotland to bed down good casework practice. Although the Project has the remit to work across Scotland, distance to other cities with long travel times and the staff's capacity to take on cases are limiting factors in terms of its geographical expansion.

As stated earlier, the lack of awareness of the law relating to human trafficking amongst criminal defence solicitors is problematic with trafficking victims pleading guilty to offences when they should not. There is also a lack of other asylum and immigration practitioners in Scotland who have sufficient knowledge and/or a specialism in advising in trafficking cases[3]. In addition to these victim-protection related obstacles, the lack of adequate or safe housing for children and women who have been trafficked is a challenge since NASS[4] accommodation is not always suitable and, together with welfare concerns that might arise, these are barriers to effective rehabilitation. The launch of the guardianship pilot for unaccompanied children, which is discussed in detail below, has been very helpful with obtaining better disclosure from children and so child protection issues have been flagged up sooner than was previously the case. The guardians have been essential during litigation in providing support and intervening when necessary to ensure that the best interests of the child are always at the forefront.

[1]   Interview with LSA senior solicitor Kirsty Thompson on 15 April 2011.
[2]   The Project has contributed to the report, '*Child Trafficking in Scotland*' commissioned by Scottish Commissioner for Children and Young People and has given evidence to the Equality and Human Rights Commission Human Trafficking Inquiry.
[3]   The majority of solicitors in Scotland specialising in immigration and asylum law are based in Glasgow. Solicitors in Scotland do not need to be accredited in immigration and asylum law with the Law Society to practice and the public funding regime is administered through the Scottish Legal Aid Board under a different system to that in England and Wales.
[4]   The National Asylum Support Service (NASS) is a section of the UK Border Agency (UKBA). It is responsible for supporting and accommodating people seeking asylum while their cases are being dealt with.

NON-STATUTORY SERVICES

7.6 Glasgow Community Safety Services is a charitable organisation formed by Glasgow City Council and Strathclyde Police to prevent crime, tackle anti-social behaviour and promote community safety in Glasgow. In the summer of 2003, Glasgow City Council established an Inter-Agency Working Group to explore the issue of trafficking in women for the purposes of commercial sexual exploitation and two years later the Trafficking Awareness Raising Alliance (The TARA project) was set up in Glasgow and is funded by Glasgow City Council and the Scottish Government[1]. It has a staff of six, three full-time and three part-time staff members, and its remit is to provide support services for adult women who have been trafficked into commercial sexual exploitation across Scotland, which includes domestic servitude where there has been sexual exploitation. TARA is founded on the principle of a feminist, human rights based approach. TARA is a first responder in the NRM scheme and it accepts referrals from NGOs, the Scottish Refugee Council's one stop advice service, the police, health services and solicitors. Victims themselves can self refer to TARA. It offers a holistic service to women and operates on a multi-agency approach with the aim of raising awareness of the issue of trafficking, to better understand victims' needs, to continue to develop and provide a specialised support service and to provide existing organisations with advice and information so they can better support women to socially and vocationally integrate or reintegrate into their chosen communities.

Every woman referred is assessed for eligibility and a risk assessment is carried out. There is no specialised or safe accommodation like the Poppy Project in London provides but TARA can negotiate with NASS in terms of where women should be housed and if they require single and not shared accommodation. For those women who do not qualify for NASS, TARA has the resources to accommodate them in local hotels where it will be difficult for them to be traced and to provide them with subsistence. After a woman is referred she is seen daily for two weeks so that a proper assessment of her needs can take place. An individual care plan is then drawn up with regular reviews with support workers. 70–80% of the women who are seen at TARA have met with the police[2] who take statements at the offices of TARA if the women wish to disclose information about their trafficking. Due to capacity issues TARA does not write reports for immigration, criminal or civil cases but does provide letters of support. Staff can accompany women to their screening and substantive asylum interviews and act as a watching brief as well as accompanying them to court.

In 2010 TARA had 56 referrals, a substantial increase from just two referrals in 2005, and to date has an active caseload of between 35–40 women[3], Nigeria and China being the most frequent nationalities of the women who were referred. TARA has acted as First Responder for 15 women and received a positive reasonable grounds decision in all cases and a positive conclusive decision in six cases Where they have supported a case but have not been the First Responder there has been reasonable grounds decisions granted in six of the 12 cases referred with five of those cases being granted a positive conclusive decision[4].

The main barrier to effective representation for victims is the lack of training for frontline workers who come into contact with victims, the need for more lawyers specialised in human trafficking together with immigration and asylum law, the lack of awareness within the criminal defence community on trafficking issues and the scale of the problem being countrywide with most services Glasgow based. There continues to be difficulties with regional UKBA acting as the Competent Authority, with negative conclusive decisions served at the same time as negative asylum decisions, with the Competent Authority decision-maker commenting on the lack of credibility of the victims' accounts in both decisions, most often written by the same UKBA case worker[5].

Migrant Helpline provides support to adult men trafficked for sexual exploitation and anyone trafficked for forced labour and domestic servitude[6]. Since beginning work on 1 April 2009, in their first year Migrant Helpline assisted 60 potential victims of trafficking, of whom six have been granted reasonable grounds decisions under the NRM. Of these there were no victims of sexual exploitation, three victims of domestic servitude, 54 victims of forced labour and three dependents of victims. 36 were male and 24 female. They came from the Slovak Republic, Zimbabwe, Nigeria, Kyrgyzstan, Lithuania and India. Routes that traffickers have used have been via Stranraer from Northern Ireland, via Glasgow and Edinburgh's airports and across the border from England[7].

Both TARA and Migrant Helpline are members of the Scottish Government's Human Trafficking Stakeholder Group which has been set up to focus on the practical issues of the NRM and to develop a national protocol for the safety, human rights and best interests of victims in Scotland. TARA is also involved in a number of steering groups and advisory panels across the UK and was a key contributor to the Anti-Trafficking Monitoring Board's research in 2010 on trafficking in Scotland.

[1]   TARA (2010) Equal Opportunities Committee Inquiry into Migration and Trafficking: written submission received from Glasgow Community and Safety Services http://www.scottish.parliament.uk/s3/committees/equal/inquiries/migration/subs/MT16TARA.pdf .

[2]   Interview with Broangh Andrew, Assistant Operations Manager, TARA on 15 March 2011.

[3]   As of 15 March 2011.

[4]   Statistics from TARA period 1 April 2009 to 31 December 2010.

[5]   Please see the Chapters on 'Identification' in this Handbook for further details on the conflict that is inherent in this approach.

[6]   http://www.migranthelpline.org.uk/migrant_helpline_services/volunteering_ready_programme.cfm.

[7]   Migrant Helpline (2010) Equal Opportunities Committee Inquiry into Migration and Trafficking: written submission http://www.scottish.parliament.uk/s3/committees/equal/inquiries/migration/subs/MT06MigrantHelpline.pdf.

EHRC INQUIRY INTO HUMAN TRAFFICKING IN SCOTLAND

7.7 Baroness Helena Kennedy QC is leading the Equality and Human Rights Commission's Inquiry into Human Trafficking in Scotland that began on 9 February 2010 and is still ongoing[1]. The terms of reference for the Inquiry are:

'1.   To inquire into the extent and nature of human trafficking in relation to Scotland, focusing mainly but not exclusively on trafficking for the purpose of commercial sexual exploitation.

2.   To inquire into the causes of human trafficking relating to Scotland focusing especially on the role of demand for commercial sexual exploitation.

3.   To inquire into domestic and international good practice on the prevention and prohibition of human trafficking, the criminal prosecution of traffickers, and the protection of its victims.

4.   To inquire into policy and practice in Scotland measured against anti-trafficking human rights standards especially in respect of:

   i.   the identification and treatment of trafficking victims in the asylum and immigration system

   ii.   monitoring for, and the investigation and prosecution of, traffickers, especially for trafficking crime; and

   iii.   the extent and quality of statutory and specialist services and accommodation for victims.'[2]

The Inquiry has heard evidence from both statutory and non-statutory bodies, NGOs and civil society. The Inquiry is expected to report its finding in the

Autumn of 2011. The purpose of the Inquiry is to, 'try and identify the nature of human trafficking and estimate its extent in Scotland in order to understand its underlying influences and causes to see where policy and practice needs to improve.'[3] The trafficking that will be examined is not restricted to sexual exploitation but will also cover forced labour and other forms of trafficking. The Inquiry is taking a particular interest in policy and practice against human trafficking in Scotland in the areas of asylum, law investigation and enforcement, and in services and accommodation for the victims of human trafficking.

[1] 'Formal Inquiry opened into Human Trafficking in Scotland', Equality and Human Rights Commission news release, 9 February 2010
http://www.equalityhumanrights.com/media-centre/2010/february/formal-inquiry-opened-into-human—trafficking-in-scotland.

[2] http://www.equalityhumanrights.com/scotland/projects-and-campaigns-in-scotland/inquiry-into-human-trafficking-in-scotland/terms-of-reference/.

[3] http://www.equalityhumanrights.com/scotland/projects-and-campaigns-in-scotland/inquiry-into-human-trafficking-in-scotland/about-the-human-trafficking-inquiry/.

CHALLENGES TO EFFECTIVE PROTECTION OF ADULTS AND CHILDREN VICTIMS

7.8 The Anti-Trafficking Monitoring Group met with 10 participants from statutory and non-statutory agencies in Scotland in November 2009 to discuss the implementation of the Trafficking Convention and its impact in Scotland, especially in terms of victim care and support. The findings were reported in June 2010[1]. The key issues that arose from the report were: the challenges faced in identifying victims outside of Glasgow, as the main expertise was in the Glasgow-based TARA project which has limited resources to travel far; that more focus was required on victims of trafficking for forced labour and domestic servitude; that the lack of training for frontline police officers particularly outside Glasgow to identify victims and facilitate disclosure was an obstacle to protection (and in some cases led to trafficking victims being charged with criminal offences). Key issues with the NRM in Scottish cases were the delays in the issuing of conclusive decisions by regional UKBA Competent Authority decision makers who did not have the capacity to deal with NRM referrals efficiently due to their parallel asylum/immigration casework and when they did make decisions these were made in isolation without seeking expertise of the First Responder (FR) if the FR was not the UKBA. As FRs, regional UKBA staff appeared to lack the requisite skilled knowledge of human trafficking and were therefore ineffective as FRs. The insufficient provision of support services for trafficked persons in Scotland in particular for interpreting and counseling was also highlighted[2].

[1] Anti-Trafficking Monitoring Group '*Wrong Kind of Victim? One year on: an analysis of UK measures to protect trafficked persons*' (2010) London, Anti-Trafficking Monitoring Group.

[2] Anti-Trafficking Monitoring Group '*Wrong Kind of Victim? One year on: an analysis of UK measures to protect trafficked persons*' (2010) London, Anti-Trafficking Monitoring Group at page 108, which states that 'In Glasgow COMPASS Asylum Seekers and Refugee Mental Health Liaison Team has expertise in working with trafficked persons but their service is oversubscribed and there are very long waiting lists.'

CHILDREN WHO ARE TRAFFICKED

7.9 Statutory services are bound by the Children (Scotland) Act 1995. This encompasses all children irrespective of their immigration status and whether they are accompanied or unaccompanied and local authorities have a duty to safeguard and protect the welfare of the child found or living in their area who are in need. '*Getting it Right for Every Child*'[1] is a Scottish Government program that aims to improve outcomes for children and young people when services work together to assess and plan to meet their needs.

The Children's Commissioner for Scotland and the Centre for Rural Childhood, Perth College UHI, published research in February 2011[2] that found that at least 80 children may have been trafficked in 2009/10 for domestic servitude, benefit fraud, forced labour and sexual exploitation. The report found that as there had not been any criminal prosecutions together with a poor response to the children's needs, Scotland was attractive to traffickers. 850 relevant professionals in health, police, social services, teachers and voluntary organisations were involved in the research. The lack of awareness for child trafficking was high and this was the root cause of children not being identified and referred to relevant agencies.

Between April 2009 and August 2010 there were 14 referrals to UKBA while the research found that there was at least 80 potential referrals in the same time period. Age disputes, grooming within foster care and the closed nature of some communities were of concern as well as the perception that trafficking was an urban and not a rural issue. Between 1 April 2009 and 15 January 2010, Glasgow City Council and Moray Council made referrals of children who may have been trafficked into their respective areas during this period, but it was not clear how many children were involved, the type of exploitation they were trafficked for or the decisions made in each case by the Competent Authorities[3].

In February 2007[4] research was conducted by the Child Protection Committee in Glasgow. This was a retrospective study of records kept by the social work asylum assessment team concerning 75 individual unaccompanied asylum-seeking children in Glasgow. Of these, 23 children were identified as having possibly been trafficked either having been exploited on the way to the UK or being at continued risk of future exploitation, with a further nine cases indicating 'suspicions' of trafficking. During Operation Pentameter I and II[5] there were no trafficked children found. The Scottish Government in February 2009 published '*Safeguarding Children in Scotland who may have been Trafficked*'[6]. The guidance recommended Child Protection Committees[7], of which there are 30 in Scotland, to adopt a multi-agency approach to safeguarding. Following on from this the Children, Young People and Social Care Directorate of the Scottish Parliament sent a letter on 31 March 2009 to all Chairs and Lead Officers of the Child Protection Committees to inform them of the NRM as well as of the assessment framework for children and to encourage them to let their staff know of a series of events organised by the Scottish Government in May 2009 to raise awareness on the new procedures[8].

The Glasgow Child Protection Committee published their Inter-Agency Guidance for Child Trafficking in September 2009 with instructions about the NRM[9]. The Committee prepared this protocol to provide information and guidance to all those working with children in Glasgow, including police, schools and health professionals, so that they would be able to identify trafficked children and to provide them with the necessary protection and support. The Scottish Government published a practice document and assessment toolkit[10] for practitioners working with children whom they suspect may have been trafficked. Glasgow City Council was one of 13 local authority areas involved in the UK pilot monitoring the implementation of an assessment framework for child trafficking. The child trafficking toolkit[11], which includes an assessment framework and guidance, was developed by the London Safeguarding Children Board. The pilot ran across the UK from 2009–2010 to monitor and trial the toolkit. The toolkit was used as a basis of making decisions to refer children suspected of being trafficked to the NRM. Feedback from the pilot programme suggests that the toolkit has helped raise awareness of child trafficking and mainstreamed child trafficking as a child[12].

The Council of Europe Trafficking Convention requires the provision of guardianship for unaccompanied children who have been trafficked[13]. The UK Government has yet to establish a guardianship system. In Glasgow, since June 2010, an inter-agency, child-centered model of guardianship developed by the Scottish Refugee Council and run in partnership by the Aberlour Childcare Trust for unaccompanied asylum seeking children is being piloted[14]. The service will offer advice for existing separated children and the services that work with them and:

> 'All separated children newly arrived in Scotland will be allocated a guardian who will be their consistent point of contact to act as a link between all services and professionals that are involved in their life, help the young person to understand the roles and responsibilities of these professionals, assist the young people in understanding the complex immigration and welfare processes and enable them to fully participate in their claims for status and support, help the young person to present their case in their claim for asylum and develop tools and techniques to support them and their workers and advocate on their behalf and ensure young people's voices are heard.'[15]

The pilot will run for 30 months and has appointed four Guardians. The service was set up to improve separated children's experience and understanding of the welfare, immigration and asylum system. The pilot is funded by the Big Lottery Fund, Paul Hamlyn and the Scottish Government.

The pilot was initiated to focus on children claiming asylum but children who have been trafficked and/or are age disputed can also access the service. It is a Scotland wide service available to any child presenting in one of the 32 local authority areas. The Guardians themselves are not guardian ad litems and are not a statutory service. They act as a link to the children and the services they are accessing and ensure that the voice of the child is heard and that children participate in the decision making that affects them. The Guardians can also offer professional advice to other professionals working with separated children.

Children who have been trafficked are referred by Glasgow City Council's UASC[16] asylum assessment team but the guardians are not First Responders under the NRM, the UASC team are. The Guardians help young people understand what trafficking actually means. Trafficking victims can attend dancing and drama groups which the guardians have found to be therapeutic allowing space for victims to be children first and foremost. The Guardians have a current caseload of 29 separated children of which seven have had an NRM submitted. Predominantly the victims come from Nigeria, Vietnam and Somalia[17]. The victims have solicitors but for cases outside Glasgow it has posed a challenge to find specialist solicitors.

The only specialist counselling service for children is the COMPASS Asylum Seekers and Refugee Mental Health Liaison Team in Glasgow which has expertise in working with asylum seekers, refugees and trafficked persons[18]. It is the only mental health service that offers therapeutic rehabilitation for trafficking victims but there is a long waiting list. The children involved in the guardianship service who have made asylum, and/or human rights claims have reported that the delay in decision making by UKBA has placed considerable stress on them with some children waiting more than six months for their substantive asylum interview from the time they claimed protection. The Guardian's experience is that with the asylum process being time consuming and complex it is challenging to make the experience better for those children affected. There is a further problem with the absence of specialist accommo-dation for trafficking victims and dispersal all over Glasgow means the Guardian's time is taken up with accompanying the children who can't commute by themselves to appointments. Specialist health examinations/social work reports/age assessments/interviews with the police all potentially mean that children have several interviews where they must repeat their trafficking experience, as well as having to recount it to decision makers. In practice UKBA will only delay an asylum interview if a medical report is submitted. UKBA do not interview children at the Guardian's office unlike the police who take statements from adult trafficking victims at TARA's offices.

Scottish Refugee Council's Children's Policy Officer and the policy officer at Aberlour, work on policy issues affecting separated children. The Scottish Refugee Council has given evidence to both the EHRC'S ongoing Trafficking Inquiry[19] in 2011 and the Scottish Parliament's inquiry into migration and trafficking in 2010 and were involved with the Scottish Children's Commis-sioner's report into trafficking 2011. The guardianship service is being evaluated by Dr Heaven Crawley[20] and Dr Ravi Kohli[21] and is a potential model for similar services across the UK in the future.

The UASC asylum assessment team which is part of Glasgow Asylum Support Services is where unaccompanied trafficking victims may be referred to if they are seeking asylum. It is known as the de facto specialist trafficking service in Scotland for unaccompanied children. The team consists of two social workers and two support workers with a current caseload of 140 unaccompanied children, of which 10 have been identified as trafficked[22]. Pre-NRM the team had instituted a practice of calling a multi-agency meeting with the police, legal representatives, child protection specialists, UKBA, health services and any other relevant professionals where a case would be discussed and views sought from the professionals on the case. If an asylum statement had been drafted, the police would receive a copy with the child's consent for the purposes of investigating the trafficking so that the child would not have to give another statement. Since the introduction of the NRM, multi-agency meetings still take place with UKBA as the Competent Authority invited. The UASC team as First Responders can refer any case to the NRM if appropriate.

Young males aged 16–18 are supported in specialist accommodation – the Campus Project[23], however young women who are seeking asylum and have been trafficked who are over 16 are housed in hostels and hotels as there is no specialist accommodation for victims of trafficking in Scotland. The Campus Project has limited resources and provides no specialist services for trafficking victims. Children who are younger than 16 years are usually placed in children's homes where the staff are not necessarily trained on trafficking issues. Most of the trafficking victims which the UASC team has worked with have come from England where they have escaped from the traffickers. The experience of the team is that child victims have not been recognised as refugees and instead been granted discretionary leave to temporarily remain in the UK on the basis that they are unaccompanied and there are no adequate reception arrangements for them in their country of origin. Age assessments are carried out by this team.

The absence of an equivalent of TARA for children is hugely problematic as the UASC asylum assessment team, which is under-resourced, is struggling to meet the needs of trafficked children who are referred to it. The team members are also called by Social Services around the country for advice and guidance on how to support trafficked children and are often asked if the children can be transferred to Glasgow as whatever services there are in Scotland, are based there. There are no specialist children's NGOs in Scotland for trafficked children: many of the domestic children's NGOs do not include trafficking victims within their remit.

1   http://www.scotland.gov.uk/gettingitright.
2   SCCYP, *'Scotland: A Safe place for child traffickers?'* (2011).
3   Freedom of Information request submitted by ECPAT UK answered on 11 February 2010.
4   Rigby, P, *'Child Trafficking in Glasgow: Report of a Case File Analysis of Unaccompanied Asylum Seeking Children '* – Glasgow Child Protection Committee 14 (2009).
    http://www.glasgowchildprotection.org.uk/NR/rdonlyres/F4470FF7-1586-4ADB-8217-03A0
    E45EA07A/0/GCPC_child_traffic_2009.pdf.
    Rigby, P *'Child Trafficking in Glasgow 2: The Views of Professionals' Glasgow Child Protection Committee* (2010).
    http://www.glasgowchildprotection.org.uk/NR/rdonlyres/C3597A7A-8D4C-4F98-B846-76A
    6F7CB1D1C/0/GCPC_child_traffic_research2010.pdf.
5   Operation Pentameter I was a UK policing operation that involved eight police forces in Scotland and the Scottish Crime and Drug Enforcement Agency and ran between February 2006 and 2007. Operation Pentameter II ran between October 2007 and March 2008.
6   Scottish Government, *'Safeguarding Children in Scotland Who May Have Been Trafficked'* (2009) http://www.scotland.gov.uk/Publications/2009/02/18092546/0.
    Guidance adapted to the Scottish context and derived from its equivalent produced by the Home Office and the Department for Children, Schools and Families for England.
7   http://www.scotland.gov.uk/Topics/People/Young-People/children-families/17834/10238.
8   Scottish Government, 'The National Referral Mechanism - letter to CPC Chairs 31/3/09' (2009) http://www.scotland.gov.uk/Resource/Doc/254429/0080167.pdf
9   Glasgow Child Protection Committee, Inter-Agency Guidance for Child Trafficking. (National Referral Mechanism form and risk assessment framework), (September 2009) http://www.gl asgowchildprotection.org.uk/NR/rdonlyres-/AADFD622-A183-4B96-9D5E-D6F3C2C37A79 /0/GLASGOWCHILDTRAFFICKINGGUIDANCESept09.pdf.
10 Scottish Government, *'Safeguarding Children in Scotland Who May Have Been Trafficked'* (2009) http://www.scotland.gov.uk/Publications/2009/02/18092546/0.
11 http://www.londonscb.gov.uk/trafficking/.
12 http://www.ecpat.org.uk/sites/default/files/child_trafficking_in_the_uk_a_snapshot.pdf.
13 Article 10(4)(a). As soon as an unaccompanied child is identified as a victim, each party shall provide for representation of the child by a legal guardian, organisation or authority which shall act in the best interests of that child.
14 http://www.aberlour.org.uk/newguardianshipservicelaunched.aspx.

[15] http://www.aberlour.org.uk/scottishguardianshipservice.aspx.

[16] Unaccompanied Asylum Seeking Children.

[17] Interview with Catriona McSween, Guardianship Service Manager, 10 May 2011. Two girls and five boys. The youngest age disputed boy is 12 years and the others boys are aged between 15 and 18.

[18] http://www.nhsggc.org.uk/content/default.asp?page=home_compass.

[19] http://www.scottishrefugeecouncil.org.uk/policy_and_research/responding_to_policy/policy_and_research_2011.

[20] Director of the Centre for Migration Policy Research, Swansea University.

[21] Head of Department of Applied Social Studies, University of Bedfordshire.

[22] Interview with team leader Chris Perkins, UASC Asylum Assessment Team, Glasgow City Council, 15 April 2011.

[23] http://www.themungofoundation.org.uk/documents/CampusProject.pdf.

CONCLUSION

7.10 The impediments to effective protection for trafficking victims lie in the small number of specialist statutory and non-statutory services in Scotland which are based mostly in Glasgow and have limited capacity and resources to meet the demands from around the country. The Scottish Government is fully committed to fulfilling its obligations under the Trafficking Convention however what is desperately needed is, for example, further quantitative and qualitative research on all forms of human trafficking in Scotland, more training on the identification of trafficking victims for staff in statutory and non-statutory organisations[1] and further funding and resources for existing services. Only by adopting a dynamic and multi-faceted approach will we be able to fully understand why children and adults are trafficked into Scotland, why they are vulnerable to being exploited whilst living in Scotland and what are the best ways to protect and support them.

[1] And also the legal profession in Scotland as a whole.

8

HUMAN TRAFFICKING IN NORTHERN IRELAND

Lois Hamilton and Catherine Robinson

'Human trafficking is a vile and wicked crime. The degree of brutality, misery and suffering involved is difficult to grasp, and sadly, it exists in Northern Ireland. Let's also call it for what it is – human trafficking is human slavery – whether it be for sexual exploitation, labour exploitation or domestic servitude.'

[1]   David Ford, Minister of Justice, speaking to the NI Assembly, 21 September 2010, reported at http://www.dojni.gov.uk/northern-ireland-must-open-its-eyes-to-human-trafficking-ford.

INTRODUCTION

8.1 The aim of this chapter[1] is to explain what is currently known about human trafficking in Northern Ireland (NI) and also to highlight some of the regional differences in NI in comparison to the rest of the UK.

[1]   The opinions and interpretations set out in this chapter are strictly confined to personal viewpoints of the authors and in no way reflect the view of Law Centre (NI) or others.

THE NI INFRASTRUCTURE

8.2 On 21 September 2010 the NI Assembly formally condemned human trafficking, noted with grave concern the growing prevalence of trafficking for the sex trade, domestic servitude and labour exploitation in NI and voted to make NI a 'hostile place for human traffickers.'[1]

The Northern Ireland Act 1999 provides the basis for devolution in NI. A devolution order, approved by Westminster in 1999 under the Act, provided for the transfer of certain powers from central Westminster Government to the NI Assembly. The NI Assembly was established as part of the Belfast Agreement/Good Friday Agreement in 1998 and, along with the NI Executive, has full legislative and executive authority for all matters that are the responsibility of the NI Government departments. Since 1999, devolution has been suspended on a number of occasions with the re-imposition of Direct Rule, however, devolved powers were restored on 8 May 2007[2].

The Northern Ireland Act effectively apportions Government matters into three different categories of legislative competence: 'excepted' matters are matters deemed to be of national importance and remain the responsibility of HM Government and Westminster, eg, international relations, defence, taxation, immigration and nationality; 'reserved' matters are broadly UK-wide issues such as telecommunications – although the Assembly has power to legislate on these matters, it requires the formal consent of the Secretary of State for NI; 'transferred' matters include anything that is not considered 'reserved' or 'exempted' – the Assembly does not require consent to legislate on these matters. Transferred matters are often referred to as 'devolved'. Most recently, the previously 'reserved' matters of policing and criminal justice were transferred to NI on 12 April 2010.

Employment is a transferred/devolved matter and therefore employment is the responsibility of the Minster for Employment and Learning. By comparison, immigration remains an excepted matter.

Tackling perpetrators of human trafficking and raising awareness of the issue is being taken forward by the Organised Crime Task Force (OCTF) of the Department of Justice (DOJ). In particular, its Immigration and Human Trafficking Expert Group promotes intelligence sharing and partnership working between stakeholders and identifies emerging trends and barriers to effective investigation. The Group includes representatives of Police Service of NI (PSNI), An Garda Síochána[3], the UK Border Agency (UKBA), the Serious Organised Crime Agency (SOCA) and NI government departments[4,5].

Since 2008 around 35 people have been rescued from exploitation in NI but no-one has yet to be convicted of the offence of trafficking[6].

The Blue Blindfold campaign was officially launched in NI on 23 February 2010 with the aim of raising awareness of the problem of human trafficking[7]. Blue Blindfold is an international campaign designed by the UK Human Trafficking Centre. The campaign has received support from the 'All Party Parliamentary Group on Trafficking in 2008'.

Speaking at the launch Paul Goggins, the then Minister of State said: 'through the Blue Blindfold information campaign, we are raising awareness of the issue. The most valuable asset in combating crime is information and we are asking everyone to open their eyes to the fact that human trafficking is happening in Northern Ireland'[8]. The Blue Blindfold campaign was re-launched to run for three months by David Ford, the NI Justice Minister on 18 January 2011. A public awareness campaign was launched in Dublin on the same day. David Ford concluded: 'I welcome the opportunity for both Northern Ireland and the Republic of Ireland to launch campaigns on this important issue at the same time. Human trafficking knows no borders and it is important that we work together to highlight and detect this crime'[9].

The Irish Baptist Network held a conference on human trafficking on 22 March 2011[10]. Speaking at this conference, Mr Ford welcomed the fact that two potential victims of human trafficking were rescued the day before by the PSNI. He stated that the Blue Blindfold campaign had helped to raise awareness of human trafficking across NI, that during 2009/10 the PSNI had identified 25 victims of human trafficking, that there had been 20 cases of human trafficking in 2010/11 and there were currently a number of charges for human trafficking offences going through the criminal justice system[11,12].

In October 2010 the 'Visitor or Victim campaign' was launched, which features a multilingual poster and leaflet[13] to make victims of trafficking aware of the support that is available[14].

The PSNI is 'currently developing a policy on human trafficking'[15]. Recent DOJ research also states that the majority of frontline PSNI officers do not receive any formal training on human trafficking as part of their overall training[16]. However there is an initiative in place to train a number of specialised police officers within each police district to recognise potential indicators of human trafficking[17].

NI has separate and distinct issues by virtue of its geographical and strategic location. The lack of a border between the North and South results in an ease of movement of victims for traffickers[18]. NI has been shown as a transit route between Dublin and the rest of the UK in both directions. Bi-lateral co-operation between the UK Home Office, the UK Human Trafficking Centre, the NI DOJ, the PSNI, An Garda Síochána and the Irish Department of Justice and Law Reform continues and officials meet regularly to monitor operations and exchange information on developments and best practice[19]. However there is little or no cross border sharing of information between NGOs, lawyers and statutory bodies by way of an all Ireland specialist Trafficking Group[20].

[1] David Ford, Minister of Justice, speaking to the NI Assembly, 21 September 2010, reported athttp://www.dojni.gov.uk/northern-ireland-must-open-its-eyes-to-human-trafficking-ford 'human trafficking for the sex trade, domestic servitude and labour exploitation in Northern Ireland; further notes that men, women and children are victims of human trafficking and that human trafficking exists because of local demand; and calls on the Minister of Justice and the Executive to raise awareness of human trafficking among the public in order to assist the authorities in securing prosecutions against those who carry out this modern form of slavery and to ensure that Northern Ireland is a hostile place for traffickers; and further calls on the Minister of Justice to work closely with the Irish Government and the European Union to ensure that Northern Ireland is part of an all-island, European-wide response to this serious issue.' The full debate is available at http://www.theyworkforyou.com/ni/?id=2010-09-21.7.1.

[2] Devolution was initially established in 1999 following the Good Friday Agreement 1998 but was suspended, only to be restored in May 2007 following the St Andrews Agreement.

[3] The Police in the Republic of Ireland.

[4] Information provided by Marie Patterson of the Department of Justice on 20 May 2011.

[5] As well as the OCTF initiatives, there are a number of Government-led working groups involved in human trafficking issues but we are unclear about how frequently they meet and the exact remits of these groups. The groups include – the Immigration Sub Group set up under the Office for the First Minister and the Deputy First Minister's (OFMDFM) Racial Equality Forum. It is convened by OFMDFM, chaired by Law Centre (NI) and attended by a number of voluntary and statutory representatives including from Department for Employment and Learning (DEL).The DEL chairs the Migrant Workers Thematic Sub-Group which consists of almost 50 members. It includes most NI departments, relevant UK departments, statutory and non-Governmental organisations, which seek to represent the interests of migrant workers. There are different groups within the Sub-Group – for example, one that deals with information and publications and one that deals with enforcement. We have also found reference to a Human Trafficking Social Care Group made up of the DOJ, UKBA, PSNI, Woman's Aid, Migrant Helpline and the Department of Health, Social Services and Public Safety; however, its terms of reference are unclear.

[6] These were the numbers stated during the NI Assembly debate on 21 September 2010 and subsequently reported in a BBC News article entitled 'MLAs say NI 'hostile place for human traffickers' dated 21 September 2010, see http://www.bbc.co.uk/news/uk-northern-ireland -11376024.

[7] See press release of Organised Crime Task Force dated 23 February 2010 at http://www.oct f.gov.uk/News/Launch-of-Blue-Blindfold.aspx.
The Blue Blindfold logo is fast becoming an internationally recognised symbol of help for victims. Further information can be found at http://www.blueblindfold.co.uk.

[8] See press release of Organised Crime Task Force dated 23 February 2010 at http://www.oct f.gov.uk/News/Launch-of-Blue-Blindfold.aspx.

The blue blindfold logo is fast becoming an internationally recognised symbol of help for victims. Further information can be found at http://www.blueblindfold.co.uk.

[9] See press release of the Northern Ireland Executive dated 18 January 2011 at http://www.northernireland.gov.uk/index/media-centre/news-departments/news-doj/news-releases-doj-january-2011/news-doj-180111-ford-launches-campaign_.htm.

[10] Recordings of the speeches from this conference are available at http://www.ibnetworks.org/human_trafficking_conference.html.

[11] See press release of the Northern Ireland Executive dated 22 March 2011 at http://www.northernireland.gov.uk/index/media-centre/news-departments/news-doj/news-doj-220311-ford-addresses-human.htm?WT.mc_id%3Drss-news.

[12] There was a Workshop on Human Trafficking 22 June 2011. An event funded under Priority 1.1 of the Peace III programme for NI and the Border Region.

[13] These are available in English, Mandarin, French, Romanian, Lithuanian, Russian, Thai, Czech and Albanian.

[14] *'Research paper investigating the issues for women in Northern Ireland involved in prostitution and exploring best practice elsewhere'*, Department of Justice (January 2011) at p 50.

[15] *'Research paper investigating the issues for women in Northern Ireland involved in prostitution and exploring best practice elsewhere'*, Department of Justice (January 2011) at p 29.

[16] *'Research paper investigating the issues for women in Northern Ireland involved in prostitution and exploring best practice elsewhere'*, Department of Justice (January 2011) at p 29. In addition, we have been informed that in 2009, a potential victim of trafficking and an Asylum Support worker from Bryson One Stop Service were turned away from a Belfast police station because police officers informed them that it was 'an immigration matter' and treated them with contempt. UKBA officials also sent the case away, stating that the PSNI were the relevant First Responders [under the NRM]. In another incident a police detective left an interview telling other professionals that a potentially trafficked woman was telling 'a very common story' that they didn't accept. Information provided by Edie Shillue, Bryson One Stop Service, Asylum Advice and Support Worker on 25 May 2011.

[17] *'Research paper investigating the issues for women in Northern Ireland involved in prostitution and exploring best practice elsewhere'*, Department of Justice (January 2011) at p 44.

[18] Martynowicz, A, Toucas, S and Caughey, A *'The Nature and Extent of Human Trafficking in Northern Ireland, A Scoping Study'* by the Institute for Conflict Research commissioned by Northern Ireland Human Rights Commission and Equality Commission for Northern Ireland (2009) at p 33.

[19] Walsh, M, Anti Human Trafficking Unit, Article in The Researcher (March 2011) at p 9; see http://www.legalaidboard.ie/lab/publishing.nsf/content/The_Researcher_March_2011_Article_1Human Trafficking.

[20] The Cross Border Organised Crime Assessment 2010 includes commentary on immigration crime from a cross border perspective and a case study on a successful joint policing operation by PSNI and An Garda Síochána on sham marriages but also states from a cross border perspective that 'neither PSNI nor An Garda Síochána have seen any evidence of human trafficking although there is evidence of a number of people smuggling operations taking advantage of the border from the Republic into Northern Ireland allowing freer movement onwards to the UK Mainland' – at p 14.

HUMAN TRAFFICKING IN NI

8.3 Human trafficking is still perceived as a relatively new problem in NI and documented numbers remain fairly low in comparison to other parts of the UK. Notwithstanding this, the lack of regional monitoring or recording of data results in only a partial picture of the reality of human trafficking in NI[1].

To date NI has seen examples of forced labour through domestic servitude, exploitation of labour, sexual exploitation, the use of victims for cannabis cultivation and the abuse of children from a variety of countries including China, India, Afghanistan, Nigeria and Gambia.

Unlike Scotland and the rest of the UK, NI was not included in Pentameter I[2]. At the close of Pentameter II, preliminary reports were that five victims had been rescued in NI (four of them as victims of sexual exploitation and one of forced labour); six people were arrested for controlling prostitution and people smuggling; nine properties were searched and £5,500 was confiscated[3,4]. While the results of Pentameter II indicated that a number of women had been smuggled or trafficked into NI, exact numbers have still not been established and the one trafficking conviction was subsequently overturned[5].

Operation Gull[6] deserves special mention as it remains unclear how this potentially affects victims. It is a joint operation between An Garda Síochána, PSNI and the UKBA. The operation has been running since at least mid to late 2005. It targets migrants entering NI on domestic flights from South East England and on boats from Stranraer. Those targeted are questioned and if it is suspected they are entering NI with a view to entering the Republic of Ireland illegally or are suspected of another immigration offence they will be detained and removed. It remains an 'unpublished' policy and there is no way of knowing how Immigration Officers have been instructed to deal with potential victims of trafficking that they encounter. It runs on an irregular basis. When it is in operation upwards of 50 individuals have been believed to be detained in one weekend. The speed and secrecy under which Operation Gull is carried out results in individuals being unable to access independent legal advice. There is no independent, transparent, oversight of the operation. The legal basis of the operation has never been formally stated and its operation and scope has not, to date, been tested in law[7].

1   BBC News article entitled 'Seedy underworld of human trafficking' dated 18 May 2010, http://seenews.bbc.co.uk/1/hi/northern_ireland/8675275.stm.

2   Martynowicz, A, Toucas, S and Caughey, A 'The Nature and Extent of Human Trafficking in Northern Ireland, A Scoping Study' by the Institute for Conflict Research commissioned by Northern Ireland Human Rights Commission and Equality Commission for Northern Ireland (2009) at p 32. Pentameter I and II were sustained police operations involving a number of agencies. Both Pentameter Operations comprised hundreds of raids. Pentameter 1 focused on sexual exploitation, Pentameter II on sex trafficking but also forced labour. Pentameter II, which included NI, was launched in October 2007 and ran for six months. Nationwide, 167 victims were recovered and 528 criminals were arrested.

3   Martynowicz, A, Toucas, S and Caughey, A *'The Nature and Extent of Human Trafficking in Northern Ireland, A Scoping Study'* by the Institute for Conflict Research commissioned by Northern Ireland Human Rights Commission and Equality Commission for Northern Ireland (2009) at p 33, footnote 32 citing Irish Times, 2 July 2008. These figures are also stated at p 42.

4   The Anti-Trafficking Monitoring Group*'Wrong Kind of Victim? One year on: an analysis of UK measures to protect trafficked persons'* (June 2010) – see Appendix 6: Issues in Northern Ireland, Scotland and Wales.

5   Martynowicz, A, Toucas, S and Caughey, A *'The Nature and Extent of Human Trafficking in Northern Ireland, A Scoping Study'* by the Institute for Conflict Research commissioned by Northern Ireland Human Rights Commission and Equality Commission for Northern Ireland (2009) at p 33 with a reference to Northern Ireland Women's European Platform (2008) Submission to the Committee on the Convention for the Elimination of Discrimination against Women, 6th Periodic Report of the United Kingdom, Shadow Report at http://www2.ohchr.org/english/bodies/cedaw/docs/ngos/NIWEPUK41_1.pdf.

6   See Report of Department of Justice, Equality and Law Reform and An Garda Síochána Working Group on Trafficking in Human Beings (2006), at page 16 see http://www.justice.ie/en/JELR/THBreport.pdf/Files/THBreport.pdf and an ongoing topic with UKBA and LCNI.

7   Information provided by Elizabeth Griffith at LCNI.

Research available

8.4 In May 2006 in the Republic of Ireland (ROI) the Department of Justice, Equality and Law Reform and An Garda Síochána Working Group on Trafficking in Human Beings published its report on the nature and extent of trafficking of human beings into ROI for the purposes of sexual exploitation[1]. The value of this report is that it comprehensively sets out the Irish criminal legislative landscape as regards the types of offences that human trafficking in Ireland could engage at the time and it also provided a summary of what was known about human trafficking in the EU and the south of Ireland at that time. It also detailed law enforcement measures in place in Ireland and made recommendations based on its conclusion that although not believed to be a widespread problem the ROI continued to be at risk of human trafficking. The report only refers to NI very briefly in relation to Operation Gull and the potential for cross-border co-operation in the fight against human trafficking between law enforcement agencies North and South[2].

The Anti-Human Trafficking Unit of the Department of Justice in the Republic of Ireland established in February 2008 was set up to ensure the Irish State's response to human trafficking was comprehensive, co-ordinated and holistic. It has now implemented a data strategy based on systems being developed at EU level. The goal is to collect information on cases from a variety of organisations having regard to the definition of trafficking as contained within the ROI's specific Criminal Law (Human Trafficking) Act 2008 enacted on 7 June 2008[3].

On the 21 June 2010 in ROI, the Minister for Justice and Law Reform, Mr Dermot Ahern, T.D. announced that ROI had ratified the UN Convention against Transnational Organised Crime and the Protocol to Prevent, Suppress, and Punish Trafficking in Persons, especially Women and Children.

A Special High Level Meeting on Transnational Organized Crime was held at the United Nations General Assembly to celebrate the 10th Anniversary of the adoption of the UN Convention and its additional protocols. Ms Marion Walsh, Executive Director of the Anti Human Trafficking Unit represented Ireland at that event. Ireland's instruments of ratification of the Convention and Protocol were deposited with the UN Secretary General to coincide with that Anniversary[4].

The first main piece of research relating specifically to NI was published jointly by the NI Human Rights Commission (NIHRC) and Equality Commission in 2009[5]. This report noted 'To date, as elsewhere, there is no clear data on the number of victims of trafficking in Northern Ireland. However, Government agencies and organisations working with victims noticed signs of increased activity in trafficking. Our own findings would concur with this'[6]. This report also noted the limited and ad-hoc nature of the provision of services for victims[7]. It made a number of recommendations in relation to: service provision to victims; victim identification; the training of law enforcement agencies; the criminal justice sector; data collection; and further work that the NIHRC and Equality Commission could undertake[8].

Secondly, the Anti-Trafficking Monitoring Group's (ATMG) report of June 2010 was written following a study into whether the UK was meeting its obligations under the Trafficking Convention and followed a series of seminars and interviews undertaken across the UK including NI. The ATMG report was critical of the practices in NI and made a number of recommendations[9]. When the report was released Amnesty International in NI called for a stronger response and stated that the 'identification system is clearly not fit for purpose, and we need the Assembly Government to take a strong lead in this area in order to establish an All Northern Ireland Human Trafficking Group, bringing together devolved and non-devolved departments, the PSNI, Health and Social Care Trusts and all other relevant statutory and non statutory agencies to establish an integrated approach to trafficking and thus adequately safeguard people at risk in Northern Ireland'[10].

In a letter dated 10 February 2011[11], David Ford responded positively to the ATMG and to the recommendations outlined in the ATMG report. He highlighted the re-launch of the Blue Blindfold campaign in 2011 and he confirmed that support has been available for victims of trafficking since 1 April 2009. He explained that the Public Prosecution Service (PPS) have a draft policy regarding human trafficking cases which will be issued for consultation soon. He also referred to the co-operation between different agencies and departments under the OCTF. However, we highlight that there is no victim representation on this group and there are shortcomings such as access to trauma counselling for victims in NI. We also dispute David Ford's reference to 'immigration crime' when talking about human trafficking. Clearly trafficking is primarily an issue of human rights violations. Preparation of a detailed response to the Minister is ongoing between Amnesty International in NI, the NI Law Centre and Woman's Aid.

Thirdly the scope of recent DOJ research paper on 'investigating the issues for women in NI involved in prostitution and exploring best practice elsewhere' included human trafficking in recognition that women may have been trafficked into NI and forced into prostitution. The report emphasises that 'women, or indeed men, who have been trafficked are not "prostitutes" even though they are forced to work in the industry'[12]. It stated that the research indicates that NI is a destination country as well as a transit country for victims of trafficking for sexual exploitation and that it is common for these victims to be moved across the border from NI to ROI and back again[13]. It said that human trafficking for sexual exploitation is becoming an increasing problem in NI and recommended the need for 'the DOJ, Probation Board for NI and the NI Prison Service to develop a close working relationship with the Organised Crime Branch of the DOJ, which sponsors the OCTF's Pilot to support victims of trafficking'[14]. It also called for a consistent police response to prostitution and human trafficking (see above) and for the need to raise awareness and educate the public in identifying indicators of human trafficking or prostitution[15]. The DOJ have indicated that it intends to organise a round table seminar with all relevant groups in Autumn 2011.

Finally John Vine[16] released a report in May 2011 entitled 'Inspection of the UK Border Agency in Scotland and Northern Ireland: Countering Abuse of the Common Travel Area'[17]. It is critical about the way immigration control is conducted between NI and Scotland. The report also identified problems in the way the UKBA managed the risks associated with people landing in the ROI and travelling on to the UK. It states that the UKBA were operating on intelligence which was more than two years' old[18]. It seems likely that the response to this will be an increase in enforcement and this may well have a negative impact on identifying victims of trafficking.

In June 2011 the Institute for Conflict Research in partnership with the South Tyrone Empowerment Programme, the Law Centre NI, An Munia Tober/Multi-Cultural Resource Centre and Gems NI released a report on forced labour in NI following a detailed study into forced labour among new migrants to NI. The report finds that some migrants are being seriously exploited and are subjected to working conditions which include elements of forced labour[19]. The report specifically addresses the exploitation of migrant workers in the mushroom industry, fishing industry and in the Roma community in NI and it makes a number of recommendations, an important number of which are directed at improving the identification of cases of forced labour in NI[20].

---

1. See Report of Department of Justice, Equality and Law Reform and An Garda Síochána Working Group on Trafficking in Human Beings (2006) at www.justice.ie/en/JELR/THBreport.pdf/Files/THBreport.pdf.

2. The Working Party did not engage NGOs in NI in investigating human trafficking in NI. Instead it engaged exclusively with the experiences of the Garda. The Report found: 'Garda operations have uncovered a small number of trafficking cases. These indicate the involvement of eastern European nationals, in particular nationals of Bulgaria, Romania and Lithuania, in trafficking and attempted trafficking activity. The Gardai have encountered a small number of cases of eastern European women being trafficked to Ireland for the purpose of sexual exploitation within their own ethnic communities. Two Chinese nationals (previously resident in the ROI) have been charged with serious offences in NI and in connection with alleged trafficking for the purposes of prostitution'.

3. For the most recent figures, see Anti-Human Trafficking Unit, Department of Justice and Equality, *'Annual Report of Trafficking in Human Beings in Ireland'* (2010), at page 8 it states that 'During 2010, 69 cases of alleged trafficking in human beings involving 78 alleged victims were reported to An Garda Síochána' at http://www.justice.ie/en/JELR/AHTU%202010%20Annual%20Report.pdf/Files/AHTU%202010%20Annual%20Report.pdf.

4. http://www.justice.ie.

5. Martynowicz, A, Toucas, S and Caughey, A *'The Nature and Extent of Human Trafficking in Northern Ireland, A Scoping Study'* by the Institute for Conflict Research commissioned by Northern Ireland Human Rights Commission and Equality Commission for Northern Ireland (2009).

6. Martynowicz, A, Toucas, S and Caughey, A *'The Nature and Extent of Human Trafficking in Northern Ireland, A Scoping Study'* by the Institute for Conflict Research commissioned by Northern Ireland Human Rights Commission and Equality Commission for Northern Ireland (2009) at p 32.

7. Martynowicz, A, Toucas, S and Caughey, A *'The Nature and Extent of Human Trafficking in Northern Ireland, A Scoping Study'* by the Institute for Conflict Research commissioned by Northern Ireland Human Rights Commission and Equality Commission for Northern Ireland (2009) at p 7.

8. Martynowicz, A, Toucas, S and Caughey, A *'The Nature and Extent of Human Trafficking in Northern Ireland, A Scoping Study'* by the Institute for Conflict Research commissioned by Northern Ireland Human Rights Commission and Equality Commission for Northern Ireland (2009) at pp 8–10. The recommendations included a call for a co-ordinated, multi-agency approach to be established to co-ordinate services for victims and provision of services for children and young people arriving unaccompanied and who may be at risk of internal trafficking to be given priority. It also called for an information campaign to be organised by the PSNI and specialist training to be given to the relevant organisations including the PSNI and the PPS. It called for a consultation regarding data collection. It also called for mechanisms to address forced labour within all sectors of the economy.

9. The Anti-Trafficking Monitoring Group *'Wrong Kind of Victim? One year on: an analysis of UK measures to protect trafficked persons'* (June 2010) – see Appendix 6: Issues in Northern Ireland, Scotland and Wales. The report called for the establishment of an all NI Human Trafficking Group across devolved and non-devolved, statutory and non-statutory agencies. It also called for NGOs with experience of working with victims of trafficking to be appointed

as First Responders and for the establishment of a localised NRM structure. It called for guidance from the Public Prosecution Service to improve the level of convictions of traffickers and also guidance on the non-criminalisation of trafficked persons. It called for an evaluation of the Blue Blindfold campaign and also the training available to frontline practitioners and the support available to victims. It called for an information sharing protocol across devolved and non-devolved departments. It also called for the appointment of a specific individual who would have 'lead' responsibility on the issue of trafficking. Finally it recommended that guidance continue to be issued and adequately disseminated.

[10]   Amnesty International Press Release: Trafficking in Northern Ireland: Call for stronger response dated 16 June 2010 at http://www.amnesty.org.uk/news_details.asp?NewsID= 18821.

[11]   This letter is unpublished but was circulated by Sarah Edwards of the ATMG by email dated 8 March 2011.

[12]   'Research paper investigating the issues for women in Northern Ireland involved in prostitution and exploring best practice elsewhere', Department of Justice (January 2011) at p 1 of the Executive Summary.

[13]   *'Research paper investigating the issues for women in Northern Ireland involved in prostitution and exploring best practice elsewhere'*, Department of Justice (January 2011) at p 1 of the Executive Summary.

[14]   *'Research paper investigating the issues for women in Northern Ireland involved in prostitution and exploring best practice elsewhere'*, Department of Justice (January 2011) at p 4 of the Executive Summary. The OCTF's Pilot to support victims of trafficking was how Women's Aid and Migrant Helpline were initially funded to provide support to victims.

[15]   *'Research paper investigating the issues for women in Northern Ireland involved in prostitution and exploring best practice elsewhere'*, Department of Justice (January 2011) at p 4 of the Executive Summary.

[16]   The Independent Chief Inspector of the UK Border Agency who was appointed to his post by the Home Secretary in 2008.

[17]   John Vine 'Inspection of the UK Border Agency in Scotland and Northern Ireland: Countering Abuse of the Common Travel Area – April 2010 – December 2010' http://(2011)icinspector. independent.gov.uk/wp-content/uploads/2011/05/Scotland-Northern-Ireland_Countering-abu se-of-CTA.pdf.

[18]   BBC article entitled *'UK Border Agency operations criticised in report'* dated 20 May 2011 at http://www.bbc.co.uk/news/uk-scotland-13463036.

[19]   Institute for Conflict Research *'Forced Labour in Northern Ireland: Exploiting Vulnerability'*, published by the Joseph Rowntree Foundation in June 2011 and can be found at http://ww w.jrf.org.uk. The Report finds, at page 56 'the exploitation through forced labour that we encountered was not particularly associated with human trafficking. Rather people's vulnerability to exploitation through forced labour was more likely to be associated with factors such as an individuals' legal status, their English language skills, a lack of access to advice and information and to an absence of community-based support networks. Furthermore, being subjected to forced labour conditions may further increase an individual's marginalisation and vulnerability.'

[20]   Institute for Conflict Research *'Forced Labour in Northern Ireland: Exploiting Vulnerability'*, published by the Joseph Rowntree Foundation in June 2011 – the recommendations contained in this report include that the remit of the Gangmasters' Licensing Authority be extended to include all forms of labour providers, that the research should be considered in conjunction with the ATMG's recommendations, that OFMDFM should review its funding strategy to ensure that issues of forced labour are included within their priorities, that DEL should establish a working group to address the issues associated with forced labour, that there should be a campaign to raise awareness of the issue of forced labour, there should be funding for an organisation to act as the primary point of contact for anyone reporting cases of forced labour, migrant workers who become undocumented as a result of being subjected to forced labour should be given support to re-secure their legitimate working status, there should be a working group within the trade union movement to raise awareness of forced labour issues, there also needs to be awareness of the issue amongst employers and the business community. There are also specific recommendations for each of the industries considered in the report.

THE NRM PROCESS IN NI

First Responders

8.5 The identification and referral of potential victims of trafficking in NI remains a problem. Confusion as to who can refer cases to the Competent Authority from NI remains largely unresolved. As a general rule with adult victims it is the PSNI/UKBA who act as First Responders. Migrant Helpline are also First Responders but to date it is our understanding that they have not made any referrals in NI. There are other NGOs available who would be well placed to act as First Responders such as: Bryson One-stop Service for Asylum Seekers and Woman's Aid (see below)[1]. Children in the care of social services will normally be referred by the responsible social worker usually in close collaboration with the PSNI. Frequently individuals or statutory bodies who believe that someone may be a victim have no idea what to do or who to call despite the awareness raising through the Blue Blindfold campaign.

When referrals are made, the huge backlog within UKBA means that it can take months before a reasonable grounds decision is made[2]. This results in real difficulties for the PSNI, immigration lawyers, service providers and victims alike. A senior police officer in NI disclosed to us that in cases involving nationals of the European Union the reasonable grounds decisions are taken within five days because this is done by the UKHTC but in all other of the 25 referrals made by the PSNI it has taken UKBA six months or more[3].

[1]   Neither Bryson One-stop Service nor Women's Aid are first responders for NI cases that are referred into the NRM which is different to mainland Britain where the Poppy Project and Kalayaan are first responders.

[2]   The timeframes for decisions are set out in the UKBA's guidance on Victims of Trafficking: Guidance to frontline staff, see www.ukba.homeoffice.gov.uk/sitecontent/documents/policyan dlaw/asylumprocessguidance/specialcases/guidance/trafficking-guidance?view=Binary at page 5 it states that 'the expectation is that this decision will be made within five working days of referral. If the Competent Authority finds there are reasonable grounds to believe someone is a potential victim of trafficking, they will be granted a minimum of 45 calendar days for recovery and reflection... Following a positive reasonable grounds decision, Competent Authorities are required to make a second identification decision which is to conclusively decide if the individual is a victim of trafficking. The expectation is that a conclusive grounds decision will be made in 45 calendar days.'

[3]   Our source has requested that he remain anonymous (disclosure made on 25 May 2011).

Service Provision

8.6 Woman's Aid is the lead agency providing support services and accommodation to female victims of human trafficking in NI alongside Migrant Helpline who now have the overarching responsibility for victims here[1]. Funding is provided by the Organised Crime Branch of the DOJ from the time the victims are identified in the NRM process.

Difficulties in the past have arisen where victims have been identified by service providers but not yet recognised by the Competent Authority and this has at times impeded access to appropriate accommodation and services[2].

Male victims of trafficking in NI fall outside the remit of Woman's Aid and are supported directly through Migrant Helpline. Up until very recently Migrant Helpline had no physical presence in NI at all. Its headquarters are based in

South East England. The fact that a regional office is now set up in Belfast is a welcome development but we understand that contact with Migrant Helpline still needs to be made in the first instance through its main office in Dover[3].

Once a positive conclusive decision under the NRM has been reached a victim will be expected to survive alone[4]. This can result in difficulties in relation to obtaining accommodation either privately or through the NI Housing Executive as often there is limited availability and most is frequently but not exclusively restricted to central Belfast. Given NI is a relatively small place this often poses problems for victims who fear their location may become known to their trafficker or owing to the risk of stigma or shame they perceive from their own ethnic/religious or cultural communities. It is because the communities in NI are so small that issues regarding safety and confidentiality are so very important.

Unaccompanied and separated children who are victims of trafficking[5] are supported and accommodated through the four regional Health and Social Care Trusts in NI governed by the Department of Health and Social Services (DHSSPS). Again the exact numbers of child victims of trafficking in NI is unclear[6]. Policy guidance to social services was finally issued in February 2011 after considerable delay[7]. Prior to this guidance being issued interim care orders had been obtained by the relevant NI Health Trust from the NI Family Courts[8] for unaccompanied children in individual cases and had been extremely beneficial for children who may also be victims of trafficking. This is reflected in the fact that care orders will trigger extensive support services along with the beneficial appointment of the Official Solicitor and Guardian ad Litem Agency in NI[9]. A Care Order will also carry weight in an appeal before the First Tier Tribunal (Immigration and Asylum Chamber)[10] when the UKBA are seeking to remove a child from the NI jurisdiction and back to their country of origin[11]. However, the guidance of February 2011 does not seem to specifically recommend this course of action in future.

Until fairly recently the issue of age assessment remained in stalemate. The previous two qualified Social Workers in age assessments in NI moved out of their posts leaving a vacuum for a considerable period of time. This resulted in lengthy delays where a child presented to the UKBA as being older than 18 years. The department has finally trained a number of social workers in conducting 'Merton compliant' age assessments[12].

As in the rest of the UK disappearances of potentially trafficked children at port, and whilst in social services care, has occurred and the provision of hostel/B&B type accommodation for children aged 16 and17 remains a concern[13,14].

[1] According to the DOJ, 'Comprehensive care and support services for rescued victims of human trafficking are available in Northern Ireland. Funded by DOJ and delivered by Women's Aid Federation (NI) and Migrant Helpline, the package offers access to secure accommodation, healthcare and counseling for victims of human trafficking. It also provides assistance with living expenses and full access to legal advice and translation services.' See: http://www.dojn i.gov.uk/index/media-centre/ford_addresses_human_trafficking_conference.htm.

[2] Most women Edie Shillue has met have never received the 45 day temporary admission and positive reasonable grounds decision in writing. Information provided by Edie Shillue, Bryson One Stop Service, Asylum Advice and Support Worker on 25 May 2011.

[3] Information provided at a DEL Migrant Workers Sub-Group on Friday 25 March 2011 at which Migrant Helpline gave a presentation on their work. They are now operating in NI and are principally working on trafficking issues. The lead person in NI is Roger McVicker but as

he is not employed full time in NI with Migrant Helpline he suggests that contact with Migrant Helpline should in the first instance be through Dover: http://www.migranthelpline.org.uk and 01304 203977 (Information confirmed by Roger McVicker on 15 June 2011).

4   Except where an asylum claim has been made, independently of the NRM referral, in which case accommodation and support will be provided by NASS.

5   By way of written Parliamentary question, Mark Durkan MP asked the following question: To ask the Secretary of State for the Home Department what estimate her Department has made of the number of *(a)* confirmed and *(b)* suspected cases of trafficking of children of each (i) gender and (ii) age group in or through each parliamentary constituency in Northern Ireland in each of the last three years. Damian Green MP, Minister of State for Immigration, responded:

> ' . . . [S]ince 1 April 2009 <u>eight children have been referred to the NRM by First Responders in Northern Ireland.</u> One child has been conclusively identified as a victim of trafficking for the purposes of the Trafficking Convention, four children have been found not to be victims of trafficking, in one case the child has gone missing, in another case the decision is pending and the remaining case was withdrawn.' [Emphasis underlined]. Written answer of 28 May 2011.

See http://www.publications.parliament.uk/pa/cm201011/cmhansrd/cm110328/text/110328 w0004.htm.

6   Geraghty,T, McStravick, C and Mitchell, S.'*New to Northern Ireland A study of the issues faced by migrant, asylum seeking and refugee children in Northern Ireland*' NCB Northern Ireland, (March 2010) at p 18 http://www.gulbenkian.org.uk/pdffiles/NTNI_final.pdf.

7   DHSSPS and PSNI, '*Working Arrangements for the Welfare and Safeguarding of Child Victims of Human Trafficking*', (February 2011) http://www.dhsspsni.gov.uk/oss_working_a rrangements_for_the_welfare___safeguarding_of_child_victims_of_human_trafficking.pdf.

8   The Children (NI) Order 1995.

9   The Official Solicitor is appointed to provide legal representation to people who do not have capacity to instruct a solicitor and have no-one acting on their behalf. The court has discretion in any proceedings to appoint the Official Solicitor and is often appointed in Family proceedings where a court is of the view that a child should be separately represented. The Guardian ad Litem is appointed by the court as per Article 60 of the Children Order (NI) 1995 in 'specified proceedings' being, an application for a care or supervision order, where a court has given a direction under Article 56 of the Children Order (NI)1995, on an application to vary or discharge a care or supervision order, an application under Article 58(4) of the Children Order to replace a care order with a supervision order, where the court is considering a residence order for a child who is subject to a care order, in respect of contact between a person and a child who is subject to a care order, proceedings under Part VI of the Children Order, and appeals and variations in respect of the above. This information was provided by Liam Mackle of the Children's Law Centre on 9 June 2011.

10   http://www.judiciary.gov.uk/media/tribunal-decisions/immigration-asylum-chamber.htm. On 15 February 2010, Immigration and Asylum Chambers were established in both tiers of the Unified Tribunals framework created by the Tribunals, Courts and Enforcement Act 2007. The new chambers replace the existing Asylum and Immigration Tribunal. The Upper Tribunal (Immigration and Asylum Chamber) is a superior court of record dealing with appeals against decisions made by the First-tier Tribunal (Immigration and Asylum Chamber).

11   UKBA Policy on Family members found in Chapter 8 of the Immigration Directorate Instructions (IDIs) Section 5a Annex M.

12   *R (on the Application of B) v Merton London Borough Council* [2003] EWHC 1689 (Admin), [2003]4 All ER 280, [2005] 3 FCR 69.

13   Martynowicz, A, Toucas, S and Caughey, A '*The Nature and Extent of Human Trafficking in Northern Ireland, A Scoping Study*' by the Institute for Conflict Research commissioned by Northern Ireland Human Rights Commission and Equality Commission for Northern Ireland (2009) at p 47.

14   Geraghty,T, McStravick, C and Mitchell, S. '*New to Northern Ireland A study of the issues faced by migrant, asylum seeking and refugee children in Northern Ireland*' NCB Northern Ireland, (March 2010) at p 42 http://www.gulbenkian.org.uk/pdffiles/NTNI_final.pdf.

Specialists, practitioners and lawyers in NI

8.7 Although immigration is an expanding and growing area of legal work in NI there is still no co-ordinated and holistic provision of free legal advice and agreed good practice for all victims of trafficking in NI. Should a potential victim be identified by an acting legal advisor 'out of hours' or during the weekend the adviser may often have no specialist knowledge of the complex law and nature of trafficking or any of the related implications involved at such an early stage. The delay in providing or offering specialist immigration advice at the earliest possible opportunity remains a serious problem in NI. Frequently victims of trafficking are not provided with the 'victims leaflet' about the NRM process[1] nor given an opportunity to seek specialist advice on this and other related immigration matters until very late in the day or not at all. As a result, legal practitioners are often left with limited control over outcomes. Ill-founded perceptions that the appointment of an immigration lawyer early on will delay things or result in obstacles to the criminal process still clearly prevail according to the professionals with whom we have spoken.

Similarly like the rest of the UK the fact that a victim may be subject to a number of separate legal processes remains a serious problem. Victims may inadvertently expect the immigration lawyer to provide advice and support well beyond their remit. This is one of the major flaws in the current legal system and legislative and policy-based processes that apply in trafficking cases. This deficiency in ensuring a coordinated and holistic approach very often results in wasted time, inefficient use of public funds, duplication, re-traumatisation of the victim and at times a failure to provide both trafficking-related protection and restorative justice. Many solicitors in NI do not provide casework that covers criminal, asylum, immigration, employment, civil and family law for an individual case and yet frequently trafficking cases involve many of these aspects. Furthermore, the chance that a victim could end up losing out on compensation[2] is alarming yet very probable. Training, awareness-raising and communication between NI lawyers who represent victims is still at present inadequate and there is a lack of sufficient mechanisms and monitoring in place in NI to enable good practice and ideas to be routinely shared.

Cross-border sharing of information between lawyers is generally limited to individual governance. The Law Centre in NI convenes a North/South Forum twice yearly to try to encourage sharing of information and good practice. However, its remit is not limited to issues such as trafficking and as a result only one forum to date has focused on the issue.

[1] Guidance to UKBA staff in referring cases is found at http://www.ukba.homeoffice.gov.uk/site content/documents/policyandlaw/asylumprocessguidance/specialcases/guidance/trafficking-gu idance –specifically section on what to do when a potential victim has been identified – victims leaflet.

[2] Article 15 of the Trafficking Convention establishes the right to compensation. See **CHAPTERS 15** to **18** of this Handbook which address in detail compensation for victims of trafficking.

Location of the victim

8.8 Despite the fact that there have been at least 35 victims rescued in NI it still is not clear what has happened to these individuals in many of the cases.

Some victims have been transferred out of NI for their own protection with limited data available on what subsequently occurs. Others may have been repatriated home, voluntarily or forcibly we do not know, and no publicly accessible information is available on whether or not an opportunity was provided to them to claim asylum in the UK, consent to be referred into the NRM process or seek financial compensation as a result of restorative justice. Information indicates that to date the Law Centre NI has been involved in at least 13 cases of human trafficking, some of which involve only the NRM process but others contain combinations of asylum, the NRM process and the civil litigation processes[1]. These have included sexual exploitation, forced labour, domestic servitude and exploited children from varying backgrounds and nationalities. Many of these cases, and others which are represented by other legal advisors in NI remain pending in the various legal systems referred to above but data in NI remains fragmented, inaccessible and unreliable[2].

[1]   In one case in NI a victim in domestic servitude was successful in obtaining a NI County Court Judgment for breach of contract for non-payment of wages but unfortunately the judgment was unenforceable as the trafficker had fled the NI jurisdiction leaving no assets and enforcement overseas was not a viable option. To the authors' knowledge no cases have been brought in the employment tribunals in Northern Ireland for forced labour. In addition it appears that no victim in NI has ever received compensation as a result of a successful criminal trial against a trafficker or through the criminal injuries compensation scheme. Information provided by LCNI on 13 June 2011.

[2]   Institute for Conflict Research 'Forced Labour in Northern Ireland: Exploiting Vulnerability', published by the Joseph Rowntree Foundation in June 2011 and can be found at www.jrf.org.uk. – see conclusions and recommendations section.

Interpreters

8.9 There are real concerns about the limited access and availability of independent and professional interpreting services in NI. Interpreters frequently provide services for UKBA, PSNI, legal representatives and Health Trusts alike. Issues around confidentiality and safety for victims remain. In addition minority groups in NI tend to be located in specific areas in NI where communities are small. Reliance is placed on members of the community to assist when there are no professional interpreters available for a particular language. This raises difficulties if victims are afraid of reprisals which may follow any disclosure about their location and their case to their traffickers and/or the repercussions from their own community. At times victims are advised to move out the local jurisdiction to avoid this and this raises further distress to the victim and representative alike. In addition the UKBA often obtains the services of interpreters flown over from the mainland presumably at a hefty cost to the taxpayer.

Availability of statistics and monitoring

8.10 Statistics collected by statutory agencies on trafficking victims are collated on a UK-wide basis and are not broken down regionally. Furthermore regional statistics are not recorded when an asylum claim in the UK involves an element of trafficking but the victim has not, for whatever reason, opted to go through the NRM process. Statistical data on the incidence rate of trafficking-related appeals that are heard, allowed or dismissed by the First

Tier Tribunal (Asylum and Immigration Chamber) in Belfast is to date unavailable. Neither the DOJ nor the NI Assembly collect or publish data on human trafficking in NI aside from information provided to them from the PSNI. This ultimately results in a partial picture of the extent and nature of human trafficking in NI.

THE CRIMINAL JUSTICE PROCESS IN NI

8.11 In practice any entitlement to assistance through the criminal justice process is extremely limited, ad-hoc and at times simply non-existent. There are three distinct aspects to this. First, the victim as an injured party, secondly as the witness for the prosecution against the trafficker/s and last, but certainly not least, as a defendant in the criminal justice process:

(1) The Victims as an Injured Party

Victims subjected to sexual exploitation in NI face a lengthy and traumatising time if they have alleged rape. In NI immigration lawyers acting for the victim are prohibited from attending with their clients during the interviewing process at PSNI trauma centres. This is despite the fact that any evidence the victim gives during a police interview may be used against her at a later date in other legal processes such as during any consideration of their asylum claim/appeal or NRM referral and clearly this can have implications for the victim's immigration status in the UK. Investigating officers in a rape allegation in NI are distinct from those who conduct the trafficking investigation. The current system results in a lack of adequate protection for the victim[1]. The disclosure of PSNI witness statements during a criminal investigation where the victim has alleged rape is not guaranteed and while some police officers in NI are willing to disclose copies of these statements to assist lawyers who are acting for the victim through NRM, it is frequently some time after the initial interview. This can inhibit comprehensive immigration advice and cause unnecessary delays in relation to consideration of other possible related legal claims such as asylum and/or access to compensation. In addition, disclosure of information between the PSNI and UKBA may raise problems for the victim whose account to the police and that provided to the UKBA will be compared and her credibility attacked for any differences between them, when the point of the two interviews were of course entirely distinct. This may well lead to further trauma for a victim who has no faith in anyone or anything as a result of her experiences as a trafficking victim[2].

Delay in the criminal process in NI leads to delays in conclusive decisions by the Competent Authority and where appropriate decisions about an asylum claim. UKBA frequently refuses to take decisions in relation to the trafficking identification until the criminal process is complete. Victims can be left for months without knowing what is happening in their criminal case. Certainly to the authors' knowledge there is no weekly/fortnightly or even monthly contact between victims and the PSNI. A lack of communication results in victims feeling isolated and confused and prohibits attempts by support services from providing the necessary victim support. One woman in NI who was subject to trafficking and forced prostitution was unable to avail herself of the trauma counselling organised through Woman's Aid on account of her acute distress at the lack of information provided to her in her criminal case by the PSNI.

(2)   Trafficking Victims as Prosecution Witnesses

Trafficking victims who have co-operated with the PSNI in order to investigate their traffickers have yet to obtain compensation or restorative justice by seeing their trafficker convicted under NI's criminal law. To date there have been no successful prosecutions of traffickers in NI except for those taken by the PPS under the Sexual Offences Act 2003 for offences relating to 'controlling prostitution'. Many victims never make it to give evidence against their captors or controllers in court as they are often taken into protective custody or returned to their country of origin long before the criminal case slowly plods to court. In one case involving a victim of forced labour who had been exploited in conditions of domestic servitude in NI the PPS refused to prosecute on evidential and public interest grounds despite a lengthy investigation and a recommendation to prosecute by the PSNI. The PPS has produced draft legal guidance on human trafficking to all prosecutors but it is still not finalised and no consultation or publication has taken place[3].

(3)   Trafficking victims as defendants

One barrister in NI who has prosecuted in several cases 'involving' human trafficking elements was able to shed some light on the current situation[4]. In a nutshell victims of trafficking who are working as prostitutes in NI are never prosecuted for offences under the Sexual Offences Act 2003. The cases are normally only prosecuted if they can be made out on the police evidence, which can include them posing as customers. Generally these cases will fail on public interest grounds.

Regarding the link between trafficking and cannabis cultivation, in one recent case a potential victim was identified in a cannabis factory in NI. The person was screened and made allegations which were investigated but could not be substantiated. She was referred to the NRM and a negative decision by UKBA was received. She was then prosecuted for drug cultivation offences and after lengthy investigations, prosecution proceedings and court preparation, which lasted over a year, the Crown Court trial commenced. On the first day of the trial, the case was immediately stopped and the judge made comment in court that the defendant was quite obviously a victim of trafficking before dismissing the charges. This individual was in custody for over a year and now remains in immigration detention[5]. This case clearly shows not only a huge waste of much needed resources but, over and above that, a gross failure by the NI authorities to protect the rights of that victim in accordance with the Convention[6].

Another significant case is that of SK, an asylum seeker who claimed to have been imprisoned and raped daily for four months at an unknown location in Belfast. She had alleged that up to five different men carried out sex assaults on her after she arrived in NI to avoid a forced marriage in her native Guinea. The PSNI did not believe her and she was charged with perverting the course of justice and wasting police time after medical examinations allegedly failed to back up her account. Bail was granted on the basis of SK being tagged and placed under a curfew. She was heavily pregnant at the time. The judge in the High Court in Belfast who heard the bail application, Lord Justice Girvan, pointed out that her asylum request must be processed separately through the normal immigration tribunal system. He added: 'She may have no claim for asylum and it may be that her claim of trafficking will be shown to be false'. It was also conceivable, but not noted by the judge, that her trafficking claim might of course have been true. It was an extraordinary decision on the part of the PPS to go ahead and prosecute this woman while the trafficking identification matter in particular remained outstanding. The woman has now given birth. The PSNI have dropped the charges against her. The negative reasonable grounds decision by UKBA remains[7].

[1] The Anti-Trafficking Monitoring Group '*Wrong Kind of Victim? One year on: an analysis of UK measures to protect trafficked persons*' (June 2010) – see Appendix 6: Issues in Northern Ireland, Scotland and Wales.
[2] Guidance to UKBA staff in referring cases is found at www.ukba.homeoffice.gov.uk/sitecont ent/documents/policyandlaw/asylumprocessguidance/specialcases/guidance/trafficking-guidan ce. It specifically addresses the fact that information at the referral stage of the NRM process should be comprehensive to avoid re-traumatisation of victims given their vulnerability in having to repeat their story.
[3] In David Ford's letter to the ATMG dated 10 February 2011 he states, 'The PPS has produced in draft form a policy on cases of Human Trafficking for prosecutors. This is being reviewed and when finalised will issue for consultation' (this letter is unpublished).
[4] This information has been provided by Philip Henry, Bar Library Belfast.
[5] Information provided by a Senior Police Officer of the PSNI on 25 May 2011.
[6] Such as the right to be identified as a victim of trafficking under Article 10 of the Trafficking Convention and the right to be afforded assistance under Article 12, both taken with the non-punishment provision under Article 26 of that Convention. See the relevant chapters on Identification and on Trafficked Victims in the Criminal Justice System in this Handbook.
[7] Belfast Telegraph article entitled 'Refugee's rape claims "untrue"' dated 25 January 2011 http://www.belfasttelegraph.co.uk/news/local-national/northern-ireland/refugeersquos-rape-cl aims-lsquountruersquo-15063529.htmland information confirmed by LCNI.

JUDICIAL REVIEW IN NI

8.12 As far as the authors are aware there have been at least four Judicial Reviews (JRs) in the High Court in Belfast in trafficking cases, two heard and two pending the outcome. There have also been at least two cases in the First Tier Tribunal (Immigration and Asylum Chamber) in Belfast adjourned because of extant JRs in the High Court. The first two JRs involved a 'root and branch' challenge to the NRM process and were heard by Treacy J in the summer of 2010. (*Xai Xai Weng 2009 No. 06992/01 & Meng Ting Xu*). The cases took issue with the legality of the NRM and raised fundamental questions about whether or not the Trafficking Convention was even justiciable in a domestic court as it has not yet been incorporated into domestic law unlike the European Convention of Human Rights (ECHR). The cases also challenged the NRM policy approach to the very definition of who could be a 'victim' under Article 4(e) of the Trafficking Convention. Both cases concerned young Chinese women who had consented to travel to the UK but who had been subjected to slavery, forced labour and/or sexual exploitation during transit and upon arrival in the UK. Both women managed to extricate themselves from the traffickers and live 'free' lives in the UK for some time until detected by the authorities when they claimed they were victims. As the book was going to print the authors were informed that the lead application for leave to apply for JR in the case of *Xai Xai Weng & Meg Ting Xu*[1] was dismissed on all grounds in a judgment by Treacy J on 7 September 2011. All other JRs sitting behind this lead trafficking case were adjourned pending consideration of the judgment. At this stage it is anticipated that the matter is to be appealed to the Court of Appeal.

[1]   TRE 8283(2) 2011.

SUMMARY

8.13 Human trafficking in NI is a growing problem and there is increasing recognition that this needs to be dealt with, as evidenced by the debate in the NI Assembly in September 2010 and following the ATMG's recommendations in their report. The Justice Minister's response to this is to be commended, but, there is still much to be done in terms of guaranteeing early access to specialist legal advice, adequate victim support and protection, collecting accurate data, establishing a multi-agency inclusive and victim-focused group, developing an efficient cross-border information-sharing protocol, improving the NRM system, and requiring frontline PSNI officers to be properly trained in identifying and working with victims of trafficking. It is also imperative that the PPS publishes its draft guidance for prosecutors on human trafficking, and opens this up for public consultation, as a matter of high priority.

Part III

PERSPECTIVES ON SUPPORTING VICTIMS

Contents

9

ON THE SAFE SIDE: PROVIDING CHILDREN WHO HAVE BEEN TRAFFICKED WITH SAFE ACCOMMODATION IN THE UK

Christine Beddoe, Kayte Fairfax and Andrew Howard

INTRODUCTION

9.1

> 'When you are trafficked, you need to be moved as far as possible from where you're living before, that would be the first step to safety. The second is to make sure the place is safe so that there's no way that people can just walk in and out, or put you with a foster carer who doesn't really care much about your safety. Safety [has]to be taken seriously. I think it should be the main priority [as], there's no future when you're not safe.'(Young person, ECPAT UK youth group)

Every year hundreds of children are trafficked into and within the UK. Many children who are trafficked or suspected as having been trafficked are placed in accommodation provided by local authorities. The quality of this accommodation varies significantly and as ECPAT UK has identified there are no commonly agreed safety and protection standards for the placement of children who are suspected or known to be trafficked across the UK. As a result, children are left vulnerable to going missing and the risk of being re-trafficked is increased.

ECPAT UK is highly concerned about the number of child victims of trafficking who go missing from local authority care and become vulnerable to further exploitation. The 2007 report, *Missing Out: A Study of Child Trafficking in the North-West, North-East and West Midlands*[1], found that a high number of separated children thought to be trafficked were going missing from local authority care, never to be found again. Of the 80 cases of known or suspected child victims identified in the report, 52 children (64%) went missing from social services care, of which only four were located.

These concerns were picked up in political circles. In 2009, the Home Affairs Select Committee report on human trafficking raised concerns about suspected child victims in local authority care who go permanently missing. The Committee was particularly alarmed by accounts that traffickers may be using the 'care home system for vulnerable children as holding pens for their victims until they are ready to pick them up'[2]. In May 2009, the then Prime Minister, Gordon Brown, described the situation of potentially trafficked children going missing as 'completely unacceptable'[3]. Recent research conducted by CEOP[4] has also confirmed that the numbers of trafficked children who go missing from local authority care is significant.

In the light of ECPAT UK's findings in 2007 and to help support efforts to find safe accommodation options for children who have been trafficked, ECPAT UK began to explore the issues around what makes accommodation safe for children who may have been trafficked. During 2010 and early 2011 face-to-face interviews and a roundtable discussion were held with professionals from local authority children's services, the police, NGOs and organisations accommodating child victims. The interviews and roundtable both sought to answer two key questions: what makes accommodation safe for trafficked children and what makes them feel safe. ECPAT UK is committed to young people's participation and has made every effort to include comments and opinions of children and young people who have been trafficked to the UK. Members of the ECPAT UK Youth Group for child victims of trafficking have input into our work on safe accommodation.

This is an extract of a more comprehensive report to be published in Summer 2011. It outlines 10 child-centred principles around safe accommodation that emerged from ECPAT UK's research. These 10 principles are intended to guide professional practice on the provision of accommodation and support to children who have been trafficked. They are not intended to form a definitive list, but aim to contribute to a wider national discussion about quality standards of care for some of the most vulnerable children in the UK. Safe accommodation is central to all other protection measures and prevention strategies for children who are at risk of going missing.

[1]   ECPAT UK, *Missing Out: A Study of Child Trafficking in the North-West, North-East and West Midlands* (2007).

[2]   The Trade in Human Beings: Human Trafficking in the UK, Home Affairs Select Committee, (May 2009) http://www.publications.parliament.uk/pa/cm200809/cmselect/cmhaff/23/2302. htm.

[3]   492 HC Official Report (6th series) col 853, 13 May 2009 http://www.publications.parliam ent.uk/pa/cm200809/cmhansrd/cm090513/debtext/90513-0003.htm.

[4]   The Child Exploitation and Online Protection Centre's (CEOP) Strategic Threat Assessment, *Child Trafficking in the UK*, published in December 2010, focussed on data collected from 1 March 2009 to 28 February 2010. During this time CEOP identified 287 potential child victims of trafficking in the UK. Many of these children went missing from local authority care: 42 children were still recorded as missing by the end of the study. CEOP found that '[t]he number of potential victims of trafficking who go missing from local authority provided care continues to be a major theme. Sixty-seven per cent (28) were Vietnamese nationals and 17% (7) were Chinese [the remaining children were from other countries]. A number of Vietnamese children who went missing were rediscovered in cannabis factories. Local authority provided care is sometimes failing to prevent victims returning to exploitation, although there are cases where supportive care has prevented this.' Executive Summary, page 6.

SAFE ACCOMMODATION – 'BRINGING SAFETY TO THE CHILD'

9.2

> 'Safety has to be taken seriously. It should be the main priority . . . there's no future when you're not safe, there's nothing there if you're not safe.' (Young person, ECPAT UK youth group)

As ECPAT UK outlined in *Missing Out* (2007), safe accommodation involves more than just the provision of accommodation in a confidential location. It also spans the range of specialised responses to the child's physical, psychological, legal, language and security needs. Most importantly, it must include the child's own perception of safety – ie, how safe any measure or accommodation option makes *them* feel. A child-centred approach to safe accommodation 'brings safety to the child' through a range of integrated supports provided by local authorities and specialist agencies. It takes their particular set of needs as a starting point, uses a multi-agency approach where possible and recognises that what constitutes safe accommodation can differ from one child to the next, and can change over time.

In practice human trafficking is not well understood across all local authority areas and very few children are housed in what could be termed 'safe accommodation'. Instead they can end up in any one of a vast array of accommodation types across the UK. These include generic emergency or longer-term foster care; general children's homes or residential units; reception and assessment centres for unaccompanied young people; specialised but limited 'trafficking-aware' foster care (with some specialist training and/or support related to trafficking); and residential units for separated children. Children aged 16 to 18 years can be placed in semi-independent accommodation for children[1], emergency accommodation in Bed and Breakfast (B&B) or hostel accommodation.

In 2008, the UK Government ratified the Council of Europe Convention on Action against Trafficking in Human Beings ('the Trafficking Convention') which, amongst other protections for victims of trafficking, promotes the recovery of victims including the provision of 'appropriate and secure accommodation, psychological and material assistance'[2]. The Trafficking Convention entered into force in the UK on 1 April 2009.

The Explanatory Report to the Trafficking Convention states that:

> '164. Under Article 12(2) each Party must take due account of victims' safety and protection needs. Victims' needs can vary widely depending on their personal circumstances. They may arise from matters such as age or gender, or from circumstances such as the type of exploitation the victim has undergone, the country of origin, the types and degree of violence suffered, isolation from his or her family and culture, knowledge of the local language, and his or her material and financial resources. It is therefore essential to provide measures that take victims' safety fully into account. For example, the address of any accommodation needs to be kept secret and the accommodation must be protected from any attempts by traffickers to recapture the victims.'

More recently, in March 2011, the UK committed itself to opt into the EU Directive on Preventing and Combating Trafficking in Human Beings and Protecting Victims[3]. The Directive amongst other things requires the UK Government to provide child victims with assistance, support and protection and that in providing these requirements 'the child's best interests shall be a primary consideration'[4]. Moreover the Directive requires the Government to assist and support 'the physical and psycho-social recovery' of child victims of trafficking, based on the special, individual circumstances of each child victim and by taking into account the child's views, needs and concerns with a view to finding a durable solution for the child[5]. The Directive also introduces the requirement that in certain circumstances a guardian or representative for a child victim of trafficking must be appointed from the moment the child is identified by the authorities to ensure the child's best interests are met[6].

[1]   Such shared housing rented by the local authority either directly or through a provider, where several young people aged over 16 live together, each with an allocated worker from the local authority, and sometimes extra support staff where a provider is used.

[2]   Trafficking Convention, Article 12. See too the Preamble to the Trafficking Convention which confirms that 'all actions or initiatives against trafficking in human beings must be non-discriminatory, take gender equality into account as well as a child-rights approach'.

[3]   Directive 2011/36/EC of the European Parliament and of the Council of 5 April 2011 on preventing and combating trafficking in human beings and protecting its victims, and replacing Council Framework Decision 2002/629/JHA. The Directive will enter into force in April 2013.

[4]   Directive 2011/36/EC of 5 April 2011, Article 13.

[5]   Directive 2011/36/EC of 5 April 2011, Article 14.

[6]   Directive 2011/36/EC of 5 April 2011, Article 15.

10 Principles of safe accommodation for children who have been trafficked

9.3   Child trafficking is a complex form of child abuse that requires a robust safeguarding response within a child protection framework. ECPAT UK proposes the following 10 principles to guide professional practice on the provision of accommodation and support to children who may have been trafficked. It is not intended to be a definitive list, but aims to contribute to a national discussion about quality standards of care for some of the most vulnerable children in the UK.

Principle 1: The best interests of the child should be at the centre of all decisions regarding the provision of accommodation and related supports

9.4   Children who have been trafficked are amongst the most vulnerable group of children in the UK, even after they are identified and placed in care. It is therefore imperative that their best interests are at the forefront of decisions taken to safeguard them and to ensure that the supports they receive are comprehensive and assist them to recover. The UN Convention on the Rights of the Child (UNCRC), which the UK ratified in 1991, supports this view, stating that the best interests of the child should be a primary consideration in all actions concerning children, whether undertaken by public or private social welfare institutions, courts of law, administrative authorities or legislative bodies[1].

ECPAT UK believes that placing the best interests of the child at the centre of all decisions regarding the provision of accommodation and related supports to children who have been trafficked is fundamental to keeping the child safe.

Taking this approach requires a multi-agency response, with a high level of co-ordination and agreement between all services which provide care and support, including accommodation providers, local authorities, police, health professionals and lawyers. It must also involve the child being made aware of their rights and participating as much as possible in decisions taken on their behalf.

[1] UN Convention on the Rights of the Child, Article 3(1).

Principle 2: Children should be asked about what makes them feel safe

9.5 The UN Convention on the Rights of the Child enshrines the right for children to participate in decision-making processes that affect their lives and to influence decisions taken on their behalf[1]. This reflects the belief that children are people who have the right to express their views about situations that affect them and to have those views taken into account. While this does not mean that a child's views will automatically be acted upon, it provides for a process during which the child can gain an understanding of why certain decisions are being taken.

ECPAT UK believes that children who have been trafficked should be fully involved in discussions that impact upon their lives. Asking a child about what would make them feel safe and involving them in decisions relating to their accommodation and support can help them regain a sense of control in their life, and thereby help to reduce their risk of going missing and potentially being re-trafficked.

It is also imperative that children who have been trafficked are given the right support and encouragement over the long term to help them understand and feel able to express what would make them feel safe. This process must be undertaken by professionals who have a clear understanding of the serious obstacles that these children face when trying to articulate their feelings and needs.

[1] UN Convention on the Rights of the Child, Article 12.

Principle 3: Safe accommodation should be understood as multi-faceted, involving physical and psychological elements, with particular recognition of the impact of trauma on a child's perceptions and behaviour

9.6 Children who have been abused and exploited have been through traumatic experiences that can impact on their sense of safety and behaviour. But the trauma of trafficking, particularly for children trafficked from abroad, has extra layers of complexity relating to the experience of multiple abuse over what can be many years, including the loss of family and identity. The psychological impact of trafficking and exploitation on women and children is well documented[1], and can include the development of post-traumatic stress disorder (PTSD) and other physical and mental health conditions. This will impact on the child's needs and their perceptions of safety and can influence a child's behaviour in ways that carers and other professionals can struggle to understand and respond appropriately to. Yet an understanding of trauma is essential to undertake accurate risk and needs assessments as accommodating a child safely includes creating an environment where they can recover from trauma and rebuild a sense of safety and control.

ECPAT UK believes that safe accommodation for children must address the complex interrelationship between a child's physical security needs and any emotional or psychological issues that impact on their behaviour and perceptions of safety. Trauma in particular can make a child feel extremely unsafe, even when the actual risk from their traffickers is reduced.

Children need to be accommodated in a placement, with a range of safety measures in place that are appropriate to the child's needs and level of risk. The accommodation should incorporate a broad range of supports, including counselling that reflects an understanding of the fact that children who have been trafficked have often suffered tremendous physical, sexual or psychological abuse.

[1] C. Zimmerman et al, *'Stolen smiles: The physical and psychological health consequences of women and adolescents trafficked in Europe'* London School of Hygiene and Tropical Medicine (2006).

Principle 4: A child's accommodation and safety needs will change over time and should be regularly assessed

9.7 Every child who has been trafficked is an individual with a unique history, set of circumstances, experience of abuse, grief and trauma, and hopes for the future. They have their own understanding of trafficking and exploitation, feelings about being a victim, and perceptions of risk and safety. As a child grows older and begins to recover a sense of safety and rebuild their life, their needs will invariably change. Risks to the child or their family from traffickers can also develop unpredictably at any point of a child's care, such as when a child is a witness at their trafficker's trial or the trafficker is released from prison. These factors all create a unique set of needs and level of risk for each child that must be regularly assessed to ensure that the most appropriate accommodation and support package is being provided to a child at any point in time.

ECPAT UK believes it is crucial to treat children as individuals and that their accommodation and safety needs and the level of risk they are at, or perceive themselves to be at, must be assessed on a regular basis so as to provide them with the most appropriate level of care and support. While children should not be expected to direct their care, asking them about what makes them feel safe should be a critical part of any assessment and ongoing reassessments. This can help professionals avoid making assumptions about a child's needs based on a broad-brush understanding of trafficking or factors such as a child's cultural background, age, gender or type of exploitation.

It is also imperative that children transitioning from childhood to adulthood at 18 are supported appropriately, addressing the current and future risks and needs as a victim of trafficking. An assumption must not be made that just because they have turned 18 they no longer require support.

Principle 5: Safety measures should be implemented to reduce a child's risk of going missing, especially within 24 to 72 hours after first contact with the child

9.8 Children who have been trafficked can face incredible pressure to return to their traffickers. When their journey is interrupted by a referral to the police, local authority or other agency, they and their families can face serious reprisals from their traffickers. Children found in transit areas like a port authority or airport are especially likely to run away as their intended destination is elsewhere in the UK. The first 24 to 72 hours after first contact with a child is therefore a critical time to give a child information about the risks facing them and to implement 'safety measures' to help protect a child from their traffickers and prevent them going missing. This period of time is sometimes referred to as the 'golden hour' or 'golden day'. Many professionals have reported using safety measures, and increasingly they are incorporating them into protocols, safety plans and good practice guides. However, debate exists as to how to strike the right balance between 'care and control' in trying to maximise a child's safety and minimise their risk, and how to best work with children to help them understand why certain actions are being taken to try and keep them safe. The decision to accommodate a child outside of the area where they were exploited can be an important early step in attempting to reduce the chance of the child being re-trafficked and/or going missing.

ECPAT UK believes that safety measures must be part of a robust and integrated plan that manages risks around the child and at the same time reduces their risk of going missing. These must be implemented immediately on first contact with a child and the child must be involved in discussions about the measures taken to keep them safe. Crucially, children must be informed of the risks they face if they go missing. This must, however, be done sensitively, with an appreciation of the pressure that the children might be facing to return to their traffickers or to simply run away from what they perceive to be an unsuitable environment.

It is also imperative that children are removed as far as possible from the area where they were found to be exploited. In this sense, ECPAT UK would like to see the development of reciprocal placement arrangements between local authorities.

Principle 6: A child should not feel punished or overly restricted by measures taken to help keep them safe in accommodation

9.9 Trafficking is a form of child abuse that often takes away a child's sense of control over their life and greatly restricts their freedom of movement. Some child victims of trafficking have never had a sense of their own identity and many have not been able to make their own decisions or choices. It is important, therefore, that efforts to keep children safe do not mirror the child's experience of being controlled in any way that replicates their trafficking experience.

ECPAT UK believes that children who have been trafficked should not be made to feel punished or overly restricted by the security measures taken to keep them safe in accommodation. While a balance must clearly be found between safety and freedom, care providers must be at pains not to replicate the child's past experience of being controlled.

Where possible a child's safety plan should be developed in consultation with the child. This can help professionals to understand what the child's needs and perceptions of risk are at that point in time, including how certain measures could potentially impact on a child's level of trauma. It can also help the child understand how and why certain safety measures are being implemented, and for what period of time, and give them the option to opt-in to certain measures, for example, the non-use of mobile phones[1]. Any safety plan should take an individual approach that develops an accommodation and support package appropriate to the needs and level of risk unique to that child at that point in time.

[1] The link between the trafficker and a trafficked child is often maintained via mobile phone, internet or agency contact. This risk is well established. Indeed, as CEOP found in its Strategic Threat Assessment, 'Child Trafficking in the UK' 2010, 'It has been demonstrated that monitoring the child's use of phone and internet communication and not allowing unsupervised visits from strangers will decrease the likelihood of children running away since communication with the trafficker is broken.' (at page 21).

Principle 7: A child should be given access to a range of psychological, educational, health, social, legal, financial and language support that 'brings safety to the child' and helps them recover

9.10 Safe accommodation involves many more elements than finding a child a secure placement in a secret location. Children who have been trafficked also need a range of integrated supports provided by local authorities and specialist agencies that address their psychological, educational, health, social, legal, financial, language, cultural and religious needs amongst others. These supports are essential to a child's development and recovery, and many are also basic human rights. In order to be able to recover from the abuse of trafficking, children need stability, consistency and access to a range of services that meet their developmental needs and address the impacts of abuse. A multi-agency, multi-disciplinary approach can be a particularly effective way of 'bringing safety to the child' and minimising the chance of overlooking risks to their safety.

A child's safety plan should also assess the risk of all service provision outside the placement, including all potential points of access that a potential trafficker could have to the child.

Safe accommodation is the foundation on which other specialist agencies rely on to ensure that the child is in the best environment for recovery and stability.

Principle 8: Everyone working with children who have been trafficked should be trained to recognise and respond appropriately to their needs

9.11 Trafficking is a highly complex form of child abuse that requires a robust and informed safeguarding response. To accommodate children safely, professionals need knowledge about trafficking indicators, the trafficking process and the impact of exploitation and trauma on a child's development, behaviour and sense of safety. They need to be able to undertake ongoing risk assessments prior to and during a placement; identify a child's needs and know how to respond to them; develop individualised safety plans to minimise the risk of children going missing; and work with other agencies in the child's best interests to bring safety to the child. Most of the accommodation providers that ECPAT UK spoke to as part of this research were using specialist trainers including ECPAT UK, while others were developing in-house training and/or building trafficking into existing child protection training. However they identified gaps around the type and level of training being provided.

Carers need to be trained on range of issues to become 'trafficking aware' in a way that helps the young person feel protected, secure and comfortable. Issues identified by professionals and young people in ECPAT UK's youth group include:

(i)   *Awareness and sensitivity:* of the child's trauma/past experience including trauma, and what the child needs to feel safe and recover;

(ii)   *Autonomy:* awareness of the level of autonomy and independence that a child may have had prior to being trafficked;

(iii) *Confidentiality and privacy:* not being 'gossiped' about by the carer; not being introduced to other people as a victim of trafficking;

(iv)   *Fairness:* being treated with same level of respect and attention as other children in the family. Children have felt singled out and badly treated as the 'trafficked child' in a residential unit or foster family;

(v)   *Freedom:* not feeling overly restricted or punished by security measures used to keep them safe;

(vi)   *Support:* Having someone 'on their side'.

ECPAT UK believes that training is essential for all those people who work with trafficked children in a residential or foster care setting. They should be trained on range of issues, particularly on the impact of trauma, to become 'trafficking aware' in a way that helps children feel protected, secure and comfortable. The quality of this 'trafficking aware' training is also very important in that it can have a major impact on the development of personal relationships between such children and their carers, which can be so important to the children's sense of feeling safe, secure, supported and understood.

Principle 9: Children should be given sufficient information to help them make informed decisions about their accommodation and care

9.12 This is a core principle that should underscore any effort to involve children in discussions about their care including asking about what makes them feel safe (Principle 2) and designing appropriate support (Principle 7). Professionals have shared with ECPAT UK that children do not always see themselves as a trafficking victim or understand the risks facing them, especially if they return to their traffickers. Children also face enormous challenges in navigating highly complex bureaucracy involved in welfare and immigration systems.

ECPAT UK believes that for children to engage meaningfully in decisions about their own accommodation and care, they need to be kept informed about their current circumstances, what may have happened to them (the trafficking process), their care and placement plans, the immigration process, any ongoing criminal investigations with respect to their traffickers, and their human rights and entitlements. While all professionals should strive to implement this principle, an independent guardian or advocate for the child can be especially useful in this regard.

Whilst respecting the child's wishes and feelings, it is incumbent on professionals to understand that the child may be still in the control of the trafficker, or influenced by threats and coercion. The wishes of the child may in fact be the result of grooming by the trafficker or fear of retribution. In this situation a 'best interest' determination may not be what the child wants or immediately feels comfortable with, however whatever the circumstances the child needs to know exactly why decisions are being made and have information provided to them about the decision making process.

Children should also be given information in their own language with access to trained interpreters, using concepts that are appropriate to their age and culture, and at a pace that is sensitive to their level of trauma and ability to learn.

Principle 10: Efforts to keep children safe should involve the wider community

9.13 A number of Local Authorities through their Local Safeguarding Children Board, have developed a 'trafficking subgroup' to develop a multi-agency approach to capacity building, sharing resources and policy development that involves wider community networks and sources of community 'intelligence'. Sharing relevant information about the risks of child trafficking across the local community can increase crime reports, establish new networks for information gathering and breakdown the culture of disbelief that can prevent vulnerable children from getting access to appropriate support and safe accommodation.

Practice points shared by professionals

9.14 The following practice points have been shared with ECPAT UK by child welfare professionals based on their learning around what helps keep trafficked children safe and helps them to feel safe. Some points have also arisen from comments made by young people in ECPAT UK's youth group for children who have been trafficked. Like the set of 10 principles, these practice points are not intended to be a definitive list, but aim to add to a growing national body of knowledge on promising and good practice around the provision of safe and supported accommodation for children who may have been trafficked.

Principle 1

9.15 The best interests of the child should be at the centre of all decisions regarding the provision of safe accommodation and related support

- Professionals should meet face to face as soon as possible after first contact with a child to: (a) help reach a shared determination of the child's best interests; (b) seek and include the child's own views on what makes them feel safe; and (c) seek to establish how the child prioritises their own needs.
- Keep the child's needs at the forefront of decision making regarding their accommodation to reduce the risk of making resource-led decisions that do not meet the child's needs.
- Information-sharing about a child's case should be on a 'need to know' basis.

Principle 2

9.16 Children should be asked about what makes them feel safe

- Ask the child about what emotional, physical, environmental and other factors would help them to feel safe but with an understanding that the child may not know. Feed this information into the ongoing trafficking assessment process and care planning.
- Give the young person information about what has helped other young people feel safe.
- Speak with the child regularly about their placement and in an environment where they feel able to speak freely, eg, away from foster carers. Consider using an independent reviewer.
- Ask the child questions in a sensitive way that does not 'assume a right to go and question children' or that could further traumatise them.
- Be sensitive to the child's level of comfort with their interpreter and ability to understand them.
- Keep a record of what the child says, and check its accuracy with the child.

Principle 3

9.17 Safe accommodation should be understood as multi-faceted, involving physical and psychological elements, with particular recognition of the impact of trauma on a child's perceptions and behaviour

- Be sensitive when discussing a child's case when they can hear (eg discussion between foster carers and social worker on home visit). Think about the child's needs, views and wishes when selecting a placement. Avoid assumptions about culture, religion and gender – children may have other needs that are a higher priority. Give the child access to independent representation where possible, eg independent guardian or advocate who has a specific knowledge of the child's history.
- Be sensitive and understanding to the child's needs and feelings.

Principle 4

9.18 A child's accommodation and safety needs will change over time and should be regularly assessed

- Regularly review the placement with input from the carer, social worker, where relevant the police and of course the child.
- Question children away from their carer in a place where they feel able to speak freely.
- Assess whether the placement has or could become compromised. Assess whether the placement is working, any new risks to the child, whether there has been any contact with traffickers or other people known to the child, the safety of the child's use of technology (eg mobile phone, internet).
- Change the placement if the placement becomes compromised or the child needs to change it. Have a rapid-response contingency plan already worked out.
- Build a 'reducing safety net' into the care plan that responds to a reduction in risk and any increase in a child's desire for more autonomy and independence.
- Engage adult services sufficiently early in the child's care to ensure a child's needs are met when making the transition from being looked after to living as an independent adult.
- Train Emergency staff to identify trafficking indicators and be able to link suspected child victims into specialist professional support and police investigation.

Principle 5

9.19 Safety measures should be implemented to reduce a child's risk of going missing, especially within 24 to 72 hours after first contact with the child

- Where possible use safe accommodation out of the area in which the child was exploited.
- Multi-agency planning will help to identify security measures linked to local police.
- Keep the location of the child's placement confidential (other than to the police).
- Give the child information in first 24 hours about risks of going missing and how to come back (eg laminated contact cards with an emergency telephone number).
- Ask the child what helps make them feel safe and explain to the child why and how safety measures are being used.
- Take immediate practical steps to establish the child's identity on first contact and to keep the child safe (ie photograph child, CCTV, escorted movement, removal of mobile phone/sim cards).
- Develop a local practice guide based on the most effective safety actions to take in the first 24–48 hours after first contact with a child – and update it regularly.
- Develop an individualised 24/7 safety plan for each child. Consider inclusion of voluntary 'opt-in' elements for the child (eg agreeing to not use their mobile phone). Involve the foster carer, schools and other service providers where relevant.
- Consider which rooms would be safest for child victims, eg rooms on upper floors, away from main entry/exit doors.

- Train foster carers to watch out for risks in areas surrounding the placement, eg for loitering persons or cars driving up and down the road. Foster carers should be aware of people approaching or making contact with the child and report any concerns.
- Observe and act on early warning signs that the child might go missing – build knowledge of early warning indicators and feed these into the development of safety plans and 'golden hour' safety measures.
- Consider the risks to the child of the behaviour and possessions of other children in placements, eg the lending of phones. When two children are referred together, consider that one may be a chaperone or in contact with the trafficker.

Principle 6

9.20 A child should not feel punished or overly restricted by measures taken to help keep them safe in accommodation

- Give the child a detailed explanation of why and how safety measures are being used and for how long. Regularly review the use of safety measures as part of a 'reducing safety net' built into a child's safety plan that responds to a reduction in risk and any increase in a child's desire for more autonomy and independence.
- Give the child their own room where possible, with a door that locks from the inside.
- Find ways to help the child stay in contact with their friends and family of origin where it is safe to do so particularly where the care plan involves removing the child's mobile phone.
- Consider the inclusion of voluntary 'opt-in' elements in the child's safety plan (eg agreeing to not use their mobile phone and no visits without supervision).

Principle 7

9.21 A child should be given access to a range of psychological, educational, health, social, legal, economic and language support that 'brings safety to the child' and helps them recover

- A child's safety plan should address the risk of all service provision outside the placement, including all potential points of access that a potential trafficker could have to the child.
- Provide accommodation in locations which also can provide the child with access to education and appropriate health care necessary for the health and well-being of children who have experienced trauma and violence, such as specialist counselling.
- Provide long term (ie permanent) carers who are available 24 hours a day as this can provide the child with the possibility of developing personal relationships.
- Provide young people with independent legal advice concerning their welfare and immigration matters.

Principle 8

9.22 Everyone working with children who have been trafficked should be trained to recognise and respond appropriately to their needs

- Conduct multi-agency training for all staff that are involved in identification, assessment and accommodation provision. Review and update training.
- Inform the police that the placement is accommodating a child at risk and ask them what additional measures could be put in place to make it a safe placement.
- Train foster carers to be aware of indicators or risk and what to do about it.

Principle 9

9.23 Children should be given sufficient information to help them make informed decisions about their accommodation and care

- Wherever possible, give children access to documents that are written about them (for example, their personal files and care plans) at all times. Use language and concepts they understand and provide access to interpreters.
- Explain to children about what happened to them (ie the trafficking process) and they are a victim of crime and the risks they face if they return to their traffickers.
- Explain to children how various accommodation options will impact on their day-to-day life, especially the differences between shared and independent living.
- Help children understand their statutory entitlements and rights.
- Let children know they are entitled to change their mind, express their feelings and ask for more support or a different placement.
- Update, share and explain care plans/pathways to young people that map out what accommodation and support will be provided to assist them towards independent living.
- Explain professional relationships to children such as the relationship between their foster carer and social worker.

Principle 10

9.24 Efforts to keep children safe should involve the wider community

- Local Safeguarding Children Boards should ensure they have a child trafficking sub-group or focal point that allows relevant information to be shared with and from the community networks on child trafficking.

CONCLUSION

9.25 In the UK there are no official quality standards for 'safe accommodation' for children who may be trafficked. There are pockets of good practice emerging, but no regulatory framework or inspection regime to ensure children are guaranteed a particular standard of 'safeness'. Accommodation provision for all separated children should be based on the fundamental principle of what is in the best interests of the child. However, when a child has been harmed, or is still at risk of harm, professionals need to understand how key factors relevant to that child's situation can render accommodation unsafe. Safe accommodation is integral to recovery and stability but it is also essential to the prevention of re-trafficking. It is poor professional judgment to believe that just because a trafficked child is taken out of an immediate situation of danger (eg a brothel, a cannabis factory or a situation of servitude) that they are no longer at risk of harm. Children can still be under the control of traffickers or feel threatened by traffickers while they are in local authority care. Accommodation should not be viewed as a one-size-fits-all approach: the benefits of any particular form of accommodation must depend on the particular child's personal needs and circumstances, including their relationship to their trafficker/s and others who may threaten or harm them. Also of crucial importance is the need to address the young person's sense of personal autonomy and their ability to live independently and safely. Above all it is important to ask children what makes them feel safe: but to be aware that they alone must not be expected to direct the process of keeping themselves safe.

SAFETY AND SUPPORT FOR VICTIMS OF TRAFFICKING FOR SEXUAL EXPLOITATION IN ENGLAND AND WALES

Silva Hove and Sally Montier

INTRODUCTION

10.1 There are no generally agreed upon estimates of the scale of trafficking into England and Wales for the purposes of sexual exploitation. In 2010 ACPO published findings from Project ACUMEN[1] which suggested that of an estimated 17,000 migrant women involved in off-street prostitution 2,600 are trafficked and a further 9,600 are considered to be vulnerable[2]. Due to the covert nature of trafficking and the many barriers to women both in coming to the attention of services and disclosing trafficking, it is difficult to give an accurate picture of the scale of trafficking for sexual exploitation into the UK.

Eaves Housing for Women – a charitable feminist organisation providing accommodation and support to women in London who have experienced gender violence for many years, began receiving referrals of female victims of trafficking in 2001. These women presented with horrific tales of abuse and sexual exploitation often possessed no documentation or legal status in the UK and, having no right or recourse to public funds, therefore lacked access to safe housing[3]. They also faced an immigration system which most often did not recognise their need for protection. Eaves started lobbying the Government for recognition of a gap in service provision and for a need for support for this emerging group of vulnerable women with no entitlements.

In February 2002, the Government published the White Paper 'Secure Borders Safe Havens', which highlighted a need for provisions for victims of trafficking[4]. In 2003 the Government agreed to fund a pilot project – the Poppy Project to provide support for victims of trafficking but with limited criteria for support[5]. From the outset it was necessary to challenge the limitations of these criteria to reflect the true needs of those women who were being encountered and supported: based on an understanding that women are often unable or unwilling to access support immediately or shortly following their escape, Poppy advocated that support should not be dependent on co-operation with police, that victims needs are complex, requiring longer term specialist support and that, for many victims, returning to their country of origin is not a safe option.

Since its inception, the Poppy Project has received hundreds of referrals of potential victims of trafficking for sexual exploitation[6] to the UK from over 90 different countries and has witnessed changes and fluctuations such as in the main countries of origin that women are trafficked from, the methods of travel and documentation used to traffick them, and the types of places in which they are exploited in prostitution. For example, in 2004, 70% of women supported by the Poppy Project were from former Soviet States/Eastern Europe[7] and many women accessing the project had been brought into the UK undocumented, via clandestine routes and forced to work in massage parlours, saunas and walk-up flats. In 2011 the Project is seeing much higher numbers of women trafficked from West Africa who may be trafficked using their own documents or false documents arranged by the traffickers and who are forcibly prostituted in private houses and via hotels and nightclubs. There has also been a significant increase in referrals of women from China[8]. The locations of exploitation have also shifted from being less London-centric to spanning cities and towns across the length and breadth of the UK. The Poppy Project recognises the diversity of women's experiences of trafficking and that the variety of backgrounds of different groups of victims necessitates the need for a range of support services that acknowledge and are tailored to meet these differences.

Knowledge gained from the pilot project, pressure from human rights groups and NGOs and the diligence of legal professionals in challenging Government decisions which had failed to protect or further violated the rights of victims has been integral to influencing trafficking-related policy and strategies[9]. The UK Government's Action Plan 2007[10] recognised trafficking for the purposes of sexual exploitation as a form of gender-based violence and emphasised a real need to utilise shelters that are experienced in supporting vulnerable women. The national provision for victim care was increased and the Poppy Project expanded its provision both geographically[11] and in terms of capacity. The Action Plan advocated national guidance for minimum standards in victim care[12] and the Poppy Project was recognised as providing a model of best practice on a national and international level.

The UK's ratification in December 2008 of the Council of Europe Convention on Action against Trafficking in Human Beings (referred to hereafter as the Trafficking Convention), which came into force in the UK in April 2009, brought with it obligations to identify and protect victims and safeguard their rights, and established the minimum standards of service provision[13]. This also led to the creation of a National Referral Mechanism (NRM). However, the model which was introduced in the UK in many ways appeared to be a step backwards in terms of best practice for victim care, especially regarding the limited timescales that were to be implemented for reflection and recovery[14]. A significant concern for the Poppy Project was also the fact that victims who were not recognised by the Competent Authority within UKBA as victims of trafficking would be denied access to support and that these formal decisions were to be made by immigration services, disregarding the expertise of NGOs such as the Poppy Project in identifying victims of trafficking and, most alarmingly, denying a right to appeal against poor decision-making.

In order to improve responses to victim care and protection for sexually exploited victims it is important to understand both the underlying factors that make women vulnerable to trafficking, the barriers to seeking assistance and the continued vulnerabilities that they face on escape.

1   ACUMEN was commissioned to gain an understanding of the nature and extent of trafficking of foreign nationals for sexual exploitation in England and Wales. The findings are published in the document Kevin Jackson, Jon Jeffrey and George Adamson, *'Setting the Record: The Trafficking of Migrant Women in England and Wales Off-Street Prostitution Sector'* ACPO (August 2010).

2   Research methodology for ACUMEN drew on the ILO operational indicators of trafficking system and adhered to the UN definition of trafficking. For those who were considered to be vulnerable the report states 'Although they have elements of vulnerability to trafficking, most are likely to fall short of the trafficking threshold. There may be cultural or financial factors which prevent them from exiting prostitution (or seeking help to do so) but they tend to have day to day activities, and although they may have large debts they generally do not consider themselves to be debts-bonded'. Kevin Jackson, Jon Jeffrey and George Adamson, *'Setting the Record: The Trafficking of Migrant Women in England and Wales Off-Street Prostitution Sector'* ACPO (August 2010) at p 5.

3   Prior to Home Office funding in March 2003, Eaves Housing supported such women from emergency funds.

4   Whilst acknowledging the need for specialist support for victims the Paper focused on the need for support to be provided in direct relation to co-operation with the authorities and envisaged that the majority of victims would require short term support before being assisted to repatriate to their country of origin.
Home Office, *'Secure Borders Safe Havens; Integration with Diversity in Modern Britain'* (February 2002).

5   Women had to have been exploited within the past 30 days. Following a four week reflection period the victim was expected to co-operate with the police in order to secure a 16 week period of accommodation and support. It was expected that the majority of victims would then return via a reintegration programme. Criteria barring women from accessing services if claiming asylum were dropped shortly after the project's implementation.

6   Between March 2003 and March 2011, of 1869 referrals received by the Poppy Project, 1055 of those were for women who had been trafficked and exploited in prostitution.

7   Gina Taylor, *'Evaluation of the Victims of Trafficking Pilot Project – Poppy Summary Findings'*, (2004) Home Office Research, Development and Statistics.

8   Whilst the number of women from China referred to the Project as potential victims makes up the second largest referral group, take up of support is comparatively low. Chinese women may frequently not identify themselves as victims of trafficking as their family would be liable for the 'debt' owed to the traffickers and they may have also taken out loans from loan sharks to enable their family members to travel to the UK.

9   A consultation for UK Action Plan in 2006 highlighted inadequacies remaining in victim protection and called for the protection of victims and their human rights to be at the core of the Action Plan. Gaps in provision included those victims who had escaped the exploitative situation more than 30 days prior to accessing support, the need for protection to be independent of co-operation with the authorities and better quality of immigration decision-making, emphasising the need for further guidance on the risks faced by victims on return. The majority of respondents expressed the need for the UK to sign up the Council of Europe Trafficking Convention.
See: Home Office and Scottish Executive, *'Tackling Human Trafficking – Summary of Responses to the Consultation on Proposals for a UK Action Plan'* (June 2006).

10 Home Office and Scottish Executive, *'UK Action Plan on Tackling Human Trafficking'* *(March 2007)'* Ref 5545552.

11 The Project was expanded to cover England and Wales, with nine bed spaces based in Sheffield, with an outreach worker covering the north of England and five bed spaces based in Cardiff with outreach capacity for Wales.

12 There is currently no formal procedure in place to make adherence to minimum standards a prerequisite for providing services to victims of trafficking, nor are the standards enforceable.

13 The support must include at a minimum: safe and secure accommodation; access to medical, social, and psychological support; legal services; and assistance in acquiring identification documents, as well as the facilitation of voluntary repatriation or resettlement.
Council Of Europe Convention on Action against Trafficking in Human Beings 2005.

[14] For example, limiting the Reflection and Recovery period to 45 days (although extendable to 90 days) did not reflect what had been learned about the needs of victims in terms of rehabilitation and our practical experience has shown that the main reasoning behind the issuing of the Residence Permit is to enable victims who are potential or actual prosecution witnesses to remain in the UK. There has been no recognition of the fact that the majority of victims require longer term care, regardless of whether they are co-operating with the police.

THE VULNERABILITY TO TRAFFICKING AND PRE-TRAFFICKING EXPERIENCES OF GENDERED VIOLENCE

10.2 Trafficking is a crime that disproportionately affects women and girls. Poverty is frequently cited as being a major push factor in leading victims of trafficking to accept an offer of travel from recruiters, hoping to escape poverty and seek new opportunities. 58% of women accessing services at the Poppy Project described their standard of living prior to being trafficked as 'poor' or 'very poor'[1]. However, on further exploration of their experiences prior to trafficking, multiple push factors emerge. Many women accessing services for victims of trafficking have previously experienced a number of forms of gender-based violence, discrimination and inequality. In a study by the Poppy Project, half of the trafficked women questioned disclosed previous experiences of violence, including sexual violence: this is twice the global average[2]. Social isolation, stigmatisation, lack of family support, previous exploitation and displacement are also frequently disclosed as part of the pre-trafficking narrative. These experiences will impact not only on the support needed to aid recovery from the abuse suffered in the trafficking situation but also on the victim's ability to seek assistance and the risks faced on return to their country of origin.

The effects of the feminisation of poverty are apparent in the backgrounds that victims describe. Women cite having been taken out of education and having limited access to job opportunities because of their gender status. Women in developing countries who had lost one or both parents, particularly the loss of their father, described finding themselves in dire poverty, often with the responsibility of providing for their surviving parent and siblings[3]. In traditionally patriarchal societies women also found themselves targeted by traffickers, as they were perceived as having no male family members to protect them.

Gender-based violence and/or harmful traditional practices feature as both a pre-trafficking experience of trauma and as triggering the need to flee, thus making women vulnerable to offers of recruitment. Several women have cited fleeing FGM and forced marriage as the main push factors for leaving their homes, having faced the risk of stigmatisation, societal rejection, violence and even death for refusing to conform to gender and cultural expectations. Victims accessing services have also witnessed and experienced rape as a weapon of war, suffered multiple rapes from soldiers and seen family members raped and murdered in front of them.

Child exploitation in domestic servitude, forced labour and prostitution feature in the pre-trafficking experience of a number of victims, with some women having long histories of being held in slave-like conditions. In these cases women may have been sold into slavery as children and trafficked internally and internationally over a number of years prior to being trafficked to the UK. Some women and children may have been sold by family members in order to pay off debts owed[4].

Family violence, both sexual and physical and experiences of domestic violence not only leave women vulnerable to recruitment, exacerbated by the failure of the authorities to respond appropriately or protect them generally as a gender group or individually, but can also affect women's trust in the UK authorities to treat them as victims of crime when making the decision whether to approach the police to report the trafficking experience. Zimmerman has highlighted the particular vulnerabilities of women who have experienced sexual abuse to being targeted by traffickers[5].

It is also important to remember that not all women who fall victim to traffickers share a background of traumatic experiences, and that all women's circumstances are unique. However, when supporting victims, the trauma of the abuse inflicted in the trafficking situation cannot be treated in isolation; the impact of previous violations on the individual's health and sense of self will affect how and when women seek support, the kind of treatment they require and the length of support needed to aid recovery and rehabilitation.

[1]   The Poppy Project, 'Routes In Routes Out: Quantifying the Gendered Experience of Trafficking to the UK'(August 2008), at p 9.
[2]   The Poppy Project, 'Routes In Routes Out: Quantifying the Gendered Experience of Trafficking to the UK' (August 2008), at p 5.
[3]   Several women accessing services have also experienced rejection from the family home of both themselves and their mothers when their fathers have taken second or third wives, leaving them displaced and without financial and social support.
[4]   In some cases this transaction is overt but in other cases the complicity between parents and traffickers may be less obvious to the victims and any risks to remaining in contact with their family once they have escaped needs to be carefully assessed.
[5]   'Research suggests that sexual abuse among pre-adolescent girls is associated with low self-esteem, feelings of shame, vulnerability, and unworthiness, and that young girls who come from poor, dysfunctional or abusive families are extremely vulnerable to traffickers'. Moreover, traffickers reportedly target girls who they perceive to be distressed or who reveal family problems.
       Zimmerman, C. et al, *'The health risks and consequences of trafficking in women and adolescents. Findings from a European study'* London: London School of Hygiene & Tropical Medicine (LSHTM) (2003).

UNDERSTANDING THE FEARS AND CONCERNS OF VICTIMS

10.3 The decision for victims of trafficking to attempt to escape the situation is not always straightforward. For many victims of trafficking it is not simply that they are locked in or constantly monitored (although this is the experience of the majority of women) that keeps them from escaping. Traffickers employ many control mechanisms to keep victims within their power which range from severe physical violence to more subtle forms of manipulation.

The strongest fear expressed by the majority of victims on considering escaping from the trafficking situation is the immediate risk of severe physical harm and death, to themselves and family members. Other factors, such as a lack of faith in the authorities, the absence of a place of safety to escape to, financial pressures and acute fear of arrest and removal are also widely cited. Victims who have undergone ritual oaths prior to being trafficked may also believe that they will die if they attempt to defy their traffickers or reveal to anyone their circumstances[1]. Where victims are held in debt-bondage, escape from the trafficking-related exploitation also carries with it real risks to the safety, welfare and livelihood of their families.

Women report having made failed attempts to escape, resulting in brutal, life-threatening beatings, further rape and acts of humiliation and degradation. Severe physical punishment and threat of death emphasises the idea that there is no possible way to escape the traffickers alive. Threats of exposure to family and community[2], which can carry very real risks of honour-based violence and social isolation, are also exploited by traffickers to deter women from seeking to escape.

Fear and distrust of the authorities can be a significant barrier to seeking assistance. Many women have experienced police corruption in their home country, poor responses to previous reports of violence (for example, being to told that domestic violence is a family, not a criminal, matter), and sexual and physical violence inflicted by the police[3]. Fear of the UK immigration authorities is often a major concern for women which can keep them in the exploitative situation and this fear is frequently manipulated by the traffickers. Not only do women fear being found by their traffickers and relocated, ie re-trafficked, by them but they also fear a return to the violent circumstances from which they fled, as outlined above.

[1] For more information regarding the use of juju rituals in controlling victims of trafficking see Siddharth Kara *Inside The Business of Modern Slavery*(2009), Columbia University Press.
[2] During rehabilitation women will often speak of feeling that strangers will look at them and know what has happened to them; that they are forever 'marked out', and will never be able to fit into 'normal' society.
[3] More than one service user accessing the Poppy Project disclosed that when they approached the police in their home country to report rape and trafficking offences they were subjected to rape by the police officers themselves.

BARRIERS TO DISCLOSURE AND ACCESSING SERVICES

10.4 Several women accessing support services had previously been forced to work in brothels where police raids had been carried out, often on more than one occasion, but who did not identify themselves as trafficking victims when questioned by the police and immigration services[1]. Women have identified the fact that traffickers or their associates were present in the brothel at the time of the raid, or that other women working there were also controlled by the same gang and so could report back to the traffickers if they alerted the police. The experience of women that the Project has supported, who did not disclose their trafficking status and were removed back to their home countries as illegal entrants and then subsequently re-trafficked into the UK tells us that these fears are not unfounded.

Potential victims of trafficking can find themselves disbelieved by the Competent Authorities and UKBA case owners if it is known that they have had prior contact with the police or immigration authorities but failed to disclose that they were trafficked.

Many victims of trafficking lack the information and knowledge that there is support available for them, however even if they are aware there is assistance available they may distrust support services. This may be because they have had negative experiences of social welfare services in their country of origin, have previously asked for assistance but been turned away due to their immigration status[2] or fear being judged. This may be particularly true of women who have had children, either as a result of, or after, the trafficking experience. Some women fear that they may be viewed negatively by social services for having been involved in prostitution. We have found this fear is not unfounded[3].

[1] 'B was trafficked from the Balkan region to the UK. Whilst being forced to work in a sauna the police raided the premises and she was taken to a police station. The police asked her whether she had been forced in prostitution but she denied this. She later stated that she had been too scared to disclose what had happened as she had heard of victims being sent back to her home country where they were imprisoned. The parents of those women had to pay a fine in order to get their daughters released. When parents refused to go, due to the social and cultural stigmas associated with prostitution and trafficking, the last option was that the women would call their traffickers to ask them to get them released. Ms B was aware that a lot of those women were already re-trafficked in the UK. When B was released by the police she returned to her traffickers. She was later arrested in a second raid and detained in an immigration removal centre. It was only at this time that she disclosed that she had been trafficked and accessed support via the Poppy Project'.
Comment by women on the Poppy Project submitted in Memorandum to the Home Affairs Committee The Trade in Human Beings: Human Trafficking in the UK, Home Affairs Committee Publications(May 2009).

[2] This also applied to EU nationals who, although they do not risk removal are limited in their recourse to public funds and also therefore a number of vital services including housing and financial support.

[3] In two cases supported by Poppy, social services teams in two different boroughs threatened to take children into care because the women involved had been exploited in prostitution until Poppy intervened.

CONTINUED VULNERABILITIES ON ESCAPE OF BOTH SUPPORTED AND UNSUPPORTED VICTIMS

10.5 Due to the fears and concerns of many victims of trafficking and the barriers to disclosure, a number of victims do not access support services on escape from the trafficking situation, including some who may have come into contact with the authorities. This can result in women remaining vulnerable to further exploitation and abuse. Some women will seek assistance from clients, maids, and others who they come into contact with whilst in the sex industry such as drivers or security guards. Although this assistance can lead to a successful escape, in our experience it can also lead to further exploitation abuse[1].

Victims who have escaped but do not access services may seek to find employment in the black market as informal, undocumented workers, leaving them further open to the risk of abuse but of a different kind, namely labour exploitation. Others may try to get a regulated job by using false documents. There is also evidence of former victims being targeted by agents offering documents for a fee. This exposes the women to the risk of arrest and also leads to judgments by the Competent Authorities that they are not in need of assistance as they had managed to survive 'perfectly well' without the need for a recovery period. Having been the victim of very serious crimes in the UK, victims may find themselves being treated as criminals.

Some victims of trafficking, left undocumented or with little means to support themselves continue to work in the sex industry following escape. That victims of trafficking continue to engage in prostitution can lead to assumptions by the authorities that they are not 'credible' victims. In the Poppy Project's experience, it is not uncommon for victims of trafficking who have not come to attention of specialist support services to return to prostitution after escape, as women continue to remain in a vulnerable situation with few other options[2]. The decision of victims of trafficking to survive through selling sex, despite their traumatic experiences, reflects how far their options have been curtailed[3].

In Poppy's experience, women who have been supported by the project who escaped their traffickers several months and sometimes years before accessing services, do not necessarily present with significantly lower needs than those who accessed support immediately or shortly after escape. In fact, that their health needs had gone untreated and that they had often been subjected to further exploitation and abuse and been further entrenched in prostitution meant that some women presented with considerably higher needs. It is therefore essential that barriers to victims accessing services are reduced wherever possible and that they are offered equal access to high-quality specialist services.

[1] The Poppy Project has received a number of trafficking-related referrals from domestic violence services where victims have, after escaping from the trafficking situation, experienced violence perpetrated by those individuals who assisted them: 'J disclosed to one of her regular clients in the brothel that she had been trafficked and needed help. He agreed to try to assist her. Without her knowledge he approached her traffickers to try to buy her. The traffickers agreed. The client took J to a rented flat where he kept her locked in. He would visit regularly with food and toiletries and to have sex with her. He told her that she did not have to worry about all the other clients or the traffickers. J managed to escape and approached the police.' Internal case study, The Poppy Project.

[2] For some women, working for oneself after escape can feel like a way of regaining some level of control. Women find themselves with no means to support themselves, no legal status in the UK, no family or friends to rely on for support, no knowledge of support services and systems in the UK, little English language skills, and with sometimes long histories of having been involved in the sex industry. Working for themselves can be the only solution for some women in this situation.

[3] Financial pressures to support family members, including children, back in the country of origin, means that some women who are accessing support schemes will continue to engage in prostitution. This engagement may be sporadic and for limited period only. It is vital that these women are not discriminated against by support services and that they have equal access to assistance, including support around exiting prostitution, if requested. This will require support services to carefully manage the heightened risk that continued involvement in prostitution presents.

KEY PRINCIPLES IN SUPPORTING VICTIMS

10.6 Given the complexity of the problems victims of trafficking experience, real progress in assisting recovery very much depends on having comprehensive response strategies in place. At the centre of these strategies is the understanding that trafficking is a gross violation of an individual's rights, attacks the core of a person and affects the person's being, sense of self worth and identity. Any support provided to victims should seek to restore and defend the victim's rights and ensure that their rights are observed in all circumstances while giving them power over decisions that affect their lives. It is vital that victims are given information about their rights in a language that they understand[1] and are kept up to date with any developments in immigration and criminal matters relating to them.

Confidentiality and building trust are key to enabling disclosure. Victims often fear that revealing their trafficking experience without an assurance of confidentiality will have serious consequences; for example reprisals from the perpetrators, prosecution for having participated in illegal activities or immediate expulsion from the destination country. Faced with this dilemma victims may either remain silent or recount their experiences only very selectively. Explanations for eliciting information, the scope of what needs to be discussed and the potential risks and benefits of disclosing information must be given to victims in order for them to make an informed decision on whether to engage[2]. When providing support, it is important to be guided by the victim's own wishes, expectations and concerns. Support services should understand their role as empowering and supporting victim's choices and advocating on their behalf and not making choices for them.

A critical factor in providing support to a victim is that the support should be both comprehensive and integrated. Assistance with accommodation, medical, psychological, legal services, education and training will not exist satisfactorily in isolation. The Poppy Project works in partnership with other providers to ensure that victims are able to access all the relevant services, including health care and all other forms of support they need. This includes working with agencies that can assist victims through the immigration and criminal justice systems[3]. However, as highlighted below there remain a number of challenges to achieving co-ordinated and appropriate responses to victims' needs from a number of agencies.

Building on 10 years of directly supporting female victims of trafficking from a wide range of backgrounds and with diverse experiences, the Poppy Project[4] has used our understanding of the needs of women who have experienced gender-based violence to create a victim-centred, multi-agency approach which provides a support model for victims. Key to the support that we offer has been creating an environment where women feel not only physically safe but also that they are aware that staff are advocating for their rights when dealing with systems that may not acknowledge their needs and may disbelieve them. Ensuring that women are given rightful access to the care and protection that they need is a fundamental part of our support work and requires us to challenge Government failures which undermine victims' rights to protection and respect under the Trafficking Convention and the Human Rights Act 1998.

[1]   Victims of trafficking can remain highly vulnerable even after they have been referred to services if these services are in a language they do not understand. Clear information should be available to victims in their own language using reputable accredited interpreters and policies and procedures must be in place to protect the confidentiality of the victim. In Poppy's experience there exist challenges among some communities such as the Chinese and Albanian communities where victims were sometimes reluctant to talk to an interpreter from their own communities citing fear of being judged or reported back to their trafficker.

[2]   Services should have a policy on recording and sharing information and agreed information sharing protocols with partner agencies especially when dealing with law enforcement. Written consent or documented verbal consent should be obtained from the victim before sharing personal information with third parties – the purpose of any information sharing must be clearly defined.

[3]   Poppy has long-established service level agreements with almost all the support services that are crucial to the women's recovery from specialist sexual health clinics, to counsellors, to

local GPs and specialist solicitors who can instruct expert barristers. We have memoranda of understanding with the police, the UK Human Trafficking Centre (UKHTC). This not only ensures that each agency is clear about their role and responsibilities but it also means that they have been able to develop a good understanding of working with victims through our training and feedback.

4   At the Poppy Project the service itself also reflects this diversity. Poppy has a staff team from diverse backgrounds and policies that monitor and prohibit discrimination proactively address any discriminatory practices.

Safety and Risk Management

10.7 Victims who have escaped or have been rescued from their traffickers are in danger of reprisals because their escape challenges the control of the traffickers and presents a loss to their 'business'. It is therefore very important that they are immediately protected. Initial information such as a victim's danger areas, their immediate health concerns and the risk of self harm or suicide should be ascertained within the first 12 hours, and before placing the victim in accommodation or leaving the victim alone.

The Trafficking Convention requires that victims of trafficking be given access to 'appropriate and secure accommodation'[1]. For the Poppy Project this means providing women-only housing for female victims of trafficking for sexual exploitation[2]. Safety of accommodation includes not only the security of the houses, such as having intercom systems and CCTV cameras and 24 hour access to support staff, but also ensuring that the victims are clear about their own responsibility in maintaining their safety. It is Poppy's experience that women who have been trafficked can develop attachments to their traffickers or exploiters (Stockholm syndrome). This means that risks of re-trafficking may remain even after a woman has escaped. Reducing this risk can be achieved by ensuring the woman understands that she plays a key role in keeping herself safe and that she recognises the risks involved in contacting anyone associated with her trafficking, and appreciates that this may include family members.

Whilst being aware of maintaining safety it is also crucial to be aware that the women will most often have had nowhere they identify as being their home for some time and will have had little control over their living conditions. They may have had to sleep in the brothel they were forced to work in, to share rooms with their trafficker(s) and/or other victims and may have been frequently moved from house to house. It is important that women accessing services are able to create their own private space within the housing scheme. Staffed accommodation, where victims cannot leave unless accompanied, may be well intended but it is Poppy's experience that highly controlled environments can perpetuate the experiences from their trafficking situation instead of fostering recovery.

1   Council of Europe Convention on Action against Trafficking in Human Beings, Article 12, Section 1.
2   As female victims of trafficking for other forms of exploitation may also have experienced gender-based violence then they should also be afforded access to gender appropriate housing.

Accessing health services

10.8 The majority of victims of trafficking for sexual exploitation often have urgent medical needs[1] which need to be addressed immediately upon escape. They may have physical injuries or have been exposed to the risks of diseases from unsafe sexual practices which increase the risk of contracting HIV/AIDS and or other sexually transmitted diseases[2]. The majority of women accessing Poppy support have been forced to have sex with between 10–20 clients per day, to 'work' throughout menstruation, often with no day off[3]. Women may also present with unwanted pregnancies, either as a direct result of rape in the trafficking situation or as a result of subsequent relationships, and will require access to undergo a termination.

The majority of victims have mental health problems[4] resulting from the traumatic experiences they have been made to endure. These can range from PTSD and depression to psychosis, schizophrenia and personality disorders. In our experience there can be a lack of understanding from mental health services regarding the needs of victims which can be exacerbated by women's reluctance to identify mental health needs due to stigma and negative experiences of mental health services in their home country. In the UK all victims who are formally identified as victims can receive free NHS treatment[5]. However this is not widely known and in cases where a victim has not yet been identified they may be charged for treatment. In these cases it is necessary to advocate on behalf of the service user. Other difficulties include a lack of provision of interpreters at medical appointments meaning that women are not able to fully discuss their symptoms and may be prescribed anti-depressant and anti-psychotic medication without an understandable explanation of their purpose.

Access to counselling for victims is a requirement under the Trafficking Convention and the Poppy Project works closely with a number of therapeutic providers[6]. In the experience of the Poppy Project there are a number of women who are reluctant to engage with counselling on escape and some for whom it would be detrimental to begin the process so soon. There is a concern that many women will not be ready to (or unable to) access counselling within 45 days and also that the Competent Authorities may question their level of psychological distress if they are not accessing services. It is our opinion that the 45 day reflection period is woefully inadequate to address the needs of the vast majority of sexually exploited victims. In our experience many women accessing support are unable to access counselling until they feel safe and stable enough to discuss their trauma and this is often only once they have been assured of protection in the UK.

[1] Zimmerman, C. et al, *'The health risks and consequences of trafficking in women and adolescents. Findings from a European study.'* London: London School of Hygiene & Tropical Medicine (LSHTM) (2003). In this study of 207 victims of trafficking in a number of European countries of which the UK was one, over 57% of victims reported 12 or more physical health symptoms that caused them pain in the first 14 days following escape.
[2] Zimmerman, C. et al, 'The health risks and consequences of trafficking in women and adolescents. Findings from a European study.' London: London School of Hygiene & Tropical Medicine (LSHTM) (2003). 44% reported having been diagnosed and treated for an STI and 2% had contracted HIV.
[3] The Poppy Project, 'Routes In Routes Out: Quantifying the Gendered Experience of Trafficking to the UK '(August 2008), at page 18.

[4]   Zimmerman, C. et al, '*The health risks and consequences of trafficking in women and adolescents. Findings from a European study.*' London: London School of Hygiene & Tropical Medicine (LSHTM) (2003). 70% of victims reported 10 or more mental health symptoms associated with depression anxiety and hostility in the first 14 days after escape.

[5]   The statutory instrument which sets out this amendment to the Regulations can be found at http://www.opsi.gov.uk/si/si2008/pdf/uksi_20082251_en.pdf.
The NHS (Charges to Overseas Visitors) Regulations 1989, SI 1989/306 have been amended to provide a new exemption from charge category for anyone who the 'Competent Authorities' of the UK:
(i)   have identified as a victim of human trafficking, or
(ii)   consider that there are reasonable grounds to believe is a victim of human trafficking for whom a 'recovery and reflection' period has not yet expired.
Victims of trafficking prior to the entry into force of the Trafficking Convention in the UK in April 2009 and amendment of the Regulations had great difficulties accessing health services as they needed to show proof of identity which they did not have and could not provide previous addresses or details of previous GP as they would not have had access to one while in the trafficking situation.

[6]   Poppy had to set up service level agreements with a number of medical support services including specialist counselling services such as Women and Girls Network, The Helen Bamber Foundation, the Medical Foundation for the Care of Victims of Torture and the Traumatic Stress Clinic in order to facilitate access and to reduce the delay in receiving these crucial services.

Working with the police and supporting women through the Criminal Justice System

10.9 Successful prosecution of traffickers is often a critical element in the recovery of victims as they can feel that they have been believed and have been vindicated. Criminal justice authorities owe it to victims to make all possible efforts to effectively prosecute and sentence traffickers. However, in the experience of the Poppy Project it is only a small minority of victims who ultimately act as witnesses in successful prosecutions against their traffickers. It is clear that acting as a witness can have far-reaching effects on the witness's life. Since proceedings against sex traffickers typically involve individuals linked to organised crime, witnesses and their families in home countries are frequently in danger. As a result, every victim should be able to decide, without duress, on whether or not they co-operate with the criminal justice system, being both aware of potential benefits and risks. In Poppy's experience the police do not always give room for victims to consider risk factors and the consequences of their choices. Testifying may increase the risk of harm to them and their families and women may decide that the risk is too high to take. Often protection from authorities in many source countries is seriously inadequate; in reality leaving victims who may return there vulnerable after they have reported their traffickers to the police and victims should in such cases be given the opportunity to give intelligence only[1].

It has been Poppy's concern that sometimes victims of trafficking are seen primarily – or even exclusively – as a tool or instrument to identify and prosecute criminals by the police/Government which often leads to unfair treatment in a number of ways. For example a woman's account in her immigration case is often discredited if she is not co-operating with the police. There can also appear to be a disparity in the way that women are treated if they are reporting an individual trafficker rather than a criminal network (especially if the police are already aware of the network and view the witness as being of value to their case). Other challenges include victims being subjected to intensive and repetitive interrogation by the police before support is offered or without consideration of the victim's mental state and often without provision of adequate legal advice and assistance. This can lead to inconsistencies in accounts that may be problematic in the course of the case.

It is essential in assisting women through the criminal justice system that every care is taken to not traumatise victims anew. Interviewing victims soon after they have escaped and for long hours, before they have had a chance to process what has happened to them can be damaging[2]. It is Poppy's experience that successful prosecutions happen in cases where women have been allowed to get support, have had the chance to have the process explained to them, and where they have been given support for their immediate needs such as safety, health and have built good and trusting relationships with the support agency and police first. Allowing the victim to stabilise can contribute to a clarification in the victim's mind about what they have experienced. In the course of this process, the victim can then make an informed decision about whether they want to pursue a criminal case. Should they decide not to however, this should not be grounds for excluding them from the support structures. It is the Poppy's experience that providing support to victims increases the likelihood that they will be willing to assist with investigations.

The most effective way to enable victims to access the justice system is if there is co-operation between support providers and the police. At times the police appear to view NGOs as interfering when they are advocating for the rights of the victim. It is therefore essential for there to be trust between these actors wherein the police place value on the assessment of support providers as to the readiness of a victim to give evidence at any given time. Having specialist teams in place and regular exchange of views and information has helped Poppy improve collaborative working and to an extent contributed to the increase in number of prosecutions[3].

[1]   Nigeria is a case in point. In 2010 it was placed by the United States' State Department on Tier 1 in the Trafficking in Persons country report. This was based on reports by the Nigerian Government on the efforts it was making in prosecuting traffickers and providing support for victims yet in reality there still remained huge gaps in service provision, documented evidence of corruption and ill treatment of victims as evidenced in, for example, the Human Rights Watch reports of that year.

[2]   Statutory agencies, namely the police, have targets and their own priorities and in the majority of cases these will often take precedence over a victim's needs. A recent referral to the Poppy Project of M is a case in point. M was encountered in a raid on a private property where she was being exploited at 10pm. She was referred to Poppy right away from the advice given by UKHTC however she was not taken to accommodation until 3.30am. Upon arrival at Poppy a risk assessment was conducted and M disclosed that she was in a lot of pain and that she been in pain from the time she was found by the police. She had had this pain for some time. M was taken to hospital by the Poppy worker where she was kept overnight to do further tests that revealed that she had gynecological complications. M said no one had checked if she was OK. Instead she was subjected to a lengthy interview before she was given relevant support. The fact that it was late was not given consideration. (Poppy Case study – unpublished). This is but one of several cases where the police place priority on the criminal justice process over the welfare of victims.

[3]   Between 2003 and August 2011, the Poppy Project has supported 42 women to testify against 62 perpetrators for human trafficking-related offences, securing a total of 416 years' imprisonment in sentencing terms. (Internal data, The Poppy Project, June 2011).

Supporting women through the National Referral Mechanism (NRM) and Asylum Process

10.10 It is Poppy's experience that the granting of leave to remain in the UK for victims of trafficking is one of the most important elements in securing the safety and rehabilitation of victims of trafficking. Indeed the majority of the women we have supported have not been able to engage with the full range of services available to them until they have been granted some form of status. It is essential that a victim of trafficking is granted leave for at least a year in the destination country for them to be able to meaningfully recover and assess their situation. It is also vital to recognise the serious and life-threatening risks that victims may face on return. If victims are returned to their countries without these issues addressed they remain vulnerable to re-trafficking, further exploitation and serious harm.

Victims of trafficking for sexual exploitation may be subject to both the NRM system and the asylum system. The purpose of the NRM is to identify whether they have been trafficked and whether they require a residence permit and the asylum system is to assess whether they meet the threshold for protection in the UK. In the experience of the Poppy Project there are serious flaws in the decision-making processes for both systems[1].

There is evidence of a lack of understanding of the methods, complexities and impacts of trafficking by the Competent Authorities[2] and despite the fact that the Trafficking Convention requires that 'Each Party shall adopt such legislative or other measures as may be necessary to identify victims as appropriate in collaboration with other Parties and relevant support organisations'[3] it remains the case that the expertise of organisations such as the Poppy Project are not taken into account during the initial decision-making, despite the wealth of supporting information that is provided to the UKBA/NRM case owner in order to inform the decision. Poor quality of decisions and the fact that there is no formal appeal process against negative NRM findings mean that valuable support resources are spent on preparing and submitting informal reconsideration requests to the UKBA and supporting judicial reviews against negative NRM decisions. The fact that the vast majority of these decisions, when reconsidered are changed to positive outcomes prior to judicial review hearings suggests an acknowledgement of the flaws in the system.

The role of the Poppy Project as providing advocates in women's cases and in preparing detailed reports for asylum appeals are also an extremely vital part of the service. A report produced by the Poppy Project showed that 80% of negative asylum/humanitarian protection decisions were overturned on appeal in the asylum tribunal for women who were accessing the services of the project[4]. This is far higher than the average and significantly higher than women's asylum appeals in general[5]. Support staff work intensively with victims and are able to build up trust in order to gain important insight into both their case and their ongoing support needs. This, coupled with extensive knowledge gained from supporting hundreds of victims of trafficking as a project, needs to be acknowledged by decision-makers in order to reduce the severe distress caused to women who receive negative decisions and the costs to the public purse of successfully challenging decisions.

Far too often many defenceless victims of trafficking go unidentified due to lack of training and knowledge among First Responders including immigration officers. In a few cases Poppy has worked with victims who have been regarded as perpetrators, and have been criminalised[6]. Some are removed to their countries before the true circumstances are investigated or in other circumstances victims are not identified as victims; their revelations of trafficking often dismissed as fabrications mostly because the accounts of trafficking are disclosed late which shows a lack understanding of the effects of trafficking on victims. After escaping from their captors, trafficked persons are recurrently held in detention centres or jails[7].

Whilst the Poppy Project recognises and supports the efforts of the UK Government to tackle trafficking into the UK for sexual exploitation, as evidenced by the ratification of the Trafficking Convention, the establishment of the NRM, the provision of free NHS health services for identified victims and the provision of funding for national specialist accommodation and support service for victims, we must also urge that the UK strives not to just adhere to minimum requirements but to surpass them and to commit to this not only in rhetoric but in practice. The UK's commitment to dealing with trafficking should be reflected in policies that are not entrenched in immigration and border control but instead should acknowledge in policy, practice and priorities that trafficking is a gross violation of an individual's human rights which necessitates the absolute need for comprehensive assistance that has not yet been addressed by the UK. The attitude among officials charged with identification of potential victims needs change to be more positive. Raising awareness and training especially for law enforcement agencies and immigration staff needs to be prioritised. Also the body charged with identifying victims ought to be truly multi-agency and this role ought not, and must not, be placed solely within immigration or police structures.

From the success achieved by Poppy in advocating for victims of trafficking and ensuring that all agencies involved in the support of victims of trafficking worked to a set standard, a centralised support service to which all potential victims are referred is essential. Such a service should have oversight not only of referrals of victims, but of the adequacy of support provisions, monitor the involvement of all the other agencies engaging with victims, including immigration and the criminal justice officials, and feedback into policies and procedural guidance documents governing the work of all agencies working with victims. Priority needs to be given to addressing the issue of trafficking with a focus on effective and open inter-agency working for key agencies involved in dealing with trafficking in a way that is truly responsive to victims' needs and which recognises the importance of the NGOs contribution to this process.

[1] In the case of non-EU nations the decision-making for both will lie with UKBA, often with the same case owner making a decision as the Competent Authority case owner in the NRM and on behalf of the Home Secretary in the asylum case.

[2] For example, one woman was discredited and given a negative decision under the NRM because she had knowledge of the pricing structures at the brothel she was forced to work in.

[3] European Convention on Action against Trafficking in Human Beings, Article 10, Section 2.

[4] Sarah Richards, Poppy Project, Mel Steel and Debora Singer, Asylum Aid 'Hope Betrayed: An Analysis of Women Victims of Trafficking and Their Claims for Asylum'(February 2006).

[5] The Refugee Council found that 28% of asylum appeals in general were overturned on appeal in 2009. Asylum Aid very recently found that 50% of women's negative decisions were overturned.

'Unsustainable: the quality of initial decision making in women's asylum claims Asylum Aid' January 2011.

6   Such as victim in the landmark non-punishment trafficking related criminal appeal of *R v O* [2008] EWCA Crim 2835, (2008) Times 2 October whose criminal conviction was overturned in the Court of Appeal. In a separate case three women were initially charged by the police for controlling prostitution. Poppy got involved and found that the women were themselves victims and had been used by traffickers to control other women for supposedly more favourable treatment. They were each charged and imprisoned for some time until Poppy advocated for their release and for recognition of the women as victims. Through assistance of committed solicitors, Poppy worked closely with these women and the charges were later dropped. The barristers representing the women had very little understanding of trafficking and the dynamics of control within the trafficking situation and one of them had actually advised the victim to plead guilty. The victims received support from Poppy and they felt able to give evidence of against their traffickers who were sentenced to a total of 66 years.

7   The Poppy Project has supported a number of cases of victims arrested for and charged with using a false instrument and who were only identified as trafficking victims by befriending organisations which work with women in prisons or in detention centre spending removal for overstaying or some other immigration offences. See also 'Detained: Prisoners with no crime' The Poppy Project 2008.

PROTECTING THE NEEDS OF VICTIMS OF DOMESTIC SERVITUDE IN THE UK

Jenny Moss and Kate Roberts

'Migrant domestic workers [in the UK] are particularly vulnerable to trafficking and forced labour and consequently to abuses of their human rights . . . . Migrant domestic workers are dependent on their employer for their accommodation, their work, and their immigration status. They have no local network of support and are isolated in the house of their employer with no access to trade unions. Often migrant domestic workers do not speak English and/or have their movement restricted meaning they have to rely on their employer for any information about their rights in the UK. These issues create a dramatic power-imbalance between employer and employee and this is manipulated by unscrupulous employers to exploit workers. Those same employers use intimidation and threats such as telling migrant domestic workers they will become "illegal" if they leave their position or that they will be "arrested and deported".'[1]

[1] Kalayaan submission to the Special Rapporteur on Contemporary Forms of Slavery, 4 June 2010.

DOMESTIC SERVITUDE IN THE UK

11.1 Like many other forms of human trafficking, trafficking for domestic servitude involves the elements of movement and recruitment and either deception or coercion[1] for an end purpose of holding someone in forced labour; in this case in a domestic work setting[2]. Domestic work is, of course, not always exploitative or unlawful: if it is work that is properly paid with the provision of decent working and living conditions it does not equate with domestic servitude.

In some cases, the point at which lawful domestic work becomes unlawful domestic servitude may be difficult to define, as was recently recognised by the UN Special Rapporteur on contemporary forms of slavery, including its causes and consequences:

'24.   The line between domestic work, albeit accompanied by serious violations of fair labour standards, and domestic servitude and slavery is difficult to draw. In practice, there is a wide spectrum ranging from domestic workers engaged in labour relationships that follow applicable labour and human rights standards to victims of domestic servitude and slavery. Owing to the criminal and hence clandestine nature of servitude and slavery, it is impossible to determine what percentage of domestic workers are actually victims thereof.

25. Slavery and servitude have in common that the victim is economically exploited, totally dependent on other individuals and cannot end the relationship at his or her own volition. In cases of slavery, as classically defined by the Slavery, Servitude, Forced Labour and Similar Institutions and Practices Convention of 1926, the perpetrator puts forward a claim to "own" the victim that is sustained by custom, social practice or domestic law, even though it violates international law. In servitude and slavery-like practices, no such claim to formal ownership exists. This does not mean that servitude is the lesser human rights violation: the humiliation, exploitation and suffering can be equally or more intense depending on the nature of the individual case.

26. Domestic servitude and domestic slavery can be distinguished by the fact that the exploitation takes place primarily in or around the household of the perpetrators. In many cases, these phenomena go hand in hand with other forms of servitude and slavery. Beyond having to do household chores, for instance, a victim might be forced to work in agriculture, in the market or engage in prostitution.'[3]

What is clear is that migrant domestic workers ('MDWs') in the UK are particularly vulnerable to abuse, exploitation and trafficking because of the nature of their work. As recognised in research conducted by the Home Office, migrant domestic workers in the UK are most often isolated in a private household with no co-workers for support or to inform them of their rights, working in an under-regulated sector, and dependent on their employer for their work, accommodation, immigration status and for any information about their rights in the UK[4].

In our experience at Kalayaan[5], domestic servitude in the UK is mostly characterised by the withholding of identity documents by the employer, by the use of threats and humiliation, the imposition of excessive working hours with no proper rest breaks or days off and by payment that is below what is promised and often dramatically below the national minimum wage.

The following table shows the levels of abuse that have been reported by migrant domestic workers newly registering with Kalayaan:

Table 2: Types of abuse and exploitation experienced by clients registering with Kalayaan[1]

Type of abuse/ exploitation	2008	2009	2010
Control			
Not allowed out unaccompanied	63% (n^2 =340)	56% (n=240)	60% (n=284)
Passport was withheld	59% (n=92)[3]	68% (n=319)	65% (n=290)
Abuse			
Psychological abuse	59% (n=344)	60% (n=319)	54% (n=285)
Physical abuse/assault	16% (n =342)	15% (n=316)	18% (n=283)

Type of abuse/ exploitation	2008	2009	2010
Sexual abuse/harassment	5% (n=273)	5% (n=265)	3% (n=239)
Did not receive regular/sufficient food	22% (n=336)	27% (n=311)	26% (n=279)
Did not have own room (e.g. sleeping on kitchen or living room floor)	43% (n=340)	46% (n=311)	49% (n=281)
Exploitation			
Working seven days a week with no time off	60% (n=340)	67% (n=317)	67% (n=287)
Had to be available 'on call' 24 hours	67% (n =239)	76% (n=264)	58% (n=239)
Worked 16 hours a day or more per day	50% (n =322)	51% (n=282)	48% (n=252)
Received a salary of £50 or less per week	56% (n =315)	59% (n=281)	56% (n=238)

[1]   Lalani M, Kalayaan, 'Ending the Abuse: Policies that work to protect migrant domestic workers, May 2011', p10 http://www.kalayaan.org.uk/documents/Kalayaan%20Report%20 final.pdf.

[2]   The 'n' number (total number of individuals answering each question related to their experience of abuse/exploitation) varies due to the fact that not all migrant domestic workers answer each question.

[3]   Data for this criterion only began to be collected in September 2008, so the n number is lower than in subsequent years. Prior to September 2008, MDWs registering with Kalayaan were asked the question 'Who has your passport?'.

The link between trafficking and domestic servitude is well-established, although the covert nature of trafficking for domestic servitude may present obstacles to its identification. The Special Rapporteur on contemporary form of slavery has recognised this:

'59.   Trafficking is one path into domestic servitude. International law defines trafficking as the recruitment, transportation, transfer, harbouring or receipt of persons, by means of the threat or use of force or other forms of coercion, of abduction, of fraud, of deception, of the abuse of power or of a position of vulnerability or of the giving or receiving of payments or benefits to achieve the consent of a person having control over another person, for the purpose of exploitation. Slavery, practices similar to slavery and servitude are among the worst forms of exploitation that can result from trafficking; the victim's "consent" to such exploitation is immaterial.

60.   While links with other forms of organized violent crime cannot be excluded, trafficking into domestic servitude usually takes places under the cover of activities that seem legal or enjoy widespread social acceptance. Agents recruiting domestic workers become perpetrators of trafficking, if

191

they deliberately deceive their clients about the conditions of work or engage in illegal practices of control (such as the withholding of passports), while knowing that such practices will result in the exploitation of their recruits.'[6]

Most of Kalayaan's expertise is regarding workers, sometimes but not necessarily trafficked persons, who have come to the UK on the overseas domestic worker visa or the 'domestic workers (diplomat)' visa[7]. Increasingly, however, Kalayaan has supported individuals who have been brought, sometimes trafficked, to the UK on visit visas, false documents or as family members.

Kalayaan's figures show that the rate of trafficking via these routes and via the diplomatic domestic worker route is far greater than through the domestic worker visa route of entry into the UK whereby the worker has certain protections in law[8].

Home Office data show that each year approximately 16,000 domestic workers enter the UK on a domestic worker visa[9]. Of these, only 6% go on to renew their visas, indicating, we believe, that most are treated well and return with their employers to their employer's home country. We cannot give a clear estimate of how many of those entering on the visa are victims of trafficking, as is discussed later. Individuals who find themselves as victims of domestic servitude are predominantly but not exclusively women; approximately 92% of individuals identified as trafficked by Kalayaan in 2010 were female[10]. Migrating to do domestic work is often viewed as the only way out of poverty for women in countries where there are limited or no employment opportunities, with extended families relying on the remittances of one female worker. Most of the migrant domestic workers identified as trafficked by Kalayaan were Filipino, Indian and Indonesian, with a significant minority coming from Nigeria and Sri Lanka[11].

Migrant domestic workers find Kalayaan predominantly through word of mouth. Typically they have fled a house, sometimes with no money, no water and without proper clothes, and someone who speaks their language has found them and helped them. In some cases migrant domestic workers have been helped to escape from their abusive employer by a member of the public or by hotel staff who were concerned about them.

[1] Kalayaan's work involves adults and not children: of course there is no legal requirement to prove that coercion or deception was used in the case of a trafficked child.
[2] Usually in a private household.
[3] Report of the Special Rapporteur UN Special Rapporteur on contemporary forms of slavery, including its causes and consequences, 18 June 2010, A/HRC/15/20.
[4] Marsh, K, Sarmah, R, Davies, P, Froud, E, Mallender, J and Scalia, E 'A review of the literature on the abuse/ exploitation of overseas domestic workers in the UK Home Office Research Report', (2007 – unpublished), released in draft in June 2009 by the UKBA.
[5] Kalayaan is a registered charity working with migrant domestic workers in the UK. Until 2009 our remit was to work only with those migrant domestic workers who had entered the UK on the overseas domestic worker visa either with a private or diplomatic household. We have now extended that remit to include individuals trafficked to the UK for domestic servitude, even if that worker was brought via a different immigration route. Approximately 350 new migrant domestic workers register at Kalayaan each year. These migrant domestic workers register for different reasons such as immigration advice, help retrieving a passport withheld by an employer, employment rights advice, emergency accommodation, English class and others. Some of these workers report having been exploited and/or abused by their employers.

6   Report of the Special Rapporteur UN Special Rapporteur on contemporary forms of slavery, including its causes and consequences, 18 June 2010, A/HRC/15/20.

7   In November 2008, the domestic worker (diplomat) route was abolished and diplomats were instead to bring domestic workers to the UK under the 'Tier 5 International Agreement' route. The UK Government had, however, already agreed to maintain the existing rights of diplomatic domestic workers and as such they have slightly different visa rights to others entering under Tier 5 International Agreement, most notably the right to settlement.

8   See below section on domestic workers who accompany diplomats for more details of differential trafficking rates.

9   Figures obtained through requests directly to Home Office from their management information systems.

10   Kalayaan database – queried 6 April 2011.

11   This is more likely to reflect the communities in which Kalayaan is well known rather than necessarily rates of trafficking.

PROTECTION FOR MIGRANT DOMESTIC WORKERS IN THE UK

11.2 Kalayaan[1] was formed by domestic workers themselves in 1988 who understood that while they could offer each other informal support upon escaping abusive employers the structural abuse of migrant domestic workers in the UK would never change until migrant domestic workers had an independent immigration status in the UK and corresponding protections in law. Kalayaan was formed to campaign for this legal recognition of migrant domestic workers.

The need for specific protections for migrant domestic workers has been recognised in the UK for some time and it was because of this that a concession was introduced in 1998, which was then formally incorporated into the immigration rules in 2002 in order to provide basic protections in the form of a recognised independent immigration status. The 'Overseas domestic worker' visa was created by the Government in recognition of the vulnerability to exploitation of migrant domestic workers in the UK. This visa recognises migrant domestic workers as workers and confers on them the same rights in law as other employees. Importantly the visa allows domestic workers to change employers (not sectors) without losing their immigration status. This is crucial to the ability of migrant domestic workers to secure redress for violations of their human and working rights, as without independent status they would be powerless to leave the employer or pursue justice. This visa and the 'portability' of the permission to work have been instrumental in enabling migrant domestic workers to come forward and seek justice through the police and the employment tribunals. Many migrant domestic workers have compelling reasons why they feel they cannot return home, including but not limited to debts they have taken out to migrate and find work, money needed for family illness or raising children, family violence and the proximity of their employer's families to their own. The visa allows people to move on with their lives and continue supporting their families whilst also enabling the worker to remain visible within the immigration system and so can contribute to the UK economy.

Prior to 1998 there was no formal immigration route for migrant domestic workers to enter the UK. The result was that such workers entered informally, accompanying wealthy employers whose entry the UK encouraged. At this time migrant domestic workers were issued visit visas, despite entering for the purpose of work, or a stamp stating that they were 'to work with' and naming the employer. Although they were unlikely to come into contact with the UK authorities whilst employed, any worker who left their employer, or ran away, in order to escape abuse was seen as a being 'illegal' with no immigration status and no protection under UK law. Although at the time there was no system to identify whether any of these workers were victims of trafficking, it is clear to us that many indeed had been trafficked, and that the lack of a formal route to enter the UK together with the absence of any corresponding or specific protection encouraged this.

Key to the protections provided by the MDW visa is the right to change employer, so allowing a worker to escape abuse without jeopardising their immigration status[2]. While migrant domestic workers may still remain vulnerable to exploitation at the hands of their employers, this visa has provided substantial protections against trafficking and forced labour[3]. Also significant is the recognition as a worker which provides protection through UK employment law[4].

In March 2006, in the context of the introduction of the Points Based System for immigration to the UK, the UK Government announced that it would end the existing route of entry for migrant domestic workers, and that instead workers in private households would enter the UK as 'domestic assistants' on an 'amended business visitor visa'[5]. As such they would no longer have the right to change employers (no matter what their treatment), would not be considered workers in the UK so would not be protected by UK employment law and would not be able to apply to renew their visa after the initial six months had expired. There was significant opposition to the proposals based on the fact that proposed changes would facilitate trafficking and slavery.

In response, in June 2008 the Home Office Minister announced that migrant domestic workers would maintain their current rights and that the Government was 'committed to ensuring that future arrangements concerning overseas domestic workers minimise any risk of abuse or exploitation'[6]. In spite of the Government again recognising the particular vulnerabilities of domestic work in a private household, domestic workers who enter the UK in the employment of diplomats were still not granted the right change employers and so escape abuse.

As of the time of writing[7], the migrant domestic worker visa is again under review by the UK Government. It proposes to remove the visa route entirely or to restrict the visa to a six–12 month non-renewable visa without the right to change employer[8]. The first of these suggestions is likely to lead to an increase in trafficking via unlawful routes as evidence already shows that wealthy employers bring their staff on visit visas, false documents, or as family members[9], sometimes with the knowledge of the British Embassy[10]. Workers brought via these routes will have no rights under employment legislation and no possibility to move on and support themselves. They will be reliant on government support under trafficking legislation, the effectiveness of which has been questioned by NGOs[11], and which has been shown not to work for migrant domestic workers[12].

The alternative proposal, to allow employers to bring their staff to the UK but to tie the worker to that employer with no right to change employer and no right to renew the visa will facilitate trafficking and forced labour[13]. The proposal is in direct contradiction to what has been found important internationally in preventing trafficking[14] and, if implemented, has the potential to undermine trafficking prevention efforts in the UK. The Home Affairs Select Committee in their 2008-09 inquiry into Human Trafficking in the UK[15] found '"To retain the existing Migrant Domestic Workers visa and the protection it offers to workers is the single most important issue" in preventing the forced labour and trafficking of such workers'. We at Kalayaan are staggered at the new proposals for 2011, which represent such a fundamental step backwards.

1   'Kalayaan' means 'freedom' in Tagalog, a language of the Philippines.
2   In addition a requirement of a 12 month pre-existing employment relationship was imposed as part of the application process.
3   As found by the House of Commons Home Affairs Committee Inquiry 'The Trade in Human Beings: Human Trafficking in the UK'. Sixth Report of Session 2008-09 Volume 1, at p 26.
4   See further **CHAPTER 17** by Jamila Duncan-Bosu on Employment Tribunal claims.
5   Kalayaan Campaign Statement April 2007 'Migration must work for workers too' http://www.kalayaan.org.uk/documents/Kalayaan%20Campaign%20statement%20with%20supporters.pdf accessed 21.4.11.
6   UK Border Agency (2008) Government response to the consultation on visitors http://www.ukba.homeoffice.gov.uk/sitecontent/documents/aboutus/consultations/closedconsultations/visitorsconsultationpaper/visitorsconsultationrespon.PDF accessed on 24/04/09.
7   Early June 2011.
8   UK Border Agency Consultation on Employment-related settlement 9 June 2011 http://www.ukba.homeoffice.gov.uk/sitecontent/documents/policyandlaw/consultations/employment-related-settlement/ accessed 13 June 2011.
9   Lalani M, Kalayaan, 'Ending the Abuse: Policies that work to protect migrant domestic workers, May 2011', p23 http://www.kalayaan.org.uk/documents/Kalayaan%20Report%20final.pdf.
10   Kalayaan Database.
11   The Anti Trafficking Monitoring Group Briefing: Assistance to Trafficked People, January 2011.
12   Lalani M, Kalayaan, 'Ending the Abuse: Policies that work to protect migrant domestic workers, May 2011', p 22–30 http://www.kalayaan.org.uk/documents/Kalayaan%20Report%20final.pdf
13   'Unprotected Work, Invisible Exploitation: Trafficking for the Purpose of Domestic Servitude' OSCE 2011, p16.
14   2010 Trafficking in Persons Report, US Department of State, June 2010, p 24 http://www.state.gov/g/tip/rls/tiprpt/2010/.
15   House of Commons Home Affairs Committee Inquiry 'The Trade in Human Beings: Human Trafficking in the UK. Sixth Report of Session 2008-09 Volume 1, p 26.

DEVELOPMENT OF PROTECTIONS FOR VICTIMS OF TRAFFICKING

11.3 Until 2008 there remained no formal mechanism for trafficked migrant domestic workers to be identified as such. In December 2008 the UK Government ratified the Council of Europe Convention on Action against Trafficking in Human Beings ('the Trafficking Convention'). Implementation in the UK has been based around the establishment of a National Referral Mechanism (NRM) whereby named 'First Responders'[1] can refer individuals who they suspect may have been trafficked. Referrals go to the 'Competent Authority'[2] in order that it can make a decision as to whether it accepts that person has indeed been trafficked. In theory the UK authorities are then responsible for ensuring that accommodation and support services are available for recognised victims[3]. This should include legal advice[4], although making referrals for trafficked victims to receive legal advice has not been the practice of the Competent Authority in the UK.

Despite much optimism from organisations in the UK who work with victims of trafficking following the ratification of the Trafficking Convention, there has been significant disappointment with its implementation and much criticism of the fact that so much of the focus has been around crime prevention with little attention given or checks made as to the provision or quality of victim care[5]. There has also been a dire lack of co-ordination across Government departments concerning preventing trafficking and the protection of victims. This includes migration policies (proposed or existing) that may potentially facilitate trafficking, as is discussed above in relation to the private household visa for domestic workers and below with regard to domestic workers who accompany diplomats. This lack of co-ordination is also seen in the lack of safe accommodation for recognised victims of trafficking, as discussed below, and the fact that in spite of all victims being entitled to counselling and information including legal advice[6], there has been no supplement to legal aid for any identified trafficking victims. If proposed reforms go ahead many will have no access to legal advice at all[7].

One of the main benefits of the Trafficking Convention to migrant domestic workers who are identified as trafficked is that they should be provided with safe housing[8]. As the existing domestic worker visa contains a stipulation that the holder has 'no recourse to public funds' this makes a vital difference to workers who, upon escaping an employer and often knowing no one in the UK, would otherwise be at risk of destitution or further exploitation. For those with an irregular immigration status a positive 'reasonable grounds' decision by the Competent Authority also provides a short reflection period (usually 45 days) during which the individual will not be removed from the UK, on the basis that this allows time to seek appropriate advice and make decisions on their situation.

In practice even where positive identifications have been made under the NRM, Kalayaan has found that if the individual is not making an asylum claim, there is often no accommodation available or it is only available outside of London, away from the migrant worker's support networks and most potential new jobs. For domestic workers, many of whom are illiterate in all languages and might, in some cases, only speak a relatively uncommon community language, being dispersed or sent by the UKBA to a new area where they know no one can be isolating and traumatic. This is particularly significant since it is often isolation that forms the bedrock of the exploitative trafficking experience for migrant domestic workers. The NRM system in the UK also does not include any provision to ensure that, once any positive identification has been made, all other appropriate referrals, such as to legal advice, counselling, medical care and support for any compensation, take place, and there are no quality standards for accommodation and support[9].

We have additional concerns that where there is no one advocating on their behalf migrant domestic workers are not being correctly identified as trafficked even when coming into contact with authorities, for example when reporting the theft of their passports by employers. We have found that identification is unlikely even when supported by an advocate from Kalayaan and attempting to specifically report trafficking. Out of 37 domestic workers who, accompanied by a staff member from Kalayaan, attempted to report trafficking to the police during a period between May 2008 and August 2010, the police only recorded the crime as trafficking in 12 of these cases. In 14 cases there was reported to have been no crime committed[10]. There is increasing awareness of trafficking for forced labour and domestic servitude in the UK but for many trafficking is still synonymous with sexual exploitation: domestic servitude is too often mistaken for irregular migration, or simply that a person has been employed by a bad employer in a bad job.

In cases where domestic workers are undocumented, identification as trafficked victim does not automatically provide for any right to remain the UK. Trafficked domestic workers often enter on a valid domestic worker visa but become undocumented either because they entered in the employ of a diplomat and are prevented by the immigration rules from switching employers, even where there is evidence of severe abuse including trafficking, or because their employer kept their passport from them and never renewed their visa or deliberately let it expire in order to increase their power over the worker. In other cases they are bought to the UK by employers on visit visas or family member visas.

Provision for a renewable annual Residence Permit was introduced upon ratification of the Trafficking Convention[11] but practice has shown that this can really only be applied for by the police in order for the victim to assist with an ongoing investigation[12]. One impact of the inadequacies of the NRM is that many migrant domestic workers who have been identified by Kalayaan as having been trafficked chose not to be referred into it as they simply do not see a referral as being in their interest. Figures from Operation Tolerance[13] (May to September 2008) and from April 2009 (when the Trafficking Convention came into force in the UK) to December 2010, show that 102 out of the 157 migrant domestic workers who Kalayaan identified as trafficked chose not to be referred to the NRM[14]. One of the reasons for this is the risk that a referral into the NRM, followed by any co-operation with the authorities may lead to their employer being arrested whilst the victim has no right to remain in the UK and so could be returned to their home country where they and their family are once again vulnerable but additionally so, as they may be placed at additional risk of reprisals from the worker's former employer and/or his family.

In April 2010, the Coroners and Justice Act 2009, s 71, brought into force in the UK a new criminal offence of holding someone in slavery, servitude, or forcing them to perform forced or compulsory labour. This is an important development in enabling the criminal conviction and punishment of those who traffic domestic workers and exploit them in the UK[15] but unfortunately the focus obviously is, as a piece of criminal legislation, entirely on the prosecution of the new crime and as such it does not materially improve the provision of victim support.

One issue that has been often overlooked in the UK has been access to compensation, either for damage or harm suffered during the course of the trafficking or for unpaid wages[16]. Many trafficked migrant domestic workers will have incurred large debts during the process of migration and the difficult decision to migrate has usually been made due to the desperate need to earn money to support family members. It is not unusual for a trafficked migrant domestic worker not to have been paid for several years, or to have been paid a tiny amount. It is clear that anyone in this position, who has been identified as trafficked, should receive help to apply for compensation for their treatment and at minimum for their unpaid wages. The long hours that migrant domestic workers work mean that even National Minimum Wage employment claims that do not include a damages claim are potentially very large. However taking a claim to the Employment Tribunal is problematic for a number of reasons, including to the hidden nature of domestic work, the fact that the work may be hard to quantify, and that there is so little evidence other than one side's word against the other. The Family Worker Exemption[17] also means that employers frequently claim that the worker was living and working as a 'member of the family' in order to avoid National Minimum Wage liabilities. Individuals who do not have a valid visa, may face insurmountable obstacles in taking their claims to an Employment Tribunal or pursuing other forms of compensation. Remaining in the UK to receive specialist advice and to apply for compensation is not an option if the trafficked worker has nowhere to live and no means of supporting themselves. These individuals are effectively being denied the rights under the Trafficking Convention[18]. Broadening the existing Residence Permit to allow for individuals to pursue compensation claims would address this.

[1]   Kalayaan is a first responder.
[2]   The named 'Competent Authorities' in the UK are the UKBA and the UKHTC.
[3]   The Government reply to the Sixth Report from the Home Affairs Committee Session 2008–09 HC 23 'The Trade in Human Beings: Human Trafficking in the UK'. Presented to Parliament by the Secretary of State for the Home Department by Command of Her Majesty August 2009.
[4]   Article 12, Chapter IV of the Trafficking Convention includes provision for standards of care and livelihood capable of sustaining the victim. These standards encompass at least: appropriate accommodation as well as medical and mental health assistance, education, access to medical treatment, translation and interpretation services as well as counselling and information, in particular as regards their legal rights and the services available to them.
[5]   For more detail see The Anti-Trafficking Monitoring Group *'Wrong kind of victim? One year on: an analysis of UK measures to protect trafficked persons'* June 2010.
[6]   Trafficking Convention, Article 12 (Chapter IV).
[7]   Ministry of Justice Proposals for the Reform of Legal Aid in England and Wales Consultation Paper 12/10 November 2010.
[8]   Article 12, Chapter IV of the Trafficking Convention includes provision for standards of living capable of ensuring [the victim's] subsistence, through such measures as appropriate and secure accommodation, psychological and material assistance.
     Council of Europe Convention on Action Against Trafficking, Warsaw, 16 May 2005. http://conventions.coe.int/Treaty/EN/Treaties/Html/197.htm accessed 7 June 2011.
[9]   The Anti-Trafficking Monitoring Group Briefing: Assistance to Trafficked People, January 2011.
[10] 'Ending the Abuse; Policies that work to protect migrant domestic workers'. Lalani, M. Kalayaan, May 2011 at p 25.http://www.kalayaan.org.uk/documents/Kalayaan%20Report%20final.pdf.
[11] Residence permits fall under the Trafficking Convention, Article 14.
[12] There is also the possibility to apply for the residence permit for 'personal circumstances' but in practice, and to our knowledge, the UKBA has only ever granted a residence permit on this basis to two migrant domestic workers.
[13] The UK Border Agency pilot project to support victims of trafficking for labour exploitation.
[14] Lalani, M, 'Ending the Abuse; Policies that work to protect migrant domestic workers' Kalayaan, May 2011 at p 27. http://www.kalayaan.org.uk/documents/Kalayaan%20Report%20final.pdf.
[15] Notably the new s 71 offence takes place irrespective of whether the victim has been trafficked.
[16] Please see the various chapters on compensation in this Handbook where the right to compensation, and the obstacles to obtaining it, is discussed in more detail.

¹⁷ National Minimum Wage Regulations 1999, SI 1999/584, reg 22, 'Definition of Worker'.
¹⁸ Article 15 of the Trafficking Convention provides for the right to compensation.

EXPERIENCES OF MIGRANT DOMESTIC WORKERS AND THE JUSTICE SYSTEM IN THE UK

11.4 It seems that in formulating policies to protect and support victims of trafficking and domestic servitude, policy makers and professionals have not fully understood the perspectives of the individuals themselves. There has been a lack of recognition in the UK of domestic workers' own ideas regarding their priorities and needs, namely the need to work again to support their families. As described, the systems established ostensibly for the benefit of victims of trafficking focus entirely on their co-operation with authorities (be they criminal, immigration, legal) and may often leave domestic workers without the right to work for months or in some cases years whilst their cases are being decided, thus denying them the ability to support their families in the short term and offering no answer to paying off debts in the future. This can sometimes increase the stress suffered by victims rather than relieve it.

> 'I feel so worried, I don't know what is going to happen – this worries me more. My solicitor is still waiting for the Home Office. Sometimes I wake up in the middle of the night and I'm crying, I just want to know what is happening with my case . . . I keep thinking when is this going to be over.'[1]

There are some victims of domestic servitude who are so deeply traumatised by their experience that they cannot contemplate working again[2]. They may have acute mental and physical health needs and certainly the perspectives of these individuals are different from those domestic workers who are desperate, and physically and mentally able, to work again. For the former category of individuals trauma-based therapy, rest and recovery can be essential. However, most of the domestic workers that Kalayaan see, feel very strongly that they are workers not victims. The status of 'victim of trafficking' often holds very little resonance with women and men who not only do not understand the concept but even once they do, see no advantage in acquiring such a label. Their primary need, as they see it, may only be for proper conditions of work that are conducive to decent living standards for themselves and their children.

Another difficulty migrant domestic workers face is navigating and understanding the systems designed to protect them. It is difficult to understand what trafficking means as a legal concept and understanding what rights are triggered from being recognised as a 'victim' and how the different authorities can help in pursuing different types of justice is complicated. An individual might have more than one immigration case, at the same time be acting as a witness in a criminal investigation, as a claimant in the an Employment Tribunal and in some cases might also have a claim against the police for the mishandling of their investigation, or lack of it, in their case. Understanding the implications and potential outcomes of all these cases, and on what basis the different claims are being pursued, can be very challenging. The rules and processes by which each of the different authorities operate can also be opaque, even to the professionals who are involved in helping the trafficked individuals navigate them. It is unsurprising therefore that domestic workers are left confused at why one authority may find their trafficking claim has substance and merit whilst a different authority might find the contrary. One victim of trafficking who won her Employment Tribunal claim but was refused a residence permit could not comprehend why the two things were not linked:

'. . . the employment tribunal told them [the UKBA] they should give me my residence permit; they should have given it'[3].

In most cases trafficked migrant domestic workers choose not to pursue cases against their employers and traffickers or even be referred into the NRM. There are many reasons for this, some of which have been described earlier. In summary, for those who do not have a valid immigration status in the UK and desperately need to work they may fear making the authorities aware of their presence in the UK. Some domestic workers may not want to pursue redress because they fear reprisals against them or their family, particularly if they were recruited in their own village and thus their homes are known to the agents or employer. Victims also sometimes have strong emotional ties to the young children and elderly people they looked after in their exploitative employment in the UK. Some state that they do not want to cause trouble for employers in case this negatively affects the employer's children. There have also been cases where domestic workers have been pressured by their own families to drop claims against their traffickers because the trafficker knows the family and the family fears them. On the other hand in Kalayaan's experience some victims of domestic servitude simply want to move on to a new job where conditions are better and choose not to pursue their traffickers because they wish to forget about what has happened and leave justice 'to God'.

Often when domestic workers do wish to take action, they talk in terms of the wages that they worked for and were not paid and about not having been treated properly at work. One domestic worker told Kalayaan:

'I am only asking for my wage arrears, nothing else. I am not claiming anything illegal; I just want what is rightfully mine.'[4]

The fact that there is no threat of jail for their employers may make the Employment Tribunal feel like a safer option in terms of potential reprisals[5] and monetary compensation is important; returning home can be unthinkable when the domestic worker has debts to family members, or even worse to agents, and many feel like they have failed their families. Compensation could mean the worker has 'something to show' for their time away. This is very important to domestic workers and may also decrease their vulnerability to re-trafficking.

The Employment Tribunal process has not always proved successful, not least in the area of enforcement. In the past two years a total of £786,548 has been awarded to domestic workers in successful Employment Tribunal decisions[6]. Whilst there have been very few problems in getting the settlement monies[7], none of the actual sums awarded by the Employment Tribunal itself have ever been paid. Domestic workers who have won their cases in the Employment Tribunal have mixed feelings about this. They describe being extremely happy that they had won their case, 'I felt very happy. I couldn't sleep for three nights afterwards because I was so overjoyed'[8] but of feeling unhappy and frustrated that they had not received the money. However in response to the question 'What would you do if your friend experienced the same problems with her employer?' they almost universally answered that they would tell them to get advice and pursue justice: 'I would tell them to go to court and say the truth. The truth will come out. I would tell them to fight for their rights'[9]. The legal process has certainly empowered some domestic workers to believe in the law: one who settled their claim saying 'At least now they will know that the law is for everyone, not just for the rich people with money'[10].

In terms of criminal cases there have also been very few successful cases which can provide strong examples of the kind of justice that can be achieved and compensation for the victim has not, until very recently, featured in criminal cases against traffickers. To date there have been no successful criminal prosecutions for trafficking for domestic servitude. This provides little encouragement for trafficked domestic workers to pursue justice through the criminal courts.

[1] Interview with a domestic worker, whose case involved an NRM decision and an asylum claim. Lalani, M, 'Ending the Abuse; Policies that work to protect migrant domestic workers'. Kalayaan, May 2011 at p 26. http://www.kalayaan.org.uk/documents/Kalayaan%20Report%20final.pdf.

[2] Please refer to **CHAPTER 4** in this Handbook.

[3] Interview with a migrant domestic worker, March 2011. Reported in Kalayaan Final Progress Report to the Barrow Cadbury Trust (8 March 2011). It is unlikely that the Employment Tribunal commented on the policy of the UKBA with regards to the issuing of residence permits, which further exemplifies the domestic worker's confusion over the roles of the authorities.

[4] Interview with male domestic worker with an ongoing case in the employment tribunal, February 2011.

[5] In fact this is not necessarily the case; there have been cases of reprisals against family members and the victims themselves in a number of cases. Predominantly these have taken the form of threats, but individuals have been followed home, and in some cases police in other countries have arrested a victim's family members on spurious grounds. On the reverse, one domestic worker told Kalayaan that the threats had only stopped once her employer had been served by the solicitors (interview with female domestic worker, February 2011).

[6] Kalayaan Final Progress Report to the Barrow Cadbury Trust (8 March 2011). Note that these are not all victims of trafficking. Some of these cases are migrant domestic workers who have had their employment rights violated. We do know of one migrant domestic worker who received her judgment before this two year period and did receive the monies awarded by the Tribunal. There are other cases where enforcement is ongoing.

[7] £268,865 has been paid in settlement monies, namely where a case has been settled prior to the Employment Tribunal substantively hearing the claim.

[8] Interview with a migrant domestic worker, March 2011. Reported in Kalayaan Final Progress Report to the Barrow Cadbury Trust (8 March 2011).

[9] Interview with a migrant domestic worker, March 2011. Reported in Kalayaan Final Progress Report to the Barrow Cadbury Trust (8 March 2011).

[10] Informal conversation between migrant domestic worker and Kalayaan caseworker, February 2011.

PARTICULAR VULNERABILITY OF DOMESTIC WORKERS IN DIPLOMATIC HOUSEHOLDS

11.5 One specific group of migrant domestic workers has been consistently ignored by the UK Government's policies for victims of trafficking. Since the introduction of the overseas domestic worker visa in 1998, domestic workers who come to the UK with diplomats have been treated differently to those who come with private household employers. Diplomats can recruit domestic workers directly from overseas either through personal contacts or a recruitment agent. There are little in the way of checks on either the diplomat or the recruitment agency used[1]. It appears to be simply assumed that the diplomat will treat the worker with respect and follow UK employment laws; they are not even required to provide a contract to the UKBA. Once in the UK the domestic worker can only work for diplomats in that particular mission.

In practice this has meant that domestic workers who work with diplomats have been made more vulnerable to abuse, exploitation and trafficking for forced labour. When comparing the number of referrals of trafficked domestic workers into the National Referral Mechanism to the number of workers entering the UK, there is a rate of trafficking of approximately 3.8 per cent in diplomatic households, compared to 0.2 per cent in private households[2]. Amongst those individuals identified as trafficked by Kalayaan (most of whom are not referred into the Government's NRM system), the figures are 7.4 per cent for diplomatic households and 0.54 per cent for private households[3].

The power imbalance already inherent in a relationship where a worker is isolated and very dependent on their employer is greatly exacerbated where an employer has immunity (whether presumed or real) to prosecution. If the domestic worker also cannot withdraw her/his labour then the individual has no way of negotiating better terms and conditions. Their choice is simply to either remain with the employer and thereby continue to suffer ill-treatment, or flee and lose their accommodation, their right to work, their ability to support their family and in so doing become a criminal, an 'illegal'.

The phenomenon of trafficking by diplomats has been reported across Europe[4] and in the USA[5] and is receiving worldwide attention, including by the OSCE[6]. Recently the US Government has, in its 2010 Trafficking in Persons report, made recommendations that States should increase the oversight of this diplomat/worker employment relationship and should create an independent migration status for domestic workers giving them the right to change their employer[7].

Diplomatic Immunity is a difficult and sensitive issue. There are good reasons for international laws on immunity to protect diplomats from rogue regimes or vengeful arrests. However professionals dealing with the issue, including some police officers in the UK[8] feel that the use of immunity to cover a diplomat who violates the basic human rights of an individual is unacceptable.

In the UK there have been at least 12 domestic workers who have reported to the police that their diplomat employer trafficked to them to the UK[9]. To our knowledge, in only two of these cases did the police ask the Foreign and Commonwealth Office to request a waiver of immunity from the embassy concerned, which was needed in order to continue the police investigation and not be prevented from doing so on the basis of diplomatic immunity. In one of these cases the diplomat was asked to leave the UK. In another case, the diplomat's embassy refused to waive immunity, the diplomat remained in post and Kalayaan were later approached by a different domestic worker, who was identified by Kalayaan as having been trafficked, claiming to have been mistreated by the same diplomat[10].

Various lawyers in the UK have argued that the civil courts and Employment Tribunal must first consider whether immunity applies in the treatment of domestic workers by diplomats. The business or commercial activities of a diplomat are not included within the scope of diplomatic immunity in the

Vienna Convention on Diplomatic Relations 1961[11] and there is some debate over whether profiting from an individual's unpaid or underpaid labour is effectively a commercial activity and thus is not covered by diplomatic immunity[12].

Even if immunity is not considered to apply, once a domestic worker has a judgment against a diplomat then of course there is the further difficulty of how to enforce this judgment. In the UK there has been a successful Employment Tribunal case against a diplomat. The diplomat did not answer the Tribunal and therefore the issue of immunity was not raised. A default judgment was issued in the claimant's favour for a sum of approximately £80,000 for claims including unpaid wages, and damages for aggravated damages for sexual discrimination[13]. The domestic worker has not been able to enforce the award because the diplomat returned to his country of origin.

If the UK courts and tribunals do not consider that they have jurisdiction in these cases because diplomatic immunity is seen to apply then it remains to be seen as to whether the UK Immunity Acts[14] are compatible with the ECHR[15]. Internationally, NGOs are also calling for the Vienna Convention on Diplomatic Relations of 1961[16] to be re-examined with a view establishing whether the articles on immunity are still fit for purpose[17].

Leaving immunity aside, it is clear that domestic workers who accompany diplomats to the UK find it extremely difficult to obtain justice, not least because after leaving their employer they have no right to remain in the UK. Moreover it is likely that the binding of their visa to their employer may well prevent them from leaving an abusive situation in the first place.

The UK is potentially failing in its obligation to suppress forced labour[18] as the rules governing diplomats' ability to bring domestic staff to the UK are not sufficiently robust to prevent forced labour and in fact the restrictive nature of the visa may facilitate trafficking for domestic servitude. The ability to withdraw one's labour is the only negotiating power that a migrant domestic worker can have: without it she/he has no viable options but to remain and suffer. If the UK's Immigration Rules were amended to allow migrant workers to escape trafficking by diplomats without losing their immigration status, these trafficked persons could move on to new non-exploitative work and continue supporting their families. Whilst doing so they would have adequate breathing space to consider trying to pursue criminal and civil redress against their employers.

[1]   Currently under the Tier 5 international agreement route the embassy must have a sponsorship licence. This is the only real check used.

[2]   For the period covering pilot project to protect victims of trafficking 'Operation Tolerance' (May–September 2008), and the period from 1 April 2009 when NRM was introduced to 31 December 2010. 'Ending the Abuse: Policies that work to protect migrant domestic workers', Kalayaan, May 2011.

[3]   For the period covering first year of operation of the NRM – 1 April 2009 to 31 March 2010. Migrant Domestic Workers who accompany diplomats, Kalayaan. August 2010.

[4]   Kartush, A. 'Rights Violations and Access to Justice of Domestic Workers in the context of Diplomatic Immunity: Research into Practice in Six European Countries'. Deutsche Institut fur Menschenrechte. Draft report. Discussed at Berlin Roundtable, 2 May 2011.

[5]   US Government's efforts to address alleged abuse of Household workers by foreign diplomats with immunity could be strengthened. United States Government Accountability Office, July 2008.

[6]   'Unprotected Work, Invisible Exploitation: Trafficking for the Purpose of Domestic Servitude', OSCE, 2011.

[7] 2010 Trafficking in Persons Report, US Department of State, June 2010, p 38. http://www.s tate.gov/g/tip/rls/tiprpt/2010/.

[8] Conversation between specialist police officer and Kalayaan caseworker, March 2011 and conversation with territorial police officer in October 2009.

[9] Kalayaan data – accessed 26 April 2011.

[10] http://www.bbc.co.uk/programmes/b00srp6v.

[11] Vienna Convention on Diplomatic Relations 1961, United Nations, Article 31(c). http://untre aty.un.org/ilc/texts/instruments/english/conventions/9_1_1961.pdf accessed 26 April 2011.

[12] See for example Eileen Denza, *Diplomatic Law, Commentary on the Vienna Convention on Diplomatic Relations* (3rd edn, 2008), p 311 cited in Kartusch, A, 'Rights Violations and Access to Justice of Domestic workers in the Context of Diplomatic Immunity'. Deutsche Institut fur Menschenrecthe. See also Amicus Brief of American Civil Liberties Union, Asian American Legal Defense and Education Fund and 11 others in support of Plaintiff-Appellee-cross-Appellant http://www.aclu.org/files/assets/2010_02_16_Amicus_Brief_of_ACL U_AALDEF_and_11_Other_Organizations.pdf accessed 26 April 2011.

[13] The Tribunal case cannot be referenced as the domestic worker has requested that Kalayaan continue to protect her identity.

[14] These are the Diplomatic Privileges Act 1964 (http://www.legislation.gov.uk/ukpga/1964/81) accessed 7 June 2011 and the Consular Relations Act 1968 (http://www.legislation.gov.uk/u kpga/1968/18) accessed 7 June 2011.

[15] Articles 3, 4 and 6. European Convention on the Protection of Human Rights and Fundamental Freedoms 1950 (http://www.echr.coe.int/NR/rdonlyres/D5CC24A7-DC 13-4318-B457-5C9014916D7A/0/ENG_CONV.pdf) accessed 26 April 2011.

[16] http://untreaty.un.org/ilc/texts/instruments/english/conventions/9_1_1961.pdf , accessed 7 June 2011.

[17] 'Recommendations on the Situation of Domestic Workers who Work for Diplomats'. February 2011. Ban Ying (Berlin), BliNN (Amsterdam) CCEM (Paris) Kalayaan (London), Lefö (Vienna) Migrants Rights Centre Ireland (Dublin) and Pag.Asa (Brussels).

[18] Article 1, Forced Labour Convention No 29. 1930, International Labour Organisation.

CONCLUSION

11.6 As explained in this chapter, domestic work is not inherently exploit-ative. The majority of the migrant domestic workers known to Kalayaan, including some who are trafficked, are able to leave bad employment and find domestic work which entails reasonable hours and working conditions for which they are paid according to UK laws and for which they feel valued. The provision within their visa to withdraw their labour without jeopardising their immigration status means that many migrant domestic workers are able to negotiate good working conditions. Kalayaan's experience of working with migrant domestic workers who have had the option to switch employers and with those who, for immigration reasons cannot, makes clear that this and other basic protections provided by the independent overseas domestic worker visa are vital to prevent far more widespread trafficking and other abuses of migrant domestic workers in the UK and have also been recognised by the International Labour Organisation (ILO) as an example of good practice[1].

The UK's trafficking protections do not work for migrant domestic workers and need a great deal of improvement particularly in terms of providing appropriate support and ongoing protection that is based on the needs of trafficked persons themselves, including safe accommodation, residence per-mits where the trafficking has resulted in the migrant domestic worker becoming undocumented, and better access to compensation, including through the enforcement of tribunal and court judgments. Urgent attention is needed to address the particularly vulnerable situation of domestic workers who accompany diplomats to the UK who, at an absolute minimum, need an option within the immigration rules to escape an abusive employer without becoming undocumented. The UK Government's recent proposals to either remove or restrict the rights associated with the domestic worker visa are likely to facilitate and exacerbate trafficking to the UK for domestic servitude and will be strenuously challenged by all of us who work to prevent trafficking and protect its victims.

[1]   Draft ILO Multilateral Framework on Labour Migration Non-binding principles and guidelines for a rights-based approach to labour migration, Geneva, 31 Oct–2 Nov 2005. Annex II 'Examples of best practise, VI Prevention of and protection against abusive migration practises', Pt 82.

Part IV

PERSPECTIVES ON THE LEGAL RECOGNITION OF RIGHTS AND DUTIES

Contents

CHILD TRAFFICKING IN THE UK IN THE CONTEXT OF INTERNATIONAL LEGAL PROTECTION

Nadine Finch

CHILD TRAFFICKING AS A PHENOMENON

12.1 UNICEF estimates that 1.2 million children are the victims of child trafficking in any one year[1]. The numbers of children trafficked into and within the United Kingdom is not known and any statistics which do exist are no more than snapshots of this abuse which have come to light through the work of statutory authorities, such as the police[2], or Non-Governmental Organisations such as ECPAT UK[3] or Anti-Slavery International[4]. The major difficulty is that the trafficking and exploitation of children largely takes place behind closed doors and as they are often assumed to be with parents or relatives no suspicions of abuse are raised. The discovery of their true situation may be a bi-product of unrelated police investigations as was the case in the 2007 Operation Pentameter II[5] when over a six month period brothels and saunas thought to be exploiting migrant women who had been trafficked were raided by various police forces in the UK. During these raids 164 victims of sex trafficking (including 13 children) and five victims of labour exploitation (including three children) were recovered. The ages of the children who were found ranged from 13 to 17 years old[6].

The Government's National Referral Mechanism (NRM), which has operated since 1 April 2009 to identify victims of trafficking in the UK, also provides figures for the number of trafficked children who were referred to it between 1 April 2009 and 31 December 2010[7]. According to ECPAT UK's analysis of those NRM statistics[8], 215 (26%) of the 843 cases of potential victims of human trafficking referred under the NRM related to children, with Vietnamese children accounting for over a quarter of all children referred. Of the total number of children referred, 97 were potential victims of labour exploitation, including domestic servitude. Thirty five children were under 13 at the date of referral.

In contrast, figures published by the Child Exploitation and Online Protection Centre[9] (CEOP) in its *Strategic Threat Assessment: Child Trafficking in the UK 2010* showed that in the 12 month period from 1 March 2009 to 28 February

2010, CEOP identified a total of 287 children from 47 countries as being potential victims of trafficking in the UK. CEOP found:

> 'Most were from Vietnam (58), Nigeria (40), China (24) and a significant number of Roma children (32) were also identified. Where the type of exploitation was identified (219 cases), 35% (76) of children were sexually exploited, most of whom were female. Eighteen per cent (39) were exploited for cannabis cultivation, 11% (25) were exploited for domestic servitude, 11% (23) for benefit fraud, 9% (19) for labour exploitation, 9% (20) for street crime, 4% (8) for servile marriage, 2% (4) for illegal adoption and 2% (5) for various other types of exploitation.'

One of the important characteristics of child trafficking is that children are exploited for a far greater range of purposes than adults. A failure to recognise this has impeded the successful identification of such children and the development of international law and national services to provide them with the sustainable protection they require.

[1] The State of the World's Children Special Edition, Executive Summary, UNICEF (2010) at p 9.

[2] Such as through the work of the Child Exploitation and Online Protection agency (CEOP), the United Kingdom Human Trafficking Centre (UKHTC) which currently exists under the Serious Organised Crime Agency (SOCA) and the work of the Metropolitan Police's Paladin team.

[3] End Child Prostitution, Child Pornography and the Trafficking of Children for Sexual Purposes UK.

[4] A non-governmental organisation working at local, national and international levels to eliminate all forms of slavery around the world.

[5] ECPAT UK, 'The trafficking of children for sexual exploitation' (2009). Pentameter II focussed on sex trafficking but also forced labour. Pentameter II was launched in October 2007, ran for six months and involved 35 police force areas across the UK.

[6] UK Pentameter II Statistics of Victims recovered and the Suspects arrested during the operational phase, available at http://www.soca.gov.uk/about-soca/about-the-ukhtc/statistical -data.

[7] Not all trafficked children in the UK are referred into the NRM.

[8] ECPAT UK, 'Child Trafficking in the UK: A Snapshot' (October 2010).

[9] A specialist unit of the UK police.

Benefit fraud

12.2 For example, children as opposed to adults are regularly trafficked for the purpose of benefit fraud. It is very difficult to estimate the true extent of this phenomenon but in one small survey CEOP identified 19 children who had potentially been trafficked for this purpose between 1 April 2008 and 31 March 2009[1]. The CEOP report went on to state that the most common nationalities and ethnicities of these children were Nigerian, Somali and Roma and that their exploiters were of the same nationality and ethnic background[2]. As it was happening within specific communities and amongst populations which were fluid and where members of extended families may be living in the same household the identification of these children was particularly difficult.

The report also noted that the majority of these children were aged 12 or under and suggested that this was because they could be exploited for a longer period of time[3]. It also noted that these children were moved between different addresses and passed from adult to adult, which raised serious safeguarding issues[4]. In addition, it suggested that one child may be being used as a commodity by traffickers to form the basis of a number of different fraudulent claims.

1   CEOP, *'The trafficking of children into and within the UK for the benefit fraud purposes'* (October 2010), paragraph 2.1 at page 4.
2   CEOP, *'The trafficking of children into and within the UK for the benefit fraud purposes'* (October 2010), at paragraph 2.2.
3   CEOP, *'The trafficking of children into and within the UK for the benefit fraud purposes'* (October 2010), at paragraph 2.3.
4   CEOP, *'The trafficking of children into and within the UK for the benefit fraud purposes'* (October 2010), at paragraph 2.5.

Forced criminality

12.3 In addition, children are trafficked into and within the United Kingdom by criminal networks for forced criminality covering a range of crimes, including street crime such as DVD selling, bag snatching, ATM theft, pick-pocketing and forced begging[1]. Adults can be trafficked for the same purposes but it appears that criminal gangs prefer to use children. ECPAT UK has suggested that this may be because 'these children will be "invisible" to the wider community until they come to the notice of the authorities because of the crimes they have committed'[2]. In addition, 'children under the control of adults, particularly those related to them, will be reluctant to come forward and ask for help'[3]. CEOP also concluded that some of these children were being placed in private fostering[4] arrangements, which were a cover for benefit fraud.

Investigations have also disclosed that this form of child trafficking, namely for the purposes of enforced criminality, has characteristics which correlate with the child's country of origin. One example quoted by ECPAT in their Discussion Paper[5] involved Roma children. It noted that from 2007–2010 Operation Golf, a specialist Joint Investigation Team (JIT) between the Metropolitan Police and the Romanian National Police, investigated organised crime networks involved in the trafficking of children from the Romanian Roma community into London for forced criminality. According to Operation Golf, over 1,000 children from one Romanian town were found to be trafficked into Western Europe for labour (and sexual) exploitation over a four-year period[6].

In another example referred to in its *'Strategic Threat Assessment: Child Trafficking in the UK 2010'* CEOP identified the trafficking of Vietnamese children into and within the UK as being 'the largest and most significant trend' in 2009–2010[7]. It also stated that the most frequently identified potential victims of trafficking identified by the National Referral Mechanism during this period were under the age of 18, were Vietnamese and had been exploited in cannabis farms[8]. This trend was also confirmed by ECPAT UK. It noted that between 1 April 2009 and 30 June 2010, 27% (or 59 of the 215) of the children referred under the NRM were Vietnamese[9].

The CEOP Strategic Threat Assessment went on give more detail about this child specific form of trafficking when it stated that:

'All of the children identified in cannabis factories worked as "gardeners", tending and watering the cannabis plants. As might be expected for a child, this is the "bottom rung" position within the criminal enterprise. Often children were isolated, locked in the property alone and sleeping in the premises. One child stated that he slept on a quilt on the floor. It is unclear if the children were locked in to prevent escape or as a measure of security, as other criminal networks have been known to force entry to disrupt rival operations. Many stated they remained in the residence for the entirety of their exploitation. Those who did venture outside stated that they would be accompanied by a member of the criminal network'[10].

The same report highlighted the ongoing criminalisation of Vietnamese trafficked children who are found by the police following raids on cannabis farms in the UK[11].

In all cases of trafficking which involve the use of a child for criminal activity, be it for the sale of illegal DVDs, handbag thefts, benefit fraud or cannabis cultivation the key to understanding the rights of a trafficked child is that under Article 3 of the Palermo Protocol[12] and Article 4 of the Council of Europe Convention on Action against Trafficking in Human Beings[13] (the Trafficking Convention) a child cannot consent to their own exploitation. It follows that such children are entitled to protection under the law as victims of crime and not to be prosecuted as criminal offenders.

[1] ECPAT UK Discussion Paper, '*Child Trafficking for Forced Criminality*' (Winter 2010). See also, generally, the CEOP report '*Strategic Threat Assessment: Child Trafficking in the UK 2010*'.
[2] ECPAT UK Discussion Paper, '*Child Trafficking for Forced Criminality*' (Winter 2010).
[3] ECPAT UK Discussion Paper, '*Child Trafficking for Forced Criminality*' (Winter 2010).
[4] Section 66 of the Children Act 1989 defines a privately fostered child as a child under 16 who is being cared for and being provided with accommodation by an adult who is not a close relative (grandparent, brother, sister, uncle or aunt or step-parent) for 28 days or more. In such situations the foster carer should inform the appropriate local authority who will then ensure that the privately fostered child's welfare is satisfactorily safeguarded and promoted. For further information on the risks to trafficked children of private fostering arrangements see ECPAT's Understanding Paper '*Child Trafficking and Private Fostering*' (February 2011).
[5] ECPAT UK Discussion Paper, '*Child Trafficking for Forced Criminality*' (Winter 2010).
[6] ECPAT UK Discussion Paper, '*Child Trafficking for Forced Criminality*' (Winter 2010). See further **CHAPTER 22**.
[7] '*Strategic Threat Assessment Child Trafficking in the UK 2010*', (December 2010), at p 6 and at p 23, para 10.1.
[8] '*Strategic Threat Assessment Child Trafficking in the UK 2010*', (December 2010), at p 23, para 10.1.
[9] ECPAT UK, '*Child Trafficking in the UK: A Snapshot*',(18 October 2010),p 3.
[10] '*Strategic Threat Assessment Child Trafficking in the UK 2010*', (December 2010), at p 25, para 10.5.
[11] '*Strategic Threat Assessment Child Trafficking in the UK 2010*', (December 2010), at pp 25–26, para 10.7.
[12] United Nations Convention against Transnational Organized Crime – Protocol to Prevent, Suppress and Punish Trafficking in Persons, Especially Women and Children 2000.
[13] Council of Europe Warsaw, 16.V.2005.

Forced marriage

12.4 Forced marriage is yet another form of trafficking and exploitation which is often child-specific. Such marriages are often a form of recruitment into sexual exploitation but may also be 'servile marriages'[1]. There are no official statistics on the extent of this practice in the United Kingdom but in 2007 ECPAT UK identified seven Somali girls who had been trafficked into the country for forced marriages and it estimated that there were some 300 cases of forced marriages each year and that 30% of these involved children[2].

The UN Convention on the Elimination of all Forms of Discrimination against Women[3] (CEDAW) (1979) calls on Governments to ensure that the engagement and marriage of children are not accorded legal standing. On a domestic level, the Forced Marriage (Civil Protection) Act 2007[4] was brought into force and the Government also issued statutory guidance[5] on how to combat this phenomenon and established the Forced Marriage Unit[6]. In the statutory guidance a forced marriage is defined as 'a marriage in which one or both spouses do not (or, in the case of some vulnerable adults, cannot) consent to the marriage and duress is involved. Under this Guidance, duress can include physical, psychological, financial, sexual and emotional pressure'[7]. In the UK it is legal for older children between 16 and 18 to marry where they and those with parental responsibility for them all consent. However, when forced marriage takes place as a form of human trafficking it will not be necessary to show that a child who is legally of an age to marry has not consented to that marriage or has been subjected to some form of duress. The Palermo Protocol[8] makes it very clear that children are trafficked whether or not they consent or are coerced.

[1] The UN Supplementary Convention on the Abolition of Slavery, and the Slave Trade and Institutions and Practices Similar to Slavery (1956) defines a servile marriage as a being where a woman (minimum age not defined) does not have the right to refuse being given in marriage in exchange for monetary payment or in kind gain benefiting her family or any other person or group.

[2] ECPAT UK Discussion Paper, '*Child Trafficking for Forced Marriages*'(Winter 2008).

[3] Ratified by the UK in April 1986.

[4] The 2007 Act was passed in order to protect victims of forced marriages by empowering the courts to make Forced Marriage Protection Orders, which are injunctive orders aimed at protecting the victim or potential victims of a forced marriage and will assist in removing them from their situation of duress. The Act was passed to make provision for protecting individuals against being forced to enter into marriage without their free and full consent and for protecting individuals who have been forced to enter into marriage without such consent.

[5] '*The Right to Choose: Multi-agency statutory guidance for dealing with forced marriage*'(November 2008).

[6] A joint initiative between the Foreign and Commonwealth Office and the Home Office.

[7] 'The Right to Choose: Multi-agency statutory guidance for dealing with forced marriage' (November 2008).

[8] United Nations Convention against Transnational Organized Crime: Protocol to Prevent, Suppress and Punish Trafficking in Person, Especially Women and Children 2000, Article 3.

Sexual exploitation

12.5 Children are also trafficked into or through the United Kingdom for all forms of sexual exploitation, from child pornography to child prostitution. In April 2009 CEOP reported[1] that it had identified 325 children who it knew or suspected had been trafficked in the UK between March 2007 to February 2008. ECPAT UK also believes that trafficking for sexual exploitation remains the most common form of child trafficking to the United Kingdom[2]. Many young girls from Africa are bought from impoverished families by other family members or members of their community and then sold on to brothel owners in Europe. Consequently it is common to see young African girls as prostitutes in the streets of Italy, Spain and the Netherlands[3]. Some of these girls are also brought into or through the United Kingdom and CEOP has recently found that the trafficking of West African children, predominantly from Nigeria, into the United Kingdom for many exploitative purposes continues to be a major trend[4].

CEOP found:

> 'Of all the profiles identified, West African children had the most diverse age range, with potential victims aged between two and 17 when first trafficked to the UK. Again, this is reflective of the exploitation type. Girls who were sexually exploited had reached puberty and were aged between 14 and 17 and children exploited for benefits were between four and 15, with most aged below 10. Children exploited for benefits may be younger when first trafficked into the UK so the benefits can be claimed for longer, up until adulthood. Children exploited in domestic servitude were trafficked into the UK as young as eight.'[5]

In the same report CEOP also noted that unlike elsewhere African traffickers accompanied the child victims in to the UK, were often female and purported to be related to or known to the child victim so as to enable the child to be brought into the United Kingdom as 'a member of their family'[6]. CEOP concluded:

> 'By attempting to establish a valid link to the child, traffickers hope to pass border controls with greater ease or provide an explanation as to why the child is in their care'.[7]

Other girls, particularly from Eastern Europe, are trafficked for sexual exploitation into the United Kingdom by 'boyfriends' who promise to marry them but then force them into prostitution[8].

[1] CEOP, *'Strategic Threat Assessment on Child Trafficking in the UK'*(2009), at p 9.
[2] ECPAT UK Discussion Paper, *'The trafficking of children for sexual exploitation'*(2009).
[3] *'What is Child Trafficking? Safeguarding African Children in the UK'* Series 2 AFRUCA at p 10.
[4] CEOP, *'Strategic Threat Assessment: Child Trafficking in the UK'* (2010), at p 29.
[5] CEOP, *'Strategic Threat Assessment: Child Trafficking in the UK'* (2010), at p 29.
[6] CEOP, *'Strategic Threat Assessment: Child Trafficking in the UK'* (2010), at p 29.
[7] CEOP, *'Strategic Threat Assessment: Child Trafficking in the UK'* (2010), at p 29.
[8] Farhat Bokhari, ECPAT UK, *'Stolen Futures: Trafficking for Forced Child Marriage in the UK'*(2009) at p 19.

TRAFFICKING INTO SLAVERY

12.6 Notwithstanding all detailed discussions about the different forms of child exploitation and *modus operandi* of groups of traffickers from different countries one must never lose sight of the fact that the end result of human trafficking is the reduction of the victim to modern day slavery.

Kevin Bales, one of the world's leading experts on contemporary slavery estimated that as far back as in 1999[1] there were 27 million slaves being held around the world. Significantly he went on to describe them as being 'enslaved by violence and held against their wills for purposes of exploitation'. This description also aptly fits the victims of child trafficking.

However today, as in the past, reference to human trafficking and slavery conjures up history book descriptions of the 'Slave Trade' and many people believe that it only occurs elsewhere in the world as it was abolished here.

It is true that historically this was more accurate and that the international human rights conventions were focussed on activities taking place abroad. The signatories of the General Act of the Brussels Conference of 1889–90 declared a firm intention to put an end to the traffic in African slaves. After the end of the First World War the Council of the League of Nations appointed a Temporary Slavery Commission. This in turn led to the adoption of a Slavery Convention in 1926[2].

In this early Convention the slave trade was said to include 'all acts involved in the capture, acquisition or disposal of a person with intent to reduce him to slavery'. The States that ratified the Convention undertook to prevent and suppress the slave trade[3].

However, shortly afterwards the definition of slavery was broadened to include forced or compulsory labour in the International Labour Organisation Convention (No 29) of 1930 concerning Forced or Compulsory Labour[4] in recognition that increased international trade and communication was also extending the scope of this phenomenon.

Then after the Second World War in the last century[5] there was an international wave of human rights instruments[6] formulated in an attempt to ensure that the atrocities of that period were not repeated. These Conventions recognised that certain groups of individuals were rendered more vulnerable to harm and discrimination by race or circumstance. These Conventions also recognised human slavery as a fundamental breach of individual human rights. In particular the Universal Declaration of Human Rights 1948[7] boldly declared that 'no one shall be held in slavery or servitude and the slave trade shall be prohibited in all their forms'.

Whilst setting the need for human rights protection in concrete terms, these instruments were largely aspirational and left individual countries to evolve the means by which to ensure that the principles contained in the conventions were upheld. This is a trend which has continued until today and has meant that the paper protection enshrined in these treaties may be of little practical use to many victims of human trafficking. Also, where a country has translated the need for protection into tangible rights via its domestic law this rights-based approach has also meant that a victim needs to have the means and understanding to assert his or her rights or find a lawyer to advocate on his or her behalf.

The principles contained in the Universal Declaration of Human Rights were used by the Council of Europe as a blueprint for its own European Convention for the Protection of Human Rights and Fundamental Freedoms two years later[8]. In its Article 4 it was also declared that no-one shall be held in slavery or servitude or required to perform forced or compulsory labour which was not connected to a term of imprisonment or national service.

However, it was not until nearly 50 years later, on 9 December 1998, that the need for a more specific convention was recognised which would tackle the breadth of the phenomenon of modern human trafficking and slavery. It was then that the United Nations General Assembly[9] decided to establish an open-ended *ad hoc* committee for the purpose of developing an international convention combating organised crime and human trafficking.

This resulted in the adoption of the United Nations Convention against Transnational Organized Crime 2000 and its supplementary Protocol to Prevent, Suppress and Punish Trafficking in Person, Especially Women and Children[10].

1.   Bales, K, *'Disposable People: New Slavery in the Global Economy'*(University of California Press 1999).
2.   League of Nations 25 September 1926 – entered into force 9 March 1927.
3.   Article 2 of the Slavery Convention.
4.   Adopted by the General Conference of the International Labour Organisation on 28 June 1930 – entered into force on 1 May 1932 – ratified by the United Kingdom on 3 June 1931.
5.   1939–1945.
6.   Such as the International Covenant on Civil and Political Rights and the International Covenant on Cultural Social and Economic Rights, both in 1966.
7.   General Assembly of the United Nations December 10 1948, Article 4.
8.   Council of Europe (Rome, 4 November 1950).
9.   General Assembly Resolution 53/111.
10.   Adopted by the UN General Assembly in its resolution 55/25 of 15 November 2000.

CHILD TRAFFICKING

12.7 It was this supplementary protocol, which became known as the 'Palermo Protocol', which laid down the definition[1] of human trafficking now generally adopted by States and by NGOs. What is significant in relation to children is that the definition goes on to provide that the 'recruitment, transportation, transfer, harbouring or receipt of a child for the purposes of exploitation shall be considered "trafficking in persons" even if it does not involve the threat or use of force, abduction, fraud, deception or the abuse of power or a position of vulnerability[2].

Article 6 goes on to provide that States ratifying the Protocol shall take into account the special needs of child victims in terms of housing, education and care. However, this was not a mandatory obligation.

Meanwhile on 17 June 1999 the General Conference of the International Labour Organisation had adopted the 'Convention concerning the Prohibition and Immediate Action for the Elimination of the Worst Forms of Child Labour'[3]. Article 3 defined the worst forms of child labour to include all forms of slavery, including the sale and trafficking of children, debt bondage, forced recruitment of child soldiers, the use of children for prostitution and pornography and drug trafficking and manufacture. This was a step forward in acknowledging that child trafficking could take many forms. Although it is noteworthy that it did not mention trafficking for the purposes of forced marriage or benefit fraud it appears likely that the links between trafficking and these two latter forms of exploitation were only identified internationally at a later date.

On 25 May 2000 the General Assembly of the United Nations also adopted the 'Optional Protocol to the Convention on the Rights of the Child on the sale of children, child prostitution and child pornography'[4]. The preamble to the Optional Protocol noted the significant and increasing international traffic in children and also recognised that girl children were disproportionately represented amongst children who were sexually exploited.

In addition, the preamble to the Optional Protocol usefully recognised the very wide factors which had led to the increase in the human trafficking of children and listed them as being: underdevelopment, poverty, economic disparities, inequitable socio-economic structure, dysfunctional families, lack of education, urban-rural migration, gender discrimination, irresponsible adult sexual behaviour, harmful traditional practices and armed conflict.

Importantly the Optional Protocol also imposed an obligation[5] on parties ratifying it to submit a report to the United Nations Committee on the Rights of the Child on the measures it had taken to implement the Protocol within two years of ratification. This is a welcome addition as many previous Conventions did not have any mechanism for international intervention if the high standards recommended in those conventions were not achieved on a national level.

However, despite the efforts of the ILO and others, the trafficking of children between and within countries worldwide and in the United Kingdom for domestic servitude has continued on a very large scale. There has now been a very recent and significant development in the international field of seeking to introduce measures to combat the employment of children in domestic work and also their consequent deprivation of educational opportunities. The ILO has opened for signature the Convention Concerning Decent Work for Domestic Workers 2011 which aims to achieve decent work for domestic workers[6]. Signatories are required to eliminate all forms of forced or compulsory labour, child labour, and discriminatory employment and occupation practices (Article 3). In addition, the Convention requires the establishment of a minimum age for domestic workers consistent with the 1973 Minimum Age Convention and the 1999 Worst Forms of Child Labour Convention and to ensure that work by child domestic workers above that age does not interfere with their education. An accompanying Recommendation urges Governments to limit strictly the working hours of child domestic workers and to prohibit domestic work that would harm their health, safety, or morals. More generally, the Convention states that domestic workers around the world who care for families and households, must have the same basic labour rights as those recognised for other workers, such as reasonable hours of work, weekly rest for at least 24 consecutive hours, a limit on payment in-kind, clear information on the terms and conditions of employment, as well as respect for fundamental principles and rights at work, including freedom of association and the right to collective bargaining. This Convention was adopted at the 100th Annual Conference of the International Labour Organisation on 16 June 2011 by a vote of 396 to 16, with 63 abstentions[7] and an accompanying Recommendation[8], which was passed by 434 votes to eight, with 42 abstentions.

[1]   Article 3(a) states that '"trafficking in persons" shall mean the recruitment, transportation, transfer, harbouring or receipt of persons, by means of the threat or use of force or other forms of coercion, of abduction, of fraud, of deception, or the abuse of power or of a position of vulnerability or of the giving or receiving of payments or benefits to achieve the consent of a person having control over another person, for the purposes of exploitation. Exploitation shall include, at a minimum, the exploitation or the prostitution of others or other forms of sexual exploitation, forced labour or services, slavery or practices similar to slavery, servitude or the removal of organs.'

[2]   Palermo Protocol, Article 3(c).

[3]   C 182 Worst Forms of Child Labour Convention 1999 – came into force on 19 November 2000 – ratified by the United Kingdom (pre-entry into force) on 22 March 2000.

⁴ Resolution A/RES/54/263 – entered into force on 18 January 2002 – ratified by the United Kingdom on 20 February 2009.
⁵ Article 12 of the Optional Protocol.
⁶ Gulnara Shahinian, the United Nations Special Rapporteur on contemporary forms of slavery has said of the Convention: 'Children are particularly vulnerable to domestic servitude, especially if they live with their employers and/or migrate on their own to find domestic work. The majority of these children are girls. As with many other forms of slavery, domestic servitude occurs in the shadows of many informal economies. This is the first time that the protection of rights is being extended to work that has been regarded as informal. Speedy ratification of the convention will restore dignity to the many men, women and children doing such work, and to the work they perform.' Statement of 20 June 2011. See http://www.ohch r.org/EN/NewsEvents/Pages/DisplayNews.aspx?NewsID=11171&LangID=E.
⁷ The UK abstained from the vote. Of Governments, only Swaziland voted against the Convention. The UK was joined in abstaining by only one other EU country, the Czech Republic, and six other States: El Salvador, Malaysia, Panama, Thailand, Singapore and Sudan.
⁸ Recommendation Concerning Decent Work for Domestic Workers.

THE CONVENTION ON THE RIGHTS OF THE CHILD

12.8 The United Nations Convention on the Rights of the Child 1999[1] itself is also of central importance in protecting the rights of children, including those who have been trafficked. The strength of the international obligations, which it contains has been emphasised in recent case law. Most importantly in *ZH (Tanzania) v Secretary of State for the Home Department*[2]. Lady Hale, giving judgment on behalf of the Supreme Court of England and Wales, confirmed that Article 3 of the United Nations Convention on the Rights of the Child, which provides that in all actions concerning children the best interests of the child shall be a primary consideration was a binding obligation in international law[3] (even though this Convention has not been incorporated into domestic law).

This was a very important acknowledgement by the Supreme Court of the centrality of international law in the protection of the rights of migrant children[4], including those who have been trafficked. In its 2008 report[5] on the United Kingdom, the United Nations Committee on the Rights of the Child said that it was concerned that the principles of the Convention were not taken into account in all pieces of domestic legislation and that the Convention had still not been incorporated into domestic law. However the Convention was relied upon in the case of *D v the Home Office (Bail for Immigration Detainees intervening)*[6] by the Court of Appeal when it found that the detention of children with their parents in Yarl's Wood Immigration Removal Centre was not compatible with Article 37(b) of the Convention on the Rights of the Child, which stated that a child should only be detained as a measure of last resort and for the shortest appropriate period of time. The Court of Appeal also found that a failure to take this Article into account could render a period of immigration detention unlawful.

ZH (Tanzania)[7] also acknowledged the connection between the best interests principle contained in Article 3 of the Convention on the Rights of the Child and the Borders, Citizenship and Immigration Act 2009, s 55. In particular Lady Hale found that the duty under s 55 had translated the spirit, if not the precise language, of Article 3 of the Convention into domestic law.

Section 55 imposes on all those working in the UK Border Agency a duty to have regard to the need to safeguard and promote the welfare of any child in the United Kingdom in reaching any immigration-related decisions. It came into force on 2 November 2009 and was a significant advance in the protection of the rights of migrant children, including those who had been trafficked, as up until then the similar duty in the Children Act 2004, s 11, applied to all other authorities working with children in the UK but not to the UK Border Agency.

In relation to trafficked children, Article 35 of the Convention on the Rights of the Child states that States must make every effort to prevent the sale, trafficking and abduction of children. The trafficking-related criminal legislation[8] now passed by the UK Government, together with the UK Action Plan[9] and the establishment of the UKHTC[10] and the National Referral Mechanism[11] indicates that the Government has taken some steps to implement its duty under this Article.

However, serious concerns have been raised about the ability of the National Referral Mechanism to protect child victims of trafficking. ECPAT UK has said that 'the professionals who make vital decisions about whether a child is trafficked are usually immigration officials, not police or child protection specialists. Local authorities, police and immigration officials are requested to refer children suspected as being trafficked to the NRM to be 'formally' identified. It is unacceptable that Border Agency officials, with perhaps one or two days' training on human trafficking and virtually no specialist training on children, are making decisions about a criminal act against a child even before a police investigation has been completed'[12].

In addition, full compliance with the Trafficking Convention also depends on the Government ensuring that it protects trafficked children who have been wrongly age disputed. Children who have been trafficked may well have arrived in the United Kingdom without any form of identification to confirm that they are under 18. In other cases they will have been supplied with passports or identity cards, which purport to show that they are adults to make it easier[13] for them to be taken out of their country of origin by traffickers and brought into the United Kingdom.

The UK Government has now acknowledged that the leading case on the age assessment of children is that of *R (on the application of A) v Croydon London Borough Council, R (on the application of M) v Lambeth London Borough Council*[14]. In this case the Supreme Court held that the assessment was a matter of fact and should be decided by the court assessing any dispute between a child and a local authority or the UK Border Agency. However, the case did not consider the very specific position of trafficked children. In particular, it did not take into account the fact that when the United Kingdom brought the Council of Europe Convention on Action against Trafficking in Human Beings[15] ('the Trafficking Convention') into force on 1 April 2009 it agreed to apply a different test in relation to age assessment to that which it had adopted in relation to migrant children in general. In particular, Article 10.3 of the Trafficking Convention states that:

> 'When the age of the victim is uncertain and there are reasons to believe that a victim is a child, he or she shall be presumed to be a child and shall be accorded special protection measures pending verification of his/her age'.

This provides children who are suspected to have been trafficked additional protection whilst an assessment of their age is being undertaken. In contrast the test[16] applied to other migrant children states that where there is little or no evidence to support the person's claimed age they should be treated as an adult if their physical appearance or demeanour very strongly suggests that they are significantly over 18 years or age.

The Trafficking Convention also contains another very important protection for trafficked children. Article 16.7 states that 'child victims shall not be returned to a State, if there is an indication, following a risk and security assessment, that such return would not be in the best interests of the child'. This is an important safeguard as the decision in our domestic law in *ZH (Tanzania)*[17] goes no further than stating that the best interests of a child will be a first consideration. It does not give it the paramountcy in relation to returns suggested by the wording in the Trafficking Convention and this is something that has yet to be determined by a higher court of England and Wales since, although *ZH (Tanzania)* is highly instructive in terms of the UK's duties towards the rights and best interests of the child, the case was not itself a child trafficking case and as such no consideration was given to the special rights of trafficked children in the UK under either the Trafficking Convention or under Article 4 ECHR.

However the mere fact that the United Kingdom has ratified the Trafficking Convention and the United Nations Convention on the Rights of the Child does not ensure complete compliance. This is because the actual implementation of each of the Conventions is left to the National State authorities. An example, of the consequences of this is contained in the United Nations Committee on the Rights of the Child 2008 Report[18] on the United Kingdom's compliance with the Convention on the Rights of the Child. In this report the Committee welcomed what was then the United Kingdom's intention to ratify the Trafficking Convention and its adoption of a domestic Action Plan to combat trafficking. However the Committee expressed its concern that 'the necessary resources to implement [the Trafficking Convention] are not being provided, including those needed to ensure the provision of high quality services and safe accommodation for trafficked children'. Three years later in 2011 these resources have not yet been made available and there is still no system of safe accommodation for trafficked children. In CEOP's most recent risk assessment[19] it found that 53 (or 18%) of the children who had been identified as having been potentially trafficked had gone missing from social services foster care or accommodation and that 42 (or 15%) were still missing. It also found that most went missing within a week and many within 48 hours. These findings beg the question, in the absence of the provision of safe local authority accommodation how can a trafficked child be safe?

[1] Ratified by the UK on 16 December 1991.
[2] [2011] UKSC 4 at para 23, [2011] 2 All ER 783, [2011] 2 WLR 148.
[3] See also Article 18 of the Vienna Convention on the Law of Treaties 1969, which obliges a State which has signed or ratified a treaty to refrain from acts which would defeat the object and purpose of a treaty.
[4] The reservation which meant that the Convention did not apply to immigration related decisions relating to children which was lodged when the United Kingdom ratified the Convention on 16 December 1991 was removed with the UK's agreement on 18 November 2008.
[5] Concluding observations on United Kingdom of Great Britain and Northern Ireland CRC/C/GBR/CO/4 20 October 2008 para 10.
[6] [2005] EWCA Civ 38, [2006] 1 All ER 183, [2006] 1 WLR 1003.

7   [2011] UKSC 4 at para 23, [2011] 2 All ER 783, [2011] 2 WLR 148.
8   Nationality, Immigration and Asylum Act 2002, s 145; Sexual Offences 2003, ss 57 and 59; Asylum and Immigration (Treatment of Claimants etc) Act 2004, s 4.
9   Home Office and Scottish Executive, '*UK Action Plan on Tackling Human Trafficking*' (March 2007).
10 United Kingdom Human Trafficking Centre is a multi-disciplinary unit that provides a point of co-ordination for the development of expertise and cooperation to combat trafficking in human beings, which is now part of the Home Office Serious Organised Crime Agency.
11 The present framework in the United Kingdom for identifying victims of trafficking and providing them with a recovery period and in a few cases a temporary residence permit.
12 ECPAT UK, '*Child Trafficking in the UK: A Snapshot*'(18 October 2010) at p 4.
13 For example, para 46A of the United Kingdom's Immigration Rules imposes additional requirements on children wishing to enter the United Kingdom as visitors. The Immigration Rules were last updated in August 2011. See http://www.ukba.homeoffice.gov.uk/policyandlaw/immigrationlaw/immigrationrules/.
14 [2009] UKSC 8, [2010] 1 All ER 469, [2009] 1 WLR 2557.
15 Council of Europe Treaty Series – No. 197, Warsaw 16.V.2005 – in force in the United Kingdom since 1 April 2009.
16 UK Border Agency, Asylum Process Guidance '*Assessing Age*' at para 2.2. Article 13.2 of the EU Directive 2011/36/EU on preventing and combating trafficking in human beings and protecting its victims now includes the same presumption in relation to age as that contained in the Trafficking Convention and therefore the UKBA's guidance is likely to be amended once the Directive is adopted by the UK.
17 [2011] UKSC 4 at para 23, [2011] 2 All ER 783, [2011] 2 WLR 148.
18 Concluding observations on United Kingdom of Great Britain and Northern Ireland CRC/C/GBR/CO/4 20 October 2008 para 75.
19 CEOP, '*Strategic Threat Assessment: Child Trafficking in the UK 2010*' at p 21.

The trafficked child's right to be heard

12.9 Article 12.1 of the Convention on the Rights of the Child also provides that:

> 'States Parties shall assure to the child who is capable of forming his or her own views the right to express those views freely in all matters affecting the child, the views of the child being given due weight in accordance with the age and maturity of the child'.

Of the 527 people referred into the National Referral Mechanism (NRM) in 2009, 27% were children[1]. The Anti Trafficking Monitoring Group[2] undertook research into the first year of the operation of the NRM. It concluded that the result of the United Kingdom not appointing a guardian for children suspected of having been trafficked meant that no-one was necessarily responsible for guiding the child through the NRM process or for ensuring that a child's best interests were met[3]. This in turn had an obviously negative impact on the child being able to make his or her voice heard and being able to disclose the full extent of the abuse and exploitation he or she may have suffered. The UK Government's announcement in March 2011 that it will seek to opt-in to the EU's new Trafficking Directive[4], which amongst other protections for trafficked persons introduces a scheme for trafficked children to be provided with a guardian or representative who will ensure that their best interests are taken into account, is a very welcome development.

In addition, it is relevant to note that despite the Convention on the Rights of the Child expressing a strong commitment to children having the right to make their own views known, children do not yet have an individual right of petition to the United Nations Committee on the Rights of the Child if they believe any of their rights within that Convention have been breached. This is a right accorded in many similar human rights conventions, such as under the European Convention on Human Rights 1950 and the International Covenant on Civil and Political Rights 1966.

In 2009 the United Nations Human Rights Council established a working group to explore the possibility of creating a complaints procedure for the Convention on the Rights of the Child. The Chairperson-Rapporteur of the Open-ended Working Group on an Optional Protocol to the Convention produced a draft proposal on 14 January 2011 and this was then subjected to a process of negotiation[5]. At a meeting of the working group in February 2011 it became apparent that many countries, including the United Kingdom, were not happy about the proposal to introduce a collective complaints mechanism[6]. This was championed by many international NGOs but it was not included in the final draft proposal. The final text also permits States to make reservations in relation to various aspects of the complaints procedures. The UN Human Rights Council[7] adopted the Optional Protocol to the Convention on the Rights of the Child on a communications procedure on 17 June 2011. It will now be transmitted to the UN General Assembly for discussion and adoption in December 2011. It remains to be seen whether the United Kingdom could enter into any reservation in the light of its duty to safeguard and promote the welfare of children under the Borders, Citizenship and Immigration Act 2009, s 55 and the importance accorded to discovering a child's own views by the Supreme Court in *ZH (Tanzania) v Secretary of State for the Home Department*[8].

[1] The Anti Trafficking Monitoring Group Briefing *'Trafficked Children'* (2010).
[2] A coalition comprised of nine organisations: Anti-Slavery International UK, Anti-Slavery International, ECPAT UK, the Helen Bamber Foundation, the Poppy Project, the Immigration Law Practitioners Association, Kalayaan, the TARA Project and UNICEF UK.
[3] The Anti-Trafficking Monitoring Group, *'Wrong kind of victim? One year on . . . an analysis of UK measures to protect trafficked persons'* at pages 44–52. See also Summary Report of the Anti-Trafficking Monitoring Group which is included in the Appendices to this Handbook.
[4] Directive 2011/36/EU of the European Parliament and of the Council of 5 April 2011 on preventing and combating trafficking in human beings and protecting its victims, and replacing Council Framework Decision 2002/629/JHA.
[5] Child Rights Information Network 20 January 2011.
[6] This would have allowed complaints to be submitted without naming specific individual victims and was though to be essential to protect children who had suffered extreme violations of their rights, such as child victims of trafficking.
[7] An inter-Governmental body within the UN system made of 47 States responsible for strengthening the promotion of human rights around the world. It was created by the UN General Assembly on 15 March 2006.
[8] [2011] UKSC 4 at paragraph 34, [2011] 2 All ER 783, [2011] 2 WLR 148.

Durable solutions

12.10 Article 3 of the Convention on the Rights of the Child's Optional Protocol[1] on the sale of children, child prostitution and child pornography also obliges the United Kingdom to take all feasible measures to ensure that child victims are given the necessary assistance to reintegrate into society and make a full physical and psychological recovery.

To date children who have been recognised as victims of trafficking have generally been expected to apply for asylum and have either been granted asylum on the basis of an established risk on return to their home country or discretionary leave to remain here on the sole basis of their age. In either case the need to safeguard and promote their welfare in terms of the services provided to them will primarily fall on the local authority in whose area they live. It will be that local authority which will have to assist their physical and psychological recovery. There is no national resource, which they can call upon to assist in this task and therefore there is a wide discrepancy between the levels of service provided to trafficked children across the UK. The lack of a national resource has also meant that expertise in assisting such recovery has not been developed and shared.

[1]   Adopted and opened for signature, ratification and accession by General Assembly resolution A/RES/54/263 on 25 May 2000 and entered into force on 18 January 2002.

Compensation for trafficked children

12.11 Article 9.4 of the Protocol also places the United Kingdom under a duty to ensure that child victims can access the necessary procedures to obtain compensation from their traffickers and abusers. A right to compensation for all trafficked persons, including children, is also contained within Article 15 of the Trafficking Convention. Again as yet there is no mechanism in the UK by which anyone, let alone a child who has been trafficked, can obtain compensation solely on account of their status as a victim of trafficking, and thereby a victim of crime. Instead they have to fall back on the more general remedies available in the civil courts for false imprisonment and assault or seek assistance from the Criminal Injuries Compensation Authority as victims of a crime[1] or bring an Employment Tribunal claim against their trafficker. In the cases of children and adults these avenues of possible redress pose substantial obstacles to securing redress as some of the chapters in this Handbook identify.

[1]   For a detailed discussion of this see Janice Lam and Klara Skrivankova, Anti-Slavery International' *Opportunities and Obstacles: Ensuring access to Compensation for trafficked persons in the UK*' (2009).

Prosecutions of Child Traffickers

12.12 ECPAT UK noted that although 215 children in total had been referred into the NRM by the time it completed its report in 2010, very few prosecutions for child trafficking had been instigated and that these prosecutions were not uniform across the country.

CONCLUSION

12.13 More is now known about the great variety of reasons for children being trafficked across and within national borders. The need to identify these children and the exploitation they suffer is also now increasingly recognised. However States still generally fail to provide trafficked children with the durable status they need in the countries in which they have sought protection.

Therefore they remain at risk of being re-trafficked or suffering further exploitation in their countries of origin.

States, including the United Kingdom, also continue to fail to provide them with the practical support and services they need to recover from this most serious form of human rights abuse. Safe accommodation, appropriate psychological and psychiatric services and the provision of a legal guardian are just some of the services which have yet to be provided despite these needs being recognised in international law.

13

ECHR AND EU PROTECTION FOR VICTIMS OF TRAFFICKING IN THE UK

Saadiya Chaudary and Adam Weiss

INTRODUCTION: EUROPE'S TWO LEGAL ORDERS

13.1 The purpose of this chapter is to familiarise readers with the provisions of European law relevant to the protection of victims of trafficking in human beings. This chapter is intended for lawyers and non-lawyers alike, including those with little experience of European law.

There are two European legal orders: European Union law and Council of Europe law. These were originally two distinct regional legal orders which now have an expanding interface, and provisions of both legal orders apply to victims of human trafficking.

The Council of Europe, based in Strasbourg, has 47 European Member States[1] and its objective is to ensure respect for its fundamental values – human rights, democracy and the rule of law – throughout the whole continent. The European Union ('EU'), based in Brussels with its Court in Luxembourg, is formed of only 27 Member States[2], all of whom are also members of the Council of Europe. The objective of the EU is primarily to further the aim of a single market within the Union through, inter alia, the strengthening of economic and social cohesion, to strengthen the protection of the rights and interests of the nationals of its Member States through the introduction of a citizenship of the Union, to maintain and develop the Union as an area of freedom, security and justice, in which the free movement of persons is assured in conjunction with appropriate measures with respect to external border controls, asylum, immigration and the prevention and combating of crime[3]. The European Union's purposes and values have expanded considerably over the years, and also include respect for fundamental rights.

The primary legal instrument of Council of Europe law is the European Convention on Human Rights ('ECHR'), respect for which is overseen by the European Court of Human Rights ('ECtHR'). Victims of violations of the Convention who have exhausted the remedies available to them in the domestic legal system without getting effective redress can send individual applications to the ECtHR, which can make findings of violations of the Convention and award a sum of money by way of just satisfaction. The primary legal instruments of European Union law are the Treaty on European Union ('TEU'), the Treaty on the Functioning of the European Union ('TFEU') and the Charter of Fundamental Rights. The judicial bodies of the EU are the General Court and the Court of Justice of the European Union ('CJEU'); however, unlike the ECtHR, there is no right of direct petition to the General Court or the CJEU when an EU Member State has violated a provision of EU law (including a fundamental rights obligation). Instead, the CJEU will get involved in such cases only when the European Commission, another EU body, brings legal proceedings against a Member State for a breach of EU law (Article 259 TFEU) or the court of a Member State refers questions for a preliminary ruling to the CJEU (Article 267 TFEU).

In brief, for a trafficking victim who claims that her rights have not been respected under the EHCR, it may be appropriate to take a case to the European Court of Human Rights once she has exhausted the remedies available to her in the domestic legal system. It may also be appropriate, if she has been a victim of a violation of EU law, to make a complaint to the European Commission[4] and/or encourage the domestic courts dealing with her case to refer questions to the CJEU.

The EU Charter of Fundamental Rights contains many rights which correspond to those contained in the ECHR. It also contains other rights and principles, including an explicit prohibition on human trafficking (discussed below)[5]. However, while the ECHR has a long history and a long line of jurisprudence – from both the ECtHR and the domestic courts (which was incorporated in the UK through the Human Rights Act 1998) – the Charter of Fundamental Rights only became justiciable (that is, effective in the courts) on 1 December 2009. The Charter itself states that it applies to EU Member States 'only when they are implementing Union law'[6]. Furthermore, there is an ambiguous Protocol to the treaties which may further restrict the application of the Charter to the United Kingdom and Poland, and which is currently being litigated before the Court of Justice of the European Union[7].

The Treaty on European Union requires, and the European Convention on Human Rights permits, the EU to accede – that is, become a party to – the ECHR. Negotiations are currently underway in this process. It is not clear what this will look like or whether it will have a significant impact on the rights of victims of human trafficking.

[1] These States are: Albania, Andorra, Armenia, Austria, Azerbaijan, Belgium, Bosnia and Herzegovina, Bulgaria, Croatia, Cyprus, Czech Republic, Denmark, Estonia, Finland, France, Georgia, Germany, Greece, Hungary, Iceland, Ireland, Italy, Latvia, Liechtenstein, Lithuania, Luxembourg, Malta, Moldova, Monaco, Montenegro, Netherlands, Norway, Poland, Portugal, Romania, Russia, San Marino, Serbia, Slovakia, Slovenia, Spain, Sweden, Switzerland, The Former Yugoslav Republic of Macedonia, Turkey, Ukraine, and the United Kingdom. Correct as at 28 June 2011.

[2] States forming the European Union: Austria, Belgium, Bulgaria, Cyprus, Czech Republic, Denmark, Estonia, Finland, France, Germany, Hungary, Ireland, Italy, Latvia, Lithuania, Luxembourg, Malta, Netherlands, Poland, Portugal, Romania, Slovenia, Slovakia, Spain, Sweden and the United Kingdom. Correct as at 28 June 2011.

[3] Treaty on the European Union, art 2.

[4] Article 35(2)(b) of the Convention prevents the ECtHR from dealing with any matter that is 'substantially the same as a matter that . . . has already been submitted to another procedure of international investigation or settlement and contains no relevant new information'. However, in *Karoussiotis v Portugal* (judgment of 1 February 2011) the ECtHR found

that a complaint to the European Commission is not 'another procedure of international investigation or settlement', so it is possible, for example, for a trafficking victim to have a complaint pending with the European Commission about a violation of her EU law rights and an application being considered by the European Court of Human Rights.

5   EU Charter of Fundamental Rights, art 5(3).
6   EU Charter of Fundamental Rights, art 51(1).
7   *Case C-411/10 NS v Secretary of State for the Home Department* (referred from the Court of Appeal of England and Wales).

COUNCIL OF EUROPE ANTI-TRAFFICKING LAW

13.2 This section deals with the following subjects:

* The Trafficking Convention;
* ECHR, arts 4 and 6;
* Applying the Trafficking Convention – particularly ECHR, arts 10–16 via art 4.

Council of Europe law creates obligations on States. Victims of trafficking cannot use provisions of Council of Europe law directly against their traffickers[1]; rather, trafficking victims can claim that the State has violated their rights under Council of Europe law, for example, by failing to carry out an effective investigation of the traffickers or by returning them to another country where there is a real risk the victim will be re-trafficked or otherwise subjected to ill treatment.

The prohibition of trafficking in human beings is not explicitly mentioned in the European Convention on Human Rights, which was drafted in 1951. In 2005, however, the Council of Europe took firm steps towards prohibiting trafficking and providing for the protection of victims of trafficking through the Convention on Action against Trafficking in Human Beings 2005 ('the Trafficking Convention'). This is the most comprehensive international instrument currently in force which deals with human trafficking. The Convention is split into 10 Chapters, the most important of which, for the purposes of victims' rights, are Chapter II (Prevention, co-operation and other measures), Chapter III (Measures to protect and promote the rights of victims, guaranteeing gender equality) and Chapter IV (Substantive criminal law). Chapters V to VII deal with investigation and monitoring mechanisms[2]. This section will primarily focus on the protection provisions contained in Chapter III as very often these provisions are the most difficult to access and secure by victims of trafficking. This is particularly the situation in the UK which has ratified the Convention (which entered into force in the UK in April 2009) but has not implemented parts of the Convention, including the protection provisions, into national law. This is important because unlike most other European countries, in the UK international treaties do not automatically become part of the domestic legal system when they are ratified; steps must be taken (eg an Act of Parliament transforming the treaty into domestic law) in the UK legal system to make the treaty enforceable. Virtually no such steps have been taken in relation to the Trafficking Convention. As a result, it is unclear to what extent victims of trafficking who are denied or unable to access their rights as provided for by Chapter III of the Trafficking Convention can rely directly on the Convention in proceedings before domestic courts[3]. One argument open to victims of trafficking is reliance on Article 18 of the Vienna Convention on the

Law of Treaties which provides that States must refrain from acts which would defeat the object and purpose of a treaty when they have signed or ratified that treaty. Arguments relying on the Trafficking Convention have also been made under Articles of the ECHR, such as Article 4 (discussed below) and Article 6[4].

Trafficking in human beings is defined in the Convention in substantially the same terms that it is defined in the Palermo Protocol: '"Trafficking in human beings" shall mean the recruitment, transportation, transfer, harbouring or receipt of persons, by means of the threat or use of force or other forms of coercion, of abduction, of fraud, of deception, of the abuse of power or of a position of vulnerability or of the giving or receiving of payments or benefits to achieve the consent of a person having control over another person, for the purpose of exploitation. Exploitation shall include, at a minimum, the exploitation of the prostitution of others or other forms of sexual exploitation, forced labour or services, slavery or practices similar to slavery, servitude or the removal of organs.'[5] Where the victim is a child, it is not necessary to prove any of the means, such as threat, deception, coercion etc[6].

The Convention therefore covers all forms of trafficking, including the protection to be afforded to victims. The principal protection provisions provided for include the following:

The right to be identified (or the positive obligation to identify trafficking victims) – Article 10 – identification of victims of trafficking must be undertaken by trained and qualified persons. This includes the obligation to take into account the special situation of women and child victims of trafficking, and provides that a person shall not be removed from the State until the identification process as a victim of an offence (provided for in Article 18) has been completed and shall likewise ensure that that person receives the assistance provided for in Article 12, paragraphs 1 and 2.

The right to support – Article 12 – victims on the territory of a Member State have a right to assistance to aid their physical, psychological and social recovery, including appropriate and secure accommodation, psychological and material assistance, access to emergency medical treatment, counselling and information about their legal rights, access to education for children and access to the labour market and vocational training for victims lawfully present in the State. In addition any assistance measures should not be made conditional on a victim's willingness to act as a witness.

The right to a recovery and reflection period – Article 13 – a recovery and reflection period of at least 30 days must be given when there are reasonable grounds to believe that the person concerned is a victim of trafficking to allow the victim to recover and escape the influence of traffickers and/or to take an informed decision on co-operating with the competent authorities. The Convention however specifically provides that this provision does not need to be observed if victim status has been claimed improperly or if grounds of public order prevent it.

The right to a residence permit – Article 14 – a State must issue a renewable residence permit to victims if this is necessary owing to their personal situation, or if their stay is necessary for the purpose of their co-operation with authorities in investigation or criminal proceedings. This residence permit should be granted without prejudice to the right to seek and enjoy asylum.

The right to information – Article 15 – victims have the right to information on relevant judicial and administrative proceedings in a language which they can understand, the right to legal assistance and to free legal aid for victims under the conditions provided by its internal law and the right to compensation from the perpetrators. This compensation should be guaranteed to victims by law, through for example the establishment of a fund for victim compensation or measures or programmes aimed at social assistance and social integration of victims. The Convention also suggests that the fund for compensation should be funded by the assets seized from perpetrators of trafficking in human beings.

Rights in the context of repatriation – Article 16 – the Convention provides protection for victims of trafficking who are being repatriated or returned. Under Article 16, a victim of trafficking who wants to be repatriated to her country of origin must be able to do so without undue or unreasonable delay. For victims who are being returned to another State, the returning State must pay due regard to their rights, safety and dignity and the status of any legal proceedings relating to their situation of trafficking. Where the victim of trafficking is a child, (s)he should not be returned to a State 'if there is indication, following a risk and security assessment, that such return would not be in the best interests of the child'[7].

As noted earlier, the above protection provisions have not been incorporated into domestic law in the UK and consequently it is very difficult for victims of trafficking to rely directly upon these provisions. A route to enforcement of Articles 10–16 may be said to have emerged through recent case law of the European Court of Human Rights ('the Court') on Article 4 of the ECHR.

The ECHR applies directly in the UK, through the Human Rights Act 1998. Article 4 states so far as relevant that 'no one shall be held in slavery or servitude . . . No one shall be required to perform forced or compulsory labour'. This is the only Article in the ECHR that closely reflects a situation of trafficking[8], even though trafficking is not explicitly included within its text. Case law on Article 4 is sparse in comparison to other articles of the Convention and there is no definition of the prohibitions contained in the Article to assist interpretation or in the *travaux préparatoires*. Clarity in interpreting Article 4 is crucial, as it is one of the most fundamental Articles in the Convention: as the Court has stated:

> ' . . . Article 4 enshrines one of the fundamental values of democratic societies. Unlike most of the substantive clauses of the Convention and of Protocols Nos. 1 and 4, Article 4 makes no provision for exceptions and no derogation from it is permissible under Article 15 § 2 even in the event of a public emergency threatening the life of the nation . . . '[9].

In the three main judgments on Article 4, the Court has developed a practice of using other relevant international instruments and the definitions contained therein to interpret the scope and application of Article 4. In *Van der Mussele v Belgium*[10], one of the first cases to consider forced and compulsory labour, the Court referred to the definition contained in the International Labour Organisation Convention No 29. Article 2(1) of that Convention defines forced or compulsory labour as 'all work or service which is exacted from any person under the menace of any penalty and for which the said person has not offered himself voluntarily'[11]. The Court noted the similarity between the language used in ECHR, art 4 and the ILO Convention No 29 and found that the definition contained in the ILO Convention could therefore 'provide a starting-point for interpretation of Article 4 of the European Convention'[12].

This approach was also adopted by the Court when considering the case *Siliadin v France*[13] which concerned a 15 year old girl from Togo who had been trafficked to France for the purposes of being forced into domestic work where she was required to work 15 hours a day, seven days a week for no pay and was also required to live and remain in her employer's house. The Court used the definitions contained in the Slavery Convention to ascertain whether the applicant in this case had been subjected to either slavery or servitude:

> 'The Court notes at the outset that, according to the 1927 Slavery Convention, "slavery is the status or condition of a person over whom any or all of the powers attaching to the right of ownership are exercised" . . . With regard to the concept of "servitude", it "prohibits a particularly serious form of denial of free-dom" . . . It includes, "in addition to the obligation to provide certain services to another . . . the obligation of the "serf" to live on the other's property and the impossibility of changing his status" . . . for Convention purposes "servitude" means an obligation to provide one's services that is imposed by the use of coercion, and is to be linked with the concept of "slavery" described above . . . '[14].

The Court adopted the definition of 'forced labour' in accordance with its findings in the *Van der Mussele* case and applied all three definitions to the applicant to ascertain whether the treatment she suffered came under one of the three heads of Article 4. The Court found in this case that the applicant had been subjected to forced labour, and also to servitude in violation of ECHR, art 4 and that because those who had subjected the applicant to this treatment had not been adequately punished, due to deficiencies in French law, there had been a violation of Article 8 ECHR[15].

The next substantive protection case to be communicated to the Government under ECHR, art 4 was *M v the United Kingdom*[16]. This case concerned a Ugandan national who was sexually exploited in Uganda and was then brought to the UK where she was again forced into prostitution. She escaped and claimed asylum however her asylum and human rights claim was refused and she faced removal back to Uganda. The Court communicated the case, specifically asking the Government to comment on whether M's rights under Article 4 would be violated if she were removed to Uganda[17]. The case did not however result in a judgment; instead, it was resolved by means of a friendly settlement under the terms of which the applicant was granted three years leave to remain in the UK[18].

Given the history of interpretation of Article 4 through other international instruments, it is perhaps unsurprising that the Court continued this practice when faced with its next trafficking case. In *Rantsev v Cyprus and Russia*[19] the Court used the Palermo Protocol and the Trafficking Convention to expand its interpretation of the scope of Article 4. Prior to *Rantsev* the Court had taken the approach of assessing whether the situation of the victim of trafficking could be defined as either slavery, servitude or forced or compulsory labour in order for the victim to be able to benefit from the rights and protections contained in ECHR, art 4 (as in *Siliadin*). This assessment has become obsolete for trafficking cases following the *Rantsev* judgment.

The applicant in *Rantsev* was the father of Ms Rantseva, a Russian national who had entered Cyprus on an *artiste* visa. This visa was widely known to be used to bring women into the country for purposes of forced prostitution in nightclubs. Ms Rantseva escaped from the club where she was working, but her 'employers' found her and brought her to a police station in order to have her deported for violating the terms of her visa. She spent several hours at the police station; the police, not intending to deport her, contacted the alleged traffickers to come and pick her up, which they did. Several hours later Ms Rantseva was found dead on the pavement outside the apartment building of one of the men concerned. In this case, Ms Rantseva's father complained principally about the failure to investigate the allegations of human trafficking and his daughter's death, as well as the failure of the Cypriot authorities to protect his daughter. In its judgment, the Court found a violation of Article 2 by Cyprus of the procedural obligation to carry out an effective investigation; of Article 4 by Cyprus of the procedural obligation to put in place an appropriate legislative and administrative framework and of the positive obligation to take protective measures, and a further violation by both Cyprus and Russia of the procedural obligation to investigate human trafficking. The Court also found a violation of Article 5(1) of the Convention by Cyprus arising out of Ms Rantseva's detention in the police station until the alleged traffickers came to get her and her subsequent detention in the apartment before her death.

The Court's judgment in *Rantsev* has become the key instrument for enforcing the Trafficking Convention, including provisions not incorporated into domestic law and the crucial parts of the judgment are set out below:

The Court recognised in *Rantsev* that:

> 'trafficking in human beings as a global phenomenon has increased significantly in recent years . . . In Europe, its growth has been facilitated in part by the collapse of former Communist blocs. The conclusion of the Palermo Protocol in 2000 and the Anti-Trafficking Convention in 2005 demonstrate the increasing recognition at international level of the prevalence of trafficking and the need for measures to combat it'

and further decided that:

> '[in] light of the proliferation of both trafficking itself and of measures taken to combat it, the Court considers it appropriate in the present case to examine the extent to which trafficking itself may be considered to run counter to the spirit and purpose of Article 4 of the Convention such as to fall within the scope of the guarantees offered by that Article without the need to assess which of the three types of proscribed conduct are engaged by the particular treatment in the case in question'.[20]

This is an extremely important development for individuals who have been trafficked for the purposes of exploitation but who have escaped from their traffickers before actually being forced into exploitation which can be categorised as slavery, servitude or forced or compulsory labour. Having found that trafficking itself comes within the scope of ECHR, art 4, the Court makes specific mention of the positive obligation on States under ECHR, art 4 to have in place adequate protection measures for victims of trafficking and for **potential** victims:

'The Court considers that the spectrum of safeguards set out in national legislation must be adequate to ensure the practical and effective protection of the rights of victims or potential victims of trafficking. Accordingly, in addition to criminal law measures to punish traffickers, Article 4 requires member States to put in place adequate measures regulating businesses often used as a cover for human trafficking. Furthermore a State's immigration rules must address relevant concerns relating to encouragement, facilitation or tolerance of trafficking . . . member States are required to put in place a legislative and administrative framework to prohibit and punish trafficking. The Court observes that the Palermo Protocol and the Anti-Trafficking Convention refer to the need for a comprehensive approach to combat trafficking which includes measures to prevent trafficking and to protect victims . . . The extent of the positive obligations arising under Article 4 must be considered within this broader context'[21].

In summary, the Court found that Council of Europe States have three positive obligations towards trafficking victims:

- to have in place a legislative and administrative framework designed to punish human traffickers;
- to protect individuals who have been or are at risk of becoming trafficking victims; and
- to investigate acts of human trafficking and, where possible, prosecute the traffickers.

Following the Court's explicit reference to the Trafficking Convention for the purpose of informing the positive obligations of States under Article 4 towards victims of trafficking, it is possible to argue that these three positive obligations encompass, at a minimum, the obligations found in Articles 10–16 (Chapter III of the Trafficking Convention). This means that the obligation to identify victims of trafficking (Article 10), to provide material support to victims present in the UK (Article 12) and to only return victims to other States with due regard for their rights, safety and dignity (Article 16(2)) apply directly under ECHR, art 4.

The *Rantsev* judgment also informs the content of some of those rights. For example, in relation to the right to be identified, or the positive obligation to identify trafficking victims as victims, found in Article 10 of the Trafficking Convention, the Court in *Rantsev* found that States' positive obligations towards trafficking victims begin when:

'the State authorities were aware, or ought to have been aware, of circumstances giving rise to a credible suspicion that an identified individual had been, or was at real and immediate risk of being, trafficked or exploited'[22].

It can be inferred that where the authorities ought to have been aware that someone was a victim of trafficking but did not identify her as such, there has been a violation of Article 10 of the Trafficking Convention and ECHR, art 4. The question of whether the authorities 'ought to have known' should be answered by reference to whether a trained person would have identified the victim, since Article 10 requires States to provide their competent authorities (eg police, prosecutors, immigration authorities, judges) with people trained in identifying victims[23].

Under the Human Rights Act 1998, s 7 ('HRA 1998'), an individual can bring a claim before the UK courts if her/his rights under the ECHR have been violated. This claim can also include a request for damages or compensation under HRA 1998, s 8. An example of this type of litigation is the recent case of *OOO v the Commissioner of the Police for the Metropolis*[24], the claimants were young Nigerian women who were brought into the UK from Nigeria illegally and then subjected to slavery, domestic servitude and physical and emotional abuse (in contravention of ECHR, arts 3 and 4). The Metropolitan police failed to investigate the claimants' complaints about their treatment and exploitation and the claimants therefore sought a declaration that the lack of investigation was a violation of the procedural obligations under ECHR, arts 3 and 4. They also sought damages under HRA 1998, s 8. The court carried out a detailed assessment of the ECtHR's findings in *Rantsev*[25] in relation to the duty to investigate under Article 4 and adopted the ECtHR's principles in relation to this, finding:

> 'If the principles identified from *Rantsev* are incorporated into the domestic law of England and Wales it would follow that the police would be under a duty to carry out an effective investigation of an allegation of a breach of Article 4 once a credible account of an alleged infringement had been brought to its attention. The trigger for the duty would not depend upon an actual complaint from a victim or near relative of a victim. The investigation, once triggered, would have to be undertaken promptly'[26].

The court found in *OOO* that the duty to investigate under Articles 3 and 4 had been breached and each claimant was awarded £5,000.

This case illustrates the importance of the ECtHR's judgments in bringing provisions of the Trafficking Convention to life. They can also be applied in the same way to the common situation of a victim who is facing return to her/his country of nationality, which very often is the country from which (s)he was first trafficked, without any assessment of the risk or hardship the person may face on return. That victim can claim a violation of her/his rights under ECHR, art 4 as the State has not fulfilled its positive obligations under Article 4 which include the requirement to make such an assessment in accordance with the Trafficking Convention, art 16.

Similarly, the court's finding in *Rantsev* has also opened the doors for victims to take their cases to Strasbourg once domestic remedies have been exhausted, where there is excessive delay in domestic remedies or where urgent interim measures are necessary, for example to prevent removal or return, under Rule 39 of the Council of Europe Rules of Court for the European Court of Human Rights.

[1]   Unless, that is, if the traffickers are themselves State agents. This might be the case for example where police or immigration officials are complicit in acts of trafficking.

[2]   Article 36 of the Trafficking Convention provides for the establishment of a Group of Experts on action against Trafficking in Human Beings (GRETA) who will monitor implementation of the Convention.

[3]   There have been some suggestions by UK judges that international treaties that have been ratified may indeed have some force in the UK legal system, even if not transformed into domestic law. See, eg, Lord Steyn's speech in *In re McKerr*, para 51 (referring to the special status of human rights treaties, of which the Trafficking Convention is certainly one).

[4]   See for instance *R v O* [2008] EWCA Crim 2835, (2008) Times, 2 October. In this case the protection provisions for victims of trafficking under the Trafficking Convention (which at that stage had only been signed by the UK and not ratified) were successfully litigated under ECHR, art 6, the right to a fair trial. The case concerned an appeal against a conviction of possessing a false identity card with the intention of using it, by a victim of trafficking.

[5]   Trafficking Convention, art 4(a).

[6]   Trafficking Convention, art 4(c).

[7] Trafficking Convention, art 16(7).

[8] Although Article 3 may also encompass relevant protection.

[9] *Siliadin v France (Application 73316/01)* [2005] ECHR 545 at para 112, (2005) 43 EHRR 287, 20 BHRC 654, ECtHR.

[10] *Van der Mussele v Belgium (Application 8919/80)* (1983) 6 EHRR 163, [1983] ECHR 8919/80, ECtHR.

[11] The court expanded on this definition in *Siliadin v France (Application 73316/01)* finding that the definition contained in Article 2(1) ILO Convention No. 29 'brought to mind the idea of physical or mental constraint' (at para 117).

[12] *Van der Mussele v Belgium (Application 8919/80)* (1983) 6 EHRR 163 at para 32, [1983] ECHR 8919/80, ECtHR.

[13] *Siliadin v France (Application 73316/01)* [2005] ECHR 545, (2005) 43 EHRR 287, 20 BHRC 654, ECtHR.

[14] *Siliadin v France (Application 73316/01)* [2005] ECHR 545 at paras 122–124, (2005) 43 EHRR 287, 20 BHRC 654, ECtHR.

[15] *Siliadin v France (Application 73316/01)* [2005] ECHR 545, (2005) 43 EHRR 287, 20 BHRC 654, ECtHR – see discussion of court at paragraphs 112–129.

[16] *M v the United Kingdom (Application 16081/08)* [2009] ECHR 1229.

[17] *M v the United Kingdom (Application 16081/08)* [2008] ECHR 522. Statement of Facts, ECtHR, 10 June 2008.

[18] *M v the United Kingdom (Application 16081/08)* [2009] ECHR 1229. Decision to strike out the case, ECtHR, 29 January 2010.

[19] *Rantsev v Cyprus and Russia (Application 26965/04)* (2010) 28 BHRC 313, [2010] ECHR 25965/04, ECtHR.

[20] *Rantsev v Cyprus and Russia (Application 26965/04)* (2010) 51 EHRR 1 at para 278–279, (2010) 28 BHRC 313, [2010] ECHR 25965/04, ECtHR.

[21] *Rantsev v Cyprus and Russia (Application no. 26965/04)* (2010) 51 EHRR 1 at paras 284–285, (2010) 28 BHRC 313, [2010] ECHR 25965/04, ECtHR.

[22] *Rantsev v Cyprus and Russia (Application 26965/04)* (2010) 51 EHRR 1 at para 286, (2010) 28 BHRC 313, [2010] ECHR 25965/04, ECtHR.

[23] Under the National Referral Mechanism, set up in the UK in accordance with the Trafficking Convention to identify victims of trafficking, the only competent authorities which can conclusively identify a victim of trafficking are the UK Human Trafficking Centre and the UK Border Agency. This is clearly narrower than the requirement under the Trafficking Convention, art 10 for the competent authorities to include all public authorities which may have contact with victims of trafficking (see Explanatory Report to the Trafficking Convention at paragraph 129) and judges and prosecutors.

[24] *OOO v the Commissioner of the Police for the Metropolis* [2011] EWHC 1246 (QB).

[25] *OOO v the Commissioner of the Police for the Metropolis* [2011] EWHC 1246 (QB) at paras 148–168.

[26] *OOO v the Commissioner of the Police for the Metropolis* [2011] EWHC 1246 (QB) at para 154.

EUROPEAN UNION LAW

13.3 This section deals with the following subjects:

- The Framework Decisions and the Residence Permit Directive;
- The new Trafficking Directive and what this means for protection of victims of trafficking in the UK;
- Ways in which EU law can make things worse for trafficking victims.

European Union law originated in the creation of a common market, with free movement of goods, services, labour and capital. It has since expanded to cover fundamental rights and the creation of an area of freedom, security and justice. EU law measures relating to trafficking in human beings can be seen as a counter-measure to other provisions of EU law that may facilitate human trafficking, including, for example, the free movement of persons within the

EU with reduced or non-existent border controls, which, in the absence of a harmonised system of criminal law enforcement at EU level, may facilitate cross-border criminal activity in the Union. This section looks first at the provisions of EU law designed to prevent human trafficking and protect and support victims, and then at the provisions of EU law which may, in subtle ways, facilitate human trafficking or make things worse for trafficking victims.

Until April 2011, EU Anti-Trafficking law was made up of three instruments of EU law: Council Directive 2004/81/EC[1] on the residence permit issued to third-country nationals who are victims of trafficking who co-operate with competent authorities, Council Framework Decision 2002/629/JHA of 19 July 2002 on combating trafficking in human beings and Council Framework Decision 2001/220/JHA of 15 March 2001 on the standing of victims in criminal proceedings. These three instruments lacked the application, enforcement and comprehensive approach necessary to prevent trafficking and protect victims.

Directives are legal instruments of the EU that require EU Member States to attain certain goals, but leave open to them the means by which they will alter their legal system (ie 'transpose the Directive') in order to reach those goals[2]. However, if a provision of a Directive confers rights on individuals in a clear and precise way, and the deadline for its implementation has passed, an individual can invoke the Directive directly in a court of law against the authorities of the State (but not against private individuals)[3]. Council Directive 2004/81/EC's deadline for transposition has already passed. However, it is extremely limited as it applies only to third-country (ie non-EU) nationals, and not to nationals of EU countries who may have been trafficked, and in addition, in order to obtain the residence permit provided for by the Directive, the victim of trafficking must co-operate with the competent authorities, including the police, prosecution and judicial authorities. This places victims of trafficking in serious difficulties if they are unable or unwilling to talk about their experiences, or if there is no hope of pursuing their traffickers regardless of their level of co-operation. The Directive also does not apply in the United Kingdom, Ireland or Denmark. The Directive, which is still in force, was complemented by the two Framework Decisions set out above, the first of which (2001/220/JHA) does not specifically relate to victims of trafficking, who may require specialised support, but to all victims involved in criminal proceedings. The second Framework Decision (2002/629/JHA) only presents steps to be taken to combat trafficking (through investigation and prosecution) and does not contain any protection provisions. Framework Decisions are legislative tools which could be unanimously adopted by the EU Council of Ministers to approximate the laws and regulations of member States of the EU in areas of criminal law[4]. However they lack direct effect[5], meaning they cannot be invoked at national level if they have not been incorporated by the Member State into domestic law[6]. With the entry into force of the Treaty of Lisbon in December 2009, Article 34 of the Treaty on the European Union (TEU) was repealed and Framework Decisions can no longer be adopted. Any legislation must now be adopted in the form of either Directives or Regulations[7]. In accordance with this, the European Union has taken steps towards codifying its trafficking law into a binding Directive – Directive 2011/36/EU – which incorporates and replaces Framework Decision 2002/629/JHA on combating trafficking in human beings and also provides rights and protections for victims of trafficking.

Directive 2011/36/EU entered into force on 15 April 2011. Member States to the Directive, including the United Kingdom, now have two years (until 6 April 2013) in which to transpose the provisions of the Directive into national law. During this time, the Directive is in force but its provisions do not yet have 'direct effect', meaning victims of trafficking cannot yet rely on them directly to challenge State action in the courts. However Member States must nevertheless ensure that until the Directive is adopted into national law, or if the two year period has passed and it has not been transposed, no measures are adopted which 'seriously compromise the attainment of the result prescribed by the directive'[8]. After 6 April 2013, those provisions of the Directive that are clear, precise and unconditional will have direct effect. In terms of the protection of victims of trafficking, this means that victims should be given assistance and support, in the form of appropriate and safe accommodation, material assistance, any necessary medical treatment, counselling and information, before, during and for a period of time after the conclusion of criminal proceedings[9]. In addition, victims must be given access to legal counselling and representation and this must be free of charge where the victim does not have sufficient financial resources[10].

The Directive also brings in new provisions (not reflected in the Council of Europe Convention on Action against Trafficking in Human Beings) extending the protection to be given to child victims. Under Directive 2011/36/EU, art 14(2), Member States shall 'appoint a guardian or a representative for a child victim . . . from the moment the child is identified by the authorities, where . . . the holders of parental responsibility are . . . precluded from ensuring the child's best interests and / or from representing the child'. Where the child is unaccompanied, the same obligation to appoint a guardian applies under art 16(3) of the Directive.

The Directive also defines a 'position of vulnerability' (one of the means of trafficking)[11] as 'a situation in which the person concerned has no real or acceptable alternative but to submit to the abuse involved'[12] bringing further definition to international trafficking legislation. In addition, the Directive extends the definition of trafficking to include 'other behaviour such as illegal adoption or forced marriage in so far as they fulfil the constitutive elements of trafficking in human beings'[13]. Victims should be given access to compensation[14] and those whose rights have not been respected under the Directive may be able to get damages[15].

The text of the preamble to Directive 2011/36/EU states that Council Directive 2004/81/EC on residence permits to be issued to third country national victims of trafficking who co-operate with competent authorities and Framework Decision 2001/220/JHA on the standing of victims in criminal proceedings must be taken into account when applying the Directive[16]. The result is an 'integrated, holistic and human rights approach to the fight against trafficking in human beings'[17], although this is still limited in the UK due to its opt out from Council Directive 2004/81/EC.

It is also important to highlight the EU Charter of Fundamental rights, art 5(3) (the Charter applies only when implementing Union law), which simply provides that 'Trafficking in human beings is prohibited'. This is probably a 'principle' as opposed to a 'right', which means that it is 'judicially cognisable only in the interpretation of such acts and in the ruling on their legality'[18]. In other words, victims probably cannot rely on it directly but can invoke it when arguing for a favourable interpretation, for example of Directive 2011/36/EU, an instrument which must be interpreted, it can be argued, in order to prohibit human trafficking.

EU law can also leave people vulnerable to trafficking or make things for trafficking victims worse. Three examples are: restrictions on new EU citizens' right to work; EU asylum law; and EU law governing cross-border co-operation in criminal matters.

There were two waves of accession of new EU Member States in the past decade: 10 countries joined in 2004 and another two, Bulgaria and Romania, in 2007. Of the 10 that joined in 2004, eight were located in Central and Eastern Europe. The citizens of these countries ('A8 nationals') had all the same free movement rights as other EU citizens to free movement – that is, they could travel to any other Member State for a short stay and stay longer to study, be self-employed or simply to live off their own resources – but unlike other EU citizens the 'old' Member States could restrict their right to work for seven years; this just ended on 1 May 2011.The same restrictions apply to Bulgarian and Romanian nationals, and may remain in place until 1 January 2014. These transition arrangements may leave some accession nationals vulnerable to trafficking: they can travel to other EU Member States without any controls but may not be able to work, a potentially profitable combination for traffickers. In the UK, for example, from 1 April 2009 to 31 March 2010, 105 of the 706 trafficking victims referred to the National Referral Mechanism for identifying victims of trafficking were EU migrants[19], all of them from the accession States to which work restrictions applied. EU nationals are rarely faced with expulsion from the United Kingdom, but may have difficulty accessing benefits. They are however eligible for residence permits in accordance with the Trafficking Convention, art 14.

Because asylum seekers may travel from one EU Member State to another, creating confusion about who is responsible for examining that person's claim, the EU has created rules for deciding which Member State is responsible for examining those claims. The instrument is called the Dublin II Regulation[20]. It is predicated on a fiction: that the standards for receiving asylum seekers and processing their claims all meet minimum human rights standards across the EU. The European Court of Human Rights exposed that fiction in a recent judgment finding that Belgium had violated the ECHR by returning an asylum seeker to Greece under Dublin II, where he faced inhuman and degrading living and detention conditions and a real risk of onward return to Afghanistan, his country of origin, without proper consideration of his asylum claim[21]. The Dublin II Regulation is meant to provide an expedited mechanism for returning asylum seekers to the EU Member State responsible for them. In addition to the problem of returning asylum seekers to EU Member States that generally do not respect asylum seekers' rights, there is also the problem that these expedited proceedings may not permit adequate identification of victims. It may be, for example, that a victim was trafficked to and within Europe and then escaped to another EU Member State; returning her to the last Member State she was in may leave her vulnerable to her traffickers and is likely to re-traumatise her. Trafficking victims may also have made false asylum claims under the influence of their traffickers in other EU Member States, in order to get them temporary permission to work. If those same Member States consider their asylum claims, they may find them not credible. Many trafficking victims may also be receiving psycho-social and medical support in the State where they have most recently lodged an asylum claim, making it inappropriate to send them to another Member State where such services might not be available.

In order to counterbalance the opportunities in the EU's internal market for cross-border criminal activity – with the massive border-free Schengen Zone[22] and free movement of people, goods, service and capital – the EU has developed legislative instruments designed to facilitate co-operation between criminal investigators, prosecutors and judges in different Member States. One such instrument is a framework decision that introduced the European Arrest Warrant ('EAW')[23], which allows for expedited extradition of criminal suspects or those who have time to serve behind bars. The problem is that many trafficking victims, from within and outside the EU, find themselves in EU prisons charged with offences committed in the course of their trafficking. They may be facing return to another EU Member State which does not respect minimum human rights standards for trafficking victims and may face re-traumatisation, re-trafficking or worse if returned to face criminal justice in another EU Member State.

What these three examples show is how EU law can leave people more vulnerable to trafficking. Authorities, lawyers and NGOs must be vigilant to ensure that those dealing with individuals subject to these provisions are properly identified as trafficking victims and that the obligation to protect them overrides the aims of EU law.

---

1   This Directive is not applicable in the UK as the UK, along with Ireland and Denmark, took a decision to opt-out of the Directive. Council Directive 2009/52/EC of 18 June 2009 providing for minimum standards on sanctions and measures against employers of illegally staying third-country nationals can also apply to victims of trafficking, however the UK has also opted out of this.

2   Treaty on the Functioning of the European Union, art 288.

3   See *Grad v Finanzamt Traunstein: 9/70* [1970] ECR 825, [1971] CMLR 1, ECJ; *Pubblico Ministero v Ratti: 148/78* [1979] ECR 1629, [1980] 1 CMLR 96, ECJ; *Marshall v Southampton and South-West Hampshire Area Health Authority (Teaching): 152/84* [1986] QB 401, [1986] 2 All ER 584, ECJ.

4   Under the Treaty on the Functioning of the European Union, art 67 (TFEU) – previously TEU, art 29 – 'The Union shall endeavour to ensure a high level of security through measures to prevent and combat crime, racism and xenophobia, and through measures for coordination and co-operation between police and judicial authorities and other competent authorities, as well as through the mutual recognition of judgments in criminal matters and, if necessary, through the approximation of criminal law'.

5   Treaty on the European Union, art 34(2)(b) (TEU) (pre-Treaty of Lisbon).

6   The European Court of Justice (ECJ, now the CJEU (Court of Justice of the European Union)) have nonetheless confirmed that when 'applying national law, the national court that is called upon to interpret it must do so as far as possible in the light of the wording and purpose of the framework decision in order to attain the result which it pursues and thus comply with Article 34(2)(b)' *Pupino (criminal proceedings against): C-105/03* [2006] QB 83, [2005] ECR I-5285, ECJ.

7   Regulations are like ordinary legal instruments: they apply automatically and directly after they are adopted, without needing to be transposed into the legislation of the Member State. There are no Regulations that apply directly to victims of human trafficking.

8   *Mangold v Helm: C-144/04* [2005] ECR I-9981 at para 28, [2006] All ER (EC) 383, ECJ.

9   Directive 2011/36/EU, art 11(1) and (5).

10 Directive 2011/36/EU, art 12(1) and (2).

[11] Under Directive 2001/36/EU, art 2(1) the offences listed include '[t]he recruitment, transportation, transfer, harbouring or reception of persons, including the exchange or transfer of control over those persons, **by means of** the threat or use of force or other forms of coercion, of abduction, of fraud, of deception, of the abuse of power or of a position of vulnerability or of the giving or receiving of payments or benefits to achieve the consent of a person having control over another person, for the purpose of exploitation'.

[12] Directive 2011/36/EU, art 2(2).

[13] Recital 11 to Directive 2011/36/EU.

[14] Directive 2011/36/EU. art 17.

[15] *Francovich and Bonifaci v Italy: C-6/90 and C-9/90* [1991] ECR I-5357, [1993] 2 CMLR 66, ECJ.

[16] See the Preamble to Directive 2011/36/EU, paras (7), (13) and (19).

[17] Preamble to Directive 2011/36/EU, para (7).

[18] Charter of Fundamental Rights, art 52(5).

[19] Data available at http://www.soca.gov.uk/about-soca/about-the-ukhtc/statistical-data.

[20] Regulation 343/2003/EC.

[21] *M.S.S. v Belgium and Greece* (Grand Chamber judgment of 21 January 2011). Belgium was found to have violated ECHR, arts 3 and 13, as was Greece.

[22] This is a zone without internal border controls, covering every EU Member State except the UK and Ireland, as well as Bulgaria and Romania (who are set to join soon) and also including Iceland, Norway and Switzerland.

[23] Framework Decision 2002/584/JHA.

CONCLUSION

13.4 Council of Europe law bolsters the rights of trafficking victims. Its advantage is that it is rooted in respect for human rights and the rule of law and there are mechanisms – the European Court of Human Rights for the ECHR being the most important – for enforcing those rights if States fail to do so. Council of Europe rights need to be part of the language the police, prosecutors, judges, NGOs and lawyers use when dealing with each trafficking case. The Trafficking Convention in particular is a comprehensive framework for fighting trafficking and protecting victims and needs to be relied on, invoked through the lens of the ECHR if necessary.

EU law is more ambivalent. EU anti-trafficking law is as much about cross-border co-operation, mutual trust between States and maintaining the integrity of the EU's internal market as it is about victim protection. The most significant shift in both legal orders is in the increased awareness of the need to protect victims of trafficking. Previously, the emphasis in both the Council of Europe and the European Union was on the need to prevent trafficking and prosecute perpetrators. Now, however, we have two comprehensive instruments, the Trafficking Convention and Directive 2011/36/EU, and an essential judgment of the ECtHR in *Rantsev v Cyprus and Russia (Application 26965/04)*[1] all of which establish and set out the duty to protect and support victims of this crime.

[1] (2010) 28 BHRC 313, [2010] ECHR 25965/04, ECtHR.

14

RESIDENCE FOR VICTIMS OF TRAFFICKING IN THE UK: HUMANITARIAN, ASYLUM AND HUMAN RIGHTS CONSIDERATIONS

Parosha Chandran and Nadine Finch

'Following a reflection and recovery period, trafficked persons should be provided with temporary or permanent residence status on certain grounds. Firstly, trafficked persons should be entitled to remain in the country where remedies are being sought for the duration of any criminal, civil or . . . administrative proceedings . . . [Article] 7 of the Palermo Protocol . . . should be interpreted to encourage States to provide trafficked persons with temporary residence status for the purpose of seeking remedies. Secondly, trafficked persons should be granted temporary or permanent residence status on social or humanitarian grounds. Such grounds may include, for instance, the inability to guarantee a safe and secure return, the fears of reprisals and retaliation by traffickers, the risk of being re-trafficked, or the return is otherwise not in the best interests of the trafficked person. Another factor that should be taken into account is the obligation of States not to return trafficked persons to States where they have a well-founded fear of persecution. Some victims or potential victims of trafficking may fall within the definition of a refugee contained in article 1(A)(2) of the 1951 Convention relating to the Status of Refugees and may therefore be entitled to international refugee protection. In these circumstances, temporary or permanent residence status may in itself become a substantial form of remedy.'[1]

[1] *Report of the UN Special Rapporteur on trafficking in persons, especially women and children, Joy Ngozi Ezeil*, to the Human Rights Council of the UN General Assembly, 13 April 2011, at para 51. In this report the Special Rapporteur provides her thematic analysis on the right to an effective remedy for trafficked persons.

INTRODUCTION

14.1 In many cases, victims of human trafficking in the United Kingdom who escape or are rescued from their traffickers fear that they will be re-trafficked by the same individuals or criminal gangs or face retribution and punishment if they are returned to their countries of origin. In other cases they believe that if they are returned home and to the same socio-economic or cultural conditions which rendered them vulnerable to trafficking in the first place, such as poverty, age, gender or family circumstances, they will be re-exposed to the same or increased risks of trafficking and exploitation at the hands of other individuals or organised criminals. There are also some victims who simply cannot face the prospect of return, either because they might have lost all links and bonds with their home countries on account of having been trafficked abroad many years previously and have no idea what might await them there or, owing to illness, they are highly reliant on support structures and medical assistance in the UK for their ongoing ability to survive and function and, in the cases of some extremely vulnerable victims, removing them from the UK may raise a real risk of suicide.

In all cases, the onset of trafficking and exploitation-based trauma which may take the form of single or multiple mental illness(es)[1], may materially exacerbate their existing vulnerabilities if removed to the country of origin and leave the victims much more susceptible to the risks of harm by others and less able to fend for themselves in the absence of family, community or economic support, particularly where there is a lack of any durable State protection, including specialist medical treatment, shelter and rehabilitation.

[1] Which in the authors' experience is often Post Traumatic Stress Disorder, sometimes in its complex form if correctly diagnosed, and major depressive disorder. For an understanding of trauma in victims of trafficking please see **CHAPTER 4** on Identifying and Treating Trauma in Victims of Trafficking and Exploitation.

TEMPORARY RESIDENCE UNDER THE TRAFFICKING CONVENTION

14.2 The Council of Europe Convention on Action against Trafficking in Human Beings[1] (the Trafficking Convention) offers a renewable, temporary period of residence[2] to victims of trafficking if the competent authority[3] considers that their stay is necessary owing to their personal situation[4] or for the purpose of their co-operation with those authorities in criminal investigations or proceedings[5]. However, the renewable residence permits which may be granted under this Convention are primarily designed to prevent the return home of a former victim of trafficking until the end of any police or court activity or to provide the individual with a short period of leave to remain in the country of destination so they can obtain any necessary medical or psychiatric treatment, complete a period of education or training or possibly bring a trafficking-related claim[6]. The grant of a residence permit does not therefore represent international protection, nor reflect recognition that the victim is likely to face persecution, serious harm or further exploitation if they are removed to their country of origin in the future[7].

[1] Warsaw, 16.v.2005.
[2] A residence permit under Article 14 of the Convention. Under UK policy the renewable residence permit, where granted, is a year. For more comment on the residence permit and the conditions in which it is to be granted see further **CHAPTER 2** on Identification at para **2.3**.
[3] Which in the UK is the United Kingdom Border Agency (UKBA) or the United Kingdom Human Trafficking Centre (UKHTC).
[4] Trafficking Convention, Article 14(1)(a).
[5] Trafficking Convention, Article 14(1)(b).
[6] See too the opinion of the UN Special Rapporteur, cited above, that the scope of a residence permit under the Palermo Protocol should cover . . . 'the duration of any criminal, civil or administrative proceedings', *Report of the UN Special Rapporteur on trafficking in persons, especially women and children, Joy Ngozi Ezeil'*, to the Human Rights Council of the UN General Assembly, 13 April 2011. By analogy to a victim's rights under the Palermo Protocol, a residence permit under the Trafficking Convention should be granted to enable a victim of trafficking to remain in the UK to seek, for example, compensation or civil/employment

proceedings against the trafficker: the conditions for granting the residence permit must not be limited only to the victim's co-operation with the police. See for example the Explanatory Report to the Trafficking Convention: '183. Thus, for the victim to be granted a residence permit . . . either the victim's personal circumstances must be such that it would be unreasonable to compel them to leave the national territory, or there has to be an investigation or prosecution with the victim co-operating with the authorities . . . '[Emphasis added]. The wording as underlined provides the test for a residence permit under Article 14(1)(a). And further the Explanatory Report provides, '184. The personal situation requirement takes in a range of situations, depending on whether it is the victim's safety, state of health, family situation or some other factor which has to be taken into account.' [Emphasis added]. Compensation, civil or employment claims are surely therefore materially relevant 'other factors' that are covered by the expressed 'personal circumstances' grounds for the grant of a residence permit under Article 14(1)(a) of the Trafficking Convention.

7   And note: Trafficking Convention, Article 10(5) expressly provides: 'Having regard to the obligations of Parties to which Article 40 of this Convention refers, each Party shall ensure that granting of a permit according to this provision shall be without prejudice to the right to seek and enjoy asylum.' Article 40(4) provides: 'Nothing in this Convention shall affect the rights, obligations and responsibilities of States and individuals under international law, including international humanitarian law and international human rights law and, in particular, where applicable, the 1951 Convention and the 1967 Protocol relating to the Status of Refugees and the principle of *non-refoulement* as contained therein.'

PERMANENT RESIDENCE UNDER THE PALERMO PROTOCOL

14.3 Furthermore, and notwithstanding a person's right to claim a residence permit under the Trafficking Convention or their right to claim asylum under the Refugee Convention 1951, the possibility of a grant of permanent residence to a victim of trafficking by the State in which he or she is identified (which will often be the destination State, known formally as 'the receiving State') is suggested in Article 7 of the Palermo Protocol as being an appropriate measure[1]. This has also been suggested by the Organisation for Security and Co-operation in Europe (OSCE)[2] and, as expressed above by the UN Special Rapporteur on Trafficking, may constitute a significant effective remedy for a victim of trafficking.

In her 2011 report the UN Special Rapporteur on Trafficking[3] also advises that:

'23 . . . returning a trafficked person to his or her country of origin may not be an appropriate form of remedy where he or she has lost legal, cultural or social ties with the country of origin and it is no longer in his or her best interest to return to it. For instance, it is conceivable that a child who is trafficked to another country and perpetuated in this situation over decades may lose his or her social and cultural identity in the country of origin. In this case, it would be difficult to justify that "restitution" in a traditional sense alone would be an appropriate, victim-centred remedy. Where these factors exist, restitution may involve reintegration of the trafficked person into the host community or resettlement in a third country.'

1   Palermo Protocol, Article 7: *Status of victims of trafficking in persons in receiving States* '1. In addition to taking measures pursuant to [the assistance measures under article 6 of this Protocol], each State Party shall consider adopting legislative or other appropriate measures that permit victims of trafficking in persons to remain in its territory, temporarily or permanently, in appropriate cases. 2. In implementing the provision contained in paragraph 1 of this article, each State Party shall give appropriate consideration to humanitarian and compassionate factors.'

2   See further: OSCE report, *Analysing the business model of trafficking in human beings to better prevent the crime*, May 2010, at p 80.

[3] *Report of the Special Rapporteur on trafficking in persons, especially women and children, Joy Ngozi Ezeilo*, to the Human Rights Council of the UN General Assembly, 13 April 2011, at paras 51 and 52.

PERMANENT RESIDENCE IN THE UK FOR REFUGEE VICTIMS OF TRAFFICKING: THE IMPLICATIONS OF THE CASE OF *YUSUF AND OTHERS* [2006] EWHC 3513 (ADMIN)

14.4 A discussion of asylum claims by victims of human trafficking is to be found later below at paras **14.7–14.17**.

The duration of the grant of leave that is provided by any State to those who have been recognised as refugees or humanitarian protection is a matter for the State to determine.

In respect of the duration of refugee leave, the UNHCR Handbook on Procedures 1992 advises at para 135:

'135 . . . A refugee's status should not in principle be subject to frequent review to the detriment of his sense of security, which international protection is intended to provide.'[1]

In the UK, until 2005, the Secretary of State for the Home Department (SSHD) operated a policy by which indefinite leave to remain (ILR) (ie permanent settlement[2]) was granted to individuals who were recognised by the SSHD or the UK's courts and tribunals as a refugee. That policy was amended. Under the new policy, operative from 30 August 2005 to date, a successful claim for asylum or humanitarian protection will entitle the individual to an initial period of five years' leave to remain, after which an application for ILR may be made.

The impact of this policy change on a highly vulnerable victim of trafficking was highlighted in a judicial review in 2006 which sought to challenge the grant of five years leave to remain as opposed to ILR in four linked cases[3]: see the judgment of Davis J in *Yusuf and Others (on the application of) v Secretary of State for the Home Department*[4]. In Yusuf's case it was argued she had a legitimate expectation that she would be granted ILR as a recognised refugee as her refugee claim crystallised prior to the policy change[5] and, in the alternative, that her mental health illnesses which stemmed as a direct result of having been trafficked and exploited were so severe that the grant of only five years' leave to remain left her, subjectively and objectively, without any enduring protection against removal from the UK. For her the limited grant of leave was akin to having the sword of Damocles hanging over her head: she remained in a state of anticipatory fear of harm and was thereby unable to enter into any meaningful recovery from her horrific experiences[6].

Dismissing the applications of all four applicants Davis J did make favourable comments regarding the distinct mental health arguments that had been advanced on Miss Yusuf's behalf and stated that the new medical evidence relied on[7] was capable of forming the basis of fresh representations for ILR to the SSHD[8]. Referring to the judge's comments, these representations were made to the SSHD and in November 2007 Miss Yusuf was granted indefinite leave to remain in the UK directly on account of the trafficking-based harm, and the mental health consequences of this that she had received as a victim of trafficking and sexual exploitation.

1   This advice is expressed by the UNHCR in the context of cessation via a change of circumstances in the country of origin but has wider application.

2   ILR constitutes 'settlement' in the United Kingdom, giving *inter alia* in general a right to permanent residence in the UK, subject to exceptions (Immigration Act 1971, s 7). There is eligibility for naturalisation or registration as a British Citizen (British Nationality Act 1981, ss 4 and 6). Settlement enables a parent to qualify her child for British Citizenship if the child is born in the UK (British Nationality Act 1981, ss 1(1) and 50(4)).

3   The claims were summarised by Davis J at para 2: 'The claimants in these four claims for judicial review complain that delay in the handling of the consideration of their claims for asylum, and in particular in the handling of and giving effect to their successful appeals, meant that they were only formally granted the benefit of the recognition of refugee status after 30 August 2005; and in consequence were only granted leave to remain in the United Kingdom for an initial period of five years. They say that, without such delay and in accordance with their successful appeals, their cases would and should have been disposed of earlier and a formal grant of leave to enter or remain would and should have been made before 30 August 2005. In consequence, the argument goes, they would and should have been granted indefinite leave to remain.' Of these four claimants one was a victim of human trafficking, Yusuf.

4   [2006] EWHC 3513 (Admin) (21 December 2006).

5   This argument was not accepted by the High Court

6   The mental health arguments that were advanced were novel: it was argued that there were 'exceptional circumstances' which warranted the grant of ILR on the facts of the applicant's case, despite there being no written UK law or policy which supported this. The applicant's case was supported by detailed, expert medical evidence from the Helen Bamber Foundation.

7   Which had arisen in the course of the judicial review proceedings and not in advance of them.

8   See *Yusuf and Others (on the application of) v Secretary of State for the Home Department* [2006] EWHC 3513 (Admin) at para 76: 'Ms Chandran did also object that the Secretary of State had failed to give individual consideration to the exceptional circumstances said to apply to Miss Yusuf in deciding whether or not to grant indefinite leave to remain, and had rigidly and wrongly fettered his discretion. The arguments here went rather further than the arguments advanced in respect of the other claimants on this particular point (which in substance had been in those other cases simply a variation of their primary argument): because in the present case Ms Chandran very eloquently referred to the asserted psychological consequences to Miss Yusuf of even the possibility of being returned to Nigeria, which possibility of course at least exists in the light of the decision to grant five years' leave to remain. However, it transpired that much of this, including the reference to psychological evidence, has emerged since the decision to grant five years' leave to remain. At the time the original decision was made, it seems to me to have been a perfectly valid and reasonable decision to have been made as matters then stood. Accordingly, that point cannot be a basis for acceding to this claim for judicial review in these proceedings: although it perhaps may be a basis for those acting for Miss Yusuf hereafter to make further representations to the Secretary of State for him to consider whether, in his discretion, to grant indefinite leave to remain on the basis of the exceptional circumstances now being advanced, including any psychiatric or psychological evidence' and at para 127 'MR JUSTICE DAVIS: You will convey to Ms Chandran, will you, that the particular point she was urging on behalf of Miss Yusuf, which does not apply to the other cases, about the particular psychological hardship, does seem to be capable of further formal representations accompanied by evidence. That is not so in the other cases that I am aware' and at para 128 'MISS FINCH: My Lord, I note that.'

PERMANENT RESIDENCE FOR VICTIMS OF TRAFFICKING AND TORTURE: EU LAW AS INTERPRETED IN UK POLICY

14.5 As to the possibility of a victim of trafficking obtaining permanent settlement in the UK under EU law, the principle that permanent protection may be appropriate in the cases of vulnerable individuals is recognised under Council Directive 2004/83/EC of 29 April 2004[1] on minimum standards for the qualification and status of third country nationals or stateless persons as refugees or as persons who otherwise need international protection and the content of the protection granted, (otherwise known as 'the EU Qualification Directive'). This Directive expressly recognises that victims of severe persecution may need a more durable form of protection than the Directive's minimum grant of three years[2] provides to refugees and those entitled to humanitarian protection.

The EU Qualification Directive provides, under Chapter VII, as follows:

'CHAPTER VII
CONTENT OF INTERNATIONAL PROTECTION
Article 20
General rules

1.   This Chapter shall be without prejudice to the rights laid down in the Geneva Convention.
2.   This Chapter shall apply both to refugees and persons eligible for subsidiary protection unless otherwise indicated.
3.   When implementing this Chapter, Member States shall take into account the specific situation of vulnerable persons such as minors, unaccompanied minors, disabled people, elderly people, pregnant women, single parents with minor children and persons who have been subjected to torture, rape or other serious forms of psychological, physical or sexual violence.
4.   Paragraph 3 shall apply only to persons found to have special needs after an individual evaluation of their situation.'

The recognition under Article 20 of the EU Qualification Directive that there may be some vulnerable persons with special needs for whom temporary protection is inadequate was eventually incorporated into the SSHD's Asylum and Policy Instructions (API) on Refugee Leave in August 2008[3]. It is still so incorporated[4]:

'2.2 Vulnerable persons with special needs
Article 20(3) of the Qualification Directive states that when implementing Chapter VII of the Directive, "Member States shall take into account the specific situation of vulnerable persons such as minors, unaccompanied minors, disabled people, elderly people, pregnant women, single parents with minor children and persons who have been subjected to torture, rape or other serious forms of psychological, physical or sexual violence."
Article 20(4) of the Qualification Directive states that paragraph 20(3) "shall only apply to persons found to have special needs after an individual evaluation of their situation."
The Qualification Directive specifies that three years leave is the minimum period that can be given to those with refugee status. Five years leave to remain [under UK policy] will be a sufficient grant of leave save in the most exceptional of circumstances. However, in accordance with Article 20, where, in light of the specific situation of a vulnerable person with special needs a longer period of leave to remain is considered appropriate, the advice of a Senior Caseworker must be sought.'

In late 2008 in the unreported case of *R v SSHD, ex parte Q*[5] a judicial review was brought on behalf of a victim of trafficking who had requested ILR from the SSHD shortly after her receipt of five years' refugee leave. Similarly to the applicant in *Yusuf*, Miss Q was in dire mental ill-health as a result of trafficking-based harm and exploitation and medical experts had concluded that, in order for her to engage in effective recovery this would necessitate a form of more durable protection than five years' leave to remain could provide. The SSHD replied that in the absence of any stated 'trigger for review' in the

API[6] her ILR request would have to await the expiry of her five years' leave. Placing reliance on (1) *Yusuf*, (2) Article 20 of the EU Qualification Directive and (3) para 2.2 of the SSHD's API on Refugee Leave[7], a judicial review application was lodged on behalf of Q in which she challenged the lawfulness of the SSHD's decision. Very shortly afterwards, and before the permission application was considered by the High Court, the SSHD offered to reconsider the medical evidence and the legal representations made and by agreement the judicial review application was withdrawn. The SSHD subsequently agreed to grant Q indefinite leave to remain in the UK on the basis of her need for permanent protection owing to her serious mental ill health as a victim of trafficking[8].

In both cases of *Yusuf* and *Q* the victims of trafficking had obtained refugee recognition and, in view of the severity of their mental suffering[9], their claims to convert their existing five years' leave to remain into ILR were successful[10]. The principal test is that under Article 20(3) and 20(4) of the EU Qualification Directive[11], which could also arguably be taken together with Article 7 of the Palermo Protocol[12] as establishing the need for permanent settlement in the UK for certain highly vulnerable victims of trafficking[13].

[1]   The transposition date of the Council Directive 2004/83/EC was 10 October 2006. The UK's Refugee or Person in Need of International Protection (Qualification) Regulations 2006 entered into force on that date but the UK's obligations under Article 20 of the Council Directive were not reflected in Home Office policy until nearly two years later in August 2008 when it was recognised in the UKBA's revised Asylum Policy Instructions Version (API) 2.0.

[2]   The UK's grant is five years. UKBA API on Refugee Leave, at para 2.1 provides: '"2.1 Summary of changes to Refugee Leave" The Five Year Strategy for Asylum and Immigration, published in February 2005, provided that most categories of immigrants should be subject to a minimum five year residency requirement before becoming eligible for permanent settlement. This includes refugees. Where the requirements in paragraph 334 of the Immigration Rules are satisfied, refugees should normally be granted five years Leave to Enter/Remain (LTE / LTR) under paragraphs 330 or 335 of the Immigration Rules rather than being given immediate Indefinite Leave to Enter or Remain (ILE/ILR) as previously.'

[3]   API on Refugee Leave, Version 2.0 of 11.08.08.

[4]   API on Refugee Leave, Version 3.0 of 26.2.09 [current], accessed 1 August 2011. Available at: http://www.ukba.homeoffice.gov.uk/sitecontent/documents/policyandlaw/asylumpolicyinstructions/apis/refugeeleave.pdf?view=Binary.

[5]   Case No. CO/11827/2008 (unreported), lodged on 5 December 2008.

[6]   Which might, for example, have included cessation as a refugee where there was a significant change in the country of origin. The current API on Refugee Leave at para 2.1 under the heading 'Summary of Changes to Refugee Leave' provides: 'Reviews during the course of the leave may be triggered by the actions of the individual or on the basis of a significant and non-temporary change in the conditions in a country which has produced refugees (see Trigger 2 below). The nature of the review will vary depending on the particular trigger.
If it is found following review that a refugee no longer requires, or is no longer entitled to, protection in the UK, the person's refugee status will cease and leave will be curtailed under paragraph 323 of the Immigration Rules, unless he qualifies for leave on another basis, in which case leave may be varied.
At the end of five years limited leave, subject to the outcome of any review and to the policies in place at the time, a refugee will be eligible to seek ILR.'

[7]   Version 2.0, relevant parts extracted above in the body of para **14.5**.

[8]   The solicitor in *Yusuf* and in *Q's* case was Rachael Despicht at Birnberg Peirce solicitors in London.

[9]   And indeed the quality of the medical evidence relied upon.

[10] The *Yusuf* judicial review was lodged in the High Court some months before the transposition date of the EU Qualification Directive in October 2006. *Yusuf* was heard in December 2006. One and a half years later, in August 2008 the API on Refugee Leave was amended to include the UK's obligations under Article 20 of the EU Qualification Directive. The *Q v SSHD*

judicial review was brought shortly after the API was amended to reflect this: the judicial review application in Q was withdrawn in December 2008 by consent and Q was granted ILR by the SSHD in early 2009.

[11] Supported by the API on Refugee Leave.

[12] Particularly in view of the Special Rapporteur's advice on the scope of Article 7 in her 2011 report.

[13] Where the case involves a recognised refugee or a person recognised as being eligible for HP, where the medical evidence is strong in terms of the individual's need for permanent protection in the form of ILR and they fall into the following categories of case under Article 20 (which many victims of trafficking will – but of course Article 20 is not limited to trafficked cases) then such an application for ILR should be made: 'vulnerable persons such as minors, unaccompanied minors, disabled people, elderly people, pregnant women, single parents with minor children and persons who have been subjected to torture, rape or other serious forms of psychological, physical or sexual violence.' The outcomes of the *Yusuf* case and the *Q* case might be prayed in aid.

ARTICLE 8 ECHR

14.6 Where a trafficked victim has been refused asylum by the SSHD and appeals on asylum and human rights grounds, it is worth recalling that another theme of the UN Special Rapporteur on Trafficking's 2011 report is that a right of temporary residence in a country on humanitarian[1] grounds may form an effective remedy for trafficking and exploitation-related harm. This general principal was recognised by Sedley LJ in 2007 as falling within the nature and scope of Article 8 ECHR[2] in his permission ruling in the *PO (Nigeria) case*[3] when it was first appealed to the Court of Appeal. The core facts were summarised by Sedley LJ in the following way:

'1. The applicant . . . is a young Nigerian woman who was brought into this country by a man who I think can be briefly and accurately described as a Nigerian gangster, for the purposes of enforced prostitution. After months of repeated rape she escaped and, with the help of the Poppy Project, sought refuge and protection here. Her reward has been a decision of the Home Office to send her back to Nigeria.'

Having granted permission to appeal on several of the grounds advanced, which related principally to the second AIT's dismissal of the appellant's asylum appeal[4], Sedley LJ considered the grounds which related to the appellant's right to respect for her private life in the UK under Article 8 ECHR and found:

'9. There is, however, in my judgment, another reason for granting permission to appeal. This woman was brought to this country by a criminal who should not have been allowed in, and was compelled by force to provide sexual services to men living here. Her reward, now that she has finally escaped, is to be returned to a country where she will certainly be without social or familial support, will be expected to move to a strange region and try to find work there and might still be at risk from the same predator. Some might think she is owed better than this. This court is not a court of morals, but it is a court which, in my view, will want to look with great care at an outcome such as was arrived at here . . . '5

He concluded:

'10. I would add this. The test applied by the second immigration judge was the test of exceptionality which is now known to be an incorrect application of [A]rticle 8(2) [ECHR] . . . it may be that the moral case which I have mentioned would have been accorded to rather more weight if the correct exercise of assessing not exceptionality but proportionality had in fact been gone through. This too may deserve attention.'

It follows that in arguing for human rights protection under Article 8 ECHR against removal from the UK on behalf of a victim of trafficking, practitioners are advised to plead all the relevant facts, historical and present, which relate to the circumstances which led to the individual being trafficked, the treatment they received as a victim of trafficking, the personal impact of such treatment on them and their vulnerabilities on return in the trafficking, and any wider, context. Such factors ought to be material considerations for the Immigration Judge when assessing the proportionality of removal and in conducting the lawful balancing exercise that is required. Relevant too in cases of international trafficking[6] will be to highlight that it was the trafficker's actions via his control over the victim which caused any breach of UK immigration control, not the actions of the victim[7]. Accordingly any reliance by the State on 'the interests of immigration control' argument as justifying the proposed interference with the individual's private of family law rights under Article 8 ought, rationally, to be nullified.

[1] And hence human rights grounds.

[2] Which is a qualified right under the European Convention on Human Rights and protects, amongst other things, an individual's right to respect for his or her private life and family life in the host state.

[3] *PO (Nigeria) v Secretary of State for the Home Department* [2007] EWCA Civ 1183 (24 October 2007).

[4] When it had been won in front of the first AIT.

[5] *PO (Nigeria)* has a long history and some readers might be aware that it was concluded in the Court of Appeal in February 2011: *PO (Nigeria) v Secretary of State for the Home Department* [2011] EWCA Civ 132 where it was held, amongst other things, that the burden of proving that an individual was trafficked by a gang does not fall on the victim. Following Sedley LJ's decision to grant permission to appeal to the Court of Appeal on several grounds in 2007, the Secretary of State for the Home Department (SSHD) agreed that the decision of the Asylum and Immigration Tribunal (AIT) to reject PO's asylum and human rights appeals was flawed and the parties consented that PO's case should be remitted back to the AIT, as it was then called, for a new hearing to take place: a consent order was signed by the parties to that effect. That new hearing, which was limited to particular issues which included risk on return for PO (on asylum and Article 3 ECHR grounds) and the right to respect for PO's private life under Article 8 ECHR (which was argued on the basis of Sedley LJ's ruling in 2007, above), took place over three days in late 2008 and early 2009. The original Immigration Judge's finding that 'women in Nigeria' formed a particular social group under the Refugee Convention 1951 was preserved in the terms of the Court of Appeal remittal order and hence that finding was, and is, preserved. The AIT promulgated its decision in November 2009 by which it dismissed PO's asylum and the human rights appeals: *PO (Trafficked Women) Nigeria CG* [2009] UKAIT 00046. That decision was appealed to the Court of Appeal in 2010 (heard in 2011) Just before the appeal was lodged the appellant was granted indefinite leave to remain (ILR) in the UK (ie permanent residence) by the SSHD for reasons unconnected with her appeal (ie on account of the SSHD's policy to grant ILR to particular asylum seekers with unresolved cases under the 'legacy' scheme). As such PO retained no personal interest in the outcome of her appeal before the Court of Appeal but on account of the fact the AIT decision in her case had been designated as being Country Guidance on trafficked women from Nigeria, and was therefore continuing to affect all asylum protection claims by Nigerian victims of trafficking in the UK, she instructed her lawyers to proceed in the Court of Appeal and funding was granted by the Legal Services Commission. As the appeal had become academic it was not possible therefore to continue to argue the Article 8 ECHR issue as this was of course a fact-dependent exercise. Hence the Court of Appeal in hearing the academic appeal in *PO (Nigeria)* in January 2011 did not hear any Article 8 ECHR argument. It follows that Sedley LJ's decision to grant permission in 2007 on the 'moral case' that may have to form part of the balancing exercise in deciding on the proportionality of removal continues to be relevant and may form the basis of Article 8 ECHR

representations and argument on behalf of other victims of human trafficking who have suffered on account of their trafficking and exploitation in the UK.

⁶ That is across a country's border as opposed to within it.

⁷ If a practitioner is in any doubt about the irrelevance of an adult victim's consent to trafficking where any of 'the means' under the Palermo Protocol and Trafficking Convention definition of human trafficking were used by the trafficker to obtain that consent please see for clarification **CHAPTER 2** at paras **2.5** and **2.7**. Practitioners are also reminded that in children's cases, under the human trafficking definition a child cannot consent in law to their trafficking in any circumstances – see **CHAPTER 2** at para **2.8**.

ASYLUM

14.7 In 2005 the UNHCR advised that:

'An estimated 100-500,000 persons are trafficked annually into Europe. Trafficking into, out of or within Europe is done overwhelmingly for the purpose of sexual exploitation.

Human trafficking in general is on the increase. New EU and external border countries have become important transit routes and are increasingly becoming destination countries as well. The phenomenon of re-trafficking has also been reported as a growing trend. While the great majority of persons trafficked to and within Europe are women and girls for the purpose of sexual exploitation, the trafficking of children includes boys for begging and street vending, and men for other types of exploitative labour.'[1]

¹ *UNHCR's role in combating human trafficking in Europe*, by Malika Floor, Senior Regional Adviser (Refugee Women and Children) Europe Bureau, UNHCR. Summary Report. The full report, *Combatting Human Trafficking: Overview of UNHCR Anti-Trafficking Activities in Europe, 2005* is available at http://www.unhcr.org.

(1) Introduction to Asylum

14.8 Neither the Palermo Protocol nor the Trafficking Convention precludes a victim from seeking protection under other international human rights instruments, including the Refugee Convention 1951. Indeed both instruments, by expressly preserving the right of a trafficked individual to seek and enjoy asylum[1], implicitly recognise that a trafficking victim may be recognised as a refugee, provided his or her case falls under the scope of the 1951 Convention[2].

If a victim has a fear of persecution on return it is possible that he or she will be able to seek asylum under the 1951 Convention of the Status of Refugees ('the Refugee Convention') and its 1967 Protocol. The usual dictionary definition of 'asylum' is the provision of refuge, shelter or protection and Article 14 of the Universal Declaration of Human Rights 1948 refers to there being a right to 'seek and enjoy asylum from persecution'. However the definition used by the Refugee Convention is far more precise.

Article 1(2) of the Refugee Convention limits its protection to those who are outside their country of origin or habitual residence and who have a well-founded fear of being persecuted for reasons of race, religion, nationality, membership of a particular social group or political opinion. The same article also requires a prospective victim of persecution to show that he or she would be unable, or because of their fear of future persecution be unwilling, to seek the protection of the authorities in their country of origin or habitual residence[3].

Both potential and actual victims of trafficking could have valid claims for asylum. As explained by the UNHCR's Guidelines On International Protection: The application of Article 1A(2) of the 1951 Convention and/or 1967 Protocol relating to the Status of Refugees to victims of trafficking and persons at risk of being trafficked ('the UNHCR Trafficking Guidelines') a claim for refugee status can arise in a number of circumstances[4]:

(1)   The victim may have been trafficked abroad, may have escaped her or his traffickers and may seek the protection of the State where she or he now is[5];

(2)   The victim may have been trafficked within national territory, may have escaped from her or his traffickers and have fled abroad in search of international protection;

(3)   The individual concerned may not have been trafficked but may fear becoming a victim of trafficking and may have fled abroad in search of international protection.

It is important to note that not all victims or potential victims of trafficking are eligible for refugee status:

'In order to be recognized as a refugee, an applicant must satisfy all of the elements of the refugee definition. He or she must prove a well-founded fear of persecution based on one or more of the Refugee Convention grounds: race, religion, nationality, membership in a particular social group or political opinion. He or she must also establish that the state of origin is unwilling or unable to protect him or her.'[6]

In considering scenario (1) as described above, the connection between trafficking and smuggling must also be appreciated:

'In some respects, trafficking in persons resembles the smuggling of migrants, which is the subject of another Protocol to the Convention against Transnational Crime. As with trafficking, the smuggling of migrants often takes place in dangerous and/or degrading conditions involving human rights abuses. It is nevertheless essentially a voluntary act entailing the payment of a fee to the smuggler to provide a specific service. The relationship between the migrant and the smuggler normally ends either with the arrival at the migrant's destination or with the individual being abandoned en route. Victims of trafficking are distinguished from migrants who have been smuggled by the protracted nature of the exploitation they endure, which includes serious and ongoing abuses of their human rights at the hands of their traffickers. Smuggling rings and trafficking rings are nevertheless often closely related, with both preying on the vulnerabilities of people seeking international protection or access to labour markets abroad. Irregular migrants relying on the services of smugglers whom they have willingly contracted may also end up as victims of trafficking, if the services they originally sought metamorphose into abusive and exploitative trafficking scenarios.'[7]

Moreover, in addition to understanding the definition of human trafficking[8], the nature of the human trafficking process must also be appreciated both by practitioners in terms of seeking best evidence for asylum applications and appeals and by decision makers. As the Trafficking Guidelines explain:

'10. An important aspect of..[the human trafficking] definition is an understanding of trafficking as a process comprising a number of interrelated actions rather than a single act at a given point in time. Once initial control is secured, victims are generally moved to a place where there is a market for their services, often where they lack language skills and other basic knowledge that would enable them to seek help. While these actions can all take place within one country's borders, they can also take place across borders with the recruitment taking place in one country and the act of receiving the victim and the exploitation taking place in another. Whether or not an international border is crossed, the intention to exploit the individual concerned underpins the entire process.'

If a victim of trafficking can meet the requirements contained in Article 1(2) they will be protected against '*refoulement*', which is any attempt to return a victim to a place where their life or liberty would be at risk. This principle of *non-refoulement* would be applied if a victim feared persecution or other serious harm in his or her country of origin.

[1] Palermo Protocol, Article 14(1): 'Nothing in this Protocol shall affect the rights, obligations and responsibilities of States and individuals under international law, including international humanitarian law and international human rights law and, in particular, where applicable, the 1951 Convention and the 1967 Protocol relating to the Status of Refugees and the principle of non-refoulement as contained therein.' Trafficking Convention, Article 40(4) contains the exact same saving clause.

[2] See, UNHCR, *Considerations on the issue of Human Trafficking from the Perspective of International Refugee Law and UNHCR's Mandate, Second meeting of National Authorities on Human Trafficking (OAS), March 2009, Buenos Aires, Argentina* at page 7, footnote 7.

[3] Article 1A(2) of the Refugee Convention as amended defines a 'refugee' for purposes of the Convention as any person who 'owing to well-founded fear of being persecuted for reasons of race, religion, nationality, membership of a particular social group or political opinion, is outside the country of his nationality and is unable or, owing to such fear, is unwilling to avail himself of the protection of that country; . . . ' In many cases the applicant for asylum in trafficking cases will be a refugee *sur place*. As the UNHCR's Trafficking Guidelines of 2006 explain: '25 . . . The requirement of being outside one's country does not, however, mean that the individual must have left on account of a well-founded fear of persecution.24 Where this fear arises after she or he has left the country of origin, she or he would be a refugee sur place, providing the other elements in the refugee definition were fulfilled.'

[4] UNHCR Trafficking Guidelines, para 13. See too Special Issues in Refugee Status Determination, Victims of Trafficking, Anna Marie Gallagher, 2011, available at http://www.srlan.or g/beta/index.php?option=com_content&view=article&id=768&Itemid=210

[5] Aside from any reported or unreported trafficking cases which are already mentioned in the text of this chapter, recent trafficking-related UK jurisprudence (which covers issues of law and evidence which may assist practitioners in preparing asylum applications and appeals on behalf of victims of trafficking in the UK) include: *PO (Nigeria) v Secretary of State for the Home Department* [2011] EWCA Civ 132, [2011] NLJR 327, (2011) Times, 19 April; *AZ (Trafficked women) Thailand CG* [2010] UKUT 118 (IAC); *AM and BM (Trafficked women) Albania CG* [2010] UKUT 80 (IAC).

[6] Special Issues in Refugee Status Determination, Victims of Trafficking, Anna Marie Gallagher 2011, at page 2, available at http://www.srlan.org/beta/index.php?option=com content&view =article&id=768&itemid=210. This paper is an excellent resource for practitioners who are representing victims of trafficking in their asylum claims and appeals.

[7] UNHCR Trafficking Guidelines, para 4.

[8] See para **14.5**, footnote 5, below. See too all the Identification chapters of this book, particularly **CHAPTER 1** on Interpreting Human Trafficking.

(2) Well-founded fear of persecution

(i) *General*

14.9 The fear of persecution by a victim of trafficking could be manifested as reprisals from traffickers or criminal networks, re-trafficking, harassment, threats or intimidation, particularly when the trafficked victim's escape from the trafficker will have meant that the target earnings expected by the trafficker, or the work that was expected to have been done, will not have been fulfilled. It is also often the case that the victims of trafficking fear stigma and intimidation from their home communities making it highly difficult for them to live safely in their home area without severe discrimination and/or punishment by the authorities.

(ii) *The future risk of persecution*

14.10 The standard of proof which is applied by the courts when deciding whether a person is entitled to protection under the Refugee Convention is low. In the leading case of *Sivakumaran*[1] the House of Lords held that the appropriate test was whether there was a 'serious possibility' or 'reasonable likelihood' of persecution in the future. This test is much lower than the 'balance of probabilities' civil standard. Trafficking and re-trafficking may both constitute acts of persecution according to the UNHCR Trafficking Guidelines 2006, set out at para **14.11** below. The mere fact that a victim has suffered persecution in the past does not however mean that this test is made out or that he or she is necessarily entitled to protection under the Refugee Convention in the future. However, paragraph 339k of the Immigration Rules does state that:

> 'the fact that a person has already been subject to persecution or serious harm, or to direct threats of such persecution or such harm, will be regarded as a serious indication of the person's well-founded fear of persecution or real risk of suffering serious harm, unless there are good reasons to consider that such persecution or serious harm will not be repeated.'

The leading Court of Appeal case on past persecution, *Demirkaya v Secretary of State for the Home Department*[2] which pre-dated the insertion of this rule, reflects the same principle. In *Demirkaya* the Court of Appeal had to consider whether the Tribunal's failure to have regard to a history of previous persecution when assessing future risk amounted to an error of law. Having taken into account the views of various leading academic texts on this issue, together with Berwick LJ's findings in the House of Lords in *Adan*[3], the Court held that the treatment a person had been subjected to before leaving his country of origin was very relevant to the question of whether that person had a well-founded fear of persecution on his return. This may obviously be very relevant in trafficking cases where the victims fear may largely depend upon their past experiences of being trafficked. Furthermore, the Court held that in the absence of a 'significant change' in the country of origin there may be a real risk of persecutory treatment on return.

Applying the above, in trafficking cases where the country of origin has been ranked at the same tier or lower by the US State Department Trafficking in Persons (TIP) Report since the year in which the individual was trafficked this will evidence, in *Demirkaya* terms, a likelihood that the risk of re-trafficking, either internationally or internally, is real. Where however the country has been given a higher ranking since the time of the original trafficking the authors suggest that this will not constitute a 'significant change' under the *Demirkaya* principle without more. It is recalled that the TIP reports are short and produced annually. If there are objective and expert reports which question the ranking of the country in the TIP and expose the protection flaws that the State might have in practical terms of protecting a particular victim of trafficking against the risk of re-trafficking or serious harm[4], then the incidence of past persecution remains linked to the prospect of persecution in the future despite any higher TIP ranking. Evidence on the prevalence of the trafficking of victims of particular nationalities into the UK, such as can be possibly gleaned from the statistics of the National Referral Mechanism in the UK[5], may also be relevant in terms of demonstrating that the home country has a continuing porous border in spite of its increasing efforts to combat trafficking.

These issues should encourage the courts to place greater emphasis on a careful analysis of the current prevalence of trafficking in the victim's country of origin and the steps being taken by the authorities there to effectively combat this trade and protect victims of trafficking against the risks described above. Does the Government, for example, fund long term shelters or provide medically trained specialist trauma counsellors to victims of trafficking or provide any durable forms of assistance and measures similar to those described in the Palermo Protocol or the Trafficking Convention?[6] In many cases the key area of dispute will be the risk on return and the availability of protection in the country of origin. However, as suggested above, in some cases the very fact that the individual has previously been trafficked from that country can suggest a porous border, an inability by that state to protect its nationals from being trafficked and a well-founded fear of persecution on account of the individual.

When considering the risk faced in that country it is still useful to rely on the definition of trafficking[7] provided in the Palermo Protocol and the Trafficking Convention, as this explains the many different forms that trafficking can manifest itself in and indicates that many different individuals may be involved in the trafficking process. Therefore it is not just the case that the victim of trafficking will be desperately seeking to avoid the actual individual who may have trafficked him or her out of the country, but he or she may be also be at risk from numerous unidentified persons who were involved in the trafficking of that person[8].

---

1   *R v Home Secretary, ex parte Sivakumaran* [1988] AC 958.
2   [1999] Imm AR 498, CA.
3   [1999] 1 AC 293.
4   Such as the State being unable to provide long term or durable shelter for the victim of trafficking, or providing no rehabilitation services or any specialist medical help to enable the victim recover from the trafficking-related harm they have suffered or being unable to protect the victim from the risk of harm at the hands of unidentified players in the trafficking gang. On medical and rehabilitation services in NAPTIP shelters in Nigeria see, for example the Court of Appeal's guidance in *PO (Nigeria) v Secretary of State for the Home Department* [2011] EWCA Civ 132 at paras 12–29.
5   The NRM statistics are available at http://www.soca.gov.uk/about-soca/about-the-ukhtc/statistical-data.
6   UNHCR Trafficking Guidelines: '22. Whether the authorities in the country of origin are able to protect victims or potential victims of trafficking will depend on whether legislative and administrative mechanisms have been put in place to prevent and combat trafficking, as well as to protect and assist the victims and on whether these mechanisms are effectively implemented in practice. Part II of the [Palermo] . . . Protocol requires States to take certain steps with regard to the protection of victims of trafficking, which can be of guidance when assessing the adequacy of protection and assistance provided. Measures relate not only to protecting the privacy and identity of victims of trafficking, but also to their physical,

psychological and social recovery. Article 8 of the [Palermo] . . . Protocol also requires State Parties, which are facilitating the return of their nationals or permanent residents who have been trafficked, to give due regard to the safety of the individuals concerned when accepting them back. The protection measures set out in Part II of the [Palermo] . . . Protocol are not exhaustive and should be read in light of other relevant binding and non-binding human rights instruments and guidelines.' See too therefore the Trafficking Convention, Article 16, which requires certain safeguards to be in place before a victim can be returned to their home country. Article 16(2) provides: 'When a Party returns a victim to another State, such return shall be with due regard for the rights, safety and dignity of that person and for the status of any legal proceedings related to the fact that the person is a victim, and shall preferably be voluntary.' As for child returnees, Article 16(7) requires that: 'Child victims shall not be returned to a State, if there is indication, following a risk and security assessment, that such return would not be in the best interests of the child.' The ramifications of the UK having ratified the Trafficking Convention in December 2008 were made clear by the Court of Appeal in *R v LM* [2010] EWCA Crim 2327, [2011] 1 Cr App Rep 135, [2011] Crim LR, when Hughes LJ, Vice-President of the Court of Appeal Criminal Division, stated: '2 . . . Now . . . this country has ratified the [Trafficking] Convention . . . it is fully bound by it.'

7 'Trafficking in persons' shall mean the recruitment, transportation, transfer, harbouring or receipt of persons, by means of the threat or use of force or other forms of coercion, of abduction, of fraud, of deception, of the abuse of power or of a position of vulnerability, or of the giving or receiving of payments or benefits to achieve the consent of a person having control over another person, for the purpose of exploitation. Exploitation shall include, at a minimum, the exploitation of the prostitution of others or other forms of sexual exploitation, forced labour or services, slavery or practices similar to slavery, servitude or the removal of organs.

8 UNHCR Guidelines, para 27: '[E]ven where the exploitation experienced by a victim of trafficking occurs mainly outside the country of origin, this does not preclude the existence of a well-founded fear of persecution in the individual's own country. The trafficking of individuals across international borders gives rise to a complex situation which requires a broad analysis taking into account the various forms of harm that have occurred at different points along the trafficking route. The continuous and interconnected nature of the range of persecutory acts involved in the context of transnational trafficking should be given due consideration. Furthermore, trafficking involves a chain of actors, starting with those responsible for recruitment in the country of origin, through to those who organize and facilitate the transport, transfer and/or sale of victims, through to the final "purchaser". Each of these actors has a vested interest in the trafficking enterprise and could pose a real threat to the victim. Depending on the sophistication of the trafficking rings involved, applicants may thus have experienced and continue to fear harm in a number of locations, including in countries through which they have transited, the State in which the asylum application is submitted and the country of origin. In such circumstances, the existence of a well-founded fear of persecution is to be evaluated in relation to the country of origin of the applicant.' See too on the evidential issues regarding trafficking by gangs in the Court of Appeal's guidance in *PO (Nigeria) v Secretary of State for the Home Department*[2011] EWCA Civ 132 at paras 30–45.

(iii) *Well-founded fear*

14.11 As indicated above, the Refugee Convention protects potential victims from future persecution if they are removed to their country or origin. 'Persecution' also has a particular meaning for the purposes of the Refugee Convention. The UNHCR Trafficking Guidelines explain that:

'14. What amounts to a well-founded fear of persecution will depend on the particular circumstances of each individual case. Persecution can be considered to involve serious human rights violations, including a threat to life or freedom, as well as other kinds of serious harm or intolerable predicament, as assessed in the light of the opinions, feelings and psychological make-up of the asylum applicant[1].
15. In this regard, the evolution of international law in criminalizing trafficking can help decision-makers determine the persecutory nature of the various acts associated

with trafficking. Asylum claims lodged by victims of trafficking or potential victims of trafficking should thus be examined in detail to establish whether the harm feared as a result of the trafficking experience, or as a result of its anticipation, amounts to persecution in the individual case. Inherent in the trafficking experience are such forms of severe exploitation as abduction, incarceration, rape, sexual enslavement, enforced prostitution, forced labour, removal of organs, physical beatings, starvation, the deprivation of medical treatment. Such acts constitute serious violations of human rights which will generally amount to persecution.'

And further:

'17. Apart from the persecution experienced by individuals in the course of being trafficked, they may face reprisals and/or possible re-trafficking should they be returned to the territory from which they have fled or from which they have been trafficked. For example, the victim's cooperation with the authorities in the country of asylum or the country of origin in investigations may give rise to a risk of harm from the traffickers upon return, particularly if the trafficking has been perpetrated by international trafficking networks. Reprisals at the hands of traffickers could amount to persecution depending on whether the acts feared involve serious human rights violations or other serious harm or intolerable predicament and on an evaluation of their impact on the individual concerned . . . In view of the serious human rights violations often involved, as described in paragraph 15 above, re-trafficking would usually amount to persecution.'

---

[1] See too UNHCR Guidelines: '19. The forcible or deceptive recruitment of women and children for the purposes of forced prostitution or sexual exploitation is a form of gender-related violence, which may constitute persecution. Trafficked women and children can be particularly susceptible to serious reprisals by traffickers after their escape and/or upon return, as well as to a real possibility of being re-trafficked or of being subjected to severe family or community ostracism and/or severe discrimination.'

(iv) *Actors of protection*

14.12 Article 4 of the Refugee or Person in Need of International Protection (Qualification) Regulations 2006 (the Qualification Regulations) explains that it is only State authorities or a party or organisation[1] which controls the State or a substantial part of the territory of the State and controls the legal and criminal justice system of a State which can provide State protection. In particular it provides that:

'(1)   In deciding whether a person is a refugee or a person eligible for humanitarian protection, protection from persecution or serious harm can be provided by:
(a)   the State; or
(b)   any party or organisation, including any international organisation, controlling the State or a substantial part of the territory of the State.

(2)   Protection shall be regarded as generally provided when the actors mentioned in paragraph (1)(a) and (b) take reasonable steps to prevent the persecution or suffering of serious harm by operating an effective legal system for the detection, prosecution and punishment of acts constituting persecution or serious harm, and the person mentioned in paragraph (1) has access to such protection.

(3)   In deciding whether a person is a refugee or a person eligible for humanitarian protection the Secretary of State may assess whether an international organisation controls a State or a substantial part of its

territory and provides protection as described in paragraph (2).' [Emphasis underlined]

It follows that NGOs are not 'actors of protection' for the purposes of the Refugee (Qualification) Regulations. Hence the mere existence of NGOs in a country which can provide some support or shelter to victims of trafficking will not constitute effective State protection under the Refugee Convention in the assessment of the whether an individual's fears on return are well-founded. This is particularly relevant in trafficking-related asylum cases where it is often argued by the host Government, such as the UK, that the trafficked individual will be able to obtain adequate protection and services from NGOs in the country of origin. In fact, as highlighted above, the enquiry must in fact be related to what protection the State, which will usually be the Government in the country of origin, can actually provide to victims of trafficking in terms of durable and effective protection[2]. If an NGO is predominantly funded by the State such that it is effectively State-run and there is sufficient evidence to demonstrate that it can provide durable protection to a trafficked individual then this might arguably meet the State protection test.

Indeed, as to the assessment of State protection generally the UNHCR Trafficking Guidelines advise:

'22. Whether the authorities in the country of origin are able to protect victims or potential victims of trafficking will depend on whether legislative and administrative mechanisms have been put in place to prevent and combat trafficking, as well as to protect and assist the victims and on whether these mechanisms are effectively implemented in practice . . .
23. Many States have not adopted or implemented sufficiently stringent measures to criminalize and prevent trafficking or to meet the needs of victims. Where a State fails to take such reasonable steps as are within its competence to prevent trafficking and provide effective protection and assistance to victims, the fear of persecution of the individual is likely to be well-founded. The mere existence of a law prohibiting trafficking in persons will not of itself be sufficient to exclude the possibility of persecution. If the law exists but is not effectively implemented, or if administrative mechanisms are in place to provide protection and assistance to victims, but the individual concerned is unable to gain access to such mechanisms, the State may be deemed unable to extend protection to the victim, or potential victim, of trafficking.'

---

[1] Such as the multinational troops in Iraq: see the judgment of the European Court of Justice in *Salahadin Abdulla (Area of Freedom, Security and Justice)* [2010] EUECJ C-175/08.
[2] This concurs with the findings of the House of Lords in *Horvath v SSHD* [2000] UKHL 37 where per Lord Hope: 'The primary duty to provide the protection lies with the home state. It is its duty to establish and to operate a system of protection against the persecution of its own nationals. If that system is lacking the protection of the international community is available as a substitute . . . '.

(v) *Agents of persecution*

14.13 In trafficking cases it is more likely that the process of trafficking will not directly involve State agents, although in some countries, particularly where corruption is prevalent there are direct links between State officials and trafficking[1]. The UNHCR Trafficking Guidelines provide:

'21. There is scope within the refugee definition to recognize both State and non- State agents of persecution. While persecution is often perpetrated by the authorities of a country, it can also be perpetrated by individuals if the persecutory acts are "knowingly tolerated by the authorities or if the authorities refuse, or prove unable to offer effective protection". In most situations involving victims or potential victims of trafficking, the persecutory acts emanate from individuals, that is, traffickers or criminal enterprises or, in some situations, family or community members. Under these circumstances, it is also necessary to examine whether the authorities of the country of origin are able and willing to protect the victim or potential victim upon return.'

1   See UNHCR Guidelines para 24: 'There may also be situations where trafficking activities are de facto tolerated or condoned by the authorities or even actively facilitated by corrupt State officials. In these circumstances, the agent of persecution may well be the State itself, which becomes responsible, whether directly or as a result of inaction, for a failure to protect those within its jurisdiction. Whether this is so will depend on the role played by the officials concerned and on whether they are acting in their personal capacity outside the framework of governmental authority or on the basis of the position of authority they occupy within governmental structures supporting or condoning trafficking. In the latter case, the persecutory acts may be deemed to emanate from the State itself.'

(vi) *The causal link*

14.14 In order to satisfy the refugee definition under the Refugee Convention a victim or potential victim of trafficking will have to prove that his/her well-founded fear of persecution is 'for reasons of' one or more of the Convention grounds: race, religion, nationality, membership in a particular social group or political opinion. The Trafficking Guidelines recognise that the difficult issue for adjudicators in assessing claims related to trafficking is often the link between the persecution and a Convention ground and so the Guidelines explain the causal link in readily understandable terms:

'29 . . . In relation to asylum claims involving trafficking, the difficult issue for a decision-maker is likely to be linking the well-founded fear of persecution to a Convention ground. Where the persecutor attributes or imputes a Convention ground to the applicant, this is sufficient to satisfy the causal link.
30. In cases where there is a risk of being persecuted at the hands of a non-State actor for reasons related to one of the Convention grounds, the causal link is established, whether or not the absence of State protection is Convention-related. Alternatively, where a risk of persecution at the hands of a non-State actor is unrelated to a Convention ground, but the inability or unwillingness of the State to offer protection is for reasons of a Convention ground, the causal link is also established.'

(vii) *The Convention Grounds*

14.15 The UNHCR Guidelines provide:

'32. Members of a certain race or ethnic group in a given country may be especially vulnerable to trafficking and/or less effectively protected by the authorities of the country of origin. Victims may be targeted on the basis of their ethnicity, nationality, religious or political views in a context where individuals with specific profiles are already more vulnerable to exploitation and abuse of varying forms. Individuals may also be targeted by reason of their belonging to a particular social group. As an example, among children or women generally in a particular society some subsets of children or women may be especially vulnerable to being trafficked and may constitute a social group within the terms of the refugee definition. Thus, even if an individual is not trafficked solely and exclusively for a Convention reason, one or more of these Convention grounds may have been relevant for the trafficker's selection of the particular victim.'

(viii)   *Particular social group*

14.16 For the purpose of this chapter, detailed consideration will only be given to the Convention reason, particular social group (PSG).

The UNHCR Trafficking Guidelines advise:

'37. Victims and potential victims of trafficking may qualify as refugees where it can be demonstrated that they fear being persecuted for reasons of their membership of a particular social group. In establishing this ground it is not necessary that the members of a particular group know each other or associate with each other as a group. It is, however, necessary that they either share a common characteristic other than their risk of being persecuted or are perceived as a group by society. The shared characteristic will often be one that is innate, unchangeable or otherwise fundamental to identity, conscience or the exercise of one's human rights. Persecutory action against a group may be relevant in heightening the visibility of the group without being its defining characteristic. As with the other Convention grounds, the size of the purported social group is not a relevant criterion in determining whether a social group exists within the meaning of Article 1A(2). While a claimant must still demonstrate a well-founded fear of being persecuted based on her or his membership of the particular social group, she or he need not demonstrate that all members of the group are at risk of persecution in order to establish the existence of the group.'

In 1999 in the landmark case of *Shah and Islam*[1] the House of Lords for the first time gave detained consideration to the particular social group definition in the Refugee Convention 1951 and approved the definition of a particular social group contained in *Re Acosta*[2] where it held that:

'Applying the doctrine of ejusdem generis, we interpret the phrase 'persecution on account of membership of a particular social group' to mean persecution that is directed toward an individual who is a member of a group of persons all of whom share a common, immutable characteristic. The shared characteristic might be an innate one such as sex, color [sic], or kinship ties, or in some circumstances it might be a shared past experience . . . The particular kind of group characteristic that will qualify under this construction remains to be determined on a case-by-case basis . . . '[3] [Emphasis underlined]

Three years later in 2002 the UNHCR's Particular Social Group Guidelines[4] were published. According to those Guidelines:

'[A] particular social group is a group of persons who share a common characteristic other than their risk of being persecuted, or who are perceived as a group by society. The characteristic will often be one which is innate, unchangeable, or which is otherwise fundamental to identity, conscience or the exercise of one's human rights' [Emphasis underlined]

The above UNHCR definition was considered in detail albeit *obiter* by the House of Lords in 2006 in the second particular social group case to require its detailed consideration: *K and Fornah v Secretary of State for the Home Department*[5]. Significance was given by their Lordships to whether the UNHCR definition above accorded with the EU Council Directive 2004/83/EC of 29 April 2004, effective as of 10 October 2006, and later transcribed into domestic law by the Refugee or Person in Need of International Protection (Qualification) Regulations 2006[6] and the UNHCR definition was approved by the majority of their Lordships[7].

There are some examples of particular social groups which have been recognised by the UK courts and tribunals and which may have a bearing on the protection claim by a victim of trafficking.

For example, where the victim is a woman and women have an inferior position in the home country she may be able to assert that she is at risk of future persecution as a woman in that country. In *K and Fornah*[8] Baroness Hale stated that:

'86 . . . the world has woken up to the fact that women as a sex may be persecuted in ways which are different from the ways in which men are persecuted and that they may be persecuted because of the inferior status accorded to their gender in their home society. States Parties, at least if they are also parties to the International Covenant on Civil and Political Rights and to the Convention on the Elimination of All Forms of Discrimination against Women are obliged to interpret and apply the Refugee Convention compatibly with the commitment to gender equality in these two instruments'.

Indeed, the UNHCR Trafficking Guidelines have recognised that various particular social groups might apply to asylum claims by victims of trafficking:

'38. Women are an example of a social subset of individuals who are defined by innate and immutable characteristics and are frequently treated differently to men. As such, they may constitute a particular social group. Factors which may distinguish women as targets for traffickers are generally connected to their vulnerability in certain social settings; therefore certain social subsets of women may also constitute particular social groups. Men or children or certain social subsets of these groups may also be considered as particular social groups. Examples of social subsets of women or children could, depending on the context, be single women, widows, divorced women, illiterate women, separated or unaccompanied children, orphans or street children. The fact of belonging to such a particular social group may be one of the factors contributing to an individual's fear of being subjected to persecution, for example, to sexual exploitation, as a result of being, or fearing being, trafficked.'

In the case of children, age has been held to be an immutable characteristic by the Asylum and Immigration Tribunal. In *LQ (Age: immutable characteristic) Afghanistan*[9], the Tribunal found that a child could be a member of a particular social group for the purposes of the Refugee Convention:

'6. We think that . . . age is immutable. It is changing all the time, but one cannot do anything to change one's own age at any particular time. At the date when the appellant's status has to be assessed he is a child and although, assuming he survives, he will in due course cease to be a child, he is immutably a child at the time of assessment.'

In the case of *SB (PSG-Protection Regulations – Art 6) Moldova CG*[10] the Asylum and Immigration Tribunal (AIT) accepted that 'former victims of trafficking' or 'former victims of trafficking for sexual exploitation' are capable of being members of a particular social group because of their shared common background or past experience of having been trafficked[11]. However the Tribunal went on to find that in order for 'former victims of trafficking' or 'former victims of trafficking for sexual exploitation' to be members of a particular social group, the group in question must also have a distinct identity in the society in question[12]. The Tribunal's finding that both a protected (ie immutable) characteristic and a social perception approach or characteristic (such as the group having a distinct identity in society) must be present for the PSG to exist, as opposed to either one being present, is highly controversial and is contrary to the House of Lords' approval in in *Shah and Islam* of the PSG definition in *re Acosta*, the UNHCR's 2002 definition of particular social group[13], the House of Lords approval of that definition in *K and Fornah* and their Lordship's reasoning in *Fornah*, albeit *obiter*, for approving that definition. Notwithstanding this controversy, the appellant in *SB* won her asylum appeal, which had been brought on a test case basis as being one with potentially wide significance to asylum claims by victims of trafficking in the UK, and in the process her case helped to develop trafficking law and policy in the UK[14].

Indeed the UNHCR Trafficking Guidelines 2006 had earlier recognised that former victims of trafficking can fall within membership of a particular social group: it is the past experience of having been trafficked which forms the innate characteristic shared between members of the group.

As the UNHCR Trafficking Guidelines advise:

'39. Former victims of trafficking may also be considered as constituting a social group based on the unchangeable, common and historic characteristic of having been trafficked. A society may also, depending on the context, view persons who have been trafficked as a cognizable group within that society. Particular social groups can nevertheless not be defined exclusively by the persecution that members of the group suffer or by a common fear of persecution. It should therefore be noted that it is the past trafficking experience that would constitute one of the elements defining the group in such cases, rather than the future persecution now feared in the form of ostracism, punishment, reprisals or re-trafficking. In such situations, the group would therefore not be defined solely by its fear of future persecution.'

[1] *Islam v Secretary of State for the Home Department (United Nations High Comr for Refugees Intervening)* [1999] 2 AC 629, [1999] 2 All ER 545, HL.
[2] (1985) 19i & N.211.
[3] (1985) 19i & N.211.
[4] UN High Commissioner for Refugees, Guidelines on International Protection No. 2: 'Membership of a Particular Social Group' Within the Context of Article 1A(2) of the 1951 Convention and/or its 1967 Protocol Relating to the Status of Refugees, 7 May 2002.
[5] [2006] UKHL 46, [2007] 1 AC 412, [2007] 1 All ER 671.
[6] SI 2006/2525.
[7] See *K and Fornah* per Bingham LJ at paras 15–16, Hale LJ at paras 99–103 and Browne LJ at para 118.
[8] [2006] UKHL 46, [2007] 1 AC 412, [2007] 1 All ER 671.
[9] [2008] UKAIT 00005.
[10] [2008] UKAIT 00002, at paras 53–56 and conclusions at 112.
[11] In so finding the Tribunal overturned para 95 of the reported case of *MP (Trafficking-sufficiency of protection) Romania* [2005] UKIAT 00086 *(SB(PSG-Protection Regulations – Art 6) Moldova CG* [2008] UKAIT 0002 at paras 61 and 112(c) – see also para 60, 15 and 16) and found that para 18 of *JO (internal relocation-no risk of re-trafficking) Nigeria* [2004] UKIAT 00251 was similarly wrongly reasoned.
[12] *SB(PSG-Protection Regulations – Art 6) Moldova CG* [2008] UKAIT 0002, at paras 56, 74 and conclusions at 112 for example.
[13] '[A] particular social group is a group of persons who share a common characteristic other than their risk of being persecuted, or who are perceived as a group by society'
[14] Although the *SB* Tribunal's findings on the either/or PSG definition aspect of the case were lengthy, as a matter of fact the Tribunal heard no oral legal argument in reaching its own conclusion that both the 'protected' (ie immutable) characteristic and the 'social' perception

characteristic had to be present: there was no dispute between both Counsel who were involved in the case as to the correctness of the UNHCR definition of PSG as approved by the House of Lords in *Fornah*. Consequently the appeal had proceeded on the agreed presumption between Counsel that the UNHCR definition as approved *obiter* in *Fornah* was correct. Hence there is no record in the AIT's *SB* determination of Treasury Counsel arguing that the *Fornah obiter* findings on the UNHCR definition were wrong: he did not argue this. When the Tribunal promulgated its determination some months later and allowed SB's asylum appeal, finding that both characteristics had to be, and were satisfied on the basis that former victims of trafficking have an innate shared historical characteristic of having been trafficked, and that former victims of trafficking in Moldova have a distict identity in society in Moldova, the Appellant did not appeal that decision since the Tribunal had found a Convention reason applied, had allowed her appeal and had accepted she was a refugee. The principal finding by the AIT, namely that 'former victims of trafficking' are capable of forming a particular social group was very important as not only did this overturn bad law (see footnote 11 above) but it was a finding that itself would later inspire a change in Home Office policy: before *SB* every claim for refugee protection by a victim of trafficking in the UK was routinely rejected by the SSHD on the basis that AIT precedents had established that no Refugee Convention reason applied to their case. After the *SB* determination this type of blanket refusal could no longer apply.

(viii)   *Internal relocation*

14.17 Even where it is the case that a victim of trafficking would be at risk in the home area of his or her country of origin and he or she would not be provided with sufficient protection by the authorities in that area, it may be asserted that they could live safely in another part of that country.

Paragraph 339O of the Immigration Rules states that:

'(i)   The Secretary of State will not make:
   (a)   a grant of asylum if in part of the country of origin a person would not have a well founded fear of being persecuted, and the person can reasonably be expected to stay in that part of the country".
(ii)   In examining whether a part of the country or origin or country of return meets to the requirements in (i) the Secretary of State, when making his decision on whether to grant asylum . . . .., will have regard to the general circumstances prevailing in that part of the country and to the personal circumstances of the person'

Therefore it will be necessary for any victim to demonstrate that the proposed area of relocation will not be safe or that it would be unreasonable to expect him or her to live there. This may necessitate the obtaining of up to date and detailed information about conditions in other parts of their countries of origin and the safety of any proposed route to such a part of the country.

The law on this form of 'internal relocation' was confirmed by the House of Lords in *AH (Sudan) v Secretary of State for the Home Department*[1]. At paragraph 5 of his judgment in *AH (Sudan)* Lord Bingham of Cornhill recalled that he had found in *Januzi v Secretary of State for the Home Department*[2] that:

'The decision-maker, taking account of all relevant circumstances pertaining to the claimant and his country of origin, must decide whether it is reasonable to expect the claimant to relocate or whether it would be unduly harsh to expect him to do so.'

Lord Bingham then continued at paragraph 5 by stating that:

'It is, or should be, evident that the enquiry must be directed to the situation of the particular applicant, whose age, gender, experience, health, skills and family ties may all be very relevant. There is no warrant for excluding, or giving priority to, consideration of the applicant's way of life in the place of persecution. There is no warrant for excluding, or giving priority to, consideration of conditions generally prevailing in the home country. I do not underestimate the difficulty of making such decisions in some cases. But the difficulty lies in applying the test, not in expressing it. The humanitarian object of the Refugee Convention is to secure a reasonable measure of protection for those with a well-founded fear of persecution in their home country or some part of it . . . '

Particular considerations are likely to arise when considering removing a woman who is the victim of trafficking to her country of origin. For example when assessing whether the findings of fact reached by the House of Lords in *AH (Sudan)* applied to the case of the vulnerable female appellant in *AA (Uganda) v Secretary of State for the Home Department*[3] the Court of Appeal in *AA* recalled that the factual case in *AH (Sudan)* was 'significantly different' to that of *AA*, not least because the slum and general conditions in Kampala considered by the House in *AH(Sudan)* affected 'everyone' returning there, whereas the specific characteristics of *AA* herself were very different as, in Kampala, she was:

' . . . faced not merely with poverty and lack of any sort of accommodation, but with being driven into prostitution'.[4]

In the view of Buxton LJ in *AA (Uganda)*, reaching his conclusion on whether it would be unduly harsh to return young women to Kampala generally:

'17 . . . Even if that is the likely fate of many of her fellow countrywomen, I cannot think that either the AIT or the House of Lords that decided AH (Sudan) would have felt able to regard enforced prostitution as coming within the category of normal country conditions that the refugee must be expected to put up with. Quite simply, there must be some conditions in the place of relocation that are unacceptable to the extent that it would be unduly harsh to return the applicant to them even if the conditions are widespread in the place of relocation.
18. This was a case that called for an enquiry as to whether the conditions in Kampala fell into that category . . . In this case, and relying only on the evidence that was before the AIT, I would hold for the reasons already indicated that it would be unduly harsh to return AA to Kampala'.

The Court of Appeal in *AA* had also considered whether relocation would be rendered unduly harsh 'on the particular facts' of AA's case. In this regard the court recalled that AA had no formal qualifications and that she was traumatised and suffering from anxiety and depression. The evidence before the Court established that not just qualifications but connections were required to obtain any sort of formal employment in Kampala and the Court found the AIT had given no weight to such evidence[5]. These types of considerations might also be very relevant to trafficking-based asylum cases.

[1]   [2007] UKHL 49, [2008] 1 AC 678, [2008] 4 All ER 190.
[2]   [2006] UKHL 5, [2006] 2 AC 426, [2006] 3 All ER 305.
[3]   [2008] EWCA Civ 579.
[4]   [2008] EWCA Civ 579 at para 17.
[5]   [2008] EWCA Civ 579 at para 24'. Practitioners reading this chapter should note that the subsequent AIT decision in *FB (Lone women, PSG, internal relocation, AA (Uganda) considered) Sierra Leone* [2008] UKAIT 00090 (27 November 2008), by which the Tribunal sought to restrict the scope of the Court of Appeal's findings in *AA* was appealed by *FB* to the Court of Appeal. The Court of Appeal granted her permission to appeal and the SSHD

conceded the case by granting her asylum in the UK. The AIT decision in *FB* is therefore unsafe and it ought not to be followed by decision makers.

ARTICLE 3 AND 4 ECHR

14.18 Where a victim of trafficking is not a refugee they may be entitled to Humanitarian Protection if there are substantial grounds for believing they will face a risk of 'serious harm' under Immigration Rules, paragraph 339C or to human rights protection if there is a 'real risk' their removal would engage a breach of the ECHR. Articles 3 and 4 impose an absolute prohibition on Member States, such as the United Kingdom, from imposing any treatment which would breach these Articles or failing to act to protect an individual from such treatment, which would include the risk of reprisals or re-trafficking by a trafficker or the risk of serious harm, including forced labour or other forms of exploitation, from others. Returning a former victim of trafficking to his or her country of origin where there was a serious risk that the receiving State would breach or would permit a breach to occur would therefore engage the United Kingdom's obligations under Articles 3 and 4 ECHR.

The text of Article 3 states that 'no one shall be subjected to torture or to inhuman or degrading treatment or punishment'. In order to rely on the protection of Article 3 a victim of trafficking would have to show that they were was a serious risk that they would suffer treatment, which could be said to fall within Article 3. The European Court of Human Rights has repeatedly held, following its judgment in *Ireland v UK*[1], that the benchmark for the necessary minimum level of severity required to prove torture or inhuman and degrading treatment is relative, and depends on factors including the duration of the treatment, its physical or mental effects, and the age, sex, vulnerability and state of health of the victim[2].

Therefore in trafficking cases it will usually be necessary for submissions to be made that the victim's personal situation brings his or her anticipated suffering above the Article 3 threshold and this may be achieved by providing objective and/or expert evidence to show that it is likely he or she will face such treatment if removed from the United Kingdom.

If the decision maker, court or tribunal decides that it would be a breach of Article 3 to remove a victim of trafficking from the United Kingdom, he or she is likely to be granted by the SSHD Humanitarian Protection for five years (under Immigration Rule 339C) or three years Discretionary Leave on medical grounds and in the latter case they will be able to apply for further such leave in the future if their removal would still give rise to a breach of Article 3.

In the context of protection claims by victims of trafficking the European Court of Human Rights (ECtHR) has found that Article 4 ECHR prohibits human trafficking, forced and compulsory labour, servitude, slavery and slavery-like practices. In *Rantsev v Cyprus and Russia (Application No 25965/04)*[3], judgment of 7 January 2010, the ECtHR held:

'281. The Court considers that trafficking in human beings, by its very nature and aim of exploitation, is based on the exercise of powers attaching to the right of ownership. It treats human beings as commodities to be bought and sold and put to forced labour, often for little or no payment, usually in the sex industry but also elsewhere . . . . It implies close surveillance of the activities of victims, whose movements are often circumscribed . . . . It involves the use of violence and threats against victims, who live and work under poor conditions. It is described by Interights and in the explanatory report accompanying the Anti-Trafficking Convention as the modern form of the old worldwide slave trade . . . '

And further:

'282 . . . There can be no doubt that trafficking threatens the human dignity and fundamental freedoms of its victims and cannot be considered compatible with a democratic society and the values expounded in the Convention'.

In finding that a State's positive obligations to protect arise under Article 4 ECHR the Court held:

'286. As with Articles 2 and 3 of the Convention, Article 4 may, in certain circumstances, require a State to take operational measures to protect victims, or potential victims, of trafficking . . . In order for a positive obligation to take operational measures to arise in the circumstances of a particular case, it must be demonstrated that the State authorities were aware, or ought to have been aware, of circumstances giving rise to a credible suspicion that an identified individual had been, or was at real and immediate risk of being, trafficked or exploited within the meaning of Article 3(a) of the Palermo Protocol and Article 4(a) of the Anti-Trafficking Convention. In the case of an answer in the affirmative, there will be a violation of Article 4 of the Convention where the authorities fail to take appropriate measures within the scope of their powers to remove the individual from that situation or risk.'

It follows that where there is an identifiable risk of a victim of trafficking being re-trafficked on return to their country of origin or indeed a risk of being exposed to any of the prohibited conditions identified by the ECtHR at para 281 above the individual ought to be entitled to succeed to the grant of Humanitarian Protection on the basis of Article 3 ECHR, taken together with Article 4 ECHR.

[1]   (1980) 2 EHRR 25.
[2]   In cases where the victim of trafficking is suffering from severe mental health illness as a result of the trafficking-based exploitation or harm that he or she has received and where expert medical evidence establishes that returning the individual to their home country raises a real risk of suicide (whether the individual's fear of return is objectively based or not), practitioners are referred to the highly significant Court of Appeal judgment in *Y (Sri Lanka) v Secretary of State for the Home Department* [2009] EWCA Civ 362, (2009) Times, 5 May for an explanation and understanding of the legal and evidential requirements that such an Article 3 ECHR medical claim will engage.
[3]   (2010) 28 BHRC 313, [2010] ECHR 25965/04, ECtHR.. See also **CHAPTER 14** on the return-related rights that arise under Article 16(2) of the Trafficking Convention.

CONCLUDING REMARKS

14.19 The above is but an analysis, in some places detailed in other places less so, of the protection and residence rights that might be available to victims of trafficking in the UK. This chapter is not at all intended to be an exhaustive guide on the application of such law, policy and practice in the UK but instead is a starting point to highlight issues for consideration and discussions which may hopefully enable practitioners and all others who are interested in these matters to work towards assisting victims of trafficking receive equal and fair treatment and protection in the UK.

Part V

PERSPECTIVES ON THE RIGHT
TO COMPENSATION BY VICTIMS

Contents

15

THE RIGHT TO COMPENSATION FOR TRAFFICKED PERSONS: AN OVERVIEW

Klara Skrivankova

'Compensation is an important mechanism to restore the dignity of a person and to bring the access to justice.'
Ms Gulnara Shaninian, UN Special Rapporteur on Contemporary Forms of Slavery[1]

[1] In a film by the German institute for Human Rights, November 2010. http://www.institut-fu er-menschenrechte.de/, accessed 17 April 2011.

EFFECTIVE REMEDIES IN ADDRESSING TRAFFICKING IN HUMAN BEINGS

15.1 The focus of this chapter is on compensation for trafficked persons. Rather than analysing the routes for claiming compensation that are available within the legal framework in the UK and the technicalities of putting forward a claim for damages (which are dealt with in other chapters of this book), this chapter addresses the principal importance of compensation as an effective remedy and its significance for combating trafficking in human beings.

Within the international human rights legal framework, the right to an effective remedy has been well established. Under international human rights standards, a person whose rights have been violated is entitled to obtain an effective remedy, which includes reparation, as a consequence of such violations. Full and effective reparation for those who have suffered violations may take a variety of forms, including: restitution, including rehabilitation; compensation; satisfaction and guarantees of non-repetition[1].

Trafficking in human beings is recognised not just as a serious crime committed against a person, but more importantly as a gross violation of fundamental rights. The right of trafficked persons to compensation and consequently the obligations of the UK are established by international legislation[2] against trafficking and more recently European[3] legislation against human trafficking. In the context of the interpretation of EU law, human trafficking is also explicitly prohibited under Article 5(3) of the Charter of Fundamental Rights of the European Union.

Consequently, every trafficked person possesses the right to an effective remedy – regardless as to whether they have been identified or formally recognised as such[4]. With regards to compensation (as one of the forms of effective remedies), this is often understood as being derived from the fact that a trafficked person had been subjected to the crime of trafficking[5] and hence is entitled to compensatory measures as a victim of crime. Albeit, it is important to point out that effective remedies extend well beyond compensation.

In each and every case of trafficking the individual's personal circumstances should be considered (such as whether the trafficked person is fit enough or wishes to pursue a claim for compensation), as well as the needs of the victim in determining what form of remedy is the most appropriate for that trafficked person, considering both the likelihood and impact of a positive outcome and how difficult it will be for the person to go through the claim process.

Upholding the right to an effective remedy for those who have suffered violations is an obligation carried by States, not only in terms of ensuring that there is effective and equal access to justice which should enable adequate reparation of the suffered harm, but also with regard to introducing and implementing measures that are required to guarantee access to an effective remedy[6].

It is those measures which have often been found lacking or inadequate in States, resulting in a failure to deliver equal opportunities for accessing remedies to trafficked persons. For example, for victims who originate from outside the European Union, being formally granted leave to enter or remain in this country to seek compensation for the trafficking and exploitation they have suffered here ought to be a pre-requisite to enable them to access remedies in the first place. Without the ability to remain lawfully in the UK to seek compensation, many trafficked persons would be wholly deprived of their right to an effective remedy in the form of financial reparation.

It is also notable that in some cases, the provision of safe and durable, as distinct to temporary, residence status will be appropriate and may constitute a full and effective remedy in itself. For very vulnerable trafficked persons, such as those who are at a high risk of re-trafficking, in danger of their lives or who have suffered significant injuries[7] whilst being trafficked or exploited for which they may be receiving specialist treatment, remedy in the form of permanent right to reside in the UK might be the only viable option for restoring their human rights, abating their fears and ensuring the non-repetition of the violations[8].

As stated above, there must be various forms of effective remedies available. Other chapters will deal with remedies such as the prosecution and punishment of traffickers or assistance and services for trafficked persons. This chapter will focus on a particular remedy, that of compensation.

Contextually, the concept of compensation seems to be rather well understood and unlike other areas of the anti-trafficking discourse, it is quite non-controversial. In the experience of the COMP.ACT coalition, general agreement seems to have been reached by various actors involved in combating trafficking that ensuring compensation for trafficked persons is a 'good thing'[9].

Compensation for those trafficked can be sought for both general damages and special damages that are suffered by victims of crime. General damages compensate the trafficked person for non-material aspects of the harm suffered, including physical or emotional pain and suffering. Special damages compensate for the material, quantifiable monetary loses, including medical expenses, repair or replacement of damaged property, lost earnings and unpaid wages[10].

Whilst in cases of trafficking for sexual exploitation, the examples of losses and injuries suffered by the victims are quite clear and widely understood, in cases of trafficking for forced labour (in all its forms) it may be much more difficult however to agree on what was the actual harm done and how to quantify it (for the purposes of compensation), other than as an assessment related to the non-payment of wages.

It is well known amongst anti-trafficking specialists that traffickers are resorting more and more to subtler forms of coercion, using sophisticated methods of psychological violence, pressure, control and implicit, rather than explicit threats.

Examples of the more subtle psychological consequences of the abuses suffered by victims of trafficking for forced labour include: loss of dignity following treatment as a worthless slave; mental health illness as a result of psychological pressure and fear; loss of confidence and the ability to act autonomously as a consequence of constant control; continuing fear that was instilled through the trafficker's use of voodoo and juju practices.

The loss of honour and position in one's community/society is also very important, particularly in cases of trafficked men who, on account of having been exploited for their forced labour, will not have been able to provide income to their families in their role as the bread-winner: this labels them as being unable men or as 'losers' within their whole society and the psychological consequences of this shame must not be underestimated.

However, the fact that often no physical violence is suffered in cases of forced labour, where traffickers have resorted to more sophisticated methods of coercion and deceit (a pertinent example being the implicit threats by traffickers – having weapons on display, fight dogs present at sites or planting stories of workers being beaten up for complaints), means that in practice many victims trafficked for forced labour will be excluded from obtaining compensation through the UK's well established fund for victims of crime, namely the Criminal Injuries Compensation Scheme (CICS). As explained in the chapter by Hogan Lovells in this book, under the CICS the injury must be a 'criminal injury' as defined in paragraphs 8 and 9 of the Scheme, meaning that the injury must be caused by a 'crime of violence'.

Notwithstanding this however, if one takes a broad formal view, the UK could be regarded as meeting its obligation to provide access to compensation via the existence of legal avenues which enable trafficked persons to seek compensation. Hence, in theory, trafficked persons in the UK have several options of seeking compensation within the courts or by alternative means, namely:

- The law allows for a compensation order to be made as a part of the criminal proceedings against traffickers;
- Victims of crimes (including trafficked persons) can submit an applications to the Criminal Injuries Compensation Authority (CICA);
- Trafficked persons can take a civil claim for damages against the traffickers;

- Those trafficked for domestic servitude may be able to bring their cases before an Employment Tribunal[11].

However, as the relevant chapters on each of these systems demonstrate, each of these four avenues of legal redress suffer from significant protection gaps through which a majority of compensation claims will, often fatally, fall.

Hence, there is still a long way to go in this country from the position of recognising in theory that compensation for trafficked victims is legally and morally important to actually seeing it being awarded and received by trafficked persons: in practical terms the actual award and receipt of a compensation payment by a trafficked person is extremely rare in the UK and the right to compensation remains one of the weakest protected rights of trafficked persons when it comes to accessibility[12].

It is therefore still critical to enable the effective operation of existing, or new, systems by which trafficked persons can effectively exercise their rights to claim compensation.

To realise this right fully, certain prerequisites need to be in place that facilitate access to justice and remedies.

[1] See, for example, Basic Principles and Guidelines on the Right to a Remedy and Reparation for Victims of Gross Violations of International Human Rights Law and Serious Violations of International Humanitarian Law, adopted and proclaimed by General Assembly resolution 60/147 of 16 December 2005.

[2] The Protocol to Prevent, Suppress and Punish Trafficking in Persons, especially Women and Children, supplementing the UN Convention on Transnational Organised Crime (2000).

[3] The Council of Europe Convention on Action against Trafficking in Human Beings 2005, ratified by the UK in December 2008 and brought into force on 1st April 2009; Directive 2011/36/EU of the European Parliament and of the Council of 5 April 2011 on preventing and combating trafficking in human beings and protecting its victims, and replacing Council Framework Decision 2002/629/JHA.

[4] Conclusions of the Expert Consultation on 'The Right to an Effective Remedy for Trafficked Persons', convened by the UN Special Rapporteur on trafficking in persons, especially women and children, Ms. Joy Ngozi Ezeilo, November 2010.

[5] With particular reference to laws in England, Wales, Scotland and Northern Ireland: See CHAPTER 19 on Trafficking-related Criminal Legislation.

[6] Background Paper on State Practices, Concrete Strategies and Implementation of the Right to an Effective Remedy for Trafficked Persons, Consultation of the Special Rapporteur on Trafficking in Persons, Especially Women and Children, Joy Ngozi Ezeilo (November 2010).

[7] Psychiatric or physical harm.

[8] This ought not to be as controversial as it first might sound. See further: OSCE report 'Analysing the business model of trafficking in human beings to better prevent the crime', May 2010, at page 80. See too 'Report of the Special Rapporteur on trafficking in persons, especially women and children, Joy Ngozi Ezeilo', to the Human Rights Council of the UN General Assembly, 13 April 2011, at paras 51 and 52.

[9] Country initiative lead by Anti-Slavery International and La Strada International, http://www w.compactproject.org.

[10] See COMP.ACT, http://www.compactproject.org.

[11] The author is unaware of any examples of successful ET claims that have been brought by victims of forced labour, as distinct to cases concerning domestic servitude.

[12] See further: 'Compensation for Trafficked and Exploited Persons in the OSCE Region', OSCE/ODIHR, Warsaw 2008, pp 126–128.

ACCESS TO JUSTICE

15.2 Access to justice is a process whereby an individual receives judicial protection of their rights by exercising their right to seek a remedy before a court of law or a tribunal for the wrongdoing they have suffered. Access to justice can be seen as the operational process of the attainment of remedies[1] – without which effective remedies cannot be spoken of.

In relation to trafficking, access to justice means enabling a trafficked person to overcome the harmful trafficking experience by seeking remedies through the justice system for grievances according to basic human rights principles and standards[2]. In many trafficking cases the direct link between an award of compensation and the trafficked person's ability to prevent its recurrence must be appreciated, particularly if poverty was a key cause of their vulnerability to trafficking. However, in order for a trafficked person to obtain justice in the form of a concrete remedy, certain prerequisites need to be in place.

The first and perhaps the most important one is the existence of a legal framework. While there is no specific UK domestic legislation on compensation to trafficked persons, the four possibilities within the law described above can be used by trafficked persons to seek compensation. However, as briefly noted above and later below, those four systems each contain major flaws in terms of the protection of the right to compensation which will leave a very high percentage of trafficked persons without any compensatory redress in the UK.

Legal provisions allowing for compensation are the fundamental element of effective remedies. Nevertheless, the existence of a law itself does not mean that access to those remedies exists in practice. Exercising the right of trafficked persons to compensation and their actual access to the remedy requires further facilitating measures.

Research by Anti-Slavery International[3] and by the OSCE/ODIHR[4] in 2008 showed that the receipt of compensation by trafficked persons in the UK is unlikely, despite the existence of laws, and this is due to procedural and systematic obstacles preventing effective access to those remedies. Even the introduction of a Government system of victim assistance (the National Referral Mechanism) in 2009 did not seem to have improved the situation according to the Anti-Trafficking Monitoring Group[5].

Furthermore, experiences from practice and examples collected in this book show that for some victims, namely adult women trafficked for sexual exploitation or adults trafficked for domestic servitude, access to justice, and compensation in particular, might be more attainable than for other victims (notwithstanding the existing obstacles).

The fact that trafficking is not included in the tariffs of the Criminal Injuries Compensation Scheme effectively precludes nearly half of people trafficked in the UK (ie those trafficked for forced labour[6]) from accessing remedies through this scheme, because the majority of victims of labour trafficking will not have been exposed to direct physical violence (as described above). Hence, despite trafficking being repeatedly being described and accepted by the Government and in international for a as a serious crime, a violation of human rights and an offence to human dignity, it is not presently considered by the UK as being serious enough to allow all those who have been trafficked to claim compensation for being victims of the crime of trafficking.

Those trafficked for forced labour can further be precluded from bringing their claims to the Employment Tribunals. While for certain categories of victim the issues of irregular immigration status and illegality of contract have been successfully resolved (see **CHAPTER 17** on taking domestic servitude cases to the Employment Tribunal), many victims of forced labour in non-domestic servitude situations will be unable to access this route either on the grounds of their irregular status (for example in cases of people smuggled into the UK who were subsequently trafficked within the UK, ie internally, for forced labour), or because they do not fall into the category of an employee or worker (such as those on a visitor visa or the self-employed).

Additionally, those trafficked into forced labour outside of regular industries (victims trafficked for forced begging, forced criminal activities, benefit fraud etc) would not be able to access either the Employment Tribunal or the CICA scheme (unless they were subject to physical violence and sustained injury as a result and in the case of the CICA scheme were additionally prepared to make a formal report against their trafficker/exploiter to the police)[7].

In cases of child trafficking the lack of clarity over who (ie which authority) should be the legal guardian (in the absence of a parent) to initiate a compensation claim on behalf of the child effectively negates the trafficked child's right to access compensation. When a child victim of trafficking is identified, he/she is commonly placed in the care of the local authority. If a child victim was to seek compensation for example from the Criminal Injuries Compensation Scheme, the child's legal representatives would have to be instructed by that local authority. However, establishing the appropriate individual within any local authority to give the instructions to a lawyer has proven extremely difficult in practice and this one of the key obstacles which prevents access to justice for child victims, as has been identified by legal representatives[8].

In addition, other pre-requisites will need to be established in order to bring about the actual implementation of the right to access justice and compensation. The next section will explore some of them.

[1]   Fancioni, F., *Access to Justice as a Human Right* (2007), Oxford University Press, p 3.
[2]   Lam, J., Skrivankova, K., *Opportunities and Obstacles: Ensuring access to compensation for trafficked persons in the UK* (2009) Anti-Slavery International.
[3]   Lam, J., Skrivankova, K., *Opportunities and Obstacles: Ensuring access to compensation for trafficked persons in the UK* (2009) Anti-Slavery International.
[4]   OSCE/ODIHR, 'Compensation for Trafficked and Exploited Persons in the OSCE Region', (Warsaw 2008).
[5]   Anti-Trafficking Monitoring Group, London 'Wrong kind of victim? One year on . . . an analysis of UK measures to protect trafficked persons' (2010).
[6]   According to the data of the National Referral Mechanism nearly half of those referred were presumed victims of labour trafficking: http://www.soca.gov.uk/about-soca/about-the-uhtc.
[7]   In order to obtain a crime reference number, which is a prerequisite for a claim to be accepted under the CICA Scheme.
[8]   Further information and details about how to claim compensation on behalf of child victims can be found in **CHAPTER 18** on the Criminal Injuries Compensation Scheme.

(1) A victims' rights culture

15.3 The existence and promotion of a victims' rights culture is an essential prerequisite, not solely in terms of the recognition of the right to compensation but also as regards victims' rights to have their full complement of entitlements under the Trafficking Convention respected, including the right to be identified, to safe and appropriate accommodation, to necessary medical treatment, to protection against re-trafficking in this country and abroad, to non-punishment for crimes committed whilst trafficked, to protection when acting as a witness in criminal proceedings and to non-refoulement.

The stronger the victims' rights culture[1] in a country, the better the chance that these rights will be formalised and incorporated into the existing victim assistance programmes, such as the UK's National Referral Mechanism and the criminal justice system.

Like many other European countries, in the UK there is currently no victims' rights culture to speak of. A particular indicator of this is the limited use and success of compensation orders being granted by criminal courts (in all cases of violent crimes, not just in cases of trafficking) as found in research by Anti-Slavery International[2]. It appears that any consideration of victims' rights in terms of their right to compensation for harm done has not yet entered into the psyche of the prosecutors of traffickers in such cases, whose duty it is to recommend to a judge that a compensation order be made, nor indeed the judges themselves, who having often heard the victim's horrific testimony, pass down sentences on traffickers convicted in their criminal courts without considering any further the interests of the victim. The high incidence rate of confiscation orders[3] being ordered as part of criminal sentencing, whereby the trafficker's money is confiscated and placed in the hands of the State, may be said to illustrate that the primary concern of the Crown is not, upon convicting a wealthy trafficker, to compensate the victim. When victims' interests and rights remain under-represented, either in criminal proceedings or in other areas of access to justice, the chances of trafficked persons being able to obtain a financial compensatory remedy are minimal. The fact that victims of crime do not have a standing as a *damaged party*[4] in criminal proceedings in the UK and also that their right to an effective remedy does not form a statutory obligation which is assigned to a concrete body can be considered as representing other contributory factors.

Furthermore, there are no specific provisions which entitle trafficked persons in the UK to obtain any special measures in relation to compensation other than those which apply generally to victims of crime. This becomes relevant when it is recalled that, as already explained, the rate of compensation awards that are granted to victims of crime in the UK by criminal courts is nil.

In contrast to this, in the USA a so-called 'restitution order' (similar to the compensation order in the criminal courts in the UK) is issued mandatorily for victims of all trafficking offences and all crimes of violence[5]. Aside from the actual monetary value of such restitution, there is a significant restorative value for the victims in the US system whereby an acknowledgement of the wrongdoing and suffering is embodied in the obligation of the court to issue a compensation order in every trafficking case.

279

For those representing trafficked persons in the UK, either as service providers or as legal representatives, the promotion of the right of each trafficked person to be recognised as being a victim of crime is vital to ensuring their access to compensation. A useful background for this is provided by the 1985 UN Declaration by which the international community agreed Basic Principles of Justice for Victims of Crime and Abuse of Power according to which victims should:

- be treated with respect and recognition;
- to be referred to adequate support services;
- receive information about the progress of the case;
- to be present and give input to the decision-making;
- have a right to counsel;
- have a right to protection of physical safety and privacy;
- have a right of compensation, from both the offender and the State[6].

[1] A victims' rights culture for these purposes can be described as being the awareness in society of the right of those trafficked to be recognised as being victims of serious human rights abuses, for which they should, like another victim of serious crime, receive compensation as a recognition of their suffering.

[2] Lam, J., Skrivankova, K., *Opportunities and Obstacles: Ensuring access to compensation for trafficked persons in the UK* (2009) Anti-Slavery International.

[3] As opposed to the very low incidence rate of compensation orders.

[4] See the system in the USA which is described further below.

[5] OSCE/ODIHR, '*Compensation for Trafficked and Exploited Persons in the OSCE Region*', (Warsaw 2008), p114.

[6] http://www.un.org/documents/ga/res/40/a40r034.htm, accessed on 17 April 2011.

(2) The role of compensation in combating trafficking

15.4 Secondly, compensation needs to be considered as an important means of combating trafficking. It is indeed a significant instrument of anti-trafficking law and policy which serves multiple purposes: restorative, punitive and preventative.

For victims, the restorative justice function of compensation is important for the process of recovery – this will be further discussed below. Enabling, and more importantly facilitating, access to compensation is the recognition of the right of trafficked persons to a remedy for the violations of their human rights, as required by international human rights standards. Victims who achieve financial autonomy through compensation are more empowered and in a stronger position to support themselves and their families – a factor that has been well documented to significantly reduce the risk of re-trafficking.

In particular, compensation that is paid by the trafficker to their victim, such as from his/her confiscated assets, carries more than just the face value of punishment and has ramifications over and above the single act of taking away money from the criminals and giving it to their victims. Instead, if the trafficker is deprived of their money as a direct consequence of his/her criminal actions, namely to traffick and exploit, this constitutes a strong deterrent mechanism which can impact on and contribute to the prevention of trafficking-related crime. Trafficking is a crime committed for the benefit of traffickers and it generates huge sums in profit every year. Unfortunately trafficking still remains a low-risk, high-profit crime. To reverse this equation we would need to see more focus on the confiscation of the trafficker's criminal assets and, as a direct corollary to this, the award of compensation for victims.

Importantly, in the past five years, the importance of compensation for trafficked persons has gained momentum. To pinpoint the significance of compensation in combating trafficking, compensation was explicitly included as an express right for trafficked persons in the Council of Europe Convention on Action against Trafficking in Human Beings (Article 15), in force in the UK since 1 April 2009, and in the new EU Directive 2011/36/EU (Article 17) which has yet to take force in the EU and the UK. Still, the number of victims compensated remains negligible and the significance given to compensation in the international framework needs to be translated into practice in the UK and embedded into anti-trafficking policy and assistance programmes.

(3) The need for practical and special measures to ensure access to compensation

15.5 Practical measures facilitating and translating the right to compensation into practice and acknowledging its importance forms the third pre-requisite to access to justice. The obligation to put in place some special measures to facilitate access to compensation for trafficked persons is anchored in the Council of Europe Convention on Action against Trafficking in Human Beings:

> 'Article 15 (1): Each Party shall ensure that victims have access, as from their first contact with the competent authorities, to information on relevant judicial and administrative proceedings in a language which they can understand.
> (2) Each Party shall provide, in its internal law, for the right to legal assistance and to free legal aid under the conditions provided by its internal law.'

Some of these provisions have yet to be complied with, in particular the UK's duty, via its Competent Authorities, to provide information to a victim of trafficking about the right to compensation in a timely and appropriate manner.

It is unlikely that victims will be aware of their rights to compensation and the specific measures the UK is obliged to take to ensure their access to this right. People cannot claim their rights if they are unaware of them. Currently, the correspondence received by trafficked persons from the Competent Authorities within the UK's National Referral Mechanism does not contain any mention of the right to compensation or how such compensation may be sought. It is known that the police have, in some cases, been able to raise the issue of compensation with trafficked victims whose evidence has led to the conviction of their trafficker however the right to compensation is far broader than this and even in cases where the police have assisted by explaining compensation-related information to victims this role ought to involve a public authority other than the police as there is a danger of the defence of inducement being used by the traffickers' defence lawyers at trial.

In the absence of a statutory mechanism informing trafficked persons about their rights to compensation, it falls upon those who provide the assistance to the trafficked persons – either the service providers or the legal representatives – to ensure that victims are provided with information on their right to compensation, that the processes for seeking it are carefully explained and that the victims are supported in lodging their claims.

In addition to the provision of information regarding the right to seek compensation trafficked persons need to be able to firstly remain in the UK for a sufficient period of time to consider, lodge and pursue a claim. The inability to remain in the country in order to pursue compensation was identified as one of the key obstacle in accessing justice by both Anti-Slavery International[1] and OSCE/ODIHR[2] and has been raised by the UN Special Rapporteur on trafficking in persons, especially women and children, Ms Joy Ngozi Ezeilo in her thematic report on effective remedies, presented to the UN Human Rights Council in April 2011[3]. In relation to this issue the Special Rapporteur has made the following findings and recommendations:

'49. The ability of trafficked persons to claim remedies hinges upon possibilities to remain in countries where remedies are sought, as it would be difficult for them to obtain remedies if they were at risk of expulsion or had already been expelled from the countries. In many instances, however, trafficked persons are misidentified as irregular migrants and detained in immigration detention centres, or immediately deported without being given any opportunities to seek compensation . . .

51. Following a reflection and recovery period, trafficked persons should be provided with temporary or permanent residence status on certain grounds . . . .trafficked persons should be entitled to remain in the country where remedies are being sought for the duration of any criminal, civil or administrative proceedings. In this regard, article 7 of the Palermo Protocol should be read in conjunction with the mandatory requirements under article 6, paragraphs 2(b) and 6. As it would be almost impossible for trafficked persons to seek compensation through legal proceedings if they are unable to lawfully remain in the country, article 7 should be interpreted to encourage States to provide trafficked persons with temporary residence status for the purpose of seeking remedies.'[4]

The importance of allowing trafficked persons to stay in a country in order to pursue compensation is further stressed in paragraph 192 of the Explanatory Report to the Council of Europe Trafficking Convention, whose Article 14 provides for such residence permit possibility.

In the UK, the National Referral Mechanism put in place in April 2009 does not contain any significant aspects which facilitate access to compensation. Neither does the policy that governs the issuing of residence permits for identified trafficked persons foresee granting those specifically to allow trafficked persons to seek compensation[5].

Several trafficked persons have been able to obtain temporary permission to stay in the UK in order to seek compensation though the Employment Tribunal. Albeit they were only able to do so thanks to the strong support and advice mechanisms available to them from service providers and lawyers.

It seems obvious that the UK's residence permit policy under the NRM should be amended to allow for the possibility of a trafficked person to remain in the country to pursue a claim for compensation and to ensure that their right to an effective remedy is upheld.

---

[1] Lam, J., Skrivankova, K., *Opportunities and Obstacles: Ensuring access to compensation for trafficked persons in the UK* (2009) Anti-Slavery International.

2 OSCE/ODIHR, '*Compensation for Trafficked and Exploited Persons in the OSCE Region*' (Warsaw 2008).

3 Joy Ngozi Ezeilo, '*Report of the Special Rapporteur on trafficking in persons, especially women and children*' (13 April 2011), A/HRC/17/35.

4 Joy Ngozi Ezeilo, '*Report of the Special Rapporteur on trafficking in persons, especially women and children*' (13 April 2011), A/HRC/17/35.

5 *Briefing: Compensation for trafficked persons*, Anti-Trafficking Monitoring Group, January 2011.

COMPENSATON AS A FORM OF RESTORATIVE JUSTICE

15.6 To experience justice and be given the sense of acknowledgement of the wrongdoing is very important to the recovery process of victims of trafficking. The restorative function of justice is to assist victims to overcome what they have been through and to focus on their needs. It is a process whereby a victim becomes the subject of justice rather than an object of it – he or she is not just a passive actor in a process of bringing perpetrators to justice.

Many trafficked persons have expressed frustration with the process of criminal proceedings and have said that they felt used by the criminal justice system only to testify against the traffickers. Once their role as witnesses ended and they were no longer useful for the prosecution they were simply sent home as their residence permit was issued only for the duration of the criminal proceedings. Some of them expressed that this felt like being punished, rather than their suffering being acknowledged[1].

Residence permit and adequate assistance are prerequisites to seeking compensation and fall right inside the principle of restorative justice. The provision of Article 11 of the EU Directive 2011/36/EU will be important in asserting access to justice in the course of criminal proceedings. The Article states that assistance and support should be provided 'to victims before, during and for an appropriate period of time after the conclusion of criminal proceedings in order to enable them to exercise the rights set out . . . in this Directive' [which includes the right to seek compensation].

Every trafficked person has the right to compensation and should be informed about it and assisted in exercising this right. However, it should be pointed out that not every trafficked person will be interested in seeking compensation.

Some will want to move on and forget about the experiences of abuse, others will feel that the trauma and suffering they have endured is not commensurable with monetary value. Many trafficked persons will be preoccupied with more pressing problems, such as their fear of reprisals from their trafficker on return to their home countries, and many trafficked persons will be in need of counselling so that they will be unable to even consider compensation. Consequently, not every trafficked person will pursue compensation, but many may not do so both because they are unaware of the possibility or because they do not receive appropriate support in order to do so[2].

A colleague from La Strada International[3] once said: 'Cash is an effective remedy'. Payment of compensation monies whether for unpaid wages or for the harm and suffering caused by traffickers has a huge significance in providing victims with financial autonomy and empowering them to take their lives back into their own hands.

Albeit it would not be true to conclude that trafficked persons only wish to pursue compensation in instances where there is a prospect that the actual payment will materialise. Even in cases where the perpetrator is unable to pay, or the judgment against the trafficker is difficult to enforce, there may be a significant psychologically rehabilitative effect on trafficked persons as a consequence of having experienced justice.

Some trafficked persons who brought claims against their abusers in the Employment Tribunals in the UK were able to see judgments of significant value against the traffickers awarded, however with a little chance of receiving the actual money. Many nevertheless expressed to their support workers and legal representatives their satisfaction at being able to experience justice and receive a formal acknowledgement that harm was done to them and the person who did it was condemned[4]. The significance of the victim being the one initiating the process, and hence being the 'driving force', is very well described in **CHAPTER 17** on seeking redress for victims of domestic servitude in the Employment Tribunals.

Furthermore, such a positive experience of justice can contribute to empowering trafficked persons to seek further remedies – for example by instigating criminal proceedings against a trafficker after a successful Employment Tribunal claim.

A similar positive experience could be achieved by taking a civil action against (convicted) traffickers. However, as it can be seen from **CHAPTER 16** on civil claims for damages, this route is the least accessible one for trafficked persons, both because of its cost (and the dire limits on legal aid to bring such a claim) and fact that it is unlikely to yield any payment due to difficulty of enforcing the judgment against the traffickers.

Furthermore the complexity and changing nature of trafficking requires us to look for more flexible and creative ways of seeking compensation for those who have been trafficked. For instance, in cases where people have been compelled to commit a crime – and may have been prosecuted, convicted and imprisoned before being identified as trafficked – compensation should be considered not only for the trafficking experience, but also for the specific criminal consequence attributed to this particular form of exploitation. The victim's reputation, honour and dignity might have been destroyed as a consequence of having served a prison sentence for a crime for which he/she should not have been punished as the criminal act itself was the very purpose of their trafficking. Such a victim should be compensated for these aspects as well, with the aim to, for example, restore their status which was damaged by having been convicted and imprisoned.

In accordance with international law, a person should be recognised as a victim of a human rights violation from the moment he or she suffers harm and not on the basis of the application of prohibitively high criteria for having such status 'conferred' onto him or her. States also have related obligations to: exercise due diligence in the identification of trafficked persons; to apply the principle of non-criminalisation of trafficked persons; and to explicitly recognise that neither a trafficked person's immigration status nor their decision on whether or not to participate in criminal proceedings against their traffickers should be seen as in any way limiting their right to receive respect for their human rights, including that of an effective remedy[5].

1   These views of trafficked persons were facilitated by their support workers.
2   Lam, J., Skrivankova, K., *Opportunities and Obstacles: Ensuring access to compensation for trafficked persons in the UK* (2009) Anti-Slavery International, p 13.
3   A European Network against Trafficking in Human Beings, http://www.lastradainternationa l.org.
4   See further **CHAPTER 11** by Kalayaan in this Handbook.
5   Background Paper on State Practices, Concrete Strategies and Implementation of the Right to an Effective Remedy for Trafficked Persons, Consultation of the Special Rapporteur on Trafficking in Persons, Especially Women and Children, Joy Ngozi Ezeilo (November 2010).

CONCLUDING REMARKS

15.7 Victims, most of the time, do not know about their rights. The legal system surrounding them is complicated and is highly intelligible to them and also because of many other pressing needs, compensation is often not on their minds. With the State often failing in its role as the facilitator for the victim's access to justice, the duty is upon those who support trafficked persons to assume the role of facilitators to assist in this role, in particular the service providers and lawyers. Needless to say the majority of the trafficked persons who have been able to obtain compensation in the UK (at least in a form of an award from a court or tribunal, if not the actual payment) did so only because of the dedicated support of service providers and lawyers – the latter often working pro bono, the former often working beyond their regular responsibilities.

Compensation is not a specialty or a luxury that should be viewed as an add-on or an extra to the basic assistance that must be provided to trafficked person. It is a right, like many other rights, including that of a shelter. Consequently, the consideration about compensation should not come last. It needs to be incorporated into the process of assistance early on, so that the trafficked person has enough information to think about it, to take steps to obtain a residence permit if need be and to instruct a legal representative to assist him/her with a claim.

Early consideration of compensation is also important as for some of the avenues of redress time limits apply (such as for the Employment Tribunal or the CICS). Furthermore, evidence will need to be gathered so that it can be presented with the claim. Much of the information needed will be the same as the information that will have been gathered by the support services or possibly the police. Where a victim is co-operating with the police, she/he should seek supporting evidence from the police for the purposes of a compensation claim (notably, in some of the cases submitted to CICA the police had assisted in the claims). Furthermore, the victim's legal representatives might be able to also request that the assets of the perpetrators be frozen so as to prevent the trafficker from transferring them onto another person and claiming bankruptcy. The service provider could request that the prosecutor asks the judge to order a compensation order if the trafficker is convicted: until there is a functioning mechanism for reparation for victims of trafficking in the criminal justice system that is embedded in the minds of the police, the prosecutors and the courts the need for third parties to assist victims of trafficking in securing their rights will continue.

Instead of a conclusion, the end of this chapter offers eight non-exhaustive points to think about when dealing with a case of a trafficked person:

(1) Compensation is a crucial tool in combating trafficking and has a restorative, preventative and punitive function;

(2) Each trafficked person has the right to an effective remedy, including compensation. There is an obligation on the State to inform the victim about his/her right to compensation and to ensure that all victims have equal access to the remedies the law provides;

(3) There are certain prerequisites to ensure access to this right –many of these are also rights – and knowing what they are will help assist victims in seeking compensation;

(4) Compensation is not an add-on to basic services – it is a right of itself and it needs to be considered early – some decisions and evidence-collection cannot wait and physical injuries will need to be documented when they are still visible given the time limits for making a claim to the Employment Tribunal or to the CICS or to the civil courts;

(5) The restorative justice function of compensation stretches beyond monetary remedy – trafficked persons ought to be made aware of the reality where it is unlikely an actual payment will be received, but should not be discouraged from seeking compensation regardless and given the opportunity to experience justice;

(6) The fact that trafficking is not included in the tariff of the CICS precludes a large number of trafficked persons from obtaining compensation. One must question whether this is consistent with the UK's obligations under European Union and Council of Europe law?

(7) The right to compensation is not reserved for adults only;

(8) The link between the confiscation of criminal assets and the right to compensation for victims must be strengthened in the criminal courts of the UK.

16

DAMAGES CLAIMS AGAINST TRAFFICKERS IN THE UK COURTS FOR HARM ASSOCIATED WITH TRAFFICKING

Jawaid Luqmani

INTRODUCTION

16.1 This chapter will examine:

- The scope and availability of compensatory claims whether in criminal or civil proceedings;
- The anatomy of a claim in the civil courts arising from legal wrongs in the trafficking context[1];
- Obstacles in the way of pursuing such claims;
- Difficulties regarding enforceability of successful monetary claims.

---

[1] This chapter, which directs itself to the route to compensation against traffickers in the civil courts was initially written before the Administrative Court's decision in *OOO v Commissioner of Police for the Metropolis* [2011] EWHC 1246 (QB), judgment of 20 May 2011. That case concerned a civil claim, including a claim for damages, against the police for failing to investigate the traffickers of four claimants who had been victims of trafficking and domestic servitude in the UK. The successful claimants were each awarded damages of £5,000 for the police's breaches of Art 4 ECHR.

SCOPE AND AVAILABILITY OF COMPENSATORY CLAIMS

16.2 The availability of claims to the Criminal Injuries Compensation Authority (CICA) and in the Employment Tribunal are dealt with elsewhere within this Handbook. This chapter focuses on the availability of court-based financial compensation within either the criminal or civil courts of England and Wales, including where the wrongdoer has been convicted (or, in the case of civil proceedings, at the very least prosecuted within the criminal justice system). It is unlikely that the recovery of financial redress will necessarily be an adequate recompense for what may have been weeks, months or even years of the systematic violation of an individual's rights, but for some victims of trafficking the initiating of compensatory claims may be to either draw a line over past events or to attempt to assert a voice, particularly when the highly exploitative nature of trafficking relied primarily upon fear and intimidation, actual or threatened violence and demanded from the victims their silence, submission and total obedience.

Criminal courts, compensation, confiscation and deprivation orders

16.3 The Powers of Criminal Courts (Sentencing) Act 2000 (PCC(S)A 2000), s 130 empowers a criminal court on conviction to impose a compensation order in favour of any person for personal injury, loss or damage arising from the offence for which the individual was convicted or any other offence which is taken into consideration by the court in determining sentence. The level that can be awarded is at the discretion of the sentencing court having regard to representations received from the defendant or the prosecutor. A crown court has no upper limit but there are restrictions on the powers of a magistrates' court[1].

Although this form of penalty does not envisage an opportunity for a victim to directly enforce payment by the convicted defendant, it enables such an award to be made[2] and enforced by the court. Whilst there is nothing within the PCC(S)A legislation itself that appears to require the victim's circumstances to be taken into account by the court when deciding whether to make such an award, or even what level of award should be made, in practice one would anticipate that these issues ought properly to be the subject of representations made by the prosecution[3].

Hence, in *R v Pola*[4] the Court of Appeal, in dismissing an appeal against the making of a compensation order, recalled that the trial judge had been presented with medical evidence of injuries to the victim and the court found no fault in his assessment of the order by reference to that evidence and also a statement from the victim's family (the victim in that case having suffered severe head injuries).

The Proceeds of Crime Act 2002 (POCA 2002) enables a confiscation order to be made by the Crown Court if a defendant has benefitted from their criminal conduct. It applies to offences of all descriptions committed on or after 23 March 2003, and is not limited to human trafficking or related offences. The POCA 2002, s 13 describes the effect of a confiscation order on the court's other powers. Under this section, where confiscation applies it always takes precedence over compensation[5]. As with compensation orders, it is important to appreciate that this provision does not give the victim of crime an enforceable right directly against a defendant. The power will apply only where a request is made by the CPS (or the Director of the Asset Recovery Agency) or by the court of its own motion[6].

It is important to distinguish between the purpose of these two sorts of orders. Compensation orders, are intended to compensate persons identified as victims of crime whereas confiscation orders, are designed to ensure that convicted persons should not be entitled to profit from criminal conduct. The former is thereby concerned with the possible restitution for victims; the latter is an element of crime prevention and punishment to ensure that crime does not pay.

The legislation and the courts themselves appear to be alive to the possibility that, in some if not many cases, the amount that is capable of being recovered will be insufficient to discharge both orders in full.

Hence, where the crown court makes both a confiscation order under the POCA 2002 and a compensation order under the PCC(S)A 2000, s 130 and where it appears to the court that the convicted person will not be able to make full payment to satisfy both orders, then the court must direct that a specific amount of the confiscation order be used to satisfy the part of the compensation order that the court believes will not be recoverable owing to the insufficiencies of the convicted person's means[7].

However, this approach does not necessarily reflect current practice and certainly the Home Office has stated in written correspondence[8] that, where a criminal court is considering the imposition of a compensation order and a confiscation order, the maximum amount available to satisfy a compensatory order as against realisable assets would be 50% of the total amount recoverable. This approach[9] conflicts with the POCA 2002, s 13(6) in so far as the policy seeks to read into the legislation a minimum percentage that is preserved for the purposes of satisfying a confiscation order. This approach also potentially conflicts with the POCA 2002, Part 2, s 6(6), which provides that if the sentencing court believes that the victim has started or intends to start civil proceedings for loss, injury or damage the court's duty to make a confiscation order is converted into a power to do so, presumably on the basis that any confiscated funds should be held for any civil claims that a victim might bring.

There is also a third kind of ancillary order that can be made by the court upon convicting a trafficker, namely a deprivation order[10]. This order can be made to deprive the offender of property[11] (for example, his premises) that was used or intended to be used to commit or facilitate the commission of 'any offence' and not necessarily the offence for which the offender was convicted[12]. It is the duty of the prosecutor to request the court to consider making such an order[13] and, since the court must have adequate supporting evidence to justify making such an order, the prosecutor's application must be fully prepared[14]. Where such a deprivation order is made, the proceeds arising from the disposal of the property can be awarded to the victim where the offence resulted in personal injury, loss or damage[15] and where the court believes the offender's means are inadequate to justify the ordering of a compensation order[16]. It is not known whether the criminal courts have made any deprivation orders upon the conviction of traffickers but where the trafficker's own premises[17] were used in trafficking or exploiting a victim, and where his means are limited, the making of a deprivation order by the court would seem to be a very appropriate mechanism by which to punish the trafficker and also ensure that a victim is recompensed for the wrongs that he/she was subjected to at the trafficker's hands or whilst under his control.

---

[1]   Where a compensation award is made in a magistrates' court, there is a statutory limit of £5,000 per charge by virtue of the Powers of Criminal Courts (Sentencing) Act 2000, s 131 but it is not envisaged that trials of such magnitude as trafficking prosecutions would be routinely disposed of in the magistrates' courts.

[2]   It is also notable that, according to s 130(3) of the PCC(S)A 2000, '[a] court shall give reasons, on passing sentence, if it does not make a compensation order in a case where this section empowers it to do so.'

3 The CPS's Legal Guidance on 'Sentencing and Ancilliary Orders', updated September 2010, and available online, includes that: 'The prosecutor should be ready to assist the court to reach the appropriate decision as to sentence, which includes drawing the court's attention to its powers to award compensation and inviting them to make such an order where appropriate.' See: http://www.cps.gov.uk/legal/s_to_u/sentencing_and_ancillary_orders_applications/#a02.

4 [2009] EWCA Crim 655, [2010] Cr App Rep (S) 32, [2009] Crim LR 603. This was a non-trafficking case, but provides relevant guidance.

5 POCA 2002, s 13(2) and (3).

6 POCA 2002, s 6(3).

7 POCA 2002, s 13(6) as amended.

8 Letter from Home Office to Luqmani, Thompson & partners 13 September 2010.

9 The CPS is not bound by the Home Office's letter however.

10 PCC(S)A 2000, s 143. The provision requires that the court must have regard to the value of the property and the likely financial and other effects of the making of the order on the offender.

11 Ie it deprives the offender of his title to property. Hence this type of order is distinct to a confiscation order which does not deprive title but instead confiscates the proceeds of crime.

12 The deprivation order will be limited to any property seized from the offender on arrest or any property which was controlled by him at that time.

13 CPS Legal Guidance: Sentencing — Ancillary Orders. See http://www.cps.gov.uk/legal/s_to_u/sentencing_and_ancillary_orders_applications/.

14 *R v Pemberton* (1982) 4 Cr App R (S) 328, [1983] Crim LR 121, CA.

15 PCC(S)A 2000, s 145(1)(a).

16 PCC(S)A 2000, s 145(2).

17 But note that where the property is in multiple ownership or subject to encumbrances, it might be appropriate for the court to consider an increased financial penalty instead: *R v Troth* 1 Cr App R (S) 341, CA; *R v Khan* [1982] 3 All ER 969, [1982] 1 WLR 1405, CA.

The significance of compensation orders

16.4 In theory the availability of compensation orders *per se* within criminal proceedings, would appear to be a very satisfactory way of ensuring redress for victims of trafficking: the order is purely directed at compensating the victim, it is made at the request of a prosecutor, the evidence can be tendered to demonstrate to a sentencing judge the assets of a convicted trafficker and the loss and harm suffered by a victim, and the enforcement of this order is also managed through the court.

It is telling that by November 2010[1], not a single application for a compensation order had been made on behalf of a victim by a prosecutor following a trafficking conviction, even in cases where a victim might have to have been persuaded to give evidence to secure the trafficker's conviction. In those same cases however, confiscation proceedings would have almost inevitably followed[2] as it is recognised that significant sums of money are generated by this crime, human trafficking is a 'lifestyle offence' under POCA and the motive behind this offence is the enormous profit that can be generated and indeed achieved by traffickers. At least one of the claimants in *AT v Dulghieru and another*[3] was issued with a witness summons after expressing grave reservations as to giving evidence at the criminal trial, yet no attempt was made to secure financial redress for her despite the fact that the police had seized considerable assets from the defendant at the time of arrest.

1 As discussed by delegates (including a representative from the CPS) at a conference, 'Human Trafficking: routes to effective enforcement', 5 November 2010, Freshfields Bruckhaus Deringer LLP/Aire Centre, London.

2 Indeed, as the OCSE found in its report, 'Compensation for trafficked and Exploited Persons in the OSCE Region', 2008 '[i]n general there is much greater emphasis [on UK] police and

prosecutors to use their...powers to restrain and seize assets than there is to ensure that the victim receives compensation from those same proceeds' (at para 5.7.2.3).

3   [2009] EWHC 225 (QB).

Civil remedies

16.5 As observed above, often there is a failure on the part of those involved in conducting criminal prosecutions to adequately consider or address the availability of remedies that would directly compensate victims, or where such consideration is given, the desire of the State to confiscate assets may be prioritised given that the costs of initiating investigations and mounting prosecutions can be significant.

Whilst the expansion and codification of the criminal law in this area has been rapid, there have not been corresponding developments within the civil law and so far there is no specific tort of people trafficking.

Consequently victims of trafficking will need to have regard to the armoury of existing torts that are recognised by the courts as best fitting their circumstances. Tort is an actionable breach of a civil law duty engaging a right to seek damages for injury or other loss. Much of the law of tort is concerned with actions for negligence, but the torts that this chapter is concerned with are those which are intentional. There are a number that are likely to be of relevance in bringing a civil claim for damages against a trafficker and the fact that they may be overlapping does not inhibit their use.

Such torts are likely to include: false imprisonment, harassment, assault, battery, intimidation and, where there is a gang of traffickers involved, unlawful means conspiracy[1].

In order to pursue a claim in the civil courts it may be sensible to try and identify the *modus operandi* of the traffickers in order to establish which torts are likely to have been committed, and by whom, although this may be easier in theory than in practice as one aspect of trafficking that is particularly prevalent is the number of different individuals operating at different levels, with the result that distance is generally kept between those responsible as primary organisers and those who are trafficked.

Although many if not most readers will be familiar with the term 'trafficker' and the term 'victim of trafficking', in the civil court context the participants would be defendant and claimant. The remainder of this chapter will utilise that terminology.

Despite the availability of numerous torts that may enable a civil claim to be commenced against a trafficker, there remain a number of obstacles in terms of pursuing civil claims. Some are practical, some technical and in the absence of a specific tort covering this growing phenomenon it is likely that litigants and the courts will need to find, wherever possible, creative solutions to overcome some of these obstacles in order that justice may be done for those whose rights have been violated by being trafficked.

These problems include the following:

16.5 Damages claims against traffickers

(i)   As regards intentional torts generally, due to the fragmented structures and levels within a trafficking organisation, it may be difficult for a claimant to show that those at the top of the organisation had direct knowledge that is sufficient to establish an intentional tort against that claimant;

(ii)   Evidence of physical injury, to support an action in tort, may be rare, either because the defendant will have avoided direct physical harm to the claimant, or due to the passage of time;

(iii)   Although damages are available for psychiatric injury, they are not likely to be available for distress, which may be relevant if the claimant is able to evade those responsible for trafficking her/him at a relatively early stage.

In terms of potential defences to civil claims, apart from the defendant claiming that she/he had no knowledge of the claimant or of the torts inflicted, it would not be open to a defendant to rely upon consent as a defence where it has been established that the claimant had been trafficked. Article 3(b) of the Palermo Protocol[2] is unequivocal in stating:

> 'The consent of a victim of trafficking in persons to the intended exploitation set forth in subparagraph *(a)*[3] of this article shall be irrelevant where any of the means set forth in subparagraph *(a)* have been used'.

Furthermore where a defendant has already been successfully prosecuted by a criminal court, the existence of that conviction may be relied upon by a claimant in civil proceedings to establish liability and imposes a burden on the defendant in civil proceedings to establish that s/he was not responsible[4].

Even where an individual is acquitted, or their conviction overturned on appeal, it does not mean that a civil suit is prevented, as the burden of proof between a criminal prosecution and a civil suit is different. Securing a conviction requires evidence beyond reasonable doubt, whereas civil liability is established on the balance of probabilities.

However, given the nature of the association between claimant and defendant it is unlikely that civil proceedings could be even be contemplated by such a claimant unless the defendant had been imprisoned or the claimant had some other secure means of protecting him/herself against the consequences of initiating a civil claim against the defendant.

[1]   A conspiracy to act together with others to make gain from unlawful actions.
[2]   Protocol to Prevent, Suppress and Punish Trafficking in Persons, especially Women and Children, supplementing the United Nations Convention against Transnational Organized Crime.
[3]   '*(a)* "Trafficking in persons" shall mean the recruitment, transportation, transfer, harbouring or receipt of persons, by means of the threat or use of force or other forms of coercion, of abduction, of fraud, of deception, of the abuse of power or of a position of vulnerability or of the giving or receiving of payments or benefits to achieve the consent of a person having control over another person, for the purpose of exploitation. Exploitation shall include, at a minimum, the exploitation of the prostitution of others or other forms of sexual exploitation, forced labour or services, slavery or practices similar to slavery, servitude or the removal of organs.'
An identical definition is to found in Article 4 of the Council of Europe Convention on action Against Trafficking in Human Beings which entered into force in the UK on 1 April 2009.
[4]   Civil Evidence Act 1968, s 11.

Bringing a civil claim

16.6 There are a significant number of reference sources available for the initiation of proceedings in the civil courts in the UK, one the most authoritative being the Civil Court Practice[1] in addition to numerous text books and articles on the subject.

The process of a civil claim inevitably involves a series of points of contact, serving and responding to legal documents even before any date for trial. In this particular field this will be a particular obstacle, given the desirability of the claimant being able to avoid the defendant for fear of potential reprisals.

To date the first and as yet only case that has been initiated by a claimant against trafficker defendants in this context is that of *AT v Dulghieru and another*[2] and it may be instructive to consider some of the issues that the litigation in that case highlighted.

The facts of that case are by no means untypical of the circumstances of many trafficking operations. The claimants were lured to travel to the UK with the promise of work and study and the journey to the UK was through unconventional means. Upon arrival the claimants were forced to work in the sex industry and threats were made against them and against family members in their home country if they failed to co-operate.

What was different in this case was that the claimants were able to escape from the defendants (without police assistance) and they were later contacted by the police and asked to act as prosecution witnesses against two defendants who were subsequently arrested. Their premises had been under surveillance and targeted in an undercover operation.

The defendants were tried in criminal proceedings, with one of the defendants entering a guilty plea and the other being been tried and later convicted of some but not all of the charges, including money laundering. Both of the defendants (in respect of whom civil claims were pursued) were sentenced to terms of imprisonment but these men were by no means the only persons involved in the trafficking operation. A confiscation order was made, but this was appealed. No compensation order was made by the court and it is not known if the court even considered the grant of a deprivation order.

Following the defendants' convictions, it was felt that the potential claimants had not received redress for the harm they had experienced, given the absence of any grant to them of compensation by the criminal court. Hence as with most civil claims, pre-action correspondence was initiated on behalf of the prospective claimants to the prospective defendants. There was a failure on the part of one prospective defendant to engage with the process at all. The other denied responsibility and, in so far as a defence was raised, it consisted of repeated requests for the identification of the prospective claimants both at the pre-action stage and during the proceedings in order that the defendant could answer definitively whether he had indeed been culpable of the torts alleged.

Measures needed to be put in place to avoid the defendant learning of the identity of the claimants and certainly the claimants were understandably anxious not to take any steps that would enable them to be identified as they feared that they and their families remained at risk of reprisals and harm.

Eventually after a series of preliminary hearings, judgment was entered in default of a proper defence as it was clear that: (i) the existence of the criminal convictions, and (ii) the fact that the claimants had been asked to give statements for the purposes of securing convictions, with at least two of those anonymised statements having been disclosed to the defendant within the criminal proceedings, enabled the court to be satisfied that there was no proper defence[3].

The remainder of the proceedings were concerned with the assessment of damages, but even in relation to that assessment, the same consideration regarding the need to ensure the anonymity of the claimants was preserved for fear that reprisals would follow not necessarily from the imprisoned defendants but potentially by their associates.

At a damages assessment hearing that lasted beyond a day, judgment was reserved and damages were later assessed by Treacy J as amounting to a total of more than £600,000 divided between the four claimants, with the amounts being slightly different as the incidents during their incarceration, the length of time for which they had been falsely imprisoned and levels of psychiatric injury differed as between the claimants. Live evidence was considered at the damages hearing and the defendants had been given notice of the hearing and were both entitled and invited to participate in what was an open court.

Although the claimants claimed that being identified and/or confronted by the defendants would be exposing them to greater harm and the consequent possibility of being re-traumatised, the High Court was keen to ensure that the Article 6 ECHR rights to a fair trial of the defendants were preserved and was not prepared to agree to a series of case management suggestions proposed by the claimant's solicitor to avoid direct communication between the defendants and the claimant, which included the need to submit questions either through a representative, or that the questions be posed to the claimant's solicitor in the first instance.

In essence, although measures may be available to minimise the level of contact, to reduce the likelihood of the defendant discovering the identity of the claimant, the court was unwilling, and one suspects will remain unwilling, to reduce the defendants' participation to a level whereby the defendant's rights under Article 6 would be compromised.

This is likely to be an important consideration in the pursuit of a civil claim as certainly two of the claimants had indicated in very clear terms that, despite the measures that had been taken to avoid them being identified, they were not willing to participate in proceedings that would involve the defendants being able to question them directly. Balancing the competing rights of claimant and defendant and ensuring that neither party's ability to litigate is impaired may prove a significant disincentive to potential claimants as the root cause of the claim relates to the relationship of control and power that the defendant had held over the claimant.

In terms of the protective measures that were permitted to enable the identity of the claimants to remain anonymous the court did agree to the following:

(i)   A pre-action application for the proceedings to be brought anonymously with the name, address and other detail of the claimants to be lodged with the court and not to be opened without leave of the court;

(ii)   A screen to avoid direct eye contact between the claimants and other participants in the assessment process other than the judge;

(iii)   The claimants were permitted by prior arrangement to enter the building other than through the public entrance and to remain in part of the court to which the public did not have access during the hearing when not giving evidence.

Furthermore, recognising the potential harm that might flow from disclosure of any details that would enable the claimants to be identified, the judge conducting the assessment hearing asked persons in the public gallery to identify themselves.

¹   Civil Court Practice 2011 (Lexis Nexis).
²   [2009] EWHC 225 (QB).
³   See Civil Procedure Rules (CPR), 12.3 and 24.2.

OTHER OBSTACLES

16.7 The need to preserve anonymity, the likely antagonism from defendants, the difficulty in ensuring that the safety of the claimant's identification is preserved, the lack of a definable tort specifically encompassing this scenario: all these represent some of the myriad of problems facing potential claimants seeking to pursue damages claims.

To that list may be added issues regarding the availability of funding to pursue the claim.

In the case of *AT v Dulghieru*[1] funding was granted by the Legal Services Commission (LSC) but was subject to very strict limitations since the litigation was considered unlikely to succeed by the LSC and the probability of enforcing any damages award was considered even less likely.

The funding of the claim was to a large extent undertaken *pro bono* by AT's solicitors but also with an extremely significant contribution by Faisal Saifee, Counsel for all of the claimants. The cost limitation imposed by the LSC meant that very little of the work undertaken by either solicitor or counsel will be remunerated even at the limited legal aid rates, but it was believed both then and now, that the claim represented an opportunity for a breakthrough in what had hitherto been regarded as an area where the civil courts would simply not provide a remedy[2].

Further changes to the availability of legal aid to pursue civil cases are likely to reduce rather than increase the possibility of potential claimants having an effective remedy within civil proceedings[3].

As with any civil proceedings, a claim will become time-barred unless proceedings are issued within the time limits set by statute. The Limitation Act 1980 requires any action founded in tort to be commenced within six years[4], but where the claim relates to intentional sexual assault the period is reduced to three years under s11 following the decision in *Av Hoare*[5]. There is discretion to extend time under s 33 of the Limitation Act 1980, but for these purposes the date is from the injury to the individual and not from the date of conviction which may be several years later[6].

For some claimants, enduring the anguish of re-telling an account of events in the civil courts may prove too difficult, especially when an account may have been given for the purposes of criminal proceedings and the claimant may have been challenged via cross-examination by the defendant's lawyer within those proceedings. Even where the defendant has been convicted in criminal proceedings in which the claimant has not given evidence, the defendant may question, when civil proceedings against him are brought, whether s/he was involved in trafficking this particular claimant. Furthermore, even the fact of liability being established does not mean that the claimant will not face questioning by or on behalf of the defendant.

Often there may be a range of potential defendants only some of whom have been encountered in the UK, others being based either in the country from which the claimant was trafficked to the UK, or in countries *en route* to the UK. It is possible to start proceedings and serve the claim form on a defendant who is abroad but provisions regarding the service of claims in overseas jurisdictions differ depending upon whether the individual being served is within or outside the EEA[7]. A further factor will be the need to consider whether the acts committed outside of the UK as part of the process of bringing the claimants to the UK are matters that are actionable in the UK, or actionable overseas. This is quite apart from the potential difficulty of being able to identify or trace those involved as it will be an uncommon feature of any trafficking arrangement that a claimant will know all the players who participated in the trafficking and exploitation process.

Another aspect to consider is the requirement of disclosure within any civil proceedings[8]. Failure to give proper and full disclosure may give rise to an action for contempt[9]. Many claimants will feel vulnerable and very uncomfortable that they are being required not only to disclose what is likely to be extremely sensitive material about themselves, but includes material which may adversely affect their own case[10]. It may be that information given to the police in interviews will be inconsistent with statements taken for the purposes of the civil litigation. This may arise for a variety of reasons including fear of the authorities, fear of reprisals, shame, stigma or trauma and/or the fact that the interview to gather evidence for a criminal prosecution may have been focused on some matters and not others. Such interviews, which may not necessarily have been relied upon in the successful prosecution (as the claimant may not have been called to give evidence), may also contain details about the claimant's past or personal elements that would enable him/her to be identified.

Although the Civil Procedure Rules contain provisions enabling the withholding of documents in the public interest[11], this proviso would not encompass claimants in such cases. A separate application would have to be made and there is no reason to assume that such an application will necessarily be granted. It is probable however that redacted versions of interview records may be considered more acceptable than no disclosure at all, but this may necessitate an application being made to the court without notice to the defendant[12].

Ensuring that neither party is prejudiced and that the rights of the defendant are adequately protected may be an obstacle that many potential litigants will consider too significant to enable them to participate within such proceedings.

¹ [2009] EWHC 225 (QB).
² See **CHAPTER 15** on Compensation by Klara Skrivankova. See too J Lam and K Srivanakova, *'Opportunities and Obstacles: ensuring access to compensation for trafficked persons in the UK'* (Anti Slavery International 2009).
³ Proposals for the Reform of Legal Aid in England and Wales Consultation paper C10/12 Ministry of Justice.
⁴ Limitation Act 1980, s 2.
⁵ [2008] UKHL 6, [2008] 1 AC 844, [2008] 2 All ER 1.
⁶ The power to extend time is a matter of wide discretion, broad and unfettered and the prejudice to the claimant caused by not extending time was considered in *Cain v Francis* [2008] EWCA Civ 1451, [2009] 2 All ER 579, [2009] 3 WLR 551 which concluded that the length of delay was not of itself a deciding factor but needed to be considered together with other aspects including whether a defendant knew that there might be a claim.
⁷ CPR Part 6 Section IV and Practice Direction 6B.
⁸ CPR Part 31.
⁹ CPR 31.23.
¹⁰ CPR 31.6.
¹¹ CPR 31.19.
¹² It may be for example that a claimant issuing proceedings is one of a number of witnesses in criminal proceedings and particular aspects of the evidence given within those proceedings would enable a defendant in civil proceedings to identify that litigant. In balancing the competing interests of claimant and defendant, a court may be reluctant to grant every application designed to protect a claimant's anonymity where it might be said that to do so would compromise a defendant's entitlement to properly resist any civil suit.

ASSESSING DAMAGES

16.8 In view of the fact that there have been no previous claims brought, the court in *AT and others v Dulghieru and another*¹, AT was required to evaluate in financial terms the harm done to the individual claimants without reference to clearly defined principles and consequently established a framework for future cases. As observed earlier, this assessment took place with the claimants giving evidence and, although they wished to adopt their own detailed witness statements, the assessing judge insisted that the witnesses be taken through their statements in detail. This was for all of the claimants a painful experience, particularly as, despite objections raised, this remained an open hearing albeit some protective steps were taken to preserve the anonymity of the claimants.

This is a consideration that will need to be drawn to the attention of a prospective claimant who may be unwilling or unable potentially to face the defendant or submit to rigorous examination by a judge of the account given. Even where liability has been determined, this does not prevent an examination by the court of the extent of the harm claimed or of the circumstances giving rise to damages.

In *AT v Dulghieru* the court's mechanism for quantifying the level of damages to be awarded was by reference to previous civil claims in the context of sexual assault cases, where more often than not the claimants were either child sex abuse victims or claimants who had pursued civil actions for damages arising from rape. Neither of these were necessarily apt comparators but in the absence of other guidelines their cases were adopted to give assistance in establishing what the level of damages would be set at.

Some of the comparator claims related to civil actions pursued through the civil courts and some related to claims made to the CICA. In general it should be noted that the statutory CICA scheme has fixed amounts and is not necessarily set at rates that are appropriate as a comparator.

To many, this approach of assessing damages for harm arising from trafficking and exploitation may appear to be too arbitrary, and to some attempting to put a financial figure on the types of injuries sustained by the claimants may seem distasteful. The problem courts face is that attempting to quantify the harm suffered is to try and normalise and rationalise the extent and nature of the injuries sustained. That there are no apt comparators reflects not only that there have been no other such damages claims pursued in the civil courts (and very few compensation awards made in criminal proceedings) but also that an understanding of the complex nature of trafficking-related damages claims has yet to filter down into all parts of the legal consciousness. This may reflect the fact that legal recognition of the phenomenon of human trafficking is relatively new in the UK, but the briefest of glances at human history reminds us that the exploitation of individuals within and across borders has been with us for many years.

In this undeveloped area of law there are problems quantifying and justifying both main categories of damages: general (for suffering and other losses) and special (for other losses that are readily quantifiable and calculable). In assessing the level of general damages recoverable the claimant is required to specify his or her loss according to definable heads of damage which include pain and suffering, loss of amenity, aggravated damages and exemplary damages. In *AT*, Treacy J concluded that the claimants were entitled to recover damages under all heads of general damages and allowed aggravated and exemplary damages. However he disallowed the claims for special damages (losses that must be specifically identified) on the basis that insufficiently clear evidence had been put forward to justify the costs of therapeutic treatment[2].

[1]   [2009] EWHC 225 (QB).
[2]   The amounts claimed were less than £2,000 per claimant. In another claim detailed costs estimates of treatment might enable a claimant to recover under this head also. In AT's case the figures were referred to within the expert reports but had not been fully costed.

ENFORCING DAMAGES CLAIMS

16.9 Although a successful claimant may be able to establish liability, and may be able to present evidence enabling a court to quantify the level of compensation that should be made, the question of enforceability will in many cases prevent a litigant from achieving restitution or just satisfaction.

As observed earlier, the proceedings may be brought for a variety of reasons that include the need for the claimant to be heard, not merely the possibility of a financial claim being satisfied. However, whether a claimant is willing to endure a highly traumatic process without recovering any funds is a factor to consider. It is also highly likely that any arrangements to secure funding for the litigation either on a no-win no-fee basis or under legal aid funding will be extremely difficult unless it can be shown that a successful outcome will result in monies being recovered.

Difficulty arises from a combination of factors which include:

(i)   A desire on the part of the State to ensure that any assets recovered are used to further the work of Government which will doubtless include tackling criminal gangs operating in this field;

(ii)   The lack of any effective mechanism to enforce damages claims against monies recovered through civil courts, as opposed to compensation awards made under the PCC(S)A 2000, s 130[1];

(iii)   The fact that any monies or assets seized by the police/CPS will be proceeds of crime and in principle, and as such, those sums would not ordinarily be available to satisfy a judgment debt[2].

In many cases, the criminal profits made in such activities will have been transferred to third parties or have been removed from the jurisdiction and the likelihood of there being assets available to satisfy a judgment debt will be the exception rather than the rule.

Part 74 of the Civil Procedure Rules provides a mechanism for the enforce-ability of judgments in other jurisdictions with different mechanisms in operation depending upon the country in which enforcement is sought. The rules are complex and differentiate between enforceability within or outside the European Union[3].

It is possible to seek to enforce judgment against a third party[4] but being able to prove that the third party is holding assets belonging to the judgment debtor is not straightforward. Although the rules relate primarily to funds held by a bank or building society, the rule is certainly not restricted to such institutions. However, for the third party debt order to be made, the third party must be within the jurisdiction[5]. In many cases, the judgment debtor will either have ensured that funds have been moved out of the jurisdiction or will have passed funds to third parties whose identity cannot be established. It will be rare for funds to be held in a UK clearing bank (or indeed in other property in the UK) and, if so, it is highly likely that any such assets will already have been seized as part of confiscation proceedings commenced under the POCA 2002, s 13.

The claimants in *AT v Dulghieru* are continuing to consider whether the State is entitled to prevent them enforcing part of the judgment debt against assets seized from the defendants at the time of arrest. Even if all such assets were utilised to discharge the judgment debt, it would still not be sufficient to discharge the full extent of the damages otherwise available. Once the judgment debtor has left the jurisdiction, the claimants have no realistic belief that further funds will become available to enable that claim to be satisfied. and enforcing the debt against an impecunious prisoner will be unlikely to yield further sums.

---

[1]   There are mechanisms to enforce judgment against property held in the name of the defendant or to attach a judgment debt to a bank account or to earnings in the UK but the availability of these remedies apply in limited circumstances where property or bank accounts can be identified and are not already subject to confiscation proceedings.

[2]   Although the POCA 2002, s 6(6) enables money to be set aside where civil claims are contemplated, often the possibility of bringing a civil action will not have been considered until after the conclusion of the criminal proceedings.

[3]   See CPR 74.27.

[4]   CPR Part 72 (Third party Debt Orders).

[5]   CPR 72.1.

OTHER POSSIBLE REMEDIES

16.10 The disruption of the activities of a trafficking gang will only have been achieved after a significant period of investigation and surveillance. There may be a desire on the part of the State not to initiate a raid or otherwise to alert gang members until the State has sufficient evidence to ensure that successful prosecutions of as many key players as possible can be achieved. In the meantime it is inevitable that, in the desire to ensure that those responsible are held accountable in criminal courts, the State may have tolerated some activities of the gang members, possibly including the assault, battery, false imprisonment, harassment and intimidation of trafficked individuals. Knowing that these crimes are being perpetrated and failing to take immediate action to ensure that they are not continued will arguably give rise to a breach of a State's positive obligations to protect an individual against trafficking-related harm under both Articles 3 and 4 ECHR.

'Tolerated' within this context might be regarded as an inapt expression, but it is difficult to explain in some cases why the State, aware of the criminal and civil wrongs perpetrated, does not act sooner. A justification might be said to be the need to gather more information so as to enable the arrest, charge and prosecution of all the criminal players in the network, including those at the top of it and not just at the bottom, but all of those involved. However, for each day that passes, further crimes will be committed, further torts will continue, quite possibly with more individuals being brought into the trafficking operation.

The recent judgment of Wyn Williams J in the High Court in *OOO v Commissioner of Police for the Metropolis*[1] has now established the nature and scope of the Article 4 ECHR positive obligation which falls upon the police in investigating the perpetrators of human trafficking in the UK. The judgment recognises the right of victims of trafficking to be protected from such harm and also recognises that the State may be responsible for allowing the acts of ill-treatment by traffickers continue[2].

In light of the High Court's recent judgment in *OOO v Commissioner of Police for the Metropolis* and also the ECtHR's judgment in *Rantsev v Cyprus and Russia (Application 25965/04)*[3] the question as to who would or could be added as an appropriate defendant in a civil claim against a trafficker may need to be revisited, especially given the lack of effective enforcement measures against a tortfeasor and the unwillingness of the State, to date, to regularly secure compensation orders in criminal proceedings in the first place.

Importantly *OOO and others* establishes that the pursuance of that Article 4 duty does not depend upon an actual complaint, but arises once the potential infringement of Article 4 has come to the State's attention and that once established, the duty is to investigate promptly and/or with reasonable expedition. There is however a distinction between the failure to adequately investigate (the situation in *Rantsev* and *OOO*) as opposed to the failure to act earlier. It remains to be seen whether the duty to prevent against Article 4 (or Article 3) breaches gives rise to a cause of action to a claimant for the failure to initiate arrests if it can be shown that the investigation was being carried out expeditiously, but that for operational reasons, decisions were taken not to make arrests until more evidence of wrongdoing had been identified.

1   [2011] EWHC 1246 (QB), judgment of 20 May 2011.
2   [2011] EWHC 1246 (QB).
3   (2010) 28 BHRC 313, [2010] ECHR 25965/04, ECtHR.

17

TAKING CASES FOR VICTIMS OF DOMESTIC SERVITUDE TO THE EMPLOYMENT TRIBUNAL

Jamila Duncan-Bosu

INTRODUCTION

17.1 At first sight, it might seem surprising that victims of trafficking would seek redress in the Employment Tribunal[1]. It is not appropriate in every case, but there are instances where the Employment Tribunal has proven to be a successful means of obtaining both justice and compensation for victims of trafficking into domestic servitude.

The Employment Tribunal has a number of factors in its favour.

In contrast to the criminal system, the trafficking victim is the driving force in the process. In criminal proceedings, the trafficked person is a witness for the Crown and not able to make decisions or sometimes even be informed of progress. Civil proceedings permit the trafficked person to be involved from the outset, determining whether proceedings are started, which claims are brought and pursued and it is their decisions which drive the process throughout. This sense of ownership of the legal proceedings can be significant to a person who may need to re-establish their sense of self determination. Some victims, especially if they have cared for children, may be unwilling or too intimidated to consider criminal proceedings.

Employment Tribunal proceedings can be a catalyst to criminal proceedings. If there has been no police prosecution, a successful Employment Tribunal judgment can be used to persuade the police and CPS to investigate and prosecute. Following success in the Employment Tribunal, legal proceedings can even be brought against the police if necessary for failure to investigate; so an Employment Tribunal claim can be a powerful weapon in persuading or helping the police to act. Further a victim who has been through the Employment Tribunal may later be more willing to consider criminal proceedings.

The Employment Tribunal, relatively speaking, has a simpler and more straightforward user friendly procedure than most other legal proceedings to obtain redress against the trafficker/forced labour exploiter. However, it is important to understand that it is still legal proceedings which can be most

303

intimidating and complex for the uninitiated. Public funding can be obtained in order for workers to be legally assisted in issuing claims at the Tribunal, but this funding is limited to the preparation of the claim. No public funding is available for representation at the hearing[2].

The worker will also be subject to close cross-examination. The facts in complaints of domestic servitude will undoubtedly be emotive and hotly disputed. The employer will often produce large numbers of witnesses to refute the worker's claims and to attack the worker's credibility. More often than not the employers will be professional individuals who would appear to the Tribunal as wholly reputable and believable[3]. For this reason the difficulty in successfully bringing a claim at the Tribunal should not be underestimated.

Tribunal time limits are extremely strict; even a claim made a day late will be rejected. However, that is not to say that missing this time limit is always fatal. Where the delay in issuing is due to the worker not being aware or unable to access legal advice and assistance then there is scope for extending time and the complaint being heard, particularly in discrimination complaints. But there is no guarantee that an extension will be obtained, so the deadline should never knowingly be missed.

---

[1]   The OSCE's 'Compensation for Trafficked and Exploited persons in the OSCE region' (2008) and 'Anti – Slavery International Rights & Recourse – A Guide to Legal Remedies for Trafficked Persons in the UK' (2010) both contain useful discussions in relation to the use of the Employment Tribunal for victims of trafficking. (Readers should note that there have been developments in case law since these guides were published). This chapter builds upon these guides. The focus is on domestic servitude as it is in the main, these instances of trafficking that are taken to the Employment Tribunal. A complaint from a claimant who had been trafficked for the purposes of sexual exploitation was issued in March 2010 at the London Central Employment Tribunal, but was subsequently withdrawn due to the claimant's fear of having to re-count her treatment.

[2]   In theory the worker would therefore have to represent themselves at the hearing. In practice, a referral should be made to the Free Representation Unit (http://www.thefru.org.uk) or the Bar Pro Bono Unit http://www.barprobono.org.uk/ – under the proposed cuts to Legal Aid non discrimination employment disputes would be removed from the scope of Legal Aid assistance.

[3]   In the matter of *Asuquo v Gbaja* 3200383/2008 heard in the Tribunal in October 2008, the employer went to great lengths to refer to the fact that she was a practicing solicitor. In fact her failings in relation to payment of tax and National Insurance, provision of payslips etc were highlighted all the more. Evidence was adduced on the employer's behalf from numerous witnesses who gave oral evidence. In contrast the Claimant called only one other witness to give evidence in support of her claim. The Tribunal in upholding the Claimant's claims commented on the consistency and credibility of her account. As such, a claimant's ability to be clear and consistent should be more of a concern than the apparent status and standing of the employer.

WHO CAN USE THE TRIBUNAL?

17.2 Anyone who is an employee or worker can use the Employment Tribunal. Some claims can only be brought by an employee such as a complaint of unfair dismissal. Others such as under discrimination legislation can be brought by both a worker and an employee. It is for this reason that many employers will argue that the claimant is a worker in an attempt to reduce their liability. In practice the primary position should always be that those trafficked for the purposes of domestic servitude are employees. The question as to whether a claimant is an employee or worker is one for the Tribunal having heard evidence as to how the claimant's role was carried out.

THE CONTRACT

17.3 Complaints to the Employment Tribunal are of course premised on the basis that a contract (whether of employment or for services) has been entered into between the parties whether expressly, or implied. There is certainly an argument that in severe cases of trafficking and forced labour the basic requirements of a contract are not present. However, in the writer's experience this has not to date proven to be an insurmountable problem. Possibly because these workers are trafficked into recognisable employment scenarios. Indeed, even in cases of extreme abuse amounting to forced labour, there has been no suggestion that the dispute before the Tribunal did not arise from a contract.

Another issue that sometimes arises in ET cases is when employers seek to argue that the Employment Tribunal has no jurisdiction to hear the complaint as the contract of employment was formed outside of the UK. For example many workers travel in and out of the UK with their employer perhaps remaining for several months at a time. In such cases the worker would be entitled to bring claims regarding breaches occurring within the UK[1].

---

[1] *Saikh v Sheikh Khalid & Sheika Fawaghis Saqr Bin Alqasim* 2201318/2010 heard on 9 June 2011. For a further discussion of the scope of territorial jurisdiction see *Lawson v Serco Ltd* [2006] UKHL 3, [2006] 1 All ER 823, [2006] ICR 250 HL.

IMMIGRATION STATUS

17.4 The claimant's immigration status will also affect the claims brought on their behalf. Many claimants will have the appropriate permissions to live and work in the UK. In the case of a domestic worker this will be a valid migrant domestic worker visa. But a significant number of claimants will not have any legal status in the UK. A common means of exerting control over a worker is to ensure their visa status is irregular or unknown.

It is often suggested that illegality is an absolute bar to a complaint being brought at the Employment Tribunal[1]. However, the Tribunal enjoys considerable discretion. Key will be whether the worker is complicit in the illegality. This has been taken to mean more than knowledge of illegality, but actual participation.

A claimant will need to give detailed evidence as to the steps taken in obtaining the role and travelling to the UK; what were they told, what documents did they see if any, what did they know about their immigration status and when? If the claimant has been referred under the National Referral Mechanism (NRM) and has received a positive conclusive decision from the Competent Authority[2] by which the claimant is formally recognised as being a victim of human trafficking[3], it is well worth raising this in evidence and on submissions. Whilst the Tribunal is not automatically bound by the Council of Europe Convention on Action against Trafficking in Human Beings[4] ('the Trafficking Convention'), reminding the Tribunal that the element of consent should be disregarded where the claimant is a victim of trafficking may have persuasive value. In the matter of *Roucou v Esparon & Frederick*[5] the claimant had at no time had a valid visa enabling her to work in the UK. The claimant was aware that she had travelled on a tourist visa but had been led to believe that steps would be taken to regularise her status. The Tribunal held that the claimant although having knowledge of her illegal status had not been complicit. Therefore, the contract, albeit tainted, was not void for illegality and the contractual complaints should succeed[6].

However, in view of the Tribunal's recent position in *Zarkasi v Anindita* to disregard the Trafficking Convention's principles, it is vital that the Tribunal's role in the Convention's machinery is clarified. The Employment Tribunals are often wary of what can be seen as an attempt to use another jurisdiction to bind them[7].

In practice, the Tribunal is far more willing to uphold a claim on behalf of an illegal worker under discrimination legislation than any other. As such, it is important (where it is appropriate to do so) to also plead all breaches of employment law as acts of discrimination. Under the discrimination statutes[8], legal rights do not flow only from employment status and the contract of employment: a broader public policy approach is taken. The Tribunal will consider whether the claim being brought is so linked to the illegality that to compensate the worker would amount to condoning and benefitting illegal behaviour[9].

A useful illustration of this point can be found in the case of *Hougna v Allen*[10]. The claimant had been promised an education in return for acting as a 'nanny' to the employer's two children. The claimant was asked to sign documents stating that she was older than 14 in order that a visa could be obtained. The Tribunal concluded that the claims under the contract[11] could not be upheld, but that under discrimination legislation[12], the claims should succeed and illegality should not be a bar to a legal remedy. The claimant was given compensation for race discrimination[13].

As such, the claimant's position will always be that it is in the interests of public policy that compensation for acts of discrimination be awarded, despite any ostensible illegality. For the Tribunal to decline to make an award because of illegality would reward the employer for breaking both criminal and immigration law. It would serve to prevent a victim of trafficking from obtaining any substantive remedy and send entirely the wrong signal to employers. Employers might rationally conclude that it is better to bring in illegal workers and not pay them and mistreat them, rather than employ people who can work in the UK legally.

Arguments in relation to illegality and the application of the trafficking convention are likely to grow in importance, in the event that the Government's proposals to remove the domestic worker visa altogether, or replace it with a non-renewable six–12 month visa with no right to change employer, come into effect. It is likely that such a proposal will increase the number of employees working without immigration status. Where such arguments fail workers will be left with no rights at all.

[1] *Vakante v Governing Body of Addey and Stanhope School (No 2)* [2005] ICR 279.
[2] Which is either the UKBA or the United Kingdom Human Trafficking Centre (UKHTC).
[3] For the purposes of the Trafficking Convention, Article 10.
[4] Which entered into force in the UK on 1 April 2009.
[5] 1100332/2010 decided on 4 August 2010.
[6] Unfair dismissal, unlawful deduction of wages, failure to provide statement of terms and conditions, failure to provide paid annual leave, failure to provide payslips. In addition, complaints of race discrimination were brought and upheld.

[7] 2303671/2009, decided on 14 April 2011. The Tribunal found that in effect the Claimant's claims were tainted by illegality because of her complicity in, or consent to, the arrangements, so that they could not be heard. In so doing, it defeated the object and purpose of Article 15 of the Trafficking Convention, which requires signatory states to 'ensure' access of victims (consenting or otherwise) to the right to compensation. Arguably, the Claimant's status as a victim of trafficking meant that the Tribunal should have construed the doctrine of illegality so as to allow expression of the Claimant's rights under the Trafficking Convention. In other words the Claimant's status as victim of trafficking should have led the Tribunal to disregard any consent or complicity in her actions. An appeal has now been raised to the Employment Appeal Tribunal.

[8] The Equality Act 2010, which renders discrimination on the grounds of prohibited characteristics such as gender, race, age, religion and sexual orientation unlawful.

[9] *Hall v Woolston Hall Leisure Ltd* [2000] IRLR 579 CA.

[10] (UKEAT/0326/10/LA) [2011] All ER (D) 250 (Apr), EAT.

[11] Unfair dismissal, failure to provide paid annual leave, breach of contract – unpaid wages.

[12] The Race Relations Act 1976, ss 1, 1A and 3A.

[13] The claim was issued at a time that the statutory dispute resolution procedures were in force. This meant that there was a requirement to serve a grievance prior to issuing a complaint at the Tribunal. In this case it was not possible as initially the respondents' whereabouts were unknown. An exception to the requirement to serve a grievance was relied on. The Tribunal did not agree the exception applied. So the client was compensated for having suffered a discriminatory dismissal – grievance procedures did not apply to dismissal. Discriminatory acts other than dismissal were subject to the grievance procedures so the client was not compensated for these acts. This decision is now being appealed. The grievance procedures were repealed in 2009, so such a situation is unlikely to arise again. This case is of importance as it demonstrates that illegality will not automatically negate a discrimination complaint.

IMMUNITY

17.5 Where a claimant has been employed by an employer working at an embassy, diplomatic or consular immunity may be invoked as a bar to the proceedings.

Where an employer purports to have immunity their status should be verified with the relevant Embassy and/or via the Protocol Directorate at the Foreign and Commonwealth Office (FCO)[1]. The FCO holds a register of all diplomats and consular officials in post in the UK.

The information provided by the FCO will assist in determining whether the employer is a diplomat or a consular official[2]. The distinction is an important one since the exceptions to immunity are considerably broader in respect of consular than in respect of diplomatic immunity[3]. Where immunity is genuinely found to apply and it is neither waived nor any exception is found to be available[4], there may be some scope for using human rights arguments, as in the recent case of *Cudak v Lithuania (Application No 15869/02)*[5] in which it was found by the European Court of Human Rights that the Lithuanian court's determination that state immunity prevented a claimant from bringing a claim against her employers (the Polish embassy in Vilnius) amounted to a 'disproportionate interference' with the claimant's Article 6 right to a fair trial. However, the practical impact of this judgment for clients in the UK's domestic courts is unclear as the immunities enshrined in the relevant international instruments are implemented by primary legislation in the UK.

[1] http://www.fco.gov.uk/en/about-us/what-we-do/protocol/.

[2] Diplomats represent and negotiate on behalf of their countries, as well as doing functions performed both by diplomats and consuls such as building mutual relations, reporting about host countries and issuing visas etc. Consuls do not represent or negotiate for their countries.

[3] The relevant provisions are found in the Vienna Convention on Diplomatic Relations 1961, Article 31, enacted in the UK by Diplomatic Relations Act 1964, and the Vienna Convention on Consular Relations 1963, Article 43 as enacted by Consular Relations Act 1968. In the case of a consular official, the immunity is expressly stated in Article 43 to apply only to those acts of the consular official which are performed in the exercise of their consular functions. The US Court of Appeal in the case of *Park v Shin* (No 01-16805) found that employing a domestic servant fell outside of the relevant consular official's consular functions. At the date of going to press, the matter is due to be tested in the UK High Court in the case of *Namusoke v Chinkanda*.

[4] Immunity may be waived by agreement or by action, such as serving a detailed response to the Tribunal complaint.

[5] (2010) 30 BHRC 157, ECtHR.

CLAIMS

17.6 Common grievances are that workers have received little or no salary, for excessively long hours. It is not uncommon for workers to report that they work a 14 hour day and are also then on call throughout the night. Many workers report inadequate living accommodation, often sleeping on the floor and/or sharing a room with small children.

Freedom of movement may also be heavily restricted; many report that they are not allowed to leave the house unaccompanied or at all. Threats of arrest and of removal or deportation are often used to ensure compliance with the traffickers.

Most victims of trafficking and victims of domestic servitude will not have been provided with a written contract of employment or statement of terms and conditions.

Many report verbal, physical and sexual abuse. In these cases the main concern will be whether the claimant wishes to raise the issue at the Tribunal: it is important that allegations of abuse are raised as soon as possible.

The majority of claimants report that their passport is not in their possession or control. Again, this is a means of the trafficker or exploiter exerting control: many workers are told that if they are found without their passport that they can and will be arrested.

All of the above, are matters for which the Employment Tribunal can award compensation. Below, is a summary of the main claims that are likely to be brought on a claimant's behalf.

UNLAWFUL DEDUCTION OF WAGES

17.7 The failure to pay a salary in line with the National Minimum Wage, (or at all) is brought as a claim for unauthorised deduction of wages under the Employment Rights Act 1996, s 13.

For the majority of victims of domestic servitude, this claim will be the most important financially.

Time limits

17.8 This claim must be brought within three months (less a day) of the last deduction or the last in a series of deductions. Usually this means the start of the limitation period should be calculated from the date of termination of employment. This date would include the date on which the victim escaped or ran away.

Workers are entitled to the National Minimum Wage (NMW), which is implied into all contracts of employment by the National Minimum Wage Act 1998, s 17. Any arguments that a particularly low salary was due to an agreement between the parties, or because salary is paid abroad in the workers home country, are irrelevant; it is not possible to contract out of the NMW.

Some employers will suggest that the value of the provision of accommodation, food, clothes etc should be counted as salary, but this incorrect. Unless, the claimant is actually given cash, any benefit does not count towards the NMW. The only exception is that an employer can deduct no more than £4.61 per day for accommodation[1].

An employer is also under a duty to keep records of payments in line with the NMW; indeed the failure to keep these records can amount to a criminal offence[2].

The provisions of the National Minimum Wage Act 1998 and related Regulations[3] require the Tribunal to begin with the assumption that the claimant has *not* received the NMW. The employers' record-keeping duties further suggest that it is for the employer to demonstrate that they have paid a salary in line with the NMW. It is worth reminding the Tribunal of this and carefully taking the Tribunal through the relevant provisions.

[1] National Minimum Wage Regulations 1999, SI 1999/584, reg 36(1) – £4.61 is the current rate. The accommodation offset increases annually as does the NMW.
[2] National Minimum Wage Act 1998, s 31(2).
[3] National Minimum Wage Regulations 1999, SI 1999/584.

Evidence

17.9 Whilst the burden is on the employer to show that they have paid the NMW, in practice, the claimant needs evidence of the hours worked. Many employers will contend that the claimant's hours were very low in order to assert that the salary paid was in line with the NMW.

Domestic workers rarely have documentary evidence of the hours they have worked. In the absence of a diary or witnesses to the hours worked and tasks undertaken, the claimant will need to give detailed evidence as to how their time was spent. One means of doing this is to prepare a schedule of activities, setting out both timing and activities, eg 'Preparing breakfast 30 minutes, bathing two children 60 minutes'. It is a good idea to prepare the schedule as soon as possible before the claimant's memory of events fades. This schedule will be central to the minimum wage case. It is important that time and attention is given to preparing the schedule as the workers credibility will be at issue.

A request under the Data Protection Act 1998 should be made to HMRC in order to ascertain whether tax and National Insurance have been paid in respect of the claimant[1]. It is not uncommon for cases where employers produce payslips detailing deductions for tax and NI for the worker and yet there is no record of these sums having been paid to Her Majesty's Revenue and Customs (HMRC).

A request should also be made in the course of document disclosure for the employers' bank records. Even if the employer suggests that payments of the claimant's salary were made in cash, bank records would need to show regular withdrawals capable of satisfying the claimant's salary.

In nearly every case of domestic servitude the claimant will be entitled to bring a complaint regarding the failure to pay the NMW. However, there is no minimum wage for children under 16[2]. Therefore, a claimant who was trafficked as a child cannot claim the minimum wage for years worked under the age of 16.

In these circumstances a claim may be brought arising out of the contract of employment (which does not have to be in writing), with an implied term of the contract being that the child would be paid and this payment should be either at a commercial rate or in line with the NMW.

[1] Data Protection Act 1998, s 7.
[2] National Minimum Wage Act 1998, s 1(2); National Minimum Wage Regulations 1999, SI 1999/584, reg 13(1).

Regulation 2(2): the Family Worker Exemption

17.10 The Regulations[1] are secondary legislation made under the National Minimum Wage Act. They exclude certain workers from the NMW.

Under the exemption an employer can lawfully pay no salary at all, or a salary below the NMW, if they are able to demonstrate that the claimant is treated as a member of the family. This is an absolute defence, so the exemption will be raised in almost every case, however implausibly.

The family worker exemption should be construed narrowly. It was originally put in place to cater for au pairs, whose main purpose for being in the UK was cultural exchange. In those cases, bed, board and an allowance are given for fixed hours of work. The British Au Pair Society suggests that au pairs should work no more than 25–35 hours per week[2].

This is entirely different to those who are trafficked or who travel to the UK to support themselves and their families abroad.

The exemption was not intended to permit employers to employ migrant domestic workers for very low pay. Particular attention should be paid to ensure that the relationship is not a shield for exploitation, and that the individual is genuinely being treated as a member of the family unit. The exemption should be construed narrowly and it is for the employer to demonstrate that the worker was treated as a member of the family.

It is often necessary to remind the Tribunal that being employed and living in the family household does not automatically make the worker a member of the family. After all, the Queen's butler may work in the royal household, but that does not mean he is a member of the royal family.

The Tribunal will take into account a number of factors, including whether or not the claimant had access to their passport or whether they genuinely participated in social events. Many employers will produce photographs of the worker at family events as evidence of their treatment as a member of the family; such photos need be examined closely – was the worker engaged in their duties such as caring for the children when the photo was taken?

Other factors to be considered are whether the worker had adequate living space – a bedroom and a bed to themselves[3] – and whether they ate with the family.

There is no standard definition or test that the Tribunal will apply in looking at treatment as a member of the family. In some cases the Tribunal has taken an objective approach in looking at how an actual member of the family would be treated. The matter of *Awan v Shariff*[4] usefully sets out some of the factors to be considered, looking at the claimant's level of autonomy and control over her/his movements. Notably, in that case the Tribunal found, in contrast to the family members of the household, that the claimant was a grown woman who did not have control of her own passport and required permission to leave her employers' home at any time: these were indicative of the fact that she was not treated as a member of the family. The Tribunal considered that there should be parity of treatment with the actual family members.

In the matter of *Genova v Allin*[5] the Tribunal looked at treatment as a member of the family within the context of the claimant's role and whether there was any involvement in family life, concluding that although the claimant and respondents did not equally share tasks and socialised only on a handful of occasions, within the context of the role undertaken the claimant had been treated as a member of the family.

To date, all of the Tribunal decisions regarding the application of the family worker exemption under the National Minimum Wage Regulations 1999, SI 1999/584, reg 2(2) have been at first instance[6]. It is envisaged that appeals to the Employment Appeal Tribunal which are due to be heard in late 2011[7], will provide a unified approach to the concept of treatment as a member of the family.

[1] National Minimum Wage Regulations 1999, SI 1999/584.
[2] Guidelines for Au Pairs & Host Families — http://www.bapaa.org.uk.
[3] Many victims of trafficking for domestic servitude have told us that they were forced to sleep on the floor and to eat leftovers.
[4] 3302759/2007.
[5] 2328552/2009.
[6] Ie, not on appeal.
[7] *Jose v MSL Julio & Others* UKEAT/0597/10.

Challenging the family worker exemption

17.11 The exemption itself (rather than its application in any individual case) is being challenged on the grounds that it offends against the principle of equal treatment between men and women, enshrined in EU legislation – and thus must be disregarded.

Those employed in a private household are more likely to be female than male, and thus the exemption bars more women than men from receiving the NMW. The argument that the Employment Tribunal should disregard the exemption is live in Tribunals and it remains to be seen as to how the Tribunals will deal with this argument.

Compensation

17.12 Where the Tribunal finds that a claimant should have received the NMW, it will go on to calculate the compensation. The claimant receives the shortfall between the NMW and the sum actually paid (if any).

The National Minimum Wage Act 1998 contains a punitive provision in that the shortfall is calculated at the rate applicable at the date of hearing[1]. The NMW increases on a yearly basis – at present the rate applicable for adults over 21 is £5.93 increasing to £6.08 in October 2011.

In addition, it is always worth considering whether a complaint should be brought under any express contract. Where the claimant was employed under a migrant domestic worker visa, it is necessary to file alongside the visa application a statement of terms and conditions. The UKBA will not in practice grant a visa if no statement of terms and conditions is provided. Often the sum stated here is the same as the NMW or is in any event greater than that the claimant has actually been receiving. Bringing a claim under the express contract provides a backup should the claim in relation to the national minimum wage fail.

---

[1]   National Minimum Wage Act 1998, s 17. The amount of underpayment is divided by the rate applicable at the time underpayment occurred. It is then multiplied by the rate in force at the date of Tribunal determination.

UNFAIR DISMISSAL

Time limits

17.13 Where the claim is dismissed (or thrown out)[1], a complaint of unfair dismissal can be brought if the worker had been continuously employed for over a year. Under the Employment Rights Act 1996, s 215, employment outside the UK with the same employer will count towards continuity of service.

A complaint to the Tribunal must be made within three months (less a day) of termination. The Tribunal's discretion to hear a late unfair dismissal claim is very limited. Unless the claimant can show that they could not possibly have issued in time (it was not reasonably practicable to do so), then the claim will not be accepted. Take the example of a claimant who has delayed issuing a claim in order to deal with their visa status. However understandable this may be, the Tribunal is unlikely to extend time, as there was no actual bar to the claim being issued earlier.

In order to defend an unfair dismissal complaint the employer must show that the dismissal was for one of the six permitted reasons – capability, conduct, redundancy, retirement, illegality and some other substantial reason[2].

The employer must further show that the dismissal was carried out for a fair reason with a fair procedure being followed[3].

Many employers will seek to justify dismissal by suggesting that the claimant's performance had been poor, that there was no further need for a domestic worker or – commonly – that the claimant was dismissed for theft. Persuading the Tribunal otherwise, will often come down to the claimant's credibility and the careful preparation of witness statements. For example, if the claimant has long service or steps had been taken by the employer to renew a visa this should be flagged up to refute allegations of misconduct.

[1] The situation of where a claimant ran away or escaped is discussed further below.
[2] Employment Rights Act 1996, s 98(2).
[3] Employment Rights Act 1996, s 98(4). See also *Iceland Frozen Foods Ltd v Jones* [1983] ICR 17, [1982] IRLR 439, EAT and *Polkey v AE Dauton (or Dayton) Services Ltd* [1988] AC 344, [1987] 3 All ER 974.

Constructive unfair dismissal

17.14 In many cases the claimant will have run away from their employer or have been rescued. In those circumstances the complaint to the Tribunal would be for constructive unfair dismissal[1]. In this case the claimant would need to demonstrate that the employer had acted to fundamentally breach their contract of employment, leaving them with no choice but to leave. A Tribunal is likely to agree that the treatment commonly reported – failure to pay salary etc – amounted to a fundamental breach of contract.

[1] Employment Rights Act 1996, s 95(1)(c).

Compensation

17.15 Compensation is made up of a basic award which is calculated with reference to age and length of continuous service. This can add up to several thousand pounds if the claimant has many years service. The claimant will also receive a compensatory award to compensate them for loss of earnings. If the claimant had been unemployed for six months by the date of hearing, then they would be awarded six months' salary. Salary will be awarded at the NMW rate[1].

The claimant will need to account for earnings post dismissal. This may be problematic if the claimant is now employed in contravention of their immigration status, for example a migrant domestic worker working in a restaurant as opposed to a private household. Often the claimant's new employer is not wholly adhering to employment legislation so the claimant will be unable to produce evidence of their employment.

The claimant is also required to demonstrate they have tried to mitigate their loss, by attempting to find new employment. The failure to demonstrate mitigation can result in a compensatory award being reduced. For this reason the claimant's evidence on mitigation should detail any matters which would hinder their ability to find new employment. For example, those under a domestic worker visa being restricted to employment in a private household or a claimant having limited English[2].

1   *Paggetti v Cobb* [2002] IRLR 861, (2002) Times,12 April, EAT.
2   *Wang v Beijing Ton Ren Tang (UK) Ltd* (2009) UKEAT/0024/09/DA, [2010] All ER (D) 84 (Jan).

RACE DISCRIMINATION UNDER THE EQUALITY ACT 2010

17.16   There are three advantages to a claim for race discrimination. Firstly the discrimination jurisdiction is a more forgiving environment for workers with technical problems with their claims such as bringing a late claim or having worked illegally. Secondly, the Employment Tribunal can award compensation for injury to feelings. Finally, it can be argued that the other claims – wages, dismissal etc – are but symptoms of the disease whereas race discrimination names the disease itself – mistreatment linked to someone's national origins or nationality.

It is important to plead everything that the employer did as a specific act of discrimination. This does not just apply to matters such as physical abuse which can only be brought under the Equality Act 2010[1]. Every other complaint (failure to pay the NMW, dismissal etc) should be pleaded as an act of discrimination. Therefore, if any single complaint was to fail (perhaps because the claimant was working illegally), the claimant can still recover under the Equality Act 2010.

Further, under the Equality Act 2010, the claimant may be awarded aggravated and/or exemplary damages, in addition to awards for loss of earnings, injury to feelings and personal injury. Aggravated damages would be awarded where the claimant's feeling of injury is 'justifiably heightened by the manner in which, or motive for which the wrongful act was committed.'[2]. In the case of claimants' complaining of domestic servitude, this is taken to mean high-handed or oppressive conduct[3]. Exemplary damages are awarded to punish a wrongdoer. However, the circumstances in which an award would be made are narrowly defined[4]. The case of *Kuddus v Chief Constable of Leicester Constabulary*[5] suggests that exemplary damages can be awarded in respect of discrimination in employment.

1   Equality Act 2010, s 13 (direct race), s 18 (indirect race).
2   *Alexander v The Home Office* [1988] 2 All ER 118, [1988] 1 WLR 968.
3   In *Guilbena v Al Salawi & Another* 2205472 heard on 17 February 2010, Judge Etherington also considered the length of time the employer's conduct lasted, the failure to acknowledge the claimant's statements of disquiet and the maintenance of a state of servility as being reasons for an aggravated damages award.
4   Oppressive, arbitrary or unconstitutional action by Government servants; where defendants conduct has been calculated to make a profit which otherwise exceeds the compensation payable, statute specifically prescribes it.
5   [2001] UKHL 29, [2002] 2 AC 122, [2001] 3 All ER 193. See also *Fletcher v Ministry of Defence* (UKEAT/0044/09/JOJ) [2010] IRLR 25 where the ET awarded exemplary damages. The decision was overturned on appeal UKEAT/0044/09.

Time limits

17.17 A complaint for discrimination must be brought within three months (less a day) of the act of discrimination complained of. Usually it is argued that the worker has suffered an act of discrimination which has continued throughout the course of employment.

The Tribunal's discretion as to whether to accept a late complaint is significantly wider under discrimination legislation[1]. The Tribunal considers whether it is just and equitable to extend time and hear the claim[2]. Therefore, if the limitation has been missed and a reasonable explanation as to why is given, the tribunal is more likely to extend time.

A discrimination complaint is not brought to suggest that the employers had any particular antagonism to people of the claimant's race or nationality (many traffickers are of the same origins as their victims). But rather that they sought to take advantage of the worker because of their race, nationality etc and no British worker would have been treated in the same way.

Prior to 1 October 2010 a complaint of direct discrimination would be raised on the grounds of racial, ethnic and/or national origins – as discrimination against workers in a domestic household was (due to a loophole in the law) lawful on the grounds of nationality and colour[3]. This has now been remedied by the Equality Act 2010 and discrimination on the grounds of nationality in a private household is now unlawful[4].

Discrimination claims operate by comparing the treatment of the claimant with that of another individual from a different racial group, nationality etc. It is important to check whether there are any actual comparators to whom that the claimant can be compared: are there other workers in the household, either British or from the European Union, whose treatment was different, for example British domestic workers paid the NMW, or who do not have their passports removed from them? Equally, it is wise to check that there were no British workers treated as poorly as the claimant as this would undermine the assertion that the claimant's treatment was because they are not a British worker.

In the absence of an actual comparator, the Employment Tribunal will construct a hypothetical comparator. That is, had there been a British worker in the household, would they have been treated better? If the Tribunal is persuaded that the claimant's status as a migrant worker/victim of trafficking allowed the employer to offer poorer terms of employment than would have been given to a British worker – essentially to treat the claimant without due regard for British employment law norms – a race claim is likely to succeed.

The Tribunal should be referred to the Employment Appeal Tribunal case of *Mehmet v Aduma*[5]. This is authority for the legal proposition that if no British worker would have been treated the same way as the claimant, then the race claim should succeed.

If the Employment Tribunal does not accept this argument, it is also possible to argue that the claimant has suffered indirect race discrimination. In practice, this is rarely necessary – if the Employment Tribunal believes the worker's account and accepts that their migrant/trafficked status was linked to their mistreatment, the Employment Tribunal will find that they are a victim of direct race discrimination.

Indirect discrimination is complex and hard to argue in practice. It occurs when there is equal treatment of all employees, but the effect of a provision, criterion or practice imposed by the employer has an adverse impact disproportionately on one group. For example, the employer refuses to employ anyone without a beard: this provision will have a disproportionate adverse impact on women as opposed to men and, unless the employer can justify it (ie there is a good reason for the beard rule), the employer will be liable for indirect sex discrimination.

The big difference with an indirect claim is that one is not comparing a British and non-British worker (as in the direct claim). The comparison is between everyone of the claimant's nationality in the national workforce and everyone else.

An indirect discrimination complaint is, as has been described, by no means straightforward. It is necessary to argue that the employer had a practice of mistreating workers who are trafficked or on a migrant domestic worker visa, irrespective of their nationality. The crucial element is establishing that such a practice was more likely to impact on workers of the claimant's nationality. The difficulty is in establishing that people from the claimant's country (say, India) are more likely to be trafficked into domestic servitude, as opposed to the rest of the UK working population. The Tribunal would normally expect to see statistical evidence that the group the claimant belongs to is most likely to be trafficked. This may be easier in some cases, for instance, Nigeria where there has been considerable study[6].

An indirect claim should be pleaded in the alternative: detailed submissions are only appropriate where a Tribunal is particularly legalistic and concludes that it is the circumstances around being a victim of trafficking, eg including illegal employment, which is/are the cause of mistreatment. This can be a hard call to make in the heat of an Employment Tribunal hearing.

[1]   Equality Act 2010.
[2]   Equality Act 2010, s 123.
[3]   Race Relations Act 1976, s 4(3).
[4]   Equality Act 2010, s 9.
[5]   UKEAT/0573/06.
[6]   http://www.womenconsortiumofnigeria.org, http://www.who.int/en/www.antislavery.org.

Compensation under the Equality Act 2010

17.18 Where there has been a dismissal on the grounds of race, the Tribunal can award compensation for lost salary from the date of the dismissal going forwards. This is useful where there has been no unfair dismissal complaint under the Employment Rights Act 1996.

The Tribunal may also make an award for injury to feelings and it is in this way that the claimant can obtain compensation for verbal and physical abuse. The award is at the Tribunals discretion but made with reference to the Vento scale[1] the lower band of Vento sets compensation between £500–£6,000, the middle band £6,000–£16,000 and the upper band £16,000–£35,000 (these figures may be adjusted for inflation).

Where the claimant has suffered a discriminatory dismissal, any award should be within at least the middle band[2]. Where the claimant has suffered abuse or other extreme treatment the Tribunal should be asked to consider an award within the upper band. There is as yet no case law or legal authority from the Employment Tribunal or the Employment Appeal Tribunal which states that human trafficking in itself means that an award must be in the higher band so each case is judged on its merits.

Where the claimant has suffered actual injury (including mental injury or sexual assault) because of their treatment, then the Tribunal can also make an award for personal injury. In these cases, a medical report will be necessary to demonstrate the cause and any long term effect of the injury.

The Tribunal can also make an award of aggravated damages which is intended to deal with cases where the injury was inflicted by conduct which was high-handed, malicious, insulting or oppressive[3]. In most cases if the Tribunal has found that the claimant was kept in a state of domestic servitude, they will be minded to make such an award.

It should be emphasised that only under discrimination legislation can the Tribunal compensate for injury to feelings and personal injury[4].

[1]   *Vento v Chief Constable of West Yorkshire Police* [2002] EWCA Civ 1871, [2003] ICR 318, [2003] IRLR 102.
[2]   *Voith Turbo Ltd v Stowe* UKEAT/0675/04/CK.
[3]   *Scott v IRC* [2004] EWCA Civ 400, [2004] ICR 1410, [2004] IRLR 713.
[4]   Equality Act 2010, s 124(2).

OTHER DISCRIMINATION COMPLAINTS

17.19 Sex discrimination complaints work in the same fashion as race discrimination, except the claimant will compare themselves to a male comparator.

It is possible to plead all of the treatment suffered as both race and sex discrimination: it is then for the Tribunal to decide the reason for any less favourable treatment. However, this approach should be considered carefully as it can undermine the claimant's credibility and the strength of the legal submissions.

As a rule of thumb, it is better to bring a claim of discrimination under one strand only (usually race) unless there is a good reason for doing otherwise – for instance, where there has been specific sexual harassment or sexual assault (including rape) or if the claimant was not permitted to practice their religion[1].

Again compensation will be awarded at the Tribunals discretion but with reference to the Vento scale.

[1]   In which case discrimination on grounds of religion should be pleaded under the Equality Act 2010, s 10.

WORKING TIME REGULATIONS 1998

17.20 Many workers report that they are required to work excessive hours with no break either during the day or in the course of the week. Similarly, many are refused paid annual or indeed annual leave at all.

Time limits

17.21 Again complaints must be brought within three months (less a day) of any breach.

Although domestic workers are not entitled to the 48 hour working week, they are entitled to daily rest breaks, weekly rest (at least one day off per week) and paid annual leave[1].

Again, demonstrating failures in relation to the working time regulations will come down to the claimant's credibility and careful preparation of witness statements.

1   Working Time Regulations 1998, SI 1998/1833, reg 10 (daily rest), reg 11 (weekly rest), reg 12 (rest breaks), reg 13 (annual leave).

Compensation

17.22 As a Tribunal may award a sum they consider just and equitable, in practice awards are unpredictable. In practice, a few thousand pounds is the most common award.

In respect of annual leave, in practice, the claim is usually limited to the claimant's last year of employment which means compensation will be for no more than five weeks pay.

OTHER CLAIMS

17.23 There are a number of other minor claims, such as in relation to the failure to provide payslips, failure to provide a statement of terms and conditions etc. Compensation is relatively low, but can amount to several weeks' salary so are still to be considered.

It is possible to bring many of the claims discussed as a breach of contract complaint in both the civil courts and the Employment Tribunal but this is usually a very bad idea. In breach of contract claims (and no other Employment Tribunal claim) an employer has the right to bring a counterclaim. Domestic workers are particularly vulnerable to counterclaims – allegations of theft, outstanding loans and the like. Compensation for breach of contract is usually either minimal or recoverable under other heads in any event.

ENFORCEMENT OF TRIBUNAL AWARDS

17.24 The difficulty in enforcing compensation awards is not a problem specific to those bringing complaints of domestic servitude. Previously, Tribunal judgments did not have the status of a county court judgment, meaning that it would first have to be registered at the county court and enforcement measures such as the use of bailiffs, charging orders on property explored. In most circumstances the worker would have little or no help in doing this. On 6 April 2010 the services of the High Court Enforcement Officer were extended to the Employment Tribunal. This means that the judgment can be referred to the HCEO who will take steps to enforce the award.

Because of the problems associated with enforcement. Investigation of the employers' means and consideration of settlement should take place at an early stage. An employer entering into settlement discussions is likely to negotiate within their means, is likely to want the matter resolved and so more likely to make payment of the agreed sum.

CONCLUSION

17.25 The Employment Tribunal has jurisdiction to deal with a complaint which emanates from the act of trafficking a worker for the purposes of domestic servitude into the UK and results in the employer exploiting the victim as a worker in a domestic household. However, there can be resistance from some judges in the Employment Tribunal for what is perceived to be an inappropriate use of the Tribunal. Some see claims for redress for the harms associated with human trafficking as matter which is only to be dealt with by the criminal law. However, it is important to remember that the main means of coercion, deception or the abuse of a person's vulnerability in instances of trafficking for domestic servitude is the promise of payment in return for labour. As such, whilst the acts of trafficking and exploitation may amount to a breach of the criminal law, they will often also amount to a breach of employment legislation. There is no reason why a victim of trafficking who has worked for many months or even years with little or no pay, should not be compensated for their labours; no-one else in our society would be expected to work for free, and victims of trafficking in the 21st century are entitled to equality before the law.

18

COMPENSATION CLAIMS BY VICTIMS OF TRAFFICKING UNDER THE CRIMINAL INJURIES COMPENSATION SCHEME

Giles Hutt and Harriet Dykes

INTRODUCTION

18.1 This chapter explains how victims of trafficking for the purpose of sexual exploitation ('sex trafficking') may in certain circumstances obtain Government compensation under the Criminal Injuries Compensation Scheme 2008 ('the Scheme')[1]. It sets out the main features of the Scheme insofar as they are relevant to trafficking, and then summarises briefly the principal applications that the authors have handled: their basic facts, key issues that arose, the outcome of each application, and any reasons given for their decision by the Criminal Injuries Compensation Authority ('CICA'), which administers the Scheme, or by the First-tier Tribunal of the Tribunals Service ('the Tribunal')[2], which hears appeals. The chapter ends by drawing conclusions from these and other (non-trafficking) applications that should assist future applicants and their professional advisers.

To protect their identity, applicants' names have been withheld, as have all but the essential details of their cases. Cross references are to paragraph and page numbers of the Scheme unless otherwise stated[3].

Although this chapter covers claims for statutory compensation for harm associated with sex trafficking, much of what it says applies equally to claims in respect of trafficking for forced labour/domestic servitude[4]. In both cases compensation is not offered under the Scheme for the basic fact of having been exploited, although it may be available in respect of specific injuries suffered (see paras **18.10** and **18.14** below)[5].

---

[1]   This is not new: it supersedes the similar criminal injury compensation schemes of 1996 and 2001. The Scheme can be accessed on the Ministry of Justice website at: http://www.justice. gov.uk/downloads/guidance/courts-and-tribunals/tribunals/criminal-injuries-compensation/Cr iminal%20Injuries%20Compensation%20Scheme%202008.pdf.

[2]   The Tribunal is a new statutory body established by the Tribunals, Courts and Enforcement Act 2007 (Criminal Injuries Compensation), but it has essentially the same form and function as its predecessor, the Criminal Injuries Compensation Appeal Panel (CICAP).

³ For readers' convenience, references are to the Scheme even where applications were in fact made under an earlier compensation scheme.
⁴ Although we are not aware of any such claims having been made under the Scheme to date.
⁵ Injuries may be physical or mental, or take the form of a disease (paragraph 9). However, an applicant who has been exploited in the domestic context may have difficulty obtaining compensation under the Scheme if her injury is exclusively mental, and not linked to a sexual offence, because the Scheme generally requires her to have been 'put in reasonable fear of immediate physical harm to . . . her own person' for compensation to be made available to her (paragraph 9(a)).

THE SCHEME

18.2 The Scheme offers limited compensation to individuals of any nationality who have suffered injury as a direct result of a crime committed in Great Britain.

History

18.3 The first British criminal injuries compensation scheme was set up in 1964 and initially administered by CICA's predecessor, the Criminal Injuries Compensation Board. The UK Government claims that 'this makes the British system of Criminal Injuries Compensation the oldest in the world'[1]. Originally compensation claims were assessed in the same way that personal injury claims were dealt with in the civil courts. However, in 1996 a tariff of injuries was introduced (see below), fixing compensation payments for each injury.

Since then, the compensation system has been revised twice[2]. When the current Scheme was introduced in 2008, it was hoped that it would make explicit provision for victims of sex (and other kinds of human) trafficking: this was, for example, the explicit recommendation of the UK Parliament's Joint Committee on Human Rights in their 26th Report of 2006:

> 'We consider that, for the avoidance of doubt, the simplest way for the Government to meet obligations relating to the provision of compensation to trafficking victims would be to clarify the Criminal Injuries Compensation Scheme rules as to the entitlement of trafficking victims to claim under the Scheme. This could be dealt with as part of the current review of the Scheme.'[3]

However, the clarification sought by the Committee was not forthcoming, and the Scheme is in many respects an imperfect means of compensating victims of trafficking (see para **18.14** below). As the Office for Democratic Institutions and Human Rights' report on Compensation for Trafficked and Exploited Persons in the OSCE Region (2008) put it:

> 'The existence of a generous state-funded scheme that pays both material and moral damages is positive. It has also demonstrated some flexibility in terms of the types of damages paid to trafficked victims. Its limitations, however, present problems for trafficking victims, especially regarding restrictive eligibility criteria and the limited categories and amounts of damages awarded.'[4]

Whether the Government will remedy this problem, given its increasing obligations towards victims of trafficking[5], remains to be seen.

¹ http://www.justice.gov.uk/guidance/compensation-schemes/cica/information-if-you-applied-b efore-3-november-2008.htm.

2   See para **18.1**, note 1.
3   Recommendation 33. See http://www.publications.parliament.uk/pa/jt200506/jtselect/jtrights /245/24502.htm.
4   Paragraph 5.7.3 of the report.
5   For example, following the entry into force in the UK on 1 April 2009 of the Council of Europe Convention on Action against Trafficking in Human Beings, which includes the right to compensation under Article 15 and under the EU's new Directive on Human Trafficking (2011/36/EU) which the UK Government declared, in March 2011, that it would opt into.

Basic criteria

18.4 For an application for statutory compensation to be successful, it is necessary to show among other things that three conditions are met.

Firstly, the injury must be a 'criminal injury' as defined in paragraphs 8 and 9 of the Scheme. For present purposes, this means that the injury must be caused by a 'crime of violence', which excludes, for example, the statutory rape of a child where she has given 'real' consent to sexual intercourse and cannot be considered a true 'victim'[1]. The 'criminal injury' may be a physical injury or (subject to certain conditions[2]) a mental injury or a disease.

Second, the injury must have been sustained in Great Britain, whether or not the applicant was resident here[3]. (In principle, at least, other countries' schemes offer compensation for injuries sustained abroad. CICA can provide information about this).

Third, the crime must generally match one of the categories of injury set out in the tariff ('the Tariff') appended to the Scheme.

1   The fact that she is below the age of consent under criminal law is irrelevant. So too is the fact that children cannot consent to trafficking under the Council of Europe Convention on Action against Trafficking in Human Beings, Article 4(c). Re consent generally, see the Court of Appeal's decisions in *R v Criminal Injuries Compensation Appeals ex parte August and R v Criminal Injuries Compensation Appeals ex parte Brown* [2000] EWCA Civ 331 and subsequent case law. See also paragraph **18.14** below re mental injury arising from rape and other sexual offences.
2   Set out in paragraph 9.
3   Where an applicant has entered the country illegally, this may be taken into account by CICA and/or the Tribunal when deciding whether or not to reduce or withhold an award under paragraphs 13(1)(d) or (e). These refer to the applicant's conduct and 'character as shown by his or her criminal convictions' – see paragraph **18.6** below. However, in applications relating to sex trafficking it is often possible to argue that these provisions are irrelevant since the applicant did not know when entering the country that she was doing so illegally, and later had no choice as to whether to leave or remain.

Levels of compensation and heads of claim

18.5 The level of compensation offered is determined by the Tariff, a 'Level 1' injury (the lowest) attracting an award of £1,000, and a 'Level 25' injury (the highest) an award of £250,000. Compensation may be claimed for up to three injuries arising from the same crime. However, for the less severe injuries only a percentage of the Tariff sum may be awarded: 30% of the Tariff sum for the second-most severe injury, and 15% of the Tariff sum for the third[1].

Additional compensation is available where the applicant has lost earnings as a result of the injury, or where 'special expenses' are incurred[2]. (The latter may include private health treatment where 'reasonable', adaptations for the disabled, the cost of transport to hospital appointments, etc[3]). One further ground for obtaining additional compensation, of particular relevance to trafficking claims, is the applicant having become pregnant or having contracted a sexually transmitted disease as a result of a sexual offence[4]. (For more details, see para **18.10** below).

A cap operates to limit overall compensation under the Scheme to £500,000[5].

1   Paragraph 27.
2   Paragraphs 30–36.
3   Paragraph 35. Private health treatment must not only be reasonable in itself, but obtained at reasonable cost (paragraph 35(1)(c)).
4   The Tariff at pages 35 and 36.
5   Paragraph 24.

Reducing and withholding compensation

18.6 Compensation that is otherwise available may be reduced or withheld altogether if an applicant's relevant 'actions, conduct [or] character' are open to criticism[1]. The underlying principle here is that it is not appropriate for public money to be handed out to individuals who fail, for example, 'to take, without delay, all reasonable steps' to inform the police or other 'appropriate' body of all the circumstances of their injury; who do not help bring the assailant to justice; or who fail to assist fully with the application process itself[2]. But the Scheme gives CICA (or the Tribunal, if the application goes to appeal) surprisingly wide discretion to reduce or refuse compensation on less specific grounds too[3]. This can make the outcome of trafficking and other atypical applications difficult to predict (see para **18.14** below).

1   Paragraphs 13–17. In principle unspent criminal convictions are taken into account here, but in practice CICA does not appear to withhold or reduce awards where convictions are unrelated to the application, provided a satisfactory explanation is given of the relevant circumstances.
2   Paragraph 13(1).
3   See, for example, the references in paragraph 13(1)(d) to the applicant's 'conduct .. before, during or after the incident' making it 'inappropriate that a full award or any award at all be made'.

Children

18.7 It is not necessary for the applicant to be an adult, either when making the application[1] or when the injury was suffered. Indeed, the Tariff makes special provision for injuries suffered by applicants when they were a child. However, applications by children are especially problematic where the issue of consent arises, in particular because of the need to establish that the claim arises from a 'crime of violence'.

In addition, practical problems arise where children are in the care of social services, as many child victims of trafficking are, having been identified through police operations. In these cases CICA 'expect the local authority to apply for compensation if they have parental responsibility.'[2] This means in effect that legal representatives need to be instructed by social services on behalf of a minor. In practical terms it can be very difficult to secure the appropriate authority from social services. Similarly, it is difficult in practice to secure the records needed to show all the circumstances of child's case.

As noted above, compensation may be reduced or withheld altogether if the victim cannot show that she has reported the circumstances of her injury to the police or other appropriate body. In the case of a child or young person, CICA may well not regard the victim's statement and a report to social services or the immigration services as sufficient for these purposes.

[1] Technically a guardian with parental responsibility makes the application on behalf of the child-victim.
[2] Guide to the Criminal Injuries Compensation Scheme 2008 at section 3, paragraph 19.

Practicalities

18.8 In principle, applications should be received as soon as possible after the incident giving rise to the injury, and within two years of the date of the incident in any event. However, this rule is flexible where 'it would not have been reasonable' to expect the applicant to meet the two year deadline, provided it is still practicable for the application to be considered[1].

Applications should be made on the relevant form, which together with the Scheme and more general guidance is available on the Ministry of Justice's website at http://www.justice.gov.uk/guidance/courts-and-tribunals/tribunals/criminal-injuries-compensation/. If an applicant indicates on the form that a claim will be made for loss of earnings and/or special expenses, she will be sent supplemental forms for these purposes. The supplemental forms must be submitted together with full supporting documentation (pay slips, expense receipts, etc). Legal aid is currently available for legal advice to assist victims of crime in making applications under the Scheme; however, this is expected to be withdrawn.

[1] Paragraph 18. The Scheme also includes a mechanism for challenging a decision to refuse an application because it is out of time – see paragraphs 58–60.

Review and appeal process

18.9 Disappointed applicants may seek a 'review' (essentially an on-paper reconsideration of the application conducted by CICA itself) and, if they are still dissatisfied, an 'appeal' (an appeal hearing before the Tribunal, a panel normally consisting of a lawyer, a medical professional and a lay member).

Interim payments are available where it is clear that a substantial sum will be awarded in any event[1], and these can be very useful, in particular, where an applicant's income has been adversely affected by her injury and she would not otherwise be able to afford to wait for the review and appeal procedure to take its course[2].

Decisions of the Tribunal (ie the outcome of an appeal) can be re-opened only in limited circumstances: in general where there has been a 'material change in the victim's medical condition [such] that injustice would occur if the original assessment of compensation were allowed to stand', or where 'the victim has since died as a result of the injury'. However, decisions more than two years old will not normally be re-opened, even where one of these conditions is satisfied[3]. In addition, it may be possible for an appellant to obtain a judicial review of a Tribunal decision where there has been an error of law.

[1] Paragraph 51 does not say this in terms, instead referring to payments being made 'where a claims officer considers this appropriate', but this is the effect of that wording. Generally it is not possible to obtain an interim payment in respect of loss of earnings, since the extent to which compensation will be provided for these is always open to question and is dependent on the relevant supporting documentation being submitted and carefully evaluated by CICA or the Tribunal.

[2] Where a substantial interim payment is not available, the applicant wants early 'closure', or she simply feels oppressed by the ongoing proceedings, she may be tempted to accept an inadequate award which could be increased on review or appeal.

[3] Paragraphs 56 and 57.

CLAIMING IN TRAFFICKING CASES

18.10 In trafficking cases the precise injury for which compensation may be provided will depend on the circumstances of the case. The applicant and her advisors must review all the injuries listed in the Tariff and identify which injuries, if any, she has suffered. These may include:

(a) **Rape**

It may be that a victim has been raped by the person or persons who trafficked her into the country or by their associates within the UK (together 'the traffickers'). In these circumstances it can be relatively straightforward to obtain compensation under the Scheme in respect of that rape, provided of course that the victim is in a position to establish that the rape(s) took place (as in the cases of A and B below). Where a victim was not raped by her traffickers, but was coerced into working as a prostitute in Great Britain, then it is arguable that she has been raped by her clients since the sexual acts in question were not truly consensual. However, this argument is not readily accepted by CICA (see D's and E's cases, below).

On the other hand, the Tribunal seems more willing than CICA to adopt an imaginative approach, sometimes departing altogether from the plain meaning of the Tariff definitions of sexual offences – see in particular the case of F, where it found that the applicant had been as good as raped since her trafficker had continuously held or monitored her, as well as having threatened to kill her family (see para **18.12** below).

Rape, described by the Scheme as 'non-consensual penile penetration of the vagina and/or anus and/or mouth', is a level 13–17 injury, attracting compensation of between £11,000 and £22,000, depending on the circumstances of the rape and its effects, both physical and mental[1].

(b) **Sexual assault**

Where a non-consensual sexual act does not amount to rape, as defined above, it may nevertheless qualify as a lesser form of sexual offence, ie a 'sexual assault', which is defined in Tariff in a number of ways[2]. As with rape, it may be possible to show that the traffickers sexually assaulted the applicant (literally or otherwise), or that the trafficker's clients sexually assaulted her while she was forced to work as a prostitute.

Sexual assault attracts compensation of between £1,000 and £22,000, depending again on the circumstances of the assault and its effects, both physical and mental[3].

(c) **Pregnancy and sexually transmitted disease**

As already mentioned, a victim of a sexual offence may be able to obtain further compensation under the Scheme if she became pregnant or contracted a sexually transmitted disease as a result. The level of additional compensation under these heads ranges from £5,500 to £22,000. The higher figure is reserved for applicants who have contracted HIV, or Hepatitis B or C, whilst a victim who contracts a lesser disease such as gonorrhoea, for example, and can expect a 'substantial recovery', will receive additional compensation of £5,500. However, in all cases compensation awarded under this head is not subject to the percentage deductions for multiple injuries referred to at paragraph **18.5** above, so is treated similarly to awards for loss of earnings and special expenses, ie, as compensation that is not awarded independently but as a supplemental sum in addition to what is offered for the (up to three) injuries themselves[4].

(d) **Physical abuse etc**

Where a victim of trafficking has not been raped or sexually assaulted, or at any rate cannot demonstrate that she has been attacked in this way, it may still be possible to show that she was physically abused by her traffickers, received 'minor injuries', or suffered one of the specific physical injuries listed in the Tariff, eg, broken bones, burns, etc.

(e) **Mental Injury and temporary mental anxiety**

In general, the Scheme treats 'mental injury' and 'temporary mental anxiety' as separate heads of claim, subject to certain conditions[5]. However, where mental injury is caused by rape or some other sexual offence, and it has been confirmed as 'permanently disabling' (see below), it is treated not as a separate injury but as one of the circumstances that determine the precise level of compensation available for those injuries[6]. A distinction is made in all cases between degrees of mental injury and/or its duration, but it must at a minimum be 'disabling', and if compensation is to be available above the basic £1,000 level (for 'temporary mental anxiety'[7]) it must also be diagnosed by a psychiatrist or clinical psychologist – so a report from a counsellor or psychotherapist, for example, will be of no use as support for an applicant's claim unless they happen to be unusually well-qualified (see para **18.14** below). Notes to the Tariff explain that:

> 'Mental illness includes conditions attributed to post-traumatic stress disorder, depression and similar generic terms within which there may be: (a) such psychological symptoms as anxiety, tension, insomnia, irritability, loss of confidence, agoraphobia and preoccupation with thoughts of guilt or self-harm; and (b) related physical symptoms such as alopecia, asthma, eczema, enuresis and psoriasis.'[8]

> 'Mental anxiety or a mental illness is disabling if it significantly impairs a person's functioning in some important aspect of her/his life, eg impaired

327

> work or school performance or significant adverse effects on social relation-
> ships or sexual dysfunction.'[9]

It is not currently possible to obtain compensation under the Scheme for trafficking as such. The Tariff does not provide for it, and although paragraph 28 of the Scheme gives CICA the power (after consulting with the Tribunal) to ask the Secretary of State to add new injuries to the Tariff, and it has been asked to do this by the authors on more than one occasion, CICA has consistently refused to make such a request in relation to trafficking. Where they have given their reasons, CICA and the Tribunal have made it clear that they understand 'trafficking' to refer to the circumstances of an injury rather than an injury as such. In any event the relevant act or acts essentially amount to tricking the victim, they argue, and this typically occurs abroad, so falls outside the scope of the Scheme.

This state of affairs is unsatisfactory insofar as it leaves applicants who are not demonstrably the victim of serious injuries such as rape, sexual assault and so on with slender or non-existent grounds for bringing a compensation claim under the Scheme. However, where specific injuries of this kind have been inflicted, the absence of trafficking *per se* as a head of claim may make relatively little difference to the overall compensation offered to the victim, given the percentage reductions made to awards for second and third injuries (see para **18.5** above).[10]

In any event, the largest sums of money are often awarded not for injuries as such, however these are defined, but in response to claims for loss of earnings (see for example the cases of A and B below). These claims, like those for 'special expenses', cannot be made independently, but have to 'piggy-back' on claims for the injuries which caused them. They are also difficult to present effectively, so that a realistic level of compensation is obtained. CICA naturally requires full documentation of past earnings (see para **18.14** below), and complicated arguments may have to be advanced regarding lost earning prospects: what the applicant would have earned were it not for the injury, taking into account wage inflation, promotions, the likely gaining of qualifications, and so on. This is an area in which applicants are least able to fend for themselves, even if their English is good and they are robust emotionally, neither of which is likely to be the case in a trafficking application. Consequently it is in relation to applications for loss of earnings that applicants are most in need of help from a solicitor or other claims professional. Ultimately, CICA or the Tribunal will award a sum based on specific formulae set out in the Scheme[11], or where it is not practicable to apply these, offer a lump sum in lieu[12].

---

[1] The Tariff at page 34. Different levels of compensation are available where the victim was a minor under the age of 18 at the time of the attack – see pages 34 and 35. The term 'rape' does not in fact appear in the Scheme, but is used here for convenience.

[2] Page 34. Different levels of compensation are available where the victim was a minor under the age of 18 at the time of the attack – see pages 34 and 35.

[3] The Tariff at page 34. Different levels of compensation are available where the victim was a minor under the age of 18 at the time of the attack – see pages 34 and 35.

[4] The Tariff at pages 35 and 36.

[5] Paragraph 9 and the Tariff at page 32. See also note 5 at page 30.

[6] Page 34. An applicant cannot obtain compensation for both a sexual offence and a resulting mental injury. If the mental injury is so serious that it attracts a higher level of compensation than the sexual offence itself (taking into account the mental element), then compensation is available for the mental injury alone – see note 5 at page 30.

⁷ Confirmed by a registered medical practitioner, usually the applicant's GP.
⁸ Note 8.
⁹ Note 11.
¹⁰ This assumes that any lost earnings or special expenses claimed can be attributed to a specific injury recognised by the Tariff rather than to the trafficking or loss of liberty in general – see the cases of A and B, below, in which this hurdle was overcome.
¹¹ Paragraphs 30–34 and Tables A–C of the Scheme.
¹² Paragraph 33.

KEY HOGAN LOVELLS CASES

Rape where trafficker convicted

18.11 The first trafficking claims handled by the authors, and it appears the first of this kind to be brought successfully under the Scheme or its predecessors, were made in 2007 by two sisters, A and B, who had been trafficked into the UK at the ages of 18 and 16 in 2002/03. They were then forced into prostitution and repeatedly raped and beaten by their traffickers.

A and B applied for compensation for a pattern of repeated rape ('non-consensual vaginal and/or anal intercourse'[1]) over a period exceeding three years in A's case, and up to three years in B's. They also sought compensation for the trafficking itself (achieved by a combination of deception and threats of violence), false imprisonment, forced prostitution and loss of earnings. The claims for trafficking, false imprisonment and forced prostitution were rejected, apparently for the reasons referred to in para **18.10** above, although CICA did not explain its reasoning and the sisters did not choose to press the point by seeking a review of its initial decision. They were however successful in their claims for rape and loss of earnings.

Apart from the fact that these were the first claims to succeed in this context, they are chiefly of interest because of the sums that were awarded to the applicants in respect of loss of earnings. As already mentioned, claims under this head can sometimes result in compensation that exceeds the money awarded in respect of the injuries themselves, and that proved to be the case here: A and B's awards for rape were £22,000 and £16,500 respectively, and their awards for loss of earnings were £40,000 and £20,000. Since neither A nor B had given up a job before they came to the UK, it was not possible to use their previous salaries as the starting point for calculations-the usual approach adopted by CICA. However, it accepted that the applicants had missed out on substantial earnings during the periods in question and should be awarded discretionary lump sums under paragraph 23 of the Scheme (a provision intended to be used only in exceptional circumstances). Crucially, CICA was also persuaded to take a broad brush approach to causation. Had it been more critical of A and B's claims, it may have rejected the applications for loss of earnings on the basis that these resulted from the trafficking generally, that is to say the applicants' loss of liberty, rather than from injuries specified in the Tariff, and so fell outside the scope of the Scheme. But without saying so in terms, CICA was content to view the losses as resulting from the 'pattern of repeated incidents'[2], ie rapes, and awarded compensation accordingly.

¹ The wording of the 2001 scheme, which was then in force.
² The language of the 2001 scheme that governed the applications of A and B.

Rape where trafficker not convicted

18.12 In the cases of A and B, and a subsequent case with similar facts involving a minor, C, it was relatively easy to obtain compensation under the Scheme because the traffickers were convicted of rape. However, in the authors' fourth case, brought in July 2008, it proved more difficult to obtain an award for the applicant (D) because her trafficker had been convicted only of lesser offences (trafficking and controlling prostitution), although charges of rape had been included on the indictment and the Scheme is careful to emphasise that 'it is not necessary for an assailant to have been convicted of a criminal offence in connection with the injury'[1]. It was also argued that for the purposes of the Scheme, if not the criminal law, D had been raped by her trafficker's clients while working as a prostitute, since the work was forced upon her. However, D's application was undermined by her having previously made a false allegation of rape to the police, though without naming an attacker (see para **18.6** above re the reduction or withholding of compensation). For all these reasons the application was refused at first instance.

On review CICA took a more liberal approach, however, awarding D £16,500 for repeated rape ('non-consensual vaginal and/or anal intercourse' –'pattern of repeated incidents over a period of up to three years'[2]) and a further £600 (30% of £2,000) for physical abuse. CICA did not explain the reasons for its volte face, so it is not known, for example, whether it accepted the authors' argument that D was raped by the clients as well as by her trafficker[3]. However, in a subsequent case handled by the authors, that of E, CICA did appear to accept this argument, that is to say it made an award of £18,480 seemingly on this basis[4] – but again, without giving full reasons.

CICA is not always predictable, however, and in F's case, which followed E's and involved broadly similar facts, the applicant failed to obtain an offer of compensation until the Tribunal accepted that she had been as good as raped by being continuously held or monitored by her trafficker and intimidated by threats to kill family members in her home country. On this basis she was awarded £16,500, which is the level of compensation given to victims of repeated rape over a period of up to three years.

---

[1] Paragraph 10.
[2] The language of the 2001 scheme that governed D's application.
[3] It was clear, though, that CICA finally considered the false allegation of rape to be irrelevant to D's claim, ie that it did not justify their reducing or withholding compensation under paragraph 13.
[4] £16,500 for rape over a period of up to three years, and £1,980 (30% of £6,600) for a severe form of sexual assault over the same period.

Failure to inform the police

18.13 A recurrent theme in sex trafficking compensation applications is the reluctance of victims to report their injuries promptly to the police, which allows CICA and the Tribunal to reduce or withhold compensation pursuant to paragraph 13 (see paragraph **18.6** above).

In G's case the applicant did in fact make a statement to the Serious Organised Crime Agency ('SOCA') shortly after escaping her traffickers, arguably satisfying the wording of paragraph 13(1)(a): 'the applicant [is obliged] to take, without delay, all reasonable steps to inform the police, or other body or person considered by the Authority to be appropriate for the purpose, of the circumstances giving rise to the injury'. However, she said to SOCA that she did not wish the matter to be reported to the police and asked that no further action be taken. This was partly because she feared reprisals, and partly because she was mistrustful of police generally, having been raped by a policeman in a third country and immediately arrested by him for illegal prostitution. As a result, there was no crime reference number allocated to the report to SOCA. Nevertheless, CICA accepted that G's statement to SOCA was sufficient to satisfy the reporting obligation set out in paragraph 13(1)(a), but found that G had still failed to comply with paragraph 13(1)(b), which obliges an applicant to 'co-operate with the police or other authority in attempting to bring the assailant to justice'. The Tribunal left open the question of whether a subsequent report to the police would be sufficient to satisfy paragraph 13(1)(b).

In H's case compensation was denied to the applicant by CICA, and then the Tribunal, partly because she had been in contact with the police on several occasions while working as a prostitute, and had assisted them on at least one occasion, but had never told them during this period that she had been trafficked or was forced to work as a prostitute. This led the Tribunal to infer that, once in the UK, she had agreed to work as a prostitute in preference to returning to her home country. H's case is interesting, in addition, because it shows how traffickers use different means to 'groom' their victims or otherwise pressure them into prostitution. Some traffickers use actual or threatened violence against the trafficked person; others threaten the victim's family-for example, in E's case her trafficker threatened to harm the young daughter she had left behind in her home country. H, who was 16 years old and therefore a minor at the time she entered the UK, claimed that her traffickers 'groomed' her by forcing her to swear a traditional African 'juju' oath which obliged her to work as a prostitute. If she broke the oath, or even reported her circumstances to the police, she believed that her 'juju' would physically harm or even kill her. In the event, neither CICA nor the Tribunal accepted this explanation, partly because it appeared inconsistent with H's willingness to make a full statement to an immigration officer that was 'full and graphic' in its description of her experiences but nevertheless contained no reference to the supposed oath[1].

---

[1]   Whether or not the Tribunal was correct in rejecting H's appeal, there is a wealth of evidence that can be adduced in similar cases regarding the impact of 'juju' oaths generally and their role in inhibiting victims of trafficking, in particular, from disclosing their circumstances to the authorities.

CONCLUSIONS

18.14 Compensation is not available under the Scheme for trafficking as such, or for the false imprisonment that it typically entails. However, CICA and the Tribunal are sometimes willing to interpret the Scheme creatively so that victims' experiences of sex trafficking are understood to come within the

Tariff's definitions of rape, even where it is far from clear that the acts in question were strictly speaking non-consensual (E's case at paragraph **18.12** above) or amounted to any form of sexual contact with the trafficker (see F's case at para **18.12** above). CICA and the Tribunal may also be willing to gloss over some difficult issues of causation when awarding compensation for loss of earnings (see the cases of A and B at para **18.11** above). This is encouraging. However, CICA and Tribunal decisions are not always explained in full, and they frequently appear inconsistent. Applications are also bound to be problematic for a number of obvious (and less obvious) reasons.

First and foremost, the applicant is likely to have limited command of the English language. Even for a native English speaker, professional assistance may be needed to fill out CICA's forms correctly and is always valuable when an applicant is preparing for an appeal hearing. Appeals are particularly difficult for an applicant to prepare for because the Tribunal Procedure Rules[1] have to be followed, and the Tribunal's Practice Statements/Guidance make detailed demands regarding, for example, the kind of evidence to be adduced in respect of financial loss[2].

Secondly, the facts of a trafficking case are invariably complicated and often difficult to match with the wording of the Tariff. Therefore applications are likely to be wholly or partly rejected at first instance and on review, and to go to appeal. This is inherently unsatisfactory, mainly because it draws out the application procedure by several months, but also because the applicant is obliged on review and appeal to prove her case all over again – it is not possible to question just one element of a CICA decision and leave the rest of the decision (and monies awarded) untouched. As a consequence it is quite possible, though probably rare, for CICA or the Tribunal to reduce on appeal the sum initially offered to an applicant. In other words, the review/appeal process cuts both ways, and is not risk-free for the victim.

In addition to these basic considerations, victims of trafficking may have difficulty giving a good account of themselves at an appeal hearing, and be extremely reluctant to participate in the hearing at all. This is because their experiences are likely to be fresh in their memories and still very painful to recall, let alone to describe to strangers in the formal context of an appeal hearing. Where, as is so often the case, the trafficking victim is suffering from a trauma-related illness, the hearing is not only painful but risks re-traumatising her in the medical sense.

Further, any claim for loss of earnings has to be supported where possible by documentation relating to the applicant's previous employment in her home country. (This obviously does not apply if the victim is a minor or for some other reason has not worked before being trafficked). Documentation of the kind required (pay slips, bank statements, and so on) may not exist in the victim's home country, and where it does exist, may be impossible to obtain.

Different kinds of difficulties may be encountered when a victim tries to claim for mental injury, either as a free-standing injury or as a factor in rape or sexual assault. The Scheme recognises both temporary and longer term mental injury, but for the latter it specifically requires a diagnosis by a psychiatrist or clinical psychologist (see para **18.10** above). However, victims have little or no control over whether they are referred to a doctor of this kind, and if so, which doctor they see and how their condition is subsequently treated. In practice, the victim's GP is much more likely to refer a victim to a therapist instead. Without funds, the victim is then reliant on the psychiatrist or clinical psychologist chosen and paid by CICA[3]. He or she will generally see the victim only once; the events described by the applicant may well have taken place some years before; and the doctor will of course be mindful of the victim's motivation in seeking a medical opinion.

Practitioners need to be aware that even if they can arrange a privately funded assessment, the resulting report may not be particularly helpful. The doctor might not be able to confirm, for example, that the victim's mental condition amounts to 'disabling mental illness' for the purposes of the Scheme, or that it was caused (entirely or at all) by the 'crime of violence' described in the application form. It is true that a doctor with extensive experience of sex trafficking victims will be more attuned than others to the trauma an applicant has experienced, and therefore more likely to submit a helpful report to CICA; however, even then there may be a reluctance to make a decisive finding in favour of the victim.

Medical practitioners may also understate the likely duration of trafficking-related mental illness, partly because of a tendency to make optimistic assumptions as to the efficacy of the treatment (usually Cognitive Behavioural Therapy) that is recommended. This can severely limit the amount of compensation awarded under the Scheme, particularly if an application is made for loss of future earnings and the Tribunal needs to know when the applicant is likely to recover sufficiently to resume full time work. Doctors' optimism is understandable given that a negative prognosis may actually hinder a patient's recovery – it can be a self-fulfilling prophecy – but it unfortunately deprives applicants of the full statutory compensation to which they are entitled. In theory it is possible, of course, to re-open cases after a Tribunal has made its decision (see para **18.9** above), but the basis for that should be an injury that materially changes over time, not one which does not improve when the medical evidence that was originally submitted indicated that it would substantially improve or heal by a certain date.

In any case, it can be difficult to claim for mental injury in trafficking cases because the Scheme explicitly provides that compensation is not available for mental injury caused by rape or sexual assault where the applicant is 'the non-consenting victim of that offence (which does not include a victim who consented in fact but was deemed in law not to have consented)', ie, compensation for mental injury will be withheld where the applicant agreed to the sexual act in question, regardless of whether or not she could give consent under the criminal law and irrespective also of whether the consent was 'real' and the applicant a true 'victim' (see para **18.4** above)[4]. The practical effect of the provision appears to be that even the very youngest of children could be denied full compensation if there is any evidence to suggest they complied with their abuse through fear or a lack of understanding, for example, or if they are actively 'groomed' by their attacker. The problem is exacerbated in trafficking cases where the age of a young applicant is disputed.

More broadly, the issue of consent is often expressly or impliedly at the heart of compensation decisions in trafficking cases, even where mental injury is not the focus of attention. This is because of the need to establish that the crime which is the basis of the claim is a 'crime of violence' (see para **18.4** above). In practice this issue does not appear to concern the Tribunal very much in claims arising from domestic sexual abuse. In that context it is often ready to assume that the victim withheld consent, even if there is no evidence to suggest this. In trafficking cases, though, the Tribunal typically adopts a stricter approach, being suspicious that the applicant consented to working in the sex industry and is therefore not a true 'victim'.

The Tribunal's approach here is clearly demonstrated in the different outcomes of F's and H's applications. In F's case the Tribunal was convinced that, through a mixture of direct control and threats against her family, she had effectively been forced to work as a prostitute; therefore compensation was awarded. In H's case, on the other hand, the Tribunal thought it more likely than not that the applicant had agreed to work as a prostitute in preference to returning to her home country, and so compensation was denied even though she was only 16 years old when trafficked into the UK (see para **18.13** above). The case starkly illustrates how far the Scheme falls short of fulfilling the UK Government's obligations to victims of trafficking under the Council of Europe Convention on Action against Trafficking in Human Beings 2005, Article 15 (3) and (4)[5], and in particular to child-victims, who as a general legal principle cannot be said to consent to their trafficking or exploitation.

Finally, as the cases of G and H show, victims are likely to have difficulty justifying their actions during and after the trafficking, and may have their awards reduced or (more often) withheld altogether under paragraph 13 of the Scheme, whatever their prima facie entitlement to compensation. Needless to say, a victim deciding how much to tell (or not to tell) the police is unlikely to understand the impact this will have on any subsequent claim for statutory compensation. Indeed she will almost certainly be ignorant of the fact that compensation is available. Even if the victim were aware of the Scheme and its requirement that victims co-operate fully with the police from the outset, the chances are that she would be unable to bring herself to disclose enough about her trafficking history to enable the police to launch a criminal investigation: her mental state and general vulnerability after escaping from her traffickers would not allow it. Apart from anything else, most victims of trafficking are fearful of approaching the authorities in case they are found to have illegal immigration status and are forcibly removed to their home countries. This in turn can lead to their being located by their traffickers and exploited again.

In addition to their frequent reluctance or inability to co-operate fully with the authorities, victims of trafficking are often used as instruments of criminal activity. For example they may find themselves caught up in or coerced to perform illegal activities such as cultivation of cannabis, credit card fraud or petty crime. In these situations, victims at first sight appear far from blameless, and given the wide discretion given to the Authority by paragraph 13(1)(d) of the Scheme to consider an applicant's conduct generally (see para **18.6** above), the prospects of success of a claim for compensation are so low that victims are effectively left without a remedy. For this reason the Scheme, as currently administered, arguably fails to meet the obligations of the State expressed in the Council of Europe Convention on Action against Trafficking in Human Beings.

All these considerations underline the need for a statutory scheme in the UK that recognises trafficking as a head of claim and does not make unrealistic demands of victims as a precondition of awarding them full compensation.

1 Tribunal Procedure (First-tier Tribunal) (Social Entitlement Chamber) Rules 2008, SI 2008/2685.
2 Practice Guidance CI-1.
3 Assuming the Tribunal is willing to direct CICA to pay for an assessment by a psychiatrist or clinical psychologist.
4 Paragraph 9(c). The meaning of this provision is not entirely clear: arguably it goes further and prevents the award of *any* compensation (not just for mental injury) in respect of a sexual offence to which the applicant has consented 'in fact' - see Clare Padley and Laura Begley, *Criminal Injuries Compensation Claims* (2005), The Law Society at paragraph 4.9.
5 Article 15 provides for the right to compensation and legal redress. Under Article 15(3): 'Each Party shall provide, in its internal law, for the right of victims to compensation from the perpetrators.' Under Article 15(4): 'Each Party shall adopt such legislative or other measures as may be necessary to guarantee compensation for victims in accordance with the conditions under its internal law, for instance through the establishment of a fund for victim compensation or measures or programmes aimed at social assistance and social integration of victims, which could be funded by the assets resulting from the application of measures provided in Article 23 [which relates to sanctions and measures against traffickers].'

VI

PERSPECTIVES ON: UK CRIMINAL LEGISLATION, THE PROSECUTION OF TRAFFICKERS AND THE CRIMINALISATION OF VICTIMS OF TRAFFICKING

Contents

TRAFFICKING-RELATED CRIMINAL LEGISLATION IN THE UK, SPECIAL MEASURES FOR VICTIMS AND SENTENCING GUIDELINES

Pam Bowen

INTRODUCTION

19.1 This section sets out the relevant statutes and criminal offences used to prosecute those who traffic and exploit their victims. It also importantly identifies the UN and EU Conventions and Directives from which UK domestic legislation and Government policy flows.

The section also considers legislation and policy which provides protection and support for victims of human trafficking before and during criminal proceedings. It sets out the sentencing powers of the criminal courts, together with relevant case precedents which provide useful guidelines in sentencing practice.

UNITED NATIONS CONVENTIONS

19.2 The UN Convention against Transnational Organized Crime was adopted and signed in Palermo, Italy in December 2000 and is the main instrument against transnational organised crime. Under this multilateral treaty, Governments were required to criminalise offences committed by organised crime groups, strengthen co-operation and develop a series of protocols to combat specific acts of transnational organised crime. The treaty was supplemented by three protocols targeting human trafficking; the smuggling of migrants by land, sea and air; and the manufacture and trafficking of firearms.

The Protocol to Prevent, Suppress and Punish Trafficking in Persons, especially Women and Children entered into force in December 2003 and provided the international legally binding instrument for preventing and combating human trafficking (generally known as the Palermo Protocol). The Protocol created unity in national approaches for establishing domestic criminal offences that supports international co-operation in investigating and prosecuting trafficking cases.

Specifically, the Protocol provided international and mutually recognised interpretation and criminalisation. It established the protection to be afforded to victims; set out the policies to be adopted by parties for prevention and bilateral co-operation and other measures including strengthening border controls and control of identity documents.

The UN Convention on the Rights of the Child adopted in 1989 seeks to protect children from all forms of sexual exploitation and abuse; this obligation extends to exploitation and abuse in the context of trafficking.

The International Labour Organisation (ILO) Forced Labour Convention No 29 was adopted in June 1930 to suppress the use of forced or compulsory labour in all its forms. It established the definition of forced and compulsory labour as 'all work or service which is exacted from any person under the menace of any penalty and for which the said person has not offered himself voluntarily'.

EU CONVENTIONS

19.3 The EU Framework Decision on trafficking in human beings was adopted in 2002 to address trafficking at EU level and introduce common EU framework provisions such as criminalisation, penalties, jurisdiction and extradition. Member states had two years in which to bring the decision into domestic effect including any legislation; it advised criminalising trafficking by 2004. An EU plan on best practice standards and procedures to combat and prevent trafficking was adopted.

In December 2010 the European Parliament adopted a directive to repeal and replace the 2002 EU Framework Decision, to expand the provisions and introduce further measures. This included more rigorous prevention and prosecution, protection of victim's rights and specific protective measures for child victims. The UK Government announced their decision to opt into the EU Council Framework Decision in March 2011, although this now is subject to Parliamentary scrutiny before a final decision is made.

The Council of Europe Convention on Action against Trafficking in Human Beings was agreed in 2005. This is a binding instrument to develop a common policy against trafficking which the UK Government ratified in December 2008 and implemented in April 2009. The Convention provided for a comprehensive framework covering prevention; national co-ordination and co-operation between different agencies; protection and assistance to victims and an obligation to criminalise trafficking. In particular the Convention required the introduction of measures to identify and support victims and establishment of a recovery and reflection period during which trafficked victims cannot be removed from the receiving state.

TRAFFICKING AND SMUGGLING

19.4 In terms of prosecutions it is important to understand the difference between persons who are smuggled and those who are trafficked; in some cases the distinction between a smuggled person and a trafficked victim will be blurred and both definitions could easily be applied. The victim may have started out being smuggled into the country, but during their journey or when they arrive at their destination it could develop into or become trafficking. It is important to examine the end situation when the victim is recovered to determine whether someone has been smuggled or trafficked.

Smuggling is normally defined as the facilitation of entry to the UK either secretly or by deception (whether for profit or otherwise). The immigrants concerned are normally complicit in the offence so that they can remain in the UK illegally. There is normally little coercion/violence involved or required from those assisting in the smuggling.

Trafficking involves the transportation of persons in the UK in order to exploit them by the use of force, violence, deception, intimidation or coercion. The form of exploitation includes commercial, sexual and bonded labour exploitation. The persons who are trafficked have little choice in what happens to them and usually suffer abuse due to the threats and use of violence against them and/or their family.

Factors which help distinguish between smuggling and trafficking are:

- **Consent** – smuggling is a voluntary act and there is normally little deception/coercion/violence involved or required from those assisting in the smuggling;
- **Exploitation** – there is no exploitation by the smugglers of their victims once they reach their destination; effectively their relationship ends on arrival at destination. Trafficking victims on the other hand are subjected to a cycle of exploitation;
- **Profits** – profits for smuggling are derived primarily from transportation and facilitation of illegal entry in another country, whereas traffickers profit primarily from the exploitation of their victims.

RELEVANT UK LEGISLATION

Smuggling Offences

Section 25 of the Immigration Act 1971 Assisting unlawful immigration to a Member State (facilitation)

19.5 This offence came into force on 1 January 1973 and applies to England, Wales, Northern Ireland and Scotland.

The Immigration Act 1971, s 25 creates an offence of assisting unlawful immigration (known as facilitation). The offence was substituted by the Nationality, Immigration and Asylum Act 2002, s 143 which came into force on 10 February 2003. This widened and extended the old facilitation provisions and covers any act facilitating a breach of immigration law by a non-EU citizen (including a breach of another Member State's immigration law) and acts covered by the old offence of 'harbouring'.

Under s 25(1) a person commits an offence if he:

'(a)   does an act which facilitates the commission of a breach of immigration law by an individual who is not a citizen of the European Union;

343

(b)   knows or has reasonable cause for believing that the act facilitates the commission of a breach of immigration law by the individual; and

(c)   knows or has reasonable cause for believing that the individual is not a citizen of the European Union.'

The offence is defined broadly enough to encompass both the old offences of assisting illegal entry (whether by smuggling someone in a vehicle or by providing false documents for presentation at a port) or assisting someone to remain by deception (for example by entering into a sham marriage) and other forms of assistance which facilitate a breach of the immigration laws.

Section 25(5) of the Immigration Act 1971, was replaced by the UK Borders Act 2007, s 30(1) which came into force on 31 January 2008. This now covers acts committed in the United Kingdom, regardless of the nationality of the perpetrator as well as acts committed overseas.

The offence is an either-way offence and the maximum sentence on indictment is up to 14 years' imprisonment. It is also a 'lifestyle offence' under the Proceeds of Crime Act 2002, Sch 2.

The leading sentencing guide case is *R v Le and Stark*[1]. This states that the most appropriate penalty for all but the most minor offences of this nature is custody. Aggravating features include repeat offending; committed for financial gain; involving strangers rather than family members; a high degree of planning/sophistication; the number of immigrants involved; and the level of involvement of the offender. For guidance on non-commercial facilitation, see *R v Panesar*[2]. In the case of commercial facilitation see *R v Brown*[3], *R v Woop*[4] and *R v Akrout*[5].

[1]   [1999] 1 Cr App Rep (S) 422, [1999] Crim LR 96, CA.
[2]   [1988] Cr App Rep (S) 457, CA.
[3]   [1997] 1 Cr App Rep (S) 112, CA.
[4]   [2002] 2 Cr App Rep (S) 65.
[5]   [2003] EWCA Crim 291.

Human trafficking offences

Section 145 of the Nationality, Immigration and Asylum Act 2002

TRAFFICKING IN PROSTITUTION

19.6 This offence came into force on 10 February 2003 but was repealed by the Sexual Offences Act 2003 (Sch 7) as of 1 May 2004[1] and substituted by offences in the Sexual Offences Act 2003, ss 57–59. This offence can thus only be charged where the acts that amount to the commission of the offence, were committed after 10 February 2003 and before 1 May 2004.

Under the Nationality, Immigration and Asylum Act 2002, s 145(1), a person commits an offence if he arranges or facilitates the arrival into the United Kingdom of an individual (the 'passenger') and:

'(a)   he intends to exercise control over prostitution by the passenger in the United Kingdom or elsewhere, or

(b)   he believes that another person is likely to exercise control over prostitution by the passenger in the United Kingdom or elsewhere.'

Section 145(2) creates an offence in similar terms where the travel is within the UK. Section 145(3) creates an offence in similar terms but for departure from the UK. Section 145(4) advises that for the purposes of subsections (1) to (3) a person exercises control over prostitution by another if for purposes of gain he exercises control, direction or influence over the prostitute's movements in a way which shows that he is aiding, abetting or compelling the prostitution.

All these offences are either-way offences and on conviction on indictment, are subject to imprisonment for a term not exceeding 14 years, to a fine or to both.

This offence is a 'lifestyle offence' for the purposes of the Proceeds of Crime Act 2002.

[1]   SI 2004/874.

Section 57 of the Sexual Offences Act 2003

TRAFFICKING INTO THE UK FOR SEXUAL EXPLOITATION

19.7 This offence applies to England, Wales and Northern Ireland and came into force on 1 May 2004.

The UK Borders Act 2007, s 31(3) inserted 'or the entry into the UK' under s 57(1) with effect from 31 January 2008.

Under s 57(1) a person commits an offence if he intentionally arranges or facilitates the arrival in or the entry into the United Kingdom of another person (B) and either:

'(a)   he intends to do anything to or in respect of B, after B's arrival but in any part of the world, which if done will involve the commission of a relevant offence, or

(b)   he believes that another person is likely to do something to or in respect of B, after B's arrival but in any part of the world, which if done will involve the commission of a relevant offence.'

A relevant offence is defined under the Sexual Offences Act 2003, s 60(1) as:

'(a)   an offence under Part 1 of the Sexual Offences Act 2003;

(b)   an offence under section 1(1)(a) of the Protection of Children Act 1978;

(c)   anything done outside England and Wales and Northern Ireland which would be an offence if done in England and Wales or Northern Ireland.'

Section 60(2) and (3) are amended by the UK Borders Act 2007, s 31(4) to apply to anything done whether inside or outside the United Kingdom, with effect from 31 January 2008.

This is an either-way offence and on conviction on indictment, is subject to imprisonment for a term not exceeding 14 years. This offence is also a 'lifestyle offence' for the purposes of the Proceeds of Crime Act 2002. This offence is likely to lead to a significant sentence on conviction. Such offences would almost certainly receive sentences over 12 months and thus should be tried in the Crown Court.

19.8 *Trafficking-related criminal legislation in the UK*

Section 58 of the Sexual Offences Act 2003

TRAFFICKING WITHIN THE UK FOR SEXUAL EXPLOITATION

19.8 This offence applies to England, Wales and Northern Ireland and came into force on 1 May 2004.

Under s 58(1) a person commits an offence if he intentionally arranges or facilitates travel within the United Kingdom by another person (B) and either:

'(a)   he intends to do anything to or in respect of B, during or after the journey and in any part of the world, which if done will involve the commission of a relevant offence, (relevant offence is defined under Section 60(1) – see above); or

(b)   he believes that another person is likely to do something to or in respect of B, during or after the journey and in any part of the world, which if done will involve the commission of a relevant offence.

Section 60(2) and (3) are amended by the UK Borders Act 2007, s 31(4) to apply to anything done whether inside or outside the United Kingdom, with effect from 31 January 2008.

This is an either-way offence and on conviction on indictment, is subject to imprisonment for a term not exceeding 14 years. This offence is also a 'lifestyle offence' for the purposes of the Proceeds of Crime Act 2002.

This offence is likely to lead to a significant sentence on conviction and thus should be tried in the Crown Court.

Section 59 of the Sexual Offences Act 2003

TRAFFICKING OUT OF THE UK FOR SEXUAL EXPLOITATION

19.9 This offence applies to England, Wales and Northern Ireland and came into force on 1 May 2004.

Under s 59(1) a person commits an offence if he intentionally arranges or facilitates the departure from the United Kingdom of another person (B) and either:

'(a)   he intends to do anything to or in respect of B, after B's departure but in any part of the world, which if done will involve the commission of a relevant offence (as stated above); or

(b)   he believes that another person is likely to do something to or in respect of B, after B's departure but in any part of the world, which if done will involve the commission of a relevant offence.'

Section 60(2) and (3) are amended by the UK Borders Act 2007, s 31(4) to apply to anything done whether inside or outside the United Kingdom, with effect from 31 January 2008.

This is an either-way offence and on conviction on indictment, is subject to imprisonment for a term not exceeding 14 years. This offence is also a 'lifestyle offence' for the purposes of the Proceeds of Crime Act 2002.

This offence is likely to lead to a significant sentence on conviction and thus should be tried in the Crown Court.

Section 4 Asylum and Immigration (Treatment of Claimants etc) Act 2004

TRAFFICKING PEOPLE FOR EXPLOITATION

19.10 This offence applies to England, Wales, Northern Ireland and Scotland (but see below for further amendments to this offence in Scotland). The offence came into force on 1 December 2004. Section 31(1) of the UK Borders Act 2007 inserted 'or the entry into the UK' into s 4(1) with effect from 31 January 2008. Section 54 of the Borders, Citizenship and Immigration Act 2009 amended s 4(4)(d) with effect from 10 November 2009.

Under s 4(1) a person commits an offence if he arranges or facilitates the arrival in or the entry into the UK of an individual, and

'(a)   he intends to exploit the person in the UK or elsewhere, or
(b)   believes another person is likely to.'

Under s 4(2) a person commits an offence if he arranges or facilitates travel within the UK of an individual in respect of whom he believes has been trafficked into the UK and he intends to exploit the person, or believes another person is likely to, whether in the UK or elsewhere.

Under s 4(3) a person commits an offence if he arranges or facilitates the departure from the UK of an individual and he intends to exploit that person outside the UK, or believes another person is likely to, outside of the UK.

Under s 4(4), as amended, for the purposes of these offences, a person is exploited if he is:

'(a)   the victim of behaviour contravening Article 4 of the ECHR (slavery or forced labour);
(b)   encouraged, required or expected to do something which would mean an offence is committed under the Human Organ Transplants Act 1989;
(c)   subjected to force, threats or deception designed to induce him:
    (i)   to provide services of any kind,
    (ii)   to provide another person with benefits of any kind, or
    (iii)   to enable another person to acquire benefits of any kind; or
(d)   a person uses or attempts to use him for any purpose within sub-paragraph i, ii or iii of paragraph c, having chosen him for that purpose on the grounds that:
    (i)   he is mentally or physically ill or disabled, he is young or has a family relationship with a person, and
    (ii)   a person without the illness, disability, youth or family relationship would be likely to refuse to be used for that purpose.'

Further guidance on what constitutes behaviour contravening Article 4 of ECHR (slavery or forced labour) under sub-s 4(a) can be found in the ECHR case of *Siliadin v France (Application 73316/01)*[1]. The evidence showed the applicant, an alien who arrived in France at the age of 16, had worked for several years for the respondents carrying out household tasks and looking after their three, and subsequently four, children for seven days a week, from 7 am to 10 pm, without receiving any remuneration. She was obliged to follow instructions regarding her working hours and the work to be done, and was not free to come and go as she pleased. The court unanimously held that there has been a violation of Article 4 of the Convention.

Under sub-s 4(c) (ii) and (iii), benefits is defined as any advantage derived by the trafficker, which could include financial gain, profit, personal benefit or privilege as well as state financial assistance.

Section 5(1) and (2) are amended by the UK Borders Act 2007, s 31(4) to apply to anything done whether inside or outside the United Kingdom, with effect from 31 January 2008.

The offences are either way. On summary conviction the maximum penalty is six months' imprisonment, a fine up to the statutory maximum or both. (After s 154 Criminal Justice Act 2003 is commenced the maximum penal sentence on summary conviction will be increased to 12 months' imprisonment). Conviction on indictment carries a maximum sentence of 14 years' imprisonment, a fine or both. This offence is also a 'lifestyle offence' for the purposes of the Proceeds of Crime Act 2002.

This offence is likely to lead to a significant sentence on conviction and thus should be tried in the Crown Court.

[1]   (2005) 43 EHRR 287, 20 BHRC 654, ECtHR.

Section 71 of the Coroners and Justice Act 2009

SLAVERY, SERVITUDE AND FORCED OR COMPULSORY LABOUR

19.11 This offence applies to England, Wales and Northern Ireland and came into force on 6 April 2010. References to s 71, below, apply equally to the s 47 offence under Scottish law.

Section 71 creates an offence of holding another person in slavery or servitude or requiring them to perform forced or compulsory labour. It should be noted, however, that the s 71 offence does not contain the element of trafficking and is not an immigration offence. It is wider and will apply irrespective of whether the victim has been trafficked and irrespective of the immigration status of the victim(s).

Under s 71:

'(1).   A person (D) commits an offence if:
    (a)   D holds another person in slavery or servitude and the circumstances are such that D knows or ought to know that the person is so held, or
    (b)   D requires another person to perform forced or compulsory labour and the circumstances are such that D knows or ought to know that the person is being required to perform such labour.
(2)   In subsection (1) the references to holding a person in slavery or servitude or requiring a person to perform forced or compulsory labour are to be construed in accordance with Article 4 of the Human Rights Convention (which prohibits a person from being held in slavery or servitude or being required to perform forced or compulsory labour).
(3)   A person guilty of an offence under this section is liable:
    (a)   on summary conviction, to imprisonment for a term not exceeding the relevant period [12 months] or a fine not exceeding the statutory maximum or both;
    (b)   on conviction on indictment, to imprisonment for a term not exceeding 14 years or a fine, or both.

(4)   In this section:"Human Rights Convention" means the Convention for the
        Protection of Human Rights and Fundamental Freedoms agreed by
        the Council of Europe at Rome on 4 November 1950;'

'The relevant period' means:

'(a)   in relation to England and Wales, 12 months; and
(b)   in relation to Northern Ireland, 6 months.'

In Scotland under s 47(3) of the Criminal Justice and Licensing (Scotland) Act
2010 the maximum term of imprisonment on summary conviction is
12 months.

Section 71 does not specifically define slavery, servitude or forced or compulsory labour, but rather refers to Article 4 of the European Convention on
Human Rights. Therefore, in interpreting s 71, police, prosecutors and the
courts will need to have regard to existing case-law on Article 4 ECHR and
international conventions to find guidance defining the parameters of each of
the terms.

In *Siliadin v France (Application 73316/01)*[1], the ECHR reaffirmed that
servitude 'prohibits a particularly serious form of denial of freedom. It
includes, in addition to the obligation to provide certain services to another,
the obligation on the "serf" to live on the other's property and the impossibility of changing his status'.

The ECHR in the case of *Van der Mussele (Application 8919/80)*[2] affirmed
that the ILO conventions were the starting point for interpreting Article 4. The
conventions, defined forced or compulsory labour as being 'all work or service
which is exacted from any person under the menace of any penalty and for
which the said person has not offered himself voluntarily'. To that end, the s 71
offence will require an element of coercion or deception between the defendant
and the victim.

[1]   (2005) 43 EHRR 287, 20 BHRC 654, ECtHR.
[2]   (1983) 6 EHRR 163, [1983] ECHR 8919/80, ECtHR.

Other legislation

19.12 Often victims of trafficking have been subjected to other offences
committed during the different stages of their journey and also during their
exploitation. For example, a victim of sexual exploitation may have also been
raped, falsely imprisoned and threatened by their trafficker over a period of
time. Or a victim of forced labour or domestic servitude may have had their
passport confiscated, been assaulted and threatened with violence or death.
This is often done as a means of gaining and maintaining control of their
victim. These offences then should be considered in addition to offences of
human trafficking or, where an offence of human trafficking cannot be
evidenced, as alternative offences.

19.13 *Trafficking-related criminal legislation in the UK*

Section 53A of the Sexual Offences Act 2003

PAYING FOR THE SEXUAL SERVICES OF A PROSTITUTE SUBJECTED TO
FORCE ETC

19.13 This offence came into force on 1 April 2010.

Whilst the offence is not directly concerned with human trafficking, it was introduced to address the demand for all forms of commercial sexual exploitation and developed, in part, to enable the UK to meet its international legal obligations to discourage the demand for sexual services in support of Conventions to suppress and prevent trafficking for sexual exploitation. The offence is most likely to arise when police are conducting brothel raids, where there is enforcement against suspects controlling or exploiting prostitution for gain and where clients are apprehended in the operation.

Section 53A provides:

'(1)   A person (A) commits an offence if:
    (a)   A makes or promises payment for the sexual services of a prostitute (B),
    (b)   A third person (C) has engaged in exploitative conduct of a kind likely to induce or encourage B to provide the sexual offences for which A has made or promised payment, and
    (c)   C engaged in that conduct for or in the expectation of gain for C or another person (apart from A or B).
(2)   The following are irrelevant –
    (a)   Where in the world the sexual services are to be provided and whether those services are provided,
    (b)   Whether A is, or ought to be, aware that C has engaged in exploitative conduct.
(3)   C engages in exploitative conduct if –
    (a)   C uses force, threats (whether or not relating to violence) or any other form of coercion, or
    (b)   C practices any form of deception.'

The offence is one of strict liability. This means that it is irrelevant whether A is, or ought to be, aware that B is subject to exploitative conduct by C.

A person guilty of an offence under this section is liable on summary conviction to a fine not exceeding Level 3 on the standard scale.

Legislation in Scotland

Section 22 of the Criminal Justice (Scotland) Act 2003

TRAFFICKING IN PROSTITUTION

19.14 Section 22 came into force on 27 June 2003 and created offences of trafficking for the purposes of sexual exploitation (control over an individual for prostitution or involvement in the making or production of obscene or indecent material). These offences apply both cross- border, into and out of the UK, and within the UK. The offences also cover behaviour out with the UK by

British Citizens, and in that event, proceedings may be brought anywhere in Scotland.

Section 46 of the Criminal Justice and Licensing (Scotland) Act 2010 came into force on 28 March 2011 to amend s 22 to extend its scope so that it refers to facilitating 'entry into' the UK as well as the 'arrival in' the UK. A new offence was created under s 22(1A) to criminalise those who traffic persons into, within or out of a country other than the UK.

The amendments will ensure that it will be an offence under Scots law where a person, regardless of his/her nationality, within or out of the UK undertakes trafficking activities and an individual is trafficked into, within or out of the UK. The extra-territorial effect of s 22(4) of the 2003 Act is extended so that it is not limited to British nationals and companies by providing that the offence applies to anything done whether inside or outside the UK by any person, no matter whether they are in any way connected to the UK. Section 22(5) of the 2003 Act is amended to clarify in statute that the sheriff court has jurisdiction, under both solemn and summary procedure, for any offence to which s 22 applies.

The maximum sentence for cases prosecuted on indictment is 14 years' imprisonment and on summary conviction, imprisonment not exceeding 12 months, a fine or both.

Section 4 of the Asylum and Immigration (Treatment of Claimants etc) Act 2004

TRAFFICKING PEOPLE FOR EXPLOITATION

19.15 This offence is the same offence applying to England, Wales and Northern Ireland (see above) but was amended by the Criminal Justice and Licensing (Scotland) Act 2010, which came into force on 28 March 2011. Amendments to s 4(2) *removed* the requirement that a person who arranges or facilitates the travel of an individual within the UK intending to exploit that individual (or believes that someone else is likely to do so) has a belief that an offence under s 4(1) may have been committed.

Section 47 of the Criminal Justice and Licensing (Scotland) Act 2010

SLAVERY, SERVITUDE AND FORCED OR COMPULSORY LABOUR

19.16 This offence is the same offence as that under the Coroners and Justice Act 2009, s 71 which applies to England, Wales and Northern Ireland (see above) but it was introduced slightly later in Scotland under the Criminal Justice and Licensing (Scotland) Act 2010, s 47 and came into force in Scotland on 28 March 2011.

SUPPORT MEASURES FOR VICTIMS OF TRAFFICKING IN THE UK

19.17 The Youth Justice and Criminal Evidence Act 1999 introduced a range of Special Measures which can be used to facilitate the gathering and giving of evidence by vulnerable and intimidated witnesses and which are likely to apply to victims of human trafficking. Having identified that the witness is vulnerable or intimidated, the police can video record the victim's evidence-in-chief for presentation at court.

The following special measures are available to facilitate the victim to give their best evidence:

- Screens to shield the witness from the defendant;
- Giving evidence through live link;
- Evidence given in private through exclusion from the court of members of the public and the press;
- Removal of wigs and gowns by judges and barristers;
- In some instances, not revealing the victim's identity when giving evidence;
- Mandatory protection of the witness from cross-examination by the accused in person;
- Restrictions on evidence and questions about the complainant's sexual behaviour.

However, whilst application can be made to the court for these measures, it is for the judge to decide whether to grant the application. In considering whether to do so, the judge will seek to balance the victim's rights against the rights of the defendant. The court will seek to act in the overall interests of justice.

Other measures which can be applied for to assist victims in giving their evidence at court include the following:

- Section 46 of the Youth Justice and Criminal Evidence Act 1999 provides for reporting restrictions to restrict media coverage of cases that reveal a witness's identity and may create safety issues.
- Section 32 of the Criminal Justice Act 1988 creates a provision for evidence to be given through television link where a victim has chosen to be repatriated to their home country and does not wish to return to the UK.

Prosecutors can also in certain circumstance use powers under the Serious Organised Crime and Police Act 2005 which came into force on 1 April 2006, to provide immunity from prosecution or sentence discounts for those who assist in the investigation, and support and co-operate with the prosecution. The power must be authorised by the Director of Public Prosecutions.

- Section 71 provides for immunity from prosecution to enable prosecutors to sign up to agreements about immunity with powers to revoke if individuals do not co-operate;
- Section 72 enables prosecutors to provide undertakings as to use of evidence that information provided will not be used in proceedings against them, although it can be subject to conditions;
- Section 73 enables prosecutors to give a written agreement that a defendant has provided assistance, for the court to consider a reduction in sentence to co-operating defendants;

- Section 74 enables prosecutors to refer a sentence to court if sentence was reduced on the basis that the defendant would assist but subsequently does not.

SENTENCING POWERS OF THE COURT

Useful Sentence Guideline Cases

19.18 Sentencing guidelines have been included under the relevant statutory offences, but the following cases provide guidelines on sentencing and reflect the degree of coercion, force and violence used in the exploitation of victims.

R v Plakici, Attorney General's Reference (No 6 of 2004)[1] dealt with a series of individual offences that amounted to an extremely serious case of trafficking. The defendant had arranged for the illegal entry of women and young girls into this country in circumstances that involved both deception and coercion and forced them to work as prostitutes. He was charged with seven counts including facilitating unlawful immigration, which attracted sentences of five years; of living on immoral earnings for which he was sentenced to five years; of kidnapping for which he was sentenced to 10 years; and of incitement to rape three girls and sentenced to eight years imprisonment; those sentences to run concurrently which amounted to a sentence of 10 years' imprisonment. The court upheld the sentences but indicated that they should all run consecutively. A total sentence of 23 years' imprisonment was substituted.

R v Maka[2]. Sentences totalling 18 years' imprisonment were upheld, on a guilty plea, in the case of a man who trafficked a 15 year old girl into the UK and repeatedly sold her to others for the purposes of prostitution. The court endorsed the comment of the sentencing judge that human trafficking was a degrading activity producing untold misery around the world and that the case had echoes of slavery with the girl being sold from one procurer to another. It added that the offence was intended to embrace a wide variety of different forms of conduct, identified as trafficking for sexual exploitation.

R v Roci and Ismailaj[3]. In this case the appellants were concerned in the importation and the control in this country of prostitutes from Lithuania. While the women came to this country willingly, they were then coerced to work in unpleasant circumstances and ways contrary to their wishes and to pay over most of their earnings. The sentence for the appellant who was concerned in all these matters was reduced from 11 years to nine years' imprisonment.

R v Makai (Atilla)[4]. The appellant appealed against a sentence of 40 months' imprisonment imposed following his plea of guilty to conspiracy to traffic into the UK for sexual exploitation. He was involved in recruiting and arranging for Hungarian girls to come to the UK and work as prostitutes in brothels. He posted advertisements on Hungarian websites inviting girls to contact them and then passed the girls on to other men more closely involved in the trade. The Crown accepted that the girls would have known the kind of work for which they had been recruited. The basis of plea was that the girls came to the UK of their own free will, were above the age of consent, had entered the UK legally, knew prostitution was not illegal in the UK, and that his role had been limited to introducing them to others that placed them in the brothels. Appeal allowed and 30 months' imprisonment substituted.

A-G's Reference (Nos 37, 38 and 65 of 2010), R v Khan, Khan and Khan[5]. The defendants were convicted of charges of conspiracy to traffic for labour exploitation. The family owned a restaurant business and over a period of four years they recruited nine men from India to work at the restaurant. The men had been deceived by the promise of attractive wages, had been subjected to conditions of neglect, abuse, deprivation and economic exploitation. Their passports and other confidential personal documents were confiscated by the defendants and they were discouraged from leaving the restaurant or speaking with customers. They were each sentenced to three years' imprisonment. A sentence of four years' imprisonment was substituted for two of the three defendants.

[1]   [2005] 1 Cr.App.R.(S.) 19.
[2]   [2006] 2 Cr.App.R.(S.) 14.
[3]   [2006] 2 Cr.App.R.(S.) 15.
[4]   [2008] 1 Cr.App.R.(S.) 73.
[5]   [2010] EWCA Crim 2880, [2011] 2 Cr App Rep (S) 186, [2011] Crim LR 336.

PREFACE TO THE CRIMINAL PROSECUTION OF TRAFFICKERS

Parosha Chandran

INTRODUCTION TO THE CHAPTERS

20.1 The next three chapters provide descriptions of some of the investigation techniques that have been used by different teams of the Metropolitan Police Service to identify victims of trafficking, to identify the human traffickers responsible for their trafficking and exploitation and to bring those people to account for the serious crimes they had committed.

Serious Crime Directorate 9 (SCD9): The Work of the Human Exploitation and Organised Crime Command

20.2 This chapter summarises the work of SCD9, the Human Exploitation and Organised Crime Command of the Metropolitan Police and some of its key cases and Operations. The authors highlight examples of the kinds of deception that are used by traffickers to trick their victims and descriptions are given as to how the victims' vulnerability is increased and maintained by the traffickers' methods of control over their actions and movements. In terms of victim identification the chapter explains that this is often not straightforward. Hence, in one case an individual who appeared to be a criminal offender was in fact one of a group of victims of trafficking who were being forced to commit crimes by dangerous traffickers: the authors explain how this victim, who had been subjected to serious harm at the hands of the traffickers, eventually wanted to be caught by the police so as to be identified and how he and others were rescued by the police and treated as victims of crime, while the traffickers have been prosecuted. The authors also highlight the significant impact that trauma can have on victims' disclosure, the corresponding length of time that may be needed before a victim feels safe enough to provide disclosure and the vital role of partnerships with NGOs to enable this to take place:

> 'The vast majority of victims encountered by SCD9 are highly traumatised and often suffer from symptoms of severe post-traumatic stress disorder. Some have taken over 12 months to gain the confidence to disclose their stories to police. Obtaining this

information from individuals in these cases is often testament to the relationship formed between the victims, the investigating officers and our NGO partners'[1].

[1] **CHAPTER 21** 'Serious Crime Directorate 9 (SCD9): The Work of the Human Exploitation and Organised Crime Command', at para **21.2**.

Operation Golf: a UK and Romania Joint Investigation Tackling Romanian Organised Crime and Child Trafficking

20.3 This chapter provides a detailed description of the work of Operation Golf, the first UK Police Joint Investigation (JIT) to be established under the EU framework decision on 'Mutual Legal Assistance' and the first JIT in Europe to focus on human trafficking. The JIT involved the Metropolitan Police and the Romanian National Police and was aimed at tackling a specific Romanian Roma organised crime group (OCG) that trafficked and exploited children from the Romanian Roma community, one of the poorest and most disadvantaged communities in Europe. Again, the important role of partnerships is highlighted, not only with NGOs and social services in the UK but also with police in Romania. What is strikingly described in the chapter is the rapid and sustained police response to new information via the development and implementation of highly effective investigation techniques. This without question impacted on the ultimate success of Operation Golf, which concluded with 71 UK-based convictions of persons linked to the OCG, including, for example, convictions for human trafficking, money laundering and fraud. The chapter also highlights the importance of the role of partnership between police and prosecutors in securing successful prosecutions:

'With the exception of the four [defendants who were] convicted following the trial in the [child trafficking] case . . . every single suspect charged pleaded guilty at court. This is a testament to the diligence of the investigators and the careful preparation of the cases in partnership with the Crown Prosecution Service.'[1]

[1] **CHAPTER 22** 'Operation Golf: A UK and Romania Joint Investigation Tackling Romanian Organised Crime and Child Trafficking', para **22.19**.

Child Trafficking Investigations and Prosecutions

20.4 In this chapter the author describes her experiences of investigating child traffickers as a member of the Metropolitan Police Force's 'Operation Paladin'; particularly the cases of child victims of trafficking who were exploited for domestic servitude. Her careful respect for the children, coupled with her experience and insight prompted investigation techniques in the cases she personally dealt with which enabled trust to be developed between the police and the victim, and, helped by the interventions of trafficking aware-lawyers in one case[1] and council workers and social workers in others, complex histories were unravelled which enabled successful prosecutions against the traffickers to be brought. The author also explains some of the practical obstacles that were posed by requirements of the original wording of the 2004 law against trafficking for labour exploitation in the UK and how legislative amendment was required in 2009 to enable the law to become more effective. She advises us that, in her experience as a police investigator, children do not say they have been trafficked and are dependent upon professionals accurately identifying them as victims of trafficking. In her conclusion the author advises us of something we should surely all keep at the forefront of our minds, namely:

'[C]hild trafficking is not an immigration matter. Child trafficking is child abuse.'[2]

---

[1] As explained by the author of **CHAPTER 23** on Child Trafficking Investigations and Prosecutions', the police investigation by the Paladin team, which led to the successful prosecution of the trafficker Lucy Adedeji, described in the chapter at para **23.6** arose in response to lawyers, acting for a group of Nigerian young women who had been trafficked and exploited in the UK as children, bringing a civil claim for damages against the Chief Commissioner of the Metropolitan Police for historical failings by certain members of the Paladin team to investigate the victims' allegations of trafficking. The author's first involvement in the case was when she took over the investigation in 2009 which led to Adedeji's conviction. In May 2011 Wynn Williams J in the High Court gave judgment in the civil action: judgment of *OOO v The Commissioner of Police for the Metropolis* [2011] EWHC 1246 (QB) in which the court held that the police had historically acted in breach of their positive obligations under Articles 3 and 4 ECHR to investigate the credible allegations of human trafficking which had been brought to their attention. In awarding the Claimants damages, the court followed the judgment of the European Court of Human Rights (ECtHR) in *Rantsev v Cyprus and Russia (Application 6956/04)* (2010) 28 BHRC 313, [2010] ECHR 25965/04, ECtHR]. In that case the ECtHR, having taken into account the Trafficking Convention found a State has positive obligations to act to protect individuals against human trafficking and had duties to investigate trafficking allegations when: '286 . . . the State authorities were aware, or ought to have been aware, of circumstances giving rise to a credible suspicion that an identified individual had been, or was at real and immediate risk of being, trafficked or exploited'.

[2] **CHAPTER 23**, 'Child Trafficking Investigations and Prosecutions', at para **23.8**.

UNODC TOOLKIT TO COMBAT TRAFFICKING IN PERSONS: OVERVIEW OF THE CHALLENGES IN INVESTIGATING HUMAN TRAFFICKING

20.5 The UNODC, in its Toolkit to Combat Trafficking in Persons, 2008, has a chapter on Law Enforcement and Prosecution which includes a section on the Investigation of Trafficking in Persons. Tool No 5.1 of that toolkit provides a clear overview of the challenges which are involved in investigating human trafficking.

Tool 5.1 draws upon the findings reached and the recommendations made by highly respected anti-trafficking experts in the context of trafficking investigations in the USA. However the scope and content of the authors' expertise is not, in my view, geographically limited and hence Tool No. 5.1 is adopted in its full form in this Preface by reason of its relevancy to achieving successful human trafficking investigations in the UK. It will be readily apparent to the reader that many of the recommended best practices in Tool No. 5.1, below, reflect some of the descriptions of the trafficking investigations that have been carried out by or under the command of the five police authors in this book. There is also much resonance with what is said earlier in this book in **CHAPTER 6** which provides guidance on obtaining evidence from traumatised trafficked persons. There is therefore much to be learned from reading the three police prosecution chapters which follow, together with **CHAPTER 6** of this book and the UNODC's Tool No. 5.1 below.

'Overview: This tool summarizes a recent article written about the challenges of investigating human trafficking in the United States and the need for effective investigation to secure successful prosecutions.

An effective law enforcement response to trafficking is not limited merely to the application of law in individual cases, but has relevance to all dimensions of the complicated facets of trafficking. Effective law enforcement response also depends on the participation of all levels of society, from local communities and non-governmental organizations to migration officials and prosecutors.

"Investigating human trafficking: challenges, lessons learned and best practices"
by Kevin Bales and Steven Lize
FBI Law Enforcement Bulletin, April 2007, Vol. 76, No. 4
(United States Department of Justice, Federal Bureau of Investigation)
In the context of the United States, the authors considered the question: "How can investigations and subsequent prosecutions of traffickers be effectively increased?" Their key findings and recommendations are of value to investigators of human trafficking everywhere.

General considerations

- Initial actions taken in investigation are crucial to the ultimate success of prosecutions.
- Human trafficking investigations require careful treatment of victims and witnesses, upon whose testimony the prosecution depends.
- The process of interviewing the victim, collecting corroborating evidence and investigating perpetrators is more effective when the victim has continued presence in the country and accesses care and protection from a service provider as early in the process as possible.
- Successful law enforcement intervention requires rapid, sustained response. After initial interviews of suspected victims, witnesses and where possible, perpetrators, investigators begin collecting information and corroborating evidence to build the charges and the case.

Victim and witness co-operation

- The most successful results involve agents with experience in human trafficking cases, who show more sensitivity to victims and their needs, and are aware of other sources of information to corroborate evidence.
- Gaining the co-operation of victims as witnesses can be challenging. Often, because of their distrust of police in their home countries, trafficking survivors fear law enforcement agencies and are concerned that they will be treated as criminals, incarcerated or deported. These fears must be overcome in order for victims to become cooperating witnesses.
- Human trafficking survivors often do not identify themselves as victims. Law enforcement agents may therefore have difficulty in identifying victims among detainees and separating them from perpetrators.
- Investigators and prosecutors can gain the trust and cooperation of victims and witnesses by showing compassion and making them feel comfortable.

Agency roles and challenges

- Human trafficking investigation requires cooperation among many agencies. Investigators must consider their questioning strategy to elicit information about captivity, forced work, coerced sexual acts and abuse by perpetrators.
- Investigators may consider working closely with prosecutors to secure corroborating testimony from trafficking victims and witnesses, and consult with specialist NGOs that provide services and advocacy to trafficked persons. Other agencies, such as those dealing with labour, can assist law enforcers in the process of investigating and prosecuting.

Evidence collection

- Where investigators know where to look, they can gather evidence and locate victims and perpetrators. Traffickers use ordinary methods of commerce for activities in support of their crimes; reviewing records can provide valuable evidence. Other investigative methods such as surveillance, analysis of trash and correspondence, under cover operations and reviews of wire transfer records (if applicable), can also reveal pertinent information.

- Investigators are often required to work in settings unfamiliar to them and in communities which distrust law enforcement authorities (such as ethnic neighbourhoods which are socially and culturally difficult for investigators to access). Organizations experienced in working with law enforcement agencies can be an important resource during investigations in settings where trafficking occurs. The nature of these crimes requires appropriate social and cultural orientation to effectively gather criminal intelligence and arrest perpetrators. Ethnic community groups, immigrants' and workers' rights NGOs can assist in gaining access to culturally insulated communities. Law enforcement agencies should seek only the assistance of organizations with a proven record of assisting trafficking victims and collaborating with investigating authorities.

Interviewing considerations

- Investigators should work together when interviewing victims and witnesses to avoid having multiple interviews on record with conflicting information.
- Even when an interview has established trust with victims and witnesses, they may never provide a full account in a single interview. Aside from the trauma they have suffered, other sociological and psychological barriers impede the process, including sociocultural differences, language and gender.
  — Gender issues significantly affect the interviewer's capacity to obtain information. Trafficked women and children frequently suffer sexual abuse and violence and may be reluctant to seek assistance because of the shame and stigmatization which may flow from disclosing their experiences. Men, particularly those from a culture with a traditional view of masculinity, may not want to admit their victimization because they fear that their disclosure of losing control of their lives may lead to perceptions of diminished masculinity. For these reasons, men and women may perhaps be more willing to talk to law enforcement personnel and service providers of the same gender.
  — Investigators who are fluent in the language of the person they are interviewing and have cultural affinity with the person may have more success.'

The full article is available at:

http://www.fbi.gov/publications/leb/2007/april2007/april2007leb.htm,at page 24.'

SERIOUS CRIME DIRECTORATE 9 (SCD9): THE WORK OF THE HUMAN EXPLOITATION AND ORGANISED CRIME COMMAND

Detective Chief Superintendent Richard Martin (Commander of SCD9)

and Detective Chief Inspector Nick Sumner

INTRODUCTION

21.1 SCD9, the Human Exploitation and Organised Crime Command, was officially formed on 1 April 2010 following a review of the Metropolitan Police Service's response to incidents of trafficking that occurred within the Metropolis of London. This review concluded that having a specialist unit in the form of the current SCD9 was the way forward.

SCD9's powers cover the following areas of investigation and policing in London:

- Trafficking for sexual exploitation, forced labour and domestic servitude where there is a clear link to an organised criminal network;
- On and off street prostitution;
- Obscene publications, extreme pornography and sharing of indecent images of children via the Internet;
- Tackling violence and drugs supply within the night time economy;
- Tackling violence within promoted music events;
- Casino fraud and money laundering;
- Operation Maxim, which tackles and disrupts organised immigration crime in London, including human smuggling, human trafficking and counterfeit immigration documentation;
- Operation Swale, a joint ACPO/MPS/UKBA unit, focusing on those who profit from smuggling and exploiting migrants to the UK, and foreign criminals who cause harm to innocent people as a consequence of their illegal activities.

HUMAN TRAFFICKING IN THE METROPOLIS

21.2 Trafficking victims have often spent many years being abused, suffering servitude and slavery. The vast majority of victims encountered by SCD9 are highly traumatised and often suffer from symptoms of severe post traumatic stress disorder. Some have taken over 12 months to gain the confidence to disclose their stories to police. Obtaining this information from individuals in these cases is often testament to the relationship formed between the victims, the investigating officers and our NGO partners. Building trust and confidence with the victims takes time and great patience. The specially trained officers work with the individuals and our charity partner organisations to obtain the best possible evidence. In our view the needs of the victims are always paramount and any prosecution will take second place to their care.

In 2009 the MPS dealt with 29 reported cases of trafficking. One of the early priorities was to increase the reporting of cases and create a process of third party reporting whereby our key partners could identify trafficking victims to the police. During 2010 the newly formed SCD9 Unit received 73 cases of trafficking through this referral system alone. With the victims' support investigations are commenced. Each victim was sensitively interviewed to secure the very best evidence. From these debriefs the evidential foundations of the prosecution case are formed.

The operations instigated from our third party reporting process resulted in police identifying a further 60 trafficked victims who were rescued and taken to support reception centres, which are independent offices or rooms where victims can be spoken to and be provided services from NGOs as well as speak with police. These centres are designed to be less threatening/intimidating than a police station or interview suite.

Not every victim is willing or able to assist with a police investigation. Gaining the trust and confidence of victims will always remain a challenge within the complex arena of human trafficking. The officers who deal with these cases are skilled detectives with great compassion and commitment to the victims they speak to. However, this is not always enough and we rely on a series of charity-based support workers to continue the engagement process with the trafficked individuals.

Despite the increase in referrals the team has retained a proactive approach to gathering intelligence during brothel visits. This work has enabled officers to contact over 300 additional women who have shown indicators of being trafficked. All these women had been sexually exploited for gain. Some of the women have used this contact with the police to seek support either at the time of our visit or subsequently.

The majority of trafficking cases dealt with by SCD9 during 2010 involved individuals being sexually exploited. However, the MPS remains acutely aware of the hidden incidents of trafficking within London. Our officers have dealt with cases of over 20 victims of domestic servitude in 2010 and each of these engagements is a vital opportunity to build trust and demonstrate our commitment to the victims of trafficking. Over time this approach, we hope, will give other victims the strength to come forward. Working with our partners in the future we aim to reveal the true picture of trafficking within

London in whatever form that takes. Forced labour and domestic servitude offences often remain hidden within the chaos of the capital.

In trying to combat a complex crime such as trafficking you must begin to understand the profile of the victims, the offenders and the communities they come from. Only then can we effectively engage with these communities to stop trafficking at the source, within vulnerable groups across the globe. An important part of capturing that information will come from police investigations.

We will now share the stories of some of the victims whose cases have been dealt with by SCD9 officers. Their situations, cultures and backgrounds are very different but they also share some threads of commonality. In certain cases the individual details have been changed or removed to avoid prejudicing any investigation.

Case 1: Operation Parate

21.3 This first case concerns the trafficking of Russian and Eastern European females into the UK for the purpose of sexual exploitation by a Russian organised criminal network.

In the Spring of 2010 a local resident living in Chelsea had complained to the Borough police that a neighbouring residential property was being used for prostitution. In response, officers from a local Safer Neighbourhood Team visited the address and spoke with the two occupiers. An intelligence report was passed to SCD9 raising the local officers' concerns about the venue and the two occupants.

SCD9 intelligence officers researched the contents of the report. It was soon established that a Russian male in his forties, spoken to by the local officers, had for many years been concerned in the control of prostitutes. It was suspected that he may have been involved in human trafficking and evidence of this needed to be uncovered as this is rarely established by superficial inquiries. Detailed financial investigations were conducted which revealed suspicious purchases of one way flight tickets to the UK for females from a variety of Eastern European and Russian countries. Whilst still unconfirmed, it was suspected that some of these women would have been trafficked into the UK for the purpose of sexual exploitation.

Turning intelligence into useable evidence is no easy task and requires considerable detective skill. A covert investigation commenced in an attempt to evidentially link the Russian suspect to the controlling of prostitution with human trafficking and to identify the trafficked individuals. Over a three month period detectives from SCD9 ran a series of surveillance operations following the male and the prostitutes he was controlling. Undercover officers were used to prove the offer of sexual services.

This meticulous approach in our investigations transforms our suspicions into evidential fact, capable of withstanding the high scrutiny of the UK's criminal courts. The main suspect was captured controlling a series of brothels across London and profiting from this enterprise by many thousands of pounds on a weekly basis. He would regularly visit a Knightsbridge Safe Deposit Bank to secure his illegal cash fortune.

With the first stage of the investigation complete and sufficient evidence secured, the Russian male was arrested. The covert enquiries had identified a number of premises and women that we needed to speak to in order to establish their treatment at the hands of this man.

The investigations had shown a Russian and European Organised Crime Network were befriending and recruiting vulnerable young Eastern European females. A number of victims were rescued and two victims gave detailed statements to the investigating officers. Each had been snared by the traffickers through similar means but came from countries across Europe and the Russian states. Adverts in the local newspapers in their home countries offered employment as waitresses, shop assistants, dancers and escorts. Those who responded were facilitated into the UK with forged documents provided by their traffickers.

Once in the UK each victim had their travel documents taken away from them and they were informed that they were debt bonded to the sum of tens of thousands of pounds. In order to pay the debt they were forced to work as prostitutes in brothels controlled by the group. Any refusal to do so would have been met with violence against them and their families back home. Their every move was monitored by the traffickers in the UK from the moment they were first chosen for exploitation.

The traffickers were motivated by greed and power. Their criminal activity generated great wealth for themselves with officers seizing nearly £50,000 in cash from the addresses controlled by the network. A number of individuals have been charged with trafficking in this case and have offered guilty pleas to the trafficking charges. At the time of writing[1] their sentencing hearing was shortly due to take place.

The victims continue to be supported here in the UK.

[1]   13 June 2011.

Comment on newspaper adverts

21.4 The link between newspaper adverts and human trafficking, particularly for the purposes of sexual exploitation, remains a concerning and live issue, even in the UK. In our experience classified adverts in UK newspapers which are used to advertise the services of women, such as escorts and women in massage parlours, often have clear and tangible links with organised crime.

With this in mind the Commander of SCD9 wrote to Editors of London-based newspapers on 25 November 2010 in the following terms:

'As you will be aware, the Metropolitan Police Service is committed to reducing human trafficking and sexual exploitation. Recent investigations have demonstrated our commitment to ensuring London remains a hostile environment to those engaged in this type of criminality and a number of these investigations have resulted in successful prosecutions.
It is clear from a considerable number of these operations that advertising in newspapers can play a key role in facilitating the exploitation of trafficked victims.

The adverts in question often purport to be massage parlours, saunas or escort agencies, but are in reality a front for criminal networks to advertise trafficked victims for sexual services.

Consequently it is vital that we tackle this area as part of our overarching strategy to reduce trafficking in London. I am therefore seeking your support to help us address this issue by ensuring that your publications do not allow advertising space to be utilised to promote these practices. Advertisements that offer multi-national or young women; or which are sexually suggestive in tone are often the type found to be linked to the provision of sexual services and/or the presence of trafficked women. It is these types of adverts I am seeking your support in preventing. I would ask that you put in place a system to satisfy yourselves that those seeking to place advertisements are genuine concerns or businesses and not a cover for the types of criminal activity highlighted above.

As you will appreciate, criminal liability can arise in certain circumstances where evidence clearly shows that the advertising in question supports or promotes offences associated to trafficking, exploitation or proceeds of crime.'

We have yet to report on the success of this campaign.

Case 2: Operation Bluebok

21.5 This particular case captured national media attention in Autumn 2010 and quite understandably so. The four defendants hatched a plot to sell the virginity of young girls to a wealthy Arab businessman in a luxury hotel in the centre of London. In July 2009 they initiated contact by writing a letter to the owner of the five star Jumeirah Carlton Hotel in Knightsbridge, where they offered for sale the sexual services of children.

Upon receipt of the letter the hotel owners immediately contacted the Metropolitan Police and the SCD9 Trafficking Team commenced their investigation. The only way to identify the potential victims was through the gang and an undercover officer known as 'Cameron' was deployed to make contact. Over the following weeks and months the members of the crime gang were identified. In one covertly recorded meeting with 'Cameron' the gang discussed the terms of the contract and even provided photographs of the girls for sale. As this case evolved, any doubt as to the intent of the gang soon evaporated. Children as young as 14 years old were being offered for sexual services and their virginity was priced at £100,000.

The relationship between the undercover officer and the gang developed, ensuring that sufficient trust existed between them for the final part of the operation to succeed. The children needed to be rescued and the only way of achieving this was to arrange the handover of the girls in a carefully co-ordinated sting operation.

This meeting took place at the Lancaster Hotel in West London. In broad daylight the gang walked into the hotel with six victims who ranged in age from 14 to 22 years old. Officers from the trafficking team moved in, arresting two of the gang and rescuing the girls. Having already identified the other key suspects, the remaining members of the gang were arrested in raids across London and in Lancashire.

The victims in this case had been recruited from the North West of England. They comprised a mix of nationalities with some being British, Iranian and

European. The younger girls were duped into believing they were going to London to perform in dancing shows and that they would be offered cash in return.

On the 14 September 2010 Mahrookh Jamali, Fatima Hagnegat, Rasoul Gholampour and Sara Bordbar pleaded guilty at Harrow Crown Court to conspiring to traffick the six females. Each received a custodial sentence.

It is clear that had it not been for the intervention of SCD9 officers these vulnerable young women and children would have been sexually exploited and their entire lives destroyed. Judge Alan Greenwood noted in his summing up that the gang were motivated by greed and their 'purpose was to yield considerable sums for each of the conspirators and that is why wealthy customers were targeted'.

The success of this operation remains overshadowed by the harrowing nature of the crimes being committed.

Case 3: Operation Glenlivet

21.6 In this final scenario it is asserted that the victim was trafficked into the UK and forced to work as a thief. This story is something akin to the fictional acts of Fagin where his workers were trained as thieves and conducted the criminal acts in exchange for a roof over their heads. The victim's account is a harrowing case of deception, brutal beatings and callous organised criminality.

The victim is a Romanian male who was befriended by one of the traffickers near his home town in Romania. The victim could speak English and was offered employment acting as an interpreter for other Romanian workers in the UK. He agreed and within a matter of weeks the travel arrangements had been made and the victim boarded a flight from Romania with five other unwitting victims.

Upon arrival in the UK they were met by other traffickers from the same trafficking network and taken to an address in East London. The group were made to sleep in the back of transit van for the first night. The next day the deception was revealed when they were each ordered to steal £100 per day or face beatings.

Each day with almost military precision the victim was forced to steal along with the other men. On some occasions busy concert venues or nightclubs were targeted by the group and personal belongings were stolen in great volume. The victim on one such night was made to wear ladies tights under his trousers. As the group stole one mobile after the other they were placed inside the tights before the men walked out with the phones undetected.

A few weeks passed before the victim was unable to make his daily target. He was summoned into the front room of the house where he was head butted, kicked and punched by the traffickers. Once incapacitated he was pinned down on the floor and severely burnt on both arms with a cigarette.

Two days later he was again sent out to steal in Oxford Street where he intentionally got stopped by the security staff owing to an overt and hamfisted attempt at shoplifting. The staff initially wanted to simply retrieve the goods and let him go but he pleaded with them to call the police. When uniformed officers arrived he requested that they help him and disclosed his story. Such was the severity of the injuries to his arms that he was taken straight to hospital and required skin grafts for the burns.

Officers from SCD9 were alerted and instigated a trafficking investigation. A number of other victims were rescued. Working with our Romanian enforcement colleagues we have identified the trafficking network. A number of individuals have been arrested and charged with trafficking and causing grievous bodily harm.

They deny the allegations.

COMMENT ON THE CASES

21.7 The full complexity of these cases cannot be revealed in this brief chapter. However, one can begin to see the common strands that run through each case that makes trafficking such a deplorable and immoral crime. In each case a vulnerable and often quite desperate victim was recruited. The extent of the deceit or coercion by the traffickers varies but they each abused their position of power to entice the vulnerable victim. Of those victims brought into the UK, once here the traffickers' control of the victim was increased with the removal of all their identity documents and in each case the victims' movements were controlled, including their access to funds, and the prevention of communication with any third party who was outside of the traffickers' influence. The risk of threatened or actual violence played its part. All of this enabled the trafficking of the victim and, where it had occurred before our intervention, the exploitation of the individual to be sustained whether that was for sexual services, or forced labour as a thief. These are examples of the many hidden cases of trafficking and exploitation that continue to occur today.

THE VITAL ROLE OF PARTNERSHIPS

21.8 It remains the responsibility of the police to bring to justice those responsible for these heinous crimes. As trafficking-related crime is so camouflaged from society a reactive approach that solely waits for victims to come forward will merely skim the surface. We must continue to build effective partnerships with other enforcement agencies in the UK, throughout Europe and across the globe, to share intelligence. Such an international policing response will send a very clear message to all organised crime networks that there will be no hiding place for them. Wherever they base themselves we will relentlessly pursue them to achieve justice. Any policing activity, no matter how robust or effective, will only serve to disrupt and suppress trafficking activity. The solutions to this complex problem will be equally as complex and beyond the scope of policing alone.

Our charity partners are absolutely vital in identifying and supporting trafficking victims. We will continue to expand the working relationships with our NGO partners to improve the referral rate of victims to the police. The more we understand about the picture of human trafficking the more effective we will be in identifying the victims and prosecuting the offenders.

THE CHALLENGES AHEAD

21.9 The longer term challenges will be finding new and innovative ways of engaging with the communities where the victims and their traffickers are created. The Unit has recently published a free phone number for victims to call to request help (0800 783 2589). This is one number that will further demonstrate to victims of trafficking our willingness to listen to them and support them.

Our first year of operating as SCD9 has seen many successes for the team and our NGO partners in identifying and supporting victims of trafficking. However, we are not complacent and will continue to listen and learn from our experiences to improve our service to the people of London.

22

OPERATION GOLF – A UK AND ROMANIA JOINT INVESTIGATION TACKLING ROMANIAN ORGANISED CRIME AND CHILD TRAFFICKING

Bernie Gravett (Superintendent Retired) and Chief Inspector Colin Carswell

INTRODUCTION

22.1

> 'It is a sad fact that children are bought and sold around the world, trafficked into and around the UK for the profit of others. It is a complex but hidden crime that is largely unseen by broader society and unrecognised by frontline services.' (Jim Gamble former head of CEOP)

Operation Golf was the first ever UK Police Joint Investigation (JIT) set up under the European Union framework decision[1] on 'Mutual Legal Assistance' and the first JIT in Europe to focus on human trafficking. The JIT was between the Metropolitan Police (MPS) and the Romanian National Police (RNP) tackling a specific Romanian Roma organised crime group (OCG[2]) that trafficked and exploited children from the Romanian Roma community, one of the poorest and most disadvantaged communities in Europe.

The full investigation team consisted of the following partners:

- The Metropolitan Police
- The Romanian National Police
- The Romanian Prosecutors Office (DIICOT)
- The UK Crown Prosecution Service

Support was also provided by:

- Europol
- Eurojust
- United Kingdom Human Trafficking Centre
- End Child Prostitution and Trafficking UK (ECPAT UK)

This chapter will focus on the case study of 'Maria', a 13 year old Romanian Roma girl trafficked to the UK for forced labour. This case led to the first UK convictions for the trafficking of a child under the Asylum and Immigration

(Treatment of Claimants etc.) Act 2004, s 4, which deals with the crime of trafficking for the purposes of labour exploitation. It will also cover the creation of the first European Joint Investigation into human trafficking.

[1]   OJ L 162, 20.06.2002, Council Framework Decision of 13th June 2002 on Joint Investigation Teams.
[2]   An organised crime group is a working term we use. It is not a legal term.

THE FIRST INDICATION OF TRAFFICKING

22.2 In late 2006 a Czech Roma national by the name of Anna Puzova was stopped by UK Immigration entering the UK at Stansted Airport. Anna was travelling with three children who she claimed were three of her own children. Anna was the mother of eight children; however the three children with her could not communicate with her as they only spoke Romanian. Anna was arrested, the children placed into care and an investigation was commenced by the UK Serious Organised Crime Agency (SOCA). This operation was called 'Operation Girder'. SOCA quickly identified that Anna had, on a number of occasions, entered the UK with a total of 18 other children. The three recovered children were identified as coming from a town in South East Romania called 'Tandarei'.

The SOCA investigation revealed a Roma based criminal network operating in the UK which, it was believed, trafficked children here for the purposes of committing volume crime[1]. The gang's UK leader was identified as a Romanian Roma male by the name of Remus KVEC. While KVEC was based in the north west of England there were many links to addresses in London.

Anna Puzova is a Czech national with eight natural children of her own. The link with KVEC was that she is Roma, as were the victims.

She was paid £1,000 per trip. At this time the gang charged the Romanian Roma families £1,000 per child for them to be trafficked. The children were taken to Italy by the gang and from there flown with Anna to the UK before being passed back to the gang and distributed across the UK.

Puzova pleaded guilty at Chelmsford Crown Court in 2006 to six charges of facilitating the unlawful entry of children into Britain and was jailed for three years.

Of the 21 children trafficked into the UK by KVEC and Puzova only the last three were ever recovered and identified. The SOCA investigation led to the successful prosecution of eight adults for facilitating the unlawful entry of children into the UK. Remus KVEC was sentenced to eight years imprisonment. Anna Puzova pleaded guilty at Chelmsford Crown Court to six charges and was jailed for three years.

However this was only the tip of the iceberg.

[1]   Volume crime is defined as: Those crime categories of a statistically high importance and for which:
(a)   targets for reduction have been set within the organisational policing plan; or
(b)   through assessment, are determined to be of local community safety importance.
Examples of volume crime include offences against the person, burglaries, thefts and criminal damage.

OPERATION EUROPA

22.3 Operation Girder led the Romanian Prosecutors Office (DIICOT) and the Romanian National Police (RNP) to open an investigation into the trafficking from Romania of the three children. This quickly revealed the huge scale of the trafficking. This investigation identified that KVEC was responsible for only the final stage of the trafficking – there was a whole organised criminal gang (OCG) operating across Europe. Both the OCG and the children all originated from the single town – Tandarei, in South East Romania. All the victims and the gang were from the Romanian Roma community. The RNP identified that over a four year period the gang had moved (and were suspected of trafficking) 1087 identified children out of Romania into Hungary and onwards to Western Europe. The early indications were that the majority of these children had been, or were being exploited by being made to beg and steal in a number of European countries.

The RNP investigation identified a number of vehicles (cars and mini busses) being used to drive groups of children (without their parents) through two border posts into Hungary.

For a Romanian child to leave the country without either parent, the transporters need to be in possession of a 'Notary Letter'. This is a legal document giving a named person permission to transport the child across the national border for a specified time period. This document is a legal instrument drawn up by a legal professional in Romania.

In some cases the 'Notary Letter' was found to be forged but in the majority of cases the documents were genuine, signed by the parents of the child. This was an early indication of parental involvement in the potential exploitation of their own children.

The Romanian team discovered that many of the children were being arrested or detained for minor crimes across Europe, primarily in UK, Italy, Spain and France. However their challenge was that if this was to be proved as trafficking the exploitation was taking place outside Romania. All they had to go on at this stage was what they saw, which were the gang members getting richer with no visible means of income.

The most visible aspects were the building of large houses, the purchase of expensive vehicles and the possession of large amounts of disposable cash.

ACCESSION OF ROMANIA AND BULGARIA TO THE EUROPEAN UNION

22.4 In January 2007 Romania joined the EU. Within three months crime in London committed by Romanian nationals went up 786%[1]. Analysis showed the offences to be predominantly theft committed by children from within the Romanian Roma community. The Borough of Westminster was particularly affected by this rise in crime. By comparison the number of Bulgarian nationals being arrested in London grew by only 250%[2].

[1] MPS Nationality Index reports 2007.
[2] MPS Nationality Index reports 2007.

OPERATION GOLF

22.5 In April 2007 Commander Steve Allen, Commander for Westminster commissioned a small team, led by Superintendent Gravett and Chief Inspector Carswell to examine the causes behind this rise in crime. This was again given the name 'Operation Golf'.

Basic analysis revealed that many of the Romanian children found committing crime and begging in London were Roma and were from the same town of Tandarei. Through established international contacts Superintendent Gravett and Chief Inspector Carswell soon discovered that many of these children were in fact many of those same children identified by the Romanian Police as having been moved out of Romania by the gang. It was these children who were driving the huge increase in pick pocketing and theft being experienced in London.

Police research showed that 200 of the 1107 victims identified by the RNP were criminally active in London in the summer of 2007 and also they had convictions in 32 other UK Police Force areas. Traditionally child offenders in the UK operated locally; they certainly did not usually travel the length and breadth of the country. There were obviously adults controlling the children. The investigation revealed that it was the same gang as identified by the Romanian Police taking the children out of Romania.

Case study: Girl A

22.6 DOB: 01/01/1986 – now 24 years old

Girl A is one of the 1087 children taken from Romania pre-accession. She was driven out of Romania by the gang in a car with five other children. Her journey took her into Hungary and across Europe. She first came to notice in the UK in 2002 when she was 16 years old. She was arrested for theft within Westminster Borough. She received a juvenile reprimand for this offence. By 2007 she has acquired a total of 17 convictions and three cautions, with offences of shoplifting, distraction thefts and failing to answer court bail. She was arrested a further six times but the offences were not proceeded with. As a result of her extensive criminality she served a prison sentence in Holloway women's prison.

She also had a total of eight alias names and nine dates of birth. There were 43 intelligence reports on her in London. She was arrested predominantely in Westminster but also in Enfield, Camden, Hammersmith and Kensington. She was also known to commit offences in Surrey, the City of London and within the area covered by British Transport Police.

In 2006 she was moved by the gang to Spain but was returned to the UK in 2007 following accession of Romania into the EU.

She had numerous associates, all of whom had convictions and were well known to Police within the Metropolitan Police District. Throughout her time in the UK, committing crime on a large scale she remained under the control and direction of the gang and lived in poverty, gaining no benefit from her criminality.

Dipping a toe in the water: 'Operation Caddy'

22.7 In the last quarter of 2007 intelligence revealed that each day up to 50 Romanian Roma women and children travelled into London from Slough train station. The groups would then split up; begging and stealing across central London.

The intelligence showed that the group were all from Tandarei and were linked to the known gang members by family and clan allegiances. In addition many of the children being arrested or encountered committing crime in London were on the Operation Europa potential victims list.

To combat this criminal activity the MPS Operation Golf team set up an operation along with colleagues from the Thames Valley Police. The operation was given the name 'Operation Caddy'. At this early stage we believed that we would encounter members of the gang and children from the 'Europa' list but we were uncertain if we would find conclusive evidence of child trafficking. One concerning factor was that the intelligence showed that many parents of the children from the 'Europa' list were believed to have joined their children in the UK. Did this show that the parents were complicit or were being threatened or coerced by the gang?

On the 28 January 2008 the MPS team executed search warrants at 16 addresses in Slough. This resulted in the arrest of 34 people for a variety of crimes including child trafficking, child neglect, money laundering, theft and benefit fraud. Over 200 items of stolen property were recovered.

The most important aspect was that within the 16 small terraced three bedroom houses police found 211 people. Half of these were children. Ten children were taken into police protection[1] when it was found that their parents were not present.

Some houses were occupied by three families with children sleeping on the floor, on sheets and in one case a child had her bed in a bath. The operation was conducted with the full support of Slough Borough Council and Thames Valley Police. We were shocked to discover 60 children, under the age of 10, who local social services had no knowledge of. Only three children were attending school; all were the the sons of the gang leader in the town. No girls were in education.

---

[1] **Children Act 1989 Police Protection Powers** – Section 46(1) of the Children Act 1989 empowers a police officer, who has reasonable cause to believe that a child would otherwise be likely to suffer significant harm to: (a) remove the child to suitable accommodation and keep him/her there; or (b) take such steps as are reasonable to ensure that the child's removal from any hospital, or other place, in which he/she is then being accommodated is prevented. The child is considered to be in police protection when these powers have been exercised by the police. This power is limited to emergencies where the delay of applying for a section 44 Emergency Protection Order would pose significant harm to a child. The police's power to act under s 46 does not arise from a court order and hence should not be referred to as a police protection order.

Operation Caddy analysis

22.8 16 addresses;

211 people encountered;

103 adults;

60% with criminal records;

33 Juveniles;

78% criminal records;

74 minors (under 10);

47% on MPS intelligence for committing crime in London;

Prevalence in under age pregnancy some as young as 13 yrs old;

Only 3 children in education;

60 minors not known to Slough Borough Council;

54% reduction in pickpocket offences in Westminster for the following six months;

The days following the operation saw the parents of the 10 children placed into Police protection arriving from Romania and Spain. The parents had a variety of accounts as to how their children had been left with families who were exploiting them. Nine of the children were returned to their parents with care procedures put in place to protect them.

A victim's story. One child spoke out!

Maria's story

22.9 The facts of this case are as follows:

- Her father paid €200 to the OCN to have her trafficked to the UK;
- She was flown to Stansted by Busioc VASILE with the flights paid for on a corrupted USA credit card;
- Placed with an OCN family in Slough and controlled and exploited by Claudia STOICA& Vasile STOICA;
- She was told to call them Uncle and Auntie;
- She became the house slave in domestic servitude and forced labour;
- She was driven to Surrey each day and left for 12 hours to beg, sell the 'Big Issue' illegally and steal;
- She kept nothing, was beaten and searched at the end of her day;
- Her father cloned Maria's identity to exploit children in Valencia Spain;
- Four people were convicted for her trafficking into and around the UK for forced exploitation;
- In November 2008 at Reading Crown Court they were sentenced to a total of 24 years imprisonment for trafficking, child neglect and perjury;
- The urgent need for a JIT with Romania was recognised.

Maria (an alias for protection) was a 13 year old girl from Tandarei. Both she and her sister were taken from Romania to the UK by the gang. Maria was placed by the gang with a family in Slough and exploited. Her sister was never traced.

Maria gave an account of her trafficking and exploitation. This was corroborated by the police investigation. Her father flew into the UK within 24 hours of the operation and gave an account of bringing Maria to the UK for a holiday. He claimed that her had brought her here only three weeks earlier but had to return to Romania for a family emergency. The account given by her father was proven to be untrue. The investigation team quickly identified that Maria had been in the UK for a number of months and they identified those responsible for her trafficking and exploitation.

Within four days, five adults were arrested and charged with trafficking and exploiting Maria.

The charges were laid under the Asylum and Immigration (Treatment of Claimants etc.) Act 2004, s 4(1) and (2). Section 4(1) relates to the trafficking of a person into the UK for the purposes of labour exploitation and s 4(2) relates to the trafficking of a person within the UK for labour exploitation.

At the time this legislation was untested in relation to the trafficking and exploitation of children. The key element for us was our recognition that a child cannot consent to their own exploitation, not that Maria had ever given her consent. The basis of the case was that Maria had been sold to the gang and made to undertake a form of labour for the benefit of the gang members.

She was forced to be the domestic slave, doing the household chores for the family, looking after the family's young children, being forced to sleep on the floor and fed only scraps. In addition to this she was driven across county borders five days a week and made to sell the 'Big Issue' charity magazine on a suburban high street. She had been provided with a fake 'Big Issue' identity card by Busioc VASILE who had himself infiltrated the Big Issue charity as a regional co-ordinator for the Thames Valley area.

She was driven up to 40 miles each 'working' day by her controller Vasile STOICA, the man she was told to call 'Uncle'. She was made to work for up to 12 hours a day in all weathers throughout November and December. She was never provided with a coat and was never given food or drink.

The investigation revealed that members of the local community took pity on her with local shopkeepers providing her with some food and drink.

She was never paid for her 'labour' nor was she allowed to keep any of the proceeds from her begging and selling of the 'Big Issue'. In fact the copies she was made to sell were out of date.

Obtaining Best Evidence

22.10 In the detailed preparation for the 'raids'[1] on the houses in Slough it was understood that frontline officers who would be involved on the day would have little or no understanding of child trafficking. To remedy this, our briefings to staff conducted at 4 o'clock in the morning were meticulous in detail. The briefing covered Roma culture and history in detail and emphasised that we should consider all persons encountered as potential victims of exploitation or trafficking. A great deal of emphasis was placed on the aspects of child welfare and protection. Officers were provided with a prepared proforma of questions that should be asked of all children encountered.

The proforma gave a structure to officers that ensured that every child was asked the same questions about their being in the UK, who they were with, how long they had been here and what they did during their time here. It enabled officers to evidentially record 'first accounts' direct from the children through an interpreter and in the presence of social workers.

The questions covered the structure of each household and the relationships between individuals present. It provided opportunity for investigators to gain a picture of the circumstances in each house. It also went into detail concerning the activities of children living in the properties.

The results of the proforma were telephoned into the operations room that was staffed by Operation Golf staff with access to all available intelligence. From this detailed process it was quickly discovered that 25 of the children on the Europa children's list were present. However it also gave clear indications to officers that some of the children such as Maria were being exploited and potentially trafficked.

It was this process designed by the Golf team that enabled and encouraged Maria to speak out. The proforma that recorded her original account of her exploitation was later used in court to convict her abusers.

Following the initial assessment from the proforma, Maria was placed into Police Protection as we had significant concerns for her safety and we believed that she may have been the victim of trafficking. Social Services were fully involved in the early decision making and alongside the criminal investigation a parallel Section 47 (Children's Act) investigation was conducted.

Maria was subject to an Achieving Best Evidence (ABE) video interview conducted by the Thames Valley Police Child Abuse Team and local Social Services. During this interview Maria reaffirmed her first account and gave in depth detail of her exploitation and the harrowing conditions that she lived under.

The investigation was conducted thoroughly and was far-reaching. Officers travelled to Romania and Spain to collect evidence used at the trial. Strands of enquiry included searching for and recovering CCTV evidence of her movement and exploitation. Witnesses were traced from around the Thames Valley area who had seen or encountered Maria selling the Big Issue. Some statements gave great detail of how she was inappropriately dressed for the inclement weather and her general poor state.

One important evidential aspect that was covered was the utilisation of Europol to search for intelligence from other European law enforcement agencies relating to Maria. This revealed that there was a record of a girl matching Maria's details as having committed street crime and begging in Valencia, Spain.

Chief Inspector Colin Carswell and Slough social services travelled to Valencia where they contacted both the police and Social Services. There was indeed an extensive file on the 'Spanish' Maria. She had been given into the care of social services 11 times after being found by police begging or stealing on the streets of Valencia. However the investigators were shocked to find that, on examination of identity photographs of the Spanish Maria, it was not the same girl that was in care in the UK.

On closer examination it was found that Maria's real blood father, the man who had arrived in Slough attempting to 'recover' his daughter from Police

Protection, had himself taken the 'fake' Maria from Social Service's care in Spain using his own child's birth certificate and his real passport.

In the words of his defence lawyer this small piece of evidence was devastating.

This girl is still unknown and she has never been traced.

Prior to the trial and following contact over the telephone with her mother in Romania, Maria changed her story completely and withdrew her original account.

In the interests of fairness, police and social services re-interviewed Maria under ABE conditions. Her fresh account now matched the story given by her father. This effectively left the police with a victimless prosecution, but the quality of the evidence gathered and the fair treatment and balance given to Maria, allowed for an effective trial.

In September 2008 following a full trial at Reading Crown Court, four of the five adults, including Maria's Father, were convicted of her trafficking and child neglect. Her father was also convicted of attempting to pervert the course of justice.

These were the first ever convictions in the UK for trafficking a child for non-sexual exploitation under the Asylum and Immigration (Treatment of Claimants etc.) Act 2004, s 4.

This investigation highlighted the complicity of parents in the trafficking of their own children. While debt slavery is one aspect of how the gang controls the families, greed also plays a part.

[1]   The police were to be accompanied by social workers and interpreters on these planned raids.

Sentencing

22.11 One of the challenges in this case was that as this was the first conviction for the trafficking of a child for labour exploitation in the UK, there were no sentencing guidelines available to the judge for this. Whilst the media reported in its headlines that members of a trafficking gang were sentenced to 24 years' imprisonment for child trafficking, in fact on each individual trafficking charge only 18 month prison sentences were handed down. This was despite the maximum sentence for the s 4 trafficking crime being 14 years' imprisonment. Sentences of similar, short, length were given to Vasile STOICA for benefit fraud and to Maria's father for attempting to pervert the course of justice.

Maria's Care Proceedings

22.12 In addition to the criminal prosecution there was a parallel care case running concerning Maria's welfare. This was taken to the High Court with the outcome being that UK courts have to rely on the Brussels II[1] decision that a (trafficked) child must be returned to their parents in their country of origin for the authorities to manage their welfare. Subsequently Maria was repatriated to Romania and she passed into the care of Romanian Social Services. She was later reunited with her mother. While there is no evidence that she has been re-trafficked the intelligence received was that she was sold into marriage and became pregnant at age 14.

¹ Council Regulation (EC) No 2201/2003 of 27 November 2003 concerning jurisdiction and the recognition and enforcement of judgments in matrimonial matters and the matters of parental responsibility ('Brussels II') – see http://europa.eu/legislation_summaries/justice_freedom_sec urity/judicial_cooperation_in_civil_matters/l33194_en.htm.

Brussels II — Jurisdiction in relation to parental responsibility

22.13 Article 66 applies in children's cases. This is the article that relates to member states where there are two or more systems of law. Any reference to habitual residence in the member state 'shall refer to habitual residence in a territorial unit'. This implies that jurisdiction lies with the courts of the territorial unit in which the child is habitually resident. Such an interpretation would be consistent with the provisions relating to divorce. On this view, Brussels II governs the distribution of cases within the United Kingdom, as well as distribution between EU member states.

As a victim of trafficking who had only been in the UK for a few months the court decided that Maria was 'habitually resident' in Romania and that Romania had jurisdiction in matters of her welfare. This applied despite police presenting a case that she would be at risk of retribution, harm and further exploitation.

The High Court's decision was that it had to abide by Brussels II and Maria's safety and welfare was a matter for Romania.

1 SEPTEMBER 2008 THE FORMATION OF THE JOINT INVESTIGATION TEAM (JIT)

22.14 The international nature of the OCG¹ and the fact that the exploitation was occurring in the UK but the profits were realised in Romania, required a co-ordinated investigation. It needed to be a focused and efficient partnership between the MPS and Romanian Law enforcement. It was agreed that an official Joint Investigation Team (JIT) was required to combat the gang. This was the first EU JIT tackling human trafficking. In addition we were the first UK police force to set up and conduct a JIT with another EU state².

The JIT was initially 70% funded by a grant obtained from the European Commission under the Freedom, Security and Justice ISEC fund. The MPS Territorial Policing Command covered the remaining costs.

¹ Organised Criminal Gang.
² The only other case of a UK JIT was between the NCIS and the Dutch police in 2006 it lasted only three months and targeted drug trafficking.

What is a JIT?

22.15 Article 13 of the European Convention on Mutual Legal Assistance in Criminal Matters of 29 May 2000 and/or of the Council Framework Decision of 13 June 2002 on Joint Investigation Teams (JITs) provides the legal basis of the arrangements for the conduct of JITs in EU member states.

The full JIT partnership was Operation Golf (MPS), Romanian National Police, D.I.I.C.O.T. (Romanian Prosecutors Office), the United Kingdom Human Trafficking Centre (UKHTC), Crown Prosecution Service, Europol and Eurojust.

The Strategic objectives of the JIT were to successfully:

- Investigate and prosecute OCN members both in the UK and Romania;
- Disrupt their activities;
- Identify, restrain and confiscate criminal assets;
- Reduce criminality;
- Minimise the exploitation of victims;
- Improve victim identification and response to child trafficking by police and partners.

It was accepted at an early stage that the crime of human trafficking across international borders is extremely hard to prosecute. With this in mind it was agreed that the Romanian teams would focus on the main traffickers who lived in their jurisdiction while Operation Golf would seek to identify and prosecute senior gang members present in the UK whenever they were found, for any form of serious criminality.

The Golf policy was to prosecute for any serious crime discovered and not just human trafficking. This decision was based on adopting an 'Al Capone' approach[1] in the sense that when a major trafficker is in prison he is disrupted from his core business which in turn protects and saves victims from harm/exploitation.

A factor in this decision was also the sentencing powers of Romanian courts. In Romania the crime of trafficking carries a maximum sentence of 20 years and sentencing in Romania is generally more severe than sentences handed down in the UK. Romania also has a crime of 'being a member of an organised criminal gang'. This crime is not available to UK law enforcement.

This decision was also tactical. It was believed that by taking on the network in both countries, the impact on the entire network could be maximised with convictions in both countries thus undermining the ability of the gangs to function and operate.

---

[1] The use of prosecutions of dangerous people for provable crimes, no matter how minor, was the method adopted to bring down Al Capone, his criminal networks and his enterprises in the USA.

Support to Romanian Investigation

22.16 One of the main advantages of a JIT is the ability to exchange evidence and make investigative requests without the need for a Commission Rogitoire (Letter of Request).

The UK Operation Golf team supplied the Romanian investigation with a full and extensive evidential package to prove the exploitation of the children and families within the UK. This included, in an evidential format, the full offending history and surrounding circumstances of all the children identified as criminally active in the UK. This amounted to over 200 children, who had in excess of 2,000 criminal convictions between them.

The offending by these children had taken place in 41 of the 43 police forces of England and Wales. This is literally the length and breadth of the country. This element of our work was conducted with the assistance of the UK Human Trafficking Centre based at the time in Sheffield.

Operation Longship — a test of the JIT framework

22.17 A significant problem for Romania's efforts to tackle the grand scale of human trafficking is that the trafficked and exploited Romanian children are most often found in other jurisdictions. Another challenge for the team was that in Romania a child witness must be represented by a Romanian lawyer. To deal with this the Romanian team included four independent Romanian lawyers to oversee the process to allow the testimony of the children to be admissible in Romanian Law. This was the first such action of its kind in JIT history.

Because of the JIT we were able to deal with these issues by flying the Romanian investigation team to the UK for Operation Longship with the assistance of the EC funding.

The UK team identified and recovered 27 children from the Europa list. Following completion of UK Safeguarding Procedures the children and accompanying adults were then 'invited to assist in giving evidence to the Romanian team via a "Witness Hearing" under Romanian Law on UK soil, which they agreed to do'.

Along with achieving other important evidence this substantial piece of work has directly resulted in the Romanian authorities arresting and charging 26 Romanian nationals, all senior members of the gang, with trafficking 181 children to the UK for forced criminality in the form of begging and stealing. They have also been charged with money laundering and being members of an organised criminal gang. In addition, several have been charged with serious firearms offences.

Operation Europa arrest phase

22.18 The first phase of the Romanian arrest operation took place on 8 April 2010. This involved the execution of search warrants at 34 addresses in Tandarei and the arrest of 18 people for child trafficking, money laundering and being members of a criminal gang. The Romanian operation was supported by 26 members of the Metropolitan Police whose roles included command and control and 11 investigation teams to accompany RNP officers on the searches.

This was a unique operation as the MPS officers who were operating under the JIT had full investigative and search powers to assist our Romanian colleagues. They took an active role in searching for evidence for both UK and Romanian prosecutions. The team included two professional police photographers who recorded evidence and events on video for use in the UK courts.

In addition to the arrests the Romanian authorities seized four AK47 rifles, 12 hunting rifles, 12 shotguns including military grade weapons and 6 handguns.

Other items seized included 11 kilos of gold, €25,000, £25,000 and 40,000 Romanian Lei, 13 high value cars, six houses and a substantial amount of evidence linking the gang to the UK and other EU countries.

The above seizures are clear evidence of the power and wealth of this criminal gang who have made their lives comfortable and have become powerful as a direct result of profits they have acquired through the trafficking and exploitation of vulnerable Roma children and their families. The possession of the weaponry clearly shows that they control this small Romanian community by fear and force in addition to their cultural positions as heads of families and clans.

Operation Golf, with the support of specialist MPS units made extensive efforts to identify, recover and safeguard the 181 victims trafficked by the gang and exploited in the UK. At the time of writing, 35 of these victims have been identified and safeguarded. It is strongly believed that the remaining victims are no longer in the UK.

Operation Golf: Arrests to date

22.19 Since the inception of the JIT there have been a total of **71 UK based convictions** of persons linked to the OCG. The convictions have been for a variety of crimes but include:

- Human Trafficking – Immigration Act, s 4(1) (Into UK);
- Human Trafficking – Immigration Act, s 4(2) (Within the UK);
- Money laundering;
- Obtaining Benefit by Deception Immigration Act, s 106;
- Conspiracy to defraud;
- Forgery;
- Theft Act 1968, s 22(1) – Handling Stolen Goods.

With the exception of the four convicted following the trial in the case of Maria, every single suspect charged pleaded guilty at court. This is a testament to the diligence of the investigators and the careful preparation of the cases in partnership with the Crown Prosecution Service.

Significant convictions include:

- Large scale benefit fraud facilitated by UK based Roma on behalf of the OCG. All pleaded guilty at Southwark Crown Court. (£3 million fraud proved. Potential fraud, had claims not been closed was £12.9 million).
- Large scale benefit fraud, money laundering and forgery against 11 members of the OCG and two associates. All pleaded guilty in April 2011 at Southwark Crown Court. (£800,000 fraud proved potential annual loss of £4.5 million). This element of the gang provided false identities for children brought to the UK and provided false government documents used to obtain benefits.

All persons convicted in this operation have had applications for deportation, and those arrested in Romania for exclusion from the UK, submitted through UK Border Agency.

CONCLUSION

22.20 This operation concluded on 31 December 2010 as planned, and with the imprisonment of over 80% of those persons identified as being UK-based members of the organised criminal gang. This has dismantled their organisation and curtailed their ability to operate in London.

23

CHILD TRAFFICKING INVESTIGATIONS AND PROSECUTIONS

Detective Constable Sarah Wood

INTRODUCTION

23.1 My interest in the correlation between child abuse investigation, child migration and child trafficking began whilst working on a child abuse investigation team in north London. At the time, the Metropolitan Police Child Abuse Investigation Command was involved in a study of child migration into the UK via London Heathrow airport, namely Paladin Child, the executive summary of which is available online. The project was a unique partnership effort to combine the different working practices and focus of three statutory agencies: immigration, police, social services and the NSPCC. The final report[1] was a result of more than eight months of work undertaken in an attempt to define the nature of child migration from non-EU countries to the UK.

Paladin Child gathered data on all non-European unaccompanied children landing at Heathrow airport during a three month period from August to November 2003. Data gathered on these children – including the child's sponsor, their meeter/greeter, destination address, travel and document details – were obtained then assessed against six potential risk categories:

- Address already known to Paladin Child Team;
- Sponsor/greeters address already known to Paladin Child Team;
- Under 16 years old and staying more than 28 days (private fostering);
- No date of return given;
- Greeter is already known to Immigration authority;
- Concerns identified by other means.

Of a total 1,738 children who arrived during the period, 551 were deemed to be worthy of follow-up enquiries, were risk assessed as potentially trafficked and their details passed to the local authority for the area where the child was staying for an assessment by the local children's social care department. The following five nationalities accounted for a third of the children assessed as potential victims of trafficking: Nigeria (46), South Africa (38), Ghana (36), Zimbabwe (28) and Malaysia (25).

The Paladin Child executive summary stated:

'It is the firm belief . . . .that this scoping study has identified that there is sufficient concern about the numbers of unaccompanied minors transiting through Heathrow to warrant the creation of a new multi-agency response to child migration.'

Whilst the findings of Paladin Child were announced almost eight years ago they are still highly relevant today and were instrumental in bringing about changes in the way children were viewed within the immigration system.

As a result of the study, a number of recommendations were made and the Paladin Team was established in October 2003, and comprised of Detective Constables with child abuse investigation experience, and immigration officers. Although the team was small, (1 Detective Sergeant, 4 Detective Constables, and two Immigration Officers, all overseen by a Detective Inspector) the team had responsibility for safeguarding at all London ports and the Asylum Screening Unit in Croydon. As one of the founder members of the team, my introduction was a baptism of fire and I learnt a number of lessons quite quickly, particularly regarding language barriers and cultural differences. Working with staff from the UK Border Agency, safeguarding interventions were made in cases where the children, had they been allowed entry to the United Kingdom, would have faced an unacceptable level of risk and those children were duly accommodated by the local authority or returned to their parents.

As the level of experience within the team grew I became increasingly involved in delivering child trafficking awareness sessions to teams working within both the police and immigration services, and I also delivered training with ECPAT (UK) to local authority staff working within children's social care. I believe that knowledge of child trafficking is limited in many organisations which have day to day contact with children, and that confusion is rife in some areas as to who is and is not a potentially trafficked child. In my opinion a programme of education which clarifies the differences between facilitation (human smuggling) and trafficking (the movement of the child for the purposes of exploitation) and explains clearly the indicators of trafficking and exploitation, together with increased awareness around the child protection issues of private fostering[2], would be of real benefit to many professionals working with children.

In this chapter I will explore in detail three cases I have investigated which have resulted in successful prosecutions. Each relates to adults bringing children to the UK in order to exploit them or to gain benefit by their presence in the UK. None of the cases were straightforward and indeed each was highly challenging in many different ways.

---

[1] Paladin Child (The safeguarding children strand of Maxim funded by Reflex) 2003, available at http://www.mpa.gov.uk/downloads/committees/ppr/ppr-040712-14-appendix01.pdf.
[2] See ECPAT's Understanding Paper 'Child Trafficking and Private Fostering', February 2011.

R V PEACE SANDBERG, ISLEWORTH CROWN COURT, 2008

23.2 This case was instrumental in identifying a loophole in the trafficking legislation at the time.

The defendant PS was a former Kensington Housing Trust worker with dual nationality. She was Nigerian by birth and had acquired Swedish nationality by marriage. At the time of her arrest she was separated from her husband who lived in Sweden.

From January 2005 she privately rented a property for herself and her daughter in Acton, London until her eviction in June 2006 following a Court Order for her to vacate the property.

Following their eviction PS and her daughter were provided with temporary accommodation by Ealing Council's Homeless Persons Unit (HPU)[1]. However, in August 2006 the HPU became aware that PS's daughter was not living with her mother at the address. This brought PS's entitlement to that property to an end, and new eviction proceedings were instigated by the local authority. Enquiries subsequently revealed that her daughter had been sent to live in Sweden with her father.

PS then travelled alone to Nigeria in November 2006. A few weeks later she attended the British High Commission in Abuja, Nigeria, where she applied for entry clearance to the UK for a three-month-old child who she had added in her Nigerian passport as being her son. PS made a number of further false statements regarding her relationship with the infant and accommodation in the UK on her visa application for him, and she repeated these statements during her interview with the immigration officer at the British High Commission. She stated to the officer that she had travelled out to Nigeria earlier in the summer to have her baby, so as to enable him to acquire Nigerian citizenship, and that she now needed to return to the UK to take him to hospital as he was sick. Having secured a visa for the infant, PS then returned to London with the child and on arrival again told immigration officers that she was the child's mother. She then immediately went to the local authority to apply for housing on behalf of herself and her baby. Council officials were immediately suspicious due to the fact that PS had been seen at the Council offices a few months earlier and she had not been pregnant at the time. PS then changed her story and said she had adopted the child. Members of the Council's staff were still not satisfied by PS's accounts and, suspecting her of seeking to use the child to obtain Council accommodation they contacted the local authority children's social care and the police.

A criminal investigation was launched by the Paladin Team.

It appeared to those involved in investigating the case that PS's clear motive for bringing the child to the UK had been to gain for herself increased access to benefits and housing. At the time, human trafficking for the purposes of labour exploitation was a criminal offence in the UK by virtue of the Asylum and Immigration (Treatment of Claimants etc) Act 2004, s 4. Section 4(4) of the 2004 Act stated:

'For the purposes of this section a person is exploited if (and only if)—
(a)   he is the victim of behaviour that contravenes Article 4 of the Human Rights Convention (slavery and forced labour),
(b)   he is encouraged, required or expected to do anything as a result of which he or another person would commit an offence under the Human Organ Transplants Act 1989...,
(c)   he is subjected to force, threats or deception designed to induce him—
       (i)   to provide services of any kind,

(d)
      (ii)   to provide another person with benefits of any kind, or
      (iii)   to enable another person to acquire benefits of any kind, or
he is requested or induced to undertake any activity, having been chosen as the subject of the request or inducement on the grounds that—
      (i)   he is mentally or physically ill or disabled, he is young or he has a family relationship with a person, and
      (ii)   a person without the illness, disability, youth or family relationship would be likely to refuse the request or resist the inducement.'
[Emphasis underlined]

The wording of s 4(4)(d) at that time presented an insurmountable barrier to a successful prosecution of PS for child trafficking as it was considered impossible to evidence the fact that an infant could be 'requested or induced' to undertake the relevant activity. As a direct result of the legal loophole that was exposed in the PS case this wording was subsequently amended by the Borders, Citizenship and Immigration Act 2009, s 54 which removed the requirement that the victim be 'requested or induced'. The amended s 4(4)(d) of the 2004 Act now provides that:

'(d)   a person uses or attempts to use him for any purpose within sub-paragraph (i), (ii) or (iii) of paragraph (c), having chosen him for that purpose on the grounds that—
      (i)   he is mentally or physically ill or disabled, he is young or he has a family relationship with a person, and
      (ii)   a person without the illness, disability, youth or family relationship would be likely to refuse to be used for that purpose.' [Emphasis underlined]

The 2009 amendment ensures that a trafficking charge can now be brought against those who exploit a passive individual, or child too young to give evidence, in order to gain benefit[2].

Early advice was sought from the Crown Prosecution Service as this case was, to our knowledge, the first of its kind. At that time it was not deemed necessary for police officers to secure evidence in Nigeria and as a result the local authority sent social workers to Nigeria in order to try and trace the infant's family. Although this search was unsuccessful the social workers did obtain important information from a witness about how the child had been acquired by PS. Unfortunately this information, which may have assisted the prosecution case, was not obtained in an appropriate evidential format and therefore it was not admissible in the criminal court.

PS was therefore charged with the human smuggling offence under the Immigration Act 1971, s 25 – Assisting Unlawful Immigration[3]. She was found guilty at Isleworth Crown Court in April 2008 and in May 2008 she was sentenced to 26 months' imprisonment[4]. The young child in this case was made the subject of a care order and was subsequently adopted in the UK. His family in Nigeria was never traced.

---

[1]   PS knew that as a European citizen working in the UK she would be eligible for a council flat because she had a child.

[2]   The Explanatory Notes to the 2009 Act explain: '203. Section 54 expands the definition of exploitation in the offence of trafficking in section 4 of the AITCA 2004. This is to cover use or attempted use of a person for the provision of services or the provision or acquisition of benefits of any kind, where the person is chosen on the grounds of ill-health, disability, youth or family relationship. This section substitutes the existing definition in section 4(4)(d) of that Act, which provides that a person who is "requested or induced" to undertake any activity is

exploited. The effect of this amendment is to ensure the offence of trafficking captures those cases where the role of the person being exploited is entirely passive, and where the person is being used as a tool by which others can gain a benefit of any kind.'

3   An offence which was not designed to cover trafficking or exploitation, intended or otherwise.

4   Media reports include: http://news.bbc.co.uk/1/hi/uk/7404090.stm and http://www.telegraph.co.uk/news/uknews/1969292/Heartless-Nigerian-woman-buys-baby-to-qualify-for-council-fla t-in-London.html.

Comment on identification issues

23.3 Whilst there are many challenges with investigating child trafficking, two of the biggest difficulties relate to issues of identification namely:(i) identifying the child or young person as a victim of trafficking, and (ii) discovering the personal identification of the victim.

In the case of *R v Quainoo and Quainoo*, both of these issues had to be resolved.

The following brief facts outline the case.

R V SAMUEL QUAINOO & ERNESTINA QUAINOO, ISLEWORTH CROWN COURT 2008

23.4 In May 2006 a young Ghanaian female, Miss X, claiming to be 16 years old, attended the local authority offices of Hillingdon Borough Children's Social Care. She requested medical attention and told the duty social worker that she had been brought to the UK a few years earlier by her 'parents, the Qainoo's[1]', and had been used by them as a domestic slave. During a strategy discussion between a social work manager and a supervisor from the local child abuse investigation team the same day it was agreed that: a joint agency investigation, involving both the local authority and the police, under the Children Act 1989, s 47[2] ('a Section 47 Enquiry') be carried out; that X should be accommodated by the local authority; and that, subject to X's consent, a medical examination be conducted. The social worker allocated to support X gained her confidence as a result of which further information came to light. X stated that she had been brought from Ghana to London by Ernestina Quainoo in July 2004, and she now disclosed that although she had initially stated that SQ and EQ were her parents and that her name was XQ (ie that she had the same family name as the Q's) this was not correct and her name was actually XY (ie she was not related to the Q's at all). X claimed that whilst living as an unpaid servant for the Q's in the UK she was verbally abused by them, was branded a witch and was denied access to health care and education.

It should be noted at this stage of the investigation that had the case been judged solely on the initial facts, it could have been viewed as the case of a difficult teenager experiencing problems with her parents and she could have been returned to the family and the matter dealt with as a Children Act 1989, s 17[3] ('Child in Need') issue. The efforts of the social worker in gaining X's trust, together with her awareness of trafficking, prevented that from happening.

The ensuing period of evidence gathering was not without difficulties. A video interview was carried out with X which provided evidence of her life in Ghana prior to her being brought to the UK, of her journey to the UK and of events after arrival. It was clear from her account, (and subsequently confirmed during a police evidence-gathering visit to Ghana), that X had come from a very poor family. She had been given away twice by her mother who was unable to bring her up, and X had ended up, in Ghana, as street seller hawking plastic bags for a man and bread for a woman. The video interview was carried out very slowly with due regard for X's age, maturity and cognitive ability. Language had to be carefully chosen and questions phrased appropriately.

During her interview X spoke of having wanted to be looked after as a child by her mother, of running back to her mother when she had been sent away to work for others in Ghana, of wanting to stay with her, and of not wanting to come to England. Her mother gave her no choice in the matter however. And once handed over to the Qs X had no influence over what was to happen to her. Of her time in the UK, where her sole purpose in life was to cook, clean and care for the young child in the Q's household, she described feeling lonely with no friends or contacts and of constant verbal abuse and belittlement all of which drove her to contemplate suicide. X described how she was allowed out of the house as one of her duties was to take the young child to pre-school but she was denied any schooling herself. When she sought refuge at the local library to 'better' herself, the Qs banned her from bringing any books home.

A local librarian confirmed that she would sometimes see X sitting in the library alone, reading books appropriate for someone far younger than her due to her limited education.

X had few personal possessions but photographs taken of her in Ghana showed a healthy young girl which was found to be in stark contrast to the painfully thin girl we interviewed. The clothes that the Qs had given to her to wear were either highly inappropriate[4] for someone of her age or were very old and too big for her, in complete contrast to the well-fitting new clothes provided by the Qs to their own son.

During a search of the Q household, a number of items were seized including two different birth certificates, both falsely showing X to be the daughter of the Qs but with different dates of birth. X's passport was also seized and although it was a genuine Ghanaian passport it had been fraudulently obtained (but not by X).

Having gathered evidence from a number of sources, it was deemed necessary by the CPS to establish X's date of birth, thus necessitating a trip to Ghana. It was only during this trip that I fully appreciated the real vulnerability of children from countries with less effective registration systems than that in the United Kingdom.

Article 7 of the United Nations Convention on the Rights of the Child states:

'The child shall be registered immediately after birth and shall have the right from birth to a name, the right to acquire a nationality and. as far as possible, the right to know and be cared for by his or her parents.
Parties shall ensure the implementation of these rights in accordance with their national law and their obligations under the relevant international instruments in this field, in particular where the child would otherwise be stateless.'

According to the UNICEF 'The State of the World's Children' report of 2011[5], within rural areas of Western and Central Africa, only 33% of births are registered; this number drops to 27% in rural areas of Eastern and Southern Africa.

In many respects it was unsurprising therefore that we were unable to establish X's date of birth whilst in Ghana. This became an issue when considering the appropriate charges. In order to have brought a charge of child cruelty[6] against the Qs it would have required us to prove that X was under the age of 16. The other obstacle which prevented a charge of human trafficking was that the s 4 trafficking offence under the Asylum and Immigration (Treatment of Claimants) Act 2004, which includes exploitation by way of domestic servitude, was only brought into force in the UK in December 2004 but X had been trafficked into the UK before this date, in July 2004, a fact we had already established..

Owing to the inapplicability of the s 4 trafficking offence SQ and EQ were charged instead with the Immigration Act 1971, s 25 offence, namely Assisting Unlawful Immigration. The charge rested principally upon the fact that the Qs had falsely declared that X was their biological daughter in fraudulent identity documents when they had brought her into the UK.

The matter of the Q's claims regarding X subsequently became the subject of a Newton Hearing[7] at Isleworth Crown Court in July 2008 since, although the defendants both entered guilty pleas to the s 25 charge, they claimed to have effected a 'customary adoption' of X in Ghana, maintained that they treated her as part of their family in the UK[8] and denied having exploited her in any way whatsoever. X, who was still a minor at the time of the criminal proceedings, courageously gave evidence via live video link at the hearing in front of His Honour Judge Lowen. Owing to the restricted matter before him, namely the s 25 charge, as opposed to a trafficking charge, HHJ Lowen formally reminded himself that 'I have been careful not to have regard to the complaints made by (X), which could not bear upon the narrow issue which really comes to this: for what purpose did these defendants arrange for [her] to enter the United Kingdom?'

In his judgment HHJ Lowen concluded:

> 'I am required to judge the purpose these defendants had when committing this offence and I have inferred from their conduct towards (X) since her arrival in the United Kingdom, that the true purpose was to ensure a continuing employer/employee relationship and to enjoy childcare in a convenient way and at minimal cost and in reliance on the vulnerability of (X) as they exploited the illegality of the fabric of her life here; an illegality of their making and from which they derived the opportunity to abuse the trust (X) had placed in them.'

In sentencing the Qs the judge found it was 'clear that girl's entry [into the UK] was carefully planned' by the Qs and that X was 'especially vulnerable because of her dependence upon the Quainoo's for her identity'. The judge concluded that:

> 'This was a case of utter exploitation where she was entirely subservient to your will.'

Sentences of 18 months' imprisonment[9] and 12 months' (suspended) were imposed on SQ and EQ respectively. X subsequently won her asylum appeal and she lives in the UK as a recognised refugee.

1   Samuel Quainoo (SQ) was an accountant, Ernestina Quainoo (EQ) a teacher. This case hence demonstrated the exploitation of a child who was subjected to domestic servitude by professionals in the UK.
2   See http://www.legislation.gov.uk/ukpga/1989/41/section/47.
3   http://www.legislation.gov.uk/ukpga/1989/41/section/17.
4   The only clothes the Qs had bought her to wear were two t-shirts which proclaimed 'My other name is bitch'.
5   Available at http://www.unicef.org/sowc2011/.
6   Children and Young Persons Act 1933, s 1. This offence can be committed in five different ways (assaults, ill-treats, neglects, abandons or exposes).
7   A Newton hearing can be described as a trial within a trial: if, following a guilty plea, the factual dispute between the prosecution and defence versions is so different that it affects the appropriate sentence in the case, the court must hear evidence on the disputed points.
8   A defence statement on behalf at the Qs was produced during the criminal proceedings which also stated that X had brought an evil spirit to the home, endorsing the defendants' belief in voodoo.
9   EQ's sentence of imprisonment was suspended by the Judge on the basis that if she too were imprisoned at the same time as her husband their young child, having no parent left to care for him, would have had to have been taken into local authority care.

Comment

23.5 It should be noted that if a similar case was to occur now, then a prosecution for the offence of holding someone in slavery or servitude, or requiring them to perform forced or compulsory labour under the Coroners and Justice Act 2009, s 71[1] could now be considered.

1   The s 71 offence entered into force in England, Wales and Northern Ireland on 6 April 2010. The same offence was introduced in Scots law under the Criminal Justice and Licensing (Scotland) Act 2010, s 47 and entered into force in Scotland in March 2011. For detailed guidance on the s 71 offence see the Ministry of Justice's Court Circular 2010/07, available at http://www.justice.gov.uk/publications/docs/circular-07-2010-coroners-justice-act-section-71.pdf.

R V ADENIJI – ISLEWORTH CROWN COURT, JANUARY 2011

23.6 By way of background to this case, in 2008 a group of young Nigerian women commenced a civil action against the Commissioner of the Metropolitan Police claiming that their rights under Articles 3 and 4 of the European Convention for the Protection for Human Rights and Fundamental Freedoms (ECHR) had been infringed. OOA was one of these claimants whose case was successfully argued before Mr Justice Wyn Williams in the High Court in March 2011[1].

Having issued the proceedings outlined briefly above, OOA indicated to the Metropolitan Police, via her instructed solicitor, her willingness to co-operate with the police and assist with an investigation. I was tasked with this investigation and in early 2009 made contact with her solicitor to arrange to meet with OOA.

I met OOA for the first time with her solicitor in order to introduce myself and establish her views in respect of how her evidence should be obtained. We then arranged, owing to OOA's vulnerability as a witness, for a visually recorded interview to take place in line with the Achieving Best Evidence guidelines[2] at a later date.

During the interview OOA stated that she was brought to London in 1997 at the age of 11 and placed in the Adeniji household. She stated that she was used to care for LA's four children, one of whom was physically disabled and required a great deal of assistance. OOA claimed that her work would entail feeding the children, cooking, cleaning and washing clothes. She stated that her day began early in the morning, when she had to get the children up and off to school, and it finished late at night, with her often not going to bed until well after midnight. OOA was not enrolled in a school, she was denied friends and she was regularly beaten and verbally abused by LA.

As the A family moved abroad temporarily, OOA was then sent to live with another Nigerian woman and her two children in the UK[3].

OOA returned to live with Mrs A and on her return found that DO, another house girl, had also been brought from Nigeria to work for A and that Z, a 15 year old Nigerian boy, had also been used by A as a houseboy but he had run away. OOA described life in the A household as volatile: she was regularly beaten and verbally abused by LA. During one particular assault LA repeatedly hit her with a stick and OOA fell to the floor unconscious. LA then kicked OOA in the head, an act that was witnessed by DO. At around the same time OOA stated that another pastor had given a sermon at church about parental responsibility and childcare. This she claimed spurred her on to leave the A's household which she did, by running away to stay with friends. She feared that had she remained in the house LA would have killed her.

OOA stated that she subsequently returned to the A household in an attempt to collect her documents and passport and that LA denied having them. However, during a police search a number of items including OOAs birth certificate and educational certificates were subsequently found at LA's house.

Having investigated the families involved, details of a previous similar allegation came to light. Two years earlier DO, then a 17 year old female, had attended a police station where she made a report that she had been assaulted by LA and that she had fled the A house at around midnight having been stripped to her underwear and beaten with a belt. The matter had been investigated by officers at the time: DO had been medically examined and a visually recorded interview with her had been conducted. LA was arrested at that time and interviewed. She had denied the allegations. DO then gave a further statement to the police stating that everything she had put in her original statement was true, but that she did not want any further action taken.

LA was arrested and during interview she stated that she had allowed OOA to live in her house, claiming that she knew OOA was Nigerian. LA had difficulty in answering questions with regards to her own children, initially refusing to answer questions regarding how many children she had. She admitted that she had had a boy, Z living with her for two years but claimed that she had 'adopted' him as her son, that Z was Nigerian and that he had been 'willed' to her. She went on to admit that she had obtained a British Passport for him by deception by stating on her application that he was her biological son. As a result, the police applied to obtain copies of the birth certificates for LA and all her dependants as she claimed all of them, including herself, were British.

By this point in the investigation, matters had progressed from one victim alleging trafficking by LA, to the probability of LA trafficking potentially three victims for domestic servitude, together with her being potentially criminally liable for immigration offences and a fraudulent application for a British passport.

Once the British birth certificates were received, having studied them we noticed a significant discrepancy. LA was named as being the mother on all her five children's birth certificates and she herself had a British birth certificate which showed that she was born in London. However, despite the fact that the father on each of the children's birth certificates was recorded as being the same man, the certificates showed on one certificate that he was born in Nigeria, yet on the other four children's that he was born in London. It seemed strange. More enquiries were made and it soon transpired that LA had used the birth certificate of a third person in order to apply for a British passport for herself. Enquiries revealed that this third person had been at school with LA in Nigeria. LA would have been aware of the fact that this individual had been born in the United Kingdom in the 1960's, a time when she would have been entitled to British Nationality. Having obtained this person's birth certificate and passport LA then obtained several passports for her birth children by deception, and furthermore obtained British passports for DO and Z to which they were not entitled by claiming them as her dependants.

Then came the unenviable task of tracing DO and asking her if she would co-operate with our investigation. At the same time we had to notify her that we were aware that her identity had been acquired fraudulently. This was difficult. DO had tried hard to put her past behind her, had studied and gained qualifications and was beginning to build herself a new life. All of this was to be shattered by the fact that we had traced her and pulled the rug from under her feet by telling her that the passport she possessed, which she believed to be genuine, had been cancelled by the UK passport agency. DO was extremely wary of our contact, and was at first reluctant to co-operate. We provided her with details of where to seek help, of websites and of NGO's who would be in a position to offer her assistance. DO eventually agreed to support our investigation and provided us with further evidence, as did Z the young man who had lived with the family who was subsequently traced.

Once the evidence was gathered, we then considered what the appropriate charges should be and settled on charges of Child Cruelty, Actual Bodily Harm, Assisting Unlawful Entry to the UK and deceptions. Once again we were unable to proceed with trafficking charges as all of the young people had come to the UK prior to enactment of the relevant legislation[4]. These charges accurately reflected what had actually happened and the circumstances as a whole. Were we to have concentrated solely on charges directly relating to child protection related crimes, then had the victims lost confidence or refused to continue with the case, our prosecution case may have collapsed.

LA entered guilty pleas to having obtained passports for herself, for two of her children and for DO and Z and to assisting DO and Z to enter the UK unlawfully. The matters of cruelty to OOA, of assaulting both OOA and DO and of assisting unlawful entry to the UK by harbouring OOA she continued to deny. These were then heard during a three week trial at Isleworth Crown Court in January 2011. During the trial both OOA and DO gave evidence over several days. Their evidence was at times harrowing with a comment being made by HHJ Oliver during sentence that:

> 'Anyone who sat in Court during the length of the trial cannot have been affected by the evidence we heard, by the sheer hysterical pain and suffering that those girls had gone through'.

The defence picture painted of LA was one of a caring woman, a pastor in a church who had written books on infertility and childcare – one entitled Right Parenting Gods Way. This woman seemed far removed from the woman whose punishments included rubbing chilli pepper in eyes and genitalia and beatings as claimed by the victims.

The trial lasted three weeks, longer than the five to seven days anticipated. Difficulties were again encountered with one of the witnesses having two very young children who required childcare. Funding had been agreed by the CPS for childcare with a caveat that the witness had to pay up front and then reclaim the costs. Due to financial constraints the witness was unable to fund such care, and despite attempts to seek assistance from the NGO's who had offered to support the victim's children, care could not be found. Paladin team officers resorted to sharing the child care for her two small sons at court whilst their mother gave evidence. Baby sitting young children was not what I had anticipated and as a team of three we were juggling obtaining summonses, further witness statements, child care, transporting vulnerable witnesses, together with monitoring the progress of the trial. This was the first time in my career that my colleagues and I were thanked in court, not only by the victims and prosecution counsel, but also by the defence barristers. LA was found guilty. Passing sentence, HHJ Oliver began by reading from DO's victim impact statement the following paragraph:

> 'Once I realised why she had brought me to the UK to be nothing more than a slave to her and her family, I felt deceived and manipulated and felt that she had used and exploited me and my family at a time when things were very difficult for them. I felt like a commodity, worthless as a person, especially when she would beat me. It was torture. I was so fearful and frightful of Lucy Adeniji, that I never knew what she would do to me next.'

In sentencing LA HHJ Oliver directed the following findings to LA: 'You paint this picture to the world of being a caring woman. You are not. You are an evil woman. You are a woman who has used two young ladies to your own personal ends. You wanted them to act as your housemaids so you could present yourself as a loveable person to the outside world.' Regarding the evidence heard he continued, 'It was terrible, terrible evidence to hear, yet you sat in the witness box and were completely and utterly unmoved by it, which is why I say that you are a complete and utter hypocrite'.

As to the harm that LA had meted out to her two victims the Judge said:

> 'You ruined the life of [OOA], you ruined the life of [DO]. You stole [OOA's] childhood. You took girls in who trusted you, who had promises of futures and you ruined them . . . You are, as was said, shameful and shameless.'

LA was sentenced to 12 months concurrent for each of the charges relating to the fraudulent applications for British passports for herself, her two children and for DO and Z, and also for assisting in the unlawful immigration of DO and Z. With regards to sentencing for the offences for which she was found guilty at the conclusion of the trial, and in particular the child protection related charges, the sentences were far more significant. For the assaults on DO and OOA, 18 months (consecutive), for the facilitation (assisting unlawful immigration) of OOA, two and a half years (consecutive) and for cruelty in relation to OOA, five years imprisonment again to be served consecutively. A total sentence of 11 and a half years. The judge concluded with the following comment:

> 'You are an evil woman, Mrs Adeniji. This is the price that you pay for being evil for so long. Take her down please.'

1   *OOO v The Commissioner of Police for the Metropolis* [2011] EWHC 1246 (QB) (20 May 2011).
2   Achieving Best Evidence in Criminal Proceedings. The most recent form of this Guidance, published in March 2011 is available online.
3   This woman was charged with harbouring C and was found not guilty at court – therefore this chapter will solely focus on the outcome of the charges brought against LA.
4   Ie Asylum and Immigration (Treatment of Claimants, etc.) Act 2004, s 4.

Comment

23.7 The case was described in the media as being the first successful prosecution of trafficking of a child for domestic servitude. Technically that was incorrect, as although the facts of what had occurred amounted to trafficking, specific trafficking charges were not brought for reasons previously outlined. The prosecution described exactly what had happened to the victims, and of the defendants' use and abuse of the UK's immigration and passport systems. Use of alternative charges, which may not ordinarily have been considered, assisted in setting the scene.

Those of us involved in these prosecutions have learned from these cases. One of the most important lessons being the identification of those involved. Familial relationships were described in each of these cases which were subsequently disproved. PS was not the infant's birth mother as claimed. The Q's were not X's parents as claimed. LA was not OOA, DO or Z's 'mum'– a term they used for her.

CONCLUDING REMARKS

23.8 Rarely will a child or young person approach the authorities and state they have been trafficked. We are, therefore, reliant on professionals involved with the child or young person to carry out effective assessments, to understand how children may be exploited and to understand that child trafficking is not an immigration matter. Child trafficking is child abuse.

PROTECTING AGAINST THE CRIMINALISATION OF VICTIMS OF TRAFFICKING: RELEVANT CPS LEGAL GUIDANCE FOR ADULTS AND CHILDREN

Pam Bowen

EUROPEAN LEGAL FRAMEWORK

24.1 The UK is bound by the Council of Europe Convention on Action against Trafficking in Human Beings ('the Trafficking Convention'), a treaty that was ratified by the Government on 17 December 2008 and brought into force on 1 April 2009. The Trafficking Convention places specific and positive obligations upon the Council of Europe Member States which have signed and/or ratified the Trafficking Convention to prevent and combat trafficking and protect the rights of victims. The Trafficking Convention, Article 26, provides for the possibility of States not imposing penalties on victims for their involvement in unlawful activities to the extent that they have been compelled to do so, in accordance with the basic principles of its legal system.

The EU Directive of the European Parliament (2011)[1] which replaces the Council Framework Decision 2002 and which the Government has announced its intention to opt into, goes further:

'Article 8: Non-prosecution or non-application of penalties to the victim
Member States shall, in accordance with the basic principles of their legal systems, take the necessary measures to ensure that competent national authorities are entitled not to prosecute or impose penalties on victims of trafficking in human beings for their involvement in criminal activities which they have been compelled to commit as a direct consequence of being subjected to any of the acts referred to in Article 2[2].'

---

[1]   Directive 2011/36/EU of 5 April 2011 on preventing and combating trafficking in human beings and protecting its victims, and replacing Council Framework Decision 2002/629/JHA (EU Directive 2011/36/EU).

[2]   Article 2 of Directive 2011/36/EU criminalises the act of trafficking in persons, developing the Palermo Protocol and Trafficking Convention definitions of trafficking. Exploitation is also developed, and is defined under Article 2(3) of the Directive in the following way: 'Exploita-

tion shall include, as a minimum, the exploitation of the prostitution of others or other forms of sexual exploitation, forced labour or services, including begging, slavery or practices similar to slavery, servitude, or the exploitation of criminal activities, or the removal of organs'. For further discussion on the definitions of trafficking see **CHAPTER 1** and **CHAPTER 2**.

POLICY WHICH APPLIES IN ENGLAND AND WALES

24.2 Legal and policy guidance published by the Crown Prosecution Service (CPS) ('the CPS Guidance') to prosecutors on the 'Prosecution of Defendants (children and adults) charged with offences who might be Trafficked Victims' supports this obligation. This was first published in 2007 and was last revised and published on 1 June 2011.

The CPS Guidance advises prosecutors that when reviewing a case in which there are suspicions that the suspect might be a victim of trafficking, they should be pro-active in causing enquiries to be made and obtain further information about the circumstances in which the suspect was apprehended. The guidance is reproduced, in an abridged form, below.

PROSECUTION OF DEFENDANTS (CHILDREN AND ADULTS) CHARGED WITH OFFENCES WHO MIGHT BE TRAFFICKED VICTIMS

24.3 Adults and children arrested by the police and charged with committing criminal offences might be the victims of trafficking. This most frequently arises when they have been trafficked here to commit criminal offences *(some of the offences most frequently committed appear below)*:

- Causing or inciting/controlling prostitution for gain: Sexual Offences Act 2003, ss 52 and 53;
- Keeping a brothel: Sexual Offences Act 1956, ss 33 or 33a;
- Theft (in organised 'pick pocketing' gangs), under Theft Act 1968, s 1;
- Cultivation of cannabis plants, under the Misuse of Drugs Act 1971, s 6.

But trafficked victims may also be apprehended by law enforcement where they are escaping from their trafficking situation, the most obvious being immigration offences:

- using a false instrument under the Forgery and Counterfeiting Act 1981, s 3;
- possession of a forged passport or documents under the Forgery and Counterfeiting Act 1981, s 5;
- possession of a false identity document under the Identity Documents Act 2010, s 6;
- failure to have a travel document at a leave or asylum interview under the Asylum and Immigration (Treatment of Claimants, etc.) Act 2004, s 2.

When reviewing any such cases, prosecutors must be alert to the possibility that the suspect may be a victim of trafficking and take the following steps:

- Advise the senior investigating officer to make enquiries and obtain information about the circumstances in which the suspect was apprehended and whether there is a *credible suspicion* or *realistic possibility* that the suspect has been trafficked (this should be done by contacting the UK Human Trafficking Centre (UKHTC))[1];
- The police should be advised to consider referring[2] the suspect through the National Referral Mechanism (NRM) to the competent authority for victim identification and referral to appropriate support. In the case of children, this can be done by the Local Authority; where the suspect is assessed as being under 18 and has been arrested in connection with offences of cannabis cultivation, police should be referred to ACPO Child Protection: Position on Children and Young People Recovered in Cannabis Farms[3]. Prosecutors should also consider information from other sources that a suspect might be the victim of trafficking, for example from a non-Government organisation (NGO) which supports trafficked victims. That information may be in the form of medical reports (for example, psychiatrist reports) claiming post traumatic stress as a result of their trafficking experience;
- Re-review the case in light of any fresh information or evidence obtained;
- If new evidence or information obtained supports the fact that the suspect has been trafficked and committed the offence whilst they were coerced, consider whether it is in the public interest to continue prosecution. Where there is clear evidence that the suspect has a credible defence of duress, the case should be discontinued on evidential grounds (but see separate section on Children at para **24.4**).

In complying with the judgment in *R v O*[4], it is the *duty of the prosecutor* to be pro-active in causing enquiries to be made about the suspect and the circumstances in which they were apprehended. In giving its judgment the Court of Appeal highlighted a number of important issues in cases such as this:

- It required that both Prosecutors and Defence lawyers are 'to make proper enquiries' in criminal prosecutions involving individuals who may be victims of trafficking, in line with the findings of the Parliamentary Joint Committee on Human Rights report on Human Trafficking 2006, that there must be co-ordinated law enforcement in protecting the rights of victims of trafficking;
- CPS legal guidance on the prosecution of trafficked victims was recognised; the court advised that this is published more widely to ensure others are aware of it;
- The court, defence and prosecution were criticised for failing to recognise that O was a minor.

In the case of O, guidance on the prosecution of trafficked victims was not followed.

The importance of the CPS following the guidance was further re-enforced by *R v LM*[5].

Some trafficked victim's experiences are likely to be outside the knowledge and experience of prosecutors. For example young female victims may be subject to cultural and religious practices such as witchcraft and juju rituals inherent in their culture which binds them to their traffickers through fear of repercussions.

Other trafficked victims may be held captive, physically and sexually assaulted and violated, or they may be less abused physically but are psychologically coerced and are dependent on those who are victimising them.

Prosecutors should therefore have regard to these wider factors when considering whether the circumstances of the person's situation might support a defence of duress in law. In *DPP for Northern Ireland v Lynch*[6], Lord Simon said ' . . . such well grounded fear, produced by threats, of death or grievous bodily harm or unjustified imprisonment if a certain act is not done, as overbears the wish not to perform the act, and is effective, at the time of the act, in constraining him to perform it.'

The following are also factors which prosecutors might consider:

- When considering duress, was the defendant driven to do what he did because he genuinely believed that if he didn't, he or a member of his family would be killed or seriously injured?
- Might a reasonable person with the defendant's belief and in his situation have been driven to do what he did?
- Was there opportunity for the defendant to escape from the threats without harm to himself, for example by going to the police?
- Did the defendant put himself into a position in which he was likely to be subject to threats made to persuade him to commit an offence of the seriousness of the charge, eg getting involved in a criminal gang likely to subject him to threats to commit criminal offences?

For further guidance on duress refer to *Archbold 17-119 to 17-122*[7]

Even where the circumstances do not meet the requirements for the defence of duress, prosecutors must consider whether the public interest is best served in continuing the prosecution in respect of the criminal offence. The following factors are relevant when deciding where the public interest lies:

- is there a credible suspicion that the suspect might be a trafficked victim?
- the role that the suspect has in the criminal offence?
- was the criminal offence committed as a direct consequence of their trafficked situation?
- were violence, threats or coercion used on the trafficked victim to procure the commission of the offence?
- was the victim in a vulnerable situation or put in considerable fear?

Guidance has been issued to police[8] and UK Border Agency (UKBA)[9] on identification of victims and the indicators that might suggest that someone is a trafficked victim. However, all decisions in the case remain the responsibility of the prosecutor.

---

[1]   http://www.ukhtc.org.

[2]   Referral forms can be found by accessing http://www.soca.gov.uk/about-soca/about-the-ukht c/national-referral-mechanism/nrm-referral-forms.

[3]   See: http://www.ceop.police.uk/Documents/ceopdocs/externaldocs/160810_ACPO_lead's_pos ition_on_CYP_recovered_from_cannabis_farms_FINAL.pdf

[4]   [2008] EWCA Crim 2835, (2008) Times, 2 October.

5   [2010] EWCA Crim 2327, [2011] 1 Cr App Rep 135, [2011] Crim LR 425.
6   [1975] AC 653, [1975] 2 WLR 641, HL (Archbold 2011 17-120).
7   *Archbold: Criminal Pleading, Evidence and Practice* (Archbold) (2011) Sweet and Maxwell is a leading criminal law text in the UK. The paragraph numbers given refer to paragraphs in the 2011 edition of Archbold.
8   See http://www.education.gov.uk/publications/eOrderingDownload/DCSF_Child%20Trafficking.pdf.
9   See http://www.ukba.homeoffice.gov.uk/sitecontent/documents/policyandlaw/asylumprocessguidance/specialcases/guidance/competent-guidance?view=Binary.

CHILDREN

24.4 Children are particularly vulnerable to trafficking and exploitation. Recent experience has highlighted the following offences as those most likely to be committed by trafficked children:

- Cultivation of cannabis plants, under the Misuse of Drugs Act 1971, s 6;
- Theft (in organised 'pick pocketing' gangs), under the Theft Act 1968, s 1.

Prosecutors should be alert to the possibility that in such circumstances, a young offender may be a victim of trafficking and have committed the offences by being exploited by their traffickers or others controlling them. Child trafficking is first and foremost a child protection issue and they are likely to be in need of protection and safeguarding. In these circumstances, prosecutors should take the steps outlined above to make pro-active enquiries about the circumstances in which the child was apprehended.

The Protocol to Prevent, Suppress and Punish Trafficking in Persons, especially Women and Children *(Palermo Protocol)* makes it clear that for child victims, consent is irrelevant; therefore there is no requirement to show the means of trafficking (that is the threat, coercion, or deception).

When considering the evidential factors set out in the previous section, in particular the reasonableness of the defendant's belief in the likely harm which might be caused to them or to their family and the likelihood of taking up opportunities to escape the threats, proper allowance should be made for the age, vulnerability and lack of maturity of the young person.

Children who have been trafficked may be reluctant to disclose the circumstances of their exploitation or arrival into the UK for fear of reprisals by the trafficker or owner, or out of misplaced loyalty to them. Experience has shown that inconsistencies in accounts given are often a feature of victims of trafficking and should not necessarily be regarded as diminishing the credibility of their claim to be a victim of trafficking.

The child may have been coached by their trafficker to not disclose their true identity or circumstances to the authorities. In some cases, they may have been coached with a false version of events and warned not to disclose any detail beyond this as it will lead to their deportation.

In a similar way to adults, children may have been subject to more psychological coercion or threats, such as threatening to report them to the authorities; threats of violence towards members of the child's family; keeping them socially isolated; telling them that they/their family owes large sums of money and that they must work to pay this off; or through juju or witchcraft practices.

Police should work with local authorities to ensure early identification of trafficked victims before entering any suspected cannabis farm, in line with the 'Safeguarding Children Who May Have Been Trafficked' guidance[1]. Police and prosecutors should also be alert to the fact that an appropriate adult in interview could be the trafficker or a person allied to the trafficker.

Any child who might be a trafficked victim should be afforded the protection of our child care legislation if there are concerns that they have been working under duress or if their well being has been threatened. Prosecutors are also alerted to the DCSF Guidance, Safeguarding Children and Young People from Sexual Exploitation (June 2009)[2].

In these circumstances, the youth may well then become a victim or witness for a prosecution against those who have exploited them. The younger a child is the more careful investigators and prosecutors have to be in deciding whether it is right to ask them to become involved in a criminal trial.

Prosecutors are reminded of the principles contained within the CPS policy statement on Children and Young People[3] and in particular, our commitment to always consider the welfare of children in criminal cases.

[1]   See footnote 8, at para **24.3** above.
[2]   Available at http://www.education.gov.uk/publications/standard/publicationdetail/page1/DCS F-00651-2009.
[3]   See: http://www.cps.gov.uk/victims_witnesses/children_policy.pdf.

AGE DISPUTES

24.5 Young people may have no identifying information on them, their documents may be false or they may have been told to lie about their age to evade attention from the authorities. Some victims may claim to be adults when they are in fact under 18 years of age.

Where it is not clear whether the young person is a child (ie under 18 years of age) then in line with the United Nations Convention of the Rights of the Child, the benefit of the doubt should be given and the young person should be treated as a child. This is re-enforced in the Council of Europe Convention on Action against Trafficking in Human Beings[1].

Where there is uncertainty about a suspected victim's age, Children's Services will be responsible for assessing their age. The Local Authority in whose area the victim has been recovered will have responsibility for the care of the child as required by the Children Act 1989.

Where a person is brought before any court and it appears that they are a child or young person, it is the responsibility of the court to make due enquiry as to their age. Under the Children and Young Persons Act 1933, s 99 and the Magistrates' Courts Act 1980, s 150, the age presumed or declared by the court is then regarded to be their true age.

For further reference on age assessment refer to the judgment of the Supreme Court in *R (on the application of A) v London Borough of Croydon; R (M) v London Borough of Lambeth*[2]. This case concerned the duty imposed on local authorities in providing services under the Children Act 1989 in instances where the local authorities disputed age and assessed them as adults.

---

1   The Trafficking Convention, Article 10.3, which provides: 'When the age of the victim is uncertain and there are reasons to believe that a victim is a child, he or she shall be presumed to be a child and shall be accorded special protection measures pending verification of his/her age'.
2   [2009] UKSC 8. In this important judgment the Supreme Court held that the assessment of age was a matter of fact and should be decided by the court assessing any dispute between a child and a local authority or the UK Border Agency. The facts did not however involve a trafficked child or consideration of the age test under the Trafficking Convention.

SHOULD THERE BE A BLANKET POLICY OF NON-PROSECUTION OF ALL VICTIMS OF TRAFFICKING?

24.6 It is not an option for the CPS to issue a policy of not prosecuting those who are arrested or apprehended by the police, who later disclose that they have been trafficked, whether they are a youth or an adult. This is for a number of reasons:

(i)   It would be unlawful. The statutory obligations placed on the CPS by the Prosecution of Offences Act 1985 require prosecutors to review each case received from the police in accordance with the Code for Crown Prosecutors. The process of review and decision-making requires a full analysis of all the relevant facts and circumstances in each individual case. The analysis must necessarily be retrospective and case specific. It would not be lawful therefore in any category of case, potential defendants or set of circumstances for the CPS to agree to a proposal that provides prospective immunity from prosecution;

(ii)   The consequences of publishing a policy of immunity would potentially act as a pull factor to traffickers to exploit and victimise more vulnerable adults and children if they knew that they would not be prosecuted for any criminal offence committed;

(iii)   It would be difficult to confine the category of suspect, criminal offence or circumstances to which such a policy would apply. Anyone apprehended for a criminal offence might state that they are trafficked in the safe knowledge that they would not then face criminal proceedings.

Whilst there is a positive obligation on the prosecutor to cause further investigation in such cases, there is also a responsibility on the police to investigate the circumstances in which the suspect was apprehended and for the defence to raise with their client in the course of their instructions and case preparation.

A prosecutor can only take steps to re-review the case to consider whether to continue a prosecution if they have information from the police or other sources that a suspect might be a victim of trafficking and is only relevant where the criminality is as a direct consequence of the trafficking situation. There must also be consideration of the extent to which the victim was compelled to undertake the unlawful activity.

In many cases, the short timescales for prosecutors to make charging decisions means that referral through the National Referral Mechanism for a reasonable grounds decision on a suspect's trafficking status is not possible. In expediting cases to meet PACE (Police and Criminal Evidence Act 1984) timescales (24 hours) police have to interview the suspect, conduct enquiries, arrange for age assessment or Social Services attendance if the suspect is a child/youth and engage an interpreter. Full information and evidence then on the potential trafficked status of a suspect is not reaching the prosecutor in time to make an informed decision at the charging stage. The problem is exacerbated once in the criminal justice system where cases are expedited in short timescales, in some instances when a suspect is urged to enter an early guilty plea.

An intervention prior to referral to the CPS for charging decision might be an option to delay the inevitable course many cases take.

One option might be for the defence to make representations to the prosecutor to inform the prosecutor's decision. In 2009, two CPS Areas engaged in a proof of concept with the defence whereby contact was encouraged. Additional guidance was developed, under the supervision of the Director of Public Prosecutions, on how to deal with and respond to any defence representations before charge. The guidance did not require prosecutors to actively seek representations from the defence, but to assist prosecutors in the event that representations were made or the defence seek some kind of pre charge disclosure. This concept was tested during six months but take-up of the initiative by defence representatives was very low.

CONCLUDING REMARKS

24.7 Whilst there are safeguards in place which are underpinned by Treaties, Policy Guidance to Prosecutors, Guidance to Police, Law Society Practice Notes to Defence Solicitors and Court of Appeal Judgments, compliance with this important obligation of non-prosecution appears variable and inconsistent. This is likely to be influenced by a general lack of awareness of obligations and a lack of understanding of the complex issues affecting trafficked victims, leading to the non-investigation and identification of potential victims of trafficking.

PROTECTING AGAINST THE CRIMINALISATION OF VICTIMS OF TRAFFICKING: REPRESENTING THE RIGHTS OF VICTIMS OF TRAFFICKING AS DEFENDANTS IN THE CRIMINAL JUSTICE SYSTEM

Peter Carter QC and Parosha Chandran

INTRODUCTION

25.1

'Victims of trafficking must be recognised as such in order to avoid police and public authorities treating them as illegal migrants or criminals'[1].

Victims of human trafficking in the UK and elsewhere may be compelled to commit criminal offences as a result of their trafficking and exploitation. That they ought to be offered protection against their criminalisation for committing such acts is well-recognised in international and domestic law and guidance.

As succinctly explained by the Dutch National Rapporteur on Trafficking in Human Beings in her annual report on trafficking in the Netherlands in 2009:

'Victims of human trafficking sometimes commit criminal offences that are connected with the human trafficking situation. Examples can include victims who are forced to use a false passport, victims who are exploited in cannabis [factories] or victims who issue false statements under oath out of fear of the person exploiting them. There have also been cases where victims have been involved in drug smuggling, theft, fraud and assault under the influence of their trafficker.'[2]

The above findings of the Dutch National Rapporteur perfectly resonate with the situation that many victims of trafficking find themselves in as a result of their trafficking and exploitation in the UK.

[1] United Kingdom's *Trafficking Toolkit: Tackling Trafficking* published in October 2009 by the Criminal Justice System, at p 14, summarising the measures introduced by the Council of Europe Convention on Action against Trafficking in Human Beings 2005. The Trafficking Toolkit, which constitutes multi-agency guidance, has two aims: to provide advice and support

to frontline practitioners, including the police, CPS and local authorities, who may come into contact with victims and perpetrators of human trafficking and to help strategic bodies identify how tackling human trafficking can help meet local priorities.

2   *Trafficking in Human Beings*, Seventh Report of the Dutch National Rapporteur, The Hague, 2009, Ch 6, '*Victims as perpetrators and the non-punishment principle*' at p 207. The Dutch National Rapporteur is Ms CE Dettmeijer-Vermeulen.

INTERNATIONAL AND EUROPEAN LEGAL FRAMEWORK

25.2 The Palermo Protocol[1] provides that one of its three purposes is:

'To protect and assist the victims of such trafficking, with full respect for their human rights.'[2]

The Council of Europe Convention on Action against Trafficking in Human Beings 2005[3] ('the Trafficking Convention') expressly provides for the possibility of protection against criminal punishment for trafficked persons who commit offences as a result of their trafficking and exploitation. Article 26 of the Trafficking Convention provides:

'Article 26 – Non-punishment provision
Each Party shall, in accordance with the basic principles of its legal system, provide for the possibility of not imposing penalties on victims for their involvement in unlawful activities, to the extent that they have been compelled to do so.'

The recent EU Directive 2011/36/EU of the European Parliament and of the Council of 5 April 2011 on preventing and combating trafficking in human beings and protecting its victims, replacing Council Framework Decision 2002/629/JHA ('the EU Trafficking Directive') imposes a stricter obligation on Member States which opt into the EU Trafficking Directive[4] by requiring, as opposed to providing for the possibility of, that victims of trafficking are entitled to protection against both prosecution and punishment for crimes they were compelled to commit[5]. Article 8 of the Trafficking Directive provides:

'Non-prosecution or non-application of penalties to the victim
Member States shall, in accordance with the basic principles of their legal systems, take the necessary measures to ensure that competent national authorities are entitled not to prosecute or impose penalties on victims of trafficking in human beings for their involvement in criminal activities which they have been compelled to commit as a direct consequence of being subjected to any of the acts referred to in Article 2.'

Article 2 of the Trafficking Directive defines trafficking in human beings. The Recital to the Trafficking Directive leaves one in no doubt as to what the protection measures under Article 8 mean:

'Victims of trafficking in human beings should . . . be protected from prosecution or punishment for criminal activities . . . that they have been compelled to commit as a direct consequence of being subject to trafficking.'[6]

In providing this overt form of protection against the criminalisation of victims of trafficking for trafficking-dependent crimes[7] the Trafficking Directive recognises the direct link between securing this human rights-based protection for victims and obtaining witness evidence to prosecute human traffickers:

'The aim of such protection is to safeguard the human rights of victims, to avoid further victimisation and to encourage them to act as witnesses in criminal proceedings against the perpetrators.'[8]

Whilst the Palermo Protocol of 2000 is itself silent on the specific issue of the protection of victims of trafficking from prosecution or punishment for trafficking-dependent crimes, the UN's non-binding but highly authoritative Recommended Principles and Guidelines on Human Rights and Human Trafficking 2002[9] first recognised that such protection needed to be a necessary function of a democratic society. The Primacy of human rights is established by Recommended Principle 1:

'1. The human rights of trafficked persons shall be at the centre of all efforts to prevent and combat trafficking and to protect, assist and provide redress to victims.'

Recommended Principles 3 and 7 both seek to protect the rights of trafficked victims. By Recommended Principle 3, States are urged to protect victims of trafficking[10]:

'Anti-trafficking measures shall not adversely affect the human rights and dignity of persons, in particular the rights of those who have been trafficked, and of migrants, internally displaced persons, refugees and asylum-seekers.'

Recommended Principle 7 provides specific, and wide-ranging, protection against the criminalisation of victims of trafficking for trafficking-dependent crimes and provides that:

'Protection and assistance
7. Trafficked persons shall not be detained, charged or prosecuted for the illegality of their entry into or residence in countries of transit and destination, or for their involvement in unlawful activities to the extent that such involvement is a direct consequence of their situation as trafficked persons.'

Recommended Guideline 2, which relates to the crucial matter of the identification of trafficked persons, cautions that a 'failure to identify a trafficked person correctly is likely to result in a further denial of that person's rights' and finds that 'States are therefore under an obligation to ensure that such identification can and does take place.' This Guideline recalls that 'States are also obliged to exercise due diligence in identifying traffickers, including those who are involved in controlling and exploiting trafficked persons'. The Guideline specifically recommends therefore that:

'"[T]rafficked persons are not prosecuted for violations of immigration laws or for the activities they are involved in as a direct consequence of their situation as trafficked persons"[11] [and they] "are not, in any circumstances, held in immigration detention or other forms of custody."'[12]

Recommended Guideline 4 concerns 'ensuring an adequate legal framework'. Amongst other things this asks States to consider:

'Ensuring that legislation prevents trafficked persons from being prosecuted, detained or punished for the illegality of their entry or residence or for the activities they are involved in as a direct consequence of their situation as trafficked persons.'[13]

Recommended Guideline 5 reminds States that 'an adequate law enforcement response to trafficking is dependent on the cooperation of trafficked persons and other witnesses'. It advises that in 'many cases, individuals are reluctant or unable to report traffickers or to serve as witnesses because they lack confidence in the police and the judicial system and/or because of the absence of any effective protection mechanisms.' It stresses the need for law enforcement authorities and officials to be sensitive to their primary responsibility, namely 'to ensure the safety and immediate well-being of trafficked persons' and urges State to consider that:

> '[T]raffickers are and will remain the focus of anti-trafficking strategies and that law enforcement efforts do not place trafficked persons at risk of being punished for offences committed as a consequence of their situation.'[14]

Recommended Guideline 8 provides special measures for the protection and support of child victims of trafficking and highlights the need to ensure that 'procedures are in place for the rapid identification of child victims of trafficking'[15]. It recommends that:

> '[C]hildren who are victims of trafficking are not subjected to criminal procedures or sanctions for offences related to their situation as trafficked persons.'[16]

These UN Principles and Guidelines form the bedrock of an understanding of the needs and rights of victims of trafficking in the particular context of their criminalisation for trafficking-dependent crimes.

[1] Protocol To Prevent, Suppress And Punish Trafficking In Persons, especially Women And Children, Supplementing The United Nations Convention Against Transnational Organized Crime 2000.
[2] Palermo Protocol, Article 2(b).
[3] The Trafficking Convention was signed by the UK in March 2007, was ratified by it in December 2008 and entered into force in the UK on 1 April 2009.
[4] In March 2011 the UK signalled its intention to opt in to the EU Trafficking Directive.
[5] As explained in **CHAPTER 13**: 'Directive 2011/36/EU entered into force on 15 April 2011. Member States to the Directive, including the United Kingdom, now have two years (until 6 April 2013) in which to transpose the provisions of the Directive into national law. During this time, the Directive is in force but its provisions do not yet have 'direct effect', meaning victims of trafficking cannot yet rely on them directly to challenge State action in the courts. However Member States must nevertheless ensure that until the Directive is adopted into national law, or the two year period has passed, no measures are adopted which 'seriously compromise the attainment of the result prescribed by the directive'. After 6 April 2013, those provisions of the Directive that are clear, precise and unconditional will have direct effect.'
[6] Directive 2011/36/EU, Recital (14). The same Recital (14) to the Trafficking Directive explains that: 'This safeguard should not exclude prosecution or punishment for offences that a person has voluntarily committed or participated in.' The link is thereby made between the need for the crime to be trafficking-dependent as opposed to being trafficking-independent [See Authors' Note at para **25.21** which explains more precisely this new, proposed term]. The reference to 'voluntarily committed' may appear to confine the protection from prosecution to cases of or akin to those where defence of duress would apply. In fact the protection is wider than the restricted defence of duress provides – see the analysis of *R v LM* [2010] EWCA Crim 2327, [2011] 1 Cr App Rep 135, [2011] Crim LR 425 below at para **25.19**. This is necessary to ensure protection in accordance with international law. Even where duress as a defence would apply, it is a difficult defence for any vulnerable person to raise precisely because the circumstances of the coercion upon them, together with a fear of authority figures, make it unlikely that a victim of trafficking will explain the full facts when interviewed. Duress is too blunt a means of securing the protection required by international law. In cases of victims of trafficking who are children, duress should not feature because their consent cannot justify the State withholding protection and a child who consents is nevertheless a victim of trafficking (see below paras **25.11** and **25.13**.
[7] See Authors' Note at para **25.21** which explains more precisely this new, proposed term.
[8] See Authors' Note at para **25.21** which explains more precisely this new, proposed term.
[9] UN Economic and Social Council E/2002/Add.1, 20 May 2002. These have been considered and approved by numerous UN bodies and have recently formed the basis of the detailed *Commentary on the Recommended Principles and Guidelines on Human Rights and Human Trafficking*, published by the Office of the United Nations High Commissioner for Human Rights in 2010.

10   Who may, for example, be located by the police during brothel visits or drugs raids.
11   Recommended Guideline 2.5.
12   Recommended Guideline 2.6.
13   Recommended Guideline 4.5.
14   Recommended Guideline 5.5.
15   Recommended Guideline 8.2.
16   Recommended Guideline 8.3.

THE CONTINUING CRIMINALISATION OF VICTIMS OF TRAFFICKING IN THE UK

25.3 In the UK the criminalisation of some victims of trafficking for criminal acts they were forced or compelled to perform by their traffickers remains a continuing theme of our criminal justice system even though that system is supposed to protect the human rights of victims of crime and not violate them. Notwithstanding the UK's obligations under the Palermo Protocol to protect the human rights of such victims and its additional, express, obligation to do so via the possibility of not imposing punishment on victims for trafficking-dependent crimes following the entry into force of the Trafficking Convention, it remains the case that certain groups of victims of trafficking in the UK continue to be subjected to the acts of prosecution and punishment for trafficking-dependent crimes.

The current practice in the UK in this regard has been highlighted by the authoritative United States' State Department report on Trafficking in Persons [TIP] 2011[1] which, in respect of the UK, finds that:

'While the UK government has a policy of not penalizing victims for unlawful acts committed as a direct result of being trafficked, there are reports of identified trafficking victims being prosecuted for offenses they committed while under coercion of their traffickers.'

Specific concern was raised in the TIP report regarding the position of some trafficked children in the UK:

'Further, there are continued NGO reports of trafficked children in the prostitution sector, cannabis cultivation, or petty crimes; such children are subjected to criminal proceedings instead of recovery and care. In one particular case, NGOs asserted in a 2010 report that a girl in Scotland was convicted for cannabis cultivation, despite disclosing details of her exploitation to her attorney and an expert report presented during court proceedings about her trafficking experience.'

The TIP report therefore recommends that the UK must, in terms of the protection of both adult and child victims of trafficking:

'[T]ake further steps to ensure that confirmed trafficking victims are not penalized [sic] for unlawful acts committed as a direct result of being trafficked.'

Two Court of Appeal judgments, *R v O*[2] and *R v LM*[3] discussed at paras **25.18** and **25.19**, have addressed in detail, aspects of non-criminalisation from the perspectives of victims of trafficking who were prosecuted for immigration documents offences, controlling prostitution and fraud[4]. The CPS Legal Guidance represents the Crown's position as to the factors which will guide towards the Crown's discontinuance of such types of prosecutions, and other named offences, and practitioners are referred to these judgments and guidelines.

However, the ongoing criminalisation of some victims of trafficking for trafficking-dependent crimes has been recognised in numerous reports published in the UK[5]. Of particular, contemporary concern is the treatment of child victims of trafficking who have been compelled to commit illegal acts in the UK, as pointed out in the current TIP report, and we therefore highlight recent and relevant information on such cases for practitioners.

[1] Published on 27 June 2011.
[2] [2008] EWCA Crim 2835, (2008) Times, 2 October.
[3] [2010] EWCA Crim 2327, [2011] 1 Cr App Rep 135, [2011] Crim LR 425.
[4] The court has advised that it retains a power to stay a prosecution for abuse: see commentary on *R v LM* [2010] EWCA Crim 2327, [2011] 1 Cr App Rep 135, [2011] Crim LR 425, at para **25.19** below.
[5] See for recent examples ECAT UK's Understanding Paper: *Child trafficking for Forced Criminality*, 2010 and the Anti-Trafficking Monitoring Group's Briefing Paper *Criminal Justice and Trafficked People*, 2010.

CHILD VICTIMS OF TRAFFICKING

25.4 For example, the specialist UK police unit the Child Exploitation and Online Protection (CEOP) Centre observed in its report entitled *Strategic Threat Assessment: Child Trafficking in the UK*, in which it revealed its findings on data that it had collected during the period 1 March 2009 to 28 February 2010, that:

'Vietnamese and Roma children are often treated as offenders (for cannabis production and street crime offences respectively) rather than potential victims of trafficking.'[1]

[1] CEOP *Strategic Threat Assessment Child Trafficking in the UK*, December 2010, Executive Summary at p 6.

Vietnamese cannabis cases

25.5 In August 2010 the *Position from ACPO Lead[s] on Child Protection and Cannabis Cultivation on Children and Young People Recovered in Cannabis Farms* was published. Here the ACPO Lead on Child Protection and Abuse Investigation and the ACPO Lead on Cannabis Cultivation advised that police should be alert to the possibility that any person, adult or child, identified in a cannabis farm could be a victim of trafficking. They advised, with particular reference to the police's legal obligations and duties to safeguard children and young persons, that:

'1 . . . The intelligence indicates that sometimes, as a consequence of the need for more awareness of the problem, young persons are not identified as victims, statutory defences are not recognised and the individuals end up being charged, prosecuted and convicted of offences committed whilst being exploited. This is contrary to police child protection obligations where the young person has been a victim of crime. It is also contrary to responsibilities in respect of child trafficking as enumerated under the Council of Europe (COE) Convention on Action [a]gainst [Trafficking in] Human Beings, which indicates that any person under the age of 18 years cannot consent to their own trafficking.'

As to the need for statutory agencies, prosecutors and defence lawyers to ensure that victims of trafficking are not criminalised for conduct which they were forced or compelled to perform and that the age of a victim is properly considered, the ACPO Leads have advised that:

'4. No decision to progress charges against such individuals should be made until all relevant assessments have been undertaken. Prosecutors and Duty Solicitors have a duty to make full and proper enquiries in criminal prosecutions involving individuals who may be victims of trafficking and to be proactive in establishing if a suspect is a potential victim of trafficking. Therefore, information about concerns of trafficking should be fully shared with the CPS. Cases of individuals claiming to be under 18 when they are not for tactical purposes are common. However, in cases of doubt, the young person should be given the benefit of that doubt in accordance with the [Trafficking] [C]onvention until information to the contrary is available. Where official records, or other reliable evidence, are not available to confirm age, a Merton compliant age assessment should be carried out by the local authority.'

On the specific need to ensure a child welfare response is taken, the ACPO Leads have therefore advised that:

'5. On recovery of any young person in a cannabis farm s/he should be taken to a place of safety immediately . . . '

The ACPO Leads' guidance also provides in some detail the methods by which the police and local authorities are to act in conjunction to safeguard the welfare of any child who is suspected of having been trafficked and practitioners are referred to the full content of the ACPO Leads' Position of August 2010 which is reproduced as an Appendix in this book.

Of critical interest to practitioners is the fact that the May 2011 version of the CPS Legal Guidance recommends that police and prosecutors take into account the ACPO Leads' position on this issue.

The December 2010 Strategic Threat Assessment published by CEOP provided further intelligence concerning the prevalence of the trafficking of child victims for cannabis cultivation to and within the UK by organised criminal networks. The CEOP report found:

'10.1 The trafficking of Vietnamese children into and within the UK is the largest and most significant trend this period. Most victims are trafficked overland from Vietnam by lorry and enter the UK by clandestine methods via seaport. The criminal networks involved in the recruitment, transportation and exploitation of children are well organised, flexible and generate large finances, mainly from the cultivation and wholesale distribution of cannabis . . . New research commissioned by ACPO identified that white British criminals control the majority of the cultivated cannabis market in the UK, ahead of Vietnamese criminal networks. This research identified that even if farms were controlled by non-Vietnamese nationals, Vietnamese 'gardeners' were still used to cultivate the cannabis plants at the direction of these criminals . . . There has also been increased involvement and awareness-raising by the ACPO Child Protection Abuse and Investigation (CPAI) lead and many UK NGOs on the issue of children being trafficked to work in cannabis farms. There is also an increased concern that children are being prosecuted as offenders rather than protected as victims of trafficking. Many Vietnamese minors have been charged, prosecuted and sentenced for the production and supply of cannabis, but to date, there have been no convictions[1] (for trafficking offences) of criminals who have trafficked or exploited these children.'

As to the information that the trafficked children had when they were recruited by the traffickers the CEOP report found:

> '8.1 . . . Vietnamese cases: Some were told upfront they would be working in cannabis farms, with some stating they did not know that cannabis was illegal and thought they were entering legitimate work.'

An analysis by the authors of this Chapter, of CEOP's findings in relation to 'Emerging Trends' substantiates the following: that direct links exist between: (1) the absence in the UK of any prosecutions of the criminal drugs networks and traffickers which are involved in the lucrative trade of cannabis and child trafficking; (2) that home grown cannabis cultivation (as opposed to its importation) is a very low-risk high-profit crime in the UK; (3) that the modus operandi of traffickers to traffick children either to or within the UK[2] and control them within in the UK is highly successful and is done with ease. All of this has led to or otherwise encouraged a proliferation of new criminal players in the growing cannabis production industry in the UK with the result that trafficked Vietnamese children in cannabis factories in the UK are now, in 2011, likely to be at an increased risk of physical danger.

Hence, the CEOP Report found:

> '10.9. Indications are that the number of children trafficked and exploited in cannabis farms will remain at a high level. The number of cannabis farms detected by police in the UK has more than doubled within the last two years, with police now on average identifying over 500 farms in the UK per month. Whilst British criminality appears to have overtaken the dominance of Vietnamese criminal networks, there is still a demand for 'gardeners', most of whom are Vietnamese regardless of the nationality of the criminality further up the hierarchy. With demand far outstripping the supply from domestic cultivation, it is likely that criminality will seek to capitalise on the high-profit low-risk strategy of increasing home grown production rather the riskier and less profitable import of cannabis.
>
> The current methodologies used to traffic and exploit children are highly successful, with children entering largely undetected and those identified and put into care frequently going missing. Networks are still retaining victims with relative ease. It is therefore unlikely that the modus operandi currently employed will change.
>
> An increased rivalry between networks has been identified in the dataset, with children participating in attacks on other farms. The low-risk profitability has attracted the involvement of non-Vietnamese networks and this increasing level of competition will introduce an increased level of violence from rival networks, who seek to disrupt, extort or control the market. It is therefore likely that those employed as 'gardeners', including trafficked children, will be at an increased risk of physical harm from outside the network.'

---

[1] Authors' footnote: whilst it appears correct from published intelligence and information that there have not yet been any prosecutions in the UK of the traffickers or exploiters of children trafficked for cannabis cultivation, we have been reliably informed that there have been cases where UK law enforcement has co-operated with and assisted other EU agencies to investigate and prosecute for trafficking in other jurisdictions: (1) In 2009 co-operation between the UK's SOCA and a Hungarian-led investigation into the trafficking of Vietnamese victims into the UK for exploitation on cannabis farms led to the successful conviction in a Budapest Court of 17 defendants. The victims were trafficked via Moscow and Hungary and were forced to pay their debt by working in the UK in commercial cannabis cultivation. (2) In April 2011 in Budapest, Hungary, 98 people were arrested following an investigation across the EU into a human-trafficking network that brought thousands of Vietnamese nationals to Europe. Their main target was Britain where many of the victims were exploited in commercial cannabis cultivation.

[2] Some Vietnamese minors are not trafficked into the UK but become vulnerable to being trafficked once here.

Roma child cases

25.6 As to the treatment of some Roma child victims of trafficking in the UK the CEOP December 2010 *Strategic Threat Assessment Child Trafficking in the UK* found:

'[Intelligence relating to Roma child trafficking was] . . . derived from reports of criminality committed by Roma children. These children are continuously treated as offenders and not identified as potential victims of trafficking. Many Roma children caught committing or attempting petty crime are held by police until a responsible adult collects and takes them home. There are concerns that these responsible adults may be the very adults exploiting the children. The good practice established in some parts of the country (such as Operation Golf and the Hertfordshire anti-trafficking model) must be disseminated to a wider audience to increase the understanding amongst first line practitioners that these children should be safeguarded, not prosecuted.'

REMARKS

25.7 A few summary conclusions can be drawn from the above.

In short, until such a time as the advice of the ACPO Leads is thoroughly adhered to by the police and prosecutors, by which all potential trafficking victims are carefully treated by statutory agencies[1] and their human rights protected, and until such a time that defence lawyers, prosecutors, the courts and all other actors in the criminal justice system, including probation officers and youth offending teams, become aware of the protection provisions that should be available to victims of trafficking under the terms of the Trafficking Convention, and the scope of the CPS Legal Guidance, so as to properly present or represent trafficked victims' rights, human trafficking in all its forms will remain a low risk and highly profitable criminal industry in the UK, it will continue to grow, its methods will strengthen and the victims of it will be the ones harmed by the very system which is designed to protect them. The Criminal Procedure Rules 2011[2] provide:

'The overriding objective
1.1 (1) The overriding objective of this new code is that criminal cases be dealt with justly.
(2)   Dealing with a criminal case justly includes—
   (a)   acquitting the innocent and convicting the guilty;
   (b)   dealing with the prosecution and the defence fairly;
   (c)   recognising the rights of a defendant, particularly those under Article 6 of the European Convention on Human Rights . . . '

This objective does not adequately reflect the diversion of victims of trafficking from the criminal justice process. The best that can be said is that sub-paragraph (2)(c) should be deemed to incorporate the right of a defendant not to be treated as a defendant. For as long as victims of trafficking are criminalised for acts they were forced or compelled to perform, including for example cannabis cultivation, begging, shoplifting or for using false documents to seek to flee their traffickers they will be left unrecognised as victims and thereby as witness of serious crimes and, in the absence of intelligence or evidence from these victims, individual human traffickers and organised human trafficking networks will all thrive on our soil.

[1]   Which includes co-operation between the police and local authority children's services where the victim is likely to be or is potentially a child and is at risk of harm.
[2]   The Criminal Procedure Rules 2011 come into force in the UK on 3 October 2011. The Criminal Procedure Rules 2010, in force at the date of writing this chapter, contain the same wording in Rule 1(1) and (2)(a)–(c).

THE NEED FOR AWARENESS-RAISING

25.8 Since 2007 the Crown Prosecution Service has produced and published legal guidance to prosecutors on discontinuing cases against credible victims of trafficking. Originally that guidance was divided into cases concerning immigration-related offences (such as the use of false identification documents) and cases concerning young offenders (which included a number of criminal offences, including cannabis cultivation). In more recent times the updated guidance has been better, divided into cases which involve adults and those which involve children. The most recent form of the CPS legal guidance, published in May 2011, is summarised in **CHAPTER 24** and that CPS guidance is also included in a more comprehensive form as an Appendix in this book. Practitioners are advised to become fully appraised of what that guidance contains.

However, despite the existence of the CPS legal guidance since 2007[1] and the UK's express consent to respect and then be bound by the Trafficking Convention's provisions following its signature to it in 2007, its ratification of it in 2008 and then its entry into force in the UK on 1 April 2009 the unlawful criminalisation of some victims of trafficking in the UK has continued. This is thought to be due to a lack of awareness[2] of the CPS guidance and of Article 26 of the Trafficking Convention in particular by legal practitioners, including defence lawyers, prosecutors and the judiciary.

The aim of this chapter is to seek to address this.

[1]   And updated versions of it.
[2]   See for example the Court of Appeal's recognition of this lack of awareness by practitioners in *R v O* [2008] EWCA Crim 2835 at para 26, (2008) Times, 2 October; *R v LM* [2010] EWCA Crim 2327, at paras 19 and 20, [2011] 1 Cr App Rep 135, [2011] Crim LR 425.

GUIDANCE TO CRIMINAL PRACTITIONERS IN THE UK

25.9 Of vital importance to all practitioners in the criminal justice system is an understanding of:

(1)   what constitutes the act of human trafficking; and
(2)   who are the victims of such acts; and
(3)   how to fairly protect the rights of victims of trafficking who are exposed, as defendants, to criminal proceedings in the UK.

This chapter is therefore designed be read in conjunction with **CHAPTER 2**, and also with **CHAPTER 24** which sets out the CPS guidance on discontinuing cases against credible victims of trafficking and the reasons why there is no blanket ban on such prosecutions taking place[1].

In our view a legal knowledge of human trafficking is the primary essential tool by which practitioners can act to incorporate safeguards against the criminalisation of trafficked adults and children. For if one does not know what human trafficking is, how can one recognise a victim? And if one does not know what the general and specific indicators of human trafficking are, how can one act to put in place mechanisms to protect credible victims of trafficking in the UK against their criminalisation for acts which they may have been forced or compelled to perform?

---

[1] The CPS Legal Guidance of May 2011, which is included in the Appendices to this book, is not summarised in detail in this Chapter. It is suggested that **CHAPTER 24** which summarises that Legal Guidance should be referred to in full.

THE IDENTIFICATION OF VICTIMS OF TRAFFICKING: A SUMMARY

25.10 The following is a summary of what is described in **CHAPTER 2** on Identification.

The act of human trafficking

25.11 The act of human trafficking, as defined under both the Palermo Protocol 2000, Article 3, and the Council of Europe Convention on Action against Trafficking in Human Beings 2005 ('the Trafficking Convention'), Article 4[1], can be broken down into consisting of three core elements, namely being:

'(1) **The act of** the recruitment, transportation, transfer, harbouring or receipt of persons;

(2) **By means of** the threat or use of force or other forms of coercion, of abduction, of fraud, of deception, of the abuse of power or of a position of vulnerability or of the giving or receiving of payments or benefits to achieve the consent of a person having control over another person;

(3) **For the purpose of exploitation.** Exploitation includes "at a minimum, the exploitation of the prostitution of others or other forms of sexual exploitation, forced labour or services, slavery or practices similar to slavery, servitude or the removal or organs."'

With this definition in mind there are two additional legal issues that must be understood from the outset:

• The issue of the victim's consent (in the case of an adult victim of human trafficking) becomes irrelevant if any of the above 'means' have been used[2] by the trafficker to obtain that consent, ie the victim is still a victim if they consented in any of those circumstances; and

• In the case of child victims of human trafficking there is no requirement to establish that any of 'the means' were engaged for the punishable act of child trafficking to have occurred[3].

The human trafficking definition in the new EU Trafficking Directive incorporates the same three core elements[4], above, but it extends the definition of 'exploitation' to expressly include 'begging . . . or the exploitation of criminal activities'[5].

According to the Recital to the EU Trafficking Directive this broader concept of exploitation is to tackle recent developments in the phenomenon of human trafficking[6].

A common theme in the Palermo Protocol, the Trafficking Convention and the EU Trafficking Directive is that where a child is concerned, no possible consent should ever be considered valid.

The intentional act of human trafficking is a crime[7].

Under UK[8] and Scottish law there are various crimes of trafficking in respect of which a human trafficker can be prosecuted and convicted.

As summarised by the United States' Trafficking in Persons (TIP) report on the UK, June 2011:

> 'The UK prohibits all forms of trafficking through its 2009 Coroners and Justice Act, 2003 Sexual Offenses Act, and its 2004 Asylum and Immigration Act, which prescribe penalties of a maximum of 14, 14, and [14][9] years' imprisonment, respectively.'

Practitioners are specifically referred to **CHAPTER 19** on Trafficking-related Criminal Legislation for the relevant and specific country information.

1 Under Article 4(a) of the Trafficking Convention: '"Trafficking in human beings" shall mean the recruitment, transportation, transfer, harbouring or receipt of persons, by means of the threat or use of force or other forms of coercion, of abduction, of fraud, of deception, of the abuse of power or of a position of vulnerability or of the giving or receiving of payments or benefits to achieve the consent of a person having control over another person, for the purpose of exploitation. Exploitation shall include, at a minimum, the exploitation of the prostitution of others or other forms of sexual exploitation, forced labour or services, slavery or practices similar to slavery, servitude or the removal of organs.'

2 Palermo Protocol, Article 3(b); Trafficking Convention, Article 4(b); EU Trafficking Directive, Article 2(4).

3 Palermo Protocol, Article 3(c); Trafficking Convention, Article 4(c); EU Trafficking Directive, Article 2(5). The punishable acts of adult and child trafficking are subsumed within the common trafficking definition.

4 Directive 2011/36/EU Article 2(3). Article 2(1) provides that the following intentional offences of trafficking in human beings shall be punishable: 'The recruitment, transportation, transfer, harbouring or reception of persons, including the exchange or transfer of control over those persons, by means of the threat or use of force or other forms of coercion, of abduction, of fraud, of deception, of the abuse of power or of a position of vulnerability or of the giving or receiving of payments or benefits to achieve the consent of a person having control over another person, for the purpose of exploitation.'

5 Directive 2011/36/EU, Recital (11) provides that 'forced begging' should be understood as a form of forced labour or services as defined in the ILO Convention no 29 of 1930 and that 'the exploitation of criminal activities' should be understood as being the exploitation of a person to commit inter alia pick-pocketing, shop-lifting, drug trafficking and other similar activities which are subject to penalties and imply financial gain for the trafficker.

6 Directive 2011/36/EU, Recital (11).

7 Palermo Protocol, Article 5; Trafficking Convention, Article 18; EU Trafficking Directive Article 2.

8 The laws of England, Wales and Northern Ireland.

9 Authors' footnote: we have corrected this to show 14 years as the TIP report incorrectly stated 10 years instead of 14 years. With thanks to Pam Bowen of the CPS for bringing this to our attention.

Who is a victim of trafficking?

25.12 In summary, a victim of human trafficking is a person who has been subjected to the act of human trafficking. The Trafficking Convention, Article 4(e) provides:

> '"Victim" shall mean any natural person who is subject to trafficking in human beings as defined in this article.'

Practical legal tools to identify a victim

25.13

(1)   Crucial overview for practitioners:

In the context of criminal proceedings the author of **CHAPTER 24** and the two authors of this Chapter[1] suggest that often a two-stage assessment will be required to establish whether the suspect is a credible victim of trafficking and hence ought to be protected against criminalisation. Hence, it is suggested by the three authors that when the circumstances give rise to a 'reasonable suspicion'[2] that a criminal suspect was trafficked and where upon further investigation[3] there are found to be 'reasonable grounds for believing' this[4], then the suspect is a credible victim of trafficking.

The outcome of this further investigation will either confirm duress to inform the decision to discontinue on evidential grounds, or raise sufficient doubt of culpability that the prosecutor can consider whether a prosecution is required in the public interest. But sometimes this process will involve the prosecutor in further consideration, not only of the status of the suspect as a trafficked victim, but if there is sufficient evidence against them, whether the seriousness of the offence demands a prosecution.

However, there may be circumstances when this two stage assessment will be elided into a single process[5].

This final determination in the criminal context must be reached in light of a more detailed consideration of the defendant's circumstances which takes into account the facts of the suspect's case, the human trafficking definition[6], the Human Trafficking Indicators[7] which apply to their case and, if applicable, any expert reports that are obtained[8]. In such a case, where the suspect has been charged with a trafficking-dependent crime[9], an application, with submissions and/or evidence, should be made to the CPS to consider a discontinuance of the prosecution. The CPS Legal Guidance ought to be referred to in those submissions and practitioners ought to be aware that in such cases, according to the CPS Legal Guidance, the decision of the CPS to discontinue will depend on whether the criminal act was committed as a direct consequence of the suspect's trafficked status and whether and to what extent that suspect was compelled to do the act. If the CPS lawyer, having reviewed[10] the case, refuses to discontinue and the defence lawyer considers this decision to be unreasonable it ought to be recalled that the court retains the ultimate power to stay a prosecution for abuse[11] and in such circumstances an application should therefore be made to the court to obtain such a stay.

In our view it is also crucial to note that where the subjective facts and the objective indicators point to the suspect being a credible victim of trafficking the CPS must, in reviewing the public interest in whether to proceed with the prosecution, consider that it is the duty of the State to investigate the allegation of trafficking[12] once they have received a credible allegation that such an offence took place: see *OOO v The Commissioner of Police for the Metropolis* [13]. If this duty to investigate were to be properly complied with it would mean that the suspect ought to be treated as a victim[14] and, indeed, as a potential witness, of crime.

(2)   Who is an adult victim of trafficking?

Where all three of the core elements in the trafficking definition exist, the person who was subjected to such treatment is a victim of trafficking[15].

However, although there is a requirement to show that one of 'the means of' (core element 2) occurred in the case of an adult victim of trafficking in order to establish that the crime of human trafficking took place and thereby to successfully prosecute a trafficker, in terms of deciding who is an adult victim of the crime of trafficking the consent of an adult to be trafficked is irrelevant if any of the means described above in core element (2) were used by the trafficker to obtain that consent[16].

(3)   Who is a child victim of trafficking?

Where, on the facts of a case, core elements (1) and (3) in the trafficking definition exist, and the person who was subjected to such treatment was under 18 years old at the time, that person is a child victim of trafficking. In the case of child traffickers there is no requirement at all to establish that any of the means identified in the trafficking definitions were used by the trafficker(s) to enable a successful prosecution for child trafficking to take place[17]. There is no requirement to prove that a child was deceived, coerced or forced into the human trafficking scenario and the Recital to the EU Trafficking Directive confirms that:

> '[W]hen a child is concerned, no possible consent should ever be considered valid.'[18]

Hence, a child cannot consent to their own trafficking and cannot therefore consent to their own exploitation. In deciding whether a child is a victim of trafficking the following understanding is key: any child moved or recruited into a place for the purposes of exploitation is a victim of trafficking.

(4)   When are the elements of the crime of human trafficking met?

In all cases of human trafficking, the crime of human trafficking will take place before the exploitation begins, albeit the crime of human trafficking will also encompass the act(s) of the actual exploitation if the intended exploitation of the victim has already occurred[19].

---

1   This agreement between the three authors applies to both the two-stage assessment and the single process that are herein proposed.

2   This is relevant because, by analogy, it is the test which must be met for a valid arrest to be carried out.

3   The duty to investigate as part of this assessment reflects the findings of the ECtHR in *Rantsev v Cyprus and Russia* [2010] 51 EHRR 1, (2010) 28 BHRC 313, [2010] ECHR 25965/04, ECtHR regarding the positive obligations on the State when faced with circumstances which give rise to, or ought to give rise to, a credible suspicion that the person had been trafficked.

4   Relevant because, by analogy, this is the test for a decision to charge for an offence and takes into account objective factors.

5   This will occur where there are clear indicators from the outset and where the circumstances give rise to a reasonable belief that the suspect was trafficked and that the offence is a trafficking-dependent crime. This should lead law enforcement officers and prosecutors to conclude that it is likely they are a trafficked victim without the necessity of further investigation. The test must be applied sympathetically and not sceptically. It is then for the Crown Prosecution Service (or other prosecuting agency) and ultimately the courts to determine what should be the result of applying the test. Too restrictive an approach will lead to miscarriages of justice and a failure to comply with our international obligations.

6   The enquiry must begin with whether there is a reasonable suspicion that the suspect has been trafficked. This enquiry cannot be undertaken unless the practitioner is aware of the definition of human trafficking and the Human Trafficking Indicators.

7   Which, we suggest, may include both the NRM Trafficking Indicators and the UNODC Human Trafficking Indicators.

8   Which will include any trafficking identification assessment produced by an NGO and any medical evidence regarding trauma – See the relevance of such evidence as recognised in the CPS Legal Guidance which is reproduced in the Appendix.

9   See Authors' Note at para **25.21** for a definition of this term.

10   Which will involve an assessment of the evidential test and the public interest in continuing the prosecution.

11   See commentary on *R v LM* [2010] EWCA Crim 2327, [2011] 1 Cr App Rep 135, [2011] Crim LR 425 below at para **25.19**.

12   As trafficking-based harm is conduct which gives rise to potential breaches of Articles 3 and 4 ECHR.

13   In *OOO and Others v The Commissioner of Police for the Metropolis* [2011] EWHC 1246 (QB), the High Court approved the findings of the ECtHR in *Rantsev v Cyprus and Russia* [2010] 51 EHRR 1, at paras 283–289, (2010) 28 BHRC 313, [2010] ECHR 25965/04, ECtHR, as to the positive obligation on a State to take operational police measures to protect victims or potential victims of trafficking under Articles 3 and 4 ECHR once a credible allegation of trafficking is raised: see *OOO and Others v The Commissioner of Police for the Metropolis* [2011] EWHC 1246 (QB) at paras 151–164 in particular.

14   As in all cases, a victim of crime is entitled to be considered as such, regardless of whether the perpetrator is identified, apprehended, prosecuted or convicted.

15   It is relevant to note here that the National Referral Mechanism (NRM) in the UK, which has the role of formally identifying adult and child victims of trafficking in the UK, is discussed in the **CHAPTER 2** on Identification. Suffice it is to say for present purposes there will be reasonable grounds under the NRM to identify a person as a potential victim of trafficking on the basis of the test: 'I suspect but cannot prove'. A potential victim of trafficking who passes that test is entitled to protection measures in the UK including accommodation, medical and legal assistance (Trafficking Convention Article 12) and a recovery and reflection period (Trafficking Convention Article 13) of 45 days in the UK in which to begin to recover from the harmful trafficking experience. The second part of the NRM identification test, namely that of a Conclusive Decision in terms of victim identification, is at present to be reached under the NRM on the civil standard of proof, namely a balance of probabilities. Following a positive Conclusive Decision, in the context of criminal proceedings, if the victim is willing to give police evidence or intelligence against their traffickers the victim may also be eligible for a one-year residence permit in the UK (Trafficking Convention, Article 14(1)(b)).The UK's NRM is designed to trigger the protection provisions of the Trafficking Convention under Chapter III of that Convention: Chapter III does not include Article 26. The UK's NRM is not designed to direct prosecutors or the police on their investigative or prosecutorial duties of trafficker identification and victim identification. From a practical standpoint however we believe that the NRM Trafficking Indicators and the UNODC Human Trafficking Indicators will much assist defence lawyers, prosecutors and the courts in assessing whether a defendant is a credible victim of trafficking according to the 'reasonable grounds for believing' test that the authors have proposed as being relevant for victim identification in the criminal context. Both sets of trafficking indicators are included as Appendices to this book.

16   See for example, Trafficking Convention, Article 4(b) which provides: 'The consent of a victim of "trafficking in human beings" to the intended exploitation set forth in subparagraph (a) of this article shall be irrelevant where any of the means set forth in subparagraph (a) have been used'. A similar provision is included in the EU Trafficking Directive, under Article 2(4) albeit

the reference 'to the intended exploitation . . . ' in the Trafficking Convention is more precisely defined under the Directive, which instead provides 'to the exploitation, whether intended or actual . . . '.

[17] Trafficking Convention, Article 4(c), which provides: 'The recruitment, transportation, transfer, harbouring or receipt of a child for the purpose of exploitation shall be considered "trafficking in human beings" even if this does not involve any of the means set forth in subparagraph (a) of this article'. The Explanatory Report to the Trafficking Convention helpfully explains: '76. For there to be trafficking in human beings ingredients from each of the three categories (action, means, purpose) must be present together. There is, however, an exception regarding (trafficked) children: under Article 4(c) recruitment, transportation, transfer, harbouring or receipt of a child for the purpose of exploitation is to be regarded as trafficking in human beings even if it does not involve any of the means listed in Article 4(a). Under Article 4(d) the word "child" means any person under 18 years of age.'

[18] Directive 2011/36/EU, Recital (11).

[19] As the Explanatory Report to the Trafficking Convention explains: '87. Under the definition, it is not necessary that someone have been exploited for there to be trafficking in human beings. It is enough that they have been subjected to one of the actions referred to in the definition and by one of the means specified "for the purpose of" exploitation. Trafficking in human beings is consequently present before the victim's actual exploitation.'

GENERAL INDICATORS OF HUMAN TRAFFICKING

25.14 There are numerous publications in the UK and in the international domain which provide indicators that assist in the identification of victims of trafficking.

The UK's National Referral Mechanism forms[1] which are to be completed by the named First Responders in the UK[2] list many general indicators of human trafficking and these should be referred to by practitioners.

Practitioners are also referred to the 'Human Trafficking Indicators' of the United Nations Office on Drugs and Crime, published in 2010, which are reproduced in full in the Appendices to this book. This is a set of extensive lists which provide not only a detailed list of 'general indicators' that a victim of trafficking may exhibit and/or disclose but also 'specific indicators' with regard to separately identifying both child and adult victims of trafficking for the purposes of exploitation such as: domestic servitude; sexual exploitation; labour exploitation; begging and petty crime.

Relevant to all these indicators is of course a knowledge as to whether the victim comes from a country/place that is known to be a source of human trafficking victims[3] and/or whether the victim was engaged in a form of illicit activity in the UK that has links with country-specific organised crime and human trafficking[4].

It is well recognised that for a multitude of reasons victims of trafficking may be unwilling to disclose details of their trafficking and exploitation. By paying attention to the UNODC Human Trafficking Indicators practitioners will be assisted in understanding whether their clients might be potential or actual victims of trafficking and if so how to best represent their interests as defendants in the criminal justice system and prosecutors will be assisted in determining whether the defendant is likely to be a victim and witness of serious crime.

[1] There are separate NRM referral forms for adult and child victims. These are reproduced in the Appendices to this book.

[2] For a summary of the National Referral Mechanism in the UK, which is the formal identification procedure for victims of trafficking, and the involvement and names of First Responders please see **CHAPTER 2** on Identification. It is notable that in the UK Government's recently published *Human Trafficking: The Government's Strategy*, at para 27, it is stated that the NSPCC Child Trafficking Advice and Information Line (CTAIL) and Barnardo's have recently joined the NRM as First Responders. To that extent they can be regarded as expert witnesses in terms of trafficking identification.

[3] The US State Department TIP reports on particular countries might point to this, together with the NRM statistics in the UK which, albeit imperfect for the reasons given by the Anti-Trafficking Monitoring Group's 'Wrong kind of Victim' report of 2010, might indicate general trends of trafficking from countries into and within the UK.

[4] For example, reports by NGOs and by CEOP might point to this.

VICTIMS OF FORCED LABOUR AND DOMESTIC SERVITUDE

25.15 In the context of the UK it is also relevant for criminal practitioners to note that holding someone in slavery or servitude, or requiring them to perform forced or compulsory labour are now free-standing criminal offences in the UK[1] under the Coroners and Justice Act 2009, s 71 and as such any individual victim who has been subjected to any such criminal behaviour is a victim of crime and should be treated as a victim of crime regardless as to whether there is a demonstrable trafficking element (ie movement or recruitment) in their case. It is suggested by the authors of this chapter that victims of such crimes are just as much entitled to the protection of non-criminalisation as victims of trafficking, to the extent that if they were forced or compelled to commit criminal offences in their exploitation-dependent role they ought not to be treated as criminal offenders.

[1] Such crimes are committed irrespective of whether the victim was trafficked or not. The s 71 offence entered into force on 6 April 2010 in England, Wales and Northern Ireland. The same criminal offences were introduced in Scotland under the Criminal Justice and Licensing (Scotland) Act 2010, s 47 and came into force in Scotland on 28 March 2011.

TERRORISM OFFENCES

25.16 No such case seems yet to have emerged. However, the exploitation of young or vulnerable people to assist in offences of terrorism is a feature in some countries. How would such a situation fit into the scheme for protecting victims of trafficking? The question arises because of UN Security Resolution 1456 of 20 January 2003. Article 6 of that Resolution provides-

> '6. States must ensure that any measure taken to combat terrorism comply with all their obligations under international law, and should adopt such measures in accordance with international law, in particular under international human rights, refugee and humanitarian law.'

Consequently, in giving effect to its international obligation to combat terrorism, the UK must give effect to the provisions protecting victims of trafficking. No doubt it will usually be considered that participation in an offence of terrorism is too serious to justify invoking the protection for victims of trafficking. But it does need careful consideration. Some offences of terrorism do not involve acts of violence, eg offences under the Terrorism Act 2000, ss 57 and 58 (possessing or collecting information for use in terrorism or likely to be useful to a terrorist) and could easily be committed by a victim of trafficking under the control and behest of the trafficker or someone abusing the trafficked victim's vulnerability. What of a child victim of trafficking who is coerced to carry an explosive device? Duress is not a defence in law to murder or attempted murder - see *Archbold* paragraph 17-119[1] It is a defence to other terrorist offences such as causing explosions. Should the treatment by the criminal justice system of a child victim of trafficking depend on whether (s)he is charged (possibly with others) with murder or attempted murder? Would the answer be for the prosecution to charge an offence to which duress is a defence? Or does the duty to protect such victims require the prosecution and the courts to treat that person as a victim as much as the intended targets so that the high threshold of duress is avoided? Recruitment of child soldiers[2] is a war crime by virtue of Article 8.2(b)(xxvi) of the Rome Statute of the International Criminal Court, incorporated into English law by the International Criminal Court Act 2001 via s 50 and Sch 8 of that Act. These are all matters which must be taken into account should the situation arise. Let us all hope this passage remains merely hypothetical.

[1] Archbold: Criminal Pleading, Evidence and Practice, (2011) Sweet and Maxwel.
[2] For the purposes of the Article 8 of the Rome Statute a 'child soldier' is one who is under 15 years of age.

how to protect the rights of victims of trafficking who are exposed, as defendants, to criminal proceedings in the UK

25.17 Practitioners are referred to the specific guidance we have suggested in our 'Critical Overview' section, above[1]. The CPS Legal Guidance which is summarised in **CHAPTER 24** also informs practitioners as to how to protect the rights of defendants who display human trafficking indicators and may be credible victims of trafficking. Once a practitioner is aware of what the unlawful act of human trafficking entails and who, according to law, is a victim of such an act he or she will be able to decide for themselves whether their client is likely to be a credible victim of trafficking, if so whether the criminal act in respect of which they have been charged was one that was trafficking-dependent or trafficking-independent and what ought to be done.

[1] See para **25.13** above.

RELEVANT COURT OF APPEAL JUDGMENTS

(1) R v O [2008] EWCA Crim 2835

25.18 The first case to highlight the unlawful criminalisation of a victim of trafficking in the UK was the landmark non-punishment criminal appeal of *R v O*[1] in 2008 which concerned an out of time appeal against the conviction and sentence of a young Nigerian girl, a minor, who had been trafficked into the UK for the purposes of sexual exploitation. After being sexually exploited in this country she escaped her trafficker and obtained a false Spanish identity document which she used to attempt to board a coach at Dover docks that was bound for France. Her motivation was to flee her trafficker in the UK and find safety in France where she thought her uncle resided. Despite her very young appearance she was treated as an adult not only by the police who arrested and charged her under the Identity Cards Act 2006, but by all others in the criminal justice system, including her defence lawyers, the prosecutor and the sentencing judge. Despite the interest of the Poppy Project in her case and Poppy's request to O's defence lawyers that the criminal proceedings be adjourned so that Poppy could conduct a trafficking assessment of O in prison, this was ignored and O was advised to plead guilty to the criminal charge and when she did she was sentenced to eight months in an adult prison. We acted for O in her appeal, at a time when the UK had signed but not yet ratified the Trafficking Convention. In order to pray in aid the provisions of the Trafficking Convention, including its child identification provisions under Article 10 and its non-punishment provision under Article 26, we referred the court to the Vienna Convention on the Law of Treaties 1969 which provides, under its Article 18, that as a signatory state to a Treaty, namely the Trafficking Convention, the UK was obliged to refrain from acts which would defeat the object and purpose of that treaty. The Court accepted this submission. We argued that the provisions of the Trafficking Convention could be viewed clearly through the lens of the European Convention on Human Rights and that O's protected fair trial rights under Article 6 ECHR had been breached for a multitude of reasons, including that her lawyers had ignored the Poppy Project's suggestion that she might have been trafficked, had, jointly with the prosecutor, ignored the existence of the CPS Legal Guidance[2] on discontinuing cases against credible trafficked victims, that the critical issue of her minor age was also ignored and the judge had sentenced her, as an adult, on facts which pointed to her having been a child victim of trafficking who was using the identity card to escape her trafficker in the UK. In short she had been unlawfully criminalised for actions, namely her use of the false identity card, which she had been compelled to perform in order to flee her trafficker in the UK.

The Court of Appeal, on the evidence before it[3], quashed O's conviction and found that the defence lawyers, the prosecutor and the judge were all at fault for the lack of protection that was offered to O as a credible victim of sex trafficking during her process, conviction and sentence by the criminal justice system, particularly in view of her minor age. The Court found:

'18 . . . There was no consideration of any kind given to any need to protect the appellant as a child or young person.'

And further:

'25. No steps were taken by the defence to investigate the history. No consideration was given by the defence as to whether she might have a defence of duress. The possibility that she might have been trafficked was ignored. There is nothing in the transcript to suggest that any thought had been given to the State's possible duty to protect her as a young victim. . . . The judge passed what she described as an "inevitable prison sentence" of 8 months.'

The Court concluded:

'26. This appeal against conviction must obviously be allowed. We would put it most simply on the footing that the common law and Article 6 of the European Convention on Human Rights alike require far higher standards of procedural protection than were given here. There was no fair trial. We hope that such a shameful set of circumstances never occurs again. Prosecutors must be aware of the [CPS Legal Guidance] which, although not in the text books are enshrined in their Code. Defence lawyers must respond by making enquiries, if there is before them credible material showing that they have a client who might have been the victim of trafficking, especially a young client . . . We hope that this case serves as a lesson to drive these messages home.'

1   [2008] EWCA Crim 2835, (2008) Times, 2 October.
2   At that time referred to as 'the CPS Protocols'.
3   Which included but was not limited to the police custody records, the criminal solicitor's file, a note from the Defence Counsel, a full record of the sentencing hearing and a trafficking assessment report by the Poppy Project which had been commissioned by our solicitor and was subsequently admitted by the Court of Appeal as fresh evidence.

(2) R v LM [2010] EWCA Crim 2327

25.19 The principles of non-prosecution and non-punishment in *R v O* were applied and developed further by the Court of Appeal in *R v LM*[1], a joined criminal appeal by five asserted victims of sex trafficking that was heard in 2010[2].

In *LM* the Court of Appeal considered whether the UK was compliant with the non-punishment Article 26 obligation imposed under the Trafficking Convention and found that the implementation of Article 26 was achieved by three mechanisms in England and Wales:

'7 . . . First, English law recognises the common law defences of duress and necessity ("duress of circumstances"). Second, specific rules have been made for the guidance of prosecutors in considering whether charges should be brought against those who are or may have been victims of trafficking. Thirdly, in the event that the duty laid on the prosecutor to exercise judgment is not properly discharged, the ultimate sanction is the power of the court to stay the prosecution for what is conveniently, if not very accurately, termed "abuse of process".'

On the scope of Article 26 the Court held:

'13. It is necessary to focus upon what Article 26 does and does not say. It does not say that no trafficked victim should be prosecuted, whatever offence has been committed. It does not say that no trafficked victim should be prosecuted when the offence is in some way connected with or arises out of trafficking. It does not provide a defence which may be advanced before a jury. <u>What it says is no more, but no less, than that careful consideration must be given to whether public policy calls for a prosecution and punishment when the defendant is a trafficked victim and the crime has been committed when he or she was in some manner compelled (in the broad sense) to commit it.</u> Article 26 does not require a blanket immunity from prosecution for trafficked victims.' [Our emphasis]

The Court considered the content of the CPS Legal Guidance on Human Trafficking and Smuggling which existed at the time of the appellant's convictions[3] and found that the duty it imposed was wider than the consideration of the common law defences of duress and necessity[4] since the use of the word 'compelled' under Article 26 was not limited to the circumstances in which the English common law defences would be established[5]. The Court found that the effect of the CPS guidance was to impose a three-stage exercise of judgment:

'10 . . . The first is: (1) is there a reason to believe that the person has been trafficked? If so, then (2) if there is clear evidence of a credible common law defence the case will be discontinued in the ordinary way on evidential grounds, but, importantly, (3) even where there is not, but the offence may have been committed as a result of compulsion arising from the trafficking, prosecutors should consider whether the public interest lies in proceeding to prosecute or not.'

The Court recognised that:

'12. Whilst immigration offences such as using false identity documents and the like are of course offences which may very commonly be committed by trafficked victims, the obligation under Article 26 is . . . one which extends to any offence where it may have been committed by a trafficked victim who has been compelled to commit it. One of the commonest forms of trafficking is for the purpose of forced prostitution; persons trafficked for that purpose may clearly commit, under compulsion in the broad sense, offences connected with prostitution; soliciting is an obvious example. There have been cases of persons (especially youngsters) trafficked in order to be put to exploited labour in unlawful cannabis factories. There are clearly other possibilities also.'

The Court held that the application of Article 26 is fact-sensitive in every case and suggested five general propositions[6]:

'(i)   If there is evidence on which a common law defence of duress or necessity is likely to succeed, the case will no doubt not be proceeded with on ordinary evidential grounds independent of the convention, but additionally there are likely to be public policy grounds under the convention leading to the same conclusion.

(ii)   But cases in which it is not in the public interest to prosecute are not limited to these . . .

(iii)   It may be reasonable to prosecute if the defendant's assertion that she was trafficked meets the reasonable grounds test, but has been properly considered and rejected by the Crown for good evidential reason. The fact that a person passes the threshold test as a person of whom there are reasonable grounds to believe she has been trafficked is not conclusive that she has. Conversely, it may well be that in other cases that the real possibility of trafficking and a nexus of compulsion (in the broad sense) means that public policy points against prosecution.

(iv)   There is normally no reason not to prosecute, even if the defendant has previously been a trafficked victim, if the offence appears to have been committed out with any reasonable nexus of compulsion (in the broad sense) occasioned by the trafficking, and hence is outside Article 26.

(v)   A more difficult judgment is involved if the victim has been a trafficked victim and retains some nexus with the trafficking, but has committed an offence which arguably calls, in the public interest, for prosecution in court. Some of these may be cases of a cycle of abuse. It is well known that one tool of those in charge of trafficking operations is to turn those who were trafficked and exploited in the past into assistants in the exploitation of others. Such a cycle of abuse is not uncommon in this field, as in other fields, for example that of abuse of children. In such a case, the question which must be actively confronted by the prosecutor is whether or not the offence committed is serious enough, despite any nexus with trafficking, to call for prosecution. That will depend on all the circumstances of the case, and normally no doubt particularly on the gravity of the offence alleged, the degree of continuing compulsion, and the alternatives reasonably available to the defendant . . . '

Applying these to the facts of each appeal before it the Court found that in the cases of three of the appellants[7] who had been accused of having turned from victims of trafficking to the voluntary abusers of other victims[8], whilst the Article 26 duty had been in the mind of the prosecutor at the time of the original charges when the decisions to prosecute had been maintained, at a subsequent hearing when the three defendants had changed their pleas to 'guilty' on the basis that they had not used violence, threats or sexual abuse on other victims no fresh consideration was given by the prosecutor of the Article 26 duty and the three defendants were convicted on the basis that they had been pressured, short of duress, into committing the offences of controlling prostitution. The Court found that no consideration had been given to whether there was a public interest in continuing the prosecution on the new factual basis and at the appeal the Crown accepted that if the Article 26 question 'had been confronted afresh, as it should have been, there could only have been one conclusion, which was that the prosecution should have been abandoned by the offering of no evidence . . . or [as the Court observed] if it had not, an application for a stay of proceedings [by the De-fence] . . . ought to have succeeded on the grounds that any Crown decision to prosecute was one which no reasonable prosecutor could make'[9].

In the two other joined appeals before the Court, leave to appeal against conviction was refused. In one case, *Tabot*, this was because on the evidence the Court was satisfied, following an examination of all the evidence before it, that the appellant's claim to have been a victim of trafficking was in fact not credible[10]. In the other case however, *Tijani*, where the likelihood of the victim's historical trafficking was accepted, leave to appeal against her conviction was refused by the Court because the appellant's use of a false identity document and her act of fraud in producing a false national insurance case were acts which took place some months after she had been free from any exploitation as a victim of trafficking and in the Court's judgment the 'offences were not committed under the necessary nexus of compulsion (in the broad sense) with her trafficking.'[11] However, leave to appeal her sentence was granted and the appellant's sentence was reduced on appeal from nine months to four months on account of the fact an immigration judge had accepted it was likely that she had been trafficked in the past[12].

1   *R v LM* [2010] EWCA Crim 2327, [2011] 1 Cr App Rep 135, [2011] Crim LR 425.
2   It was therefore heard subsequent to the UK's ratification of the Trafficking Convention in December 2008 and the Convention's entry into force in April 2009.
3   *R v LM* [2010] EWCA Crim 2327 at para 9, [2011] 1 Cr App Rep 135, [2011] Crim LR 425.
4   *R v LM* [2010] EWCA Crim 2327 at para 8, [2011] 1 Cr App Rep 135, [2011] Crim LR 425.
5   *R v LM* [2010] EWCA Crim 2327 at para 11, [2011] 1 Cr App Rep 135, [2011] Crim LR 425.
6   *R v LM* [2010] EWCA Crim 2327 at para 14, [2011] 1 Cr App Rep 135, [2011] Crim LR 425.
7   Namely LM, MB and DG.
8   Namely under the Sexual Offences Act 2003, s 53.
9   *R v LM* [2010] EWCA Crim 2327, para 30, [2011] 1 Cr App Rep 135, [2011] Crim LR 425.
10   The appeal of *Tabot*, see *R v LM* [2010] EWCA Crim 2327 at paras 35–40, [2011] 1 Cr App Rep 135, [2011] Crim LR 425.
11   The appeal of *Tijani*. See *R v LM* [2010] EWCA Crim 2327 at para 41–47, [2011] 1 Cr App Rep 135, [2011] Crim LR 425, at para 46.
12   *R v LM* [2010] EWCA Crim 2327 at para 47, [2011] 1 Cr App Rep 135, [2011] Crim LR 425.

CONCLUSIONS

25.20 In accordance with the UK's international and domestic obligations, victims of trafficking ought to be protected against being criminalised for acts that they were compelled or forced to perform by their traffickers and for criminal conduct which arises as a direct[1] result of their having been trafficked.

The Court of Appeal has considered published versions of the CPS Legal Guidance and the UK's obligations under the Trafficking Convention and the factual situation of trafficked victims who have been criminalised for their use of false identity cards, or who have used fraud or who have controlled prostitution. Criminal convictions have been overturned where the court has found that Article 6 ECHR has been materially breached or the Article 26 duty was not properly complied with. The term of a criminal sentence has been reduced by the court where the trafficking of a victim ought to have been a relevant mitigating factor during sentencing. The court has moreover advised that it retains the power to stay a prosecution for abuse. Soon the Court will hear the appeal of a young man from Vietnam whose appeal against his conviction and sentence as a minor for an asserted trafficking-dependent crime, namely cannabis cultivation, has recently been referred to the full Court[2].

This chapter includes extracts from the TIP Report, from the relevant ACPO Leads' Position which has been specifically endorsed by the CPS in its most recent Legal Guidance and also cites objective evidence and intelligence which points towards the continuing criminalisation of some victims of trafficking, particularly young persons, in the UK today.

[1] Or indeed, in the authors' view, as an indirect result: see Authors' Note at para **25.21**.
[2] Pending appeal of *R v AVN*, Appeal Number 201101252B3, referred in July 2011 by the Single Judge of the Court of Appeal to the Full Court.

AUTHORS' NOTE

25.21 In parts of this chapter two novel terms have been used by the authors: 'trafficking-dependent crimes' and 'trafficking-independent crimes'.

The term 'trafficking-dependent crimes' is introduced and proposed by the authors of this chapter as a new term in the trafficking discourse. We propose that it shall refer to criminal conduct which is committed by a victim of trafficking when the victim of trafficking is: (1) under the control of their trafficker(s); or (2) attempting to flee the control of the trafficker(s); or (3) otherwise acting to try to protect or assist him or herself on account of their trafficked status. Where there is a clear causal nexus between the crime itself and the predicament of the perpetrator as a victim of trafficking in the ways described above, the victim of trafficking should be entitled to protection and not prosecution or punishment. To put it simply, but for victim's trafficked status the crime would not have taken place. To that extent the crime is trafficking-dependent. In some cases, particularly those which fall under categories (1) and (2) it may be obvious that the crime was trafficking-dependent. In other cases, particularly those which fall within category (3), a more searching enquiry of the facts and circumstances will be called for. It is recalled that in many cases but for a person having been a victim of trafficking and exploitation they would not be in the UK at all. Even those who escape their trafficker will often be too afraid to seek assistance from the UK police or immigration service[1] and may therefore be living 'underground', in reliance on a black market economy, involving offences such as theft, to survive. For many, this is the reality, the unprotected end consequence of their trafficked status. Hence, in category (3) cases where the causal nexus between the individual's trafficked status and the crime he or she has committed is weak, such as where a victim is arrested for using a false passport or identity card to obtain employment sometime after having escaped from the trafficker, or as stated above commits theft to survive, the nature of the crime is still arguably trafficking-dependent and this ought to go towards mitigating a criminal sentence if not obviating it.

The new term 'trafficking-independent crimes' is also proposed by the authors: these are crimes which have no nexus with the defendant's past or present status as a victim of trafficking.

We hope these new terms[2] may find a place in the developing trafficking discourse.

[1] It is also relevant that the National Referral Mechanism, the formal identification mechanism in the UK, has been found by the Anti-Trafficking Monitoring Group in its 2010 detailed report *Wrong Kind of Victim* as being not fit for purpose. The ATMG's summary of its 2010 report is included as one of the Appendices to this book.

[2] The terms have been proposed by the authors with the following in mind: that, by analogy to the rights and fundamental freedoms established under the European Convention on Human Rights, the provisions of the Palermo Protocol and the Trafficking Convention establish minimum protections for victims of trafficking and can therefore be described as constituting a floor, not a ceiling, of rights.

APPENDICES

Contents

Identification Indicators

Treaties

Multi-Agency Guidance

Guidance: other

Summary Report

Appendix 1

UNITED NATIONS OFFICE ON DRUGS AND CRIME: HUMAN TRAFFICKING INDICATORS, 2010

http://www.unodc.org/pdf/HT_indicators_E_LOWRES.pdfSimilar

"Not all the indicators listed below are present in all situations involving trafficking in humans. Although the presence or absence of any of the indicators neither proves nor disproves that human trafficking is taking place, their presence should lead to investigation.

Victims of trafficking in humans can be found in a variety of situations. You can play a role in identifying such victims.

GENERAL INDICATORS:

People who have been trafficked may:

- Believe that they must work against their will
- Be unable to leave their work environment
- Show signs that their movements are being controlled
- Feel that they cannot leave
- Show fear or anxiety
- Be subjected to violence or threats of violence against themselves or against their family members and loved ones
- Suffer injuries that appear to be the result of an assault
- Suffer injuries or impairments typical of certain jobs or control measures
- Suffer injuries that appear to be the result of the application of control measures
- Be distrustful of the authorities
- Be threatened with being handed over to the authorities
- Be afraid of revealing their immigration status
- Not be in possession of their passports or other travel or identity documents, as those documents are being held by someone else
- Have false identity or travel documents
- Be found in or connected to a type of location likely to be used for exploiting people
- Be unfamiliar with the local language
- Not know their home or work address
- Allow others to speak for them when addressed directly
- Act as if they were instructed by someone else
- Be forced to work under certain conditions
- Be disciplined through punishment
- Be unable to negotiate working conditions
- Receive little or no payment
- Have no access to their earnings
- Work excessively long hours over long periods
- Not have any days off
- Live in poor or substandard accommodations
- Have no access to medical care
- Have limited or no social interaction
- Have limited contact with their families or with people outside of their immediate environment

- Be unable to communicate freely with others
- Be under the perception that they are bonded by debt
- Be in a situation of dependence
- Come from a place known to be a source of human trafficking
- Have had the fees for their transport to the country of destination paid for by facilitators, whom they must payback by working or providing services in the destination
- Have acted on the basis of false promises

CHILDREN

Children who have been trafficked may:

- Have no access to their parents or guardians
- Look intimidated and behave in a way that does not correspond with behaviour typical of children their age
- Have no friends of their own age outside of work
- Have no access to education
- Have no time for playing
- Live apart from other children and in substandard accommodations
- Eat apart from other members of the "family"
- Be given only leftovers to eat
- Be engaged in work that is not suitable for children
- Travel unaccompanied by adults
- Travel in groups with persons who are not relatives

The following might also indicate that children have been trafficked:

- The presence of child-sized clothing typically worn for doing manual or sex work
- The presence of toys, beds and children's clothing in inappropriate places such as brothels and factories
- The claim made by an adult that he or she has "found" an unaccompanied child
- The finding of unaccompanied children carrying telephone numbers for calling taxis
- The discovery of cases involving illegal adoption

DOMESTIC SERVITUDE

People who have been trafficked for the purpose of domestic servitude may:

- Live with a family
- Not eat with the rest of the family
- Have no private space
- Sleep in a shared or inappropriate space
- Be reported missing by their employer even though they are still living in their employer's house
- Never or rarely leave the house for social reasons
- Never leave the house without their employer
- Be given only leftovers to eat
- Be subjected to insults, abuse, threats or violence

SEXUAL EXPLOITATION

People who have been trafficked for the purpose of sexual exploitation may:

- Be of any age, although the age may vary according to the location and the market
- Move from one brothel to the next or work in various locations

- Be escorted whenever they go to and return from work and other outside activities
- Have tattoos or other marks indicating "ownership" by their exploiters
- Work long hours or have few if any days off
- Sleep where they work
- Live or travel in a group, sometimes with other women who do not speak the same language
- Have very few items of clothing
- Have clothes that are mostly the kind typically worn for doing sex work
- Only know how to say sex-related words in the local language or in the language of the client group
- Have no cash of their own
- Be unable to show an identity document

The following might also indicate that . . . [people] have been trafficked [for sexual exploitation]:

- There is evidence that suspected victims have had unprotected and/or violent sex.
- There is evidence that suspected victims cannot refuse unprotected and/or violent sex.
- There is evidence that a person has been bought and sold.
- There is evidence that groups of women are under the control of others.
- Advertisements are placed for brothels or similar places offering the services of women of a particular ethnicity or nationality.
- It is reported that sex workers provide services to a clientele of a particular ethnicity or nationality.
- It is reported by clients that sex workers do not smile.

LABOUR EXPLOITATION

People who have been trafficked for the purpose of labour exploitation are typically made to work in sectors such as the following: agriculture, construction, entertainment, service industry and manufacturing (in sweatshops).

People who have been trafficked for labour exploitation may:

- Live in groups in the same place where they work and leave those premises infrequently, if at all
- Live in degraded, unsuitable places, such as in agricultural or industrial buildings
- Not be dressed adequately for the work they do: for example, they may lack protective equipment or warm clothing
- Be given only leftovers to eat
- Have no access to their earnings
- Have no labour contract
- Work excessively long hours
- Depend on their employer for a number of services, including work, transportation and accommodation
- Have no choice of accommodation
- Never leave the work premises without their employer
- Be unable to move freely
- Be subject to security measures designed to keep them on the work premises
- Be disciplined through fines
- Be subjected to insults, abuse, threats or violence
- Lack basic training and professional licences

The following might also indicate that people have been trafficked for labour exploitation:

- Notices have been posted in languages other than the local language.
- There are no health and safety notices.
- The employer or manager is unable to show the documents required for employing workers from other countries.
- The employer or manager is unable to show records of wages paid to workers.
- The health and safety equipment is of poor quality or is missing.
- Equipment is designed or has been modified so that it can be operated by children.
- There is evidence that labour laws are being breached.
- There is evidence that workers must pay for tools, food or accommodation or that those costs are being deducted from their wages.

BEGGING AND PETTY CRIME

People who have been trafficked for the purpose of begging or committing petty crimes may:

- Be children, elderly persons or disabled migrants who tend to begin public places and on public transport
- Be children carrying and/or selling illicit drugs
- Have physical impairments that appear to be the result of mutilation
- Be children of the same nationality or ethnicity who move in large groups with only a few adults
- Be unaccompanied minors who have been "found" by an adult of the same nationality or ethnicity
- Move in groups while travelling on public transport: for example, they may walk up and down the length of trains
- Participate in the activities of organized criminal gangs
- Be part of large groups of children who have the same adult guardian
- Be punished if they do not collect or steal enough
- Live with members of their gang
- Travel with members of their gang to the country of destination
- Live, as gang members, with adults who are not their parents
- Move daily in large groups and over considerable distances

The following might also indicate that people have been trafficked for begging or for committing petty crimes:

- New forms of gang-related crime appear.
- There is evidence that the group of suspected victims has moved, over a period of time, through a number of countries.
- There is evidence that suspected victims have been involved in begging or in committing petty crimes in another country."

Appendix 2

NATIONAL REFERRAL MECHANISM (NRM) REFERRAL FORMS – ADULT AND CHILDRENS' FORMS

Adults' form

**NATIONAL REFERRAL MECHANISM FOR POTENTIAL (ADULT) VICTIMS OF TRAFFICKING
REPORT TO COMPETENT AUTHORITY FOR DECISION**

Section A - Personal Details

Last name: .... First name(s): ....

Also known as: ....

D.O.B: ..../......./......... Age: .... Sex: .... Place of birth: ....

Nationality: .... Language: ....

Any English spoken: Y/N or interpreter needed: Y/N   Immigration status: ....

Other communication aids required (e.g. Sign language): Y/N Details: ....

Competent Authority referred to: UK Border Agency ☐ UK Human Trafficking Centre ☐

Home Office ref: .... Work Permit ref: ....

Any other reference numbers: ....

UK Home address/Contact Details: ....

....

Contact details of person making referral (First Responder)

Name: ....

Job title: ....

Organisation: ....

Tel: .... Mobile: ....

Email: ....

Signature and date of referral: ....

Details of encounter

Date: ..../......./......... Address (if different from above): ....

....

With access to interpreter (if applicable): Y/N

With access to legal advice: Y/N Details: ....

Consent of individual

I consent to my details including name and date of birth being submitted to the Competent Authority to assist in the identification process.

Signed: ....

435

Section B - General indicators

Please tick all relevant boxes

1. Distrustful of authorities ☐
2. Expressio! of fear or anxiety ☐
3. Signs of psychological trauma (including Post Traumatic Stress Disorder) ☐
4. The person acts as if instructed by another ☐
5. Injuries apparently a result of assault or controlling measures ☐
6. Evidence of control over movement, either as an individual or as a group ☐
7. Found in or connected to a type of location likely to be used for exploitation ☐
8. Restriction of movement and confinement to the workplace or to a limited area ☐
9. Passport or documents held by someone else ☐
10. Lack of access medical care ☐
11. Limited social contact ☐
12. Limited contact with family ☐
13. Perception of being bonded by debt ☐
14. Money is deducted from salary for food ☐
15. Threat of being handed over to authorities ☐
16. Threats against the individual or their family members ☐
17. Being placed in a dependency situation ☐
18. No or limited access to bathroom/hygiene facilities ☐
19. Any other, please provide details in Section F ☐

Where indicators are identified record full details in Section F

Section C - Indicators of forced labour

Are any of these indicators present? (Tick as applicable)
Yes ☐ please tick all relevant boxes in Section C
No ☐ continue to Section D

1. Employer or manager unable to produce documents required when employing migrant labour ☐
2. Employer or manager unable to provide record of wages paid to workers ☐
3. Poor or non existent health and safety equipment or no health and safety notices ☐
4. Any other evidence of labour laws being breached ☐
5. No or limited access to earnings or labour contract ☐
6. Excessive wage reduction ☐
7. Dependence on employer for a number of services i.e. work, transport, accommodation ☐
8. Any evidence workers are required to pay for tools, food or accommodation via deductions from their pay ☐
9. Imposed place of accommodation ☐
10. Any other, please provide details in Section F ☐

Where indicators are identified record full details in Section F

436

Section D - Indicators of domestic servitude

Are any of these indicators present? (Tick as applicable)
Yes ☐ please tick all relevant boxes in Section D
No ☐ continue to Section E

1. Living with and working for a family in a private home ☐
2. Not eating with the rest of the family ☐
3. No proper sleeping place or sleeping in shared space e.g. living room ☐
4. No private space ☐
5. Forced to work in excess of normal working hours or being "on-call" 24 hours per day ☐
6. Employer reports them as a missing person ☐
7. Employer accuses person of theft, kidnapping or other crime related to his/her escape ☐
8. Never leaving the house without employer ☐
9. Any other, please provide details in Section F ☐

Where indicators are identified record full details in Section F

Section E - Indicators of sexual exploitation

Are any of these indicators present? (Tick as applicable)
Yes ☐ please tick all relevant boxes in Section E
No ☐ continue to Section F

1. Adverts for brothels etc offering women from particular ethnic/national groups ☐
2. Sleeping on work premises ☐
3. Movement of women between brothels or working in alternate locations ☐
4. Women with very limited amounts of clothing and/or a large proportion of the clothing is 'sexual' ☐
5. Only being able to speak sexual words in local language or language of client group ☐
6. Person forced, intimidated or coerced into providing services of a sexual nature ☐
7. Person subjected to crimes such as abduction, assault or rape ☐
8. Does someone other than the victim receive the money from the client ☐
9. Health symptoms (including sexual health issues) ☐
10. Signs of ritual abuse and witch craft ☐
11. Substance misuse ☐
12. Any other, please provide details in Section F ☐

Where indicators are identified record full details in Section F

437

RESTRICTED (when completed)

Section F - Evidence to support reasons for referral (2 pages available)

Please use this section to:
- Expand on the circumstances/details of the encounter or contact, providing background to how the information was provided (e.g. On first encounter during police operation)
- Provide evidence of the indicators that you have identified in Sections B to E
- Note whether it is likely that further information will be required
- Provide any other relevant information that you consider may be important and wish to include e.g. living/working conditions, behaviour, appearance, demeanour etc
- Movements in or to the UK, including dates (if known)
- Name of agent, exploiter or trafficker (if known) and
- Any action you have taken including referral to other agencies e.g. POPPY, local authorities, children's services etc where appropriate

(If a separate sheet is required, please indicate that section F is continued and provide with referral)

Continued on next page

Section	Indicator

RESTRICTED (when completed)

POTENTIAL VICTIMS OF TRAFFICKING FORM GUIDANCE NOTES

This form should only be completed for adults where trafficking is suspected or claimed. It is for use by all agencies to record their encounters with potential victims of trafficking (PVoT). It is not to be used as an interview record but as a means for a First Responder (FR) to provide as much information as possible to the Competent Authority (CA) to enable a decision to be reached on whether the subject has reasonable grounds for being treated as a victim of trafficking. Although this is not an interview record this does not prevent an approach being made to obtain further details where appropriate. The tick box Sections (B - E) have been designed to save the FR time in completing the form by providing recognised indicators which can be marked quickly and expanded upon in Section F.

If a PVoT is to be treated as a child, the FR must use the Local Authority (LA) referral form highlighting that the child is a PVoT and submit a copy to the CA for consideration.

Section A

Complete as many of these details as possible, as more information will help the CA with their investigations, obviously the level of detail will depend on the environment in which a PVoT is encountered.

Any other reference numbers: Include any other reference numbers that are thought to be relevant here, for example: National Insurance Number, Local Authority Reference Numbers, Police Reference Numbers, your organisation's reference number. This will help where the Competent Authority needs to make further enquiries regarding the PVoT.

UK Home address/Contact details: The home address may differ from the address at which the PVoT is encountered. If provided, also include any contact numbers (landline or mobile) for them.

Contact details of person making referral: The FR should provide their work-related details here so that results of their referral can be fed back.

Details of encounter: State whether an interpreter was present during the encounter with the PVoT also note if any legal advice was provided and by whom.

Consent of individual: The PVoT **must** give their consent to this form being submitted to the CA, if they do not sign here then the form should not be referred to the CA for consideration.

Section B

To assist the FR in making a primary assessment of whether the individual they encountered is or may be a PVoT, there are 18 general indicators. These indicators are not a definitive list and there are many other indicators that may raise concerns, therefore the option to highlight "other" indicators has been included. These indicators will work in combination with those in Sections C, D and E to provide a fuller picture of the person's circumstances. It is not the case that by selecting a set number of indicators this will equate to a person being a victim; it could be just one or a combination of factors that demonstrates that the person may be a victim, each case should be considered on its own merits. Tick all relevant boxes and provide supporting evidence in Section F. After completing this section, proceed to Section C.

Sections C, D & E

To assist the FR in assessing the individual they have encountered, there are indicators of forced labour, domestic servitude and sexual exploitation; these will work in conjunction with the indicators already highlighted in section B. In each section tick any relevant boxes and provide supporting evidence in Section F.

You may also wish to consider whether the individual:

- Mentions that s/he was deceived by an agent/trafficker, i.e. false promises given such as well paid work, marriage or access to the education system
- Mentions that s/he was recruited through agents, family sold her/him etc

Tick all relevant boxes and provide supporting evidence in Section F.

Section F

The FR should begin by providing full details of the encounter, particularly when the trafficking issue was identified e.g. during a police operation, a formal interview, during a risk assessment, from a reported crime etc. This section also allows the FR to expand upon any indicators that have been highlighted in Sections B - E along with the particular circumstances that the PVoT was encountered, such as their appearance, demeanour or the condition of their surrounding environment. Where a tick box has been checked in Sections B - E, the comment in Section F should show which section and indicator it relates to. If the person has claimed to have been trafficked rather than identified by the FR, the FR should note this in Section F and whether the evidence of the indicators is being provided solely by the referred person or a person acting on their behalf or from independent sources. Note that if any other documentation has been completed separately which the FR believes to have relevance to the trafficking issue, the FR should make sure it is attached as this may assist the CA in reaching a decision.

Children's form

RESTRICTED (when completed)

**NATIONAL REFERRAL MECHANISM FOR CHILD VICTIMS OF TRAFFICKING
REPORT TO COMPETENT AUTHORITY FOR DECISION**

Section A - Personal Details

Last name: .... First name(s): ....

Also known as: ....

D.O.B (if known): ....../......./......... Age (approx. if not known): .... Sex: .... Place of birth: ....

Nationality: .... Language: ....

Any English spoken/interpreter needed:............................ Immigration status: ....

Competent Authority referred to: UK Border Agency / UK Human Trafficking Centre

Home Office ref: .... Work Permit ref: ....

Any other reference numbers including NRUC if the child is a UASC:...

UK Home address: ....

....

....

Section B - Contact details of person making referral

Name: ....

Job title: ....

Organisation and Local Authority area: ....

....

Tel: ....Fax: ....

Mobile: ....

Email: ....

Signature and date: ....

Date encountered (if relevant) or date of first agency contact: ....

Address encountered or place of first contact with your agency (if different from above): ....

....

....

Date of referral: ....

RESTRICTED (when completed)

RESTRICTED (when completed)

Section C – POTENTIAL VICTIMS OF CHILD TRAFFICKING

Child development

Exploitation	Y	S
Claims to have been exploited through sexual exploitation, criminality, labour exploitation, domestic servitude, forced marriage, illegal adoption, drug dealing by another person.		
Physical symptoms of exploitative abuse (sexual, physical etc)		
Underage marriage		
Physical indications of working (overly tired in school, indications of manual labour – condition of hands/skin, backaches etc)		
Sexually transmitted infection or unwanted pregnancy		
Story very similar to those given by others, perhaps hinting they have been coached		
Significantly older boyfriend		
Harbours excessive fears / anxieties (e.g. about an individual, of deportation, disclosing information etc)		
Movement into, within or out of the UK	**Y**	**S**
Withdrawn and refuses to talk / appears afraid to talk to a person in authority		
Significantly older boyfriend		
Other risk factors	**Y**	**S**
Shows signs of physical neglect – basic care, malnourishment, lack of attention to health needs		
Shows signs of emotional neglect		
Socially isolated – lack of positive, meaningful relationships in child's life		
Behavioural – poor concentration or memory, irritable / unsociable / aggressive behaviour in school or placement		
Psychological – indications of trauma or numbing		
Exhibits self assurance, maturity and self confidence not expected in a child of such age		
Evidence of drug, alcohol or substance misuse		
Low self image, low self esteem, self harming behaviour including cutting, overdosing, eating disorder, promiscuity		
Sexually active		
Not registered with or attended a GP practice		
Not enrolled in school		
Has money, expensive clothes, mobile phones or other possessions without plausible explanation		

Parenting capacity

Exploitation	Y	S
Required to earn a minimum amount of money every day		
Involved in criminality highlighting involvement of adults (e.g. recovered from cannabis farm / factory, street crime, petty theft, pick pocketing, begging etc)		
Performs excessive housework chores and rarely leaves the residence		
Reports from reliable sources suggest likelihood of sexual exploitation, including being seen in places known to be used for sexual exploitation		
Unusual hours / regular patterns of child leaving or returning to placement which indicates probable working		
Accompanied by an adult who may not be the legal guardian and insists on remaining with the child at all times		
Limited freedom of movement		
Movement into, within or out of the UK	**Y**	**S**
Gone missing from local authority care		
Unable to confirm name or address of person meeting them on arrival		
Other risk factors	**Y**	**S**
Accompanying adult previously made multiple visa applications for other children / acted as the guarantor for other children's visa applications		
Accompanying adult known to have acted as guarantor on visa applications for other visitors who have not returned to their countries of origin on visa expiry		
History with missing links or unexplained moves		
Pattern of street homelessness		
Unregistered private fostering arrangement		
Cared for by adult/s who are not their parents and quality of relationship is not good		
Placement breakdown		
Persistently missing, staying out overnight or returning late with no plausible explanation		
Truancy / disengagement with education		
Appropriate adult is not an immediate family member (parent / sibling)		
Appropriate adult cannot provide photographic ID for the child		

Family / environment

Exploitation	Y	S
Located / recovered from a place of exploitation (brothel, cannabis farm, involved in criminality etc)		
Deprived of earnings by another person		
Claims to be in debt bondage or 'owes' money to other persons (e.g. for travel costs, before having control over own earnings)		
Receives unexplained / unidentified phone calls whilst in placement / temporary accommodation		
No passport or other means of identity		
Unable or reluctant to give accommodation or other personal details		
False documentation or genuine documentation that has been altered or fraudulently obtained; or the child claims that their details (name, DOB) on the documentation are incorrect		
Movement into, within or out of the UK	**Y**	**S**
Entered country illegally		
Journey or visa arranged by someone other than themselves or their family		
Registered at multiple addresses		
Other risk factors	**Y**	**S**
Possible inappropriate use of the internet and forming online relationships, particularly with adults		
Accounts of social activities with no plausible explanation of the source of necessary funding		
Entering or leaving vehicles driven by unknown adults		
Adults loitering outside the child's usual place of residence		
Leaving home / care setting in clothing unusual for the individual child (inappropriate for age, borrowing clothing from older people etc)		
Works in various locations		
One among a number of unrelated children found at one address		
Having keys to premises other than those known about		
Going missing and being found in areas where they have no known links		

Y= Yes   S= Suspicion

RESTRICTED (when completed)

442

Section G - Evidence to support reasons for referral (2 pages available)

Please use this section to:
1. expand on the circumstances/details of the encounter or contact and
2. provide supporting evidence for the indicators that you have identified in the matrix
3. provide any other relevant information that you consider may be important and wish to include e.g. details of behaviour, abuse and neglect
4. movements into, within or out of the UK, including dates (if known)
5. name of any adults, exploiter or trafficker (if known)
6. and any action you have taken including referral to other agencies e.g. Police, local authorities, Missing persons, NGOs etc
7. provide any method of entry details where the subject is a foreign national,

(if a separate sheet is required, please indicate that section G is continued and provide with referral)

Appendix 3

PROTOCOL TO PREVENT, SUPPRESS AND PUNISH TRAFFICKING IN PERSONS, ESPECIALLY WOMEN AND CHILDREN, SUPPLEMENTING THE UNITED NATIONS CONVENTION AGAINST TRANSNATIONAL ORGANIZED CRIME

PREAMBLE

The States Parties to this Protocol,

Declaring that effective action to prevent and combat trafficking in persons, especially women and children, requires a comprehensive international approach in the countries of origin, transit and destination that includes measures to prevent such trafficking, to punish the traffickers and to protect the victims of such trafficking, including by protecting their internationally recognized human rights,

Taking into account the fact that, despite the existence of a variety of international instruments containing rules and practical measures to combat the exploitation of persons, especially women and children, there is no universal instrument that addresses all aspects of trafficking in persons,

Concerned that, in the absence of such an instrument, persons who are vulnerable to trafficking will not be sufficiently protected,

Recalling General Assembly resolution 53/111 of 9 December 1998, in which the Assembly decided to establish an open-ended intergovernmental ad hoc committee for the purpose of elaborating a comprehensive international convention against transnational organized crime and of discussing the elaboration of, inter alia, an international instrument addressing trafficking in women and children,

Convinced that supplementing the United Nations Convention against Transnational Organized Crime with an international instrument for the prevention, suppression and punishment of trafficking in persons, especially women and children, will be useful in preventing and combating that crime,

HAVE AGREED AS FOLLOWS:

I.

GENERAL PROVISIONS

Article 1 Relation with the United Nations Convention against Transnational Organized Crime

1. This Protocol supplements the United Nations Convention against Transnational Organized Crime. It shall be interpreted together with the Convention.

2. The provisions of the Convention shall apply, mutatis mutandis, to this Protocol unless otherwise provided herein.

3. The offences established in accordance with article 5 of this Protocol shall be regarded as offences established in accordance with the Convention.

Article 2 Statement of purpose

The purposes of this Protocol are:

    (a)   To prevent and combat trafficking in persons, paying particular attention to women and children;

(b) To protect and assist the victims of such trafficking, with full respect for their human rights; and

(c) To promote cooperation among States Parties in order to meet those objectives.

Article 3 Use of terms

For the purposes of this Protocol:

(a) "Trafficking in persons" shall mean the recruitment, transportation, transfer, harbouring or receipt of persons, by means of the threat or use of force or other forms of coercion, of abduction, of fraud, of deception, of the abuse of power or of a position of vulnerability or of the giving or receiving of payments or benefits to achieve the consent of a person having control over another person, for the purpose of exploitation. Exploitation shall include, at a minimum, the exploitation of the prostitution of others or other forms of sexual exploitation, forced labour or services, slavery or practices similar to slavery, servitude or the removal of organs;

(b) The consent of a victim of trafficking in persons to the intended exploitation set forth in subparagraph (a) of this article shall be irrelevant where any of the means set forth in subparagraph (a) have been used;

(c) The recruitment, transportation, transfer, harbouring or receipt of a child for the purpose of exploitation shall be considered "trafficking in persons" even if this does not involve any of the means set forth in subparagraph (a) of this article;

(d) "Child" shall mean any person under eighteen years of age.

Article 4 Scope of application

This Protocol shall apply, except as otherwise stated herein, to the prevention, investigation and prosecution of the offences established in accordance with article 5 of this Protocol, where those offences are transnational in nature and involve an organized criminal group, as well as to the protection of victims of such offences.

Article 5 Criminalization

1. Each State Party shall adopt such legislative and other measures as may be necessary to establish as criminal offences the conduct set forth in article 3 of this Protocol, when committed intentionally.

2. Each State Party shall also adopt such legislative and other measures as may be necessary to establish as criminal offences:

(a) Subject to the basic concepts of its legal system, attempting to commit an offence established in accordance with paragraph 1 of this article;

(b) Participating as an accomplice in an offence established in accordance with paragraph 1 of this article; and

(c) Organizing or directing other persons to commit an offence established in accordance with paragraph 1 of this article.

II.

PROTECTION OF VICTIMS OF TRAFFICKING IN PERSONS

Article 6 Assistance to and protection of victims of trafficking in persons

1. In appropriate cases and to the extent possible under its domestic law, each State Party shall protect the privacy and identity of victims of trafficking in persons, including, inter alia, by making legal proceedings relating to such trafficking confidential.

2.   Each State Party shall ensure that its domestic legal or administrative system contains measures that provide to victims of trafficking in persons, in appropriate cases:

(a)   Information on relevant court and administrative proceedings;

(b)   Assistance to enable their views and concerns to be presented and considered at appropriate stages of criminal proceedings against offenders, in a manner not prejudicial to the rights of the defence.

3.   Each State Party shall consider implementing measures to provide for the physical, psychological and social recovery of victims of trafficking in persons, including, in appropriate cases, in cooperation with non-governmental organizations, other relevant organizations and other elements of civil society, and, in particular, the provision of:

(a)   Appropriate housing;

(b)   Counselling and information, in particular as regards their legal rights, in a language that the victims of trafficking in persons can understand;

(c)   Medical, psychological and material assistance; and

(d)   Employment, educational and training opportunities.

4.   Each State Party shall take into account, in applying the provisions of this article, the age, gender and special needs of victims of trafficking in persons, in particular the special needs of children, including appropriate housing, education and care.

5.   Each State Party shall endeavour to provide for the physical safety of victims of trafficking in persons while they are within its territory.

6.   Each State Party shall ensure that its domestic legal system contains measures that offer victims of trafficking in persons the possibility of obtaining compensation for damage suffered.

Article 7   Status of victims of trafficking in persons in receiving States

1.   In addition to taking measures pursuant to article 6 of this Protocol, each State Party shall consider adopting legislative or other appropriate measures that permit victims of trafficking in persons to remain in its territory, temporarily or permanently, in appropriate cases.

2.   In implementing the provision contained in paragraph 1 of this article, each State Party shall give appropriate consideration to humanitarian and compassionate factors.

Article 8   Repatriation of victims of trafficking in persons

1.   The State Party of which a victim of trafficking in persons is a national or in which the person had the right of permanent residence at the time of entry into the territory of the receiving State Party shall facilitate and accept, with due regard for the safety of that person, the return of that person without undue or unreasonable delay.

2.   When a State Party returns a victim of trafficking in persons to a State Party of which that person is a national or in which he or she had, at the time of entry into the territory of the receiving State Party, the right of permanent residence, such return shall be with due regard for the safety of that person and for the status of any legal proceedings related to the fact that the person is a victim of trafficking and shall preferably be voluntary.

3.   At the request of a receiving State Party, a requested State Party shall, without undue or unreasonable delay, verify whether a person who is a victim of trafficking in persons is its national or had the right of permanent residence in its territory at the time of entry into the territory of the receiving State Party.

4.   In order to facilitate the return of a victim of trafficking in persons who is without proper documentation, the State Party of which that person is a national or in which he or she had the right of permanent residence at the time of entry into the territory of the receiving State Party shall agree to issue, at the request of the

receiving State Party, such travel documents or other authorization as may be necessary to enable the person to travel to and re-enter its territory.

5.   This article shall be without prejudice to any right afforded to victims of trafficking in persons by any domestic law of the receiving State Party.

6.   This article shall be without prejudice to any applicable bilateral or multilateral agreement or arrangement that governs, in whole or in part, the return of victims of trafficking in persons.

III.

PREVENTION, COOPERATION AND OTHER MEASURES

Article 9 *Prevention of trafficking in persons*

1.   States Parties shall establish comprehensive policies, programmes and other measures:

(a)   To prevent and combat trafficking in persons; and

(b)   To protect victims of trafficking in persons, especially women and children, from revictimization.

2.   States Parties shall endeavour to undertake measures such as research, information and mass media campaigns and social and economic initiatives to prevent and combat trafficking in persons.

3.   Policies, programmes and other measures established in accordance with this article shall, as appropriate, include cooperation with non-governmental organizations, other relevant organizations and other elements of civil society.

4.   States Parties shall take or strengthen measures, including through bilateral or multilateral cooperation, to alleviate the factors that make persons, especially women and children, vulnerable to trafficking, such as poverty, underdevelopment and lack of equal opportunity.

5.   States Parties shall adopt or strengthen legislative or other measures, such as educational, social or cultural measures, including through bilateral and multilateral cooperation, to discourage the demand that fosters all forms of exploitation of persons, especially women and children, that leads to trafficking.

Article 10 *Information exchange and training*

1.   Law enforcement, immigration or other relevant authorities of States Parties shall, as appropriate, cooperate with one another by exchanging information, in accordance with their domestic law, to enable them to determine:

(a)   Whether individuals crossing or attempting to cross an international border with travel documents belonging to other persons or without travel documents are perpetrators or victims of trafficking in persons;

(b)   The types of travel document that individuals have used or attempted to use to cross an international border for the purpose of trafficking in persons; and

(c)   The means and methods used by organized criminal groups for the purpose of trafficking in persons, including the recruitment and transportation of victims, routes and links between and among individuals and groups engaged in such trafficking, and possible measures for detecting them.

2.   States Parties shall provide or strengthen training for law enforcement, immigration and other relevant officials in the prevention of trafficking in persons. The training should focus on methods used in preventing such trafficking, prosecuting the traffickers and protecting the rights of the victims, including protecting the victims from the traffickers. The training should also take into account the need to consider human rights and child- and gender-sensitive issues and it should encourage cooperation with non-governmental organizations, other relevant organizations and other elements of civil society.

3.   A State Party that receives information shall comply with any request by the State Party that transmitted the information that places restrictions on its use.

Article 11 Border measures

1.   Without prejudice to international commitments in relation to the free movement of people, States Parties shall strengthen, to the extent possible, such border controls as may be necessary to prevent and detect trafficking in persons.

2.   Each State Party shall adopt legislative or other appropriate measures to prevent, to the extent possible, means of transport operated by commercial carriers from being used in the commission of offences established in accordance with article 5 of this Protocol.

3.   Where appropriate, and without prejudice to applicable international conventions, such measures shall include establishing the obligation of commercial carriers, including any transportation company or the owner or operator of any means of transport, to ascertain that all passengers are in possession of the travel documents required for entry into the receiving State.

4.   Each State Party shall take the necessary measures, in accordance with its domestic law, to provide for sanctions in cases of violation of the obligation set forth in paragraph 3 of this article.

5.   Each State Party shall consider taking measures that permit, in accordance with its domestic law, the denial of entry or revocation of visas of persons implicated in the commission of offences established in accordance with this Protocol.

6.   Without prejudice to article 27 of the Convention, States Parties shall consider strengthening cooperation among border control agencies by, inter alia, establishing and maintaining direct channels of communication.

Article 12 Security and control of documents

Each State Party shall take such measures as may be necessary, within available means:

(a)   To ensure that travel or identity documents issued by it are of such quality that they cannot easily be misused and cannot readily be falsified or unlawfully altered, replicated or issued; and

(b)   To ensure the integrity and security of travel or identity documents issued by or on behalf of the State Party and to prevent their unlawful creation, issuance and use.

Article 13 Legitimacy and validity of documents

At the request of another State Party, a State Party shall, in accordance with its domestic law, verify within a reasonable time the legitimacy and validity of travel or identity documents issued or purported to have been issued in its name and suspected of being used for trafficking in persons.

IV.

FINAL PROVISIONS

Article 14 Saving clause

1.   Nothing in this Protocol shall affect the rights, obligations and responsibilities of States and individuals under international law, including international humanitarian law and international human rights law and, in particular, where applicable, the 1951 Convention and the 1967 Protocol relating to the Status of Refugees and the principle of non-refoulement as contained therein.

2.   The measures set forth in this Protocol shall be interpreted and applied in a way that is not discriminatory to persons on the ground that they are victims of trafficking in persons. The interpretation and application of those measures shall be consistent with internationally recognized principles of non-discrimination.

Article 15 *Settlement of disputes*

1. States Parties shall endeavour to settle disputes concerning the interpretation or application of this Protocol through negotiation.

2. Any dispute between two or more States Parties concerning the interpretation or application of this Protocol that cannot be settled through negotiation within a reasonable time shall, at the request of one of those States Parties, be submitted to arbitration. If, six months after the date of the request for arbitration, those States Parties are unable to agree on the organization of the arbitration, any one of those States Parties may refer the dispute to the International Court of Justice by request in accordance with the Statute of the Court.

3. Each State Party may, at the time of signature, ratification, acceptance or approval of or accession to this Protocol, declare that it does not consider itself bound by paragraph 2 of this article. The other States Parties shall not be bound by paragraph 2 of this article with respect to any State Party that has made such a reservation.

4. Any State Party that has made a reservation in accordance with paragraph 3 of this article may at any time withdraw that reservation by notification to the Secretary-General of the United Nations.

Article 16 *Signature, ratification, acceptance, approval and accession*

1. This Protocol shall be open to all States for signature from 12 to 15 December 2000 in Palermo, Italy, and thereafter at United Nations Headquarters in New York until 12 December 2002.

2. This Protocol shall also be open for signature by regional economic integration organizations provided that at least one member State of such organization has signed this Protocol in accordance with paragraph 1 of this article.

3. This Protocol is subject to ratification, acceptance or approval. Instruments of ratification, acceptance or approval shall be deposited with the Secretary-General of the United Nations. A regional economic integration organization may deposit its instrument of ratification, acceptance or approval if at least one of its member States has done likewise. In that instrument of ratification, acceptance or approval, such organization shall declare the extent of its competence with respect to the matters governed by this Protocol. Such organization shall also inform the depositary of any relevant modification in the extent of its competence.

4. This Protocol is open for accession by any State or any regional economic integration organization of which at least one member State is a Party to this Protocol. Instruments of accession shall be deposited with the Secretary-General of the United Nations. At the time of its accession, a regional economic integration organization shall declare the extent of its competence with respect to matters governed by this Protocol. Such organization shall also inform the depositary of any relevant modification in the extent of its competence.

Article 17 *Entry into force*

1. This Protocol shall enter into force on the ninetieth day after the date of deposit of the fortieth instrument of ratification, acceptance, approval or accession, except that it shall not enter into force before the entry into force of the Convention. For the purpose of this paragraph, any instrument deposited by a regional economic integration organization shall not be counted as additional to those deposited by member States of such organization.

2. For each State or regional economic integration organization ratifying, accepting, approving or acceding to this Protocol after the deposit of the fortieth instrument of such action, this Protocol shall enter into force on the thirtieth day after the date of deposit by such State or organization of the relevant instrument or on the date this Protocol enters into force pursuant to paragraph 1 of this article, whichever is the later.

Article 18 Amendment

1.   After the expiry of five years from the entry into force of this Protocol, a State Party to the Protocol may propose an amendment and file it with the Secretary-General of the United Nations, who shall thereupon communicate the proposed amendment to the States Parties and to the Conference of the Parties to the Convention for the purpose of considering and deciding on the proposal. The States Parties to this Protocol meeting at the Conference of the Parties shall make every effort to achieve consensus on each amendment. If all efforts at consensus have been exhausted and no agreement has been reached, the amendment shall, as a last resort, require for its adoption a two-thirds majority vote of the States Parties to this Protocol present and voting at the meeting of the Conference of the Parties.

2.   Regional economic integration organizations, in matters within their competence, shall exercise their right to vote under this article with a number of votes equal to the number of their member States that are Parties to this Protocol. Such organizations shall not exercise their right to vote if their member States exercise theirs and vice versa.

3.   An amendment adopted in accordance with paragraph 1 of this article is subject to ratification, acceptance or approval by States Parties.

4.   An amendment adopted in accordance with paragraph 1 of this article shall enter into force in respect of a State Party ninety days after the date of the deposit with the Secretary-General of the United Nations of an instrument of ratification, acceptance or approval of such amendment.

5.   When an amendment enters into force, it shall be binding on those States Parties which have expressed their consent to be bound by it. Other States Parties shall still be bound by the provisions of this Protocol and any earlier amendments that they have ratified, accepted or approved.

Article 19 Denunciation

1.   A State Party may denounce this Protocol by written notification to the Secretary-General of the United Nations. Such denunciation shall become effective one year after the date of receipt of the notification by the Secretary-General.

2.   A regional economic integration organization shall cease to be a Party to this Protocol when all of its member States have denounced it.

Article 20 Depositary and languages

1.   The Secretary-General of the United Nations is designated depositary of this Protocol.

2.   The original of this Protocol, of which the Arabic, Chinese, English, French, Russian and Spanish texts are equally authentic, shall be deposited with the Secretary-General of the United Nations.

IN WITNESS WHEREOF, the undersigned plenipotentiaries, being duly authorized thereto by their respective Governments, have signed this Protocol.

Appendix 4

COUNCIL OF EUROPE CONVENTION ON ACTION AGAINST TRAFFICKING IN HUMAN BEINGS

PREAMBLE

The member States of the Council of Europe and the other Signatories hereto,

Considering that the aim of the Council of Europe is to achieve a greater unity between its members;

Considering that trafficking in human beings constitutes a violation of human rights and an offence to the dignity and the integrity of the human being;

Considering that trafficking in human beings may result in slavery for victims;

Considering that respect for victims' rights, protection of victims and action to combat trafficking in human beings must be the paramount objectives;

Considering that all actions or initiatives against trafficking in human beings must be non-discriminatory, take gender equality into account as well as a child-rights approach;

Recalling the declarations by the Ministers for Foreign Affairs of the Member States at the 112th (14-15 May 2003) and the 114th (12-13 May 2004) Sessions of the Committee of Ministers calling for reinforced action by the Council of Europe on trafficking in human beings;

Bearing in mind the Convention for the Protection of Human Rights and Fundamental Freedoms (1950) and its protocols;

Bearing in mind the following recommendations of the Committee of Ministers to member states of the Council of Europe: Recommendation No. R (91) 11 on sexual exploitation, pornography and prostitution of, and trafficking in, children and young adults; Recommendation No. R (97) 13 concerning intimidation of witnesses and the rights of the defence; Recommendation No. R (2000) 11 on action against trafficking in human beings for the purpose of sexual exploitation and Recommendation Rec (2001) 16 on the protection of children against sexual exploitation; Recommendation Rec (2002) 5 on the protection of women against violence;

Bearing in mind the following recommendations of the Parliamentary Assembly of the Council of Europe: Recommendation 1325 (1997) on traffic in women and forced prostitution in Council of Europe member states; Recommendation 1450 (2000) on violence against women in Europe; Recommendation 1545 (2002) on a campaign against trafficking in women; Recommendation 1610 (2003) on migration connected with trafficking in women and prostitution; Recommendation 1611 (2003) on trafficking in organs in Europe; Recommendation 1663 (2004) Domestic slavery: servitude, au pairs and mail-order brides;

Bearing in mind the European Union Council Framework Decision of 19 July 2002 on combating trafficking in human beings, the European Union Council Framework Decision of 15 March 2001 on the standing of victims in criminal proceedings and the European Union Council Directive of 29 April 2004 on the residence permit issued to third-country nationals who are victims of trafficking in human beings or who have been the subject of an action to facilitate illegal immigration, who cooperate with the competent authorities;

Taking due account of the United Nations Convention against Transnational Organized Crime and the Protocol thereto to Prevent, Suppress and Punish Trafficking in Persons, Especially Women and Children with a view to improving the protection which they afford and developing the standards established by them;

Taking due account of the other international legal instruments relevant in the field of action against trafficking in human beings;

Taking into account the need to prepare a comprehensive international legal instrument focusing on the human rights of victims of trafficking and setting up a specific monitoring mechanism,

HAVE AGREED AS FOLLOWS:

CHAPTER I

PURPOSES, SCOPE, NON-DISCRIMINATION PRINCIPLE AND DEFINITIONS

Article 1 Purposes of the Convention

1 The purposes of this Convention are:

    a   to prevent and combat trafficking in human beings, while guaranteeing gender equality;

    b   to protect the human rights of the victims of trafficking, design a comprehensive framework for the protection and assistance of victims and witnesses, while guaranteeing gender equality, as well as to ensure effective investigation and prosecution;

    c   to promote international cooperation on action against trafficking in human beings.

2 In order to ensure effective implementation of its provisions by the Parties, this Convention sets up a specific monitoring mechanism.

Article 2 Scope

This Convention shall apply to all forms of trafficking in human beings, whether national or transnational, whether or not connected with organised crime.

Article 3 Non-discrimination principle

The implementation of the provisions of this Convention by Parties, in particular the enjoyment of measures to protect and promote the rights of victims, shall be secured without discrimination on any ground such as sex, race, colour, language, religion, political or other opinion, national or social origin, association with a national minority, property, birth or other status.

Article 4 Definitions

For the purposes of this Convention:

    a   "Trafficking in human beings" shall mean the recruitment, transportation, transfer, harbouring or receipt of persons, by means of the threat or use of force or other forms of coercion, of abduction, of fraud, of deception, of the abuse of power or of a position of vulnerability or of the giving or receiving of payments or benefits to achieve the consent of a person having control over another person, for the purpose of exploitation. Exploitation shall include, at a minimum, the exploitation of the prostitution of others or other forms of sexual exploitation, forced labour or services, slavery or practices similar to slavery, servitude or the removal of organs;

    b   The consent of a victim of "trafficking in human beings" to the intended exploitation set forth in subparagraph (a) of this article shall be irrelevant where any of the means set forth in subparagraph (a) have been used;

    c   The recruitment, transportation, transfer, harbouring or receipt of a child for the purpose of exploitation shall be considered "trafficking in human beings" even if this does not involve any of the means set forth in subparagraph (a) of this article;

d   "Child" shall mean any person under eighteen years of age;

e   "Victim" shall mean any natural person who is subject to trafficking in human beings as defined in this article.

CHAPTER II

PREVENTION, CO-OPERATION AND OTHER MEASURES

Article 5 Prevention of trafficking in human beings

1   Each Party shall take measures to establish or strengthen national co-ordination between the various bodies responsible for preventing and combating trafficking in human beings.

2   Each Party shall establish and/or strengthen effective policies and programmes to prevent trafficking in human beings, by such means as: research, information, awareness raising and education campaigns, social and economic initiatives and training programmes, in particular for persons vulnerable to trafficking and for professionals concerned with trafficking in human beings.

3   Each Party shall promote a Human Rights-based approach and shall use gender mainstreaming and a child-sensitive approach in the development, implementation and assessment of all the policies and programmes referred to in paragraph 2.

4   Each Party shall take appropriate measures, as may be necessary, to enable migration to take place legally, in particular through dissemination of accurate information by relevant offices, on the conditions enabling the legal entry in and stay on its territory.

5   Each Party shall take specific measures to reduce children's vulnerability to trafficking, notably by creating a protective environment for them.

6   Measures established in accordance with this article shall involve, where appropriate, non-governmental organisations, other relevant organisations and other elements of civil society committed to the prevention of trafficking in human beings and victim protection or assistance.

Article 6 Measures to discourage the demand

To discourage the demand that fosters all forms of exploitation of persons, especially women and children, that leads to trafficking, each Party shall adopt or strengthen legislative, administrative, educational, social, cultural or other measures including:

a   research on best practices, methods and strategies;

b   raising awareness of the responsibility and important role of media and civil society in identifying the demand as one of the root causes of trafficking in human beings;

c   target information campaigns involving, as appropriate, inter alia, public authorities and policy makers;

d   preventive measures, including educational programmes for boys and girls during their schooling, which stress the unacceptable nature of discrimination based on sex, and its disastrous consequences, the importance of gender equality and the dignity and integrity of every human being.

Article 7 Border measures

1   Without prejudice to international commitments in relation to the free movement of persons, Parties shall strengthen, to the extent possible, such border controls as may be necessary to prevent and detect trafficking in human beings.

2   Each Party shall adopt legislative or other appropriate measures to prevent, to the extent possible, means of transport operated by commercial carriers from being used in the commission of offences established in accordance with this Convention.

3   Where appropriate, and without prejudice to applicable international conventions, such measures shall include establishing the obligation of commercial

carriers, including any transportation company or the owner or operator of any means of transport, to ascertain that all passengers are in possession of the travel documents required for entry into the receiving State.

4   Each Party shall take the necessary measures, in accordance with its internal law, to provide for sanctions in cases of violation of the obligation set forth in paragraph 3 of this article.

5   Each Party shall adopt such legislative or other measures as may be necessary to permit, in accordance with its internal law, the denial of entry or revocation of visas of persons implicated in the commission of offences established in accordance with this Convention.

6   Parties shall strengthen co-operation among border control agencies by, *inter alia*, establishing and maintaining direct channels of communication.

Article 8 Security and control of documents
Each Party shall adopt such measures as may be necessary:

a   To ensure that travel or identity documents issued by it are of such quality that they cannot easily be misused and cannot readily be falsified or unlawfully altered, replicated or issued; and

b   To ensure the integrity and security of travel or identity documents issued by or on behalf of the Party and to prevent their unlawful creation and issuance.

Article 9 Legitimacy and validity of documents
At the request of another Party, a Party shall, in accordance with its internal law, verify within a reasonable time the legitimacy and validity of travel or identity documents issued or purported to have been issued in its name and suspected of being used for trafficking in human beings.

CHAPTER III

MEASURES TO PROTECT AND PROMOTE THE RIGHTS OF VICTIMS, GUARANTEEING GENDER EQUALITY

Article 10 Identification of the victims
1   Each Party shall provide its competent authorities with persons who are trained and qualified in preventing and combating trafficking in human beings, in identifying and helping victims, including children, and shall ensure that the different authorities collaborate with each other as well as with relevant support organisations, so that victims can be identified in a procedure duly taking into account the special situation of women and child victims and, in appropriate cases, issued with residence permits under the conditions provided for in Article 14 of the present Convention.

2   Each Party shall adopt such legislative or other measures as may be necessary to identify victims as appropriate in collaboration with other Parties and relevant support organisations. Each Party shall ensure that, if the competent authorities have reasonable grounds to believe that a person has been victim of trafficking in human beings, that person shall not be removed from its territory until the identification process as victim of an offence provided for in Article 18 of this Convention has been completed by the competent authorities and shall likewise ensure that that person receives the assistance provided for in Article 12, paragraphs 1 and 2.

3.   When the age of the victim is uncertain and there are reasons to believe that the victim is a child, he or she shall be presumed to be a child and shall be accorded special protection measures pending verification of his/her age.

4.   As soon as an unaccompanied child is identified as a victim, each Party shall:

a   provide for representation of the child by a legal guardian, organisation or authority which shall act in the best interests of that child;

b   take the necessary steps to establish his/her identity and nationality;

c   make every effort to locate his/her family when this is in the best interests of the child.

Article 11 Protection of private life

1   Each Party shall protect the private life and identity of victims. Personal data regarding them shall be stored and used in conformity with the conditions provided for by the Convention for the Protection of Individuals with regard to Automatic Processing of Personal Data (ETS No. 108).

2   Each Party shall adopt measures to ensure, in particular, that the identity, or details allowing the identification, of a child victim of trafficking are not made publicly known, through the media or by any other means, except, in exceptional circumstances, in order to facilitate the tracing of family members or otherwise secure the well-being and protection of the child.

3   Each Party shall consider adopting, in accordance with Article 10 of the Convention for the Protection of Human Rights and Fundamental Freedoms as interpreted by the European Court of Human Rights, measures aimed at encouraging the media to protect the private life and identity of victims through self-regulation or through regulatory or co-regulatory measures.

Article 12 Assistance to victims

1.   Each Party shall adopt such legislative or other measures as may be necessary to assist victims in their physical, psychological and social recovery. Such assistance shall include at least:

a   standards of living capable of ensuring their subsistence, through such measures as: appropriate and secure accommodation, psychological and material assistance;

b   access to emergency medical treatment;

c   translation and interpretation services, when appropriate;

d   counselling and information, in particular as regards their legal rights and the services available to them, in a language that they can understand;

e   assistance to enable their rights and interests to be presented and considered at appropriate stages of criminal proceedings against offenders;

f   access to education for children.

2   Each Party shall take due account of the victim's safety and protection needs.

3   In addition, each Party shall provide necessary medical or other assistance to victims lawfully resident within its territory who do not have adequate resources and need such help.

4   Each Party shall adopt the rules under which victims lawfully resident within its territory shall be authorised to have access to the labour market, to vocational training and education.

5   Each Party shall take measures, where appropriate and under the conditions provided for by its internal law, to co-operate with non-governmental organisations, other relevant organisations or other elements of civil society engaged in assistance to victims.

6   Each Party shall adopt such legislative or other measures as may be necessary to ensure that assistance to a victim is not made conditional on his or her willingness to act as a witness.

7   For the implementation of the provisions set out in this article, each Party shall ensure that services are provided on a consensual and informed basis, taking due account of the special needs of persons in a vulnerable position and the rights of children in terms of accommodation, education and appropriate health care.

Article 13 Recovery and reflection period

1   Each Party shall provide in its internal law a recovery and reflection period of at least 30 days, when there are reasonable grounds to believe that the person concerned is a victim. Such a period shall be sufficient for the person concerned to recover and escape the influence of traffickers and/or to take an informed decision on cooperating with the competent authorities. During this period it shall not be possible to enforce any expulsion order against him or her. This provision is without prejudice to the activities carried out by the competent authorities in all phases of the relevant national proceedings, and in particular when investigating and prosecuting the offences concerned. During this period, the Parties shall authorise the persons concerned to stay in their territory.

2   During this period, the persons referred to in paragraph 1 of this Article shall be entitled to the measures contained in Article 12, paragraphs 1 and 2.

3   The Parties are not bound to observe this period if grounds of public order prevent it or if it is found that victim status is being claimed improperly.

Article 14 Residence permit

1   Each Party shall issue a renewable residence permit to victims, in one or other of the two following situations or in both:

    a   the competent authority considers that their stay is necessary owing to their personal situation;

    b   the competent authority considers that their stay is necessary for the purpose of their co-operation with the competent authorities in investigation or criminal proceedings.

2   The residence permit for child victims, when legally necessary, shall be issued in accordance with the best interests of the child and, where appropriate, renewed under the same conditions.

3   The non-renewal or withdrawal of a residence permit is subject to the conditions provided for by the internal law of the Party.

4   If a victim submits an application for another kind of residence permit, the Party concerned shall take into account that he or she holds, or has held, a residence permit in conformity with paragraph 1.

5   Having regard to the obligations of Parties to which Article 40 of this Convention refers, each Party shall ensure that granting of a permit according to this provision shall be without prejudice to the right to seek and enjoy asylum.

Article 15 Compensation and legal redress

1   Each Party shall ensure that victims have access, as from their first contact with the competent authorities, to information on relevant judicial and administrative proceedings in a language which they can understand.

2   Each Party shall provide, in its internal law, for the right to legal assistance and to free legal aid for victims under the conditions provided by its internal law.

3   Each Party shall provide, in its internal law, for the right of victims to compensation from the perpetrators.

4   Each Party shall adopt such legislative or other measures as may be necessary to guarantee compensation for victims in accordance with the conditions under its internal law, for instance through the establishment of a fund for victim compensation or measures or programmes aimed at social assistance and social integration of victims, which could be funded by the assets resulting from the application of measures provided in Article 23.

Article 16 Repatriation and return of victims

1   The Party of which a victim is a national or in which that person had the right of permanent residence at the time of entry into the territory of the receiving Party

shall, with due regard for his or her rights, safety and dignity, facilitate and accept, his or her return without undue or unreasonable delay.

2   When a Party returns a victim to another State, such return shall be with due regard for the rights, safety and dignity of that person and for the status of any legal proceedings related to the fact that the person is a victim, and shall preferably be voluntary.

3   At the request of a receiving Party, a requested Party shall verify whether a person is its national or had the right of permanent residence in its territory at the time of entry into the territory of the receiving Party.

4   In order to facilitate the return of a victim who is without proper documentation, the Party of which that person is a national or in which he or she had the right of permanent residence at the time of entry into the territory of the receiving Party shall agree to issue, at the request of the receiving Party, such travel documents or other authorisation as may be necessary to enable the person to travel to and re-enter its territory.

5   Each Party shall adopt such legislative or other measures as may be necessary to establish repatriation programmes, involving relevant national or international institutions and non governmental organisations. These programmes aim at avoiding re-victimisation. Each Party should make its best effort to favour the reintegration of victims into the society of the State of return, including reintegration into the education system and the labour market, in particular through the acquisition and improvement of their professional skills. With regard to children, these programmes should include enjoyment of the right to education and measures to secure adequate care or receipt by the family or appropriate care structures.

6   Each Party shall adopt such legislative or other measures as may be necessary to make available to victims, where appropriate in co-operation with any other Party concerned, contact information of structures that can assist them in the country where they are returned or repatriated, such as law enforcement offices, non-governmental organisations, legal professions able to provide counselling and social welfare agencies.

7   Child victims shall not be returned to a State, if there is indication, following a risk and security assessment, that such return would not be in the best interests of the child.

Article 17 Gender equality
Each Party shall, in applying measures referred to in this chapter, aim to promote gender equality and use gender mainstreaming in the development, implementation and assessment of the measures.

CHAPTER IV

SUBSTANTIVE CRIMINAL LAW

Article 18 Criminalisation of trafficking in human beings
Each Party shall adopt such legislative and other measures as may be necessary to establish as criminal offences the conduct contained in article 4 of this Convention, when committed intentionally.

Article 19 Criminalisation of the use of services of a victim
Each Party shall consider adopting such legislative and other measures as may be necessary to establish as criminal offences under its internal law, the use of services which are the object of exploitation as referred to in Article 4 paragraph a of this Convention, with the knowledge that the person is a victim of trafficking in human beings.

Article 20 Criminalisation of acts relating to travel or identity documents

Each Party shall adopt such legislative and other measures as may be necessary to establish as criminal offences the following conducts, when committed intentionally and for the purpose of enabling the trafficking in human beings:

a   forging a travel or identity document;

b   procuring or providing such a document;

c   retaining, removing, concealing, damaging or destroying a travel or identity document of another person.

Article 21 Attempt and aiding or abetting

1   Each Party shall adopt such legislative and other measures as may be necessary to establish as criminal offences when committed intentionally, aiding or abetting the commission of any of the offences established in accordance with Articles 18 and 20 of the present Convention.

2   Each Party shall adopt such legislative and other measures as may be necessary to establish as criminal offences when committed intentionally, an attempt to commit the offences established in accordance with Articles 18 and 20, paragraph a, of this Convention.

Article 22 Corporate liability

1   Each Party shall adopt such legislative and other measures as may be necessary to ensure that a legal person can be held liable for a criminal offence established in accordance with this Convention, committed for its benefit by any natural person, acting either individually or as part of an organ of the legal person, who has a leading position within the legal person, based on:

a   a power of representation of the legal person;

b   an authority to take decisions on behalf of the legal person;

c   an authority to exercise control within the legal person.

2   Apart from the cases already provided for in paragraph 1, each Party shall take the measures necessary to ensure that a legal person can be held liable where the lack of supervision or control by a natural person referred to in paragraph 1 has made possible the commission of a criminal offence established in accordance with this Convention for the benefit of that legal person by a natural person acting under its authority.

3   Subject to the legal principles of the Party, the liability of a legal person may be criminal, civil or administrative.

4   Such liability shall be without prejudice to the criminal liability of the natural persons who have committed the offence.

Article 23 Sanctions and measures

1   Each Party shall adopt such legislative and other measures as may be necessary to ensure that the criminal offences established in accordance with Articles 18 to 21 are punishable by effective, proportionate and dissuasive sanctions. These sanctions shall include, for criminal offences established in accordance with Article 18 when committed by natural persons, penalties involving deprivation of liberty which can give rise to extradition.

2   Each Party shall ensure that legal persons held liable in accordance with Article 22 shall be subject to effective, proportionate and dissuasive criminal or non-criminal sanctions or measures, including monetary sanctions.

3   Each Party shall adopt such legislative and other measures as may be necessary to enable it to confiscate or otherwise deprive the instrumentalities and proceeds of criminal offences established in accordance with Articles 18 and 20, paragraph a, of this Convention, or property the value of which corresponds to such proceeds.

4   Each Party shall adopt such legislative or other measures as may be necessary to enable the temporary or permanent closure of any establishment which was used to

carry out trafficking in human beings, without prejudice to the rights of *bona fide* third parties or to deny the perpetrator, temporary or permanently, the exercise of the activity in the course of which this offence was committed.

Article 24 Aggravating circumstances

Each Party shall ensure that the following circumstances are regarded as aggravating circumstances in the determination of the penalty for offences established in accordance with Article 18 of this Convention:

 a the offence deliberately or by gross negligence endangered the life of the victim;

 b the offence was committed against a child;

 c the offence was committed by a public official in the performance of her/his duties;

 d the offence was committed within the framework of a criminal organisation.

Article 25 Previous convictions

Each Party shall adopt such legislative and other measures providing for the possibility to take into account final sentences passed by another Party in relation to offences established in accordance with this Convention when determining the penalty.

Article 26 Non-punishment provision

Each Party shall, in accordance with the basic principles of its legal system, provide for the possibility of not imposing penalties on victims for their involvement in unlawful activities, to the extent that they have been compelled to do so.

CHAPTER V

INVESTIGATION, PROSECUTION AND PROCEDURAL LAW

Article 27 *Ex parte* and *ex officio* applications

1 Each Party shall ensure that investigations into or prosecution of offences established in accordance with this Convention shall not be dependent upon the report or accusation made by a victim, at least when the offence was committed in whole or in part on its territory.

2 Each Party shall ensure that victims of an offence in the territory of a Party other than the one where they reside may make a complaint before the competent authorities of their State of residence. The competent authority to which the complaint is made, insofar as it does not itself have competence in this respect, shall transmit it without delay to the competent authority of the Party in the territory in which the offence was committed. The complaint shall be dealt with in accordance with the internal law of the Party in which the offence was committed.

3 Each Party shall ensure, by means of legislative or other measures, in accordance with the conditions provided for by its internal law, to any group, foundation, association or non-governmental organisations which aims at fighting trafficking in human beings or protection of human rights, the possibility to assist and/or support the victim with his or her consent during criminal proceedings concerning the offence established in accordance with Article 18 of this Convention.

Article 28 Protection of victims, witnesses and collaborators with the judicial authorities

1 Each Party shall adopt such legislative or other measures as may be necessary to provide effective and appropriate protection from potential retaliation or intimidation in particular during and after investigation and prosecution of perpetrators, for:

 a Victims;

> b   As appropriate, those who report the criminal offences established in accordance with Article 18 of this Convention or otherwise co-operate with the investigating or prosecuting authorities;
>
> c   witnesses who give testimony concerning criminal offences established in accordance with Article 18 of this Convention;
>
> d   when necessary, members of the family of persons referred to in subparagraphs a and c.

2   Each Party shall adopt such legislative or other measures as may be necessary to ensure and to offer various kinds of protection. This may include physical protection, relocation, identity change and assistance in obtaining jobs.

3   A child victim shall be afforded special protection measures taking into account the best interests of the child.

4   Each Party shall adopt such legislative or other measures as may be necessary to provide, when necessary, appropriate protection from potential retaliation or intimidation in particular during and after investigation and prosecution of perpetrators, for members of groups, foundations, associations or non-governmental organisations which carry out the activities set out in Article 27, paragraph 3.

5   Each Party shall consider entering into agreements or arrangements with other States for the implementation of this article.

Article 29 Specialised authorities and co-ordinating bodies

1   Each Party shall adopt such measures as may be necessary to ensure that persons or entities are specialised in the fight against trafficking and the protection of victims. Such persons or entities shall have the necessary independence in accordance with the fundamental principles of the legal system of the Party, in order for them to be able to carry out their functions effectively and free from any undue pressure. Such persons or the staffs of such entities shall have adequate training and financial resources for their tasks.

2   Each Party shall adopt such measures as may be necessary to ensure co-ordination of the policies and actions of their governments' departments and other public agencies against trafficking in human beings, where appropriate, through setting up co-ordinating bodies.

3   Each Party shall provide or strengthen training for relevant officials in the prevention of and fight against trafficking in human beings, including Human Rights training. The training may be agency-specific and shall, as appropriate, focus on: methods used in preventing such trafficking, prosecuting the traffickers and protecting the rights of the victims, including protecting the victims from the traffickers.

4   Each Party shall consider appointing National Rapporteurs or other mechanisms for monitoring the anti-trafficking activities of State institutions and the implementation of national legislation requirements.

Article 30 Court proceedings

In accordance with the Convention for the Protection of Human Rights and Fundamental Freedoms, in particular Article 6, each Party shall adopt such legislative or other measures as may be necessary to ensure in the course of judicial proceedings:

> a   the protection of victims' private life and, where appropriate, identity;
>
> b   victims' safety and protection from intimidation,

in accordance with the conditions under its internal law and, in the case of child victims, by taking special care of children's needs and ensuring their right to special protection measures.

Article 31 Jurisdiction

1   Each Party shall adopt such legislative and other measures as may be necessary to establish jurisdiction over any offence established in accordance with this Convention, when the offence is committed:

a   in its territory; or

b   on board a ship flying the flag of that Party; or

c   on board an aircraft registered under the laws of that Party; or

d   by one of its nationals or by a stateless person who has his or her habitual residence in its territory, if the offence is punishable under criminal law where it was committed or if the offence is committed outside the territorial jurisdiction of any State;

e   against one of its nationals.

2   Each Party may, at the time of signature or when depositing its instrument of ratification, acceptance, approval or accession, by a declaration addressed to the Secretary General of the Council of Europe, declare that it reserves the right not to apply or to apply only in specific cases or conditions the jurisdiction rules laid down in paragraphs 1 (d) and (e) of this article or any part thereof.

3   Each Party shall adopt such measures as may be necessary to establish jurisdiction over the offences referred to in this Convention, in cases where an alleged offender is present in its territory and it does not extradite him/her to another Party, solely on the basis of his/her nationality, after a request for extradition.

4   When more than one Party claims jurisdiction over an alleged offence established in accordance with this Convention, the Parties involved shall, where appropriate, consult with a view to determining the most appropriate jurisdiction for prosecution.

5   Without prejudice to the general norms of international law, this Convention does not exclude any criminal jurisdiction exercised by a Party in accordance with internal law.

CHAPTER VI

INTERNATIONAL   CO-OPERATION   AND   CO-OPERATION   WITH CIVIL SOCIETY

Article 32 General principles and measures for international co-operation

The Parties shall co-operate with each other, in accordance with the provisions of this Convention, and through application of relevant applicable international and regional instruments, arrangements agreed on the basis of uniform or reciprocal legislation and internal laws, to the widest extent possible, for the purpose of:

- preventing and combating trafficking in human beings;
- protecting and providing assistance to victims;
- investigations or proceedings concerning criminal offences established in accordance with this Convention.

Article 33 Measures relating to endangered or missing persons

1   When a Party, on the basis of the information at its disposal has reasonable grounds to believe that the life, the freedom or the physical integrity of a person referred to in Article 28, paragraph 1, is in immediate danger on the territory of another Party, the Party that has the information shall, in such a case of emergency, transmit it without delay to the latter so as to take the appropriate protection measures.

2   The Parties to this Convention may consider reinforcing their co-operation in the search for missing people, in particular for missing children, if the information available leads them to believe that she/he is a victim of trafficking in human beings. To this end, the Parties may conclude bilateral or multilateral treaties with each other.

Article 34 Information

1   The requested Party shall promptly inform the requesting Party of the final result of the action taken under this chapter. The requested Party shall also promptly inform

the requesting Party of any circumstances which render impossible the carrying out of the action sought or are likely to delay it significantly.

2   A Party may, within the limits of its internal law, without prior request, forward to another Party information obtained within the framework of its own investigations when it considers that the disclosure of such information might assist the receiving Party in initiating or carrying out investigations or proceedings concerning criminal offences established in accordance with this Convention or might lead to a request for co-operation by that Party under this chapter.

3   Prior to providing such information, the providing Party may request that it be kept confidential or used subject to conditions. If the receiving Party cannot comply with such request, it shall notify the providing Party, which shall then determine whether the information should nevertheless be provided. If the receiving Party accepts the information subject to the conditions, it shall be bound by them.

4   All information requested concerning Articles 13, 14 and 16, necessary to provide the rights conferred by these Articles, shall be transmitted at the request of the Party concerned without delay with due respect to Article 11 of the present Convention.

Article 35 Co-operation with civil society

Each Party shall encourage state authorities and public officials, to co-operate with non-governmental organisations, other relevant organisations and members of civil society, in establishing strategic partnerships with the aim of achieving the purpose of this Convention.

CHAPTER VII

MONITORING MECHANISM

Article 36 Group of experts on action against trafficking in human beings

1   The Group of experts on action against trafficking in human beings (hereinafter referred to as "GRETA"), shall monitor the implementation of this Convention by the Parties.

2   GRETA shall be composed of a minimum of 10 members and a maximum of 15 members, taking into account a gender and geographical balance, as well as a multidisciplinary expertise. They shall be elected by the Committee of the Parties for a term of office of 4 years, renewable once, chosen from amongst nationals of the States Parties to this Convention.

3   The election of the members of GRETA shall be based on the following principles:

a   they shall be chosen from among persons of high moral character, known for their recognised competence in the fields of Human Rights, assistance and protection of victims and of action against trafficking in human beings or having professional experience in the areas covered by this Convention;

b   they shall sit in their individual capacity and shall be independent and impartial in the exercise of their functions and shall be available to carry out their duties in an effective manner;

c   no two members of GRETA may be nationals of the same State;

d   they should represent the main legal systems.

4   The election procedure of the members of GRETA shall be determined by the Committee of Ministers, after consulting with and obtaining the unanimous consent of the Parties to the Convention, within a period of one year following the entry into force of this Convention. GRETA shall adopt its own rules of procedure.

Article 37 Committee of the Parties

1 The Committee of the Parties shall be composed of the representatives on the Committee of Ministers of the Council of Europe of the member States Parties to the Convention and representatives of the Parties to the Convention, which are not members of the Council of Europe.

2 The Committee of the Parties shall be convened by the Secretary General of the Council of Europe. Its first meeting shall be held within a period of one year following the entry into force of this Convention in order to elect the members of GRETA. It shall subsequently meet whenever one-third of the Parties, the President of GRETA or the Secretary General so requests.

3 The Committee of the Parties shall adopt its own rules of procedure.

Article 38 Procedure

1 The evaluation procedure shall concern the Parties to the Convention and be divided in rounds, the length of which is determined by GRETA. At the beginning of each round GRETA shall select the specific provisions on which the evaluation procedure shall be based.

2 GRETA shall define the most appropriate means to carry out this evaluation. GRETA may in particular adopt a questionnaire for each evaluation round, which may serve as a basis for the evaluation of the implementation by the Parties of the present Convention. Such a questionnaire shall be addressed to all Parties. Parties shall respond to this questionnaire, as well as to any other request of information from GRETA.

3 GRETA may request information from civil society.

4 GRETA may subsidiarily organise, in co-operation with the national authorities and the "contact person" appointed by the latter, and, if necessary, with the assistance of independent national experts, country visits. During these visits, GRETA may be assisted by specialists in specific fields.

5 GRETA shall prepare a draft report containing its analysis concerning the implementation of the provisions on which the evaluation is based, as well as its suggestions and proposals concerning the way in which the Party concerned may deal with the problems which have been identified. The draft report shall be transmitted for comments to the Party which undergoes the evaluation. Its comments are taken into account by GRETA when establishing its report.

6 On this basis, GRETA shall adopt its report and conclusions concerning the measures taken by the Party concerned to implement the provisions of the present Convention. This report and conclusions shall be sent to the Party concerned and to the Committee of the Parties. The report and conclusions of GRETA shall be made public as from their adoption, together with eventual comments by the Party concerned.

7 Without prejudice to the procedure of paragraphs 1 to 6 of this article, the Committee of the Parties may adopt, on the basis of the report and conclusions of GRETA, recommendations addressed to this Party (a) concerning the measures to be taken to implement the conclusions of GRETA, if necessary setting a date for submitting information on their implementation, and (b) aiming at promoting co-operation with that Party for the proper implementation of the present Convention.

CHAPTER VIII

RELATIONSHIP WITH OTHER INTERNATIONAL INSTRUMENTS

Article 39 Relationship with the Protocol to prevent, suppress and punish trafficking in persons, especially women and children, supplementing the United Nations Convention against transnational organised crime

This Convention shall not affect the rights and obligations derived from the provisions of the Protocol to prevent, suppress and punish trafficking in persons, especially women and children, supplementing the United Nations Convention against transnational organised crime, and is intended to enhance the protection afforded by it and develop the standards contained therein.

Article 40 Relationship with other international instruments

1 This Convention shall not affect the rights and obligations derived from other international instruments to which Parties to the present Convention are Parties or shall become Parties and which contain provisions on matters governed by this Convention and which ensure greater protection and assistance for victims of trafficking.

2 The Parties to the Convention may conclude bilateral or multilateral agreements with one another on the matters dealt with in this Convention, for purposes of supplementing or strengthening its provisions or facilitating the application of the principles embodied in it.

3 Parties which are members of the European Union shall, in their mutual relations, apply Community and European Union rules in so far as there are Community or European Union rules governing the particular subject concerned and applicable to the specific case, without prejudice to the object and purpose of the present Convention and without prejudice to its full application with other Parties.

4 Nothing in this Convention shall affect the rights, obligations and responsibilities of States and individuals under international law, including international humanitarian law and international human rights law and, in particular, where applicable, the 1951 Convention and the 1967 Protocol relating to the Status of Refugees and the principle of *non-refoulement* as contained therein.

CHAPTER IX

AMENDMENTS TO THE CONVENTION

Article 41 Amendments

1 Any proposal for an amendment to this Convention presented by a Party shall be communicated to the Secretary General of the Council of Europe and forwarded by him or her to the member States of the Council of Europe, any signatory, any State Party, the European Community, to any State invited to sign this Convention in accordance with the provisions of Article 42 and to any State invited to accede to this Convention in accordance with the provisions of Article 43.

2 Any amendment proposed by a Party shall be communicated to GRETA, which shall submit to the Committee of Ministers its opinion on that proposed amendment.

3 The Committee of Ministers shall consider the proposed amendment and the opinion submitted by GRETA and, following consultation of the Parties to this Convention and after obtaining their unanimous consent, may adopt the amendment.

4 The text of any amendment adopted by the Committee of Ministers in accordance with paragraph 3 of this article shall be forwarded to the Parties for acceptance.

5 Any amendment adopted in accordance with paragraph 3 of this article shall enter into force on the first day of the month following the expiration of a period of one month after the date on which all Parties have informed the Secretary General that they have accepted it.

CHAPTER X

FINAL CLAUSES

Article 42 Signature and entry into force

1   This Convention shall be open for signature by the member States of the Council of Europe, the non member States which have participated in its elaboration and the European Community.

2   This Convention is subject to ratification, acceptance or approval. Instruments of ratification, acceptance or approval shall be deposited with the Secretary General of the Council of Europe.

3   This Convention shall enter into force on the first day of the month following the expiration of a period of three months after the date on which 10 Signatories, including at least 8 member States of the Council of Europe, have expressed their consent to be bound by the Convention in accordance with the provisions of the preceding paragraph.

4   In respect of any State mentioned in paragraph 1 or the European Community, which subsequently expresses its consent to be bound by it, the Convention shall enter into force on the first day of the month following the expiration of a period of three months after the date of the deposit of its instrument of ratification, acceptance or approval.

Article 43 Accession to the Convention

1   After the entry into force of this Convention, the Committee of Ministers of the Council of Europe may, after consultation of the Parties to this Convention and obtaining their unanimous consent, invite any non-member State of the Council of Europe, which has not participated in the elaboration of the Convention, to accede to this Convention by a decision taken by the majority provided for in Article 20 *d.* of the Statute of the Council of Europe, and by unanimous vote of the representatives of the Contracting States entitled to sit on the Committee of Ministers.

2   In respect of any acceding State, the Convention shall enter into force on the first day of the month following the expiration of a period of three months after the date of deposit of the instrument of accession with the Secretary General of the Council of Europe.

Article 44 Territorial application

1   Any State or the European Community may, at the time of signature or when depositing its instrument of ratification, acceptance, approval or accession, specify the territory or territories to which this Convention shall apply.

2   Any Party may, at any later date, by a declaration addressed to the Secretary General of the Council of Europe, extend the application of this Convention to any other territory specified in the declaration and for whose international relations it is responsible or on whose behalf it is authorised to give undertakings. In respect of such territory, the Convention shall enter into force on the first day of the month following the expiration of a period of three months after the date of receipt of such declaration by the Secretary General.

3   Any declaration made under the two preceding paragraphs may, in respect of any territory specified in such declaration, be withdrawn by a notification addressed to the Secretary General of the Council of Europe. The withdrawal shall become effective on the first day of the month following the expiration of a period of three months after the date of receipt of such notification by the Secretary General.

Article 45 Reservations

No reservation may be made in respect of any provision of this Convention, with the exception of the reservation of Article 31, paragraph 2.

Article 46 Denunciation

1 Any Party may, at any time, denounce this Convention by means of a notification addressed to the Secretary General of the Council of Europe.

2 Such denunciation shall become effective on the first day of the month following the expiration of a period of three months after the date of receipt of the notification by the Secretary General.

Article 47 Notification

The Secretary General of the Council of Europe shall notify the member States of the Council of Europe, any State signatory, any State Party, the European Community, to any State invited to sign this Convention in accordance with the provisions of Article 42 and to any State invited to accede to this Convention in accordance with the provisions of Article 43 of:

- a any signature;
- b the deposit of any instrument of ratification, acceptance, approval or accession;
- c any date of entry into force of this Convention in accordance with Articles 42 and 43;
- d any amendment adopted in accordance with Article 41 and the date on which such an amendment enters into force;
- e any denunciation made in pursuance of the provisions of Article 46;
- f any other act, notification or communication relating to this Convention
- g any reservation made under Article 45.

In witness whereof the undersigned, being duly authorised thereto, have signed this Convention.

Done at Warsaw, this 16th day of May 2005, in English and in French, both texts being equally authentic, in a single copy which shall be deposited in the archives of the Council of Europe. The Secretary General of the Council of Europe shall transmit certified copies to each member State of the Council of Europe, to the non-member States which have participated in the elaboration of this Convention, to the European Community and to any State invited to accede to this Convention.

Appendix 5

COUNCIL OF EUROPE CONVENTION ON ACTION AGAINST TRAFFICKING IN HUMAN BEINGS
Explanatory Report

The Treaty of Lisbon amending the Treaty on European Union and the Treaty establishing the European Community entered into force on 1 December 2009. As a consequence, as from that date, any reference to the European Community shall be read as the European Union.

I. INTRODUCTION

a. Trafficking in human beings: the phenomenon and its context

1. Trafficking in human beings is a major problem in Europe today. Annually, thousands of people, largely women and children, fall victim to trafficking for sexual exploitation or other purposes, whether in their own countries or abroad. All indicators point to an increase in victim numbers. Action to combat trafficking in human beings is receiving world-wide attention because the trafficking threatens the human rights and the fundamental values of democratic societies.

2. Action to combat this persistent assault on humanity is one of a number of fronts on which the Council of Europe is battling on behalf of human rights and human dignity.

3. Trafficking in human beings, with the entrapment of its victims, is the modern form of the old worldwide slave trade. It treats human beings as a commodity to be bought and sold, and to be put to forced labour, usually in the sex industry but also, for example, in the agricultural sector, declared or undeclared sweatshops, for a pittance or nothing at all. Most identified victims of trafficking are women but men also are sometimes victims of trafficking in human beings. Furthermore, many of the victims are young, sometimes children. All are desperate to make a meagre living, only to have their lives ruined by exploitation and rapacity.

4. To be effective, a strategy for combating trafficking in human beings must adopt a multi-disciplinary approach incorporating prevention, protection of human rights of victims and prosecution of traffickers, while at the same time seeking to harmonise relevant national laws and ensure that these laws are applied uniformly and effectively.

5. A worldwide phenomenon, trafficking in human beings can be national or transnational. Often linked to organised crime, for which it now represents one of the most lucrative activities, trafficking has to be fought in Europe just as vigorously as drug and money laundering. Indeed, according to certain estimations, trafficking in human beings is the third largest illicit money making venture in the world after trafficking of weapons and drugs.

6. In this context the *Protocol to Prevent, Suppress and Punish Trafficking in Persons, Especially Women and Children, supplementing the United Nations Convention against Transnational Organized Crime* (hereafter "the Palermo Protocol") laid the foundations for international action on trafficking. The Council of Europe Convention, while taking the Palermo Protocol as a starting point and taking into account other international legal instruments, whether universal or regional, relevant to combating trafficking in human beings, seeks to strengthen the protection afforded by those instruments and to raise the standards which they lay down.

7. The Palermo Protocol contains the first agreed, internationally binding definition

(taken over into the Council of Europe convention) of the term "Trafficking in persons" (see, below, the comments on Article 4 of the Convention). It is important to stress at this point that trafficking in human beings is to be distinguished from smuggling of migrants. The latter is the subject of a separate protocol to the *United Nations Convention against Transnational Organized Crime* (>*Protocol Against the Smuggling of Migrants by Land, Sea and Air, Supplementing the United Nations Convention Against Transnational Crime*). While the aim of smuggling of migrants is the unlawful cross-border transport in order to obtain, directly or indirectly, a financial or other material benefit, the purpose of trafficking in human beings is exploitation. Furthermore, trafficking in human beings does not necessarily involve a transnational element; it can exist at national level.

8.   There are other international instruments that have a contribution to make in combating trafficking in human beings and protecting its victims. Among United Nations instruments the following can be mentioned:

- the Forced Labour Convention (No. 29) of 28 June 1930;
- the Convention for the Suppression of the Traffic in Persons and of the Exploitation of the Prostitution of Others of 2 December 1949;
- the Convention relating to the Status of Refugees of 28 July 1951 and its Protocol relating to the Status of Refugees;
- the Convention on the Elimination of All Forms of Discrimination against Women of 18 December 1979;
- the Convention on the Rights of the Child of 20 November 1989;
- the International Labour Organisation Convention concerning the Prohibition and Immediate Action for the Elimination of the Worst Forms of Child Labour of 17 June 1999;
- the Optional Protocol to the Convention on the Rights of the Child on the sale of children, child prostitution and child pornography of 25 May 2000.

9.   Experience has shown that putting legal instruments in place at regional level valuably reinforces action at world level. In the European context, the *Council Framework Decision of 19 July 2002 on combating trafficking in human beings* and the *Council Directive 2004/81/EC of 29 April 2004 on the residence permit issued to third-country nationals who are victims of trafficking in human beings or who have been the subject of an action to facilitate illegal immigration, who cooperate with the competent authorities* regulate some of the questions concerning trafficking in human beings. The *Council Framework Decision of 15 March 2001 on the standing of victims in criminal proceedings* would also be relevant in the field of trafficking in human beings.

b. Action of the Council of Europe

10.   Given that one of the primary concerns of the Council of Europe is the safeguarding and protection of human rights and human dignity, and that trafficking in human beings directly undermines the values on which the Council of Europe is based, it is logical that finding solutions to this problem is a top priority for the Organisation. It is all the more relevant as the Council of Europe has, among its 46 member States, countries of origin, transit and destination of trafficking victims.

11.   Since the late 1980s the Council of Europe has therefore been a natural focus for work on combating trafficking in human beings[1]. Trafficking impinges on a number of questions with which the Council of Europe is concerned, such as sexual exploitation of women and children, protection of women against violence, organised crime and migration. The Council of Europe has taken various initiatives in this field and in related fields: among other things it has produced legal instruments, devised strategies, conducted research, engaged in legal and technical cooperation and carried out monitoring.

The Committee of Ministers of the Council of Europe

12.   In 1991 the Council of Europe Committee of Ministers adopted Recommendation No. R(91)11 on sexual exploitation, pornography and prostitution of, and

trafficking in, children and young adults, which was the first international instrument dealing comprehensively with these matters. In 1999 a committee of experts on protecting children against sexual exploitation was set up, in particular to revise Recommendation No. R(91)11.

13. Through the Group of Experts on traffic in women (1992–93), which reported to the Steering Committee for Equality between Women and Men (CDEG), the Council identified the most urgent areas for action from which a consultant drew up a general action plan on trafficking in women[2]. The plan suggested areas for reflection and investigation in order to draw up recommendations to the member States on legislative, judicial and punishment aspects of trafficking, on aiding, supporting and rehabilitating its victims and on programmes of prevention and training.

14. Trafficking aroused the collective concern of Council of Europe Heads of State and Government at the October 1997 Strasbourg Summit: the final declaration explicitly treats all forms of exploitation of women as a threat to citizens' security and democracy in Europe.

15. There have been various activities since the Summit. The first type of activity was concerned both with raising awareness and action. Seminars to heighten the awareness of governments and civil society to this new form of slavery[3] were organised in order to alert the different players (police, judges, social workers, embassy staff, teachers etc) to their role vis-à-vis trafficking victims and the dangers facing certain individuals.

16. In addition, member States were encouraged to draw up national action plans against trafficking. To that end, the Council prepared the above mentioned model action plan against trafficking in women in 1996 and since then has encouraged the preparation of both national and regional action plans, in particular in South-East Europe[4] and the South Caucasus[5].

17. Studies and research have also been carried out to apprehend the problem of trafficking from its many different angles. In particular the Steering Committee for equality between women and men (CDEG) prepared a study on the impact of the use of new information technologies on trafficking in human beings for the purpose of sexual exploitation.[6]

18. Furthermore, targeted seminars and meetings of experts have taken place in several member States, both providing them with the necessary technical assistance for drawing up or revising legislation in this area and helping them to take other requisite measures for combating this scourge.

19. One more recent initiative was the LARA Project supporting the reform of criminal legislation in South-East Europe as a means of preventing and combating trafficking in human beings, launched in July 2002 and completed in November 2003. This Council of Europe Project, implemented within the framework of the Stability Pact Task Force on Trafficking in Human Beings, enabled the countries concerned to adapt and review their domestic legislation in this field. As a result of this Project, nearly all those countries adopted national global action plans against trafficking in human beings, covering prevention, prosecution of traffickers and protection of the victims.

20. The awareness-raising activities led to setting up a legal framework for combating the trafficking in human beings. Two Council of Europe legal instruments were produced which specifically dealt with trafficking in human beings for sexual exploitation, most of whose victims are women and children:

– *Recommendation No. R(2000)11 of the Committee of Ministers to member States on action against trafficking in human beings for the purpose of sexual exploitation;*
– *Recommendation No. R(2001)16 of the Committee of Ministers to member States on the protection of children against sexual exploitation.*

21. These put forward a pan-European strategy taking in definitions, general measures, a methodological and action framework, prevention, victim assistance and protection, criminal measures, judicial cooperation and arrangements for international co-operation and co-ordination.

22. Finally it should be underlined that during the 5th European Ministerial Conference on Equality between Women and Men (Skopje, 22-23 January 2003) devoted to the theme: "Democratisation, conflict prevention and peace building: the perspectives and the roles of women", the European Equality Ministers agreed that the activities undertaken by the Council of Europe to protect and promote the human rights of women should be focused, among other things, on the objective to prevent and combat violence against women and trafficking in human beings

23. Trafficking in human beings may be engaged in by organised criminal groups – which frequently use corruption to circumvent the law, and money laundering to conceal their profits – but it can occur in other contexts. Consequently other Council of Europe legal instruments are also relevant to trafficking, in particular those concerned with protecting human rights, children's rights, social rights, victims' rights and personal data, those designed to combat corruption, money laundering and cybercrime, and the treaties on international cooperation in criminal matters. Thus, the following Council of Europe conventions could play a part in combating trafficking in human beings and protecting the victims of it:

- the Convention for the Protection of Human Rights and Fundamental Freedoms of 4 November 1950 (ETS No 5);
- the European Convention on Extradition of 13 December 1957 (ETS No 24) and the Protocols to it;
- the European Convention on Mutual Assistance in Criminal Matters of 20 April 1959 (ETS No 30) and the Protocols to it;
- the European Social Charter of 18 October 1961 (ETS No 35) and the Revised European Social Charter of 3 May 1996 (ETS No 163);
- the European Convention on the Compensation of Victims of Violent Crimes of 24 November 1983 (ETS No 116);
- the Convention on Laundering, Search, Seizure and Confiscation of the Proceeds from Crime of 8 November 1990 (ETS No 141);
- the European Convention on the Exercise of Children's Rights of 25 January 1996 (ETS No 160);
- the Criminal Law Convention on Corruption of 27 January 1999 (ETS No 173) and the Civil Law Convention on Corruption of 4 November 1999 (ETS No 174);
- the Convention on Cybercrime of 23 November 2001 (ETS No 185).

The Parliamentary Assembly of the Council of Europe

24. In *Recommendation 1545 (2002) on a campaign against trafficking in women* the Council of Europe Parliamentary Assembly recommended that the Committee of Ministers, among other things, draw up a European convention on trafficking in women that would be open to non-member States and based on the definition of trafficking in Committee of Ministers *Recommendation No. R(2000)11 on action against trafficking in human beings for the purpose of sexual exploitation.*

25. The Assembly returned to the question in 2003, with *Recommendation 1610 (2003) on migration connected with trafficking in women and prostitution.* This recommended that the Committee of Ministers:

"i.   begin as soon as possible the drafting of the Council of Europe convention on trafficking in human beings, which will bring added value to other international instruments with its clear human rights and victim protection focus and the inclusion of a gender perspective;

ii.   ensure that the Council of Europe convention on trafficking in human beings includes provisions aiming at:
    a.   introducing the offence of trafficking in the criminal law of Council of Europe member States;
    b.   harmonising the penalties applicable to trafficking;
    c.   ensuring the effective establishment of jurisdiction over traffickers or alleged traffickers, particularly by facilitating extradition and the

application of the principle *aut dedere aut judicare* in all cases concerning trafficking."

26. In *Recommendation 1611 (2003) on trafficking in organs in Europe*, the Parliamentary Assembly suggested developing, in cooperation with relevant organisations, a European strategy for combating organ trafficking and also suggested that drafting the future Council of Europe Convention on action against trafficking in human beings include a protocol to it on trafficking in organs and tissues of human origin.

27. Parliamentary Assembly Recommendation 1663 (2004) on domestic slavery: servitude, au pairs and mail-order brides recommended adopting the necessary measures to combat domestic slavery in all its forms. Furthermore, the Parliamentary Assembly considered that the Council of Europe must have zero tolerance for slavery, and that the Council of Europe as an international organisation defending human rights must fight against all forms of slavery and trafficking in human beings. The Assembly underlined that the Council of Europe and its member States must promote and protect the human rights of the victim and ensure that the perpetrators of such crimes are brought to justice so that slavery can finally be eliminated from Europe. Finally the Parliamentary Assembly expressed its support to the drafting of the *Council of Europe Convention on action against trafficking in human beings*.

c. The Council of Europe Convention on action against trafficking in human beings

28. At the same time as these different activities, and to follow up Committee of Ministers Recommendation No. R(2000)11, the Steering Committee for Equality between Women and Men (CDEG) took the initiative to give new impetus to the Council of Europe's work in this area and prepared a study on the feasibility of drawing up a Convention on action against trafficking in human beings.

29. The Council of Europe considered that it was necessary to draft a legally binding instrument which goes beyond recommendations or specific actions. The European public perception of the phenomenon of trafficking and the measures which need to be adopted to combat it efficiently have evolved, thus rendering necessary the elaboration of a legally binding instrument, geared towards the protection of victim's rights and the respect of human rights, and aiming at a proper balance between matters concerning human rights and prosecution.

30. Even though there are already other international instruments in this field, the Convention benefits from the more limited and uniform context of the Council of Europe, contains more precise provisions and may go beyond minimum standards agreed upon in other international instruments. The evolution of international law proves that regional instruments are very often necessary to complement global efforts. European instruments in the field of the protection of children's rights[7], money laundering or trafficking in drugs[8] have proved to have a very positive impact on the implementation of global initiatives. The drafting of a Council of Europe Convention does not aim at competing with other instruments adopted at a global or regional level but at improving the protection afforded by them and developing the standards contained therein, in particular in relation to the protection of the human rights of the victims of trafficking.

31. At a tripartite meeting in Geneva, on 14 February 2003, high-level representatives of the Council of Europe, the Organisation for Security and Cooperation in Europe (OSCE) and the United Nations stated their support for a Council of Europe convention on trafficking in human beings to improve the protection of victims and to develop pan-European action on what was an extremely serious form of criminal activity, they also backed the idea of promoting national legislation to combat trafficking.

32. The need for the Council of Europe to reinforce its action was underlined by the Foreign Affairs Ministers at the 12th (4-5 May 2003), 113th (5-6 November 2003) and 114th (12-13 May 2004) Sessions of the Committee of Ministers. Therefore, the Council of Europe launched the drafting of a Convention on action against trafficking in human beings. The convention will be geared towards the protection of victims' rights and the respect for human rights, and aim at a proper balance between matters concerning human rights and prosecution.

33. The proposal to prepare a Council of Europe Convention on action against trafficking in human beings was approved by the Committee of Ministers, at the 838th meeting of the Ministers' Deputies on 30 April 2003, when adopting the specific terms of reference setting up the Ad Hoc Committee on Action against Trafficking in Human Beings (CAHTEH). This multidisciplinary committee had the task of preparing a convention focusing on the protection of the human rights of the victims of trafficking and, balanced with this concern, the prosecution of traffickers.

34. In September 2003, the Council of Europe started negotiations on the Convention on action against trafficking in human beings. The CAHTEH held eight meetings, in September and December 2003; February, May, June/July, September/October and December 2004 and February 2005 to finalise the text.

35. The text of the draft Convention was approved by the CAHTEH during its meeting in December 2004 and transmitted to the Committee of Ministers for submission to the Parliamentary Assembly for opinion. In January 2005 the Parliamentary Assembly gave its opinion on the draft convention (Opinion n° 253 (2005), 26 January 2005) and the CAHTEH considered that opinion at its 8th and final meeting in February 2005.

36. The added value provided by the Council of Europe Convention lies firstly in the affirmation that trafficking in human beings is a violation of human rights and violates human dignity and integrity, and that greater protection is therefore needed for all of its victims. Secondly, the Convention's scope takes in all forms of trafficking (national, transnational, linked or not to organised crime, and for purposes of exploitation) in particular with a view to victim protection measures and international cooperation. Thirdly the Convention sets up monitoring machinery to ensure that Parties implement its provisions effectively. Lastly, the Convention mainstreams gender equality in its provisions.

37. The Convention contains a Preamble and ten chapters. Chapter I deals with its purposes and scope, the principle of non-discrimination and definitions; Chapter II deals with prevention, cooperation and other measures; Chapter III deals with measures to protect and promote the rights of victims, guaranteeing gender equality; Chapter IV deals with substantive criminal law; Chapter V deals with investigation, prosecution and procedural law; Chapter VI deals with international cooperation and cooperation with the civil society; Chapter VII sets out the monitoring mechanism; lastly Chapters VIII, IX and X deal with the relationship between the Convention and other international instruments, amendments to the Convention and final clauses.

II. COMMENTARY ON THE PROVISIONS OF THE CONVENTION

Title

38. The title contains the new official name of all new Council of Europe treaties. Following a decision by the Secretary General, the official name of any new treaty would be "Council of Europe Convention [or agreement] on . . . ". Therefore, this new title is adopted for the Convention.

39. Furthermore, the Convention includes in its title the term "action" in order to underline that the Convention provides not only legislative measures but also other initiatives to be taken to combat trafficking in human beings. Action against trafficking in human beings should be understood to include prevention and assistance to victims as well as criminal law measures designed to combat trafficking.

Preamble

40. The Preamble reaffirms the commitment of the signatories to human rights and fundamental freedoms. Furthermore, it underlines that the accession to the Convention is opened to other signatories other than the member States of the Council of Europe.

41. The Convention is based on recognition, already stated in the Preamble at paragraph 5 of *Recommendation N° R(2000)11 of the Committee of Ministers to member States on action against trafficking in human beings for the purpose of sexual exploitation*, that trafficking in human beings constitutes a violation of human rights and an offence to the dignity and integrity of the human being. The recognition of trafficking as a violation of human rights would have consequences for some legal systems which had introduced special protection measures in cases of infringement of fundamental rights.

42.   The recognition of trafficking in human beings as a violation of human rights appears directly or indirectly in an important number of international legal instruments and international declarations. *Recommendation Rec(2002)5 of the Committee of Ministers to member States on the protection of women against violence*, which defines violence against women as including trafficking and states that violence against women both violates and impairs or nullifies the enjoyment of their human rights and fundamental freedoms. The *Inter-American Convention on the Prevention, Punishment and Eradication of Violence against Women* affirms, in the Preamble, that violence against women constitutes a violation of their human rights and fundamental freedoms. The definition of violence against women in Article 2 of this Convention includes trafficking as a form of violence against women. The European Union, in its *Council Framework Decision on Combating Trafficking in Human Beings* of 19 July 2002 states that "trafficking in human beings comprises serious violations of fundamental human rights and human dignity . . . "(at para 3). Treaty monitoring bodies of the United Nations, including the Human Rights Committee and the Committee on the Elimination of Discrimination against Women, have also identified trafficking in human beings as a violation of human rights.[9]

43.   Furthermore, the Rome Statute of the International Criminal Court in its Article 7 states that: "For the purpose of this Statute, "crime against humanity" means any of the following acts when committed as part of a widespread or systematic attack directed against any civilian population, with knowledge of the attack: [. . .] (c) Enslavement; [. . .] which "means the exercise of any or all of the powers attaching to the right of ownership over a person and includes the exercise of such power in the course of trafficking in persons, in particular women and children".

44.   The horizontal application of the Convention for the Protection of Human Rights and Fundamental Freedoms (hereinafter ECHR) has been the subject of debate over many years. However, the case law of the European Court of Human Rights contains clear indications in favour of the applicability of the ECHR to relations between private individuals in the sense that the Court has recognised the liability of contracting States for acts committed by individuals or group of individuals when these States failed to take appropriate measures of protection. The first judgment in this sense was case X and Y v. The Netherlands[10], where the Court held that there was an obligation on the State to adopt criminal-law provisions to secure the effective protection of individuals. Culpable State failure to act on this could therefore give rise to violation of the ECHR. In the case *Young, James and Webster v. The United Kingdom*[11], the Court stated that "Under Article 1 (art. 1) of the Convention, each Contracting State " shall secure to everyone within [its] jurisdiction the rights and freedoms defined in . . . [the] Convention"; hence, if a violation of one of those rights and freedoms is the result of non-observance of that obligation in the enactment of domestic legislation, the responsibility of the State for that violation is engaged. Although the proximate cause of the events giving rise to this case was the 1975 agreement between British Rail and the railway unions, it was the domestic law in force at the relevant time that made lawful the treatment of which the applicants complained. The responsibility of the respondent State for any resultant breach of the Convention is thus engaged on this basis [. . .]" Since then[12] the liability of Contracting States for acts committed by individuals or group of individuals in violation of the ECHR has been recognised.

45.   Trafficking in human beings has become one of the Europe's major scourges. This phenomenon affecting men, women and children has reached such an unprecedented level that we can refer to it as a new form of slavery. The ECHR prohibits slavery and forced labour in its Article 4: "1. No one shall be held in slavery or servitude; 2. No one shall be required to perform forced or compulsory labour [. . .]". The definition of "trafficking in human beings" contained in Article 4 of the present Convention refers specifically to "slavery" (see comments on Article 4 below).

46.   The main added value of the present Convention in relation to other international

instruments is its Human Rights perspective and its focus on victim protection. Therefore, paragraph 5 of the Preamble states that the respect for the rights and protection of victims and the fight against trafficking in human beings must be the paramount objectives.

47. In relation to the non-discrimination principle, it should be recalled that Recommendation 1545 (2002) of the Parliamentary Assembly of the Council of Europe on a *campaign against trafficking in women*, which calls for the inclusion of a non-discrimination clause in the future Convention based on the one contained in Parliamentary Assembly Opinion 216 (2000) on Protocol No. 12 to the ECHR. (See comments on Article 3 below).

48. The Preamble of the Convention also refers to the declarations of the Foreign Affairs Ministers of the member States of the Council of Europe at the 112th, 113th and 114th Sessions of the Committee of Ministers as mentioned above.

49. The Preamble contains an enumeration of the most important international legal instruments which directly deal with trafficking in human beings in the framework of the Council of Europe, the European Union and United Nations. In particular it should be underlined that, as mentioned above, the Council of Europe through its Committee of Ministers and its Parliamentary Assembly prepared an important number of instruments to examine and combat trafficking in human beings from different perspectives. The important place that this Convention attributes to the *Protocol to prevent, suppress and punish trafficking in persons, especially women and children, supplementing the United Nations Convention against transnational organized crime* is reflected in the adoption of the definition on « trafficking in human beings » agreed upon in this Protocol. As a complement to and development of this United Nations Protocol, which emphasises the crime prevention aspect of trafficking, the Council of Europe Convention clearly defines trafficking as being first and foremost an issue of violation of human rights and emphasises the victims' protection aspect of trafficking. The aim is to improve the protection afforded by it and to develop the standards contained therein.

50. During the negotiation process of this Convention other international legal instruments relevant in this field have also been taken into account as mentioned above.

51. In conclusion it could be said that the added value of this new Council of Europe instrument in relation to the other existing international legal instruments is:

– recognition of trafficking in human beings as a violation of human rights;
– a special focus on assistance to victims and on protection of their human rights;
– comprehensive scope of application:
  – all forms of trafficking: national/transnational linked/non-linked with organised crime;
  – all trafficked persons: the Convention applies to all persons who are victims of trafficking whether they are women, children or men;
– setting up a comprehensive legal framework for the protection of victims and witnesses with specific and binding measures to be adopted;
– setting up an efficient and independent monitoring mechanism: Experience has proved that, in areas where such independent monitoring systems exist (e.g. torture and minorities), they have high credibility with the States Parties, and the cooperative nature of such mechanisms is fully understood and recognised;
– a Council of Europe Convention benefits from the more limited and uniform context of the Council of Europe, contains more precise provisions and go beyond the minimum standards agreed upon in other international instruments.

Chapter I – Purposes, scope, non-discrimination principle and definitions

Article 1 – Purposes of the Convention

52. Article 1 deals with the purposes of the Convention. Paragraph 1 states these to be:

(a) to prevent and combat trafficking in human beings, guaranteeing gender equality;

(b)   to protect the human rights of the victims of trafficking, design a comprehensive framework for the protection and assistance of victims and witnesses, guaranteeing gender equality, and ensure effective investigation and prosecution;

(c)   to promote international cooperation on action against trafficking in human beings.

53.   Paragraph 1(a) states the need for measures both to prevent and combat trafficking in human beings. At the same time it is important to bear in mind the specific needs of the victims, whether women, children or men. While applying to women, children and men, the Convention recognises that specific measures to prevent and combat trafficking in human beings also require guaranteeing gender equality and a child-rights approach to children.

54.   Gender equality means an equal visibility, empowerment and participation of both sexes in all spheres of public and private life. Gender equality is the opposite of gender inequality, not of gender difference. It means accepting and valuing equally the complementarity of women and men and the diverse roles they play in society. Equality between women and men means not only non-discrimination on grounds of gender but also positive measures to achieve equality between women and men. Equality must be promoted by supporting specific policies for women, who are more likely to be exposed to practices which qualify as torture or inhuman or degrading treatment (physical violence, rape, genital and sexual mutilation, trafficking for the purpose of sexual exploitation). These violations of women's human rights are still common and have dramatically increased in some areas of Europe. It should be noted that *Recommendation Rec(2002)5 of the Committee of Ministers to member States on the protection of women against violence* considers trafficking in human beings as a form of violence against women. The Declaration of the Committee of Ministers on Equality of Women and Men (16 November 1988) was a landmark. It affirms that the principle of equality of the sexes is an integral part of human rights, and that sex-related discrimination is an impediment to the exercise of fundamental freedoms.

55.   Here it should be noted that gender equality is not reducible to the non-discrimination principle (as laid down in Article 3) and that the CAHTEH's terms of reference asked it to take gender equality into account. A further point is that gender equality is integral to human rights and that discrimination on sex grounds is an interference with exercise of fundamental freedoms.

56.   Paragraph 1(b) reflects the multidisciplinarity necessary to combat trafficking in human beings effectively. Not only is multidisciplinarity basic to the Convention, it must also be basic to any national action on trafficking in human beings.

57.   Two of the main aims of this Convention, as set out in Article 1, are the protection of the rights of trafficked persons and the prosecution of those responsible for trafficking. The drafters recognised that the two are related to each other.

58.   Paragraph 1(c) deals with international cooperation: only by joining forces will countries overcome trafficking; on their own, they stand very little chance of success. International cooperation as referred to by the Convention is not confined to criminal matters (a field in which the Council of Europe has already adopted a number of authoritative documents – see the comments on Chapter VI) but also takes in preventing trafficking and assisting and protecting victims, and is intended to make these things central concerns of the countries which victims are trafficked from, through and into.

59.   Article 1(2) states that, in order to ensure effective implementation of its provisions by the Parties, the Convention sets up a special monitoring mechanism, the "Group of Experts on Action against Trafficking in Human Beings" (GRETA). This is a crucial element of the Convention's added value: the GRETA is a means of ensuring Parties' compliance with the Convention and is a guarantee of the Convention's long-term effectiveness (see comments on Chapter VII).

Article 2 – Scope

60.   This sets the Convention's scope. Firstly it lays down that the Convention applies to all forms of trafficking in human beings. The Convention thus applies whoever the

victim of the trafficking, man, woman or child.

61. Secondly the drafters wanted the Convention to make clear that it applied to both national and transnational trafficking, whether or not related to organised crime. That is, the Convention is wider in scope than the Palermo Protocol and, as stated in Article 39, is intended to enhance the protection which the Palermo Protocol affords. Article 1(2) of the Palermo Protocol states that the provisions of the *United Nations Convention against Transnational Organized Crime* apply *mutatis mutandis* to the protocol unless the protocol otherwise provides, and Article 3(1) of the United Nations convention states that it applies to certain offences of a transnational nature[13] and involves an organised criminal group[14]. Under Article 2 of the Convention, therefore, Chapters II to VI apply even if trafficking is at the purely national level and does not involve any organised criminal group.

62. Lastly, in the case of transnational trafficking, the Convention applies both to victims who legally entered or are legally present in the territory of the receiving Party and those who entered or are present illegally. In some cases trafficking victims are taken illegally into the country, but in other cases they enter a country legally as tourists, future spouses, artists, domestic staff, au pair girls or asylum seekers, depending on the law of the particular country. The Convention applies to both types of situations. Nevertheless, certain specific provisions (Articles 13 and 14) apply only to victims illegally present.

Article 3 – Non-discrimination principle

63. This prohibits discrimination in Parties' implementation of the Convention and in particular in enjoyment of measures to protect and promote victims' rights, which are set out in Chapter III. The meaning of discrimination in Article 3 is identical to that given to it under Article 14 of the *Convention for the Protection of Human Rights and Fundamental Freedoms* (hereafter the ECHR).

64. The concept of discrimination has been interpreted consistently by the European Court of Human Rights in its case-law concerning Article 14 ECHR. In particular this case-law has made clear that not every distinction or difference of treatment amounts to discrimination. As the Court has stated, for example in the *Abdulaziz, Cabales and Balkandali v. the United Kingdom* judgment, "a difference of treatment is discriminatory if it 'has no objective and reasonable justification', that is, if it does not pursue a 'legitimate aim' or if there is not a 'reasonable relationship of proportionality between the means employed and the aim sought to be realised'" (judgment of 28 May 1985, Series A, No.94, paragraph 72).

65. Since not every distinction or difference of treatment amounts to discrimination and because of the general character of the non-discrimination principle, it was not considered necessary or appropriate to include a restriction clause in the present convention. For example, the law of most if not all Council of Europe member States provides for certain distinctions based on nationality concerning certain rights or entitlements to benefits. The situations where such distinctions are perfectly acceptable are sufficiently safeguarded by the very meaning of the term "discrimination" as described in the above paragraph, since distinctions for which an objective and reasonable justification exists do not constitute discrimination. In addition, under the case-law of the European Court of Human Rights national authorities are allowed some discretion in assessing whether and to what extent differences in otherwise similar situations justify different treatment in law. The scope of the discretion will vary according to the circumstances, the subject-matter and its background (see, for example, the judgment of 28 November 1984 in *Rasmussen v. Denmark*, Series A, No. 87, paragraph 40).

66. The list of non-discrimination grounds in Article 3 is identical to that in Article 14 ECHR and the list contained in Protocol No.12 to the ECHR. This solution was considered preferable to others, such as expressly including certain additional non-discrimination grounds (e.g. state of health, physical or mental disability, sexual orientation and age). The reason for this was not unawareness that such grounds may be of particular importance in trafficking victims' predicament, but that such an inclusion is legally unnecessary because the list of non-discrimination grounds is not exhaustive and inclusion of any specific additional ground might give rise to unwarranted *a contrario* interpretations as regards discrimination based on grounds not so included. It is worth pointing out that the European Court of Human Rights has applied Article 14 to discrimination grounds not explicitly mentioned in that provision (see, for example, as concerns the ground of sexual orientation, the judgment of 21 December 1999 in *Salgueiro da Silva Mouta v. Portugal.*

67. Article 3 refers to "implementation of the provision of this Convention by Parties". These words seek to specify the extent of the prohibition on discrimination. In particular, Article 3 prohibits a victim's being discriminated against in the enjoyment of measures – as provided for in Chapter III of the Convention – to protect and promote their rights.

68. It should be noted that the Convention mainly places positive obligations on Parties. For example, Article 12 requires Parties to provide certain assistance to victims of trafficking, such as standards of living capable of ensuring their subsistence, through such measures as appropriate and secure housing, psychological and material assistance and access to emergency medical treatment. Similarly Article 14 provides the issuing of a renewable residence permit to victims. Under Article 3 such measures must be applied without discrimination – that is without any making of unjustified distinctions.

69. Thus Article 3 of the Convention might be contravened, even if there were no contravention of other provisions of the Convention, if the measures provided for in those articles were implemented differently in respect of particular categories of person (for example, depending on sex, age or nationality) and the difference in treatment could not be reasonably justified.

Article 4 – Definitions

Introduction concerning the Article 4 definitions

70. It was understood by the drafters that, under the Convention, Parties would not be obliged to copy *verbatim* into their domestic law the concepts in Article 4, provided that domestic law covered the concepts in a manner consistent with the principles of the Convention and offered an equivalent framework for implementing it.

Definition of trafficking in human beings

71. The Article 4 definition of trafficking in human beings is not the first international legal definition of the phenomenon. For instance, *Recommendation No. R(2000)11 of the Committee of Ministers to member States on action against trafficking in human beings for the purpose of sexual exploitation* gives a definition of trafficking, but one whose scope, unlike the definition in the present Convention, is restricted to trafficking in human beings for the purpose of sexual exploitation.

72. To combat trafficking more effectively and help its victims, it is of fundamental importance to use a definition of trafficking in human beings on which there is international consensus. The definition of trafficking in human beings in Article 4(a) of the Convention is identical to the one in Article 3(a) of the Palermo Protocol. Article 4(b) to (d) of the Convention is identical to Article 3(b) to (d) of the Palermo Protocol. Article 3 of that protocol forms a whole which needed to be incorporated as it stood into the present convention.

73. The definition of trafficking in human beings is essential in that it crucially affects implementation of the provisions in Chapters II to VI.

74. In the definition, trafficking in human beings consists in a combination of three basic components, each to be found in a list given in the definition:

–   the action of: "recruitment, transportation, transfer, harbouring or receipt of persons";
–   by means of: "the threat or use of force or other forms of coercion, of abduction, of fraud, of deception, of the abuse of power or of a position of vulnerability or

of the giving or receiving of payments or benefits to achieve the consent of a person having control over another person";
–	for the purpose of exploitation, which includes "at a minimum, the exploitation of the prostitution of others or other forms of sexual exploitation, forced labour or services, slavery or practices similar to slavery, servitude or the removal or organs".

75.	Trafficking in human beings is a combination of these constituents and not the constituents taken in isolation. For instance, "harbouring" of persons (action) involving the "threat or use of force" (means) for "forced labour" (purpose) is conduct that is to be treated as trafficking in human beings. Similarly recruitment of persons (action) by deceit (means) for exploitation of prostitution (purpose).

76.	For there to be trafficking in human beings ingredients from each of the three categories (action, means, purpose) must be present together. There is, however, an exception regarding children: under Article 4(c) recruitment, transportation, transfer, harbouring or receipt of a child for the purpose of exploitation is to be regarded as trafficking in human beings even if it does not involve any of the means listed in Article 4(a). Under Article 4(d) the word "child" means any person under 18 years of age.

77.	Thus trafficking means much more than mere organised movement of persons for profit. The critical additional factors that distinguish trafficking from migrant smuggling are use of one of the means listed (force, deception, abuse of a situation of vulnerability and so on) throughout or at some stage in the process, and use of that means for the purpose of exploitation.

78.	The actions the Convention is concerned with are "recruitment, transportation, transfer, harbouring or receipt of persons". The definition endeavours to encompass the whole sequence of actions that leads to exploitation of the victim.

79.	The drafters looked at use of new information technologies in trafficking in human beings. They decided that the Convention's definition of trafficking in human beings covered trafficking involving use of new information technologies. For instance, the definition's reference to recruitment covers recruitment by whatever means (oral, through the press or via the Internet). It was therefore felt to be unnecessary to include a further provision making the international-cooperation arrangements in the *Convention on Cybercrime* (ETS No.185) applicable to trafficking in human beings.

80.	As regards "transportation", it should be noted that, under the Convention, transport need not be across a border to be a constituent of trafficking in human beings. Similarly Article 2, on the Convention's scope, states that the Convention applies equally to transnational and national trafficking. Nor does the Convention require, in cases of transnational trafficking, that the victim have entered illegally or be illegally present on national territory. Trafficking in human beings can be involved even where a border was crossed legally and presence on national territory is lawful.

81.	The means are the threat or use of force or other forms of coercion, abduction, fraud, deception, abuse of power or of a position of vulnerability, and giving or receiving payments or benefits to achieve the consent of a person having control over another person.

82.	Fraud and deception are frequently used by traffickers, as when victims are led to believe that an attractive job awaits them rather than the intended exploitation.

83.	By abuse of a position of vulnerability is meant abuse of any situation in which the person involved has no real and acceptable alternative to submitting to the abuse. The vulnerability may be of any kind, whether physical, psychological, emotional, family-related, social or economic. The situation might, for example, involve insecurity or illegality of the victim's administrative status, economic dependence or fragile health. In short, the situation can be any state of hardship in which a human being is impelled to accept being exploited. Persons abusing such a situation flagrantly infringe human rights and violate human dignity and integrity, which no one can validly renounce.

84.	A wide range of means therefore has to be contemplated: abduction of women for sexual exploitation, enticement of children for use in paedophile or prostitution rings, violence by pimps to keep prostitutes under their thumb, taking advantage of an adolescent's or adult's vulnerability, whether or not resulting from sexual assault, or abusing the economic insecurity or poverty of an adult hoping to better their own and their family's lot. However, these various cases reflect differences of degree rather than any difference in the nature of the phenomenon, which in each case can be classed as trafficking and is based on use of such methods.

85.   The purpose must be exploitation of the individual. The Convention provides: "Exploitation shall include, at a minimum, the exploitation of the prostitution of others or other forms of sexual exploitation, forced labour or services, slavery or practices similar to slavery, servitude or the removal of organs". National legislation may therefore target other forms of exploitation but must at least cover the types of exploitation mentioned as constituents of trafficking in human beings.

86.   The forms of exploitation specified in the definition cover sexual exploitation, labour exploitation and removal of organs, for criminal activity is increasingly diversifying in order to supply people for exploitation in any sector where demand emerges.

87.   Under the definition, it is not necessary that someone have been exploited for there to be trafficking in human beings. It is enough that they have been subjected to one of the actions referred to in the definition and by one of the means specified "for the purpose of" exploitation. Trafficking in human beings is consequently present before the victim's actual exploitation.

88.   As regards "the exploitation of the prostitution of others or other forms of sexual exploitation", it should be noted that the Convention deals with these only in the context of trafficking in human beings. The terms "exploitation of the prostitution of others" and "other forms of sexual exploitation" are not defined in the Convention, which is therefore without prejudice to how States Parties deal with prostitution in domestic law.

89.   Nor does the Convention define "forced labour". Nonetheless there are several relevant international instruments, such as the *Universal Declaration of Human Rights* (Article 4), the *International Covenant on Civil and Political Rights* (Article 8), the ILO *Convention concerning Forced or Compulsory Labour* (Convention No.29), and the 1957 ILO *Convention concerning the Abolition of Forced Labour* (Convention No.105).

90.   Article 4 ECHR prohibits forced labour without defining it. The authors of the ECHR took as their model the ILO Convention concerning Forced or Compulsory Labour (No.29) of 29 June 1930, which describes as forced or compulsory "all work or service which is exacted from any person under the menace of any penalty and for which the said person has not offered himself voluntarily". In the case *Van der Müssele v. Belgium* (judgment of 23 November 1983, Series A, No.70, paragraph 37) the Court held that "relative weight" was to be attached to the prior-consent criterion and it opted for an approach which took into account all the circumstances of the case. In particular it observed that, in certain circumstances, a service "could not be treated as having been voluntarily accepted beforehand". It therefore held that consent of the person concerned was not sufficient to rule out forced labour. Thus, the validity of consent has to be evaluated in the light of all the circumstances of the case.

91.   Article 4(b) of the present Convention follows ECHR case-law in that it states that a human-trafficking victim's consent to a form of exploitation listed in Article 4(a) is irrelevant if any of the means referred to in sub-paragraph a. has been used.

92.   With regard to the concept of "forced services", the Court likewise found, in *Van der Müssele v. Belgium*, that the words "forced labour", as used in Article 4 ECHR, were to be given a broad meaning and encompassed the concept of forced services (judgment of 23 November 1983, Series A, No.70, paragraph 33). From the standpoint of the ECHR, therefore, there is no distinction to be made between the two concepts.

93.   Slavery is not defined in the Convention but many international instruments and the domestic law of many countries define or deal with slavery and practices similar to slavery (for example, the *Geneva Convention on Slavery* of 25 September 1926, as amended by the New York Protocol of 7 December 1953; the *Supplementary Conven-*

tion on the Abolition of Slavery, the Slave Trade, and Institutions and Practices similar to Slavery of 7 September 1956; the ILO *Worst Forms of Child Labour Convention* (Convention No.182)).

94. The definition of trafficking in human beings does not refer to illegal adoption as such. Nevertheless, where an illegal adoption amounts to a practice similar to slavery as defined in Article 1(d) of the *Supplementary Convention on the Abolition of Slavery, the Slave Trade, and Institutions and Practices similar to Slavery*, it will also fall within the Convention's scope.

95. The ECHR bodies have defined "servitude". The European Commission of Human Rights regarded it as having to live and work on another person's property and perform certain services for them, whether paid or unpaid, together with being unable to alter one's condition (Application No.7906/77, D.R.17, p. 59; see also the Commission's report in the *Van Droogenbroeck* case of 9 July 1980, Series B, Vol. 44, p. 30, paragraphs 78 to 80). Servitude is thus to be regarded as a particular form of slavery, differing from it less in character less than in degree. Although it constitutes a state or condition, and is a "particularly serious form of denial of freedom" (*Van Droogenbroeck* case, judgment of 24 June 1982, Series A, No.50, p.32, paragraph 58), it does not have the ownership features characteristic of slavery.

96. Exploitation also includes "removal of organs". The principle that it is not permissible for the human body or its parts as such to give rise to financial gain is established Council of Europe legal *acquis*. It was laid down in Committee of Ministers Resolution (78) 29 and was confirmed, in particular, by the final declaration of the 3rd Conference of European Health Ministers (Paris, 1987) before being definitively established in Article 21 of the *Convention on Human Rights and Biomedicine* (ETS No.164). The principle was then reaffirmed in the protocol to that convention *concerning transplantation of organs and tissues of human origin* (ETS No.186), which was opened for signature in January 2002. Article 22 of the protocol explicitly prohibits traffic in organs and tissues. It should also be recalled that the Parliamentary Assembly of the Council of Europe adopted a Report on "Trafficking in organs in Europe" (Doc. 9822, 3 June 2003, Social, Health and Family Affairs Committee, Rapporteur: Mrs Ruth-Gaby Vermot-Mangold, Switzerland, SOC) and *Recommendation 1611 (2003) on trafficking in organs in Europe*.

97. Article 4(b) states: "The consent of a victim of 'trafficking in human beings' to the intended exploitation set forth in sub-paragraph (a) of this article shall be irrelevant where any of the means set forth in sub-paragraph (a) have been used". The question of consent is not simple and it is not easy to determine where free will ends and constraint begins. In trafficking, some people do not know what is in store for them while others are perfectly aware that, for example, they will be engaging in prostitution. However, while someone may wish employment, and possibly be willing to engage in prostitution, that does not mean that they consent to be subjected to abuse of all kinds. For that reason Article 4(b) provides that there is trafficking in human beings whether or not the victim consents to be exploited.

98. Under sub-paragraphs b. and c. of Article 4 taken together, recruitment, transportation, transfer, harbouring and receipt of a child for the purpose of exploitation are regarded as trafficking in human beings. It is immaterial whether the means refers to in sub paragraph a. have been used. It is also immaterial whether or not the child consents to be exploited.

Definition of "victim"

99. There are many references in the Convention to the victim, and the drafters felt it was essential to define the concept. In particular the measures provided for in Chapter III are intended to apply to persons who are victims within the meaning of the Convention.

100. The Convention defines "victim" as "any natural person who is subjected to trafficking in human beings as defined in this Article". As explained above, a victim is anyone subjected to a combination of elements (action – means – purpose) specified in Article 4(a) of the Convention. Under Article 4(c), however, when that person is a child, he or she is to be regarded as a victim even if none of the means specified in Article 4(a) has been used.

Chapter II – Prevention, cooperation and other measures

101. Chapter II contains various provisions that come under the heading of prevention in the wide sense of the term. Some provisions are particularly concerned with prevention measures in the strict sense (Articles 5 and 6) while others deal with specific measures relating to controls, security and cooperation (Articles 7, 8 and 9) for preventing and combating traffic in human beings.

Article 5 – Prevention of trafficking in human beings

102. Trafficking in human beings takes many forms, cuts across various fields and has implications for various branches of society. To be effective, and given the nature of the phenomenon, preventive action against trafficking must be co-ordinated. The first paragraph of Article 5 is therefore concerned to promote a multidisciplinary co-ordination approach by requiring that Parties take measures to establish or strengthen co-ordination nationally between the various bodies responsible for preventing and combating trafficking in human beings. The paragraph makes it a requirement to co-ordinate all the sectors whose action is essential in preventing and combating trafficking, such as the agencies with social, police, migration, customs, judicial or administrative responsibilities, non-governmental organisations, other organisations with relevant responsibilities and other elements of civil society.

103. Article 5(2) gives a specimen list of prevention policies and programmes which Parties must establish or support, in particular for persons vulnerable to trafficking and for relevant professionals. The drafters felt that it was important that the beneficiaries of such policies and programmes include *"professionals concerned"*, namely anyone coming into contact with victims of trafficking in the course of their work (police, social workers, doctors, etc). Such measures vary in character and may have short-, medium-, or long-term effect. For example, *research* on combating trafficking is essential for devising effective prevention methods. *Information, awareness-raising and education campaigns* are important short-term prevention measures, particularly in the countries of origin. *Social and economic initiatives* tackle the underlying and structural causes of trafficking and require long-term investment. It is widely recognised that improvement of economic and social conditions in countries of origin and measures to deal with extreme poverty would be the most effective way of preventing trafficking. Among social and economic initiatives, improved training and more employment opportunities for people liable to be traffickers' prime targets would undoubtedly help prevent trafficking in human beings.

104. Under Article 5(3) Parties are to promote a human-rights-based approach. Here, the drafters took the view that it was essential that the policies and programmes referred to in paragraph 2 be based on gender mainstreaming and a child-rights approach to children. One of the main strategies for bringing about proper equality between women and men is gender mainstreaming, as described in Committee of Ministers *Recommendation R(98)14 to member States on gender mainstreaming.* Gender mainstreaming is a concept which features prominently in international documents, particularly those of the United Nations World Conferences on Women, and in European documents since its 1996 adoption by the European Commission (Commission Communication of 21 February 1996, "Incorporating equal opportunities for women and men into all Community policies and activities", COM (96) 67 final). The concept was then consolidated in the Community Framework Strategy on Gender Equality (2001–2005). The Council of Europe group of specialists on the subject defined the approach as *"the (re)organisation, improvement, development and evaluation of policy processes, so that a gender equality perspective is incorporated in all policies at all levels and at all stages, by the actors normally involved in policy making"*. Each Party is required to apply these approaches at all stages of its prevention policies and programmes – that is, in developing, implementing and evaluating them.

105. Paragraph 4 places an obligation on Parties to take appropriate measures as necessary to enable people to emigrate and immigrate lawfully. It is essential that would-be immigrants have accurate information about legal opportunities for migration, employment conditions and their rights and duties. The provision is aimed at counteracting traffickers' misinformation so that people recognise traffickers' offers for what they are and know better than to take them up. It is for each Party to decide, according to its internal functioning, which the "relevant offices" are. The drafters mainly but not exclusively had in mind visa and immigration services.

106. Paragraph 5 requires that Parties take specific preventive measures with regard to children. The provision refers in particular to creating a *"protective environment"* for children so as to make them less vulnerable to trafficking and enable them to grow up without harm and to lead decent lives. The concept of a *protective environment*, as promoted by UNICEF, has eight key components:

–   protecting children's rights from adverse attitudes, traditions, customs, behaviour and practices;
–   government commitment to and protection and realisation of children's rights;
–   open discussion of, and engagement with, child protection issues;
–   drawing up and enforcing protective legislation;
–   the capacity of those dealing and in contact with children, families and communities to protect children;
–   children's life skills, knowledge and participation;
–   putting in place a system for monitoring and reporting abuse cases;
–   programmes and services to enable child victims of trafficking to recover and reintegrate.

107. Lastly, paragraph 6 recognises the important role of non-governmental organisations, other relevant organisations and other elements of civil society in preventing trafficking in human beings and protecting and assisting victims. For that reason Parties, while responsible for meeting the obligations laid down in Article 5, must, as appropriate, involve such bodies in the implementation of preventive measures.

Article 6 – Measures to discourage the demand

108. This article places a positive obligation on Parties to adopt and reinforce measures for discouraging demand whether as regards sexual exploitation or in respect of forced labour or services, slavery and practices similar to slavery, servitude and organ removal. By devoting a separate, free-standing article to this, the drafters sought to underline the importance of tackling demand in order to prevent and combat the traffic itself.

109. The aim of measures is to achieve effective dissuasion. The measures involved may be legislative, administrative, educational, social, cultural or of other kinds.

110. The article includes a list of such minimum measures. An essential one is research on best practices, methods and strategies for discouraging client demand effectively. The media and civil society have been key agencies in identifying demand as one of the main causes of trafficking, and the measures accordingly seek to create maximum awareness and recognition of their role and responsibility in that field. Information campaigns targeting relevant groups could also be conducted, with involvement, where appropriate, of political decision-makers and public authorities. Lastly, educational measures play an important part in discouraging demand. For example, educational programmes for school children could not only advantageously tell them about the trafficking phenomenon but also alert them to gender issues, questions of dignity and integrity of human beings, and the consequences of gender-based discrimination.

Article 7 – Border measures

111. Article 7, modelled on Article 11 of the Palermo Protocol, covers a range of measures for prevention and border detection of transnational trafficking in human beings. The drafters were agreed that better management of controls and cooperation at borders would make action to combat trafficking in human beings more effective.

112. Under the first paragraph Parties have to strengthen border controls as far as

possible to ensure that people are authorised to enter or leave a Party's territory. Such measures must be without prejudice to international commitments in relation to people's freedom of movement, this requirement being particularly relevant within the European Community, where member States have developed a set of rules on control and surveillance of external borders (EC law on police and customs cooperation).

113.   Under paragraph 2 Parties must adopt legislative or other appropriate measures to prevent means of transport operated by commercial carriers from being used to commit offences established in Chapter IV.

114.   The type of measure is left to Parties' discretion. For example, paragraph 3 requires commercial carriers to check that passengers are in possession of the travel documents necessary for entering the receiving State. When passengers are not, there also have to be appropriate penalties (paragraph 4). It should be noted, however, that the obligation on commercial carriers, including any transport company or owner or operator of any means of transport, consists in checking solely for possession of documents and not on documents' validity or authenticity. The nature of the penalties to be applied in cases of contravening the paragraph 3 obligation is not specified, leaving it to Parties to decide appropriate measures according to their domestic law.

115.   Paragraph 5 is concerned with punishing persons implicated in Chapter IV offences. Each Party is required to adopt the legislative or other measures necessary so that such persons can be refused entry to their territory or their visas can be revoked.

116.   Lastly, in paragraph 6, the drafters sought to promote cooperation between border control services. Introducing new types of operational action (such as cross-border observation and pursuit, and introducing official machinery for direct exchange of information between services) has a definite place in cross-border cooperation on devising preventive law-and-order and security measures or strategies. New modes of action and intervention methods give cross-border services an important role in combating trafficking. Paragraph 6 accordingly requires Parties to consider strengthening cooperation between border-control services by, among other things, establishing and maintaining direct channels of communication.

Article 8 – Security and control of documents

117.   Under Article 8, modelled on Article 12 of the Palermo Protocol, every Party must adopt the necessary measures to ensure quality of travel and identity documents and protect the integrity and security of such documents. By "travel or identity documents" the drafters mean any type of document required to enter or leave a country's territory in accordance with domestic law or any document commonly used to establish a person's identity in a country under that country's law.

118.   It should be noted that the drafters had in mind not only cases where documents have been unlawfully falsified, altered, reproduced or issued but also those where lawfully created or issued documents have been tampered with, altered or misappropriated.

·119.   Such measures may include, for example, introducing minimum standards to improve security of passports and other travel documents, including stricter technical specifications and additional security requirements such as more sophisticated preventive features that make counterfeiting, falsification, forgery and fraud more difficult. They also include administrative and control measures to prevent illegal issue and possession, guard against improper use and facilitate detection where such documents have been falsified or illegally altered, reproduced, issued or used.

Article 9 – Legitimacy and validity of documents

120.   Travel and identity documents are essential tools in trafficking, particularly transnational trafficking. Cooperation between Parties in checking the legitimacy and validity of travel and identity documents is thus an important preventive measure.

121.   Under Article 9, modelled on Article 13 of the Palermo Protocol, Parties are required to check the legitimacy and validity of travel or identity documents which have

been issued, or supposedly have been issued, by their authorities when they are requested to do so by another Party and when it is suspected that the documents are being used for trafficking in human beings. The checking is carried out according to the rules of domestic law of the Party requested.

122.   The requested Party must verify the "legitimacy and validity" of travel or identity documents issued or purporting to have been issued in its name. By this is meant that the requested Party must check both the formal and material legality of the documents. Documents used for trafficking in human beings may be outright forgeries, and therefore not issued by the requested Party. They may also have been issued by the requested Party but later altered to produce a counterfeit. In such cases the documents are formally illegal. However, documents which neither are counterfeits nor have been altered may likewise be used for trafficking in human beings. For example, documents may have been drawn up on the basis of inaccurate or false information, or they may be perfectly valid but being used by persons other than their rightful holders. In such cases the documents are materially illegal. Article 9 places a duty on Parties to cooperate in detecting all such situations.

123.   It should be noted in particular that Parties have a duty to proceed expeditiously and that the Party requested must provide a reply to the requesting Party within a reasonable time, which will of course vary according to the complexity of the checks which the request involves. Nevertheless, it is essential that the reply be received in time for the requesting Party to take any measures necessary.

Chapter III – Measures to protect and promote the rights of victims, guaranteeing gender equality

124.   Chapter III contains provisions to protect and assist victims of trafficking in human beings. Some of the provisions in this chapter apply to all victims (Articles 10, 11, 12, 15 and 16). Others apply specifically to victims unlawfully present in the receiving Party's territory (Articles 13 and 14) or victims in a legal situation but with a short-term residence permit. In addition, some provisions also apply to persons not yet formally identified as victims but whom there are reasonable grounds for believing to be victims (Article 10(2), Article 12(1) and (2) and Article 13).

125.   This chapter is an essential part of the Convention. It is centred on protecting the rights of trafficking victims, taking the same stance as set out in the United Nations *Recommended Principles and Guidelines on Human Rights and Trafficking in human beings*: "The human rights of trafficked persons shall be at the centre of all efforts to prevent and combat trafficking and to protect, assist and provide redress to victims"[15].

126.   Chapter III has eight articles. Article 10 deals with identification of victims of trafficking as being essential if they are to be given the benefit of the rights laid down in the Convention. Article 11 deals with protection of their private life. Article 12 specifies the assistance measures to which trafficking victims are entitled. Articles 13 and 14 lay down a recovery and reflection period to which victims illegally present in a Party's territory are entitled and provide for issue of a residence permit. Article15 deals with compensation of trafficking victims for harm suffered and Article 16 with repatriation or return. Article 17 deals with gender equality.

Article 10 – Identification of the victims

127.   To protect and assist trafficking victims it is of paramount importance to identify them correctly. Article 10 seeks to allow such identification so that victims can be given the benefit of the measures provided for in Chapter III. Identification of victims is crucial, is often tricky and necessitates detailed enquiries. Failure to identify a trafficking victim correctly will probably mean that victim's continuing to be denied his or her fundamental rights and the prosecution to be denied the necessary witness in criminal proceedings to gain a conviction of the perpetrator for trafficking in human beings. Through the identification process, competent authorities seek and evaluate different circumstances, according to which they can consider a person to be a victim of trafficking.

128.   Paragraph 1 places obligations on Parties so as to make it possible to identify

victims and, in appropriate cases, issue residence permits in the manner laid down in Article 14 of the Convention. Paragraph 1 addresses the fact that national authorities are often insufficiently aware of the problem of trafficking in human beings. Victims frequently have their passports or identity documents taken away from them or destroyed by the traffickers. In such cases they risk being treated primarily as illegal immigrants, prostitutes or illegal workers and being punished or returned to their countries without being given any help. To avoid that, Article 10(1) requires that Parties provide their competent authorities with persons who are trained and qualified in preventing and combating trafficking in human beings and in identifying and helping victims, including children and that they ensure that those authorities cooperate with one other as well as with relevant support organisations.

129. By "competent authority" is meant the public authorities which may have contact with trafficking victims, such as the police, the labour inspectorate, customs, the immigration authorities and embassies or consulates. It is essential that these have people capable of identifying victims and channelling them towards the organisations and services who can assist them.

130. The Convention does not require that the competent authorities have specialists in human-trafficking matters but it does require that they have trained, qualified people so that victims can be identified. The Convention likewise requires that the authorities collaborate with one another and with organisations that have a support-providing role. The support organisations could be non-governmental organisations (NGOs) tasked with providing aid and support to victims.

131. Even though the identification process is not completed, as soon as competent authorities consider that there are reasonable grounds to believe that the person is a victim, they will not remove the person from the territory of the receiving States. Identifying a trafficking victim is a process which takes time. It may require exchange of information with other countries or Parties or with victim-support organisations, and this may well lengthen the identification process. Many victims, however, are illegally present in the country where they are being exploited. Paragraph 2 seeks to avoid their being immediately removed from the country before they can be identified as victims. Chapter III of the Convention secures various rights to people who are victims of trafficking in human beings. Those rights would be purely theoretical and illusory if such people were removed from the country before identification as victims was possible.

132. The Convention does not require absolute certainty – by definition impossible before the identification process has been completed – for not removing the person concerned from the Party's territory. Under the Convention, if there are "reasonable" grounds for believing someone to be a victim, then that is sufficient reason not to remove them until completion of the identification process establishes conclusively whether or not they are victims of trafficking.

133. The words "removed from its territory" refer both to removal to the country of origin and removal to a third country.

134. The identification process provided for in Article 10 is independent of any criminal proceedings against those responsible for the trafficking. A criminal conviction is therefore unnecessary for either starting or completing the identification process.

135. Even though the identification process may be speedier than criminal proceedings (if any), victims will still need assistance even before they have been identified as such. For that reason the Convention provides that if the authorities "have reasonable grounds to believe" that someone has been a victim of trafficking, then they should have the benefit, during the identification process, of the assistance measures provided for in Article 10(1) and (2).

136. The point of paragraph 3 is that, while children need special protection measures, it is sometimes difficult to determine whether someone is over or under 18. Paragraph 3 consequently requires Parties to presume that a victim is a child if there are reasons for believing that to be so and if there is uncertainty about their age. Until their age is verified, they must be given special protection measures, in accordance with their rights as defined, in particular, in the *United Nations Convention on the Rights of the Child*.

137. Paragraph 4 provides for measures which must be taken by the Parties when they

deal with cases of child victims of trafficking who are unaccompanied children. Hence, Parties must provide for the representation of the child by a legal guardian, organisation or authority which is responsible to act in the best interests of that child (a); take the necessary steps to establish his/her identity and nationality (b); and make every effort to locate his/her family when this is in the best interests of the child (c). The family of the child should be found only when this is in the best interests of the child given that sometimes it is his/her family who is at the source of his/her trafficking.

Article 11 – Protection of private life

138.   Article 11 protects trafficking victims' private life. Protection is essential both for victims' physical safety, given the danger from their traffickers, but also (on account of the feelings of shame and the stigmatisation risk that attach to the trafficking, both for the victim and the family) to preserve their chances of social reintegration in the country of origin or the receiving country.

139.   The first sentence of paragraph 1 states the objective of the article as a whole: to protect victims' private life and identity. The remainder of Article 11 lays down specific measures for achieving that objective. It should be noted that this question is also dealt with in Article 30 of the Convention, which is concerned with protection of victims' private life and identity in the specific context of judicial proceedings.

140.   Paragraph 1 also refers to the question of personal data regarding victims of trafficking. Because of the possible dangers to a victim if data concerning them were to circulate without any safeguards or checks, the Convention requires that such data be processed and stored in the manner prescribed in the *Convention for the Protection of Individuals with regard to Automatic Processing of Personal Data* (ETS No.108).

141.   Convention No.108 provides, in particular, that personal data are to be stored only for specified lawful purposes and are not to be used in any way incompatible with those purposes. It also provides that such data are not to be stored in any form allowing identification of the data subject or for any longer than is necessary for the purposes for which the data are recorded and stored. Convention No.108 likewise makes it compulsory to take appropriate security measures preventing unauthorised access to and alteration or disclosure of data. It should be noted that under Article 11(1) Parties must comply, as regards personal data of trafficking victims, with the requirements laid down in Convention No.108 regardless of whether they have ratified it.

142.   Paragraph 2 provides for special protection measures regarding children as it would be particularly harmful for their identity to be disclosed in the media or by other means. This provision likewise applies to "details enabling [. . .] identification" in that, without actually mentioning a child victim's name, the media may sometimes reveal details – such as where they are staying or, possibly, working – that might allow them to be identified.

143.   The Parties are free to decide what measures to take to prevent the identity, or details allowing identification, of child trafficking victims from being made publicly known. For that purpose the law of some countries lays down criminal penalties for making publicly known any information that might reveal the identity of victims of some offences.

144.   Paragraph 2 nonetheless allows information to be released about child victims' identity where exceptional circumstances justify doing so in order to trace relatives or otherwise secure the wellbeing and protection of the child.

145.   Finally, paragraph 3 exhorts Parties to adopt measures encouraging the media to protect victims' private life and identity. To avoid undue interference with media freedom of expression, it states that such measures must accord with Article 10 ECHR and must be for the specific purpose of protecting victims' private life and identity. "Self-regulation" is regulation by the private sector, "co-regulation" is regulation in the context of a partnership between the private sector and public authorities, and "regulation" applies to standards laid down by the public authorities independently.

Article 12 – Assistance for victims of trafficking

146.   Victims who break free of their traffickers' control generally find themselves in a position of great insecurity and vulnerability. Article 12(1) sets out the assistance

measures which Parties must provide for trafficking victims. It must be pointed out that Article 12 applies to all victims, whether victims of national or transnational trafficking. It applies to victims that have not been granted residence permit, under the conditions established in Articles 10(2) and 13(2).

147.   The persons who must receive assistance measures are all those who have been identified as victims after completion of the Article 10 identification process. Such persons are entitled to all the assistance measures set out in Article 12. During the actual identification process, in the case of someone whom the authorities have "reasonable grounds to believe" to be a victim, that person is entitled solely to the measures in Article 12(1) and (2) and not to all the Article 12 measures. During the recovery and reflection period (Article 13) such a person is likewise entitled to the measures in Article 12(1) and (2).

148.   Paragraph 1 provides that the measures concerned have to be taken by "each Party". This does not mean that all Parties to the Convention must provide assistance measures to each and every victim but that the Party in whose territory the victim is located must ensure that the assistance measures specified in sub-paragraphs a. to f. are provided to him or her. When the victim leaves that Party's territory the measures referred to in Article 12 no longer apply as Parties are responsible only for persons within their jurisdiction.

149.   Under paragraph 5 the assistance can be provided in cooperation with non-governmental organisations, other relevant organisations or other elements of civil society engaged in victim assistance. It is nevertheless the Parties that remain responsible for meeting the obligations in the Convention. Consequently it is they who have to take the steps necessary to ensure that victims receive the assistance they are entitled to, in particular by making sure that reception, protection and assistance services are funded adequately and in time.

150.   The aim of the assistance provided for in sub-paragraphs a. to f. is to "assist victims in their physical, psychological and social recovery". The authorities must therefore make arrange for those assistance measures while bearing in mind the specific nature of that aim.

151.   Although there was no legal necessity to do so, as it is always open to Parties to adopt measures more favourable than those provided for in any part of the Convention, the drafters wished to make it clear that the assistance measures referred to are minimum ones. Parties are thus free to grant additional assistance measures.

152.   Under paragraph a. victims are to be secured "standards of living capable of ensuring their subsistence, through such measures as: appropriate and secure accomodation, psychological and material assistance". The obligation on Parties is to provide victims with standards of living capable of ensuring their subsistence, but the drafters considered it necessary to refer, as an example, to appropriate and secure accommodation and to psychological and material assistance as being particularly relevant to assisting victims of trafficking.

153.   It should be noted that even though Article 31 of the *Revised European Social Charter* (ETS No. 163) recognises everyone's right to housing, the special features of the situation in which victims find themselves often calls for particular measures to assist them in their psychological and social recovery. Paragraph a. accordingly specifies that accommodation must be "appropriate and secure" as victims need adapted and protected accommodation in which they can feel safe from the traffickers.

154.   The type of appropriate accommodation depends on the victim's personal circumstances (for instance, they may be living in the streets or already have accommodation, and in the latter case it will be necessary to make sure that the accommodation is appropriate and does not present any security problems). Where trafficking in human beings is concerned, special protected shelters are especially suitable and have already been introduced in various countries. Such refuges, staffed by people qualified to deal with questions of assistance to trafficking victims, provide round-the-clock victim reception and are able to respond to emergencies. The purpose of such shelters is to provide victims with surroundings in which they feel secure and to provide them with help and stability. As a guarantee of victims' security it is very

important to take precautions such as keeping their address secret and having strict rules on visits from outsiders, since, to begin with, there is the danger that traffickers will try to regain control of the victim. The protection and help which the refuges provide is aimed at enabling victims to take charge of their own lives again.

155. In the case of children, the accommodation has to be appropriate in terms of their specific needs. Child victims of trafficking are sometimes placed in detention institutions. In some cases this happens because of a shortage of places in specialist child-welfare institutions. Placement of a child in a detention institution should never be regarded as appropriate accommodation.

156. Psychological assistance is needed to help the victim overcome the trauma they have been through and get back to reintegration into society. The Convention provides for material assistance because many victims, once out of the traffickers' hands, are totally without material resources. The material assistance provided for in sub-paragraph a. is intended to give them the means of subsistence. Material assistance is distinguished from financial aid in that it may take the form of aid in kind (for example, food and clothing) and is not necessarily in the form of money.

157. Sub-paragraph b. provides for emergency medical treatment to be available to victims. Article 13 of the *Revised European Social Charter* (ETS No.163) also recognises the right of any person who is without adequate resources to social and medical assistance. Medical assistance is often necessary for victims of trafficking who have been exploited or have suffered violence. The assistance may also allow evidence to be kept of the violence so that, if they wish, the victims can take legal action. Full medical assistance is only for victims lawfully resident in the Party's territory under Article 12(3).

158. Under sub-paragraph c. language aid is to be provided to victims when appropriate, for many victims do not speak, or barely speak, the language of the country they have been brought to for exploitation. Ignorance of the language adds to their isolation and is one of the factors preventing them from claiming their rights. In such cases language aid is needed to help them with formalities. This is an essential measure for guaranteeing access to rights, which is a prerequisite for access to justice. The provision is not limited to the right to an interpreter in judicial proceedings.

159. Sub-paragraphs d. and e. deal more specifically with assistance to victims in the form of supply of information: two common features of victims' situation are helplessness and submissiveness to the traffickers due to fear and lack of information about how to escape their situation.

160. Sub-paragraph d. provides that victims are to be given counselling and infor-mation, in particular as regards their legal rights and the services available to them, in a language that they understand. The information deals with matters such as availability of protection and assistance arrangements, the various options open to the victim, the risks they run, the requirements for legalising their presence in the Party's territory, the various possible forms of legal redress, how the criminal-law system operates (including the consequences of an investigation or trial, the length of a trial, witnesses' duties, the possibilities of obtaining compensation from persons found guilty of offences or from other persons or entities, and the chances of a judgment's being properly enforced). The information and counselling should enable victims to evaluate their situation and make an informed choice from the various possibilities open to them.

161. Such advice and information, even though it has to do "in particular [with] their legal rights", is to be distinguished from free legal aid by an appointed lawyer in compensation proceedings, which is dealt with specifically in Article 15(2).

162. Sub-paragraph e. deals with general assistance to victims to ensure that their interests are taken into account in criminal proceedings. Article 15(2) deals more specifically with the right to a defence counsel.

163. Sub-paragraph f. recognizes the right to access to education for children.

164. Under Article 12(2) each Party must take due account of victims' safety and protection needs. Victims' needs can vary widely depending on their personal circum-

stances. They may arise from matters such as age or gender, or from circumstances such as the type of exploitation the victim has undergone, the country of origin, the types and degree of violence suffered, isolation from his or her family and culture, knowledge of the local language, and his or her material and financial resources. It is therefore essential to provide measures that take victims' safety fully into account. For example, the address of any accommodation needs to be kept secret and the accommodation must be protected from any attempts by traffickers to recapture the victims.

165. Under paragraph 3 each Party is required to provide the necessary medical or other assistance to victims lawfully resident in its territory who do not have adequate resources and need the assistance. Lawfully resident victims are, in particular, nationals and persons with the residence permit referred to in Article 14. In addition Article 13 of the *Revised European Social Charter* (ETS No.163) – under which any person who is without resources and who is unable to secure such resources either by his or her own efforts or from other sources is to be granted adequate assistance, and, in case of sickness, the care necessitated by his or her condition – applies to nationals and to persons lawfully present on national territory. This medical assistance is not just a question of availability of emergency medical care, as provided for in paragraph 1(b). For example, the medical assistance might be assistance to a victim during pregnancy or with HIV/AIDS.

166. Paragraph 4 provides that each Party is to adopt the rules under which victims lawfully resident in the Party's territory are allowed access to the labour market, to vocational training and to education. In the drafters' view these measures are desirable for helping victims reintegrate socially and more particularly take greater charge of their lives. However, the Convention does not establish an actual right of access to the labour market, vocational training and education. It is for the Parties to decide the conditions governing access. As in paragraph 3, the words "lawfully resident" refer, for instance, to victims who have the residence permit referred to in Article 14 or who have the Party's nationality. The authorisation referred to need not involve issuing an administrative document to the person concerned that allows them to work.

167. As already stated, NGOs often have a crucial role in victim assistance. For that reason paragraph 5 specifies that each Party is to take measures, where appropriate and under the conditions provided for by national law, to cooperate with non-governmental organisations, other relevant organisations or other elements of civil society engaged in victim assistance.

168. The drafters wish to make it clear that under Article 12(6) of the Convention, assistance is not conditional upon a victim's agreement to cooperate with competent authorities in investigations and criminal proceedings.

169. Some Parties may decide – as allowed by Article 14 – to grant residence permits only to victims who cooperate with the authorities. Nevertheless, paragraph 6 of Article 12 provides that each Party shall adopt such legislative or other measures as may be necessary to ensure that assistance to a victim is not made conditional on his or her willingness to act as a witness.

170. It should also be noted that, in the law of many countries, it is compulsory to give evidence if requested to do so. Paragraph 6 is without prejudice to the activities carried out by the competent authorities in all phases of the relevant national proceedings, and in particular when investigating and prosecuting the offences concerned. Thus no one may rely on paragraph 6 in refusing to act as a witness when they are legally required to do so.

171. Paragraph 7 indicates that the services provided to victims should be carried out on an informed and consensual basis. It is indeed essential that victims agree to the services provided to them. Thus, for instance, victims must be able to agree to the detection of illness such as HIV/AIDS for them to be licit. In addition, the services provided must take into account the specific needs of persons in a vulnerable position and the rights of children concerning accommodation, education and health.

Article 13 – Recovery and reflection period

172. Article 13 is intended to apply to victims of trafficking in human beings who are illegally present in a Party's territory or who are legally resident with a short-term residence permit. Such victims, when identified, are, as other victims of trafficking, extremely vulnerable after all the trauma they have experienced. In addition, they are likely to be removed from the territory.

173. Article 13(1) accordingly introduces a recovery and reflection period for illegally present victims during which they are not to be removed from the Party's territory. The Convention contains a provision requiring Parties to provide in their internal law for this period to last at least 30 days. This minimum period constitutes an important guarantee for victims and serves a number of purposes. One of the purposes of this period is to allow victims to recover and escape the influence of traffickers. Victims recovery implies, for example, healing of the wounds and recovery from the physical assault which they have suffered. That also implies that they have recovered a minimum of psychological stability. Paragraph 3 of Article 13, allows Parties not to observe this period if grounds of public order prevent it or if it is found that victim status is being claimed improperly. This provision aims to guarantee that victims' status will not be illegitimately used.

174. Other purpose of this period is to allow victims to come to a decision "on co-operating with the competent authorities". By this is meant that victims must decide whether they will cooperate with the law-enforcement authorities in a prosecution of the traffickers. From that standpoint, the period is likely to make the victim a better witness: statements from victims wishing to give evidence to the authorities may well be unreliable if they are still in a state of shock from their ordeal. "Informed decision" means that the victim must be in a reasonably calm frame of mind and know about the protection and assistance measures available and the possible judicial proceedings against the traffickers. Such a decision requires that the victim no longer be under the traffickers' influence.

175. The reflection and recovery period provided for in Article 13(1) should not be confused with issue of the residence permit under Article 14(1). Its purpose being to enable victims to recover and escape the influence of traffickers and/or to take an informed decision on co-operating with the competent authorities, the period, in itself, is not conditional on their co-operating with the investigative or prosecution authorities.

176. Decision to cooperate or to not cooperate with competent authorities does not exclude the obligation to testify when it is required by a judge. Someone who is legally required to do so therefore cannot use Article 13(1) as a basis for refusing to testify. For that reason, Article 13(1) specifies that it is "without prejudice to the activities carried out by the competent authorities in all phases of the relevant national proceedings, and in particular when investigating and prosecuting the offences concerned."

177. The Convention specifies that the length of the recovery and reflection period must be at least 30 days. The length of this recovery and reflection period has to be of at least 30 days and has to be compatible with the purpose of Article 13. At present countries which have a period of that kind in their domestic law have lengths of one month, 45 days, two months, three months or unspecified. A three-month period was referred to in the declaration of the 3rd Regional Ministerial Forum of the Stability Pact for South-Eastern Europe (Tirana, 11 December 2002). The Group of Experts on trafficking in human beings which the European Commission set up by decision of 25 March 2003 recommended, in an opinion of 16 April 2004, a period of at least 3 months.

178. The words "it shall not be possible to enforce any expulsion order against him or her" mean that the victim must not be removed from the Party's territory during the recovery and reflection period. Although free to choose what method to employ, Parties are required to create a legal framework allowing the victim to remain on their territory for the duration of the period. To meet this end, in accordance with national legislation, each Party shall provide victims, without delay, with the relevant documents authorising them to remain on its territory during the recovery and reflection period.

179. To help victims to recover and stay free of the traffickers for that period, it is essential to provide appropriate assistance and protection. Article 13(2) consequently provides that victims are entitled to the measures contained in Article 12(1) and (2).

Article 14 – Residence permit

180.   Article 14(1) provides that victims of trafficking in human beings shall issue with renewable residence permits. Provision for a residence permit meets both victims' needs and the requirements of combating the traffic.

181.   Immediate return of the victims to their countries is unsatisfactory both for the victims and for the law-enforcement authorities endeavouring to combat the traffic. For the victims this means having to start again from scratch – a failure, that in most cases, they will keep quiet about, with the result that nothing will be done to prevent other victims from falling into the same trap. A further factor is fear of reprisals by the traffickers, either against the victims themselves or against family or friends in the country of origin. For the law enforcement authorities, if the victims continue to live clandestinely in the country or are removed immediately they cannot give information for effectively combating the traffic. The greater victims' confidence that their rights and interests are protected, the better the information they will give. Availability of residence permits is a measure calculated to encourage them to cooperate.

182.   The two requirements laid down in Article 14(1) for issue of a residence permit are that either the victim's stay be "necessary owing to their personal situation" or that it be necessary "for the purpose of their cooperation with the competent authorities in investigation or criminal proceedings". The aim of these requirements is to allow Parties to choose between granting a residence permit in exchange for cooperation with the law-enforcement authorities and granting a residence permit on account of the victim's needs, or indeed to adopt both simultaneously.

183.   Thus, for the victim to be granted a residence permit, and depending on the approach the Party adopts, either the victim's personal circumstances must be such that it would be unreasonable to compel them to leave the national territory, or there has to be an investigation or prosecution with the victim co-operating with the authorities. Parties likewise have the possibility of issuing residence permits in both situations.

184.   The personal situation requirement takes in a range of situations, depending on whether it is the victim's safety, state of health, family situation or some other factor which has to be taken into account.

#=6   185.">The requirement of the cooperation with the competent authorities has been introduced in order to take into account that victims are deterred from contacting the national authorities by fear of being immediately sent back to their country of origin as illegal entrants to the country of exploitation.

186.   In the case of children, the child's best interests take precedence over the above two requirements: the Convention provides that residence permits for child victims are to be "issued in accordance with the best interests of the child and, where appropriate, renewed under the same conditions" (Article 14(2)). The words "when legally necessary" have been introduced in order to take into account the fact that certain States do not require for children a residence permit.

187.   The Convention leaves the length of the residence permit to the Parties' discretion, though the Parties must set a length compatible with the provision's purpose. By way of example, the EU *Council Directive of 29 April 2004 on the residence permit issued to third-country nationals who are victims of trafficking in human beings or who have been the subject of an action to facilitate illegal immigration, who cooperate with the competent authorities* sets a minimum period of 6 months.

188.   Even though the Convention does not specify any length of residence permit it does provide that the permit has to be renewable. Paragraph 3 provides that the non-renewal or the withdrawal of a residence permit are subject to the conditions provided for in the internal law of the Party.

189.   The object of Article 14(4) is to ensure that a Party granting, under paragraph 1, a residence permit takes that into account when the victim requests another kind of residence permit. Where a victim applies for another kind of residence permit, paragraph 2 encourages Parties to have regard to the applicant's having been a victim of trafficking in human beings. However, it does not place any obligation on the Parties

to grant another kind of residence permit to persons who have received residence permit under paragraph 1.

190.   Paragraph 5 is a particular application of the principle provided for in article 40 paragraph 4 of the Convention.

Article 15 – Compensation and legal redress

191.   The purpose of this article is to ensure that victims of trafficking in human beings are compensated for damage suffered. It comprises four paragraphs. The first is concerned with information to victims. The second deals with victims' right to legal assistance. The third establishes victims' right to compensation and the fourth is concerned with guarantees of compensation.

192.   eople cannot claim their rights if they do not know about them. Paragraph 1 therefore requires Parties to ensure that, as from their first contact with the competent authorities, victims have access to information on relevant court and administrative proceedings in a language which they can understand. It is of paramount importance that they be told about any procedures they can use to obtain compensation for damage suffered. It is also essential that victims who are illegally present in the country be informed of their rights as regards the possibility of obtaining a residence permit under Article 14 of the Convention, as it would be very difficult for them to obtain compensation if they were unable to remain in the country where the proceedings take place.

193.   Reference is made to "court and administrative proceedings" so as to take into account the diversity of national systems. For example, compensation of victims can be a matter for the courts (whether civil or criminal) or so sometimes for administrative authorities with special responsibility for compensating victims of offences. In the case of illegally present victims eligible for a residence permit under Article 14, information about the procedure for obtaining the permit is likewise essential. Traditionally, grant of residence permits is an administrative matter but there may also be judicial review by means of appeal to the courts. It is important that victims be informed of all relevant procedures.

194.   Victims must be informed of relevant procedure as from their first contact with the competent authorities. By "competent authorities" is meant the wide range of public authorities with which victims may have their first contact with officialdom, such as the police, the prosecutor's office, the labour inspectorate, or the customs or immigration services. It does not have to be these services which supply the relevant information to victims. However, as soon as a victim is in touch with such services, he or she needs to be directed to persons, services or organisations able to supply the necessary information.

195.   Under paragraph 2 each Party shall provide, in its internal law, for the right to legal assistance and to free legal aid for victims under the conditions provided by its internal law. As court and administrative procedure is often very complex, legal assistance is necessary for victims to be able to claim their rights.

196.   This provision does not give the victim an automatic right to free legal aid. It is for each Party to decide the requirements for obtaining such aid. Parties must have regard not only to Article 15(2) but also to Article 6 ECHR. Even though Article 6(3)(c) ECHR provides for free assistance from an officially appointed lawyer only in criminal proceedings, European Court of Human Rights case-law (*Airey v. Ireland* judgment, 9 October 1979) also recognises, in certain circumstances, the right to free legal assistance in a civil matter on the basis of Article 6(1) ECHR, interpreted as establishing the right to a court for determination of civil rights and obligations (see *Golder v. the United Kingdom*, judgment of 21 February 1975). The Court's view is that effective access to a court may necessitate free legal assistance. Its position is that it must be ascertained whether appearance before a court without the assistance of a lawyer would be effective in the sense that the person concerned would be able to present their case properly and satisfactorily. Here the Court has taken into account the complexity of procedures and the emotional character of a situation - which might be scarcely compatible with the degree of objectivity required by advocacy in court - in

deciding whether someone was in a position to present his or her own case effectively. If not, he or she must be given free legal assistance. Thus, even in the absence of legislation granting free legal assistance in civil matters, it is for the courts to assess whether, in the interest of justice, an applicant who is without financial means should be granted legal assistance if unable to afford a lawyer.

197.   Paragraph 3 establishes a right of victims to compensation. The compensation is pecuniary and covers both material injury (such as the cost of medical treatment) and non-material damage (the suffering experienced). For the purposes of this paragraph, victims' right to compensation consists in a claim against the perpetrators of the trafficking – it is the traffickers who bear the burden of compensating the victims. If, in proceedings against traffickers, the criminal courts are not empowered to determine civil liability towards the victims, it must be possible for the victims to submit their claims to civil courts with jurisdiction in the matter and powers to award damages with interest.

198.   However, even though it is the trafficker who is liable to compensate the victim, by order of a civil court or – in some countries – a criminal court, or under a judicial or extra-judicial transaction between the victim and the trafficker, in practice there is rarely full compensation whether because the trafficker has not been found, has disappeared or has declared himself bankrupt. Paragraph 4 therefore requires that Parties take steps to guarantee compensation of victims. The means of guaranteeing compensation are left to the Parties, which are responsible for establishing the legal basis of compensation, the administrative framework and the operational arrangements for compensation schemes. In this connection paragraph 4 suggests setting up a compensation fund or introducing measures or programmes for social assistance to and social integration of victims that could be funded by assets of criminal origin.

199.   In deciding the compensation arrangements, Parties may use as a model the principles contained in the *European Convention on the Compensation of Victims of Violent Crimes* (ETS No.116), which is concerned with European-level harmonisation of the guiding principles on compensating victims of violent crime and with giving them binding force. European Union member States must also have regard to the *Council Directive of 29 April 2004 on compensation of crime victims*.

Article 16 – Repatriation and return of victims

200.   Article 16 is partly inspired by article 8 of the Palermo Protocol. It regards at the same time voluntary return as well as non voluntary return of victims of trafficking in human beings, though the drafters have specified that this return shall preferably be voluntary.

201.   Paragraph 1 of article 16 places an obligation on the Party which a victim is a national or in which the person had the right of permanent residence to facilitate and accept the return of the victim without undue or unreasonable delay. In this context it should be recalled article 13 paragraph 2 of the *Universal declaration of human rights* which provides for the right to return in its country, as well as article 3(2) of the Protocol n° 4 to the *Convention for the Protection of Human Rights and Fundamental Freedoms* which provides that "no one shall be deprived of the right to enter the territory of the State of which he is a national". Article 12(4) of the *International Covenant on Civil and Political Rights* also provides that "no one shall be arbitrarily deprives of the right to enter his own country", which includes the right to return for persons who, without being nationals of that country, had established their residence.

202.   The return of a victim of trafficking is not always without any risk. Therefore, the drafters wishes to precise in the text of the convention that the return of a victim "shall be with due regard for the rights, safety and dignity of that person". This applies to the Party which facilitates and accepts the return of the victim as well as, according to paragraph 2, to the Party which returns a victim to another State. Such rights include, in particular, the right not to be subjected to inhuman or degrading treatment, the right to the protection of private and family life and the protection of his/her identity. The return of a victim shall also take into account the status of any legal proceedings related to the fact that the person is a victim, in order not to affect the

rights that the victim could exercise in the course of the proceedings as well as the proceedings themselves.

203. The drafters considered that in this respect it was important to have in mind the jurisprudence of the European Court of Human Rights regarding article 3. Hence, in the case *Soering v United Kingdom* (7 July 1989, series A n° 161), in the context of extradition, the Court found that "such a decision may give rise to an issue under article 3 and hence engage the responsibility of that State under the convention, where substantial grounds have been shown for believing that the person concerned, if extradited, faces a real risk of being subjected to torture or to inhuman or degrading treatment or punishment". In the case *Cruz Varaz and others v Sweden* (20 March 1991, series A, n° 201) the court has decided that this principles apply also to deportation. In the case *D.v United Kingdom* (2 May 1997, compendium of judgments and decisions, 1997-III), she précised that the responsibility of States Parties is also engaged when the alleged ill treatments did not follow directly or indirectly from public authorities of the destination country.

204. Paragraphs 3 and 4 of this article deal with specific measures of international cooperation among the receiving Party and the Party of which the person is its national or had the right of permanent residence in its territory at the time of entry into the territory of the receiving Party. Hence, upon the request of the latter, the requested Party has an obligation of diligence to facilitate the return of the victim, by conducting checks in order to identify if the victim is one of its nationals or if the victim had the right of permanent residence on its territory, as well as, if these checks are positive, and if the victim no longer has the necessary documents, to deliver the travel documents or other authorisation as may be necessary to enable the victim to travel to and re-enter its territory.

205. Paragraph 5 obliges each Party to establish repatriation programmes by the adoption of legislative or other measures, aiming at avoiding re-victimisation. This provision is addressed to each Party, which is responsible for putting in place the measures provided for. At the same time, each Party should make its best efforts to favour the social reintegration of the victims. Regarding children, these programmes have to take into account their right to education and to establish measures in order to secure adequate care or receipt by the family or appropriate care structure.

206. Paragraph 6 provides that each Party shall adopt such legislative or other measures as may be necessary in order to make available to victims information on the services and organisations which could assist them upon their return. The list of these services is formulated in an exemplifying manner as they may vary according to each Party.

207. Paragraph 7 of article 16 includes in the context of repatriation and return the principle embodied in article 3 of the United Nations *Convention on the Rights of the Child*. When the authorities take a decision regarding the repatriation of a child victim, the best interests of the child must be the primary consideration. According to this provision, the authorities must undertake an assessment of the risks which could be generated by the return of the child to a State as well as on its security, before implementing any repatriation measure.

Article 17 – Gender equality

208. Trafficking in human beings, when it is carried out for the purposes of sexual exploitation, mainly concerns women, although women can be trafficked for other purposes. In this respect it should be recalled that to put an end to what was commonly known as "white slaving", two international conferences were held in Paris in 1902 and 1910. This work culminated in the signing of the *International Convention for the Suppression of the White Slave Traffic* (Paris, 4 May 1910), later supplemented by the *International Convention for the Suppression of the Traffic in Women and Children* (30 September 1921) and the *International Convention for the Suppression of the Traffic in Women of Full Age* (Geneva, 11 October 1933). *The Convention for the Suppression of the Traffic in Persons and the exploitation of the Prostitution of Others* (New York, 2 December 1949) cancelled and replaced, in parts, the provisions of the earlier international instruments.

209. The development of communications and the economic imbalances in the world have made trafficking in women, mainly for sexual exploitation purposes, more international than ever. There was first the "white slave traffic[16]", then trafficking from South to North and now there is trafficking in human beings from the more disadvantaged regions to the more prosperous regions, whatever their geographical location (but in particular to western Europe).

210.   The aim of Article 17 is not to avoid any discrimination on the grounds of sex on the enjoyment of measures to protect and promote the rights of victims which it is already contained in Article 3 of the Convention. The main aim of Article 17 is to draw the attention to the fact that women, according to existing data, are the main target group of trafficking in human beings and to the fact that women, who are susceptible to being victims, are often marginalised even before becoming victims of trafficking and find themselves victims of poverty and unemployment more often than men. Therefore, measures to protect and promote the rights of women victims of trafficking must take into account this double marginalisation, as women and as victims. In short, these measures must take into account the social reality to which they apply, mainly that society is composed of women and men and that their needs are not always the same.

211.   As mentioned above in relation to Article 1, equality between women and men means not only non-discrimination on grounds of sex but also positive measures to achieve equality between women and men. Equality must be promoted by supporting specific policies for women, who are more likely to be exposed to practices which qualify as torture or inhuman or degrading treatment (physical violence, rape, genital and sexual mutilation, trafficking for the purpose of sexual exploitation). As the Vienna Programme of Action, adopted by the World Conference on Human Rights (Vienna, 14-25 June 1993), and the Declaration on the Elimination of Violence against Women adopted by the General Assembly (December 1993) stated "member States were alarmed that opportunities for women to achieve legal, social, political and economic equality in society are limited, *inter alia*, by continuing and endemic violence against women (. . .)".

212.   For a long time gender equality in Europe was defined as giving women and men *de jure* equal rights. Nowadays, it is recognised that equality *de jure* does not automatically lead to equality *de facto*. It is true that the legal status of women has improved over the last 30 years in Europe, but effective equality is still far from being reality. Imbalances between women and men continue to influence all walks of life and it is becoming increasingly clear that new approaches, new strategies and new methods are needed to achieve gender equality. Gender mainstreaming is one of these strategies.

213.   The Council of Europe *Steering Committee for Equality between Women and Men (CDEG)*, in its 1998 report on *Gender mainstreaming: Conceptual framework, methodology, and presentation of good practices* agreed on the following definition:

Gender mainstreaming is the (re)organisation, improvement, development and evaluation of policy processes, so that a gender equality perspective is incorporated in all policies at all levels and at all stages, by the actors normally involved in policy-making.

214.   Following the adoption of this report by the CDEG, the Committee of Ministers adopted *Recommendation No. R (98) 14 of the Committee of Ministers to member States on gender mainstreaming* inviting them to draw inspiration from the CDEG's report and implement the strategy at national level. The Committee of Ministers also adopted a *Message to Steering Committees of the Council of Europe on gender mainstreaming*, encouraging them to use this strategy in their programmes of activities.

215.   Following these recommendations of the Committee of Ministers, Article 17 indicates that when developing, implementing and assessing measures contained in Chapter III, Parties to the Convention shall apply this strategy of gender mainstreaming which, as mentioned before, it is a strategy to reach the goal of gender equality.

Chapter IV – Substantive criminal law

216.   Chapter IV comprises nine articles. Articles 18, 19 and 20 are concerned with making certain acts criminal offences. This kind of harmonisation facilitates action

against crime at national and international level, for several reasons. Firstly, harmonisation of countries' domestic law is a way of avoiding a criminal preference for committing offences in a Party which previously had less strict rules. Secondly, it becomes possible to promote exchange of useful common data and experience. Shared definitions can also assist research and promote comparability of data at national and regional level, thus making it easier to gain an overall picture of crime. Lastly, international cooperation (in particular extradition and mutual legal assistance) is facilitated, for example as regards the rules on dual criminal liability.

217.   The offences referred to in these articles represent a minimum consensus which does not preclude adding to them in domestic law.

218.   The drafters likewise considered whether to introduce a provision on an offence of laundering the proceeds of trafficking in human beings. Trafficking in human beings is an extremely lucrative criminal activity and they recognised the importance of the question. Article 6 of the *Convention on Laundering, Search, Seizure and Confiscation of the Proceeds from Crime* (ETS No. 141) requires Parties to make laundering a criminal offence. However, Article 6(4) of that Convention allows Parties to restrict the offence to laundering the proceeds of certain underlying offences. As, at the time of drawing up the present convention, a Council of Europe committee of experts was drawing up a protocol to Convention No. 141 requiring that trafficking in human beings be treated as an offence underlying laundering, the drafters decided not to include such a provision in the Convention. They took the view that laundering was better dealt with in a cross-sector legal instrument – one dealing with cooperation in several areas of crime – such as Convention No.141 rather than a specific instrument like the present Convention.

219.   It should be noted that, in the case of European Union member States, Article 1 of the *Council Framework Decision on money laundering, the identification, tracing, freezing, seizing and confiscation of instrumentalities and the proceeds of crime* provides that member States are to take the necessary steps not to make or uphold reservations in respect of Article 6 of the 1990 convention as far as serious offences are concerned[17].

220.   This chapter likewise contains further provisions on criminalisation of acts dealt with in Articles 18 to 20. The provisions deal with attempt and aiding or abetting (Article 21), corporate liability (Article 22), sanctions and measures (Article 23), aggravating circumstances (Article 24) and previous convictions (Article 25).

221.   Article 26 deals with criminal non-liability of victims of trafficking.

Article 18 – Criminalisation of trafficking in human beings

222.   Article 18 seeks to have trafficking in human beings treated as a criminal offence. The obligation laid down in Article 18 is identical to that in Article 5 of the Palermo Protocol and is very similar to the one in Article 1 of the *Council Framework Decision of 19 July 2002 on combating trafficking in human beings*.

223.   Under Article 18 Parties are required to criminalise trafficking in human beings as defined in Article 4, whether by means of a single criminal offence or by combining several offences covering, as a minimum, all conduct capable of falling within the definition. It is thus necessary to use the definition in Article 4 in order to determine the ingredients of the offence or offences which Article 18 of the Convention requires Parties to establish.

224.   As explained above, trafficking in human beings is a combination of ingredients that has to be made a criminal offence, and not the ingredients taken in isolation. Thus, for example, the Convention does not create any obligation to make *abduction, deception, threats, forced labour, slavery or exploitation of the prostitution of others*, taken individually.

225.   In accordance with the definition, the offence laid down in Article 18 is constituted at an early stage: a person does not have to have been exploited for there to be trafficking in human beings. It is sufficient that they have been subjected to one

of the acts in the definition by one of the means in the definition for the purpose of exploitation. There is thus trafficking of human beings before any actual exploitation of the individual.

226. Under Article 4(b), where there is the threat or use of force or other forms of coercion or where there is abduction, fraud, deception, abuse of power or of a position of vulnerability, or giving or receiving of payments or benefits to achieve the consent of a person having control over another person, the consent of the victim does not alter the offenders' criminal liability.

227. Under Article 4(c) and (d), none of these means is necessary to the offence if a person aged under 18 is involved as a victim. Consequently, to prove trafficking in human beings the prosecuting authorities need establish only that there has been an act such as recruitment or transportation of a child for the purpose of exploitation.

228. The offence has to be committed intentionally for there to be criminal liability. The interpretation of the word "intentionally" is left to domestic law. It is nonetheless necessary to bear in mind that Article 4(a) provides for a specific element of intention in that the types of conduct listed in it are engaged in "for the purpose of exploitation". For the purposes of the Convention, therefore, there is trafficking in human beings only when that specific intention is present.

Article 19 – Criminalisation of the use of services of a victim

229. Under this provision Parties must consider making it a criminal offence to knowingly use the services of a victim of trafficking.

230. Several considerations prompted the drafters to include this provision in the Convention. The main one was the desire to discourage the demand for exploitable people that drives trafficking in human beings.

231. The provision targets the client whether of a victim of trafficking for sexual exploitation or of a victim of forced labour or services, slavery or practices similar to slavery, servitude or organ removal.

232. It could, for example, be made a criminal offence, under this provision, for the owner of a business to knowingly use trafficked workers made available by the trafficker. In such a case the business owner could not be treated as criminally liable under Article 18 – not having him/herself recruited the victims of the trafficking (the culprit is the trafficker) and not having him/herself used any of the means referred to in the definition of trafficking – but would be guilty of a criminal offence under Article 19. The client of a prostitute who knew full well that the prostitute had been trafficked could likewise be treated as having committed a criminal offence under Article 19, as could someone who knowingly used a trafficker's services to obtain an organ.

233. An important point is that Article 19 targets use of the services which are the subject of the exploitation dealt with in Article 4(a). Article 19 is intended not to prevent victims of trafficking from carrying on an occupation or hinder their social rehabilitation but to punish those, who by buying the services exploited, play a part in exploiting the victim. Similarly the provision is not concerned with using the services of a prostitute as such. That comes under Article 19 only if the prostitute is exploited in connection with trafficking of human beings – that is, when the components of the Article 4 definition are present together. As explained above, the Convention is concerned with exploitation of the prostitution of others and other forms of sexual exploitation only in the context of trafficking in human beings. It defines neither "exploitation of the prostitution of others" nor "other forms of sexual exploitation". It therefore does not affect the way in which Parties deal with prostitution in their domestic law.

234. To be liable for punishment under Article 19, a person using the services of a trafficking victim must do so "in the knowledge that the person is a victim of trafficking in human beings". In other words the user must be aware that the person is a trafficking victim and cannot be penalised if unaware of it. Proving knowledge may be a difficult matter for the prosecution authorities. Similar difficulty arises with various other types

of criminal law provision requiring evidence of some non-material ingredient of an offence. However, the difficulty of finding evidence is not necessarily a conclusive argument for not treating a given type of conduct as a criminal offence.

235.   The evidence problem is sometimes overcome – without injury to the principle of presumption of innocence – by inferring the perpetrator's intention from the factual circumstances. That approach has been expressly recommended in other international conventions. For instance, Article 6(2)(c) of the *Convention on Laundering, Search, Seizure and Confiscation of the Proceeds from Crime* (ETS No.141) states that "knowledge, intent or purpose required as an element of an offence set forth in that paragraph may be inferred from objective, factual circumstances". Similarly Article 6(2)(f), on criminalising the laundering of the proceeds of crime, of the *United Nations Convention against Transnational Organized Crime* states: "Knowledge, intent or purpose required as an element of an offence set forth in paragraph 1 of this article may be inferred from objective, factual circumstances".

236.   Aware of the value of a measure such as the one provided for in Article 19, while also acknowledging the problems of collecting evidence, it was considered that this provision should encourage Parties to adopt the measure, without making it a binding provision.

Article 20 – Criminalisation of conducts relating to travel or identity documents

237.   The purpose of Article 20 is to treat certain acts in relation to travel or identity documents as criminal offences when committed to allow trafficking of human beings. Such documents are important tools of transnational trafficking. False documents are often used to traffic victims through countries and into the countries where they will be exploited. Consequently identifying the channels through which false documents pass may bring to light criminal networks engaged in trafficking in human beings.

238.   Article 20(a) and (b) is modelled on Article 6(1) of the *Protocol against the Smuggling of Migrants by Land, Air and Sea, supplementing the United Nations Convention against Transnational Organized Crime*<. The two sub-paragraphs deal with making a fraudulent travel or identity document and procuring or providing such a document. However – unlike Article 6(1)(b)(ii) of the UN protocol, the Convention is not concerned with possession of a fraudulent document.

239.   The travel or identity documents with which Article 20 deals are official documents such as identity cards or passports. Article 3(c) of the *Protocol against the Smuggling of Migrants by Land, Air and Sea, supplementing the United Nations Convention against Transnational Organized Crime* defines "fraudulent travel or identity document" as: " . . . any travel or identity document:

(i)   That has been falsely made or altered in some material way by anyone other than a person or agency lawfully authorised to make or issue the travel or identity document on behalf of a State; or
(ii)   That has been improperly issued or obtained through misrepresentation, corruption or duress or in any other unlawful manner; or
(iii)   That is being used by a person other than the rightful holder".

240.   Clearly victims of trafficking in human beings may be given false documents by their traffickers. Like the Protocol against the Smuggling of Migrants by Land, Air and Sea (Article 5) the Convention does not make persons liable to prosecution for having been subjected to the types of conduct it deals with.

241.   Article 20(c) takes into account that traffickers very often take trafficking victims' travel and identity papers from them as a way of exerting pressure on them. The drafters felt that this could usefully be made a criminal offence in that it was relatively simple to prove and could thus be an effective law-enforcement tool against traffickers.

242.   Sub-paragraph c. – unlike sub-paragraphs a. and b. – does not refer to fraudulent documents. The reason for this is that the law of some countries gives no particular protection to fraudulent travel and identity documents, so that taking or destroying

them is not an offence. Some CAHTEH members took the view, however, that, in terms of pressure on and intimidation of the victim, the effect was exactly the same whether the documents taken from them were authentic or fraudulent. The drafters accordingly decided to delete the reference to fraudulence of documents so as to leave Parties free to decide whether to make it a criminal offence to retain, remove, conceal, damage or destroy a fraudulent travel or identity document.

Article 21 – Attempt and aiding or abetting

243. The purpose of this article is to establish additional offences relating to attempted commission of certain offences defined in the Convention and aiding or abetting commission of some.

244. Paragraph 1 requires Parties to establish as criminal offences aiding or abetting the commission of any of the offences under Articles 18 and 20 of the Convention. Liability arises for aiding or abetting where the person who commits a crime established in the Convention is aided by another person who also intends the crime to be committed. Treating the offence established by Article 19 (using a victim's services) as a form of aiding and abetting was ruled out as conceptually impossible.

245. With regard to paragraph 2, on attempt, it was likewise felt that treating the Article 19 offence as attempt gave rise to conceptual difficulties. Attempted commission of some of the acts dealt with in Article 20 was likewise considered to be too tenuous to be made an offence. Moreover some legal systems limit the offences for which attempt is punishable. Consequently Parties are required to make attempt an offence only in connection with the offences established in Articles 18 and 20(a).

246. As with all the offences established under the Convention, attempt and aiding or abetting must be intentional.

Article 22 – Corporate liability

247. Article 22 is consistent with the current legal trend towards recognising corporate liability. The intention is to make commercial companies, associations and similar legal entities ("legal persons") liable for criminal actions performed on their behalf by anyone in a leading position in them. Article 22 also contemplates liability where someone in a leading position fails to supervise or check on an employee or agent of the entity, thus enabling them to commit any of the offences established in the Convention.

248. Under paragraph 1 four conditions need to be met for liability to attach. First, one of the offences described in the Convention must have been committed. Second, the offence must have been committed for the entity's benefit. Third, a person in a leading position must have committed the offence (including aiding and abetting). The term "person who has a leading position" refers to someone who is organisationally senior, such as a director. Fourth, the person in a leading position must have acted on the basis of one of his or her powers (whether to represent the entity or take decisions or perform supervision), demonstrating that that person acted under his or her authority to incur liability of the entity. In short, paragraph 1 requires Parties to be able to impose liability on legal entities solely for offences committed by such persons in leading positions.

249. In addition, paragraph 2 requires Parties to be able to impose liability on a legal entity ("legal person") where the crime is committed not by the leading person described in paragraph 1 but by another person acting on the entity's authority, i.e. one of its employees or agents acting within their powers. The conditions that must be fulfilled before liability can attach are: 1) the offence was committed by an employee or agent of the legal entity; 2) the offence was committed for the entity's benefit; and 3) commission of the offence was made possible by the leading person's failure to supervise the employee or agent. In this context failure to supervise should be interpreted to include not taking appropriate and reasonable steps to prevent employees or agents from engaging in criminal activities on the entity's behalf. Such appropriate and reasonable steps could be determined by various factors, such as the type of business, its size, and the rules and good practices in force.

250. Liability under this article may be criminal, civil or administrative. It is open to

each Party to provide, according to its legal principles, for any or all of these forms of liability as long as the requirements of Article 23(2) are met, namely that the sanction on measure be "effective, proportionate and dissuasive" and include monetary sanctions.

251. Paragraph 4 makes it clear that corporate liability does not exclude individual liability. In a particular case there may be liability at several levels simultaneously – for example, liability of one of the legal entity's organs, liability of the legal entity as a whole and individual liability in connection with one or other.

Article 23 – Sanctions and measures

252. This article is closely linked to Articles 18 to 21, which define the various offences that should be made punishable under criminal law. In accordance with the obligations imposed by those articles, Article 23 requires Parties to match their action to the seriousness of the offences and lay down criminal penalties which are "effective, proportionate and dissuasive". In the case of an individual ("natural person") committing the offence established in accordance with Article 18, Parties must provide for prison sentences that can give rise to extradition. It should be noted that, under Article 2 of the *European Convention on Extradition* (ETS No. 24), extradition is to be granted in respect of offences punishable under the laws of the requesting and requested Parties by deprivation of liberty or under a detention order for a maximum period of at least one year or by a more severe penalty.

253. Legal entities whose liability is to be established under Article 22 are also to be liable to sanctions that are "effective, proportionate and dissuasive", which may be criminal, administrative or civil in character. Paragraph 2 requires Parties to provide for the possibility of imposing monetary sanctions on legal persons.

254. Paragraph 3 places a general obligation on Parties to adopt appropriate legal instruments enabling them to confiscate or otherwise deprive offenders (e.g. by so called "civil" confiscation) of the instrumentalities and proceeds of criminal offences established under Article 18 and Article 20(a) of the Convention. Paragraph 3 has to be read in the light of the *Convention on Laundering, Search, Seizure and Confiscation of the Proceeds from Crime* (ETS No. 141). That Convention is based on the idea that confiscating the proceeds of crime is an effective anti-crime weapon. As trafficking in human beings is nearly always engaged in for financial profit, measures depriving offenders of assets linked to or resulting from the offence are clearly needed in this field as well. As it is difficult to conceive of the types of act referred to in Articles 19 and 20(b) and (c) generating substantial proceeds or necessitating particular instrumentalities, paragraph 3 refers only to Articles 18 and 20(a).

255. Article 1 of the Laundering Convention defines "confiscation", "instrumentalities", "proceeds" and "property" as used in that article. By "confiscation" is meant a penalty or measure, ordered by a court following proceedings in relation to a criminal offence or criminal offences, resulting in final deprivation of property. "Instrumentalities" covers the whole range of things which may be used, or intended for use, in any manner, wholly or in part, to commit the criminal offences defined in Article 18 and Article 20(a). "Proceeds" means any economic advantage or financial saving from a criminal offence. It may consist of any "property" (see the interpretation of that term below). The wording of the paragraph takes into account that there may be differences of national law as regards the type of property which can be confiscated after an offence. It can be possible to confiscate items which are (direct) proceeds of the offence or other property of the offender which, though not directly acquired through the offence, is equivalent in value to its direct proceeds ("substitute assets"). "Property" must therefore be interpreted, in this context, as any property, corporeal or incorporeal, movable or immovable, and legal documents or instruments evidencing title to or interest in such property. It should be noted that Parties are not bound to provide for criminal-law confiscation of substitute assets since the words "or otherwise deprive" allow "civil" confiscation.

256. Paragraph 4 of Article 23 provides for closure of any establishment used to carry out trafficking in human beings. This measure is likewise provided for in paragraph 45 of *Recommendation No. R(2000)11 of the Committee of Ministers to member States* *on action against trafficking in human beings for the purpose of sexual exploitation* and, in the context of sexual exploitation of children, in paragraph 42 of *Recommendation (2001)16 of the Committee of Ministers to member States on the protection of children against sexual exploitation.* Paragraph 4 also allows the perpetrator to be banned, temporarily or permanently, from carrying on the activity in the course of which the offence was committed.

257.   The Convention provides for such measures so that action can be taken against establishments which might be used as cover for trafficking in human beings, such as matrimonial agencies, placement agencies, travel agencies, hotels or escort services. The measures are also intended to reduce the risk of further victims by closing premises on which trafficking victims are known to have been recruited or exploited (such as bars, hotels, restaurants or textile workshops) and banning people from carrying on activities which they used to engage in trafficking.

258.   This provision does not require Parties to provide for closure of establishments as a criminal penalty. Parties may, for example, use administrative closure measures. "Establishment" means any place in which any aspect of trafficking in human beings occurs. The provision applies to whoever has title to the establishment, be they a legal person or a natural person.

259.   To avoid penalising persons not involved in trafficking in human beings (for example, the owner of an establishment where trafficking in human beings has been carried on without his or her knowledge), the provision specifies that closures of establishments are "without prejudice to the rights of *bona fide* third parties".

Article 24 – Aggravating circumstances

260.   Article 24 requires Parties to ensure that certain circumstances (mentioned in sub-paragraphs a., b., c. and d) are regarded as aggravating circumstances in the determination of the penalty for offences established in accordance with Article 18 of this Convention.

261.   The first of the aggravating circumstances is where the trafficking endangered the victim's life deliberately or by gross negligence. This aggravating circumstance is likewise laid down in Article 3(2) of the *European Union Council Framework Decision of 19 July 2002 on combating trafficking in human beings.* The circumstance arises, for example, where the conditions in which trafficking victims are transported are so bad as to endanger their lives.

262.   The second aggravating circumstance is where the offence was committed against a child – that is, for the purposes of the Convention, against a person aged under 18.

263.   The third aggravating circumstance is where the trafficking was committed by a public official in the performance of his or her duties.

264.   The fourth aggravating circumstance is where the offence involved a criminal organisation. The Convention does not define "criminal organisation". In applying this provision, however, Parties may take their line from other international instruments which define the concept. For example, Article 2(a) of the *United Nations Convention against Transnational Organized Crime* defines "organised criminal group" as "a structured group of three or more persons, existing for a period of time and acting in concert with the aim of committing one or more serious crimes or offences established in accordance with this Convention, in order to obtain, directly or indirectly, a financial or other material benefit". *Recommendation Rec(2001)11 of the Committee of Ministers to member States concerning guiding principles on the fight against organised crime* and the *Joint Action of 21 December 1998 adopted by the Council of the European Union on the basis of Article K.3 of the Treaty on European Union, on making it a criminal offence to participate in a criminal organisation in the Member States of the European Union* give very similar definitions of "organised criminal group" and "criminal organisation".

Article 25 – Previous convictions

265.   Trafficking in human beings is often carried on transnationally by criminal organisations whose members may have been tried and convicted in more than one

country. At domestic level, many legal systems provide for a harsher penalty where someone has previous convictions. In general only conviction by a national court counts as a previous conviction resulting in a harsher penalty. Traditionally, previous convictions by foreign courts were discounted on the grounds that criminal law is a national matter and that there can be differences of national law, and because of a degree of suspicion of decisions by foreign courts.

266. Such arguments have less force today in that internationalisation of criminal-law standards – as a pendent to internationalisation of crime – is tending to harmonise different countries' law. In addition, in the space of a few decades, countries have adopted instruments such as the ECHR whose implementation has helped build a solid foundation of common guarantees that inspire greater confidence in the justice systems of all the participating States.

267. The principle of international recidivism is established in a number of inter-national legal instruments. Under Article 36(2)(iii) of the *New York Convention of 30 March 1961 on Narcotic Drugs*, for example, foreign convictions have to be taken into account for the purpose of establishing recidivism, subject to each Party's consti-tutional provisions, legal system and national law. Under Article 1 of the *Council Framework Decision of 6 December 2001 amending Framework Decision 2000/383/JHA on increasing protection by criminal penalties and other sanctions against counterfeiting in connection with the introduction of the euro*, European Union member States must recognise as establishing habitual criminality final decisions handed down in another member State for counterfeiting of currency.

268. The fact remains that at international level there is no standard concept of recidivism and the law of some countries does not have the concept at all. The fact that foreign convictions are not always brought to the courts' notice for sentencing purposes is an additional practical difficulty.

269. To meet these difficulties Article 25 provides for the possibility to take into account final sentences passed by another Party in assessing a sentence. To comply with the provision Parties may provide in their domestic law that previous convictions by foreign courts – like convictions by the domestic courts – are to result in a harsher penalty. They may also provide that, under their general powers to assess the individual's circumstances in setting the sentence, courts should take convictions into account.

270. This provision does not place any positive obligation on courts or prosecution services to take steps to find out whether persons being prosecuted have received final sentences from another Party's courts. It should nevertheless be noted that, under Article 13 of the *European Convention on Mutual Assistance in Criminal Matters* (ETS No.30), a Party's judicial authorities may request from another Party extracts from and information relating to judicial records, if needed in a criminal matter.

271. In order to stay within the framework of this Convention, the drafters of Article 25 had in mind only previous convictions based on the national implementation of Articles 18 and 20a. In cases of reciprocal criminalisation of offences covered under Article 19 and the remaining of 20, previous convictions based on these provisions can be taken into account.

Article 26 – Non-punishment provision

272. Article 26 constitutes an obligation to Parties to adopt and/or implement legislative measures providing for the possibility of not imposing penalties on victims, on the grounds indicated in the same article.

273. In particular, the requirement that victims have been compelled to be involved in unlawful activities shall be understood as comprising, at a minimum, victims that have been subject to any of the illicit means referred to in Article 4, when such involvement results from compulsion.

274. Each Party can comply with the obligation established in Article 26, by providing for a substantive criminal or procedural criminal law provision, or any other measure, allowing for the possibility of not punishing victims when the above mentioned legal requirements are met, in accordance with the basic principles of every national legal system

Chapter V – Investigation, prosecution and procedural law

275. This chapter contains provisions for adapting Parties' criminal procedure for two purposes: to protect victims of trafficking and assist prosecution of the traffickers.

276. The drafters considered whether to introduce into this chapter an article to facilitate collection of evidence by special investigative methods and on confiscating the proceeds of crime. As this matter is already dealt with in Article 4 of the *Convention on Laundering, Search, Seizure and Confiscation of the Proceeds from Crime* (ETS No.141) it was thought better not to have a similar provision in the Convention. The view was taken that any revision of the provisions of Convention No.141 dealing with the matter might result in inconsistencies with the present convention. It was therefore deemed preferable for the present specialised convention not to incorporate a provision from a convention like Convention No.141, intended to apply to a large number of offences and not to a particular area of crime.

Article 27 – *Ex parte* and *ex officio* applications

277. Article 27(1) is intended to enable the authorities to prosecute offences under the Convention without the necessity of a complaint from the victim. The aim is to avoid traffickers' subjecting victims to pressure and threats in attempts to deter them from complaining to the authorities. Some States require that crimes, which were committed out of their territories, must be the object of a claim by the victim or of a denunciation by a foreign authority in order to institute proceedings. The words « at least when the offence has been committed in whole or in part on its territory » enable these States not to modify their legislation on this matter.

278. Article 27(2) is modelled on Article 11(2) of the *European Union Council Framework Decision of 15 March 2001 on the standing of victims in criminal proceedings*. Its purpose is to make it easier for a victim to complain by allowing him or her to lodge the complaint with the competent authorities of his or her State of residence. If the competent authority with which the complaint has been lodged decides that it does not itself have jurisdiction in the matter, then it must forward the complaint without delay to the competent authority of the Party in whose territory the offence was committed. The obligation in Article 27(2) is an obligation merely to forward the complaint to that competent authority and does not place any obligation on the State of residence to institute an investigation or proceedings.

279. Under paragraph 3, each Party shall ensure to non-governmental organisations and other associations which aims at fighting trafficking in human beings or protection of human rights, the possibility to assist and/or support the victim with his or her consent during criminal proceedings concerning the offence of trafficking in human beings.

Article 28 – Protection of victims, witnesses and collaborators with the judicial authorities

280. In addition to victims, other persons may also be witness or intelligence sources in the fight against trafficking. But there are real risks to them in giving statements, acting as witnesses and/or exchanging intelligence.

281. Under Article 28 Parties must take the necessary measures to provide effective and appropriate protection to victims, collaborators with the judicial authorities, witnesses and members of such persons' families. The protection of family members is only "when necessary" in that the families themselves are sometimes involved in the trafficking. Similarly, the protection to collaborators with the judicial authorities is only « as appropriate ».

282. The question of protection for witnesses and persons collaborating with the judicial authorities was comprehensively dealt with by the Council of Europe in *Recommendation No. R(97)13 of the Committee of Ministers to member States concerning intimidation of witnesses and the rights of the defence*, adopted on 10 September 1997. The recommendation establishes a set of principles as guidance for national law on witness intimidation, whether the code of criminal procedure or out-of-court protection measures. The recommendation offers member States a list of measures which could help protect the interests both of witnesses and of the criminal justice system effectively, while guaranteeing the defence appropriate opportunities to exercise its rights in criminal proceedings. Some of these measures are referred to in Article 28(2).

283. The drafters of the Convention, basing themselves in particular on Recommendation No. R(97)13, interpreted the term "those who report the criminal offences established in accordance with Article 18 of this Convention or otherwise cooperate with the investigating or prosecuting authorities" as referring to persons who faced criminal charges or had been convicted of offences established in accordance with Article 18 of this Convention and who agreed to cooperate with criminal-justice authorities, in particular by giving information about trafficking offences in which they had taken part so that the offences could be investigated and prosecutions brought.

284. The word "witnesses" refers to persons who possess information relevant to criminal proceedings concerning human-trafficking offences under Article 18 of the Convention and it includes whistleblowers and informers.

285. Intimidation of witnesses, whether direct or indirect, may take different forms, but its purpose is nearly always to get rid of evidence against defendants so that they have to be acquitted.

286. The protection measures referred to in Article 28(2) are examples. The expression "effective and appropriate protection", as used in Article 28(1), refers to the need to adapt the level of protection to the threats to victims, collaborators with the judicial authorities, witnesses, informers and, when necessary, members of such persons' families. The measures required depend on the assessment of the risks such persons run. In some cases, for example, it will be sufficient to install preventive technical equipment, agree an alert procedure, record incoming and outgoing telephone calls or provide a confidential telephone number, a protected car registration number or a mobile phone for emergency calls. Other cases will require bodyguards or, in extreme circumstances, further-reaching witness-protection measures such as a change of identity, employment and place of residence. In addition, paragraph 3 provides that a child victim shall be afforded special protection measures taking into account the best interests of the child.

287. If protection measures are to be effective, it will very often also be necessary to ensure that the traffickers remain ignorant of these measures. Parties will then have to make sure that any information about the protection measures is safe from unauthorised access.

288. Regarding the period during which the protection measures have to be provided, the Convention aims in a non exhaustive manner the period of investigation and of the proceedings or the period following them. The period in which protection measures have to be provided depends on the threats upon the persons.

289. Protection measures should be granted only when the beneficiary persons have consented. Even though, in principle (in relation to the respect of the persons as well as for the effectiveness of the envisaged measures), the persons consent to the measures aimed at protecting them must be given, in some situations (for example some emergency situations in which the persons are in shock) protective measures must be taken even without the consent of the person to be protected.

290. Victims, witnesses, collaborators of justice and members of the families of these persons are not the only persons which could be subject to intimidation by traffickers. Often, the latter intimidate members of NGOs and other groups supporting victims of trafficking. For this reason, paragraph 4 provides that Parties must ensure appropriate protection to them, in particular physical protection, when necessary, ie. in case of serious intimidation.

291. Because trafficking in human beings is often international and some countries

are small, paragraph 5 encourages Parties to enter into agreements or arrangements with other countries so as to implement Article 28. They should make it possible to improve the protection afforded under Article 28. Thus, for example, an endangered person may need to be given a new place of residence. In a very small country, or if there is a risk of the person being easily found again by those threatening him or her, the only solution, to guarantee effective protection, is sometimes to arrange a new place of residence for them in another country. In addition, in some cases victims hesitate to bring legal proceedings in the receiving country because of the threat of reprisals by the traffickers against family members who remain in the country of origin. Effective protection of victims' families necessitates close cooperation between the country of origin and the receiving country, and this cooperation could also be brought about by bilateral or multilateral agreements as referred to in Article 28(5) between the countries concerned. In this connection, reference should be made to Recommendation No. R(97)13 of the Committee of Ministers to member States of the Council of Europe concerning the intimidation of witnesses and the rights of the defence.

Article 29 – Specialised authorities and coordinating bodies

292.   Under paragraph 1 Parties have to adopt the necessary measures to promote specialisation of persons or units in anti-human-trafficking action and victim protection. Each country must have anti-trafficking specialists. There must also be sufficient numbers of them and they need appropriate resources. The staff of specialised authorities and coordinating bodies should, as far as possible, be composed of women and men. The specialisation requirement does not mean, however, that there has to be specialisation at all levels of implementing the legislation. In particular it does not means that each prosecution service or police station has to have a specialist unit or an expert in trafficking in human beings. Equally the provision implies that, where necessary to counter trafficking effectively and protect victims, there must be units with responsibility for implementing the measures, and staff with adequate training.

293.   Specialisation can take various forms: countries can opt to have a number of specialist police officers, judges, prosecutors and administrative officers or to have agencies or units with special responsibility for various aspects of combating trafficking. Such agencies or units can be either special services set up to take charge of anti-trafficking action or they can be specialist units within existing bodies. Such units need to have the capability and the legal and material resources to at least receive and centralise all the information necessary for preventing trafficking and unmasking it. In addition, and independently of the role of other national bodies dealing with international cooperation, such specialist authorities could also act as partners to foreign anti-trafficking units.

294.   Such persons or units must have the necessary independence to be able to perform effectively. It should be noted that the independence of authorities specialising in anti-trafficking action should not be absolute: the police, the administrative authorities and the prosecution services should as far as possible integrate and co-ordinate their action. The degree of independence that specialist services need is the degree necessary for them to perform their functions satisfactorily.

295.   Trafficking in human beings is often a transnational criminal activity perpetrated by organised networks which, typically, are mobile and adapt rapidly to change (for example, changes in a country's law) by redeploying. For example, some trafficking organisations have been found to have a rotation system for the women they exploit, moving them from place to place so as to avert surveillance. To be effective, action against such organisations must be co-ordinated. Article 29(2) stresses the need to co-ordinate policy and action of public agencies responsible for combating trafficking in human beings. Such co-ordination may be performed by specially established co-ordination bodies.

296.   To combat trafficking effectively and protect its victims, it is essential that public authorities have proper training. Paragraph 3 specifies that such training must cover methods of preventing trafficking, prosecuting the traffickers and protecting the victims. To make agencies aware of the special features of trafficking victims' predicament, it is provided that training must also deal with human rights. Training

should also emphasise victims' needs, victim reception and appropriate treatment of victims by the criminal justice system.

297.   This training must be provided relevant officials engaged in prevention of and action to combat trafficking in human beings. "Relevant officials" covers persons and services liable to have contact with trafficking victims, such as law enforcement officials, immigration and social services, embassy or consulate staff, staff of border checkpoints and soldiers or police on international peace-keeping missions. The Convention seeks to take in the people likeliest to be faced with victims of trafficking in human beings, for it is extremely important that staff of the services concerned be trained in recognising signs of a trafficking offence and collecting and circulating information relevant to anti-trafficking action, and also that they be fully aware of their potential importance for identifying and helping victims.

298.   Paragraph 4 provides that Parties shall consider appointing national rapporteurs or other mechanisms for monitoring the anti-trafficking activities of State institutions and the implementation of national legislation requirements. The institution of a national rapporteur has been established in the Netherlands, where it is an independent institution, with its own personnel, whose mission is to ensure the monitoring of anti-trafficking activities. It has the power to investigate and make recommendations to persons and institutions concerned and makes an annual report to the Parliament containing its findings and recommendations.

Article 30 – Court proceedings

299.   Court proceedings in human-trafficking cases – as, often, with any serious form of crime – may have unfortunate consequences for the victims: a victim giving evidence against traffickers or claiming compensation for injury suffered is liable to come under pressure or be subjected to threats from criminal elements. Media coverage of cases is liable to worsen the problem by seriously invading victims' privacy, making it even more difficult for them to reintegrate socially.

300.   Article 30 therefore requires Parties to adapt their judicial procedure so as to protect victims' privacy and ensure their safety. The measures to be introduced under this provision are different from those provided for in Article 28. The measures provided for in Article 28 have to do with extra-judicial protection whereas the measures referred to in Article 30 are concerned with the procedural measures to be introduced.

301.   In criminal procedure there are values – defence rights on the one hand, victim and witness privacy and safety on the other – which converge and sometimes clash. In addition, procedure varies greatly from country to country: a method of victim and witness protection employed in one system may be incompatible with the basic principles of another.

302.   The drafters accordingly took the view that the only possible solution was for the Convention to contain a provision on court proceedings which was compulsory as to the objectives (safeguarding victims' private life and, if necessary, identity and guaranteeing victim safety and protection from intimidation) but which left it to the Parties to decide how to attain the objectives.

303.   The words "in accordance with the conditions defined by its internal law" underline that Parties are at liberty to employ whatever means they consider best to achieve the Convention's objectives (protecting victims' private life and, where appropriate, their identity, and ensuring victims' safety and protection from intimidation). In the case of child victims, the Convention states that Parties must take special care of their needs and ensure their rights to special protection measures as a child will usually be more vulnerable than an adult and likelier to be intimidated.

304.   The law in some countries provides for audiovisual recording of hearings of children and safeguarding such hearings by such means as: limiting the people allowed to attend the hearing and view the recording; allowing the child to request a break in recording at any time and making a full, word-for-word transcription of the hearing on request. Such recordings and written records may then be used in court instead of having the child appear in person.

305.   Some legal systems likewise allow children to appear before the court by

videoconference. The child is heard in a separate room, possibly in the presence of an expert and technicians. To limit as far as possible the psychological impact on the child of being in the same room as the accused or being with them by videoconference, the sightlines of both can be restricted so that the child cannot see the accused and/or *vice versa*. If, for instance, the child were to appear at the hearing, he or she could give evidence from behind a screen.

306. Article 30 states that measures must comply with Article 6 ECHR: care must be taken that measures maintain a balance between defence rights and the interests of victims and witnesses. In its *Doorson v. the Netherlands* judgment of 26 March 1996 (Reports of Judgments and Decisions, 1996-II, paragraph 70), the Court held:

"It is true that Article 6 does not explicitly require the interests of witnesses in general, and those of victims called upon to testify in particular, to be taken into consideration. However, their life, liberty or security of person may be at stake, as may interests coming generally within the ambit of Article 8 of the Convention. Such interests of witnesses and victims are in principle protected by other, substantive provisions of the Convention, which imply that Contracting States should organise their criminal proceedings in such a way that those interests are not unjustifiably imperilled. Against this background, principles of fair trial also require that in appropriate cases the interests of the defence are balanced against those of witnesses or victims called upon to testify."

307. The question of witness protection was dealt with in Recommendation No. R(97)13 of the Committee of Ministers to member States concerning intimidation of witnesses and the rights of the defence. European Court of Human Rights case-law should also be used as a guide to the various methods that can be used to protect victims' private life and ensure their safety. The following means can be used, in accordance with the ECHR and the Court's case-law, to achieve the objectives of Article 30:

Non-public hearings

308. The Court's case-law is that public deliberations are a fundamental principle of Article 6(1) (see *Axen v. the* FRG, 8 December 1983, Series A, No.72, paragraph 25). However the ECHR does not make that an absolute principle: Article 6(1) itself states that "the press and public may be excluded from all or part of the trial in the interests of morals . . . where the interests of juveniles or the protection of the private life of the parties so require, or to the extent strictly necessary in the opinion of the court in special circumstances where publicity would prejudice the interests of justice".

Audiovisual technology

309. Use of audio and video technology for taking evidence and conducting hearings may, as far as possible, avoid repetition of hearings and of some face-to-face contact, thus making court proceedings less traumatic. In recent years a number of countries have developed the use of technology in court proceedings, if necessary adapting the procedural rules on taking evidence and hearing victims. This is particularly the case with victims of sexual assault. However, this step has not yet been taken in all Council of Europe member States, in addition to which victims of trafficking are far from having the benefit of such protection measures, even in countries whose court system recognises the validity of these methods.

310. In addition to possible use of audio and video technology for avoiding traumatic or repeat testimony, it should be pointed out that victims can be influenced by the mental pressure of being brought face to face with the accused in the courtroom. To give them proper protection it is sometimes advisable to avoid their being present in court at the same time as the accused and to allow them to testify in another room. Whether it is the accused or the victim who is moved from the courtroom, video links or other video technology can be used to enable the parties to follow the proceedings. Such measures are necessary to spare them any unnecessary stress or disturbance when they give their evidence; the trial therefore has to be organised in such a way as to avoid, as far as possible, any unwelcome influence that might hinder establishing the truth or deter victims and witnesses from making statements.

311. Such methods are advocated in paragraph 6 of *Recommendation No. R(97)13 of the Committee of Ministers to member States on intimidation of witnesses and the rights of the defence*, Article A.8 of the *European Union Council Resolution of 23 November 1995 on the protection of witnesses in the fight against international organised crime*, and Article 24 of the United Nations *Convention against Transnational Organised Crime*.

Recordings of testimony

312. Under European Court of Human Rights case-law admissibility of evidence is primarily a matter for regulation by national law (see judgments in *Schenk v. Switzerland*, 12 July 1988, Series A, No.140 and *Doorson v. the Netherlands*, 26 March 1996, Reports 1996-II, among others) and as a general rule it is for the national courts to assess the evidence before them (see *Barberà, Messegué and Jabardo v. Spain* judgment of 6 December 1988, Series A, No.146). The Court's task under the ECHR is not to give a ruling as to whether statements of witnesses were properly admitted as evidence, but rather to ascertain whether the proceedings as a whole, including the way in which evidence was taken, were fair (see *inter alia* the aforementioned Doorson judgment).

313. The Court has ruled that the use as evidence of statements obtained at the stage of the police enquiry and the judicial investigation is not in itself inconsistent with paragraphs 3(d) and 1 of Article 6 provided that the rights of the defence have been respected. As a rule these rights require that the defendant has had an adequate and proper opportunity to challenge and question a witness against him either when the witness was making the statements or at a later stage in the proceedings. The lack of any confrontation deprives the defendant of a fair trial if the testimony obtained before the trial was the sole basis for convicting him, because of the inadmissible restriction on proper exercise of defence rights (*Saïdi v. France* judgment, 20 September 1993, Series A, No.261-C, paragraph 44, for instance). In addition, Article 6 does not confer an absolute right on the defendant to call witnesses. It is normally for the national courts to decide whether it is necessary or advisable to call a witness (*Bricmont v. Belgium* judgment of 7 July 1989, Series A, No.158).

314. In criminal cases concerning sexual violence the Court allows certain measures to be taken in order to protect the victim, provided that such measures are reconcilable with proper exercise of defence rights. To safeguard these the judicial authorities may require to take measures to compensate for the hindrances to the defence (*Doorson v. the Netherlands, ibid.*, and *P.S. v. Germany*, 20 December 2001).

315. In *S.N. v. Sweden* (judgment of 2 July 2002, Reports 2002-V) the Court held that the applicant could not be said to have been denied his rights under Article 6(3)(d) on the ground that he had been unable to examine or have examined the witnesses during the trial and appeal proceedings. "Having regard to the special features of criminal proceedings concerning sexual offences . . . this provision cannot be interpreted as requiring in all cases that questions be put directly by the accused or his or her defence counsel, through cross-examination or by other means".

316. The Court added: "The Court notes that the videotape of the first police interview was shown during the trial and appeal hearings and that the record of the second interview was read out before the District Court and the audiotape of that interview was played back before the Court of Appeal. In the circumstances of the case, these measures must be considered sufficient to have enabled the applicant to challenge M.'s statements and his credibility in the course of the criminal proceedings."

317. However, the Court made a point of reiterating, in that judgment, that evidence obtained from a witness under conditions in which the rights of the defence could not be secured to the extent normally required by the ECHR should be treated with extreme care.

Anonymous testimony

318. Anonymous testimony is an especially tricky issue in that protection for threatened persons must go hand in hand with protecting the rights of the defence. For instance the United Nations *Recommended Principles on Human Rights and Trafficking in human beings* state, in Guideline 6, that "There should be no public disclosure of the identity of trafficking victims and their privacy should be respected and protected to the extent possible, while taking into account the right of any accused person to a fair trial."

319. As regards the preliminary investigation stages, the European Commission of Human Rights held: "In the course of their duties police officers may well have occasion to take confidential information from persons with a legitimate interest in remaining anonymous; if such anonymity were to be refused and if these people were to be required to appear in court, much information needed if crimes are to be punished would never be brought to the knowledge of the prosecuting authorities" (Application No.8718/78, decision of 4 May 1979, D.R.16, p.200). The European Court of Human Rights has likewise stated several times that the ECHR does not preclude reliance, at the investigation stage of criminal proceedings, on sources such as anonymous informants but that subsequent use of anonymous statements as sufficient evidence to found a conviction is a different matter and can raise problems with regard to the Convention (see *Kostovski v. the Netherlands*, judgment of 20 November 1989, Series A, No.166, paragraph 44 and *Doorson v. the Netherlands*, judgment of 26 March 1996, Reports 1996-II, paragraph 69). Witness anonymity is therefore permissible at the investigation stage for reasons of expediency in so far as the information obtained in this way is to be used not as evidence but to enable evidence to be found.

320. As regards the trial stage, the above principle governing admissibility of evidence likewise applies. While all the evidence must normally be produced in the presence of the accused at a public hearing with a view to adversarial argument, there are exceptions to that principle, which, however, must not infringe the rights of the defence. As a general rule paragraphs 3(d) and 1 of Article 6 require that the defendant be given an adequate and proper opportunity to challenge and question a witness against him, either when he makes his statements or at a later stage (see *Ludi v. Switzerland*, judgment of 15 June 1992, Series A, No.238, paragraph 47). The Court takes the view that the use of anonymous statements to found a conviction is not in all circumstances incompatible with the ECHR (see, for example, *Doorson v. the Netherlands*, judgment of 26 March 1996, Reports 1996-II, paragraph 69 and *Van Mechelen and Others v. the Netherlands*, judgment of 23 April 1997, Reports 1997-III, paragraph 52).

321. For use of anonymous testimony to be permissible it has to be justified by the circumstances of the case (*Kok v. the Netherlands*, 4 July 2000, Reports 2000-VI, p.655). In *Doorson v. the Netherlands* the Court held: " . . . *principles of fair trial also require that in appropriate cases the interests of the defence are balanced against those of witnesses or victims called upon to testify.*" Threats to life, liberty or security potentially justify anonymity. It is for the national courts to examine the seriousness and well-foundedness of the reasons for witness anonymity in the particular case (see *Visser v. the Netherlands*, judgment of 14 February 2002, paragraph 47). In the *Doorson* judgment (paragraph 71) the Court nonetheless accepted use of anonymous testimony even in the absence of any specific threats made by the defendant. It held: " . . . the decision to maintain [the witnesses'] anonymity cannot be regarded as unreasonable per se. Regard must be had to the fact, as established by the domestic courts and not contested by the applicant [Mr Doorson], that drug dealers frequently resorted to threats or actual violence against persons who gave evidence against them".

322. Also, to safeguard the rights of the defence, the procedures followed by the judicial authorities must adequately counterbalance the handicaps under which the defence labours as a result of witness anonymity. As observed by the Court: "If the defence is unaware of the identity of the person it seeks to question, it may be deprived of the very particulars enabling it to demonstrate that he or she is prejudiced, hostile or unreliable. Testimony or other declarations inculpating an accused may well be designedly untruthful or simply erroneous and the defence will scarcely be able to bring this to light if it lacks the information permitting it to test the author's reliability or cast doubt on his credibility" (*Kostovski v. the Netherlands*, judgment of 20 November 1989, Series A, No.166, paragraphs 42 and 43). In its decision on the admissibility of Application No.43149/98 (*Kok v. the Netherlands*, 4 July 2000, Reports 2000-VI, p.657) the Court said that, to determine whether the arrangements for hearing an anonymous witness gave guarantees that adequately counterbalanced the difficulties caused to the defence, it was necessary to take into account to what extent the anonymous testimony had been crucial to the applicant's conviction. If the testimony was not crucial to conviction, then the defence is considerably less handicapped.

323. In *Doorson v. the Netherlands* the Court held that it was compatible with defence rights for an anonymous witness to have been questioned by an investigating judge who knew the witness's identity in the presence of the defendant's counsel (though not of the defendant), as the counsel had been able to ask the witness whatever questions he considered to be in the interests of the defence except questions which might have resulted in disclosure of the witness's identity (judgment of 26 March 1996, Reports 1996-II, paragraph 73). However the same interrogation approach, except that the defence counsel was not in the investigating judge's chamber and that communication was via a sound link, was held to be unsatisfactory in the circumstances of another case because it prevented the defence from observing the witness's demeanour. The Court held: "It has not been explained to the Court's satisfaction why it was necessary to resort to such extreme limitations on the right of the accused to have the evidence against them given in their presence, or why less far-reaching measures were not considered (*Van Mechelen and Others v. the Netherlands*, judgment of 23 April 1997, Reports 1997-III, paragraph 60). In this connection the Court referred to the possibilities of using make-up or disguise or preventing eye-contact. However it has since declared inadmissible a further application against the Netherlands in a case in which an anonymous witness had been heard in precisely the same way as in the Van Mechelen case, and so it can no longer be stated that Article 6, as interpreted by the Court, necessarily requires - regardless, in particular, of the decisiveness of the anonymous testimony for the conviction decision - that the defence be enabled to observe, face to face, the reactions of anonymous witnesses to its direct questions (*Kok v. the Netherlands*, decision of 4 July 2000, Reports 2000-VI).

324. A further requirement is that the trial and appeal courts have sufficient information to be able to form an opinion as to an anonymous witness's credibility. Such information must indicate how reliable and credible the witness is and why he or she wishes to remain anonymous (see *Van Mechelen and Others v. the Netherlands*, judgment of 23 April 1997, Reports 1997-III, paragraph 62 and *Doorson v. the Netherlands*, judgment of 26 March 1996, Reports 1996-II, paragraph 73).

325. Lastly, even when counterbalancing procedures are found to compensate sufficiently the handicaps under which the defence labours, a conviction should not be based either solely or to a decisive extent on anonymous statements (see *Doorson v. the Netherlands*, judgment of 26 March 1996, Reports 1996-II, paragraph 76).

326. The position, therefore, under the Court's case-law, is that the Court's task is not to give a ruling as to whether statements of witnesses were properly admitted as evidence, but rather to ascertain whether the proceedings as a whole, including the way in which evidence was taken, were fair. In addition, while evidence must, as a rule, be produced before the accused in a public hearing with a view to adversarial debate, there are some exceptions provided that measures are taken to counterbalance the handicaps to the defence.

Article 31 – Jurisdiction

327. This article lays down various requirements whereby Parties must establish jurisdiction over the offences with which the Convention is concerned.

328. Paragraph 1(a) is based on the territoriality principle. Each Party is required to punish the offences established under the Convention when they are committed on its territory. For example a Party in whose territory someone is recruited by one of the means and for one of the exploitation purposes referred to in Article 4(a) has jurisdiction to try the human-trafficking offence laid down in Article 18. The same applies to Parties through or in whose territory that person is transported.

329. Paragraph 1(b) and (c) is based on a variant of the territoriality principle. These

sub-paragraphs require each Party to establish jurisdiction over offences committed on ships flying its flag or aircraft registered under its laws. This obligation is already in force in the law of many countries, ships and aircraft being frequently considered to be an extension of a country's territory. This type of jurisdiction is extremely useful when the ship or aircraft is not located in the country's territory at the time of commission of the crime, as a result of which paragraph 1(a) would not be available as a basis for asserting jurisdiction. In the case of a crime committed on a ship or aircraft outside the territory of the flag or registry Party, it might be that without this rule there would not be any country able to exercise jurisdiction. In addition, if a crime is committed on board a ship or aircraft which is merely passing through the waters or airspace of another State, there may be significant practical impediments to the latter State's exercising its jurisdiction and it is therefore useful for the registry State to also have jurisdiction.

330.　Paragraph 1(d) is based on the nationality principle. The nationality theory is most frequently applied by countries with a civil-law tradition. Under it, nationals of a country are obliged to comply with its law even when they are outside its territory. Under sub-paragraph d., if one of its nationals commits an offence abroad, a Party is obliged to be able to prosecute if the conduct involved is also an offence under the law of the country where it took place or the conduct took place outside any country's territorial jurisdiction. Paragraph 1(d) also applies to stateless persons whose usual place of residence is in the Party's territory.

331.　Paragraph 1 litera e is based on the principle of passive personality. It is linked to the nationality of the victim and identifies particular interests of national victims to the general interests of the State. Hence, according to litera e, if a national is a victim of an offence abroad, the Partie has to have the possibility to start the related proceedings.

332.　Paragraph 2 allows Parties to enter reservations to the jurisdiction grounds laid down in paragraph 1 (d) and (e). However, no reservation is permitted with regard to establishment of jurisdiction under sub-paragraph a., b. or c. or with regard to the obligation to establish jurisdiction in cases falling under the principle of *aut dedere aut judicare* (extradite or prosecute) under paragraph 3, i.e. where a Party has refused to extradite an alleged offender on the basis of his or her nationality and the offender is present in its territory. Jurisdiction established on the basis of paragraph 3 is necessary to ensure that Parties that refuse to extradite a national have the legal ability to undertake investigations and proceedings domestically instead, if asked to do so by the Party that requested extradition under the terms of the relevant international instruments.

333.　In the case of trafficking in human beings, it will sometimes happen that more than one Party has jurisdiction over some or all of the participants in an offence. For example, a victim may be recruited in one country, then transported and harboured for exploitation in another. In order to avoid duplication of effort, unnecessary inconvenience to witnesses and competition between law-enforcement officers of the countries concerned, or to otherwise facilitate the efficiency or fairness of proceedings, the affected Parties are required to consult in order to determine the proper venue for prosecution. In some cases it will be most effective for them to choose a single venue for prosecution; in others it may be best for one country to prosecute some participants, while one or more other countries prosecute others. Either method is permitted under this paragraph. Finally, the obligation to consult is not absolute: consultation is to take place "where appropriate". Thus, for example, if one of the Parties knows that consultation is not necessary (e.g. it has received confirmation that the other Party is not planning to take action), or if a Party is of the view that consultation may impair its investigation or proceeding, it may delay or decline consultation.

334.　The bases of jurisdiction set out in paragraph 1 are not exclusive. Paragraph 5 of this article permits Parties to establish other types of criminal jurisdiction according to their domestic law. Thus, in matters of trafficking in human beings, some States exercise criminal jurisdiction whatever the place of the offence or nationality of the perpetrator.

Chapter VI – International cooperation and cooperation with civil society

335. Chapter VI sets out the provisions on international cooperation between Parties to the Convention. The provisions are not confined to judicial cooperation in criminal matters. They are also concerned with cooperation in trafficking prevention and in victim protection and assistance.

336. As regards judicial cooperation in the criminal sphere, the Council of Europe already has a substantial body of standard-setting instruments. Mention should be made here of the *European Convention on Extradition* (ETS No.24), the *European Convention on Mutual Assistance in Criminal Matters* (ETS No.30), the protocols to these (ETS Nos. 86, 98, 99 and 182) and the *Convention on Laundering, Search, Seizure and Confiscation of the Proceeds from Crime* (ETS No.141). These treaties are cross-sector instruments applying to a large number of offences, not to one particular type of crime.

337. The drafters opted not to reproduce in the present convention provisions identical to those in cross-sector instruments like the aforementioned ones. They took the view that the latter are better adapted to harmonisation of standards and can be revised to achieve better cooperation between Parties. They had no wish to set up a separate general system of mutual assistance which would take the place of other relevant instruments or arrangements. They took the view that it would be more convenient to have recourse generally to the arrangements set up under the mutual assistance and extradition treaties already in force, enabling mutual assistance and extradition specialists to use the instruments and arrangements they were familiar with and avoiding any confusions that might arise from setting up competing systems. This chapter therefore comprises only those provisions which offer special added value in relation to existing conventions. The Convention (Article 32) nonetheless requires Parties to cooperate to the widest extent possible under the existing instruments. As the Convention provides for a monitoring mechanism (Chapter VII), which, among other things, is to be responsible for monitoring the implementation of Article 32, the manner in which such cross-sector instruments are applied to combating trafficking in human beings is likewise to be monitored.

Article 32 – General principles and measures for international co-operation

338. Article 32 sets out the general principles which are to govern international co-operation.

339. Firstly the Parties must cooperate with one another "to the widest extent possible". This principle requires them to provide extensive cooperation to one another and to minimise impediments to the smooth and rapid flow of information and evidence internationally.

340. Then, Article 32 contains the general part of the obligation to cooperate: cooperation must include the prevention of and combat against trafficking in human beings (first indent), the protection of and assistance to victims (second indent) and to investigations or proceedings concerning criminal offences established in accordance with this Convention (third indent), ie. the offences established in conformity with Articles 18, 20 and 21. Taking into account the dual criminality principle, this cooperation can take place as regards the offence contained in Article 19 only between those Parties which criminalise in their internal law the acts contained in this article. The application of the dual criminality principle will limit this cooperation, as regards the offence established in Article 19 of this Convention, to the Parties having included such an offence in their internal law.

341. Lastly, cooperation is to be provided in accordance with relevant international and regional instruments, arrangements agreed on the basis of uniform or reciprocal legislation, and domestic law. The general principle is thus that the provisions of Chapter VI neither cancel nor replace the provisions of relevant *international* instruments. Reference to such instruments or arrangements is not confined to instruments in force at the time the present convention comes into force but also applies to any instruments adopted subsequently. In relation to this Convention, relevant general agreements and instruments should have precedence in matters of judicial cooperation.

342. Parties also have to cooperate with each other, in accordance with the provisions of this Convention. Thus, as regards international cooperation to protect and assist victims, Article 33 provides for special measures relating to endangered persons. Article 34(4) refers to transmission of any information necessary for providing the rights conferred by Articles 13, 14 and 16 of the Convention.

343.   As regards international cooperation in criminal matters for the purposes of investigations or proceedings, the general principle is that the provisions of Chapter VI neither cancel nor replace the provisions of relevant international or regional instruments on mutual legal assistance and extradition, reciprocal arrangements between Parties to such instruments and relevant provisions of domestic law concerning international cooperation. In this area, the relevant international instruments include the *European Convention on Extradition* (ETS No. 24), the *European Convention on Mutual Assistance in Criminal Matters* (ETS No. 30) and the protocols to these (ETS Nos. 86, 98, 99 and 182). In the case of European Union member States, the European arrest warrant introduced by the *Council Framework Decision of 13 June 2002 on the European arrest warrant and the surrender procedures between Member States* is likewise relevant. As regards cooperation to seize the proceeds of trafficking, and in particular to identify, locate, freeze and confiscate assets associated with trafficking in human beings and its resultant exploitation, the *Convention on Laundering, Search, Seizure and Confiscation of the Proceeds from Crime* (ETS No. 141) is relevant.

344.   It follows that international cooperation in criminal matters must continue to be granted under these instruments and other bilateral or multilateral treaties on extradition and mutual assistance applying to criminal matters.

345.   Mutual assistance may also stem from arrangements on the basis of uniform or reciprocal legislation. This concept exists in other Council of Europe conventions, in particular the *European Convention on Extradition* (ETS No. 24), which used it to allow Parties which had an extradition system based on "uniform laws", i.e. the Scandinavian countries, or Parties with a system based on reciprocity, i.e. Ireland and the United Kingdom, to regulate their mutual relations on the sole basis of that system. That provision had to be adopted because those countries did not regulate their relations in extradition matters on the basis of international agreements but did so or do so by agreeing to adopt uniform or reciprocal domestic laws.

Article 33 – Measures relating to endangered or missing persons

346.   This provision requires a Party to warn another Party if it has information that suggests that a person referred to in Article 28(1) (a victim, a witness, a person co-operating with the judicial authorities or a relative of such a person) is in immediate danger in the territory of the other Party. Such information might, for example, come from a victim reporting pressures or threats from traffickers against members of the victim's family in the country of origin. The Party receiving such information is required to take appropriate protection measures as provided for in Article 28.

Article 34 – Information

347.   Article 34 deals with supply of information. It has to do with all the types of cooperation dealt with in Chapter VI, i.e. not just international cooperation in criminal matters but also cooperation to prevent and combat trafficking in human beings and protect and assist victims.

348.   Article 34(1) places a duty on a requested Party to inform the requesting Party of the final result of action taken further to a request for international cooperation. It also requires that the requested Party inform the requesting Party promptly if circumstances make it impossible to meet the request or are liable to significantly delay meeting it.

349.   Paragraphs 2 and 3 are concerned with information spontaneously provided for purposes of cooperation in criminal matters. This article is derived from provisions in earlier Council of Europe instruments, such as Article 10 of the *Convention on the Laundering, Search, Seizure and Confiscation of the Proceeds from Crime* (ETS No. 141), Article 28 of the *Criminal Law Convention on Corruption* (ETS No. 173) and

Article 26 of the *Convention on Cybercrime* (ETS No. 185). It is an increasingly frequent occurrence for a Party to possess valuable information that it believes may assist another Party in a criminal investigation or proceedings, and which the Party conducting the investigation or proceedings is not aware exists. In such cases no request for mutual assistance will be forthcoming. This provision empowers the country in possession of the information to forward it to the other country without a prior request, within the limit of its internal law. The provision was thought useful because, under the laws of some countries, such a positive grant of legal authority is needed in order to provide assistance in the absence of a request. A Party is not under any obligation to spontaneously forward information to another Party; it has full discretion to do so in the light of the circumstances of the particular case. In addition, spontaneous disclosure of information does not preclude the disclosing Party from investigating or instituting proceedings in relation to the facts disclosed if it has jurisdiction.

350. Paragraph 3 addresses the fact that in some circumstances a Party will only forward information spontaneously if sensitive information is kept confidential or other conditions can be imposed on use of the information. In particular, confidentiality will be an important consideration in cases where important interests of the providing State could be endangered if the information is made public, e.g. where it is necessary not to reveal how the information was obtained or that a criminal group is being investigated. If advance enquiry reveals that the receiving Party cannot comply with a condition made by the providing Party (e.g. it cannot comply with a confidentiality condition because the information is needed as evidence at a public trial), the receiving Party must advise the providing Party, which then has the option of not providing the information. If the receiving Party agrees to the condition, however, it must honour it. It is foreseen that conditions imposed under this article would be consistent with those that a providing Party could impose further to a request for mutual assistance from the receiving Party.

351. To guarantee the effectiveness of the rights established in Articles 13, 14 and 16 of the Convention, paragraph 4 requires Parties to transmit without delay, subject to compliance with Article 11 of the Convention, requested information necessary for granting the entitlements conferred by these articles.

Article 35 – Cooperation with civil society

352. The strategic partnership referred to in this article, between national authorities and public officials and civil society means the setting up of co-operative frameworks through which State actors-fulfil their obligations under the Convention, by coordinating their efforts with civil society.

353. Such strategic partnerships may be achieved by regular dialogue through the establishment of Round-table discussions involving all actors. Practical implementation of the purposes of the convention may be formalised through, for instance, the conclusion of memoranda of understanding between national authorities and non-governmental organisations for providing protection and assistance to victims of trafficking.

Chapter VII – Monitoring mechanism

354. Chapter VII of the Convention contains provisions which aim at ensuring the effective implementation of the Convention by the Parties. The monitoring system foreseen by the Convention, which is undoubtedly one of its main strengths, has two pillars: on the one hand, the Group of Experts against trafficking in human beings (GRETA) is a technical body, composed of independent and highly qualified experts in the area of Human Rights, assistance and protection to victims and the fight against trafficking in human beings, with the task of adopting a report and conclusions on each Party's implementation of the Convention; on the other hand, there is a more political body, the Committee of the Parties, composed of the representatives in the Committee of Ministers of the Parties to the Convention and of representatives of Parties non-members of the Council of Europe, which may adopt recommendations, on the basis of the report and conclusions of GRETA, addressed to a Party concerning the measures to be taken to follow up GRETA's conclusions.

Article 36 – The Group of Experts against trafficking in human beings (GRETA)

355. As indicated above, GRETA is in charge of monitoring the implementation of the Convention by the Parties. It shall have a minimum of 10 and a maximum of 15 members.

356. Paragraph 2 of this Article stresses the need to ensure geographical and gender balance, as well as a multidisciplinary expertise, when appointing GRETA's members, who shall be nationals of States Parties to the Convention.

357. Paragraph 3 underlines the main competences of the experts sitting in GRETA, as well as the main criteria for their election, which can be summarised as follows: "independence and expertise".

358. Paragraph 4 indicates that the procedure for the election of the members of GRETA (but not the election of the members) shall be determined by the Committee of Ministers. This is understandable as the election procedure is an important part of the application of the Convention. Being a Council of Europe Convention, the drafters felt that such a function should still rest with the Committee of Ministers and the Parties themselves will then be in charge of electing the members of GRETA. Before deciding on the election procedure, the Committee of Ministers shall consult with and obtain the unanimous consent of all Parties. Such a requirement recognises that all Parties to the Convention should be able to determine such a procedure and are on an equal footing.

Article 37 – Committee of the Parties

359. Article 37 sets up the other pillar of this monitoring system, which is the more political "Committee of the Parties", composed as indicated above.

360. The Committee of the Parties will be convened the first time by the Secretary General of the Council of Europe, within a year from the entry into force of the Convention, in order to elect the members of GRETA. It will then meet at the request of a third of the Parties, of the Secretary General of the Council of Europe or of the President of GRETA.

361. The setting up of this body will ensure equal participation of all the Parties alike in the decision-making process and in the monitoring procedure of the Convention and will also strengthen cooperation between the Parties and between them and GRETA to ensure proper and effective implementation of the Convention.

362. The Rules of Procedure of the Committee of the Parties need to take due account of the specificities regarding the number of votes cast by the European Community in matters falling within its competence. It is also understood that the rules of procedure of the Committee of the Parties need to be drafted so as to make sure that the Parties to this Convention, including the European Community, will be effectively monitored under Article 38.7.

Article 38 – Procedure

363. Article 38 details the functioning of the monitoring procedure and the interaction between GRETA and the Committee of the Parties.

364. Paragraph 1 makes it clear that the evaluation procedure is divided in cycles and that GRETA will select the provisions the monitoring will concentrate upon. The idea is that GRETA will autonomously define at the beginning of each cycle the provisions for the monitoring procedure during the period concerned.

365. Paragraph 2 states that GRETA will determine the most appropriate means to carry out the evaluation. This may include a questionnaire or any other request for information. This paragraph makes it clear that the Party concerned must respond to GRETA's requests.

366. Paragraph 3 indicates that GRETA may also receive information by the civil society.

367. Paragraph 4 underlines that, subsidiarily, GRETA may organise country visits to get more information from the Party concerned. The drafters stressed that country visits should be a subsidiary mean and that they should be carried out only when necessary. These country visits have to be organised in cooperation with the competent authorities of the Party concerned and the "contact person" to be appointed by that Party.

368. Paragraphs 5 and 6 describe the drafting phase of both the report and the conclusions of GRETA. From these provisions, it is clear that GRETA has to carry out a dialogue with the Party concerned when preparing the report and the conclusions. It is through such a dialogue that the provisions of the Convention will be properly implemented. GRETA will publish its report and conclusions, together with any comments by the Party concerned. Such report and conclusions are sent at the same time to the Party concerned and the Committee of the Parties. This completes the task of GRETA with respect to that Party and the provision/s concerned. The reports of GRETA, which will be made public as far from their adoption, cannot be changed or modified by the Committee of the Parties.

369. Paragraph 7 deals with the role of the Committee of the Parties in the monitoring procedure. It indicates that the Committee of the Parties may adopt recommendations indicating the measures to be taken by the Party concerned to implement GRE-TA's conclusions, if necessary setting a date for submitting information on their implementation, and promoting cooperation to ensure the proper implementation of the Convention. This mechanism will ensure the respect of the independence of GRETA in its monitoring function, while introducing a "political" dimension into the dialogue between the Parties.

Chapter VIII – Relationship with other international instruments

Article 39 – Relationship with the *Protocol to Prevent, Suppress and Punish Trafficking in Persons,*
Especially Women and Children, supplementing the *United Nations Convention against Transnational Organized Crime*

370. The purpose of Article 39 is to clarify the relationship between the Convention and the Protocol to Prevent, Suppress and Punish Trafficking in Persons, Especially Women and Children, supplementing the United Nations Convention against Transnational Organized Crime.

371. Article 39 has two main objectives: (i) to make sure that the Convention does not interfere with rights and obligations deriving from provisions of the Palermo Protocol and (ii) to make clear that the Convention reinforces, as requested by the Committee of Ministers in the terms of reference it issued to the CAHTEH, the protection afforded by the United Nations instrument and develops the standards it lays down.

Article 40 – Relationship with other international instruments

372. Article 40 deals with the relationship between the Convention and other international instruments.

373. In accordance with the 1969 Vienna Convention on the Law of Treaties, Article 40 seeks to ensure that the Convention harmoniously co-exists with other treaties – whether multilateral or bilateral – or instruments dealing with matters which the Convention also covers. This is particularly important for international instruments which ensure greater protection and assistance for victims of trafficking. Indeed, this Convention intends to strengthen victims' protection and assistance and for this reason paragraph 1 of Article 40 aims at ensuring that this Convention does not prejudice the rights and obligations derived from other international instruments to which Parties to the present Convention are also Parties or shall become Parties and which contain provisions on matters governed by this Convention and which ensure greater protection and assistance for victims of trafficking. This provision clearly shows, once more, the overall aim of this Convention, which is to protect and promote the Human Rights of victims of trafficking and to ensure the highest level of protection to them.

374. Paragraph 2 states positively that Parties may conclude bilateral or multilateral

agreements – or any other international instrument – relating to the matters which the Convention governs. However, the wording makes clear that Parties are not allowed to conclude any agreement which derogates from the Convention.

375.   In relation to paragraph 3 of Article 40, upon the adoption of the Convention, the European Community and the member States of the European Union, made the following declaration:

> "The European Community/European Union and its Member States reaffirm that their objective in requesting the inclusion of a "disconnection clause" is to take account of the institutional structure of the Union when acceding to international conventions, in particular in case of transfer of sovereign powers from the Member States to the Community.
> This clause is not aimed at reducing the rights or increasing the obligations of a non-European Union party vis-à-vis the European Community/European Union and its Member States, inasmuch as the latter are also parties to this Convention.
> The disconnection clause is necessary for those parts of the convention which fall within the competence of the Community / Union, in order to indicate that European Union Member States cannot invoke and apply the rights and obligations deriving from the Convention directly among themselves (or between themselves and the European Community / Union). This does not detract from the fact that the Convention applies fully between the European Community/European Union and its Member States on the one hand, and the other Parties to the Convention, on the other; the Community and the European Union Members States will be bound by the Convention and will apply it like any party to the Convention, if necessary, through Community / Union legislation. They will thus guarantee the full respect of the Convention's provisions vis-à-vis non-European Union parties."

As an instrument made in connection with the conclusion of a treaty, within the meaning of Article 31 paragraph 2(b) of the Vienna Convention on the Law of Treaties, this declaration forms part of the "context" of this Convention.

376.   The European Community would be in a position to provide, for the sole purpose of transparency, necessary information about the division of competence between the Community and its Member States in the area covered by the present Convention, inasmuch as this does not lead to additional monitoring obligations placed on the Community.

377.   Under paragraph 3, the provisions of the Convention do not affect the rights, obligations and responsibilities of States and individuals under international law, including international humanitarian law and international human rights law. Thus, the exercise of fundamental rights should not be prevented on the pretext of taking action against trafficking in human beings. This paragraph is particularly concerned with the 1951 Convention and 1967 Protocol relating to the Status of Refugees. The fact of being a victim of trafficking in human beings cannot preclude the right to seek and enjoy asylum and Parties shall ensure that victims of trafficking have appropriate access to fair and efficient asylum procedures. Parties shall also take whatever steps are necessary to ensure full respect for the principle of *non-refoulement*.

Chapter IX – Amendments to the Convention

Article 41 – Amendments

378.   Amendments to the provisions of the Convention may be proposed by the Parties. They must be communicated to all Council of Europe member States, to any signatory, to any Party, to the European Community and any State invited to sign or accede to the Convention.

379.   The Group of Experts on Action against Trafficking in Human Beings (GRETA) will prepare an opinion on the proposed amendment which will be submitted to the Committee of Ministers. After considering the proposed amendment and the

GRETA opinion, the Committee of Ministers can adopt the amendment. Such amendments adopted by the Committee of Ministers must be forwarded to the Parties for acceptance. Before deciding on the amendment, the Committee of Ministers shall consult with and obtain the unanimous consent of all Parties. Such a requirement recognises that all Parties to the Convention should be able to participate in the decision-making process concerning amendments and are on an equal footing.

Chapter X – Final clauses

380.   With some exceptions, the provisions in this chapter are essentially based on the Model Final Clauses for Conventions and Agreements concluded within the Council of Europe, which the Committee of Ministers approved at the Deputies' 315th meeting, in February 1980. The Articles 42 to 47 either use the standard language of the model clauses or are based on long-standing treaty-making practice at the Council of Europe. It should be noted in this connection that the model clauses have been adopted as a non-binding set of provisions. As pointed out in the introduction to the model clauses, "these model final clauses are only intended to facilitate the task of committees of experts and avoid textual divergences which would not have any real justification. A model is in no way binding and different clauses may be adapted to fit particular cases."

Article 42 – Signature and entry into force

381.   The Convention is open for signature not only by Council of Europe member States but also the European Community and States not members of the Council of Europe (Canada, the Holy See, Japan, Mexico and the United States) which took part in drawing it up. Once the Convention enters into force, in accordance with paragraph 3, other non-member States not covered by this provision may be invited to accede to the Convention in accordance with Article 43 (1).

382.   Article 42 (3) sets the number of ratifications, acceptances or approvals required for the Convention's entry into force at 10. This figure reflects the belief that a significant group of States is needed to successfully set about addressing the challenge of trafficking in human beings. The number is not so high, however, as to unnecessarily delay the Convention's entry into force. In accordance with the treaty-making practice of the Organisation, of the ten initial States, at least eight must be Council of Europe members.

Article 43 – Accession to the Convention

383.   After consulting the Parties and obtaining their unanimous consent, the Committee of Ministers may invite any State not a Council of Europe member which did not participate in drawing up the Convention to accede to it. This decision requires the two-thirds majority provided for in Article 20.d of the Statute of the Council of Europe and the unanimous vote of the Parties to this Convention.

Article 44 – Territorial application

384.   Article 44 (1) specifies the territories to which the Convention applies. Here it should be pointed out that it would be incompatible with the object and purpose of the Convention for States Parties to exclude parts of their territory from application of the Convention without valid reason (such as the existence of different legal systems applying in matters dealt with in the Convention).

385.   Article 44 (2) is concerned with extension of application of the Convention to territories for whose international relations the Parties are responsible or on whose behalf they are authorised to give undertakings.

Article 45 – Reservations

386.   Article 45 specifies that the Parties may make use of the reservation as defined in Articles 31 paragraph 2. No other reservation may be made.

Article 46 – Denunciation

387. In accordance with the United Nations Vienna Convention on the Law of Treaties, Article 46 allows any Party to denounce the Convention.

Article 47 – Notifications

388. Article 47 lists the notifications that, as the depositary of the Convention, the Secretary General of the Council of Europe is required to make, and it also lays down the entities (States and the European Community) to receive such notifications.

1. 1991 Strasbourg seminar organised by the Steering Committee for Equality between Women and Men (CDEG) on *Action against traffic in women, considered as a violation of human rights and human dignity*.

2. Plan of action against traffic in women (doc. EG (96) 2) by Ms Michèle HIRSCH (Belgium).

3. For example, an International seminar on action against trafficking in human beings for the purpose of sexual exploitation: the role of NGOs (Strasbourg, June 1998) and a Workshop on good and bad practices with regard to media portrayal of women, with reference to trafficking in human beings for sexual exploitation (Strasbourg, September 1998).

4. Within the framework of the Stability Pact for South-Eastern Europe, the Council of Europe organised an International seminar on "Co-ordinated action against trafficking in human beings in South-Eastern Europe: towards a regional action plan". At the invitation of the Greek authorities, the seminar took place in Athens from 29 June to 1 July 2000. It was organised in partnership with the United Nations High Commissioner for Human Rights, OSCE/ODIHR and the International Organisation for Migration (IOM), and with the support of Japan.

5. A seminar on "Co-ordinated action against trafficking in human beings in the South Caucasus: towards a regional action plan" was held in Tbilisi on 6 and 7 November 2002.

6. EG-S-NT (2002) 9 Fin.

7. European Convention on the exercise of children's rights of 25 January 1996 (ETS No. 160) (in relation to the 1989 UN Convention on the rights of the child).

8. Convention on Laundering, Search, Seizure and Confiscation of Proceeds of Crime of 1990 (ETS No.141) (in relation to the UN Convention against Illicit Traffic in Narcotic Drugs and Psychotropic substances of 1988);
    Council of Europe Agreement of 1995 on illicit traffic by sea, implementing Article 17 of the United Nations Convention against illicit traffic in narcotic drugs and psychotropic substances of 1995 (ETS No. 156).

9. See, *inter alia*, UN Docs: CCPR/CO/79/LVA, dated 06/11/2003 and A/53/38/rev.1, respectively. See also, The Permanent Council of the OSCE's *Decision No 557: Action Plan to Combat Trafficking in Human Beings*, 24 July 2003 Budapest, *Declaration on Public Health and Trafficking in Human Beings* of 19-21 March 2003. See also, the second paragraph of the Preamble to the *SAARC Convention on Preventing and Combating Trafficking in Women and Children for Prostitution*.

10. *Eur. Court HR, X and Y v. The Netherlands judgement of 26 March 1985*, Series A no. 91, paragraph 23.

11. *Eur. Court HR, Young James and Websters v. The United Kingdom judgement of 13 August 1981*, Series A, no. 44, paragraph 49.

12. See, *inter alia*, the following judgments: *Eur. Court HR, A v. The United Kingdom judgement of 23 September 1998*, Reports of Judgments and Decisions 1998-VI, paragraph 22; *Eur. Court HR, Z and others v. The United Kingdom judgement of 10 May 2001*, Reports of Judgments and Decisions 2001-V, paragraph 73; *Eur. Court HR, M.C. v. Bulgaria judgement of 4 December 2003*; application no. 39272/98.

13. Article 3(2) of the United Nations Convention against Transnational Organized Crime states that "an offence is transnational if:

    (a) It is committed in more than one State;
    (b) It is committed in one State but a substantial part of its preparation, planning, direction or control takes place in another State;

(c)   It is committed in one State but involves an organized criminal group that engages in criminal activities in more than one State; or

(d)   It is committed in one State but has substantial effects in another State."

14   Article 2(a) of the United Nations Convention against Transnational Organized Crime states: "'Organized criminal group' shall mean a structured group of three or more persons, existing for a period of time and acting in concert with the aim of committing one or more serious crimes or offences established in accordance with this Convention, in order to obtain, directly or indirectly, a financial or other material benefit".

15   Principles, paragraph 1.

16   Agreement on the Suppression of the Traffic in Women and Children of 18 May 1904.

17   Such offences in any event include offences which are punishable by deprivation of liberty or a detention order for a maximum of more than one year or, as regards States which have a minimum threshold for offences in their legal system, offences punishable by deprivation of liberty or a detention order for a minimum of more than six months.

Appendix 6

DIRECTIVE 2011/36/EU OF THE EUROPEAN PARLIAMENT AND OF THE COUNCIL

of 5 April 2011

on preventing and combating trafficking in human beings and protecting its victims, and replacing Council Framework Decision 2002/629/JHA

THE EUROPEAN PARLIAMENT AND THE COUNCIL OF THE EUROPEAN UNION,

Having regard to the Treaty on the Functioning of the European Union, and in particular Article 82(2) and Article 83(1) thereof,

Having regard to the proposal from the European Commission,

Having regard to the opinion of the European Economic and Social Committee [1],

After consulting the Committee of the Regions,

After transmission of the draft legislative act to the national parliaments,

Acting in accordance with the ordinary legislative procedure [2],

Whereas:

(1) Trafficking in human beings is a serious crime, often committed within the framework of organised crime, a gross violation of fundamental rights and explicitly prohibited by the Charter of Fundamental Rights of the European Union. Preventing and combating trafficking in human beings is a priority for the Union and the Member States.

(2) This Directive is part of global action against trafficking in human beings, which includes action involving third countries as stated in the 'Action-oriented Paper on strengthening the Union external dimension on action against trafficking in human beings; Towards global EU action against trafficking in human beings' approved by the Council on 30 November 2009. In this context, action should be pursued in third countries of origin and transfer of victims, with a view to raising awareness, reducing vulnerability, supporting and assisting victims, fighting the root causes of trafficking and supporting those third countries in developing appropriate anti-trafficking legislation.

(3) This Directive recognises the gender-specific phenomenon of trafficking and that women and men are often trafficked for different purposes. For this reason, assistance and support measures should also be gender-specific where appropriate. The 'push' and 'pull' factors may be different depending on the sectors concerned, such as trafficking in human beings into the sex industry or for labour exploitation in, for example, construction work, the agricultural sector or domestic servitude.

(4) The Union is committed to the prevention of and fight against trafficking in human beings, and to the protection of the rights of trafficked persons. For this purpose, Council Framework Decision 2002/629/JHA of 19 July 2002 on combating trafficking in human beings [3], and an EU Plan on best practices, standards and procedures for combating and preventing trafficking in human beings [4] were adopted. Moreover, the Stockholm Programme — An open and secure Europe serving and protecting citizens [5], adopted by the European Council, gives a clear priority to the fight against trafficking in human beings. Other measures should be envisaged, such as support for the development of general common indicators of the Union for the identification of victims of trafficking, through the exchange of best practices between all the relevant actors, particularly public and private social services.

[1] Opinion of 21 October 2010 (not yet published in the Official Journal).

[2] Position of the European Parliament of 14 December 2010 (not yet published in the Official Journal) and decision of the Council of 21 March 2011.

[3] OJ L 203, 1.8.2002, p. 1.

[4] OJ C 311, 9.12.2005, p. 1.

[5] OJ C 115, 4.5.2010, p. 1.

(5) The law enforcement authorities of the Member States should continue to cooperate in order to strengthen the fight against trafficking in human beings. In this regard, close cross-border cooperation, including the sharing of information and the sharing of best practices, as well as a continued open dialogue between the police, judicial and financial authorities of the Member States, is essential. The coordination of investigations and prosecutions of cases of trafficking in human beings should be facilitated by enhanced cooperation with Europol and Eurojust, the setting-up of joint investigation teams, as well as by the implementation of Council Framework Decision 2009/948/JHA of 30 November 2009 on prevention and settlement of conflict of jurisdiction in criminal proceedings [1].

(6) Member States should encourage and work closely with civil society organisations, including recognised and active non-governmental organisations in this field working with trafficked persons, in particular in policy- making initiatives, information and awareness-raising campaigns, research and education programmes and in training, as well as in monitoring and evaluating the impact of anti-trafficking measures.

(7) This Directive adopts an integrated, holistic, and human rights approach to the fight against trafficking in human beings and when implementing it, Council Directive 2004/81/EC of 29 April 2004 on the residence permit issued to third-country nationals who are victims of trafficking in human beings or who have been the subject of an action to facilitate illegal immigration, who cooperate with the competent authorities [2] and Directive 2009/52/EC of the European Parliament and of the Council of 18 June 2009 providing for minimum standards on sanctions and measures against employers of illegally staying third-country nationals [3] should be taken into consideration. More rigorous prevention, prosecution and protection of victims' rights, are major objectives of this Directive. This Directive also adopts contextual understandings of the different forms of trafficking and aims at ensuring that each form is tackled by means of the most efficient measures.

(8) Children are more vulnerable than adults and therefore at greater risk of becoming victims of trafficking in human beings. In the application of this Directive, the child's best interests must be a primary consideration, in accordance with the Charter of Fundamental Rights of the European Union and the 1989 United Nations Convention on the Rights of the Child.

(9) The 2000 United Nations Protocol to Prevent, Suppress and Punish Trafficking in Persons, Especially Women and Children, supplementing the United Nations Convention against Transnational Organised Crime and the 2005 Council of Europe Convention on Action against Trafficking in Human Beings are crucial steps in the process of enhancing international cooperation against trafficking in human beings. It should be noted that the Council of Europe Convention contains an evaluation mechanism, composed of the Group of experts on action against trafficking in human beings (GRETA) and the Committee of the Parties. Coordination between international organisations with competence with regard to action against trafficking in human beings should be supported in order to avoid duplication of effort.

(10) This Directive is without prejudice to the principle of non-refoulement in accordance with the 1951 Convention relating to the Status of Refugees (Geneva Convention), and is in accordance with Article 4 and Article 19(2) of the Charter of Fundamental Rights of the European Union.

(11) In order to tackle recent developments in the phenomenon of trafficking in human beings, this Directive adopts a broader concept of what should be

considered trafficking in human beings than under Framework Decision 2002/629/JHA and therefore includes additional forms of exploitation. Within the context of this Directive, forced begging should be understood as a form of forced labour or services as defined in the 1930 ILO Convention No 29 concerning Forced or Compulsory Labour. Therefore, the exploitation of begging, including the use of a trafficked dependent person for begging, falls within the scope of the definition of trafficking in human beings only when all the elements of forced labour or services occur. In the light of the relevant case-law, the validity of any possible consent to perform such labour or services should be evaluated on a case-by-case basis. However, when a child is concerned, no possible consent should ever be considered valid. The expression 'exploitation of criminal activities' should be understood as the exploitation of a person to commit, inter alia, pick-pocketing, shop-lifting, drug trafficking and other similar activities which are subject to penalties and imply financial gain. The definition also covers trafficking in human beings for the purpose of the removal of organs, which constitutes a serious violation of human dignity and physical integrity, as well as, for instance, other behaviour such as illegal adoption or forced marriage in so far as they fulfil the constitutive elements of trafficking in human beings.

[1] OJ L 328, 15.12.2009, p. 42.
[2] OJ L 261, 6.8.2004, p. 19.
[3] OJ L 168, 30.6.2009, p. 24.

(12) The levels of penalties in this Directive reflect the growing concern among Member States regarding the development of the phenomenon of trafficking in human beings. For this reason this Directive uses as a basis levels 3 and 4 of the Council conclusions of 24- 25 April 2002 on the approach to apply regarding approximation of penalties. When the offence is committed in certain circumstances, for example against a particularly vulnerable victim, the penalty should be more severe. In the context of this Directive, particularly vulnerable persons should include at least all children. Other factors that could be taken into account when assessing the vulnerability of a victim include, for example, gender, pregnancy, state of health and disability. When the offence is particularly grave, for example when the life of the victim has been endangered or the offence has involved serious violence such as torture, forced drug/medication usage, rape or other serious forms of psychological, physical or sexual violence, or has otherwise caused particularly serious harm to the victim, this should also be reflected in a more severe penalty. When, under this Directive, a reference is made to surrender, such reference should be interpreted in accordance with Council Framework Decision 2002/584/JHA of 13 June 2002 on the European arrest warrant and the surrender procedures between Member States [1]. The gravity of the offence committed could be taken into account within the framework of the execution of the sentence.

(13) In combating trafficking in human beings, full use should be made of existing instruments on the seizure and confiscation of the proceeds of crime, such as the United Nations Convention against Transnational Organised Crime and the Protocols thereto, the 1990 Council of Europe Convention on Laundering, Search, Seizure and Confiscation of the Proceeds from Crime, Council Framework Decision 2001/500/JHA of 26 June 2001 on money laundering, the identification, tracing, freezing, seizing and confiscation of instrumentalities and the proceeds of crime [2], and Council Framework Decision 2005/212/JHA of 24 February 2005 on Confiscation of Crime-Related Proceeds, Instrumentalities and Property [3]. The use of seized and confiscated instrumentalities and the proceeds from the offences referred to in this Directive to support victims' assistance and protection, including compensation of victims and Union trans-border law enforcement counter-trafficking activities, should be encouraged.

(14) Victims of trafficking in human beings should, in accordance with the basic principles of the legal systems of the relevant Member States, be protected from prosecution or punishment for criminal activities such as the use of false documents, or offences under legislation on prostitution or immigration, that

they have been compelled to commit as a direct consequence of being subject to trafficking. The aim of such protection is to safeguard the human rights of victims, to avoid further victimisation and to encourage them to act as witnesses in criminal proceedings against the perpetrators. This safeguard should not exclude prosecution or punishment for offences that a person has voluntarily committed or participated in.

(15) To ensure the success of investigations and prosecutions of human trafficking offences, their initiation should not depend, in principle, on reporting or accusation by the victim. Where the nature of the act calls for it, prosecution should be allowed for a sufficient period of time after the victim has reached the age of majority. The length of the sufficient period of time for prosecution should be determined in accordance with respective national law. Law enforcement officials and prosecutors should be adequately trained, in particular with a view to enhancing international law enforcement and judicial cooperation. Those responsible for investigating and prosecuting such offences should also have access to the investigative tools used in organised crime or other serious crime cases. Such tools could include the interception of communications, covert surveillance including electronic surveillance, the monitoring of bank accounts and other financial investigations.

(16) In order to ensure effective prosecution of international criminal groups whose centre of activity is in a Member State and which carry out trafficking in human beings in third countries, jurisdiction should be established over the offence of trafficking in human beings where the offender is a national of that Member State, and the offence is committed outside the territory of that Member State. Similarly, jurisdiction could also be established where the offender is an habitual resident of a Member State, the victim is a national or an habitual resident of a Member State, or the offence is committed for the benefit of a legal person established in the territory of a Member State, and the offence is committed outside the territory of that Member State.

(17) While Directive 2004/81/EC provides for the issue of a residence permit to victims of trafficking in human beings who are third-country nationals, and Directive 2004/38/EC of the European Parliament and of the Council of 29 April 2004 on the rights of the citizens of the Union and their family members to move and reside freely within the territory of the Member States [4] regulates the exercise of the right to move and reside freely in the territory of the Member States by citizens of the Union and their families, including protection from expulsion, this Directive establishes specific protective measures for any victim of trafficking in human beings. Consequently, this Directive does not deal with the conditions of the residence of the victims of trafficking in human beings in the territory of the Member States.

(18) It is necessary for victims of trafficking in human beings to be able to exercise their rights effectively. Therefore assistance and support should be available to them before, during and for an appropriate time after criminal proceedings. Member States should provide for resources to support victim assistance, support and protection. The assistance and support provided should include at least a minimum set of measures that are necessary to enable the victim to recover and escape from their traffickers. The practical implementation of such measures should, on the basis of an individual assessment carried out in accordance with national procedures, take into account the circumstances, cultural context and needs of the person concerned. A person should be provided with assistance and support as soon as there is a reasonable-grounds indication for believing that he or she might have been trafficked and irrespective of his or her willingness to act as a witness. In cases where the victim does not reside lawfully in the Member State concerned, assistance and support should be provided unconditionally at least during the reflection period. If, after completion of the identification process or expiry of the reflection period, the victim is not considered eligible for a residence permit or does not otherwise have lawful residence in that Member State, or if the victim has left the territory of that Member State, the Member State concerned is not obliged to continue providing assistance and support to that person on the basis of this Directive. Where necessary, assistance and support should continue for an appropriate period after

the criminal proceedings have ended, for example if medical treatment is ongoing due to the severe physical or psychological consequences of the crime, or if the victim's safety is at risk due to the victim's statements in those criminal proceedings.

1   OJ L 190, 18.7.2002, p. 1.
2   OJ L 182, 5.7.2001, p. 1.
3   OJ L 68, 15.3.2005, p. 49.
4   OJ L 158, 30.4.2004, p. 77.

(19) Council Framework Decision 2001/220/JHA of 15 March 2001 on the standing of victims in criminal proceedings [1] establishes a set of victims' rights in criminal proceedings, including the right to protection and compensation. In addition, victims of trafficking in human beings should be given access without delay to legal counselling and, in accordance with the role of victims in the relevant justice systems, to legal representation, including for the purpose of claiming compensation. Such legal counselling and representation could also be provided by the competent authorities for the purpose of claiming compensation from the State. The purpose of legal counselling is to enable victims to be informed and receive advice about the various possibilities open to them. Legal counselling should be provided by a person having received appropriate legal training without necessarily being a lawyer. Legal counselling and, in accordance with the role of victims in the relevant justice systems, legal representation should be provided free of charge, at least when the victim does not have sufficient financial resources, in a manner consistent with the internal procedures of Member States. As child victims in particular are unlikely to have such resources, legal counselling and legal representation would in practice be free of charge for them. Furthermore, on the basis of an individual risk assessment carried out in accordance with national procedures, victims should be protected from retaliation, from intimidation, and from the risk of being re-trafficked.

(20) Victims of trafficking who have already suffered the abuse and degrading treatment which trafficking commonly entails, such as sexual exploitation, sexual abuse, rape, slavery-like practices or the removal of organs, should be protected from secondary victimisation and further trauma during the criminal proceedings. Unnecessary repetition of interviews during investigation, prosecution and trial should be avoided, for instance, where appropriate, through the production, as soon as possible in the proceedings, of video recordings of those interviews. To this end victims of trafficking should during criminal investigations and proceedings receive treatment that is appropriate to their individual needs. The assessment of their individual needs should take into consideration circumstances such as their age, whether they are pregnant, their health, a disability they may have and other personal circumstances, as well as the physical and psychological consequences of the criminal activity to which the victim was subjected. Whether and how the treatment is applied is to be decided in accordance with grounds defined by national law, rules of judicial discretion, practice and guidance, on a case-by-case basis.

(21) Assistance and support measures should be provided to victims on a consensual and informed basis. Victims should therefore be informed of the important aspects of those measures and they should not be imposed on the victims. A victim's refusal of assistance or support measures should not entail obligations for the competent authorities of the Member State concerned to provide the victim with alternative measures.

(22) In addition to measures available to all victims of trafficking in human beings, Member States should ensure that specific assistance, support and protective measures are available to child victims. Those measures should be provided in the best interests of the child and in accordance with the 1989 United Nations Convention on the Rights of the Child. Where the age of a person subject to trafficking is uncertain, and there are reasons to believe it is less than 18 years, that person should be presumed to be a child and receive immediate assistance, support and protection. Assistance and support measures for child

victims should focus on their physical and psycho-social recovery and on a durable solution for the person in question. Access to education would help children to be reintegrated into society. Given that child victims of trafficking are particularly vulnerable, additional protective measures should be available to protect them during interviews forming part of criminal investigations and proceedings.

(23) Particular attention should be paid to unaccompanied child victims of trafficking in human beings, as they need specific assistance and support due to their situation of particular vulnerability. From the moment an unaccompanied child victim of trafficking in human beings is identified and until a durable solution is found, Member States should apply reception measures appropriate to the needs of the child and should ensure that relevant procedural safeguards apply. The necessary measures should be taken to ensure that, where appropriate, a guardian and/or a representative are appointed in order to safeguard the minor's best interests. A decision on the future of each unaccompanied child victim should be taken within the shortest possible period of time with a view to finding durable solutions based on an individual assessment of the best interests of the child, which should be a primary consideration. A durable solution could be return and reintegration into the country of origin or the country of return, integration into the host society, granting of international protection status or granting of other status in accordance with national law of the Member States.

---

[1]   OJ L 82, 22.3.2001, p. 1.

(24) When, in accordance with this Directive, a guardian and/or a representative are to be appointed for a child, those roles may be performed by the same person or by a legal person, an institution or an authority.

(25) Member States should establish and/or strengthen policies to prevent trafficking in human beings, including measures to discourage and reduce the demand that fosters all forms of exploitation, and measures to reduce the risk of people becoming victims of trafficking in human beings, by means of research, including research into new forms of trafficking in human beings, information, awareness-raising, and education. In such initiatives, Member States should adopt a gender perspective and a child-rights approach. Officials likely to come into contact with victims or potential victims of trafficking in human beings should be adequately trained to identify and deal with such victims. That training obligation should be promoted for members of the following categories when they are likely to come into contact with victims: police officers, border guards, immigration officials, public prosecutors, lawyers, members of the judiciary and court officials, labour inspectors, social, child and health care personnel and consular staff, but could, depending on local circumstances, also involve other groups of public officials who are likely to encounter trafficking victims in their work.

(26) Directive 2009/52/EC provides for sanctions for employers of illegally staying third-country nationals who, while not having been charged with or convicted of trafficking in human beings, use work or services exacted from a person with the knowledge that that person is a victim of such trafficking. In addition, Member States should take into consideration the possibility of imposing sanctions on the users of any service exacted from a victim, with the knowledge that the person has been trafficked. Such further criminalisation could cover the behaviour of employers of legally staying third-country nationals and Union citizens, as well as buyers of sexual services from any trafficked person, irrespective of their nationality.

(27) National monitoring systems such as national rapporteurs or equivalent mechanisms should be established by Member States, in the way in which they consider appropriate according to their internal organisation, and taking into account the need for a minimum structure with identified tasks, in order to carry out assessments of trends in trafficking in human beings, gather statistics, measure the results of anti-trafficking actions, and regularly report. Such national rapporteurs or equivalent mechanisms are already constituted in an informal

Union Network established by the Council Conclusions on establishing an informal EU Network of National Rapporteurs or Equivalent Mechanisms on Trafficking in Human Beings of 4 June 2009. An anti- trafficking coordinator would take part in the work of that Network, which provides the Union and the Member States with objective, reliable, comparable and up-to-date strategic information in the field of trafficking in human beings and exchanges experience and best practices in the field of preventing and combating trafficking in human beings at Union level. The European Parliament should be entitled to participate in the joint activities of the national rapporteurs or equivalent mechanisms.

(28) In order to evaluate the results of anti-trafficking action, the Union should continue to develop its work on methodologies and data collection methods to produce comparable statistics.

(29) In the light of the Stockholm Programme and with a view to developing a consolidated Union strategy against trafficking in human beings aimed at further strengthening the commitment of, and efforts made, by the Union and the Member States to prevent and combat such trafficking, Member States should facilitate the tasks of an anti-trafficking coordinator, which may include for example improving coordination and coherence, avoiding duplication of effort, between Union institutions and agencies as well as between Member States and international actors, contributing to the development of existing or new Union policies and strategies relevant to the fight against trafficking in human beings or reporting to the Union institutions.

(30) This Directive aims to amend and expand the provisions of Framework Decision 2002/629/JHA. Since the amendments to be made are of substantial number and nature, the Framework Decision should in the interests of clarity be replaced in its entirety in relation to Member States participating in the adoption of this Directive.

(31) In accordance with point 34 of the Interinstitutional Agreement on better law-making [1], Member States are encouraged to draw up, for themselves and in the interest of the Union, their own tables which will, as far as possible, illustrate the correlation between this Directive and the transposition measures, and to make them public.

---

[1] OJ C 321, 31.12.2003, p. 1.

(32) Since the objective of this Directive, namely to fight against trafficking in human beings, cannot be sufficiently achieved by the Member States and can therefore, by reason of the scale and effects of the action be better achieved at Union level, the Union may adopt measures in accordance with the principle of subsidiarity as set out in Article 5 of the Treaty on European Union. In accordance with the principle of proportionality, as set out in that Article, this Directive does not go beyond what is necessary to achieve that objective.

(33) This Directive respects fundamental rights and observes the principles recognised in particular by the Charter of Fundamental Rights of the European Union and notably human dignity, the prohibition of slavery, forced labour and trafficking in human beings, the prohibition of torture and inhuman or degrading treatment or punishment, the rights of the child, the right to liberty and security, freedom of expression and information, the protection of personal data, the right to an effective remedy and to a fair trial and the principles of the legality and proportionality of criminal offences and penalties. In particular, this Directive seeks to ensure full respect for those rights and principles and must be implemented accordingly.

(34) In accordance with Article 3 of the Protocol on the position of the United Kingdom and Ireland in respect of the area of freedom, security and justice, annexed to the Treaty on European Union and the Treaty on the Functioning of the European Union, Ireland has notified its wish to take part in the adoption and application of this Directive.

(35) In accordance with Articles 1 and 2 of the Protocol on the position of the United Kingdom and Ireland in respect of the area of freedom, security and

justice, annexed to the Treaty on European Union and to the Treaty on the Functioning of the European Union, and without prejudice to Article 4 of that Protocol, the United Kingdom is not taking part in the adoption of this Directive and is not bound by it or subject to its application.

(36) In accordance with Articles 1 and 2 of the Protocol on the position of Denmark annexed to the Treaty on European Union and to the Treaty on the Functioning of the European Union, Denmark is not taking part in the adoption of this Directive and is not bound by it or subject to its application,

HAVE ADOPTED THIS DIRECTIVE:

Article 1 Subject matter

This Directive establishes minimum rules concerning the definition of criminal offences and sanctions in the area of trafficking in human beings. It also introduces common provisions, taking into account the gender perspective, to strengthen the prevention of this crime and the protection of the victims thereof.

Article 2 Offences concerning trafficking in human beings

1. Member States shall take the necessary measures to ensure that the following intentional acts are punishable:

The recruitment, transportation, transfer, harbouring or reception of persons, including the exchange or transfer of control over those persons, by means of the threat or use of force or other forms of coercion, of abduction, of fraud, of deception, of the abuse of power or of a position of vulnerability or of the giving or receiving of payments or benefits to achieve the consent of a person having control over another person, for the purpose of exploitation.

2. A position of vulnerability means a situation in which the person concerned has no real or acceptable alternative but to submit to the abuse involved.

3. Exploitation shall include, as a minimum, the exploitation of the prostitution of others or other forms of sexual exploitation, forced labour or services, including begging, slavery or practices similar to slavery, servitude, or the exploitation of criminal activities, or the removal of organs.

4. The consent of a victim of trafficking in human beings to the exploitation, whether intended or actual, shall be irrelevant where any of the means set forth in paragraph 1 has been used.

5. When the conduct referred to in paragraph 1 involves a child, it shall be a punishable offence of trafficking in human beings even if none of the means set forth in paragraph 1 has been used.

6. For the purpose of this Directive, 'child' shall mean any person below 18 years of age.

Article 3 Incitement, aiding and abetting, and attempt

Member States shall take the necessary measures to ensure that inciting, aiding and abetting or attempting to commit an offence referred to in Article 2 is punishable.

Article 4 Penalties

1. Member States shall take the necessary measures to ensure that an offence referred to in Article 2 is punishable by a maximum penalty of at least five years of imprisonment.

2. Member States shall take the necessary measures to ensure that an offence referred to in Article 2 is punishable by a maximum penalty of at least 10 years of imprisonment where that offence:

    (a)   was committed against a victim who was particularly vulnerable, which, in the context of this Directive, shall include at least child victims;

(b) was committed within the framework of a criminal organisation within the meaning of Council Framework Decision 2008/841/JHA of 24 October 2008 on the fight against organised crime [1];

(c) deliberately or by gross negligence endangered the life of the victim; or

(d) was committed by use of serious violence or has caused particularly serious harm to the victim.

3. Member States shall take the necessary measures to ensure that the fact that an offence referred to in Article 2 was committed by public officials in the performance of their duties is regarded as an aggravating circumstance.

4. Member States shall take the necessary measures to ensure that an offence referred to in Article 3 is punishable by effective, proportionate and dissuasive penalties, which may entail surrender.

[1] OJ L 300, 11.11.2008, p. 42.

Article 5 Liability of legal persons

1. Member States shall take the necessary measures to ensure that legal persons can be held liable for the offences referred to in Articles 2 and 3 committed for their benefit by any person, acting either individually or as part of an organ of the legal person, who has a leading position within the legal person, based on:

(a) a power of representation of the legal person;

(b) an authority to take decisions on behalf of the legal person; or

(c) an authority to exercise control within the legal person.

2. Member States shall also ensure that a legal person can be held liable where the lack of supervision or control, by a person referred to in paragraph 1, has made possible the commission of the offences referred to in Articles 2 and 3 for the benefit of that legal person by a person under its authority.

3. Liability of a legal person under paragraphs 1 and 2 shall not exclude criminal proceedings against natural persons who are perpetrators, inciters or accessories in the offences referred to in Articles 2 and 3.

4. For the purpose of this Directive, 'legal person' shall mean any entity having legal personality under the applicable law, except for States or public bodies in the exercise of State authority and for public international organisations.

Article 6 Sanctions on legal persons

Member States shall take the necessary measures to ensure that a legal person held liable pursuant to Article 5(1) or (2) is subject to effective, proportionate and dissuasive sanctions, which shall include criminal or non-criminal fines and may include other sanctions, such as:

(a) exclusion from entitlement to public benefits or aid;

(b) temporary or permanent disqualification from the practice of commercial activities;

(c) placing under judicial supervision;

(d) judicial winding-up;

(e) temporary or permanent closure of establishments which have been used for committing the offence.

Article 7 Seizure and confiscation

Member States shall take the necessary measures to ensure that their competent authorities are entitled to seize and confiscate instrumentalities and proceeds from the offences referred to in Articles 2 and 3.

Article 8 **Non-prosecution or non-application of penalties to the victim**
Member States shall, in accordance with the basic principles of their legal systems, take the necessary measures to ensure that competent national authorities are entitled not to prosecute or impose penalties on victims of trafficking in human beings for their involvement in criminal activities which they have been compelled to commit as a direct consequence of being subjected to any of the acts referred to in Article 2.

Article 9 **Investigation and prosecution**
1. Member States shall ensure that investigation into or prosecution of offences referred to in Articles 2 and 3 is not dependent on reporting or accusation by a victim and that criminal proceedings may continue even if the victim has withdrawn his or her statement.

2. Member States shall take the necessary measures to enable, where the nature of the act calls for it, the prosecution of an offence referred to in Articles 2 and 3 for a sufficient period of time after the victim has reached the age of majority.

3. Member States shall take the necessary measures to ensure that persons, units or services responsible for investigating or prosecuting the offences referred to in Articles 2 and 3 are trained accordingly.

4. Member States shall take the necessary measures to ensure that effective investigative tools, such as those which are used in organised crime or other serious crime cases are available to persons, units or services responsible for investigating or prosecuting the offences referred to in Articles 2 and 3.

Article 10 **Jurisdiction**
1. Member States shall take the necessary measures to establish their jurisdiction over the offences referred to in Articles 2 and 3 where:
    (a)   the offence is committed in whole or in part within their territory; or
    (b)   the offender is one of their nationals.

2. A Member State shall inform the Commission where it decides to establish further jurisdiction over the offences referred to in Articles 2 and 3 committed outside its territory, inter alia, where:
    (a)   the offence is committed against one of its nationals or a person who is an habitual resident in its territory;
    (b)   the offence is committed for the benefit of a legal person established in its territory; or
    (c)   the offender is an habitual resident in its territory.

3. For the prosecution of the offences referred to in Articles 2 and 3 committed outside the territory of the Member State concerned, each Member State shall, in those cases referred to in point (b) of paragraph 1, and may, in those cases referred to in paragraph 2, take the necessary measures to ensure that its jurisdiction is not subject to either of the following conditions:
    (a)   the acts are a criminal offence at the place where they were performed; or
    (b)   the prosecution can be initiated only following a report made by the victim in the place where the offence was committed, or a denunciation from the State of the place where the offence was committed.

Article 11 **Assistance and support for victims of trafficking in human beings**
1. Member States shall take the necessary measures to ensure that assistance and support are provided to victims before, during and for an appropriate period of time after the conclusion of criminal proceedings in order to enable them to exercise the rights set out in Framework Decision 2001/220/JHA, and in this Directive.

2. Member States shall take the necessary measures to ensure that a person is provided with assistance and support as soon as the competent authorities have a

reasonable-grounds indication for believing that the person might have been subjected to any of the offences referred to in Articles 2 and 3.

3. Member States shall take the necessary measures to ensure that assistance and support for a victim are not made conditional on the victim's willingness to cooperate in the criminal investigation, prosecution or trial, without prejudice to Directive 2004/81/EC or similar national rules.

4. Member States shall take the necessary measures to establish appropriate mechanisms aimed at the early identification of, assistance to and support for victims, in cooperation with relevant support organisations.

5. The assistance and support measures referred to in paragraphs 1 and 2 shall be provided on a consensual and informed basis, and shall include at least standards of living capable of ensuring victims' subsistence through measures such as the provision of appropriate and safe accommodation and material assistance, as well as necessary medical treatment including psychological assistance, counselling and information, and translation and interpretation services where appropriate.

6. The information referred to in paragraph 5 shall cover, where relevant, information on a reflection and recovery period pursuant to Directive 2004/81/EC, and information on the possibility of granting international protection pursuant to Council Directive 2004/83/EC of 29 April 2004 on minimum standards for the qualification and status of third country nationals or stateless persons as refugees or as persons who otherwise need international protection and the content of the protection granted [1] and Council Directive 2005/85/EC of 1 December 2005 on minimum standards on procedures in Member States for granting and withdrawing refugee status [2] or pursuant to other international instruments or other similar national rules.

7. Member States shall attend to victims with special needs, where those needs derive, in particular, from whether they are pregnant, their health, a disability, a mental or psychological disorder they have, or a serious form of psychological, physical or sexual violence they have suffered.

[1] OJ L 304, 30.9.2004, p. 12.

[2] OJ L 326, 13.12.2005, p. 13.

Article 12 **Protection of victims of trafficking in human beings in criminal investigation and proceedings**

1. The protection measures referred to in this Article shall apply in addition to the rights set out in Framework Decision 2001/220/JHA.

2. Member States shall ensure that victims of trafficking in human beings have access without delay to legal counselling, and, in accordance with the role of victims in the relevant justice system, to legal representation, including for the purpose of claiming compensation. Legal counselling and legal representation shall be free of charge where the victim does not have sufficient financial resources.

3. Member States shall ensure that victims of trafficking in human beings receive appropriate protection on the basis of an individual risk assessment, inter alia, by having access to witness protection programmes or other similar measures, if appropriate and in accordance with the grounds defined by national law or procedures.

4. Without prejudice to the rights of the defence, and according to an individual assessment by the competent authorities of the personal circumstances of the victim, Member States shall ensure that victims of trafficking in human beings receive specific treatment aimed at preventing secondary victimisation by avoiding, as far as possible and in accordance with the grounds defined by national law as well as with rules of judicial discretion, practice or guidance, the following:

    (a)   unnecessary repetition of interviews during investigation, prosecution or trial;

    (b)   visual contact between victims and defendants including during the giving of evidence such as interviews and cross-examination, by appropriate means including the use of appropriate communication technologies;

    (c)   the giving of evidence in open court; and

    (d)   unnecessary questioning concerning the victim's private life.

Article 13 General provisions on assistance, support and protection measures for child victims of trafficking in human beings

1. Child victims of trafficking in human beings shall be provided with assistance, support and protection. In the application of this Directive the child's best interests shall be a primary consideration.

2. Member States shall ensure that, where the age of a person subject to trafficking in human beings is uncertain and there are reasons to believe that the person is a child, that person is presumed to be a child in order to receive immediate access to assistance, support and protection in accordance with Articles 14 and 15.

Article 14 Assistance and support to child victims

1. Member States shall take the necessary measures to ensure that the specific actions to assist and support child victims of trafficking in human beings, in the short and long term, in their physical and psycho-social recovery, are undertaken following an individual assessment of the special circumstances of each particular child victim, taking due account of the child's views, needs and concerns with a view to finding a durable solution for the child. Within a reasonable time, Member States shall provide access to education for child victims and the children of victims who are given assistance and support in accordance with Article 11, in accordance with their national law.

2. Members States shall appoint a guardian or a representative for a child victim of trafficking in human beings from the moment the child is identified by the authorities where, by national law, the holders of parental responsibility are, as a result of a conflict of interest between them and the child victim, precluded from ensuring the child's best interest and/or from representing the child.

3. Member States shall take measures, where appropriate and possible, to provide assistance and support to the family of a child victim of trafficking in human beings when the family is in the territory of the Member States. In particular, Member States shall, where appropriate and possible, apply Article 4 of Framework Decision 2001/220/JHA to the family.

4. This Article shall apply without prejudice to Article 11.

Article 15 Protection of child victims of trafficking in human beings in criminal investigations and proceedings

1. Member States shall take the necessary measures to ensure that in criminal investigations and proceedings, in accordance with the role of victims in the relevant justice system, competent authorities appoint a representative for a child victim of trafficking in human beings where, by national law, the holders of parental responsibility are precluded from representing the child as a result of a conflict of interest between them and the child victim.

2. Member States shall, in accordance with the role of victims in the relevant justice system, ensure that child victims have access without delay to free legal counselling and to free legal representation, including for the purpose of claiming compensation, unless they have sufficient financial resources.

3. Without prejudice to the rights of the defence, Member States shall take the necessary measures to ensure that in criminal investigations and proceedings in respect of any of the offences referred to in Articles 2 and 3:

    (a)   interviews with the child victim take place without unjustified delay after the facts have been reported to the competent authorities;

(b)   interviews with the child victim take place, where necessary, in premises designed or adapted for that purpose;

(c)   interviews with the child victim are carried out, where necessary, by or through professionals trained for that purpose;

(d)   the same persons, if possible and where appropriate, conduct all the interviews with the child victim;

(e)   the number of interviews is as limited as possible and interviews are carried out only where strictly necessary for the purposes of criminal investigations and proceedings;

(f)   the child victim may be accompanied by a representative or, where appropriate, an adult of the child's choice, unless a reasoned decision has been made to the contrary in respect of that person.

4.   Member States shall take the necessary measures to ensure that in criminal investigations of any of the offences referred to in Articles 2 and 3 all interviews with a child victim or, where appropriate, with a child witness, may be video recorded and that such video recorded interviews may be used as evidence in criminal court proceedings, in accordance with the rules under their national law.

5.   Member States shall take the necessary measures to ensure that in criminal court proceedings relating to any of the offences referred to in Articles 2 and 3, it may be ordered that:

(a)   the hearing take place without the presence of the public; and

(b)   the child victim be heard in the courtroom without being present, in particular, through the use of appropriate communication technologies.

6.   This Article shall apply without prejudice to Article 12.

Article 16 Assistance, support and protection for unaccompanied child victims of trafficking in human beings

1.   Member States shall take the necessary measures to ensure that the specific actions to assist and support child victims of trafficking in human beings, as referred to in Article 14(1), take due account of the personal and special circumstances of the unaccompanied child victim.

2.   Member States shall take the necessary measures with a view to finding a durable solution based on an individual assessment of the best interests of the child.

3.   Member States shall take the necessary measures to ensure that, where appropriate, a guardian is appointed to unaccompanied child victims of trafficking in human beings.

4.   Member States shall take the necessary measures to ensure that, in criminal investigations and proceedings, in accordance with the role of victims in the relevant justice system, competent authorities appoint a representative where the child is unaccompanied or separated from its family.

5.   This Article shall apply without prejudice to Articles 14 and 15.

Article 17 Compensation to victims

Member States shall ensure that victims of trafficking in human beings have access to existing schemes of compensation to victims of violent crimes of intent.

Article 18 Prevention

1.   Member States shall take appropriate measures, such as education and training, to discourage and reduce the demand that fosters all forms of exploitation related to trafficking in human beings.

2.   Member States shall take appropriate action, including through the Internet, such as information and awareness- raising campaigns, research and education programmes, where appropriate in cooperation with relevant civil society organisations and other stakeholders, aimed at raising awareness and reducing the risk of people, especially children, becoming victims of trafficking in human beings.

3. Member States shall promote regular training for officials likely to come into contact with victims or potential victims of trafficking in human beings, including front-line police officers, aimed at enabling them to identify and deal with victims and potential victims of trafficking in human beings.

4. In order to make the preventing and combating of trafficking in human beings more effective by discouraging demand, Member States shall consider taking measures to establish as a criminal offence the use of services which are the objects of exploitation as referred to in Article 2, with the knowledge that the person is a victim of an offence referred to in Article 2.

Article 19 National rapporteurs or equivalent mechanisms

Member States shall take the necessary measures to establish national rapporteurs or equivalent mechanisms. The tasks of such mechanisms shall include the carrying out of assessments of trends in trafficking in human beings, the measuring of results of anti-trafficking actions, including the gathering of statistics in close cooperation with relevant civil society organisations active in this field, and reporting.

Article 20 Coordination of the Union strategy against trafficking in human beings

In order to contribute to a coordinated and consolidated Union strategy against trafficking in human beings, Member States shall facilitate the tasks of an anti-trafficking coordinator (ATC). In particular, Member States shall transmit to the ATC the information referred to in Article 19, on the basis of which the ATC shall contribute to reporting carried out by the Commission every two years on the progress made in the fight against trafficking in human beings.

Article 21 Replacement of Framework Decision 2002/629/JHA

Framework Decision 2002/629/JHA on combating trafficking in human beings is hereby replaced in relation to Member States participating in the adoption of this Directive, without prejudice to the obligations of the Member States relating to the time limit for transposition of the Framework Decision into national law.

In relation to Member States participating in the adoption of this Directive, references to the Framework Decision 2002/629/JHA shall be construed as references to this Directive.

Article 22 Transposition

1. Member States shall bring into force the laws, regulations and administrative provisions necessary to comply with this Directive by 6 April 2013.

2. Member States shall transmit to the Commission the text of the provisions transposing into their national law the obligations imposed on them under this Directive.

3. When Member States adopt these measures, they shall contain a reference to this Directive or shall be accompanied by such a reference on the occasion of their official publication. The methods of making such reference shall be laid down by the Member States.

Article 23 Reporting

1. The Commission shall, by 6 April 2015, submit a report to the European Parliament and the Council, assessing the extent to which the Member States have taken the necessary measures in order to comply with this Directive, including a description of action taken under Article 18(4), accompanied, if necessary, by legislative proposals.

2. The Commission shall, by 6 April 2016, submit a report to the European Parliament and the Council, assessing the impact of existing national law, establishing as a criminal offence the use of services which are the objects of exploitation of trafficking in human beings, on the prevention of trafficking in human beings, accompanied, if necessary, by adequate proposals.

Article 24 **Entry into force**

This Directive shall enter into force on the day of its publication in the *Official Journal of the European Union.*

Article 25 **Addressees**

This Directive is addressed to the Member States in accordance with the Treaties.

Done at Strasbourg,   5 April 2011.

For the European Parliament
The President
J. BUZEK
For the Council
The President
GYŐRI E.

Appendix 7

TRAFFICKING TOOLKIT: TACKLING TRAFFICKING

Contents

INTRODUCTION

Aims

This toolkit has two primary aims:

- To provide advice and support to frontline practitioners who may come into contact with victims and perpetrators of human trafficking; and,
- To help strategic bodies (Local Criminal Justice Boards, Crime and Disorder Partnerships, Local Strategic Partnerships, Safeguarding Children Boards and Strategic Health Authorities) identify how tackling human trafficking can help meet local priorities.

The topics covered include:

- Defining human trafficking and legislation.
- Combating human trafficking: a national and local priority.
- Developing local anti-trafficking strategies.
- The role of the National Referral Mechanism/Identifying and referring victims into support.
- Protecting and supporting victims.
- Agency specific guidance.
- Risk management, confidentiality and data sharing.

TACKLING TRAFFICKING

What is human trafficking?

Definition

Putting it simply human trafficking is the recruitment, movement and receipt of a person, with deception or coercion, into a situation of exploitation.

The Palermo Protocol defines the trafficking in human beings as:

> "the recruitment, transportation, transfer, harbouring or receipt of persons, by means of the threat or use of force or other forms of coercion, of abduction, of fraud, of deception, of the abuse of power or of a position of vulnerability or of the giving or receiving of payments or benefits to achieve the consent of a person having control over another person, for the purpose of exploitation. Exploitation shall include, at a minimum, the exploitation or the prostitution of others or other forms of sexual exploitation, forced labour or services, slavery or practices similar to slavery, servitude or the removal of organs."

For practical purposes it is important to understand the difference between trafficking and smuggling.

Nature of the crime:

- Smuggling is primarily a crime against the State (*no victim*);
- Trafficking is primarily a crime against the individual (*victim*).

Nature of the relationship:

- Smuggling: The smuggler provides a service to the migrant, ie transportation (consent);
- Trafficking: A person is exploited by the trafficker as a commodity.

Length of relationship:

- Smuggling: Usually the relationship between migrant and smuggler is a voluntary, short-term one – coming to an end on the migrant's arrival in the destination country;
- Trafficking: Involves a longer-term exploitative *relationship* with the trafficker or trafficking network.

Nature of profit:

- Smuggling: The revenue from smuggling comes from a one-off payment by the migrant;
- Trafficking: The revenue from trafficking is ongoing, coming from the ongoing appropriation of the benefits of the person's labour/exploitation.

Borders:

- Smuggling is always across a border;
- Trafficking may be cross-border but can also be internal (within one country).

Intelligence suggests that, in the UK, the four main types of trafficking are:

Sexual exploitation

The forcible or deceptive recruitment of women, men and children, for the purposes of forced prostitution or sexual exploitation:

- Home Office analysis estimates that at any one time in 2003 there were up to 4,000 women who had been trafficked for sexual exploitation in the UK. Human trafficking is the world's third most profitable criminal enterprise. The exploitation of 4,000 women in the UK would generate profits of about £275 million;
- Data collected in the UK indicates that trafficked persons identified in this country are predominantly young women between the ages of 16-30;
- Certain factors may make individuals more susceptible to trafficking eg previous experience of violence, poverty and unemployment;
- Trafficked people have very different experiences while in the trafficking situation. Some are held captive, unremittingly assaulted and horribly violated. Others are less abused physically, but are psychologically tormented, and live in fear of harm to themselves and their family members.

Labour trafficking

Persons who are trafficked into exploitative labour situations (eg sweatshops, agriculture, construction, and into illicit activities) can be sold and resold. Persons are exploited and deprived of the most basic human rights. The European Court of Human Rights has interpreted *forced labour* as comprising two elements – involuntariness and an unjustifiable or oppressive character. Subsequent case-law adopts as a starting point the International Labour Organisation (ILO) definition:

"All work or service which is exacted from any person under the menace of any penalty and for which the person has not offered himself voluntarily."

- According to ILO data, more than 2.4 million people are victims of forced labour, 1.1 million of them as a result of human trafficking worldwide;
- Women and children are particularly vulnerable to abuse, but men are likewise affected, particularly in sectors such as construction. ILO data indicates approximately 56% of those trafficked into exploitative labour are women and girls, while 44% are men and boys[1];
- Many victims experience violence and coercion, such as physical and sexual violence, debt bondage and retention of identity documents; are forced to be excessively dependent on employers or third parties and are exposed to excessive working hours and sub-standard working and living conditions.

Domestic servitude

Employment in private homes where victims are ill treated, humiliated and subjected to exhausting working hours and other exploitation. Domestic servitude is a form of trafficking for labour exploitation.

- Many trafficked domestic workers do not speak English;
- Many trafficked domestic workers may never, or rarely, leave the house for social reasons. A victim may have no private space, or proper sleeping space;
- Some trafficked domestic workers also experience sexual exploitation, or other forms of multiple exploitation. A person who is identified as having experienced multiple forms of exploitation in a trafficking situation will be provided with services and support to meet the complex needs that will arise from their individual experience.

Child trafficking

Any child moved into a situation of exploitation, or for the purposes of exploitation, is considered trafficked whether or not they have been forced or deceived.

- Taking into account studies carried out by the Child Exploitation and Online Protection Centre (CEOP) and End Child Prostitution, Child Pornography and the Trafficking of Children (ECPAT UK) into child trafficking in 2007 and a subsequent strategic threat assessment by CEOP, it is estimated there are around 360 victims of child trafficking in the UK annually;
- Child trafficking is a form of child abuse. Children are known to be trafficked for the purpose of sexual exploitation and also to be engaged in criminal activities for the benefit of organised crime gangs;
- Children are also trafficked to become involved in sexual exploitation through prostitution, illegal adoption, under-age forced marriage, benefit fraud and child labour;
- Child trafficking works through personal and family networks, as well as through highly-organised international criminal networks.

Children can be trafficked for the purpose of:

- sexual exploitation (eg child prostitution, child abuse acts and images);
- domestic servitude (eg domestic chores, looking after young children);
- labour exploitation (eg working in restaurants, building sites, cleaning);
- enforced criminally (eg cannabis cultivation, street theft, drug dealing and trafficking;
- benefit fraud;
- Illegal adoption; or,
- servile and underage marriage.

Even though a child may have been trafficked for a purpose other than sexual exploitation, they become highly vulnerable to physical and sexual abuse once they have been trafficked. The use of trafficking for exploitative labour is often hidden within local communities and can be difficult to identify without the support of communities.

Techniques used by traffickers

A range and variety of forms of deception and coercion techniques are used by traffickers. These commonly involve:

- Debt bondage – where the trafficked person, or their family, owes the trafficker money for arranging the transport and employment and the person is not released from the situation once the debt has been paid;
- Bringing the individual to the UK under the pretence of working in a legitimate profession, whilst knowing that in reality they will be working in a different and often illegitimate trade;
- Bringing the individual to work in the UK under very different circumstances than were agreed with them before arrival into the UK (including salary, working hours, profession etc);
- Forcing individuals to work in situations which they would not undertake voluntarily;
- Removal of documentation – namely passport, identification and immigration papers;
- Limitations on personal freedom and control of movement;
- Threats to victims and/or their families; and,
- Physical, sexual and emotional abuse.

Children and young people may be recruited into trafficking in the same ways as adults. Often children, as adults, will be seeking to escape poverty, without appreciating the risks to which they are exposed. However some children are abducted or kidnapped, although most children are trapped in subversive ways. There are also specific elements that apply in the case of children relating to the contributing role played by their parents.

As a result the child may have been deliberately *sold* to the trafficker by a family member, either as a matter of simple profit or removal of an uneconomic family burden, or both. The child may or may not know the planned outcome, but the family member conducting the sale will be aware or simply reckless as to the planned exploitation.

In many situations, parents part with their children believing that they will be offered a better life or opportunities in the place they are being taken to. Parents may also be deceived into believing that their children will have a better life elsewhere.

The Trafficking of UK Nationals

This is the movement of persons of UK citizenship within the UK for the purpose of exploitation.

The UK Human Trafficking Centre (UKHTC) is taking a lead role in alerting police forces about children, mainly girls, being groomed into sexual exploitation, and wehere they are moved around within the UK.

The indicators detailed in guidance documents (eg Safeguarding Children who may have Trafficked) should not be read as a definitive list and professionals should be aware of any other unusual factors that may suggest a child might have been trafficked. They are intended as a guide, which should be included in a wider assessment of the young person's circumstances.

It is also important to note that trafficked children might not show obvious signs of distress or abuse, and this makes identifying children who may have been trafficked difficult. Some children are unaware that they have been trafficked, while others may actively participate in hiding that they have been trafficked.

Prevalence

It is difficult to provide reliable figures about the scale and extent of human trafficking as it is often covert and deceptive. This is an issue that is shared with our international colleagues.

The UKHTC has a dedicated data collection and intelligence co-ordination role, working closely with other agencies. The UKHTC is currently analysing in more detail the intelligence outcomes of Operation Pentameter 2 (a multi-agency operation aimed at combating trafficking for sexual exploitation mounted in 2007/8) to help inform a more up to date picture of the nature of trafficking for sexual exploitation.

This will contribute to an updated estimate on the nature and scale of trafficking by the end of 2009 Home Office research into organised crime markets estimated that at any one time in 2003 there were up to 4,000 victims of trafficking for sexual exploitation in the UK and that remains our current estimate.

We have furthered our understanding of labour trafficking. Between May and September 2008 UK Border Agency led Operation Tolerance, a multi-agency pilot on trafficking for forced labour. As well as shedding more light on the nature and scale of labour trafficking,

Operation Tolerance also informed the development of the NRM and victim support arrangements for labour trafficking victims, including overseas domestic workers (who are supported under the same arrangements as victims of trafficking for sexual exploitation). Operation Ruby, staged after Tolerance, was a large scale multi-agency effort aimed at combating labour trafficking.

While the picture of trafficking for forced labour is still partial, these operations are helping us gain a better understanding, which is that victims tend to be males, EEA nationals who are exploited in the agricultural sector and that often there is overlap between trafficking for forced labour and labour exploitation (which does not constitute trafficking).

In relation to child trafficking, based on the figures in a CEOP scoping study (2007), the *Missing Out* report from ECPAT UK, and CEOP's 2009 strategic threat assessment, and applying assumptions during a recent impact assessment, our best estimate is of around 360 potential child victims per annum, not all of whom are unaccompanied asylum seeking children. However the assumptions are based on very limited quantitative data which inevitably lead to figures that are not fully representative.

International legislation: UN and EU protocols

UN Protocol to Prevent, Suppress and Punish Trafficking in Persons

The most important international instrument on trafficking is the UN Convention against Transnational Crime 2000 (UNTOC) and its optional Protocol to Prevent, Suppress and Punish Trafficking in Persons, Especially Women and Children (available at http://www2.ohchr.org/english/law/protocoltraffic.htm). This Protocol (known as the Palermo Protocol) was the first international instrument to define and address the trafficking problem.

The Trafficking Protocol has three main purposes, namely to:

- Prevent and combat trafficking in persons paying particular attention to women and children;
- Protect and assist the victims of such trafficking, with full respect for their human rights; and,

- Promote co-operation among States in order to meet those objectives.

The United Nations Office on Drugs and Crime recently published an International Framework for Action: to Implement the Trafficking in Persons Protocol (available at http://www.coe.int/t/dg2/trafficking/campaugn/Source/PDF_Conv_197_Trafficking_E. pdf). This is a document to assist in the implementation and interpretation of the Palermo Protocol.

Council of Europe Convention Against Trafficking in Human Beings

The Council of Europe Convention (available at http://www.coe.int/t/dg2/trafficking/campaugn/Source/PDF_Conv_197_Trafficking_E.pdf) is a comprehensive treaty which aims to:

- Prevent trafficking;
- Protect the Human Rights of victims of trafficking;
- Prosecute the traffickers.

The Convention applies to:

- All forms of trafficking: whether national or transnational, whether or not related to organised crime;
- Whoever the victim: women, men or children;
- Whatever the form of exploitation: sexual exploitation, forced labour or services.

Measures provided by the Council of Europe Convention include:

- Awareness-raising for persons vulnerable to trafficking and actions aimed at discouraging *consumers*, are among the main measures to prevent trafficking in human beings;
- Victims of trafficking must be recognised as such in order to avoid police and public authorities treating them as illegal migrants or criminals;
- Victims of trafficking will be granted physical and psychological assistance and support for their reintegration into society. Medical treatment, counselling and information as well as appropriate accommodation are all among the measures provided. Victims are also entitled to receive compensation;
- Victims are entitled to a minimum of 30 days to recover and escape from the influence of the traffickers and to take a decision regarding their possible cooperation with the authorities. A renewable residence permit may be granted if their personal situation so requires or if they need to stay in order to cooperate in a criminal investigation;
- Trafficking will be considered as a criminal offence: traffickers and their accomplices will therefore be prosecuted;
- The private life and the safety of victims of trafficking will be protected throughout the course of judicial proceedings;
- Possibility to criminalise those who use the services of a victim if they are aware that the person is a victim of trafficking;
- The Convention provides the possibility of not imposing penalties on victims for their involvement in unlawful activities, if they were compelled to do so by their situation; and,
- Civil society has an important role to play as regards prevention of trafficking and protection of the victims. Consequently, the Convention encourages the co-operation between public authorities, non-governmental organisations and members of civil society.

Which laws are being broken?

International Law

The UK is a signatory to a number of relevant UN Conventions. The most relevant of these include:

- The United Nations (2000) Protocol to prevent, suppress and punish trafficking in persons, especially women and children, supplementing the United Nations Convention against Transnational Organised Crime. This includes a definition, a requirement to criminalise trafficking and measures that should be taken to support and protect victims.
- The Convention on the Rights of the Child (1989).
- The Convention on the Elimination of All Forms of Discrimination Against Women (CEDAW) 1979 which focuses on *Trafficking in women and exploitation of prostitution of women* in part 1, article 6.

There are also a number of non-binding international standards relating to trafficking, including:

- The UN General Assembly resolution on Trafficking in Women and Girls (11 October 2002);
- The Office of the High Commissioner for Human Rights' Recommended Principles and Guidelines on Human Rights and Human Trafficking (September 2002);
- The UN Commission on Human Rights resolution on trafficking in women and girls (16 April 2002). Within this resolution, States were called on to criminalise all forms of trafficking, to penalise all perpetrators and to ensure exploited women and girls were neither criminalised nor penalised. An encouragement to governments to adopt standard minimum humanitarian treatment to trafficked persons was reiterated.

European law

The European Union Council Framework Decision on Combating Trafficking in Human Beings was approved in 2002 and was incorporated into UK law in 2004. It contains a series of recommendations to counter trafficking and requires all member states to make trafficking a criminal offence with efficient and dissuasive penalties. An EU Directive on short term residence permits has not been adopted.

Domestic law (England and Wales)

Sexual Offences Act 2003

Sections 57, 58 and 59 of the Sexual Offences Act (SOA) 2003 came into force on 1st May 2004. They deal with trafficking into, trafficking within, and trafficking out of the UK for sexual exploitation, respectively.

The elements of trafficking within the UK for sexual exploitation are:

- A person (A) intentionally arranges, or facilitates travel, within the UK of a person (B) where A intends to do anything to, or in respect of, B that would result in the commission of a relevant offence involving B, or where he believes that another person is likely to do something to, or in respect of, B that would result in the commission of a relevant offence involving B;
- In both cases, the relevant offence must take place during, or after, the journey but may take place anywhere in the world.

The elements of the offence of trafficking out of the UK for sexual exploitation are:

- A person (A) intentionally arranges, or facilitates, the departure from the UK of a person (B) where A intends to do anything to, or in respect of, B that would result in the commission of a relevant offence involving B, or A believes that another person is likely to do something to, or in respect of, B that would result in the commission of a relevant offence involving B;
- In both cases, the relevant offence must take place after B's departure and may take place anywhere in the world.

<u>*Asylum and Immigration (Treatment of Claimants) Act 2004*</u>

Section 4 of the Asylum and Immigration (Treatment of Claimants) Act 2004 makes it an offence for a person to arrange or facilitate the arrival in the UK (subsection (1)) or departure from the UK (subsection (3)) of an individual, if he intends to exploit that individual or believes that another person is likely to do so.

A person also commits an offence under subsection (2) if he arranges, or facilitates, travel within the UK by an individual in respect of whom he believes an offence under subsection (1) may have been committed, if he intends to exploit that individual or believes that another person is likely to do so.

For the purposes of the section, a person is exploited if (and only if):

- He is the victim of behaviour which contravenes Article 4 of the European Convention on Human Rights;
- He is encouraged, required or expected to do anything as a result of which he or another person would commit an offence under the legislation on organ transplants;
- He is subjected to force, threats or deception designed to induce him to provide services or benefits (or to enable another person to acquire benefits); or,
- He is requested or induced to undertake any activity, having been selected on the grounds that he is vulnerable and where a non-vulnerable person would be likely to refuse/resist.

This is the first time that trafficking for non-sexual forms of exploitation has been the subject of specific criminal offences in the UK.

National and Local Responsibilities for Combatting Trafficking

Human trafficking is a heinous crime, where people are treated as commodities and traded for profit. It can be multi-faceted and linked to organised crime. Victims are often subjected to multiple violations (including intimidation, violence, sexual violence, psychological abuse, threats and theft). Although it is often hidden, the related impact on communities can be severe, contributing to wider criminality and anti-social behaviour.

National level

At a national strategic level, action against human trafficking is a cross-government and UK wide priority. The UK Action Plan on Human Trafficking was launched in 2007 with updates published yearly.

The UK's end-to-end strategy to tackle human trafficking is based around four key themes: Prevention; Enforcement/Investigations/Prosecutions; Protection and Support for Victims; and Child Trafficking.

Governance of the Government's strategy is through an Interdepartmental Ministerial Group on Human Trafficking. This is chaired by the Home Office with a membership comprised of numerous Government departments (Attorney General's Office; Department for Business, Innovation and Skills; Crown Prosecution Service; Department for Communities and Local Government; Department for Children, Schools and Families; Department for International Development; Department for Health; Department for Work and Pensions; Foreign and Commonwealth Office; Government Equality Office; Ministry of Justice; Northern Ireland Office; Office of the First Minister and Deputy First Minister; and the Scotland Office).

An NGO Stakeholder Group, chaired by the Parliamentary Under Secretary of State for Crime Reduction and the Solicitor General, was set up by the Office for Criminal Justice Reform to act as a consultative forum on human trafficking.

The human trafficking strategy is primarily driven by:

* Public Service Agreement 23: Make communities safer;
* Public Service Agreement 24: Delivering a more effective, transparent and responsive Criminal Justice System for victims and for the public.

It can also have an impact on the following Public Service agreements:

* PSA 3: Ensure controlled, fair migration that protects the public and contributes to economic growth;
* PSA 15: Address the disadvantage that individuals experience because of their gender, race, disability, age, sexual orientation, religion or belief;
* PSA 18: Promote better health and wellbeing for all;
* PSA 19: Provide better health and social care for all;
* PSA 21: Build more cohesive, empowered and active communities.

The Government's commitment to tackling human trafficking is highlighted in:

* The CJS Strategy for 2008-2011 (Working together to cut crime and deliver justice; A strategic plan for 2008-2011);
* The New Strategy to Tackle Serious Organised Crime (Extending our reach: A comprehensive approach to tackling serious organised crime).

Local level

Crime and Disorder Reduction Partnerships, Local Criminal Justice Boards, Local Authorities and Local Strategic Partnerships have responsibilities to address crime; and protect and support victims and communities.

How can Local Criminal Justice Boards and Crime and Disorder Reduction Partnerships set the direction?

1. Develop local human trafficking strategies

Strategic planning for a local response to trafficking in people should start with a strategic review. This should consider:

* What are the local risks?
    * Are there entry points in the local area?
    * What is the local level of prostitution (especially off-street prostitution)?
    * Are there specific at-risk local labour markets?
* What reviews of these risks have been carried out?
    * What monitoring data on the extent of any problems is available?
* What initiatives have already been taken and how effective have these been?
* Based on the above, what do we now want to achieve?

This should highlight the key elements and priorities of a strategic action plan. Such an action plan should cover the requirements for:

* Specific proactive monitoring and data collection

- Multi-agency development including:
  - Awareness raising;
  - Training;
  - Identifying, resourcing and networking of service providers; and,
  - Agreement of appropriate multi-agency protocols.

2. Consider the needs of human trafficking victims as part of your Victim and Witness strategies and delivery plans (available at http://frontline.cjsonline.gov.uk/ . . . / victims-and-witnesses/Witness%20Charter%20LCJB%20Guidance.doc)

In particular note that:

- These victims may be vulnerable and/or intimidated and eligible for special measures;
- A significant proportion of those subjected to human trafficking will be non-UK nationals and you will need to consider providing services that are accessible for minority ethnic communities. In particular you will need to consider the availability of interpretative services;
- That many of these victims will have been subjected to several forms of intimidation and/or violence (including sexual violence);
- Identify local services that may be able to support victims and help them access services (including Victim Support, refuges, Sexual Assault Referral Centres, Sexual Health Clinics, Genito-urinary Medicine Clinics etc);
- Consider that non-UK national victims/witnesses may wish to return to their home country so there will be a need to factor in appropriate communication methods for keeping the victim informed about a case.

3. Recognise how human trafficking links in with other local crime priorities

NEIGHBOURHOOD POLICING

- Addressing anti-social behaviour. For example, brothels that have exploited trafficking victims have been found in residential and commercial properties, in both urban and rural areas; contributing to noise, rubbish, intimidation of local residents; and wider criminality;
- Addressing on-street and off-street prostitution;
- Adult males resident in the UK are used by trafficking groups to commit distraction burglaries or to commit *rogue trading* type offences;
- Trafficked children are used as beggars, pick-pockets, and shop-lifters.

Tackling serious and violent crime, criminal gangs and networks including:

- Child abuse including sexual abuse/paedophile networks;
- Sexual violence and other forms of interpersonal violence and meeting the particular needs of these victims (including addressing Violence Against Women);
- Drug dealing;
- Addressing street robbery;
- Addressing begging and street crime, carried out by children from Eastern Europe and other countries, trafficked to the UK and certain other Western European countries by organised crime networks, who control the children for profit;
- Addressing hate crime. If significant numbers of victims are trafficked into forced labour situations this can lead to community tensions and hate crime.

<u>HOW DO I KNOW IF TRAFFICKING IS HAPPENING IN MY AREA?</u>

The early identification of victims is key to ensuring an end to the abuse that they suffer and to providing the assistance necessary to begin their rehabilitation programme. Alongside police officers and immigration officials, Local Authority staff may often find themselves in contact with people who could potentially be victims.

These staff include social workers, youth teams, environmental health officers and other frontline staff.

The people and places where staff from local authorities and their partner organisations may come into contact with potential victims of human trafficking during their daily duties are summarised in the tables below[2].

Child victims

Where do we look?	Who is likely to be the first point of contact?
Care homes and foster families	Foster carers Children's Services LSCBs
Private homes	Children's Services
Schools	Teachers Children's Services
Hospitals and GPs surgery	Children's Services A&E staff and GPs
Interviews with unaccompanied asylum seeking children	Children's Services
On the streets	Crime and Disorder Reduction Partnerships Youth Offending Teams

Adult victims

Where do we look?	Who is likely to be the first point of contact?
Massage parlours	Licensing officers Prostitution outreach teams
On the streets	Prostitution outreach teams Gender equality officers
Shops, restaurants and factories	Health and Safety Inspectors Environmental Health Officers Trading Standards Officers
Private homes	Housing officers Adult social services Migrant integration teams
Local Authority Premises	All council staff

A network of professionals and agencies should be involved in the identification of potential victims and should work together in order to protect victims and ensure a referral network without gaps. Local staff need to be able to identify the signs that might indicate trafficking and will need to make operational judgements as to the appropriate immediate response. Proper procedures need to be in place to ensure that all relevant actors are aware of any suspicions of trafficking, and this information must be shared quickly and confidentially.

Key agencies involved in trafficking

UK Human Trafficking Centre

The United Kingdom Human Trafficking Centre [UKHTC] is a multi-agency centre that provides a central point for the development of expertise and cooperation in relation to the trafficking of human beings [THB], working together with other stakeholders from governmental, non-governmental and inter-governmental sectors in the UK and abroad.

It plays a key role in co-ordinating work across these various stakeholders and, with its partners, delivers a diverse set of programmes, including targeted campaigns to prevent and reduce THB. Raising the awareness of THB is the primary message and the UKHTC does this by addressing the four key audiences; victims; the public; law enforcement and other professionals. The UKHTC has responsibility for a number of important actions which are set out in the UK Action Plan on Tackling Human Trafficking. The Centre conducts research, develops improved training packages, promulgates best practice and develops an improved knowledge and understanding of the way criminal enterprises that are associated with human trafficking operate.

The UKHTC promotes the development of a victim centred human rights approach to THB and by working with NGOs and other partners it aims to improve the standard of care offered to victims. The UKHTC recognises that it is imperative that all victims of THB are identified and the provision of victim identification guidance to all sectors is an ongoing priority. A necessity is to reduce the harm caused by THB and to develop solutions to combat THB. The UKHTC aims to prevent human trafficking by working with all partners to build a knowledge and understanding of THB and the harm it causes and to use this knowledge and understanding to inform the UK response.

The focus of the work of the UKHTC encompasses the following:

Prevention

There are three key areas of preventative work identified within the UK Action Plan on Tackling Human Trafficking. These are increasing our knowledge and understanding of the problem, working to identify and address the issues that impact on the supply and demand sides of human trafficking, and finally maximising the collective preventative effort.

The UKHTC contributes to work in all these areas, through its multi agency work groups:

- Research;
- Prevention;
- Operations and Intelligence.

The UKHTC is the central point for the collation of data information and intelligence on all forms of trafficking, thereby striving to improve the local, national and international knowledge base on human trafficking.

Prosecution and Enforcement

The UKHTC can provide tactical advice to investigators in respect of any trafficking investigation in the United Kingdom. Where necessary a dedicated tactical advisor will work with the senior investigator throughout the lifetime of an investigation, providing advice on operational planning and care of victims.

The UKHTC provides a central point for the development of law enforcement expertise in relation to all forms of trafficking. It is a key part of an ongoing commitment to excellence in delivering a strategic partnership and collaborative working between all UK law enforcement agencies including the Crown Prosecution Service, HM Revenue and Customs, Serious Organised Crime Agency and the UK Borders Agency.

Protection-Victim Centred Approach

The UKHTC continues to pursue the continuing development of a victim-centred human rights based approach. Through the UKHTC multi agency *Victim Care* group, victim-centred protection measures continue to be developed. The UKHTC also works with partners in developing guidance on minimum standards for *support services* for victims of trafficking and to identify options for producing and disseminating information to victims.

The UKHTC houses a Competent Authority for assessing potential victims of trafficking under the National Referral Mechanism.

Partnership Approach

The focused approach of the UKHTC is that of partnership governmental, intergovernmental and non-governmental agencies. This approach is fundamental to the successful combating of THB. It is important that key partners are actively involved in the identification of good practice, thereby contributing to the UKs holistic approach to tackling trafficking in human beings. Simplistically, without effective partnership working it is impossible to successfully prevent, prosecute and protect.

Serious and Organised Crime Agency

The Serious Organised Crime Agency (SOCA) is an Executive Non-Departmental Public Body sponsored by, but operationally independent from, the Home Office.

SOCA is an intelligence-led agency with law enforcement powers and harm reduction responsibilities. Harm in this context is the damage caused to people and communities by serious organised crime.

The Home Secretary may set SOCA strategic priorities and will judge the success of its efforts. Within that framework, SOCA plans its priorities, including how it will exercise the functions given to it by statute, and what performance measures it will adopt.

SOCA has five generic priorities:

- To build knowledge and understanding of serious organised crime, the harm it causes, and of the effectiveness of different responses;
- To increase the amount of criminal assets recovered and increase the proportion of cases in which the proceeds of crime are pursued;
- To increase the risk to serious organised criminals operating in the UK, through proven investigation capabilities and in new ways;
- To collaborate with partners in the UK and internationally to maximise efforts to reduce harm;
- To provide agreed levels of high quality support to SOCA's operational partners and, as appropriate, seek their support in return.

Gangmasters Licensing Authority

The GLA is a government agency set up to protect workers from exploitation in agriculture, horticulture, shellfish gathering and food processing and packaging.

The mission of the Gangmasters Licensing Authority is to safeguard the welfare and interests of workers whilst ensuring Labour Providers operate within the law. The mission will be achieved by:

- Introducing and operating a system to licence Labour Providers, including a publicly accessible register;
- Effective communication of the legal requirement for Labour Providers to become licensed, and to operate and remain within the formal economy;
- Imposing the least possible burden on Labour Providers and Labour Users through efficient and effective processes and procedures; Developing and promoting standards for best practice in the supply and use of temporary labour, in collaboration with stakeholders;
- Checking licence holders for continued compliance with the licence conditions;
- Taking enforcement action against those who operate illegally or who for other reasons are judged unfit to hold a licence;
- Supporting enforcement of the law, by or in conjunction with the Enforcement Authorities of other Government Departments, and others as appropriate, through shared information and joint working;
- Maintaining a continuous review of the activities of Gangmasters and the effects of the Act and the Authority on them.

The GLA is keen to hear from anyone who believes a Labour Provider is either operating in breach of Licence Conditions, or operating without a licence. In addition, contact should be made when a Labour User is using an unlicensed Labour Provider.

If you have any concerns you should contact the GLA on 0845 602 5020 (during office hours 9am – 5pm) or email them at mailto://intelligence@gla.gsi.gov.uk

The GLA has introduced a secure and confidential reporting form, this will allow:

- Anybody who has information to provide it to the GLA anonymously (if they wish);
- Anybody to provide information in Polish, Latvian, Lithuanian, Slovakian and Portuguese.

Any information provided through the reporting form is directed through a secure server, meaning that the GLA have no record or details of who provided the information (unless the information provider included these details themselves).

HM Revenue and Customs

HM Revenue & Customs (HMRC) was formed on 18 April 2005, following the merger of Inland Revenue and HM Customs and Excise Departments.

In relation to human trafficking, HMRC enforces and administers border and frontier protection and enforces national minimum wages.

Home Office Organised and Financial Crime Unit

The Organised and Financial Crime Unit (OFCU) is responsible for developing the Government's strategy against organised crime. The unit also oversees the recovery of criminal assets, and the detection and conviction of money launderers.

The objectives of OFCU include:

- Improving the strategic picture on the threat from organised crime;

- Working with the Organised Crime Strategy Group to develop a strategy to fight organised crime;
- Ensuring that agencies and forces are given a clear steer on the priorities for combating organised crime, and designing effective strategies;
- Ensuring that agencies and forces are able to generate, share and assess tactical intelligence effectively;
- Giving forces and agencies the tools they need to carry out successful operations against organised crime;
- Sponsorship of the Serious Organised Crime Agency (SOCA).

OFCU also contains the Organised Immigration Crime team (OIC). The OIC team have the overall lead on human trafficking policy. The primary focus of the OIC team is on human trafficking, through ownership of the cross-government UK Action Plan on Human Trafficking. The team is also developing policy on combating organised crime aspects of people smuggling and facilitation.

The responsibilities of the Organised Immigration Crime team include:

- UK Action Plan on Human Trafficking;
- Prevention;
- Enforcement, investigations and prosecutions;
- Knowledge and intelligence;
- Oversight and funding of the UK Human Trafficking Centre;
- International work: including priority countries; institutions (EU & UN) and international conventions;
- Secretariat for the Interdepartmental Ministerial Group;
- Policy development on people smuggling;
- Strategic liaison with law enforcement.

Office for Criminal Justice Reform

The Office for Criminal Justice Reform (OCJR) is the cross-departmental team that supports all criminal justice agencies in working together to provide an improved service to the public. As a cross-departmental organisation, OCJR reports to Ministers in the Ministry of Justice, the Home Office and the Attorney General's Office.

The key goals for the CJS are:

- To improve the effectiveness and efficiency of the CJS in bringing offences to justice;
- To increase public confidence in the fairness and effectiveness of the CJS;
- To increase victim satisfaction with the police, and victim and witness satisfaction with the CJS;
- To consistently collect, analyse and use good quality ethnicity data to identify and address race disproportionality in the CJS; and
- To increase the recovery of criminal assets by recovering £250m of assets acquired through crime by 2009-10.

The Criminal Justice Strategic Plan 2008-2011 sets out how the agencies of the Criminal Justice System (CJS) in England and Wales will work together to deliver a justice system which:

- Is effective in bringing offences to justice, especially serious offences;
- Engages the public and inspires confidence;
- Puts the needs of victims at its heart; and,
- Has simple and efficient processes.

In relation to human trafficking, OCJR is part of a Virtual Trafficking Team, which works with colleagues from across Government, the criminal justice system and the non-Governmental sector to ensure that the UK Action Plan on human trafficking and the Convention are successfully implemented and to identify future strategic priorities.

OCJR holds the policy lead for providing protection and assistance to adult victims of trafficking.

UK Border Agency

The UK Border Agency (UKBA) is responsible for securing the United Kingdom borders and controlling migration in the United Kingdom. Border control is managed for the United Kingdom using immigration and customs laws. Part of immigration management includes considering applications for permission to enter or stay in the United Kingdom, citizenship and asylum.

UK Border Agency has a crucial role to play in combating organised immigration crime. In targeting those who do the most harm, UK Border Agency is committed to breaking the chain of trafficking. UK Border Agency works closely and cohesively with other agencies to identify such crime. UK Border Agency has the necessary powers to tackle organised immigration crime and can both prevent and halt crimes against human beings.

Identifying victims and the impact of these crimes

When identifying a victim it should not be a priority to label them as one type of victim or another, and assumptions should not be made about the type of exploitation a person may be suffering based on the person's characteristics such as age, nationality, gender, or other superficial characteristics such as the physical condition of the victim.

The key principles that should be followed are:

- Think victim care and protection;
- Don't judge;
- Believe, test and confirm the victim's account; and,
- Do not harm.

It is not uncommon for victims to feel both relief at having been identified along with feelings of fear and suspicion toward an identifying front line statutory responder, particularly from the police or immigration services.

This is often linked to their fear of being returned to their trafficking situation or to another unsafe situation in their home country. Many victims will have been told by their traffickers that the authorities would simply return them should they try to escape, or that they will be subject to abuse at the hands of the police. It is also not uncommon for negative feelings (fear and suspicion) to give way to those of relief once the victim felt safe and came to trust the identifying officer.

For some victims, the identification and referral process may mimic aspects of what had happened to them during trafficking – promises of help and a good life, movement by persons they did not know, being taken to unknown locations where "everything would be fine" and "they would be taken care of".

As such, for many trafficked persons the identification process itself appears suspicious, particularly when viewed through the lens of someone who is already stressed, frightened and confused.

Individuals who are in a trafficking situation may be extremely reticent with information, and may tell their stories with obvious errors. It is not uncommon for traffickers to provide *stories* for victims to tell if approached by the authorities and the errors or *lack of reality* may be because their initial stories are composed by others and learnt.

Victims' early accounts may also be affected by the impact of trauma. In particular victims may experience Post Traumatic Stress Disorder which can result in symptoms of hostility; aggression; difficulty in recalling details or entire episodes; and difficulty concentrating.

Be prepared to encounter victims with varying English language skills or other communication barriers. You should not use family members, friends or unqualified members of the public to interpret.

Adult victims

Individuals may be reticent to perceive themselves as *victims* due to:

- A fear of retribution/reprisals from their traffickers;
- Fear and suspicion of authority figures, and a lack of awareness that these figures are in a position to help;
- Accusations from authority figures that individuals were complicit to their *trafficked* situation;
- Toleration of their situation as it is more favourable than their home circumstances;
- Being in a relationship with their traffickers;
- *Stockholm syndrome*, where due to unequal power victims create a false emotional or psychological attachment to their controller;
- Fear of discrimination from their community and families.

In addition to suspecting an individual may be a victim of trafficking from the definitions provided in this toolkit, indicators (apparent symptoms of a situation) that may highlight that an individual could be a victim of trafficking may include:

Physical indicators

- Injuries apparently as a result of assault or controlling measures;
- Neurological symptoms: headaches, dizzy spells, memory loss;
- Gastrointestinal symptoms;
- Cardiovascular symptoms;
- Musculoskeletal symptoms;
- Tattoos or other marks indicating *ownership* by exploiters;
- Work related injuries.

Psychological indicators

- Expression of fear or anxiety;
- Depression (lack of interest in engaging in activities, lack of interest in engaging with other individuals, hopelessness);
- Isolation;
- Suffering from post-traumatic stress and/or a range of other trauma induced mental or physical illnesses;
- Drug use;
- Alcohol use;
- Self harm or suicidal;
- Hostility (annoyed and easily irritated, temper outbursts);
- An attitude of self-blame, shame and a pervasive loss of control.

Sexual health indicators

- Females may be suffering from unwanted pregnancy resulting from clients or their traffickers. They may also have recently been forced to terminate a pregnancy;

- High rates of sexually transmitted diseases;
- Injuries of a sexual nature.

Situational/environmental indicators

- Distrust of authorities;
- The person acts as if instructed by another;
- Difficulty in concentrating;
- Lack of knowledge of area where located in the UK;
- Fearful of saying what their immigration status is;
- Fearful and emotional regarding family or dependents;
- Limited English, only being able to speak limited vocabularies related to the exploitation situation they are in.

These may be hard to discern during an initial meeting with a victim, where the above behaviours and expressions may not be apparent to any one individual at a given time.

Child victims

Trafficked children are not only deprived of their rights to health and freedom from exploitation and abuse – they are usually also deprived of their right to an education and the life opportunities this brings. The creation of a false identity and implied criminality of the children, together with the loss of family and community, may seriously undermine their sense of self worth. At the time they are found, trafficked children may not show any obvious signs of distress or imminent harm, they may be vulnerable to particular types of abuse and may continue to experience the effects of their abuse in the future.

Trafficked children are at increased risk of significant harm because they are largely invisible to the professionals and volunteers who would be in a position to assist them. The adults who traffic them take trouble to ensure that the children do not come to the attention of the authorities, or disappear from contact with statutory services soon after arrival in the UK, or in a new area within the UK.

As an aid to all agencies responding to the needs of child victims, the following have been produced:

- The London Child Protection Procedures (London Board, 2007): (available at http://www.londonscb.gov.uk/procedures/);
- The Safeguarding Children who may have been trafficked guidance: (available at http://publications.teachernet.gov.uk/eOrderingDownload/DCSF_Child%20Tr afficking.pdf);
- ACPO guidance on Child Abuse Investigation: (available at http://www.acpo.p olice.uk/policies.asp).

The following principles should be adopted by all agencies in relation to identifying and responding to children (and unborn children) at risk of or having been trafficked:

- Trafficking causes significant harm to children in both the short and long term; it constitutes physical and emotional abuse to children;
- The safety and welfare of children is paramount;
- Trafficked children are provided with the same standard of care that is available to any other child in the UK;
- All decisions or plans for the children should be based on good quality assessments and supported by easily accessible multi-agency services; and
- All agencies should work in partnership with members of local communities, to empower individuals and groups to develop support networks and education programmes.

Most children are trafficked for financial gain. This can include payment from or to the child's parents, and can involve the children in debt-bondage to the traffickers. In most cases, the trafficker also receives payment from those wanting to exploit the children once in the UK. Some trafficking is carried out by organised gangs. In other cases, individual adults or agents traffic children to the UK for their own personal gain. The exploitation of trafficked children may be progressive. Children trafficked for domestic work may also be vulnerable to sexual exploitation or children initially trafficked for sexual exploitation may be resold.

Working together to tackle trafficking

National Referral Mechanism

From 1 April 2009 a National Referral Mechanism (NRM) was introduced to provide a framework within which public bodies such as the criminal justice agencies, UK Border Agency, local authorities and third sector partners could work together to identify individuals who may be victims of trafficking and provide appropriate protection and support.

The Council of Europe Convention on trafficking has a two stage process for identifying victims of trafficking in which the *reasonable grounds* test acts as an initial filter to a fuller more conclusive decision. Frontline professionals in named *first responder* organisations can refer individuals who they think may be evidencing signs of being a victim of human trafficking to designated *Competent Authorities* who work with partners to make an assessment. Adults must have given their consent before being referred through the NRM.

First responders are:

- Designated Third Sector Organisations (The Poppy project, Migrant Helpline, TARA, Kalayaan);
- The police;
- UK Border Agency;
- The Crown Prosecution Service;
- Local Authority Children's Services;
- The Gangmasters Licencing Authority;
- Statutory Qualified Health Officials.

Competent Authorities (CA) are:

- A central multi-agency CA based in the UK Human Trafficking Centre (UKHTC); and
- Linked but separate CA in UK Border Agency (UKBA) to assess cases where trafficking is raised as part of an asylum claim or in the context of another immigration process.

Frontline staff in first responder organisations should refer possible victims of trafficking to the CA based in the UKHTC using an agreed format (initial target referral time is 48 hours). Where UKBA identify a potential victim, the case will be assessed by designated specialist staff within a UKBA CA which will also work with other relevant partners. Other frontline professionals (not in first responder organisations) can refer individuals to any of the organisations listed as *first responders* for advice.

Where the victim is under the age of 18 years, the first responders (apart from Children's Services) should refer that child or young person, in the first instance to their local authority Children's Services. Children's Services are the primary service provider for safeguarding and responding to the needs of a child trafficking victim. Thereafter, Children's Services should undertake relevant actions as detailed in the *Safeguarding Children who may have been Trafficked* guidance. Once all assessments have been undertaken the Children's Services should refer the case, through the NRM, to the CA.

For the referral of potential child victims, an assessment toolkit and referral form are available at: http://www.crimereduction.homeoffice.gov.uk/humantrafficking005.htm.

The tool kit incorporates a matrix of trafficking indicators to help the first responder identify whether the child is a victim of trafficking along with providing a structured set of questions to record evidence in a consistent way. Where a child is assessed to be a victim of trafficking the referral report to the CA for a decision should be sent to: mailto://nrm@ukhtc.pnn.police.uk.

Process and timescales

The Competent Authority has a target (note that this is a target and not a deadline) of five working days from the date of receipt of the referral, within which to make a decision on whether the individual has reasonable grounds for being considered as a victim of trafficking. During this period, the CA may contact the first responder and other relevant organisations for further information. Once a positive *reasonable grounds* decision is made by the CA, the individual is granted a 45 day reflection/recovery period.

The temporary status of the 'reasonable grounds' decision provides the conditions for the fuller evaluation to be made, and allows the individual to escape the influence and control of the traffickers. The officer will have the discretion to extend the validity of the temporary admission beyond 45 days where circumstances warrant. Similarly the decision maker can curtail the reflection period and immigration status where the trafficking claim is found to be fraudulent. Following any decision, the officer will contact the victim to inform them of their case.

Once the CA has reached a decision, they will notify the individual by letter on their decision. A notification letter will also be sent to the first responder informing them of the outcome.

Information sharing as part of the NRM

Victims

It is essential that frontline professionals officially record all the information passed to them by victims of trafficking. One of the main reasons for this is so that victims do not have to repeat the same information to multiple organisations, which could re-traumatise them unnecessarily.

In addition, once a victim has disclosed, they are at serious risk of reprisal from their traffickers. Victim safety is therefore paramount, and hence if you are referring an individual to another organisation, the individual's situation must be made clear to that referral agency, so that adequate provisions are put in place immediately. Security issues apply to:

- Accommodation (including consideration of emergency alarms, video cameras, immediate access to police);
- Victim behaviour;
- Secure transport to/from services/hearings etc;
- Witness protection where indicated.

First responders should refer details of all individuals identified as a victim of trafficking to the UKHTC. When an individual does not wish to engage in the NRM process, first responders should still pass on details of the case to the UKHTC for monitoring purposes, using the appropriate template. Cases where individuals do not wish to engage in the NRM will not receive an identification decision.

Protection and support for victims of human trafficking

Support provisions

Victims are a priority for the criminal justice system and our Human Trafficking strategy is firmly focused around their protection and support. The aim is to ensure that all victims receive the right support and protection:

Support for all victims of crime:

• Victims of crime are legally entitled to minimum standards of service from the criminal justice agencies under the Victims Code of Practice: http://www.home office.gov.uk/documents/victims-code-of-practice. This includes receiving information about appropriate support services in their local area; being kept informed regularly by the police (at least once a month) on the progress of their case, being informed of charging decisions if the case has gone to court.

• Victims of violent crime may be eligible for compensation under the Criminal Injuries Compensation Scheme: http://www.cica.gov.uk/

• Victims may be eligible for special measures to help give their best evidence if vulnerable or intimidated: http://frontline.cjsonline.gov.uk/_includes/downloads /guidance/victims-and-witnesses/The_Witness_Charter.pdf

• Victim Personal Statements ensure that the impact of the crime on the victim is taken into consideration: http://www.cjsonline.gov.uk/victim/coming_forward/v ictim_personal_statement/

Victim Support

Victim Support is a national charity which gives free and confidential help to victims of crime, their family, friends and anyone else affected. It is free at the point of demand, and is available across the whole of England and Wales.

Trained volunteers offer the following to victims of crime:

• Someone to talk to in confidence;
• Information on police and court procedures;
• Help in dealing with other organisations;
• Information about compensation and insurance;
• Links to other sources of help.

There are three parts to Victim Support:

Community Service	Witness Service	Supportline
Police refer victims of crime to receive emotional and practical support from staff and volunteers.	In every court providing pre-trial visits and support on the day to prosecution and defence witnesses	Freephone number staffed by volunteers.

Witness Care Units

The aim of witness care units is to provide a single point of contact for victims and witnesses, minimising the stress of attending court and keeping victims and witnesses up to date with any news in a way that is convenient to them.

Under the Code of Practice for Victims of Crime, the Witness Care Unit has a legal obligation to:

- Tell witnesses if they will be required to give evidence;
- Tell witnesses the dates of their court hearings;
- Give witnesses a copy of the *Witness in court* leaflet or other relevant leaflet, if individuals are required to give evidence;
- Tell witnesses about court results and explain any sentence given within one day of receiving the outcome from the court.

Witness care units are jointly staffed by the police and the Crown Prosecution Service.

Support for children and young people

The government's annual Victim Support grant includes providing support for young victims of crime.

- The Code of Practice for Victims of Crime sets out the services victims can expect from the criminal justice system. Victims under 17 are automatically considered to be vulnerable and therefore entitled to an enhanced service.
- In the youth justice system, Youth Offending Teams contact victims to ask if they want to be involved in a restorative justice intervention, in appropriate cases.
- Young witnesses will automatically be considered for special measures in court, such as screens, TV links or intermediaries to help young witnesses give their best evidence.

The Youth Crime Action Plan (YCAP) announced further support for all young victims, starting with five pilot projects to test the best ways to support young victims. These projects have provided information to nearly 12,500 young people through school assemblies and workshops telling them about the dangers and consequences of crime, how to keep themselves safe and how to get help if they need it. They have also provided support for those who need it, including one-to-one sessions, activity breaks to share experiences with other young victims and simply referring young victims to existing local activities that will re-build self esteem. Nearly 400 young victims have been supported in this way. Over the next year, work will continue with the YCAP priority areas so that more areas adopt the good practice from the five areas and provide better support for young victims.

Specialist Support for Adult Victims of Trafficking

- Non-UK identified victims of trafficking are granted an extendable 45 day recovery period; however this is flexible and individual circumstances can be accommodated;
- One year temporary residency permits are granted to non-UK victims who qualify: due to personal circumstances or participation in a criminal investigation;
- Victims of trafficking can access safe accommodation, advocacy, living expenses, access to counselling, support through the criminal justice process, access to independent legal advice (where required), access to interpretative services, and help with resettlement through various service providers;
  - Female victims of sexual exploitation and domestic servitude – Poppy project, TARA, Hibiscus, Salvation Army, Medaille Trust;
  - Male victims of sexual exploitation and domestic servitude – Migrant Helpline, Kalayaan;
  - Victims of forced labour – Migrant Helpline
- Victims of human trafficking can also benefit from the roll out of other initiatives like sexual assault referral centres and independent sexual violence advisors.
- Victims are exempt from the charging regulations of health care for migrants: http://www.dh.gov.uk/en/Healthcare/Entitlementsandcharges/Overseasvisitors/DH_097596;

- Victims can access asylum support and local resettlement services and these can be found on the UK Border Agency website: http://www.ukba.homeoffice.gov. uk/;
- Victims are eligible to apply for voluntary assistance returns.

Specialist Support for Child Victims of Trafficking

Responsibility for the care, protection and accommodation of child trafficking victims falls within the designated responsibilities of local authorities for safeguarding and promoting the welfare of all children under the provisions of the 1989 and 2004 Children Acts.

Separated and vulnerable children from abroad enjoy the same entitlements as all UK born or resident children. Many child victims apply for asylum (often at the behest of their trafficker) and become categorised as an unaccompanied asylum seeking child (UASC).

As an aid to all agencies responding to the needs of child victims, the following have been produced:

- The London Child Protection Procedures (London Board, 2007): (available at http://www.londonscb.gov.uk/procedures/);
- The Safeguarding Children who may have been trafficked guidance: (available at http://publications.teachernet.gov.uk/eOrderingDownload/DCSF_Child%20Tr afficking.pdf);
- ACPO guidance on Child Abuse Investigation: (available at http://www.acpo.p olice.uk/policies.asp).

Assisted Voluntary Returns for Irregular Migrants

All potential victims of trafficking should be informed of the opportunity to make a voluntary return under the Assisted Voluntary Returns for Irregular Migrants (AVRIM) programme which is particularly aimed at those who have been trafficked into the UK. This programme is run in partnership with the International Organization of Migration (IOM) who liaises with the applicant. Details of the scheme can be found at: http://www.ukba.homeoffice.gov.uk/aboutus/workingwithus/workingwithasylum/assis tedvoluntaryreturn/avrim/.

The AVRIM scheme provides IOM assistance at the port of departure in the UK and assistance with immigration upon arrival in the country of origin if requested. It also meets the cost of a flight to the applicant's country of origin and onward domestic transportation. In some cases IOM will arrange referral to appropriate NGOs in the country of origin for victims of trafficking. Certain cases may also be eligible for some reintegration assistance to help with small business start up, vocational training or further education courses. Further information can be obtained from the IOM website at http://www.iomlondon.org.

What victims should expect from you

Your attitude and approach towards the individual will be pivotal in whether the person feels able to disclose fully, and for you to direct them to the necessary sources for help.

General principles

- Think about your gender, appearance and behaviour and the effect of all three on distressed and traumatised individuals;

- Consider the location in which interviews/discussions are taking place. An individual should feel safe, secure and the dialogue should be conducted at a pace that meets the needs of the individual;
- You must also consider language and communication barriers – if you feel as though an individual is in need of support, you must ensure that independent and professional interpreters are used when interviewing the individual;
- It is important to be clear about your professional boundaries and how far your role extends;
- You can listen and support, but other staff and agencies may be better equipped to provide the specialist help needed;
- It is important to state the limits of confidentiality. In public organisations, if you have concerns about a risk of serious injury, self-harm or child protection risks these issues must be passed on to the appropriate people/agencies;
- You must consider the individuals immediate needs. Victims should be removed from their place of exploitation at the earliest opportunity and taken to a place of safety. It is also vital that victims are able to access emergency health services if required.

Identification

Many victims of human trafficking will not perceive themselves as having been trafficked. Some will have been complicit in the earlier stages of the process, and may blame themselves for the situation in which they consequently found themselves in.

If there is a risk that an interview to identify whether the individual is a victim of trafficking will cause harm or compromise their safety or mental health, the interview should not be undertaken.

One must do the utmost to ascertain the individual's psychological state and the effects that an interview may have. Very often individuals, particularly those who have escaped recently, are in a state of emotional crisis. It is not appropriate to interview someone who is in this state. Moreover an interview with them in this state would be of little use as the information disclosed will not be provided in a rational manner. It is critical that a person is in full control of their faculties when the interview is requested, and that during the interview they feel as though they have some control over the interview situation.

If you intend to refer the individual, you must obtain their informed consent to this process. They must understand what the NRM is and what information is going to passed on and to whom. You must not identify the individual as formally being a victim of trafficking, unless you are a Competent Authority.

Referral

SUPPORT SERVICES

Your initial concern when a victim is identified is assessing their physical and mental wellbeing, and in ensuring that they receive appropriate emergency support. Given the abuse that may have been suffered, and the fears that will be harboured, individuals may not be in a position to make sensible decisions about their future or to make reliable statements to the police or other authorities.

Your organisation may provide specialised support for victims of trafficking, this will be listed in the agency-specific sections of this report.

Alternatively, you may be able to direct victims to support services in the community. Victims' access to appropriate support provision should happen as quickly as possible. A list of support services is provided in the voluntary organisation section of this toolkit, and the UKHTC can provide 24 hour advice (0114 252 3891).

Victims may not wish to be supported. In these circumstances, an attempt could be made to pass on a victim of trafficking leaflet. However, it is imperative that individuals are not put at risk, and it should be ensured that others are not aware that information has been given.

NATIONAL REFERRAL MECHANISM

It is your responsibility to fully explain what processes are in place in the UK for victims of trafficking; your organisation's role in the process and what will happen to the individual should they be referred through the National Referral Mechanism. You will find specific information relating to your organisations role in this process within the dedicated sections of the toolkit.

For public organisations, if an individual has immigration issues, then these will have to be addressed. Advice is provided in the agency-specific sections of this report.

A referral form has been developed for use by all agencies when referring adults and children (http://www.crimereduction.homeoffice.gov.uk/humantrafficking005.htm). Frontline staff will need to capture as much information about the individual and circumstances and record it on the referral form.

Information sharing and record keeping

You must obtain the consent of the individual before any referral is undertaken, unless there are child protection concerns or serious concerns over harm to selves or others. If you are referring the individual on to another organisation, you must specify what details you will be passing on. It must be remembered that victims could be extremely traumatised, and having to repeat information to a multitude of organisations will be detrimental to their health and well-being.

How to deal with disclosure

Your attitude and approach towards the individual will be pivotal in whether the person feels able to disclose fully, and for you to direct them to the necessary sources for help. Think about your gender, appearance and behaviour and the effect of all three on the distressed and traumatised individuals. You must also consider language and communication barriers – if you feel as though an individual is in need of support, you must ensure that independent and professional interpreters are used when interviewing the individual.

Key principles:

- Demonstrate an acceptance of what is being disclosed;
- Do not judge;
- Believe;
- Listen and give the person time to talk, asking open and not closed questions;
- Be supportive;
- Tell them that it is not their fault; they are not to blame;
- Explain that you will want to ask a few questions about their experiences, so that you can direct them to the right help and support both in your own organisation and in the community;
- Provide information about where to go for help, and refer to relevant agencies when requested;
- Take detailed notes about the disclosure following agreement from the individual;
- If appropriate, and agreed, refer the individual through the National Referral Mechanism.

It is important to be clear about your professional boundaries and how far your role extends. You can listen and support, but other staff and agencies may be better equipped to provide the specialist help needed. It is also important to state the limits of confidentiality within your organisation; for example, within statutory agencies, if you have concerns about a risk of serious injury, self-harm or child protection risks these issues have to be referred on to the appropriate people.

Multi-agency working to support victims

The development of a multi-agency approach that is able to develop long-term approaches to addressing human trafficking will be more effective than any individual initiatives. The development of such a capability depends on raising awareness of its need, developing the appropriate organisation structures and protocols to facilitate the multi-agency approach, and putting in place monitoring and review processes. Wherever possible it is preferable to build on existing structures to extend their capability to include trafficking.

Given the nature of the trafficking problem, the crimes it involves, the expertise required to address it effectively and the multiple needs of its victims, it is essential that a multi-agency approach is taken to any initiative. Establishing a management and operational framework will involve:

- Identifying key contacts and agency representatives;
- Establishing personal links between the various agency contacts;
- Developing multi-agency training;
- Jointly assessing the local priorities and developing strategies and action plans;
- Sharing intelligence and data;
- Developing protocols for joint working;
- Agreeing management structures and processes for developing the multi-agency approach further.

Strong and effective leadership of multi-agency partnerships is of critical importance to their success.

Multi-agency partnerships should at a minimum comprise three distinct groups:

- The key agencies responsible for tackling trafficking and supporting its victims (police, immigration, CPS, social services, and NGOs with specific support services to offer);
- Any other agencies who are likely to come across trafficked victims (including refugee organisations, women's refuge organisations, HIV and drug service providers, health service providers);
- The general public.

---

[1]   Belsar, P., M. de Cock, and F. Mehran. 2005. ILO Minimum Estimate of Forced Labour in the World, Geneva: ILO page 6.

[2]   A more detailed version of this information can be found in the SOLACE report 'The role of local authorities in addressing human trafficking' (2009) which can be downloaded from the SOLACE website http://www.solace.org.uk/library.asp

Appendix 8

LONDON SAFEGUARDING TRAFFICKED CHILDREN GUIDANCE

London Safeguarding Children Board
London Councils
59½ Southwark Street
London SE1 0AL
http://www.londonscb.gov.uk/trafficking/

The London Safeguarding Children Board would like to thank the 12 LSCB areas involved in piloting this guidance and toolkit . . .

Camden Council

LB Croydon

Glasgow City Council

Harrow Council

LB Hillingdon

Hounslow Council

Islington Council

Kent County Council

Manchester City Council

Slough Borough Council

Solihull Council

Southwark Council

 . . . and the members of the London Trafficking Toolkit Monitoring Group:

ECPAT UK

Department for Education (DfE)

Home Office

United Kingdom Border Agency (UKBA)

United Kingdom Human Trafficking Centre (UKHTC)

Child Exploitation and Online Protection Centre (CEOP)

Crown Prosecution Service (CPS)

Metropolitan Police Service

Contents

1. INTRODUCTION

1.1 This document provides guidance to professionals and volunteers from all agencies in safeguarding and promoting the welfare of trafficked and exploited children.

1.2 Trafficked children are at increased risk of significant harm because they are largely invisible to the professionals and volunteers who would be in a position to assist them. The adults who traffic them take trouble to ensure that the children do not come to the attention of the authorities, or disappear from contact with statutory services soon after arrival in the UK, or in a new area within the UK.

1.3 This guidance is supplementary to, and should be used in conjunction with, the latest edition of the London Safeguarding Children Board's *London Child Protection Procedures* which can be accessed at http://www.londonscb.gov.uk/procedures/.

1.4 This guidance is linked to the London Safeguarding Trafficked Children Toolkit 2011 (referred to here as the *Trafficked Children Toolkit*), which includes a number of additional tools to assist professionals in both assessing the needs of the child and the continuing risks that they may face, and referring their case to the competent authority (UKBA will fulfil this role for asylum cases, UKHTC for all other cases).

2. DEFINITIONS

2.1 Human trafficking is defined by the UNHCR guidelines (2006) as a process that is a combination of three basic components:

- Movement (including within the UK);
- Control, through harm / threat of harm or fraud[1];
- For the purpose of exploitation

2.2 The Palermo Protocol establishes children as a special case for whom there are only two components – movement and exploitation. **Any child transported for exploitative reasons is considered to be a trafficking victim** – whether or not s/he has been deceived, because it is not considered possible for children to give informed consent. See section 2a of the *Trafficked Children Toolkit* for the Palermo Protocol and other relevant international and national legislation.

2.3 'Child' refers to children anyone below 18 years of age, including those aged 0 to 17 years and adolescents up to their 18th birthday. This definition is in accordance with the *London Child Protection Procedures*. See also <u>section 9.4 determining age</u>.

2.4 A child may be trafficked between several countries in the EU or globally, prior to being trafficked into / within the UK. The child may have entered the UK illegally or legally (i.e. with immigration documents), but the intention of exploitation underpins the entire process[2]. Child victims may be indigenous UK nationals, European Union [EU] nationals or from any country outside the EU.

2.5 'Parent' means parent or carer and 'professional' refers to any individual working in a voluntary, employed, professional or unqualified capacity, including foster carers and approved adopters. This definition is in accordance with the *London Child Protection Procedures*. See the section 2g of the *Trafficked Children Toolkit* for a glossary and acronyms.

3. PRINCIPLES

3.1 The following principles should be adopted by all agencies in relation to identifying and responding to children (and unborn children) at risk of or having been trafficked:

- Trafficking causes significant harm to children in both the short and long term; it constitutes physical and emotional abuse to children;
- The safety and welfare of the child is paramount (i.e. the nationality or immigration status of the child is secondary and should be addressed only after the child's safety is assured);
- Trafficked children are provided with the same standard of care that is available to any other child in the UK;
- All decisions or plans for the child/ren should be based on good quality assessments and supported by easily accessible multi-agency services; and
- All agencies should work in partnership local communities, to empower individuals and groups to develop support networks and education programmes.

4. THE PROBLEM OF CHILD TRAFFICKING

4.1 Why do people traffic children?

4.1.1 Most children are trafficked for financial gain. This can include payment from or to the child's parents, and can involve the child in debt-bondage to the traffickers. In most cases, the trafficker also receives payment from those wanting to exploit the child once in the UK. Some trafficking is carried out by organised gangs. In other cases, individual adults or agents traffic children to the UK for their own personal gain[3]. The exploitation of trafficked children may be progressive. Children trafficked for domestic work may also be vulnerable to sexual exploitation or children initially trafficked for sexual exploitation may be resold.

4.1.2 Children may be used for:

- **Sexual exploitation** e.g.
  - child sexual abuse
  - child abuse images
- **Domestic servitude** e.g.
  - undertaking domestic chores

  - looking after young children
- **Labour exploitation** e.g.
  - working in restaurants
  - building sites
  - cleaning

- **Enforced criminality** e.g.
  - cannabis cultivation
  - begging and pickpocketing
  - drug dealing / trafficking
  - for the purpose of benefit fraud
- **Trade in human organs**

4.1.3   This list above is not exhaustive and all cases should be treated on a case by case basis. Illegal adoption, female genital mutilation (FGM) and forced marriage could be indicators of trafficking in cases where any of the listed exploitation types in 4.1.2 have also occurred. Such cases would require careful exploration of the individual case circumstances. If a child has been trafficked for these purposes, the primary response should be to safeguard the welfare of the child. In such cases, the child may be treated as a victim of a crime under the following legislation listed (i.e. *Forced Marriage Civil Protection Act 2007; Female Genital Mutilation Act 2003 for England, Wales and Northern Ireland; Prohibition of Female Genital Mutilation (Scotland) Act 2005* and the *Adoption Act 2002*) rather than as victims of trafficking offences, unless there are clear indications of exploitation under the Convention (listed in 4.1.2). Where exploitation is present, statutory child protection and safeguarding responses should be applied, and a referral should be made to the National Referral Mechanism for a decision on the status of the potential victim of trafficking.

4.2 How are children recruited and controlled?

4.2.1   Traffickers recruit their victims using a variety of methods. Some children are abducted or kidnapped, although most children are trapped in subversive ways - e.g:

- Children are promised education or what is regarded as respectable work – such as in restaurants or as domestic servants.
- Parents are persuaded that their children will have a better life elsewhere.

4.2.2   Many children travel on false documents or enter clandestinely without documentation. Even those whose documents are genuine may not have access to them. One way that traffickers control children is to retain their passports and threaten children that should they escape, they will be deported.

The creation of a false identity for a child can give a trafficker direct control over every aspect of a child's life, for example, by claiming to be a parent or guardian.

4.2.3   Even before they travel, children may be abused and exploited to ensure that the trafficker's control continues after the child is transferred to someone else's care - e.g:

- Confiscation of the child's identity documents;
- Threats of reporting the child to the authorities;
- Violence, or threats of violence, towards the child and/or his/her family;
- Keeping the child socially isolated;
- Keeping the child locked up;
- Telling some children that they owe large sums of money and that they must work to pay this off;
- Depriving the child of money; and
- Voodoo or witchcraft, which may be used to frighten children into thinking that they and their families will die if they tell anyone about the traffickers.

4.2.4   The traffickers might be part of a well organised criminal network, or they might be individuals involved in only one of the stages of the operation, such as the provision of false documentation, transport, or places where the child's presence can be concealed.

4.3 How are children brought to the UK?

4.3.1 Any port of entry into the UK might be used by traffickers. There is evidence that some children are trafficked via numerous transit countries and many may travel through other European Union countries before arriving in the UK.

4.3.2 Some may have entered the UK legitimately under any category of the Immigration Rules, such as students or visitors. Others may have entered the UK by clandestine means believing that they were going into illegal but lucrative work. Whist others will have residence rights as a result of being EEA or UK nationals.

4.3.3 Children may enter accompanied by adult/s or as unaccompanied minors.

4.3.4 The recent learning experience from Paladin through Operation Newbridge indicated that, as checks have improved at the larger ports of entry, such as Heathrow and Gatwick airports, traffickers are starting to use smaller ports or other regional airports. Traffickers are also known to use the Eurostar rail service and ferries to UK sea ports.

Accompanied children

4.3.4 There are many legitimate reasons for children being brought to the UK, such as economic migration with their family, education, re-unification with family or fleeing a war-torn country. Some children will have travelled with their parent/s.

4.3.5 However, a number of children arrive in the UK accompanied by adults who are either not related to them or in circumstances which raise child protection concerns. For example, there may be little evidence of any pre-existing relationship or even an absence of any knowledge of the sponsor. There may be unsatisfactory accommodation arranged in the UK, or perhaps no evidence of parental permission for the child to travel to the UK or stay with the sponsor. These irregularities may be the only indication that the child could be a victim of trafficking.

4.3.6 To curb illegal migration and improve children's safeguards, global visa regulations have been in place since February 2006. A photograph of the child is now shown on the visa, together with the name and passport number of the adult/s who have been given permission to travel with the child.

4.3.7 Some accompanied children may apply for asylum claiming to be unaccompanied, after being told by their trafficker that by doing so they will be granted permission to reside in the UK and be entitled to claim welfare benefits.

Unaccompanied children

4.3.8 Groups of unaccompanied children often come to the notice of the UK Borders Agency (UKBA). Unaccompanied children may come to the UK seeking asylum (Unaccompanied Asylum Seeking Children – UASC), or they may be here to attend school or join their family. A child may be the subject of a private fostering arrangement.

4.3.9 If the child is unaccompanied and not travelling to his or her parent, or if there are some concerns over the legitimacy or suitability of the proposed arrangement for the child's care in the UK, s/he will be referred to LA children's social care by UKBA.

4.3.10 Some groups of children will avoid contact with authorities because they are instructed to do so by their traffickers. In other cases the traffickers insist that the child applies for asylum as this gives the child a legitimate right of temporary leave to remain in the UK.

4.3.11 It is suspected that significant numbers of children are referred to LA children's social care after applying for asylum and some even register at school for up to a term, before disappearing again. It is thought that they are trafficked internally within the UK or out of the UK to other European countries.

Trafficking within the UK

4.3.12   There is increasing evidence that children (both of UK and other citizenship) are being trafficked internally within the UK. The list of indicators in the risk assessment matrix of section 1b of the *Trafficked Children Toolkit* 2011 should help identify these children. Children may be trafficked internally for a variety of reasons, many of them similar to the reasons children are trafficked between countries. Where children have been violently controlled by criminal gangs for sexual exploitation, the children may in some cases have been moved between several locations to retain control of their victims. The majority of these types of victims are girls although a number may include boys.

4.3.13   Whilst evidence so far generally relates to girls, boys may also be trafficked within the UK.

4.4 The impact of trafficking on children's health and welfare

4.4.1   All children who have been exploited will suffer some form of physical or mental harm. Usually, the longer the exploitation, the more health problems that will be experienced. Although in some cases, such as contracting AIDS or the extreme abuse suffered by Victoria Climbie, fatal injuries happen very quickly.

4.4.2   Trafficked children are not only deprived of their rights to health care and freedom from exploitation and abuse, but are also not provided with access to education. The creation of a false identity and implied criminality of the children, together with the loss of family and community, may seriously undermine their sense of self-worth. At the time they are found, trafficked children may not show any obvious signs of distress or imminent harm, they may be vulnerable to particular types of abuse and may continue to experience the effects of their abuse in the future.

Physical abuse

4.4.3   This can include:

- Inappropriate chastisement, not receiving routine and emergency medical attention (partly through a lack of care about their welfare and partly because of the need for secrecy surrounding their circumstances);
- Physical beatings and rape;
- Addiction to drugs (some trafficked children are subdued with drugs, which they then become dependent on). They are then effectively trapped within the cycle of exploitation, continuing to work in return for a supply of drugs;
- Alcohol addiction;
- Stress / post traumatic stress (PTSD) related physical disorders such as skin diseases, migraine, backache etc.

4.4.4   Some forms of harm might be linked to a belief in spirit possession[4]

Emotional and psychological abuse

4.4.5   Emotional abuse is involved in all types of maltreatment of a child, including trafficking.

4.4.6   Trafficked children may:

- Feel disorientated after leaving their family environment, no matter how impoverished and difficult. This disorientation can be compounded for some children who have to assume a new identity or have no identity at all;
- Feel isolated from the local community in the UK by being kept away from school and because they cannot speak English;
- Fear both the adults who have physical control of them and the threat that they will be reported to the authorities as immigration criminals;

- Lose their trust in all adults;
- Have low self-esteem and feel the experience has ruined them for life socially and psychologically. They may become depressed and sometimes suicidal;
- Worry about people in their families and communities knowing what has happened to them, and become afraid to go home; and
- Feel like criminals as a result of the new identity forced on them, which can have long term consequences for their adult lives.

4.4.7 All children who have been exploited are likely to suffer some form of mental harm, usually the longer the exploitation, the more mental health problems that will be experienced. These can include:

- Psychological distress owing to their sense of powerlessness. In many cases involving violence and deprivation at the hands of their traffickers, which can be extreme, it will take the form of post traumatic stress disorder;
- Dependent relationships with their abusers;
- Flashbacks, nightmares, anxiety attacks, irritability and other symptoms of stress, such as nervous breakdowns;
- A loss of ability to concentrate; and
- Becoming anti-social, aggressive and angry, and/or fearful and nervous – finding it difficult to relate to others, including in the family and at work.

Sexual abuse

4.4.8 Trafficked children may be sexually abused as part of being controlled or because they are vulnerable. In many cases, sexual exploitation is the purpose of the trafficking. Children being sexually exploited are at risk of sexually transmitted infections, including HIV/AIDS; and for girls there is the risk of an unwanted early pregnancy and possible damage to their sexual and reproductive health[5].

Neglect

4.4.9 Trafficked children may also suffer neglect. In particular, they may not receive routine and emergency medical attention (partly through a lack of care about their welfare and partly because of the need for secrecy surrounding their circumstances). They may also be subject to physical, sensory and food deprivation. Trafficked and exploited children are deprived of their rights to health and freedom from exploitation and abuse, and to education and related life opportunities.

5. IDENTIFYING TRAFFICKED AND EXPLOITED CHILDREN

5.1 Role of all professionals

5.1.1 All professionals who come into contact with children in their everyday work need to be able to identify children who may have been trafficked, and be competent to act to support and protect these children from harm. They should follow the practice guidance set out below, which is in accordance with the *London Child Protection Procedures*. If working outside London and not using the *London Child Protection Procedures*, please refer to your local, regional or, in the case of Scotland, national child protection procedures.

5.1.2 Whenever a professional identifies that a child may have been trafficked, s/he should act promptly before the child goes missing and assess the child's levels of need / risk of harm as set out in this guidance.

5.1.3 Identifying trafficked children at ports of entry is likely to be difficult as they may not be showing obvious signs of distress (see section 5.2 Obstacles to self-identification, below). The ports' intelligence units have developed a profile of trafficked children to assist immigration officers (see the on-line trafficking toolkit[21]). Other resources readily available to all staff include the location of Paladin-type teams, and the local UKBA.

5.1.4 Child victims may be discovered in routine police operations to detect and disrupt trafficking networks, and during other criminal investigations both in the UK and abroad. Anyone who works with children may come into contact with a victim of trafficking.

5.1.5 All agencies working with children who may have been trafficked into and within the UK should work together to safeguard and promote their welfare, providing the same standard of care that is available to any other child in the UK. This may be the crucial intervention which breaks the cycle of the child being vulnerable to continuing or further exploitation.

5.2 Obstacles to self-identification

5.2.1 Children are unlikely to disclose they have been trafficked, as most do not have an awareness of what trafficking is or may believe they are coming to the UK for a better life, accepting that they have entered the country illegally. It is likely that the child will have been coached with a story to tell the authorities in the UK and warned not to disclose any detail beyond the story, as this would lead them to being deported.

5.2.2 Apparent collusion with the trafficker can add to confusion when attempting to identify a child as victim of trafficking[6]. The child may be reluctant to disclose their circumstances because:

- Their experience of authority in their country of origin is such that they do not trust the police or other statutory agencies (s/he may provide a statement to a voluntary and community agency).
- The identification and referral process may mimic aspects of what had happened during trafficking – promises of help and a good life, movement by persons the child did not know, being taken to unknown locations where 'everything would be fine' and 'they would be taken care of'[7].
- The circumstances, even under exploitation, in the UK may compare more favourably to the child's experiences at home[8].

5.2.3 Disclosure from a child can take time, especially where the child is within the control of a trafficker or facilitator and relies on a relationship of trust and safety being established. If a child is in the care of a local authority, measures will need to be taken to make the placement safe for child victims of trafficking. See the tools in part three of the *Trafficked Children Toolkit* for 'additional' good practice guide on safe accommodation.

5.3 Possible indicators that a child may have been trafficked

5.3.1 Indicators are symptoms of a situation. Clusters of indicators around a child can highlight concern which triggers a systematic assessment of their circumstances and experiences.

5.3.2 There are a number of indicators which suggest that a child may have been trafficked into the UK, and may still be controlled by the traffickers or receiving adults. These are as follows:

At port of entry

5.3.3 The child:

- Has entered the country illegally;
- Has no passport or other means of identification;
- Has false documentation;
- Possesses money and goods not accounted for;
- Is malnourished;
- Is unable to confirm the name and address of the person meeting them on arrival;
- Has had their journey or visa arranged by someone other than themselves or their family;
- Is accompanied by an adult who insists on remaining with the child at all times;

- Is withdrawn and refuses to talk or appears afraid to talk to a person in authority;
- Has a prepared story very similar to those that other children have given;
- Exhibits self-assurance, maturity and self-confidence not expected to be seen in a child of such age;
- Does not appear to have money but does have a mobile phone; and/or
- Is unable or reluctant to give details of accommodation or other personal details.

5.3.4   The sponsor could:

- Be a community member, family member, or any other intermediary[9];
- Have previously made multiple visa applications for other children and/or has acted as the guarantor for other children's visa applications; and/or
- Is known to have acted as the guarantor on the visa applications for other visitors who have not returned to their countries of origin on the expiry of those visas.

5.3.5   See section 7.1.3 for actions following the identification of a trafficked child by port authority staff.

Whilst resident in the UK (in addition to those listed above)

5.3.6   The child:

- Receives unexplained / unidentified phone calls whilst in placement / temporary accommodation;
- Shows signs of physical or sexual abuse, and/or has contracted a sexually transmitted infection or has an unwanted pregnancy;
- Has a history with missing links and unexplained moves;
- Has gone missing from local authority care;
- Is required to earn a minimum amount of money every day;
- Works in various locations;
- Has limited freedom of movement;
- Appears to be missing for periods;
- Is known to beg for money;
- Performs excessive housework chores and rarely leaves the residence;
- Is being cared for by adult/s who are not their parents and the quality of the relationship between the child and their adult carers is not good;
- Is one among a number of unrelated children found at one address;
- Has not been registered with or attended a GP practice;
- Has not been enrolled in school;
- Has to pay off an exorbitant debt (e.g. for travel costs) before having control over own earnings;
- Is permanently deprived of much of their earnings by another person; and/or
- Is excessively afraid of being deported.

Children internally trafficked within the UK

5.3.7   Indicators include:

- Physical symptoms (bruising indicating either physical or sexual assault);
- Prevalence of a sexually transmitted infection or unwanted pregnancy;
- Young person known to be sexually active;
- Reports from reliable sources suggesting the likelihood of involvement in sexual exploitation / the child has been seen in places known to be used for sexual exploitation;
- Evidence of drug, alcohol or substance misuse;
- Leaving home / care setting in clothing unusual for the individual child (inappropriate for age, borrowing clothing from older people);
- Phone calls or letters from adults outside the usual range of social contacts;
- Adults loitering outside the child's usual place of residence;
- Significantly older boyfriend;
- Accounts of social activities, expensive clothes, mobile phones or other possessions with no plausible explanation of the source of necessary funding;

- Persistently missing, staying out overnight or returning late with no plausible explanation;
- Returning after having been missing, looking well cared for despite having no known base;
- Placement breakdown;
- Pattern of street homelessness;
- Having keys to premises other than those known about;
- Low self-image, low self-esteem, self-harming behaviour including cutting, overdosing, eating disorder, promiscuity;
- Truancy / disengagement with education;
- Entering or leaving vehicles driven by unknown adults;
- Going missing and being found in areas where the child or young person has no known links; and/or
- Possible inappropriate use of the internet and forming on-line relationships, particularly with adults.

5.3.8 The indicators above should not be read as a definitive list and professionals should be aware of any other unusual factors that may suggest a child might have been trafficked. They are intended as a guide, which should be included in a wider assessment of the young person's circumstances as well as part of a trafficking assessment.

5.3.9 It is also important to note that trafficked children might not show obvious signs of distress or abuse and this makes identifying children who may have been trafficked difficult. Some children are unaware that they have been trafficked, while others may actively participate in hiding that they have been trafficked.

5.4 Private fostering[10]

5.4.1 Private fostering is defined in *section 66 of the Children Act 1989*. A private fostering arrangement arises when a child under 16 years (or under 18 if disabled) is to reside for more than 28 days in the care of someone who is not a parent, close relative, or someone with parental responsibility (these close relatives are defined by the Act as grandparents, brother, sister, uncle or aunt whether of the full blood or half blood or by marriage or civil partnership or step-parent).

5.4.2 Many private fostering arrangements are not notified to the local authority for a variety of reasons, not all associated with a risk of serious harm. Identifying a child who is privately fostered is not the same as identifying a child who has been trafficked. Nevertheless, some children in private fostering arrangements are vulnerable to being exploited in domestic servitude, other forms of forced labour, or even to sexual exploitation. Where indicators of child trafficking are present, a child trafficking assessment will provide a vehicle to aid in identification.

5.5 Local expertise in relation to trafficked children

5.5.1 Local authorities are recommended to nominate a local professional who can develop specialist knowledge in relation to trafficked children – a 'local trafficked children lead' – to act as an adviser to other professionals in cases where the concerns in relation to a child are related to trafficking. This postholder could support staff in more than one local authority area.

5.6 The trafficking risk assessment matrix

5.6.1 Professionals should use the Risk Assessment Matrix in section 1b of the *Trafficked Children Toolkit* to identify and assess whether there are reasonable grounds to suspect that the child is trafficked. The matrix can be used to assist initial identification or as an aid to thinking as part of the assessment process e.g. the CAF or specialist assessments.

5.6.2 The Risk Assessment Matrix is a tool to assist professionals (the term includes unqualified managers, staff and volunteers) in using the available information to focus their thinking and form the basis for discussion about the risk of harm - through trafficking - to a child. This may include deciding that the available information is not enough to form a sound judgement about the risk.

5.6.3 If a professional ticks a descriptor which indicates that a child is at risk of harm (e.g. 'physical symptoms of exploitative abuse' or 'under age marriage'), the professional should make an immediate referral to LA children's social care, in line with section 7.1 Referral to LA children's social care, regardless of whether the child may be trafficked.

5.7 Information gathering

5.7.1 Information gathering should include the child's presenting behaviours and what s/he discloses together with any known information about the child's circumstances, and expert advice about trafficked children. The expert advice (including identifying children, ensuring their safety, gaining their trust and assessing them) can be obtained from:

- The local trafficked children lead (see section 5.5, above);
- The NSPCC Child Trafficking Advice and Information Line (see section 2c of the *Trafficked Children Toolkit* additional information); and
- Another local authority with expertise in responding to trafficked children.

5.7.2 The tools for gathering information and making an assessment are:

- The Common Assessment Framework; and
- A specialist / statutory assessment (including LA children's social care initial and core assessments).

5.7.3 See the Quick guide to assessments and levels of intervention in section 1g of the *Trafficked Children Toolkit*, according to which the four levels of need which an assessment could indicate for a child are:

- Level 1: Universal
- Level 2: Vulnerable – CAF
- Level 3: Complex – CAF or LA children's social care assessment
- Level 4: Acute – LA children's social care assessment

5.7.4 When a professional is concerned that a child may be at risk of being trafficked, or has been trafficked, the child is likely to be vulnerable (level 2) or at risk of harm (levels 3 or 4).

6. USE OF THE COMMON ASSESSMENT FRAMEWORK (CAF)[11]

6.1 A common assessment should be undertaken by the service or agency which first has concerns that a child may be at risk of being trafficked. There may be a need to assess (and convene meetings) about more than one child.

6.2 Where there is an immediate need for a child protection assessment and response, professionals should contact LA children's social care directly and make a referral, rather than completing a CAF. See section 7. Children at risk of or experiencing significant harm for more information.

6.3 To assist in compiling the information required for the CAF, professionals should refer to the *Trafficked Children Toolkit*, particularly sections 1a) the assessment framework for trafficked children, 1b) the Risk Assessment Matrix and 1g) quick guide to assessments and levels of intervention (Level 2: Vulnerable – common assessment and Level 3: Complex – common assessment or LA children's social care assessments).

6.4 If one of the conclusions from the common assessment is that there are reasonable grounds to believe a child is trafficked (see section 8.3, below), then the professional must follow section 7. Children at risk of / or experiencing significant harm and refer the child to LA children's social care.

7. CHILDREN AT RISK OF OR EXPERIENCING SIGNIFICANT HARM

7.1 Referral to LA children's social care

7.1.1 To assist in compiling the information required for a referral to LA children's social care, professionals should refer to the *Trafficked Children Toolkit*, particularly sections 1a) the assessment framework for trafficked children, 1b) the Risk Assessment Matrix and 1g) quick guide to assessments and levels of intervention (Level 3: Complex – LA children's social care assessments and Level 4: Acute – LA children's social care assessments).

7.1.2 If a professional is concerned that a child could be trafficked and/or at risk of significant harm, the professional should:

- Act promptly before the child goes missing;
- Wherever possible, consult with their agency's nominated safeguarding children adviser, their manager and, if available, the local professional with specialist knowledge in relation to trafficked children (see section 5.5, above); and
- If the threshold is met at level 4 for significant harm (see section 1g, Quick guide to assessments in the *Trafficked Children Toolkit*), then a referral must be made to LA children's social care, in line with the *London Child Protection Procedures*.

Port authority professionals

GATEWAY AUTHORITES

- Kent [Dover Port]
- Hillingdon [Heathrow Airport]
- Solihull [Birmingham Airport]
- Croydon [New Arrivals claiming asylum]
- West Sussex (Gatwick Airport)
- Liverpool? not sure
- Glasgow [Glasgow City Airport
- Edinburgh [Edinburgh City Airport

7.1.3 An immigration professional who is concerned that a child may have been trafficked should act promptly, following UKBA guidance. The professional should contact LA children's social care and the police based in a local child abuse investigation unit (CAIU) by telephone, confirming the referral in writing (by fax wherever possible) within 48 hours.

7.1.4 Immigration professionals should also complete the Risk Assessment Matrix and, where child trafficking is suspected, immediately refer to their LA children's services and the police.

7.2 LA children's social care response

Referral and information gathering[12]

7.2.1 The social worker should obtain as much information as possible from the referrer, including:

- The child's name, dob, address, name of carer, address if different, phone number, country of origin, home language and whether s/he speaks English, names of any siblings or other children;
- A description of the indicators and circumstances which have identified the child to the referrer as being at risk of or having been trafficked into or within the UK illegally;
- The social worker should verify that the child is living at the address as soon as possible;

- In the case of a referral from a school or education department, the list of documentation provided at admission should also be obtained;
- A Home Office check should be completed to clarify the status of the child/ren and the adult/s caring for them.

Action after the initial information gathering

7.2.2 See also section 1d) Flowchart for safeguarding a trafficked child in the *Trafficked Children Toolkit* for clarity about the child protection process once a referral has been made to LA children's social care.

7.2.3 On completion of the initial information gathering, the social worker discusses the referral with their supervising manager to agree and plan one of four ways forward:

(a) An initial assessment to decide whether:
  - appropriate arrangements for the child have been made by her/his parents
  - there are grounds to accommodate the child
  - the child is in need of immediate protection
  - section 47 enquiries should be initiated (See section 7.2.13. s.47 enquiries)

(b) Accommodation of the child under s20 Children Act 1989 – there may be enough information at this stage to support a decision to accommodate the child. A child should be accommodated under s20 Children Act 1989 if:
  - The child is lost or abandoned
  - There is no person with parental responsibility for the child
  - The person who has been accommodating the child is prevented, for whatever reason, from providing suitable accommodation or care.

If there is reasonable cause to believe that the child is suffering or likely to suffer significant harm, the child can be accommodated on a voluntary basis or an Emergency Protection Order (EPO) may be sought. The police also have powers to remove a child, but these powers (PPO) should only be used in exceptional circumstances. If, for example, there is insufficient time to seek an EPO, or for reasons relating to the immediate safety of the child.

Emergency action addresses only the immediate circumstances of the child/ren, and should be followed quickly by section 47 enquiries;

(c) Instigation of child protection enquiries and a core assessment of need under s.47 Children Act 1989 (See section 7.2.13. s.47 enquiries, below); or

(d) No further action – if no concerns are identified, the social worker should advise the referrer within 24 hours of which plan is in place.

7.2.4 The discussion between social worker and supervising manager on completion of initial information gathering should be recorded, with tasks outlined and signed off by the manager.

7.2.5 If further action is needed, consideration should be given to involvement of the police, education, health services, the referring agency and other relevant bodies (e.g. housing, the benefits agency and immigration services). Careful consideration should be given to the effect of any action on the outcome of any investigation.

7.2.6 In undertaking any assessment and all subsequent work with the child, the social worker must ensure that they use a suitable interpreter.

Initial assessment[13]

7.2.7 The initial assessment should be led by a qualified and experienced social worker. It should be carefully planned, with clarity about who is doing what, as well as when and what information is to be shared with the parents. The planning process and decisions about the timing of the different assessment activities should be undertaken in collaboration with all those involved with the child and family. The process of initial assessment should involve:

- Seeing and speaking to the child (according to their age and understanding) and family members as appropriate;
- Drawing together and analysing available information from a range of sources (including existing records); and

- Involving and obtaining relevant information from professionals and others in contact with the child and family.

7.2.8 All relevant information (including historical information) should be taken into account. This includes seeking information from relevant services if the child and family have spent time abroad. Professionals from agencies such as health, LA children's social care or the police should request this information from their equivalent agencies in the country or countries in which the child has lived[14] [15]

7.2.9 During the initial assessment, a social worker should meet with the referrer and check all the documentation held by the referrer and other relevant agencies. Documentation should include (if available), passport, Home Office papers, birth certificate and proof of guardianship. This list is not exhaustive and all possible types of documentation should be considered. A recent or new photograph of the child should be included in the social worker's file together with copies of all relevant identification documentation.

7.2.10 When assessing any documentation, attention should be given to the details. If a passport is being checked the official should:

- Verify the date of issue;
- Check the length of the visa;
- Check whether the picture resembles the child;
- Check whether the name in the passport is the same as the alleged mother/father, and if not, why not; and
- Check whether it appears to be original and take copies to ensure further checks can be made if necessary.

7.2.11 Immigration staff will be able to give a clear explanation of the immigration process, different forms of documents, leave to enter the UK and opinions on a document's validity.

7.2.12 Even if there are no apparent concerns, child welfare agencies should continue to monitor the situation until a child is appropriately settled. The social worker should advise the referrer of their decision and the proposed plan. In each case of a child with immigration issues UKBA should be informed so that they can co-ordinate the immigration processes with the child's protection plan.

Strategy meeting / discussion as part of section 47 enquiries[16]

7.2.13 Once the relevant information has been gathered, social worker and supervising manager, together with the police, should decide whether to convene a strategy discussion.

7.2.14 LA children's social care must convene a strategy meeting within two working days of:

- The child becoming looked after; or
- Arrival in the borough where intending to reside, if s.47 enquiries are appropriate.

7.2.15 The strategy meeting must:

- Share information – this should involve the Child Abuse Investigation Team, UKBA and the local police and any other relevant professionals;
- Develop a strategy for making enquiries into the child's circumstances, including consideration of a video interview;
- Develop a plan for the child's immediate protection, including the supervision and monitoring of arrangements (for looked after children this will form part of the care plan);
- Agree what information can be given about the child to any enquirers; and
- Agree what support the child requires.

Interview as part of section 47 enquiries[17]

7.2.16 The decision to conduct a joint interview with the child and, if necessary, with the child's carers will have been taken at the strategy meeting. The interviews must be conducted in line with the *London Child Protection Procedures*[18]. In particular, the child should be seen alone and in a safe environment.

7.2.17 Planning and undertaking the interview/s could involve the Child Abuse Investigation Team, the UKBA and/or the local police. It may be helpful to involve immigration officials in this decision-making as outstanding immigration concerns may need resolving. In the longer-term, information gathered at an interview might help to resolve the child's immigration status. Intelligence gathered from the interview may also be helpful in preventing other children being trafficked from overseas.

7.2.18 Professional interpreters, who have been approved and CRB checked, should be used where English is not the child's preferred language. Under no circumstances should the interpreter be the sponsor or another adult purporting to be a parent, guardian or relative[19]. Every child should be given ample opportunity to disclose any worries away from the presence of the sponsor.

7.2.19 The interview should focus on the following areas:

- The child's family composition, brothers, sisters, ages;
- The child's parents' employment;
- Tasks done around the house;
- Length of time in this country;
- Where they lived in their country of origin;
- Where they went to school in their country of origin; and
- Who cared for them in their country of origin.

7.2.20 The adults in the family should be interviewed separately, covering the same areas. A comparison can then be made between the answers to ensure they match.

7.2.21 All documentation should be seen and checked. This includes Home Office documentation, passports, visas, utility bills, tenancy agreements and birth certificates. Particular attention should be given to the documentation presented to the school at point of admission. It is not acceptable to be told that the passport is missing or that the paperwork is missing. It is extremely unlikely that a person does not know where their paperwork / official documentation is kept and this information could be considered as an indicator the child may have been trafficked.

7.2.22 The interview should be conducted as fully as possible, both to ensure accuracy and to avoid intrusion into the family for a longer period than is absolutely necessary.

On completion of section 47 enquiries

7.2.23 On completion of the section 47 enquiries, a meeting should be held with the social worker, their supervising manager, the referring agency as appropriate, the police and any other professionals involved to decide on future action. Further action should not be taken until this meeting has been held and multi agency agreement obtained to the proposed plan unless emergency action is required.

7.2.24 Where it is found that the child is not a family member and is not related to any other person in this country, consideration should be given as to whether the child needs to be moved from the household and/or legal advice sought on making a separate application for immigration status.

7.2.25 Any law enforcement action regarding fraud, trafficking, deception and illegal entry to this country is the remit of the police. The local authority should assist in any way possible. However, the responsibility for taking legal action usually remains with the criminal justice agencies (exceptions include benefit fraud, held by Department of Work and Pensions).

8. THE NATIONAL REFERRAL MECHANISM (NRM)

8.1 Overview and role of competent authority

8.1.1 In accordance with the requirements of the *Council of Europe Convention on Action against Trafficking in Human Beings*, the UK has a national referral mechanis for identifying and recording victims of trafficking and ensuring that they are provided with appropriate support wherever they are in the UK.

8.1.2 Decisions about who is a victim of trafficking are made by trained specialists in designated 'Competent Authorities'. The UKHTC and UKBA act as the UK's Competent Authorities with responsibility for the final decision on whether a frontline professional's grounds for believing that the child has been trafficked are founded (i.e. whether the child is or is not a victim of trafficking).

8.1.3 Where necessary, the Competent Authority will assist in regularising a child's immigration status, in accordance with the Council of Europe Convention on Action Against Human Trafficking.

8.1.4 As referrals are collated through the NRM process, the build up of evidence concerning child trafficking will inform policy makers and operational staff to take the necessary decisions and actions to combat child trafficking. In this sense. NRM referrals and the intelligence they provide contribute directly to UK efforts to tackle human trafficking and may ultimately lead to delivery of a reduction of children trafficked and who are ultimately safeguarded by a local authority.

8.1.5 Referrals into the NRM will provide a national picture of numbers of children trafficked, as well as supporting evidence which will assist in building up intelligence such as trends, routes of travel and details which may assist in leading to the arrest and conviction of those who commit this terrible crime.

8.1.6 NRM referrals will also help the local authority focus their approach to the appropriate response for the child by ensuring all available information can be gathered and shared quickly between partners. This will allow the child's needs to be addressed as well as certain mitigating factors taken into account such as the risk of the child going missing.

8.1.7 In addition where necessary, the Competent Authority will assist in regularising a child's immigration status. This will assist the child in accessing particular services.

8.1.8 Responsibility for the care, protection and accommodation of child trafficking victims rests with local authorities under their duty to safeguard and promote the welfare of all children. Separated and vulnerable children from abroad have the same entitlements as UK born or resident children.

8.1.9 Where a child is assessed as in need and becomes looked after by a local authority, a social worker will be responsible for putting in place an individualised care plan covering the full range of the child's needs. The social worker will also make an assessment of the type of placement which best matches the needs of the child, including the need to safeguard them from contact with traffickers.

8.1.10 National referral mechanism overview:

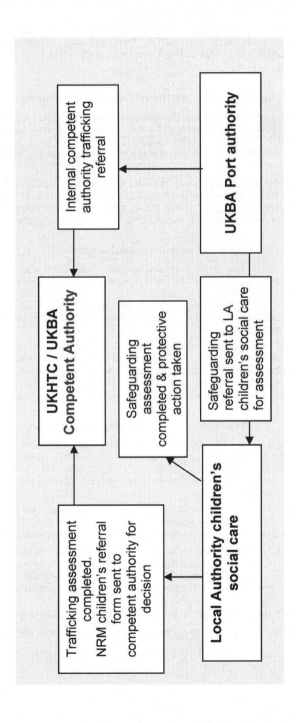

8.1.5 The national referral mechanism comprises a four stage process for establishing formally that a child is a victim of trafficking:

8.2 Stage one – safeguarding assessment

8.2.1 In the first stage a frontline professional identifies that the child may be trafficked using the indicators in <u>section 5.3</u>, and undertakes a safeguarding assessment in line with <u>section 5.7 (information gathering)</u>.

8.2.2 With support, as required, from the local trafficked children lead (see <u>section 5.5</u>, above), and using information from the safeguarding assessment, <u>the</u> professional completes the Trafficking assessment tool (section 1j in the *Trafficked Children Toolkit*).

8.3 Stage two – referral to a competent authority

8.3.1 In cases where the front line professional suspects that a child may have been trafficked, LA children's social care will refer the case to a <u>competent authority</u> by sending the child NRM referral form to UKHTC. This will <u>be in addition</u> to acting promptly before the child goes missing and initiating an assessment of the child's levels of need / risk of harm.

8.3.2 Practitioners should be aware that the safeguarding of the child takes precedence and their needs should be addressed. An NRM referral should not prevent immediate safeguarding actions taking place, although information from the NRM assessment may be helpful to those considering the safeguarding response.

8.4 Stage three – 'reasonable grounds'

8.4.1 Once the case has been formally referred, the Competent Authority will consider the details supplied on the First Responder Form along with any other evidence and apply a 'reasonable grounds' test to consider if the statement "I suspect but cannot prove" that the person is a victim of trafficking holds true. LA children's social care may be required to supply further information at this stage if there is insufficient information available.

8.4.2 The child will be granted an extendable refection and recovery period if the Competent Authority finds there are reasonable grounds to believe the child is a victim of trafficking. During this time UKBA will be asked to suspend removal action. This will allow for a fuller assessment of whether the child is a victim of trafficking. The 45 day period is also a period in which scope for criminal investigation can be explored.

8.5 Stage four – referral to competent authority

8.5.1 Following a positive reasonable grounds decision, Competent Authorities are required to make a second identification decision which is to conclusively decide if the individual is a victim of trafficking. As part of this decision, LA children's social care will be consulted and are expected to feed in any further information that may aid the decision making process.

8.5.2 LA children's social care can at any stage consider accessing assistance with reintegration available through voluntary return schemes (which are always the preferred way of carrying out any return to the child's country of origin).

8.5.3 Following a negative reasonable grounds or conclusive decision the child may still have safeguarding needs especially if they are unaccompanied. Social workers should continue to make their own assessments of a child's care needs in line with the statutory duty placed on local authorities by virtue of the Children act.

9. ISSUES TO CONSIDER WHEN WORKING WITH TRAFFICKED CHILDREN

9.1 The following services are likely to be necessary to address the child's needs:

- Appropriately trained and CRB checked independent interpreters;

- Counselling;
- Child and adolescent mental health services (CAMHS);
- Independent legal advice;
- Medical services;
- Sexual health services;
- Education;
- Family tracing and contact (unless it is not consistent with their welfare); and
- If appropriate, repatriation.

9.2   They will also need:

- Professionals to be informed and competent in matters relating to trafficking and exploitation;
- Someone to spend time with them to build up a level of trust;
- To be interviewed separately. Children will usually stick to their account and not speak until they feel comfortable;
- A safe placement - 'safe accommodation' if they are victims of an organised trafficking operation; the placement should be away from the locality where the child was recovered in order to minimise the risk to the child and reduce the risk that the child may go missing. See the Harrow Council good practice guide referenced at part three of the *Trafficked Children Toolkit* for more information.
- Their whereabouts to be kept confidential;
- Legal advice about their rights and immigration status. Professionals should make every effort to assist children to benefit from independent legal advice from a solicitor with experience in child trafficking;
- Discretion and caution to be used in tracing their families;
- A risk assessment to be made of the danger the child will face if he or she is repatriated; and
- Where appropriate, accommodation under section 20 of the children act 1989 or on application for an interim care order.

9.3   Professionals should:

- Consider interviewing children in school as they may feel more able to talk;
- Consider talking to children using the phone, e-mail, text;
- Ensure that carers are not in the proximity; and
- Ensure that interpreters are agency approved and are CRB checked.

Determining age

9.4   Assessing the age of a victim of trafficking can be necessary because a child may have documents which are fake, or belong to another child, in order to make them appear younger or older. Children are groomed (coerced) to lie about their age by the adults trafficking and exploiting them. Accordingly, information about a child provided by an accompanying adult / carer may not be accurate.

9.5   When the age of the victim is uncertain and there are reasons to believe that they are a child, either because the victim has stated they are under 18 years of age or there is documentation or information from statutory or specialist agencies that have raised concerns that they may be under 18, then s/he should be presumed to be a child and be provided with full protection as a child victim of trafficking.

9.6   Where there is concern that a child may have been trafficked and an age dispute arises, the child should be given the benefit of the doubt as to their age until his/her age is verified. This is in accordance with the Council of Europe Convention.

9.7   In circumstances where it is determined that a young victim of trafficking is an adult, professionals must follow their local Protection of Vulnerable Adults (POVA) procedure, and also contact the UKHTC.

9.8   See section 7.2.16 Interview as part of section 47 enquiries for guidance which is also relevant for interviewing children and their families / carers outside the s47 process.

Supporting child witnesses

9.9 Assessing the willingness and capacity of a child victim to support criminal proceedings at the earliest stage is critical to ensure their welfare and that the most appropriate measures are in place to provide the support they may need. The UN Convention on the Rights of the Child requires that authorities should give primary consideration to the best interests of the child.

9.10 One of the key points to recognise is that the prosecution process itself, especially the trial, can be daunting and stressful for children. There are risks of re-traumatising the child or causing the child unnecessary worry and distress. While the child may not be in any danger as a witness, he/she will still be likely to suffer from stress and worry at the thought of having to give evidence in court. It is unlikely to be possible to eliminate this altogether, but steps should be taken to reduce it to a minimum.

9.11 This also applies to the process of gathering information that might support care proceedings. Like victims of domestic abuse, the child is likely to fear reprisal from their traffickers and/or the adults with whom he or she was living in the UK if they co-operate with LA children's social care or the police

9.12 For children trafficked from abroad, an additional level of anxiety may exist because of fear of reprisals against their family in their home country. They may also fear being deported, having entered the UK illegally. Trafficked children may also have been forced to commit criminal offences while they are in a coerced situation.

9.13 The recently revised Home Office Guidance "*Achieving Best Evidence in Criminal Proceedings: Guidance for Vulnerable or Intimidated Witnesses, including Children*" [20] provides detailed recommended procedure for interviewing child witnesses. It considers planning interviews, decisions about whether the interview should be video recorded or a statement taken, preparing the witness for court and subsequent court appearances, pretrial therapy and special measures.

9.14 Children who might agree to testify in a criminal case, fear that they will be discredited in court because they were coerced into lying on their visa applications or immigration papers. No child should be coerced into testifying in court against a trafficker.

Returning trafficked children to their country of origin [safe returns]

9.15 In many cases, and with advice from their lawyers, trafficked children apply to the UKBA for asylum or for humanitarian protection. This is often because of the high risk they face of coming to harm if they are forced to return to their countries of origin. All such claims must be carefully considered.

9.16 Among the factors to consider if the child is deported is the risk of him or her being re-trafficked with the possibility of further exploitation and abuse. When considering the child's application it will be important for the social worker to gather information about the child's family, community and general conditions in the country of origin.

9.17 Local authorities have a duty of care towards children who are being returned, and this must include adequate social work checks and assessments in the country of origin to ensure that the child will be safeguarded upon their return. It is crucial that these checks are thorough and adequately address the risk of re-trafficking, taking account of specific factors relevant to the child – whether their town or village is known for trafficking children, for example, and the likelihood of the child's family allowing them to be re-trafficked.

9.18 If the child does not qualify for asylum or humanitarian protection, and adequate reception arrangements are in place in the country of origin, the child will usually have to return. The process of returning the child should be handled sensitively and will require close co-operation between the UKBA and the child's social worker. The child's social worker should ensure that the local social services department in the country of origin have been notified of the child's return.

9.19 It is important that appropriate steps are taken to minimise the possibility of the child going missing once a decision to return him or her to their country of origin has been made. Equally, the social worker may be best placed to reconcile the child to being returned, and in helping the child access the assistance with reintegration which is available through close co-operation with the social services department in the country of origin (see point 9.20, below)

9.20 Most countries have some form of reintegration support for victims of trafficking and separated children, taking account of education, health, accommodation and psychological support, details of which can be accessed through Children and Families Across Borders (CFAB, http://www.cfab.uk.net). CFAB may also be able to assist with social work checks and assessments in the child's country of origin - see section 2c of the *Trafficked Children Toolkit* for more information and contact details.

Potential prosecution of traffickers

9.18 Whether an alleged trafficker is being prosecuted may be of relevance but the decision to identify a victim (either preliminary or conclusively) is not dependent on a conviction of the perpetrators, or on whether or not the victim cooperates in the criminal proceedings.

9.19 Decision makers need to be aware that all deliberations will be subject to rules of disclosure in any subsequent prosecution for trafficking. Where an individual is being treated by the police as a potential witness, regardless of whether they are likely to be found to be victims or not, case owners should ensure lines of communication with the Senior Investigating Officer are kept open. The decision of whether someone is a victim is for the Competent Authority to make, but officers must be alert to the impact that the decision may have on the victim and other stakeholders in the criminal justice process.

10. PARTICULARLY VULNERABLE GROUPS OF CHILDREN

10.1 Trafficked children who are looked after

10.1.1 A child who may be at risk from, or has been, trafficked, may be accommodated after initial information gathering (see section 7.2.1). In these circumstances, LA children's social care will care for the child as a looked after child. The child will have a care plan (which becomes the pathway plan when s/he turns 16 and s/he will be entitled to care leaving support) based on a thorough needs assessment outlining how the local authority proposes to meet their needs.

10.1.2 The assessment of needs to inform the care plan should cover the same dimensions of need as the assessment for any other looked after child. However in addition, for children who may have been trafficked, the assessment should include:

- Establishing relevant information about the child's background;
- Understanding the reasons the child has come to the UK; and
- Assessing the child's vulnerability to the continuing influence / control of his or her traffickers.

10.1.3 Responding to this information ensures that the care plan includes a risk assessment setting out how the local authority intends to safeguard the young person so that, as far as possible, they can be protected from any trafficker to minimise any risk of traffickers being able to re-involve a child in exploitative activities. This plan should include contingency plans to be followed if the young person goes missing.

10.1.4 Given the circumstances in which potentially trafficked young people present to local authorities it will be extremely important that any needs assessments and related risk assessments are sensitively managed. It should allow for the child's need to be in a safe place before any assessment takes place and for the possibility that they may not be able to disclose full information about their circumstances immediately as they, or their families, may have been intimidated by traffickers.

10.1.5   Therefore, it will be important that:

- The location of the child should not be divulged to any enquirers until they have been interviewed by a social worker and their identity and relationship / connection with the child established, if necessary with the help of police and immigration services.
- Foster carers / residential workers should be vigilant about anything unusual (e.g. waiting cars outside the premises and telephone enquiries). See the additional good practice guide in part three of the *Trafficked Children Toolkit* for more information.
- LA children's social care should continue to share information with the police. This information may emerge during the placement of a looked after child who may have been trafficked and concern potential crimes against the child, the risk to other children, or relevant immigration matters.

10.1.6   Where adults present in this country claim a family connection to the child, then the local authority should take steps to verify the relationship between the child and these adults and exercise due caution in case they are a trafficker or a relative colluding with trafficking or exploitation of the child.

10.1.7   Anyone approaching the local authority and claiming to be a potential carer, friend, member of the family etc, of the child, should be investigated by the local authority, the police and UKBA. Normal procedures for re-uniting a child with their family should be followed. Where a child may have been trafficked it will be necessary to ensure that a risk assessment takes place prior to reunification – establishing that the adult concerned is who they say they are and is able to keep the child safe and exercise responsibility for their care.

10.1.8   It is important that no assumptions are made about young people's language skills and that assessments can call on the services of impartial translators with the necessary competences in responding to children.

10.1.9   The local authority responsible for the child should try to identify, locate and make contact with the child's parents in the country of origin, to seek their views[21]. UKBA may be able to help with this[22]

10.2 Missing children[23]

10.2.1   Research from ECPAT and CEOP (see section 2c of the *Trafficked Children Toolkit* for more information and contact details for ECPAT and CEOP) suggests that significant numbers of children who are categorised as unaccompanied asylum seeking children have also been trafficked. Some of these children go missing (back into the care of the traffickers) before being properly identified as victims of trafficking. Such cases should be urgently reported to the police.

10.2.2   Local authorities should consider seriously the risk that a trafficked child is likely to go missing and take this into account in planning that child's care. All placements should be given a copy of this guidance. A contingency plan could include contact details of agencies that should be notified if a potentially trafficked young person goes missing including the police and the UKBA. Where there are concerns that a trafficked child has been moved to elsewhere in the country away from their care placement, then it may be helpful to contact Missing People (see section 2c of the *Trafficked Children Toolkit* for more information and contact details for Missing People).

10.2.3   Missing People have a team that offers support to local authorities when young people in their care go missing and this service can advise on issues such as contact with other police forces and national publicity.

10.2.4   When the police receive the notification of a missing child they should follow the following guidance: *The Management, Recording and Investigation of Missing Persons*.

10.2.5   The guidance sets out that:

- Every missing persons report should be assessed to identify the level of risk (high, medium or low) to the missing person;
- The response should be appropriate to the level of risk;
- The risk assessment should be continuously reviewed; and
- Children who go missing from care are vulnerable and the level of risk does not diminish because of frequency of absence.

10.2.6 All local authorities should appoint a designated senior manager with responsibility for monitoring missing from care incidents, so that trends can be identified and action taken in conjunction with the LSCB to respond to the problem. Trends should also be shared with the LSCB. The designated senior manager has the potential to take an important strategic role in safeguarding children who may have been trafficked, identifying whether there are any particular patterns of children (such as unaccompanied asylum seeking children) going missing that could provide evidence suggesting that young people are being trafficked, which might be used by a local authority to inform their analysis as to how they might better safeguard these children.

10.2.7 As it is recognised that children who go missing shortly after Asylum Screening Unit (ASU) screening may have been trafficked, immigration staff should follow an agreed process to inform the appropriate authorities.

11. INFORMATION SHARING

11.1 Professionals in all agencies should be confident and competent in sharing information in line with the *London Child Protection Procedures*.

11.2 Professionals should make all efforts to share information, where appropriate, with other professionals to avoid repetition for children.

11.3 Where a professional suspects that a child may have been trafficked and/or is at risk of being trafficked, discussing concerns with the child and his/her family or carer and seeking consent to share information will place the child at increased risk of significant harm. Consent should therefore not be sought.

11.4 Professionals should talk to their agency's nominated child protection adviser, if possible, and share information with (make a referral to) LA children's social care in line with section 7. Children at risk of / or experiencing significant harm.

11.5 All agencies are empowered to share information without permission for the purpose of crime prevention under section 115 of the *Crime and Disorder Act 1998*.

12. ROLE OF LOCAL SAFEGUARDING CHILDREN BOARDS

12.1 The objective of Local Safeguarding Children Boards (LSCBs) is to co-ordinate what is done by their members to safeguard and promote the welfare of children in the local area and to ensure the effectiveness of that work. That includes addressing trafficking as well as other forms of maltreatment.

12.2 Mapping need: LSCBs should consider whether children are being trafficked into or out of their local area. Where necessary, LSCBs should undertake investigations to identify what may be a hidden problem as part of the local needs assessment and, as appropriate, make action to address this an explicit part of the LSCB business plan (which may in turn be part of the Children and Young People's Plan).

12.3 Promoting prevention: LSCBs should maintain close links with community groups and have a strategy in place for promoting awareness within the local community of the possibility that children are trafficked and exploited, and how to raise a concern. This may include public awareness work. The LSCB may publicise sources of help for child victims.

12.4 This Guidance: LSCBs should adopt this guidance as a means of supporting the professionals in all the agencies and the community their local area, to identify and respond appropriately to safeguard children who are or are at risk of being trafficked.

12.5 LSCB sub-group: LSCBs may establish a sub-group specifically to deal with trafficking issues (see section 2f for sample terms of reference).

12.6 LSCBs should also ensure that local training programmes cover trafficking issues as required, either as part of safeguarding training or as additional training.

[1] Control – to overcome or enforce consent – does not form part of the legal requirement for proof that a child has been trafficked because it is not considered possible for children to give informed consent (see the Palermo Protocol, point 2.12 in the main text).

[2] 'The application of Article 1A(2) of the 1951 Convention and/or 1967 Protocol relating to the Status of Refugees to victims of trafficking and persons at risk of being trafficked' UNHCR April 2006, p5

[3] 'Benefit' in all international legal instruments can be either monetary or non-monetary.

[4] See also the section on Spirit possession or witchcraft in the latest edition of the *London CP Procedures*.

[5] See also the *London sexual exploitation procedure (London Board, 2006)*

[6] OSCE (2007) Report on Civil Society Meeting, Warsaw, 'The NRM Approach to Trafficking and its Application to Trafficking for Labour Exploitation', p3

[7] 'Listening to Victims Experiences of identification, return and assistance in South-Eastern Europe' ICPMD, 2007 http://www.icmpd.org/768.html?&tx_icmpd_pi2[document]=593&c Hash=6688569e46 p60

[8] [Missing]

[9] Anti-Slavery International (2005) *'Protocol for identification and assistance to Trafficked Victims and Training Kit'* p7

[10] See the *London CP Procedures* for further information on private fostering.

[11] For more information on the process involved in completing a CAF, please see the *London Child Protection Procedures* and the *CAF guide for practitioners* (CWDC, 2009), available online at http://www.dcsf.gov.uk/everychildmatters/resources-and-practice/IG00063/.

[12] See the *London CP Procedures*

[13] See also the *London Child Protection Procedures*

[14] See accessing information from abroad, in the *London Child Protection Procedures*

[15] Information about who to contact can also be obtained via the Foreign and Commonwealth Office on 020 7008 1500

[16] See also sections on strategy meeting / discussion in the *London Child Protection Procedures*

[17] See the sections covering immediate protection, Section 47 enquiry thresholds and the core assessment in the *London Child Protection Procedures.*

[18] See the sections on involving parents, family members and children and visually recorded interviews / Achieving Best Evidence in the *London Child Protection Procedures.*

[19] See the sections on working with interpreters / communication facilitators in the *London Child Protection Procedures*

[20] Revised November 2007 http://www.homeoffice.gov.uk/documents/achieving-best-evidence/guidance-witnesses.pdf

[21] See also the section on accessing information from abroad in the *London Child Protection Procedures*

[22] Information about who to contact can also be obtained via the Foreign and Commonwealth Office on 0207 008 1500

[23] If a child does go missing, professionals should follow the London procedure for *Safeguarding children missing from care and home (London Safeguarding Children Board, 2006).*

Appendix 9

CROWN PROSECUTION SERVICE LEGAL GUIDANCE ON THE PROSECUTION OF DEFENDANTS (CHILDREN AND ADULTS) CHARGED WITH OFFENCES WHO MIGHT BE TRAFFICKED VICTIMS, MAY 2011

The UK is bound by the Council of Europe Treaty[1]ratified by the government on 17 December 2008 and which places specific and positive obligations upon EU States to prevent and combat trafficking and protect the rights of victims. It provides for the possibility of not imposing penalties on victims for their involvement in unlawful activities to the extent that they have been compelled to do so.

Adults and children arrested by the police and charged with committing criminal offences might be the victims of trafficking. This most frequently arises when they have been trafficked here to commit criminal offences *(some of the offences most frequently committed appear below)*

- Causing or inciting / controlling prostitution for gain: Sections 52 and 53 Sexual Offences Act 2003
- Keeping a brothel: Section 33 or 33a Sexual Offences Act 1956
- Theft (in organised "pick pocketing" gangs), under section 1 Theft Act 1968;
- Cultivation of cannabis plants, under section 6 Misuse of Drugs Act 1971

But trafficked victims may also be apprehended by law enforcement where they are escaping from their trafficking situation, the most obvious being immigration offences:

- using a false instrument under section 3 of the Forgery and Counterfeiting Act 1981;
- possession of a forged passport or documents under section 5 of the Forgery and Counterfeiting Act 1981;
- possession of a false identity document under section 6 Identity Documents Act 2010;
- failure to have a travel document at a leave or asylum interview under section 2 Asylum and Immigration (Treatment of Claimants) Act 2004.

When reviewing any such cases, prosecutors must be alert to the possibility that the suspect may be a victim of trafficking and take the following steps:

- Advise the senior investigating officer to make enquiries and obtain information about the circumstances in which the suspect was apprehended and whether there is a *credible suspicion* or *realistic possibility* that the suspect has been trafficked (this should be done by contacting the UK Human Trafficking Centre (UKHTC) *see:* http://www.ukhtc.org;
- The police should be advised to consider referring the suspect through the national referral mechanism (NRM) to the competent authority for victim identification and referral to appropriate support. In the case of children, this can be done by the Local Authority. Referral forms can be found here: referral form
- Where the suspect is assessed as being under 18 and has been arrested in connection with offences of cannabis cultivation, police should be referred to *ACPO Child Protection: Position on Children and Young People Recovered in Cannabis Farms* Prosecutors should also consider information from other

sources that a suspect might be the victim of trafficking, for example from a non-government organisation (NGO) which supports trafficked victims. That information may be in the form of medical reports (for example, psychiatrist reports) claiming post traumatic stress as a result of their trafficking experience.

- Re-review the case in light of any fresh information or evidence obtained.
- If new evidence or information obtained supports the fact that the suspect has been trafficked and committed the offence whilst they were coerced, consider whether it is in the public interest to continue prosecution. Where there is clear evidence that the suspect has a credible defence of duress, the case should be discontinued on evidential grounds *(but see separate section on **Children**)*.

In complying with the judgment in *R v O* [2008] EWCA Crim 2835, it is the *duty of the prosecutor* to be pro-active in causing enquiries to be made about the suspect and the circumstances in which they were apprehended. In giving their judgment the Court highlighted a number of important issues in cases such as this:

- It required that both Prosecutors and Defence lawyers are "to make proper enquiries" in criminal prosecutions involving individuals who may be victims of trafficking, in line with the findings of the Parliamentary Joint Committee on Human Rights report on Human Trafficking, that there must be co-ordinated law enforcement in protecting the rights of victims of trafficking;
- CPS legal guidance on the prosecution of trafficked victims was recognised; the court advised that this is published more widely to ensure others are aware of it;
- The court, defence and prosecution were criticised for failing to recognise that O was a minor.

In the case of **O**, guidance on the prosecution of trafficked victims was not followed.

The importance of following the guidance was further re-enforced by *LM, MB, DG, Betti Tabot and Yutunde Tijani v The Queen* [2010] EWCA Crim 2327

Some trafficked victim's experiences are likely to be outside the knowledge and experience of prosecutors. For example young female victims may be subject to cultural and religious practices such as witchcraft and juju rituals inherent in their culture which binds them to their traffickers through fear of repercussions.

Other trafficked victims may be held captive, physically and sexually assaulted and violated, or they may be less abused physically but are psychologically coerced and are dependent on those who are victimising them.

Prosecutors should therefore have regard to these wider factors when considering whether the circumstances of the person's situation might support a defence of duress in law. In *Lynch v DPP for Northern Ireland* [1975] A.C. 653, HL *(Archbold 2011 17-120),*Lord Simon said . . . " . . . such well grounded fear, produced by threats, of death or grievous bodily harm or unjustified imprisonment if a certain act is not done, as overbears the wish not to perform the act, and is effective, at the time of the act, in constraining him to perform it."

The following are also factors which prosecutors might consider:

- When considering duress was the defendant driven to do what he did because he genuinely believed that if he didn't, he or a member of his family would be killed or seriously injured?
- Might a reasonable person with the defendant's belief and in his situation have been driven to do what he did?
- Was there opportunity for the defendant to escape from the threats without harm to himself, for example by going to the police?
- Did the defendant put himself into a position in which he was likely to be subject to threats made to persuade him to commit an offence of the seriousness of the charge, eg getting involved in a criminal gang likely to subject him to threats to commit criminal offences?

For further guidance on duress refer to *Archbold 17-119 to 17-122*

Even where the circumstances do not meet the requirements for the defence of duress, prosecutors must consider whether the public interest is best served in continuing the prosecution in respect of the criminal offence. The following factors are relevant when deciding where the public interest lies:

- is there a credible suspicion that the suspect might be a trafficked victim?
- the role that the suspect has in the criminal offence?
- was the criminal offence committed as a direct consequence of their trafficked situation?
- were violence, threats or coercion used on the trafficked victim to procure the commission of the offence?
- was the victim in a vulnerable situation or put in considerable fear?

Guidance has been issued to police and UK Border Agency (UKBA) on identification of victims and the indicators that might suggest that someone is a trafficked victim. However, all decisions in the case remain the responsibility of the prosecutor.

CHILDREN

Children are particularly vulnerable to trafficking and exploitation. Recent experience has highlighted the following offences as those most likely to be committed by trafficked children:

- Cultivation of cannabis plants, under section 6 Misuse of Drugs Act 1971
- Theft (in organised "pick pocketing" gangs), under section 1 Theft Act 1968

Prosecutors should be alert to the possibility that in such circumstances, a young offender may be a victim of trafficking and have committed the offences by being exploited by their traffickers or others controlling them. Child trafficking is first and foremost a child protection issue and they are likely to be in need of protection and safeguarding. In these circumstances, prosecutors should take the steps outlined above to make pro-active enquiries about the circumstances in which the child was apprehended.

The Protocol to Prevent, Suppress and Punish Trafficking in Persons, Especially Women and Children *(Palermo Protocol)* makes it clear that for child victims, consent is irrelevant; therefore there is no requirement to show the means of trafficking (that is the threat, coercion, or deception).

When considering the evidential factors set out in the previous section, in particular the reasonableness of the defendant's belief in the likely harm which might be caused to them or to their family and the likelihood of taking up opportunities to escape the threats, proper allowance should be made for the age, vulnerability and lack of maturity of the young person.

Children who have been trafficked may be reluctant to disclose the circumstances of their exploitation or arrival into the UK for fear of reprisals by the trafficker or owner, or out of misplaced loyalty to them. Experience has shown that inconsistencies in accounts given are often a feature of victims of trafficking and should not necessarily be regarded as diminishing the credibility of their claim to be a victim of trafficking

The child may have been coached by their trafficker to not disclose their true identity or circumstances to the authorities. In some cases, they may have been coached with a false version of events and warned not to disclose any detail beyond this as it will lead to their deportation.

In a similar way to adults, children may have been subject to more psychological coercion or threats, such as threatening to report them to the authorities; threats of violence towards members of the child's family; keeping them socially isolated; telling them that they / their family owes large sums of money and that they must work to pay this off; or through juju or witchcraft practices.

Police should work with local authorities to ensure early identification of trafficked victims before entering any suspected cannabis farm, in line with the "Safeguarding Children Who May Have Been Trafficked" guidance. Police and prosecutors should also be alert to the fact that an appropriate adult in interview could be the trafficker or a person allied to the trafficker

Any child who might be a trafficked victim should be afforded the protection of our child care legislation if there are concerns that they have been working under duress or if their well being has been threatened. Prosecutors are also alerted to the DCSF Guidance Safeguarding Children and Young People from Sexual Exploitation (June 2009)

In these circumstances, the youth may well then become a victim or witness for a prosecution against those who have exploited them. The younger a child is the more careful investigators and prosecutors have to be in deciding whether it is right to ask them to become involved in a criminal trial.

Prosecutors are reminded of the principles contained within the CPS policy statement on Children and Young People and in particular, our commitment to always consider the welfare of children in criminal cases.

Age disputes

Young people may have no identifying information on them, their documents may be false or they may have been told to lie about their age to evade attention from the authorities. Some victims may claim to be adults when they are in fact under 18 years of age.

Where it is not clear whether the young person is a child (i.e. under 18 years of age) then in line with the United Nations Convention of the Rights of the Child, the benefit of the doubt should be given and the young person should be treated as a child. This is re-enforced in the Council of Europe Convention on Action against Trafficking in Human Beings.

Where there is uncertainty about a suspected victim's age, Children's Services will be responsible for assessing their age. The Local Authority in whose area the victim has been recovered will have responsibility for the care of the child as required by the Children Act 1989.

Where a person is brought before any court and it appears that they are a child or young person, it is the responsibility of the court to make due enquiry as to their age. Under section 99 Children and Young Persons Act 1933 and section 150 Magistrates' Courts Act 1980 the age presumed or declared by the court is then regarded to be their true age.

For further reference on age assessment refer to *R (on the application of A) v London Borough of Croydon* [2009]; *R (M) v London Borough of Lambeth* [2009] This case concerned the duty imposed on local authorities in providing services under the Children's Act 1989 in instances where the local authorities disputed age and assessed them as adults.

CHILD TRAFFICKING

Child trafficking is the practice of transporting children into, within and out of the UK for the purposes of exploitation. The exploitation can be varied and include:

- labour exploitation (e.g. construction, restaurants, etc);
- domestic servitude;
- criminal activity (e.g. cannabis cultivation, petty street crime, illegal street trade, etc);
- sexual exploitation (brothels, closed community, for child abuse images);
- application of residence
- benefit fraud;
- illegal adoption; and
- forced marriage.

Child trafficking and exploitation is often accompanied by various types of control such as violence, the threat of violence, sexual abuse, alcohol and drug abuse, emotional abuse, manipulation through twisting cultural practices and imprisonment to suppress victims and ensure their compliance. For that reason, victims may not fully cooperate with an investigation or prosecution for fear of reprisals. Offenders may also attempt to abduct or coerce the child whilst criminal proceedings are ongoing and while the child is being cared for by the local authority.

Children are sometimes forced into committing criminal acts on behalf of their trafficker. Examples include forced cannabis cultivation and organised street crime and begging. Where it is found that the child committed an offence as a direct result of trafficking prosecutors should follow the guidance on Prosecution of Defendants (children and adults) charged with offences who might be trafficked victims. If the victim states they are a child, they should be viewed as such until their age can be verified by identification or an independent age assessment carried out by the local authority or a court determination. See age disputes

INTERNAL TRAFFICKING

Whilst the UK is primarily a destination state for human trafficking, an emerging issue is the "internal trafficking" of children. This term is used to describe the trafficking of children born, or normally resident in the UK. Internal trafficking is characterised by the recruitment, grooming and sexual exploitation of young teenage girls in the UK by organised crime gangs. Investigations may arise in circumstances where a child has gone missing (often, but not limited to, children in local authority care). They may be sexually abused before being taken to other towns and cities where the sexual exploitation (prostitution) continues.

However not all cases of child sexual exploitation and abuse will be considered to be internal trafficking. Where evidence obtained by investigators supports an offence of trafficking within the UK (under section 58 Sexual offences Act 2003), then this offence should be charged. Where other serious sexual offences involving the exploitation of children are disclosed, prosecutors should refer to legal guidance on **Children as victims and witnesses**

Further guidance on investigating and evidencing such cases can be found in the NPIA Child Abuse Guidance

The Department for Education (DFE) and Home Office published guidance in December 2007 Working Together to Safeguard Children Who May Have Been Trafficked provides guidance on the roles and functions of all relevant agencies involved in identifying and supporting child victims.

[1] The Council of Europe Convention on Action against Trafficking in Human Beings 2005.

Appendix 10

POSITION FROM ACPO LEAD'S ON CHILD PROTECTION AND CANNABIS CULTIVATION ON CHILDREN AND YOUNG PEOPLE RECOVERED IN CANNABIS FARMS

1. Police should be alert to the possibility that any person, adult or child, identified in a cannabis farm could be a victim of trafficking. CEOP strategic assessments, made up of intelligence submitted by police, UKBA, children's services and NGOs, highlight cases of children and young people being trafficked into the UK and exploited in cannabis farms. The intelligence indicates that sometimes, as a consequence of the need for more awareness of the problem, young persons are not identified as victims, statutory defences are not recognised and the individuals end up being charged, prosecuted and convicted of offences committed whilst being exploited. This is contrary to police child protection obligations where the young person has been a victim of crime. It is also contrary to responsibilities in respect of child trafficking as enumerated under the Council of Europe (COE) Convention on Action Against Human Beings, which indicates that any person under the age of 18 years cannot consent to their own trafficking. The ACPO Lead on Child Protection and Abuse Investigation, and the ACPO Lead on Cannabis Cultivation have endorsed the following approach.

2. In line with the "Safeguarding Children Who May Have Been Trafficked" guidance, police should work with local authorities to ensure early identification of trafficked victims before entering any suspected cannabis farm. In the planning stage of any proactive operations or other police interventions on cannabis farms, dual operational planning should focus not only on the recovery of illegal drugs and the arrest of members of criminal enterprises, but also on the safeguarding of any children who are being exploited on the premises. Inter-agency strategies and protocols for early identification and notification should be set in place in advance in collaboration with local children's services and UKBA representatives. The police team leading on the preparation of the proactive operation should consult with the force Child Protection team and, where it is anticipated that child victims of trafficking may be present, utilise Child Protection officers in the operation to ensure that safeguarding actions take place.

3. Every individual identified as, or claiming to be, a child or young person in a cannabis farm should be assessed on a case by case basis to ascertain whether they may have been trafficked. Where circumstances give rise to reasonable suspicion that they are being exploited or abused, a child welfare response should be taken.

4. No decision to progress charges against such individuals should be made until all relevant assessments have been undertaken. Prosecutors and Duty Solicitors have a duty to make full and proper enquiries in criminal prosecutions involving individuals who may be victims of trafficking and to be proactive in establishing if a suspect is a potential victim of trafficking. Therefore, information about concerns of trafficking should be fully shared with the CPS. Cases of individuals claiming to be under 18 when they are not for tactical purposes are common. However, in cases of doubt, the young person should be given the benefit of that doubt in accordance with the COE convention until information to the contrary is available. Where official records, or other reliable evidence, are not available to confirm age, a Merton compliant age assessment[1] should be carried out by the local authority.[2]*

5. On recovery of any young person in a cannabis farm s/he should be taken to a place of safety immediately. A check on PNC or UKBA CID (Central Intelligence Database) should be undertaken to ensure that police use all available resources to find information about the young person.

6. A referral should be made to the local authority children's services for the appropriate assessments. Children's services should be prepared for this referral, having

been involved in the planning stages before entry into the premises. The local authority representative should be informed of the circumstances in which the young person was identified and the concerns around trafficking. The police should share as much information as possible to help children's services undertake the appropriate assessments. A local authority representative should attend the police station (or other place of safety where the young person is taken) within an hour of notification to undertake a joint assessment and to produce a protection plan designed to keep the young person safe. This would require an interpreter who is able to safely communicate with the young person in their own language.

7. The overall aim of the local authority and police should be to assure the young person that they are safe. Police and local authorities need to be aware that the young person is likely to be at extremely high risk of running away from care, due to continued coercion by their trafficker. Best practice has shown that supporting and supervising the child, keeping him/her updated and involved in the investigation process and providing an appropriate care package will prevent him/her from running away and going missing.

8. Any other welfare needs should be identified and responded to within a safeguarding and child protection context.

9. All assessments undertaken are to be decided between the local authority and the local police. The assessments used, should be in accordance with existing child protection standards and use the multi agency framework which is set out in the 'Working Together to Safeguard Children' guidance (2010)[3]. The assessments will be carried out by the appropriate child protection trained person in the relevant authority and should be carried out on an ongoing basis. Local authority, police and UKBA leads should meet within five days of initial joint assessment to discuss de-brief of the young person, ongoing strategy and their protection plan.

10. Once the young person is safe and within a more stable environment, the local authority children's services should undertake a trafficking assessment. The trafficking assessment can be found at http://www.crimereduction.homeoffice.gov.uk/humantraff icking005.htm. Where a concern of trafficking is confirmed by the assessment, a referral should be made to the relevant competent authorities within the National Referral Mechanism. The referral form is at the end of the Trafficking Assessment. Safeguarding and child protection processes should be put into place in accordance with the young person's needs.

11. It should be noted that the most important element of the response in identifying potential young victims of trafficking in cannabis farms is their protection plan and encouraging them to choose local authority care over absconding. Once these have been relatively secured, the NRM process can begin on a stronger footing.

12. If it is suspected that the young person is a potential victim of trafficking, it is the duty of the police, with assistance from local authorities, to investigate the trafficking allegations, according to section 47 of the Children's Act. It is important that offenders are prosecuted for trafficking crimes in order to protect future children from exploitation, and to act as a deterrent to others.

13. The above position of the ACPO lead takes the definition of child trafficking as that defined within the Council of Europe Convention on Action Against Trafficking in Persons. Namely "the recruitment, transportation, transfer, harbouring or receipt of a child for the purpose of exploitation". A "child" is any person under the age of 18 years of age.

---

[1]   See the ACPO Child Protection Lead's position on the use of age assessments.

[2]   *C412 B (Merton): R (B) v Merton London Borough Council* [2003] EWHC 1689 (Admin) [2003] 4 All ER 280 Stanley Burnton J. Granting JR, the Court gave guidance as to how a local authority should approach the question whether an accompanied asylum-seeker was aged less than 18 years old.

[3]   Safeguarding Children Who May Have Been Trafficked can be found at:

   http://publications.everychildmatters.gov.uk/default.aspx?PageFunction=productdetails&Pag

eMode=publications&ProductId=HMG-00994-2007. It is supplementary guidance to the statutory Working Together to Safeguard Children (2010) which can be found at:

http://publications.dcsf.gov.uk/default.aspx?PageFunction=productdetails&PageMode=publi cations&ProductId=DCSF-00305-2010

This position takes full account of existing guidance ACPO guidance on Investigating Child Abuse and Safeguarding Children (2009) under both ACPO and Statutory Guidance on Working Together to Safeguard Children.

Association of Chief Police Officers of England, Wales and Northern Ireland

ACPO Child Protection and Abuse Investigation Group

C/o The Child Exploitation and Online Protection (CEOP) Centre

Appendix 11

MINISTRY OF JUSTICE CIRCULAR 2010/07

TITLE Slavery, servitude and forced or compulsory labour: Implementation of section 71 of the Coroners and Justice Act 2009

From: Criminal Law Policy Unit

Issue date: 19 March 2010

Implementation date: 6 April 2010

contact:

England and Wales

Louise Douglas

mailto://Louise.Douglas@justice.gsi.gov.uk

020 3334 5013

Northern Ireland

Emma Dalton

mailto://Emma.Dalton@nio.x.gsi.gov.uk

02890 527314

Broad Subject Criminal Law

Sub Category Slavery, servitude and forced or compulsory labour

This circular is addressed to Lord Chief Justice, President of the Queen's Bench Division, Senior Presiding Judge, Justices of the Supreme Court, Lords Justices of Appeal, High Court Judges, Crown Court Judges, District Judges (Magistrates' Courts), Bench Chairmen, Clerks to the Justices, Chief Officers of Police, Chief Crown Prosecutors, Heads of Division Revenue and Customs Prosecution Office

Copies are being sent to: Judicial Studies Board, Council of Circuit Judges, Magistrates' Association, Justices' Clerks' Society, Registrar of Criminal Appeals, HMCS Area Directors, Crown Court Managers, HM Chief Inspector of Constabulary, Association of Chief Police Officers, Police Federation, Police Superintendents' Association, Chairpersons of Police Authorities, Association of Police Authorities, The Law Society, the Bar Council, the Criminal Bar Association, Whitehall Prosecutors' Group, Legal Services Commission, Law Centres, Citizens Advice Bureaux, Liberty, Anti-Slavery International, UK Human Trafficking Centre, Gangmasters Licensing Authority, Health and Safety Executive.

SLAVERY, SERVITUDE AND FORCED OR COMPULSORY LABOUR

Introduction

1. Section 71 of the Coroners and Justice Act 2009 ("the 2009 Act") introduces a new offence ("the section 71 offence") of holding someone in slavery or servitude, or requiring them to perform forced or compulsory labour.

2. The section 71 offence applies in England and Wales and in Northern Ireland. The

purpose of this circular is to give some guidance on the new offence to those working in the criminal justice system in England and Wales. This circular is for guidance only and should not be regarded as providing legal advice. Legal advice should be sought if there is any doubt about the application or interpretation of the legislation. The CPS will issue guidance to prosecutors on commencement of the new offence by way of Policy Bulletin and Legal Guidance.

3. Section 71 of the 2009 Act comes into force on 6 April 2010.

Elements of the offence

4. The section 71 offence consists of holding another person in slavery or servitude or requiring another person to perform forced or compulsory labour. The circumstances must be such that the defendant knows or ought to know that the person is being so held or required to perform such labour. The offence applies to legal persons (e.g. companies) as it applies to natural persons.[1]

5. A person can only commit the section 71 offence if they "hold" another person in slavery or servitude or "require" another person to perform forced or compulsory labour. If labour is subcontracted to another company and the employees of that other company who do the work are held in slavery or servitude or are required to perform forced or compulsory labour, then the subcontractor is the principal offender. However, if the contractor knows that the subcontractor's workers are being so held or required to perform such labour, then depending on the circumstances, they may be liable for aiding or abetting the subcontractor's offence, or for encouraging or assisting the commission of the offence under the provisions of the Serious Crime Act 2007 or for conspiring to commit the offence.

6. The terms "holds another person in slavery or servitude" and "requires another person to perform forced or compulsory labour" are defined in accordance with Article 4 of the European Convention on Human Rights. The offence of trafficking people for labour exploitation under section 4 of the Asylum and Immigration (Treatment of Claimants, etc.) Act 2004 ("the 2004 Act") is framed in similar terms and includes behaviour contrary to Article 4 as one form of prohibited exploitation. It should be noted, however, that the section 71 offence does not contain the element of trafficking and is not an immigration offence. It is wider and will apply irrespective of whether the victim has been trafficked and irrespective of the immigration status of the victim(s).

7. The exceptions under Article 4(3) of the European Convention on Human Rights, which acknowledge that forced or compulsory labour may be necessary in certain circumstances in order to ensure public safety and the rights of others, will automatically apply to the new offence. Those exceptions are work done in the course of lawful detention, military service, emergencies or life threatening situations and work or service which forms part of normal civic obligations.

8. In interpreting section 71, the courts will have regard to existing case law on Article 4 of the European Convention on Human Rights and any relevant case law on section 4 of the 2004 Act. In establishing what might constitute slavery, characteristics of ownership of the person need not be present. Servitude is much wider. Courts have been guided by Articles 1 and 7 of the 1956 UN Supplementary Convention on the Abolition of Slavery, and have stated that servitude involves a particularly serious form of denial of freedom and that "in addition to the obligation to provide services for others, [it involves] . . . the obligation for the 'serf' to live on another person's property and the impossibility of changing his condition"[2]

9. In establishing forced or compulsory labour, the section 71 offence will require an element of coercion or deception between the defendant and the victim, and the circumstances will need to be such that the defendant knew that the arrangement was oppressive and not truly voluntary, or had been wilfully blind to that fact.

10. There are a number of factors which may, depending on the circumstances, indicate that an individual is being held in servitude or subjected to forced or compulsory labour. The essential elements are those of coercion or deception, which may be demonstrated in a number of ways. The kind of behaviour that would normally,

of itself, be evidence of coercion includes (but is not limited to):-

- Violence or threats of violence by the employer or the employer's representative;
- Threats against the worker's family;
- Threats to expose the worker to the authorities (e.g. because of the worker's immigration status or offences they may have committed in the past);
- The person's documents, such as a passport or other identification, being withheld by the employer;
- Restriction of movement;
- Debt bondage;
- Withholding of wages.

11. Other factors that may be indicators of forced labour include (but are not limited to):

- The worker being given false information about the law and their employment rights;
- Excessive working hours being imposed by the employer;
- Hazardous working conditions being imposed by the employer;
- Not being provided with safety equipment and clothing, and/or being charged for the provision of such equipment that is essential to perform the work;
- Unwarranted and perhaps unexplained deductions from wages;
- The employer intentionally not paying the full tax or national insurance contributions for the worker;
- Poor accommodation provided by the employer (e.g. accommodation that is overcrowded, not licensed as a "House of Multiple Occupation" by Local Authorities, or does not have any necessary gas and electricity safety certificates);
- Intentionally poor or misleading information having been given about the nature of the employment (e.g. about the location or nature of the work);
- The person being isolated from contact with others;
- Money having been exchanged with other employers/traffickers etc for the person's services in an arrangement which has not been agreed with the person concerned or which is not reflected in his remuneration.

Penalties

12. In England and Wales and in Northern Ireland the maximum sentence on conviction on indictment for the section 71 offence is 14 years' imprisonment. The maximum sentence on summary conviction for the offence in England and Wales is six months' imprisonment.[3] The maximum sentence on summary conviction for the offence in Northern Ireland is six months' imprisonment.

Background and Context

13. It is essential that the UK has effective legislation to deal with servitude and forced labour. The behaviour can cause serious harm to individuals and to society. It creates an expectation that labour vacancies can be filled at lower than the legitimate market rate, and it creates unfair competition amongst competing businesses. The UK has a positive obligation under Article 4 of the European Convention on Human Rights to protect those within its jurisdiction from slavery, servitude and forced or compulsory labour.

14. Trading in slaves is already an offence under the Slave Trade Acts 1824-1873. However, section 71 makes clear that holding a person in slavery is also an offence. There is a range of pre-existing legislation which could cover behaviour relating to servitude and forced or compulsory labour. This includes general offences such as false imprisonment, blackmail and assault, employment legislation including offences relating to working hours, minimum wages and health and safety at work, and operating as an unlicensed Gangmaster. There are specific offences of trafficking people for labour exploitation, and offences of trafficking for sexual exploitation are provided for in sections 57-59 of the Sexual Offences Act 2003. The section 71 offence will be available in circumstances where trafficking may not have taken place or cannot be proved.

15. Because of the nature of the section 71 offence, it is possible that other offences may also have been committed alongside it, including those listed above. In circumstances where this is possible or likely, it will be for the police and the CPS to determine the most appropriate charge(s). It should be borne in mind that the elements of exploitation mentioned above may point to a wider range of offending. They might be the most obvious outward signs that there is wider criminal behaviour which requires investigation.

Sentencing guidelines

16. The Sentencing Guidelines Council's guideline, *Overarching Principles – Seriousness*, provides that where the victim is particularly vulnerable, there is deliberate targeting of vulnerable victims, or the offence is committed by a group or gang, this will be an aggravating factor in sentencing. These guidelines will apply to the section 71 offence as they do to other offences and will continue to have effect when Sentencing Guidelines Council is replaced by the Sentencing Council.

Who may be vulnerable

17. The section 71 offence will apply to all workers, although migrant workers may be particularly vulnerable. They may be vulnerable to coercion and deception for a number of reasons. They may not speak the language, they may be uncertain of their legal status in the UK, they may be distrustful of authority and they may be used to living and working conditions which are unpleasant and hazardous. They may fear being sent back to their country of origin. They may be unwilling for all these reasons to complain of their treatment, and may be even more unwilling to make a formal complaint and bear witness against their exploiters. They may have unwittingly become the victims of criminal gangs, who are threatening their safety and the safety of their families abroad.

18. The increased mobility of populations may mean that labour exploitation is continuing to increase. The section 71 offence should provide a tool to help recognise and tackle such exploitation.

Useful links

The Coroners and Justice Act 2009

http://www.opsi.gov.uk/acts/acts2009/ukpga_20090025_en_1

Explanatory notes on the Coroners and Justice Act 2009

http://www.opsi.gov.uk/acts/acts2009/en/ukpgaen_20090025_en_1

Home Office Circular 69/2004 - Asylum and Immigration (Treatment of Claimants, etc) Act 2004: Trafficking Offences

http://www.homeoffice.gov.uk/about-us/publications/home-office-   circulars/circulars -2004/069-2004/

A copy of the commencement order for the provisions addressed in this circular can be found at http://www.opsi.gov.uk/

ANNEX A

Section 71 of the Coroners and Justice Act 2009

Slavery, servitude and forced or compulsory labour

(1)   A person (D) commits an offence if—
    (a)   D holds another person in slavery or servitude and the circumstances are such that D knows or ought to know that the person is so held, or

(b)   D requires another person to perform forced or compulsory labour and the circumstances are such that D knows or ought to know that the person is being required to perform such labour.

(2)   In subsection (1) the references to holding a person in slavery or servitude or requiring a person to perform forced or compulsory labour are to be construed in accordance with Article 4 of the Human Rights Convention (which prohibits a person from being held in slavery or servitude or being required to perform forced or compulsory labour).

(3)   A person guilty of an offence under this section is liable—

     (a)   on summary conviction, to imprisonment for a term not exceeding the relevant period or a fine not exceeding the statutory maximum, or both;

     (b)   on conviction on indictment, to imprisonment for a term not exceeding 14 years or a fine, or both.

(4)   In this section—

"Human Rights Convention" means the Convention for the Protection of Human Rights and Fundamental Freedoms agreed by the Council of Europe at Rome on 4 November 1950;

"the relevant period" means—

     (a)   in relation to England and Wales, 12 months;

     (b)   in relation to Northern Ireland, 6 months.

Article 4 of the ECHR

Article 4 – Prohibition of slavery and forced labour

(1)   No one shall be held in slavery or servitude.

(2)   No one shall be required to perform forced or compulsory labour.

(3)   For the purpose of this Article the term force or compulsory labour shall not include:

     (a)   any work done in the ordinary course of detention imposed according to Article 5 of this Convention or during conditional release from such detention;

     (b)   any service of a military character or, in case of conscientious objectors in countries where they are recognised, service exacted instead of compulsory military service;

     (c)   any service exacted in case of an emergency or calamity threatening the life or well-being of the community;

     (d)   any work or service which forms part of normal civic obligations.

---

[1]   In accordance with general rules of statutory interpretation "person" includes "a body of persons corporate or unincorporated". See section 5 of and Schedule 1 to the Interpretation Act 1978

[2]   *Van Droogenbroeck v. Belgium*, no. 7906/77, Commission decision of 5 July 1979, DR 17, p. 59 &*Siliadin v France* no. 73316/01, [2005] EHRLR 660 (para 123).

[3]   On the commencement of section 154(1) of the Criminal Justice Act 2003, the maximum sentence on summary conviction in England and Wales will rise to 12 months. There are no current plans to commence this provision.

Appendix 12

THE ANTI TRAFFICKING MONITORING GROUP
WRONG KIND OF VICTIM?

One year on: an analysis of UK measures to protect trafficked persons.
Summary report
June 2010

Northern Ireland
Supriya Begum, 45
South Asia
trafficked for domestic servitude

Wales
Mikelis Đíçle, 38
Latvia
trafficked for forced labour

Scotland
Abiamu Omotoso, 20
West Africa
trafficked for sexual exploitation

England
Tuan Minh Sangree,16
Vietnam
trafficked for forced labour in cannabis farms

INTRODUCTION

In December 2008 the UK ratified the Council of Europe Convention on Action against Trafficking in Human Beings. The Convention is the first international treaty obliging states to adopt minimum standards to assist trafficked persons and protect their rights.

The Convention came into force in the UK in April 2009 but without an accompanying formal monitoring mechanism. In its absence, in May 2009 a group of nine UK-based organisations[1] set up the Anti-Trafficking Monitoring Group to monitor the implementation and to share the information they were able to gather about the UK's compliance with the Convention.

This report is a summary of the full report[2], presenting the result of the group's research to examine how the UK and its devolved administrations are meeting their obligations under the Convention. It finds that the UK Government's anti-trafficking practice is not compliant with the Council of Europe Convention on Action Against Trafficking in Human Beings and, where it relates to children, is not compliant with other aspects of UK law or best practice.

The Convention defines trafficking as acts (such as recruitment, receipt, transportation)

607

by **means** (such as threats, coercion, deception, abuse of position of vulnerability) for the purpose of **exploitation** (such as sexual exploitation, forced labour or slavery). Trafficking is defined as a crime and anyone who has been subject to the crime of trafficking should be recognised as a victim of trafficking.

The Monitoring Group identified, that in some parts of the UK, the implementation of the Convention has led to increased awareness about human trafficking[3]. Pockets of good practice seem to be developing in some areas, where stakeholders have begun to cooperate and coordinate in the absence of functioning central coordination. Such examples were seen in Bristol (where the Bristol Coalition on trafficking was created), and Wales (where a strategic lead for trafficking was created, operational points of contact were identified within the four Welsh Police forces and Gwent police convened its first consultation meeting with partner agencies including NGOs).

However in summary this report argues, based on our extensive research, that the UK is not yet meeting its obligations under the Convention. The key reasons are that, in implementing the Convention, the Government has:

- misunderstood key provisions of the Convention;
- not addressed the entirety of the Convention;
- delegated considerable authority on identification to a flawed mechanism staffed by substantially unaccountable officials;
- overlooked the necessary safeguards for child victims of trafficking in the implementation of the Convention.

The findings of this report suggest that anti-trafficking practice in the UK is not compliant with key concepts relating to the rule of law itself, specifically relating to the principle identified by Lord Bingham (2010)[4] that "questions of legal right and liability should ordinarily be resolved by application of the law and not exercise of discretion". It is a finding of this research that this principle is routinely violated in the National Referral Mechanism (NRM), the identification procedure established as part of the implementation of the Convention to help identify the victims of trafficking.

These problems, discussed in greater detail below, profoundly hamper realisation of the UK's obligations in the areas of protection and prosecution. Furthermore, there has been little to no meaningful engagement in the area of prevention.

The obligations for identification, protection, prosecution and prevention are closely intertwined. Consequently, responses also need to be linked, which implies the need for a national anti-trafficking watchdog to oversee matters. While this role is also suggested in the Convention, to date the UK Government has rejected it as unnecessary.

METHODOLOGY

The report focuses on the experience of people who have managed to escape from traffickers or who have been withdrawn from the control of others. In some cases, escape or recovery has allowed the individuals to improve their lives and heal from the trauma of trafficking. In others, the individuals who have been ill-treated by modern-day slave traders have been subject to further violations of their human rights and, in some cases, to treatment at the hands of the UK authorities which has impeded their recovery.

The report was compiled using information from public sources, from 90 interviews with professionals engaged in anti-trafficking work and by reviewing 390 individual cases. The information was obtained between September 2009 and April 2010.

SCOPE OF TRAFFICKING IN THE UK

The UK Human Trafficking Centre (UKHTC) reported in its published statistics that between April and December 2009 the cases of 527 potential victims of trafficking were referred to the National Referral Mechanism (NRM).[5] The figure was confirmed by the designated Home Office Minister during a debate in the House of Commons on 20 January 2010.[6]

Those individuals referred to the NRM came from a total of 61 countries. By far the largest source countries were Nigeria (89 people) and China (70 people). Also noticeable was Vietnam with 46 people; a significant proportion of whom are understood to have been children. The country with the next largest number of people referred was the UK itself with 37, while the next three countries (in terms of the numbers of people who were referred) were all EU countries. Out of the 527 people who were referred, 389 (74 per cent) were women or girls and 138 (26 per cent) were men or boys. Just over 140 were described as children (i.e. under 18) in the referral (26.7 per cent of the total.[7]) 195 adults (37.1 per cent) were referred as potentially trafficked for sexual exploitation and 33 per cent of total as potentially trafficked for forced labour (207).

While the data collected on the 'in' referrals to the NRM for the first time formally confirmed high proportions of presumed trafficked persons from West Africa and cases of labour trafficking, no details were published about the decisions made in response or the support offered to those found to have been trafficked. The information in this report was obtained as a result of Parliamentary Questions and Freedom of Information requests, interviews and case review. The responses to questions were essential to build up a picture of how the system was functioning.

The number of referrals is not a true reflection of the extent of trafficking in the UK or the number of individuals who have been victims of traffickers in the UK. This research collected information about **more than 130 individuals** who were identified by support organisations between 1 April 2009 and 1 April 2010 **whose cases were not referred to the system for a variety of reasons, but primarily because they did not see the benefit of being referred or were fearful of the consequences** of being brought to the attention of the authorities because of their immigration status – a paradoxical situation, as it concerns precisely the same fear that traffickers often use to control their victims.

These figures corroborate the initial concern that the nature of the NRM itself actually deters a significant proportion of the intended beneficiaries from using it; and therefore from accessing services and exercising their rights. This suggests the system is not fit for purpose.

FLAWED IDENTIFICATION SYSTEM

The principal response of the Government to their obligations as party to the Convention was the establishment of an identification system called the National Referral Mechanism (NRM). The OSCE suggest[8] that NRMs should be a multi-agency coordination system and their every stage an opportunity to help trafficked persons. The system appears to be relying excessively on the discretion of officials who receive minimal training to staff a mechanism supported by flawed legal guidance relating to who should be identified as victims of trafficking, and without a formal appeals process. This fails to consistently identify and assist people who have been trafficked. Furthermore, the system appears to be putting more emphasis on the immigration status of the presumed trafficked persons, rather than the alleged crime committed against them. The UK citizens referred were speedily identified as having been trafficked with a rate of 76 per cent of cases positively identified as trafficking, in contrast with the rate of cases positively identified as trafficked as a whole of 19 per cent. The rate of nationals from other EU states identified as trafficked was 29.2 per cent, while that of nationals from countries outside the EU was only 11.9 per cent. The different rates of positive identification should not be interpreted as evidence per se of discrimination against people originating outside the EU. However, the difference in success is startling. On this basis alone, these figures merit further investigation by the Home Office, to check that individuals from outside the EU are not being subject to discrimination in the decision-making process.

This report argues that the term 'referral' into the NRM has been misused to refer narrowly to a procedure for vetting whether individuals meet a bureaucratic standard for having been trafficked. In practice this often fails to meet the needs of people who have suffered abuse and trauma at the hands of those who trafficked and exploited them. In effect, in the UK 'referral' means that the case of an individual is being submitted to a central government authority to decide on their status, not that they are being referred to a range of specialised services.

When victims are wrongly identified this has serious consequences for the person concerned: it risks compounding the already traumatic experience of having been trafficked by setting back their recovery and removing any faith individuals may have had in the authorities and their ability to offer protection and assistance; thus undermining prosecutions and causing further breaches of individual's human rights.

The UK authorities consequently seem to have misconstrued the concept of 'competent authorities' as understood under the Convention[9] and restricted the role of identifying and referring presumed victims to a specific authority known as the Competent Authority. In the UK the Competent Authority role is fulfilled by designated officials from the UK Border Agency.

The research found that the system has not facilitated prosecutions as expected and in some instances the police were concerned that it even undermined prosecutions. No specific statistics on the total number of prosecutions or the number of successful prosecutions since April 2009 are available. In response to a Freedom of Information request[10] in January 2010, the UKHTC reported that since April 2009 a total of 36 individuals, (17 of them women), who were arrested across England and Wales on trafficking offences, had cases against them heard in court.

CHILD VICTIMS OF TRAFFICKING

Children comprised just under a third of the 527 individuals referred to the NRM in 2009. Of the 143 referred children, 85 were reported to be girls and 58 were boys; approximately half (69) were below the age of 16 and half (72) were aged 16 or 17. Of those, 45 girls and two boys were trafficked for sexual exploitation; 12 girls and seven boys were trafficked for domestic servitude; 34 boys and 13 girls were trafficked for forced labour; and in 30 cases (half boys and half girls) the form of exploitation was not known. The question explored in the course of this research with regard to children is whether the procedures introduced in April 2009 have resulted in any improvement in comparison to pre-existing systems.

The research examines in some detail the impact of the implementation of the Convention on child victims of trafficking. A strong and mature framework exists in the UK to safeguard children and the government has clearly stated that it views child trafficking as a form of child abuse. However in setting up the NRM the UK in effect decided to bypass this existing system and not to task local authority children's services to act as the primary identifier in cases of children who may have been trafficked, despite their expertise in child protection and their statutory duty to safeguard children. Instead, they are required to refer the case for decision to the NRM, which is viewed by a number of research respondents as having insufficient expertise in relation to children. Several of those concerned about the cases of trafficked children expressed the view to the Monitoring Group that it was not appropriate for the Home Office to be the government department with lead responsibility concerning trafficked children and that its place should be taken by relevant government departments responsible for children. Children are not 'mini-adults' and attempting to fit them into the system for adults is inappropriate.

The special measures for children contained in the Convention provide its added value to UK law, policy and practice, and this is where the Convention could have made a significant difference to the treatment of child victims of trafficking; augmenting the rights and safeguards already in place for children. It contains various provisions which are specific to children and confirms that procedures concerning children (or young people who might be children) must be different to those that concern adults. These special measures include that a suspected child victim should be considered a child and given the benefit of the doubt that they are a child when their age is uncertain and requires that immediately after an unaccompanied child is identified as a victim, they shall be provided with a legal guardian, organisation or authority to act in the child's best interest, before being referred into the NRM.

There are a number of challenges to the successful identification and protection of child victims of trafficking in the UK discussed in detail in the full report. Of particular significance is the need for frontline service providers to be able to identify suspected child victims of trafficking at the earliest possible opportunity. This necessitates both understanding of trafficking on the part of those agencies likely to come across child victims of trafficking and an ability to recognise children as children. A crucial issue in terms of the UK authorities viewing children as victims of trafficking concerns the locations in which a suspected child victim may be found, such as in a brothel, cannabis factory or forced into petty street crimes such as ATM theft and pick-pocketing. The report details the problems when statutory agencies do not recognise situations of exploitation as potential trafficking cases and instead identify a young trafficked person as a criminal, rather than a victim of crime.

The assessment of the age of unaccompanied and separated children arriving in the UK is a controversial issue. Children who may have been trafficked are frequently found without identification documents or with false documents and additionally may have been instructed by their traffickers to lie about their age (as well as other matters), to appear either older or younger than their actual age. This situation is exacerbated when traffickers have provided children with forged passports or other identity documents that state they are adults. The research reveals concerns by child protection organisations that the UKBA and other statutory agencies do not give young people this "benefit of the doubt", as they are required to, including by their own policy guidance, in disputed cases. This is a significant problem.

It is also of great concern that no-one is required to represent the child's best interests, as required by the Convention, since in principle children, like adults, are only likely to want their case referred if it is in their best interests. One solution here would be to appoint a legal guardian at an early stage, before a child's case is referred to the NRM.

As well as the need for a guardian to be responsible for upholding the best interest for trafficked children, the research identifies the need for safe accommodation and other services such as adequate legal representation and interpreters which are not routinely available. The lack of suitable accommodation and adequately trained supervisors or foster parents has been highlighted by the on-going scandal of children going missing from care.

FAILURE TO IMPLEMENT THE ENTIRETY OF THE CONVENTION

The 47 Articles of the Convention require a holistic approach to dealing with trafficking: namely that it requires states to take measures to protect victims, prevent trafficking, prosecute those responsible and ensure that states combat trafficking through international cooperation. However there is neither a national watchdog with the powers to ensure that this occurs, nor a National Victim Care Coordinator to ensure and monitor that all presumed trafficked persons can access their rights under Article 12 of the Convention.

As a result, access to services for identified victims of trafficking is usually patchy. Dedicated accommodation for trafficked women is, in theory, available in England, Wales, Northern Ireland, and Scotland. In practice, space in appropriate accommodation is not always available and some trafficked women have been housed in unsuitable places. Accommodation for male victims of trafficking is severely limited and NGOs often have to find resources to fund specialised services. In addition to accommodation, other services such as interpreters or legal representations are routinely not available.

Another key obligation that has not been met is in relation to access to compensation. The government is not providing information to all trafficked persons about what compensation they might be entitled to and preventing them from staying in the UK to pursue compensation.

The creation of a national anti-trafficking watchdog body with oversight of the implementation of the whole of the Convention could have prevented such gaps.

MISINTERPRETATION OF KEY PROVISIONS

The Monitoring Group found a few individual cases where the intervention of the police helped to uphold the "non-punishment clause" of the Convention. For example, in a case of an Eastern European woman, the police alerted a service provider to a woman being held in custody, after having been arrested for immigration offences and possession of stolen documents. Both the service provider and police were concerned that this woman had been trafficked. The police communicated their concerns to the court and the court decided to take no further action taken against her.

However such cases appear to be the exception rather than the rule. The analysis reveals that one of the key problems is the incorrect application of the trafficking definition when assessing who is a victim of trafficking. Too often the authorities fail to apply the Convention and do not define as victims all those who were subject to the crime of trafficking. Instead, the system creates a narrow, legally dubious, interpretation of a victim, and attaches conditions that have been proven to impede identification, and have also been found to undermine prosecution in some cases. For example, in numerous cases reviewed by the research, the authorities concluded that as the person concerned agreed to come to the UK for work, they could not have been trafficked despite the fact that the deception and abuse should, according to the Convention, render such consent irrelevant.

In recent years the police have discovered numerous cannabis farms in England, Scotland and Wales, many of them located in private houses.[11] Often the adults or children encountered by police during raids had recently arrived from other countries, notably Vietnam. There are good grounds for considering that some of these individuals were subjected to forced labour and had been trafficked. However, the prosecutions of these individuals that have resulted suggest that the UK authorities have great difficulty in identifying anyone arrested in a cannabis farm as a potential victim of trafficking.

In these cases and other similar ones, the UK authorities seem to have recognised that cannabis 'gardeners' have been subjected to pressure, but concluded that they were nevertheless responsible for their crime and should be punished. Further, the UK authorities have not protected the person concerned from the pressures exerted on them by their traffickers and/or exploiters. In other words, in a critical area the anti-trafficking system practiced in the UK does not seem to be ensuring non-punishment of victims of trafficking. Despite existing guidance from the Crown Prosecution Service, victims of trafficking are still routinely prosecuted for offences they committed when coerced. Victims are prosecuted, while the real criminals continue their profitable business.

This research suggests that the UK is creating a 'hierarchy' of victims, and allows, intentionally or not, discrimination against certain categories of victims, such as those who were trafficked before the Convention came into force (but identified after), or those coming from particular countries or regions. The research indicates that the system fails to treat those who have been trafficked as victims of crime and places too much emphasis on judging them, rather than bringing traffickers to justice.

CONCLUSION

Based on the research undertaken as part of this project the Anti-Trafficking Monitoring Group argues that in practice the UK has not established a system led by the principle that a person who has been trafficked has experienced abuse and requires time to recover before being exposed to the rigours of an immigration system that is designed to identify and remove people without entitlement to remain in the UK. The existing system is neither satisfying the provisions of the Convention nor key principles of rule of law itself. Pockets of local good practice contrast with the centralised adversarial system that lacks any formal coordination and seems to be failing to refer trafficked persons to assistance and protection. The system has so far failed to contribute significantly to either an increase in prosecution or a wider knowledge on trafficking. Further, the structures in place for children do not seem to have added any value at all and have complicated matters unnecessarily, making it more difficult to protect child victims of trafficking.

RECOMMENDATIONS

The research identified a number of areas that need improvement to ensure that the UK meets its obligation under the Convention, in particular with the upcoming review of the UK by the GRETA, the formal monitoring body of the Convention. In particular, we believe that the Government should reform the current system to:

(1)   Restructure and reduce the administrative process of the National Referral Mechanism in order to:
  - act as a multi-agency identification and referral mechanism, increasing access to services for victims;
  - introduce the right to appeal into the identification process;
  - review the application of the definition of trafficking to ensure that it reflects the UK's obligations under the Convention and is consistently applied to all victims of trafficking;
  - in cases of children embed it into the child protection system and give the services responsible for child protection the authority to make decisions;
  - give guidance on cases where the age of a young person is disputed and strictly apply the requirement of the benefit of the doubt.

(2)   Bring the system of identification and referral closer to the victims, on a devolved, regional and local level, building on the existing good practice multi-agency model.

(3)   Introduce an independent and public review of all negative decisions made by the competent authority to ensure the accountability of decision-makers and the quality of decision-making.

(4)   Ensure that no victims of trafficking are prosecuted for crimes that they committed while under coercion. In particular, stop child victims of trafficking from being prosecuted.

(5)   Uphold the best interest of the child in all decisions and introduce a system of guardianship for children with explicit responsibility to represent the child's best interest.

(6)   Appoint an independent anti-trafficking watchdog, based on the model of the Dutch National Rapporteur on Trafficking in Human Beings, with statutory powers to request information from the police, the immigration authorities, social services and NGOs and to report to the Parliament.

Front Cover

The cases on the cover refer to real cases of trafficked persons identified in the course of the research for this report. The names were changed and ages approximated to protect the identity of these individuals.

The places indicated on the map are examples of some of the locations where cases of trafficking were identified in the course of the research for this report. This is by no means an exhaustive list.

Acknowledgements

We would like to thank to all those who have contributed to this research.

Special thanks to Christine Beddoe and Hannah Pearce of ECPAT UK and Aidan McQuade and Klara Skrivankova of Anti-Slavery International for preparing this summary.

We would like to thank to Comic Relief and the City Parochial Foundation for funding this project.

The views expressed herein are those of the Anti-Trafficking Monitoring Group and in no way reflect the opinion of the funders.

ISBN: 978-0-900918-77-3

©Anti-Slavery International for the Anti-Trafficking Monitoring Group

THE ANTI TRAFFICKING MONITORING GROUP

The Anti-Trafficking Monitoring Group was formed in May 2009 and works according to a human rights-based approach to protect the well-being and best interests of trafficked persons.

This report presents the results of research undertaken to monitor the first year of implementation across the United Kingdom of the Council of Europe's Convention on Action against Trafficking in Human Beings, from 1 April 2009 to 31 March 2010.

The Anti-Trafficking Monitoring Group's Members are:

Anti-Slavery International (host)

Amnesty International UK

ECPAT UK

Helen Bamber Foundation

Immigration Law Practitioners' Association

Kalayaan

POPPY project (of Eaves)

TARA (of Glasgow Community and Safety Services)

UNICEFUK

The Anti-Trafficking Monitoring Group, c/o Anti-Slavery International
Thomas Clarkson House, The Stableyard, Broomgrove Road, London SW9 9TL, United Kingdom.
Tel. +44 (0) 207 501 8920
email: antitrafficking@antislavery.org

For further information see: http://www.antislavery.org/anti-trafficking_ monitoring_group/

---

[1] The nine organisations belonging to the Monitoring Group are: Amnesty International UK, Anti-Slavery International, ECPAT UK (End Child Prostitution, Child Pornography and the Trafficking of Children for Sexual Purposes), Helen Bamber Foundation, Immigration Law Practitioners' Association (ILPA), Kalayaan, POPPY Project (of Eaves), TARA (The Traffick-

ing Awareness Raising Alliance, of Glasgow Community and Safety Services), UNICEF UK. In addition, the Monitoring Group works closely with the Anti-Trafficking Legal Project (ATLeP).

2   The full report is available from: http://www.antislavery.org/anti-trafficking_monitoring_group/

3   Information from Northern Ireland, Scotland and Wales.

4   Bingham, T. (2010) *The Rule of Law*. London: Allen Lane.

5   By 18 January 2010, the number of referrals had risen to 557.

6   Alan Campbell MP, Parliamentary Under-Secretary of State for the Home Department, House of Commons debates, Hansard, 20 January 2010: Column 125WH, accessed on 3 March 2010 at http://www.publications.parliament.uk/pa/cm200910/cmhansrd/cm100120/halltext/100120h0009.htm

7   This information has not been published by the UKHTC, it was obtained by the research through requests made under the Freedom of Information Act 2000 and analysed.

8   Office for Democratic Institutions and Human Rights/Organization for Security and Co-operation in Europe, *National Referral Mechanisms. Joining Efforts to protect the Rights of Trafficked Persons. A Practical Handbook*, 2004, page 15, accessed on 2 March 2010 at http://www.osce.org/documents/odihr/2004/05/2903_en.pdf.

9   Under the Convention, 'competent authorities' are different authorities that come into contact with persons who might have been trafficked. The Convention places obligation on all these authorities.

10   *Freedom of Information* request 20090647 answered by UKHTC on 18 January 2010, accessed on 6 April 2010 and available at http://www.southyorks.police.uk/foi/disclosurelog/20090647-0.

11   For example, the *Daily Mail* reported on 10 March 2009 that, "Twenty-nine forces revealed that they had uncovered more of the drug being grown, including Gwent which detected no factories in 2004 but 151 last year. The largest force in the UK, London's Metropolitan Police, reported an increase from 206 to 654, while West Midlands saw a rise from 174 to 672". See, 'Police raids on cannabis factories on the rise as UK drug cultivation soars', *Daily Mail*, 10 March 2009, accessed on 25 March 2010 at http://www.dailymail.co.uk/news/article-1160845/Police-raids-cannabis-factories-rise-UK-drug-cultivation-soars.html.

Index

[all references are to paragraph number]

Index